Handbook of Individual Differences: Biological Perspectives

Wiley Psychophysiology Handbooks

Series Editor: Anthony Gale
University of Southampton

HANDBOOK OF SOCIAL PSYCHOPHYSIOLOGY
Edited by Hugh Wagner and Antony Manstead

HANDBOOK OF CLINICAL PSYCHOPHYSIOLOGY
Edited by Graham Turpin

HANDBOOK OF THE PSYCHOPHYSIOLOGY OF HUMAN EATING
Edited by Richard Shepherd

HANDBOOK OF COGNITIVE PSYCHOPHYSIOLOGY
Central and Autonomic Nervous System Approaches
Edited by J. Richard Jennings and Michael G.H. Coles

HANDBOOK OF INDIVIDUAL DIFFERENCES: BIOLOGICAL PERSPECTIVES
Edited by Anthony Gale and Michael W. Eysenck

Handbook of Individual Differences: Biological Perspectives

Edited by
Anthony Gale
University of Southampton, UK
and
Michael W. Eysenck
Royal Holloway and Bedford New College,
University of London, UK

JOHN WILEY & SONS
Chichester · New York · Brisbane · Toronto · Singapore

Other Wiley Editorial Offices

John Wiley & Sons, Inc., 605 Third Avenue,
New York, NY 10158-0012, USA

Jacaranda Wiley Ltd, G.P.O. Box 859, Brisbane,
Queensland 4001, Australia

John Wiley & Sons (Canada) Ltd, 22 Worcester Road,
Rexdale, Ontario M9W 1L1, Canada

John Wiley & Sons (SEA) Pte Ltd, 37 Jalan Pemimpin #05-04,
Block B, Union Industrial Building, Singapore 2057

Library of Congress Cataloging-in-Publication Data:

Handbook of individual differences : biological perspectives / edited by Anthony Gale and Michael W. Eysenck.
p. cm. — (Wiley psychophysiology handbooks)
Includes bibliographical references and index.
ISBN 0-471-9115-0 (cloth)
1. Psychophysiology. 2. Individual differences. I. Gale, Anthony. II. Eysenck, Michael W. III. Series.
[DNLM: 1. Individuality. 2. Psychophysiology. WL 103 H2357]
QP360.H32 1992
155.2—dc20
DNLM/DLC
for Library of Congress 91–40170
CIP

British Library Cataloguing in Publication Data:

A catalogue record for this book is
available from the British Library.

ISBN 0-471-91155-0

Typeset in 10/12pt Baskerville by Inforum Typesetting
Printed and bound in Great Britain by Biddles Ltd, Guildford and King's Lynn

Contents

List of Contributors

Kristen Joan Anderson, *Department of Psychology, Northwestern University, Evanston, Illinois, 60208, USA.*

Michael J. Apter, *Psychology Department, University of Chicago, 5848 University Avenue, Chicago, Illinois 60637, USA.*

Paul T. Barrett, *Faculty of Business, Luton College of Higher Education, Fairview House, Park Square, Luton, Bedfordshire, England LU1 3JU.*

Hans J. Eysenck, *Department of Psychology, Institute of Psychiatry, University of London, de Crespigny Park, Denmark Hill, London, England SE5 8AF.*

Michael W. Eysenck, *Department of Psychology, Royal Holloway and Bedford New College, University of London, Egham Hill, Egham, Surrey, England TW20 0EX.*

Jochen Fahrenberg, *Forschungsgruppe Psychophysiologie, Psychologisches Institut, Universität Freiburg i. Br., Belforstrasse 20, D-7800 Freiburg, Germany.*

Anthony Gale, *Department of Psychology, University of Southampton, Highfield, Southampton, Hampshire, England SO9 5NH.*

Russell G. Geen, *Department of Psychology, 209 McAlester Hall, University of Missouri-Columbia, Columbia, MO 65211, USA.*

Sarah E. Hampson, *Oregon Research Institute, 1899 Willamette Street, Eugene, Oregon 97401, USA.*

Paul Kline, *Department of Psychology, Washington Singer Laboratories, University of Exeter, The Queen's Drive, Exeter, Devon, England, EX4 4QG.*

Antony S.R. Manstead, *Department of Psychology, University of Manchester, Manchester, England M13 9PL.*

Kieron O'Connor, *Centre de Recherche, Hôpital Louis-H. Lafontaine, 7401 rue Hochelaga, Université de Montréal, Quebec, Canada H1N 3M5.*

Adrian Raine, *Department of Psychology, Seeley G. Mudd Building, University of Southern California, University Park, Los Angeles, California 90089-1061, USA.*

William Revelle, *Department of Psychology, Northwestern University, Evanston, Illinois 60208, USA.*

Robert M. Stelmack, *School of Psychology, University of Ottawa, 408B Monpetit Hall, Ottawa, Ontario, Canada K1N 6N5.*

Sven Svebak, *Department of Biological and Medical Psychology, Division of Somatic Psychology, Årstadveien 21, N-5009 Bergen, Norway.*

Steve Van Toller, *Warwick Human Chemoreception Research Group, Department of Psychology, University of Warwick, Coventry, Warwickshire, England CV4 7AL.*

Peter H. Venables, *Department of Psychology, University of York, Heslington, York, England YO1 5DD.*

Preface by Series Editor

This is the final volume in the Wiley Psychophysiology Handbook Series. Cacioppo and Tassinary (1990) in the first edition of their comprehensive introductory text in psychophysiology, begin with the following words:

> Investigations of elementary physiological events in normal thinking, feeling and interacting individuals are now quite feasible, and these investigations provide the potential for comprehensive accounts of human nature. This approach to the study of human behavior defines the discipline of psychophysiology. (1990, page ix.)

The five volumes which comprise the Psychophysiology Handbooks Series tackle each of the key aspects of psychophysiology at an advanced level, presenting a state-of-the-art account of the discipline. The *Handbook of Social Psychophysiology*, edited by Hugh Wagner and Antony Manstead, has sections covering central and peripheral processes in emotion, the biological and social contexts of emotional behaviour, and processes of social interaction. The *Handbook of Cognitive Psychophysiology*, edited by J. Richard Jennings and Michael G. H. Coles includes contributions on mental chonometry, language, memory, motor preparation, and information processing mechanisms in different age groups. In a novel and creative fashion the volume focuses on processes rather than physiological systems, drawing upon data derived from systems in a coherent and integrated approach. In the *Handbook of the Psychophysiology of Human Eating*, Richard Shepherd brings together for the first time, contributions on the determinants of human eating, the social and cultural context, developmental aspects, and consequences of nutrition for health and illness. His book has set the scene for what has recently become major governmental and research council research initiatives on nutrition; the psychophysiological approach to nutrition demonstrates how essential it is to construct a multidisciplinary approach to this crucial aspect of human existence. In the *Handbook of Clinical Psychophysiology*, edited by Graham Turpin, psychophysiology is brought to bear on the understanding of the causes of mental illness and emotional disorders, involving both central and peripheral processes, the effects of psychophysiological interventions, and the bases and treatment of the main disorders, including schizophrenia and affective disorder together with a number of specific human problems (including sexual dysfunction, hypertension and Raynaud's disease). The present and final volume in the Series introduces the final building block of Cacioppo and Tassinary's vision of psychophysiology. While the volumes on cognition, social psychophysiology and nutrition focus on general processes of thinking, feeling and human interaction and human well-being, the *Handbook of Individual Differences*, together with the *Handbook on Clinical Psychophysiology*, focus on individual differences in temperament, personality and intelligence and the ways in which individuals both vary in the expression of general processes and reveal a failure of biosocial coping mechanisms.

All five Handbooks have features in common: all the authors are international authorities working in laboratories around the globe; all offer an up-to-date and challenging account of work in their field; all volumes include critical sections on theory and method, as well as substantive chapters reviewing progress in specific fields; all have a preoccupation with the art of experimentation and the effort to capture nature in laboratory and (more rarely) field settings. It is expected that the Handbooks will constitute a major source for researchers and advanced students, not only in psychophysiology itself, but in the twin fields with which psychophysiology is combined in each volume.

Psychophysiologists are courageous scientists because they confront the full challenge to psychology: how to integrate data from four different domains: biology, behaviour, subjective experience, and social context. Gale and Edwards (1986) add what they call the fifth face of psychophysiology, namely individual differences. As well as capturing general processes, psychophysiology must recognize that individuals vary in several ways in the manner in which general processes are displayed and experienced. Unlike authorities in other areas of psychology, psychophysiology, by its very nature, does not limit itself to one domain of description. The challenge is a challenge which spans theory, method and inference. It raises major questions about the appropriate methods and contexts for research and questions also some of the traditional assumptions which underlie typically univariate statistical approaches to data analysis. Because of the need to integrate parallel data sets, which are systematically related in a dynamic fashion over time, the typical psychophysiological research study generates vast quantities of data which demand a comprehensive intellectual appraisal. Thus there is still a major preoccupation with data acquisition and analysis, perhaps at the cost of theoretical development. These Handbooks seek not only to tackle the methodological issues but also to ask searching theoretical questions which cannot be ignored by other psychologists, even although they limit their enquiries to more narrow conceptions of human nature.

The present volume summarizes research on intelligence, personality, gender and antisocial behaviour and includes consideration of genetic, biochemical, electrocortical and peripheral mechanisms in the determination of individual differences. Several chapters challenge the very assumptions underlying a biological approach and, in particular, the failure of psychophysiologists to recognize the social and personal contexts in which biological processes are expressed. Two chapters question the underlying statistical assumptions in research in the field and offer new ways of thinking about individual difference processes and constructing experiments.

I must take the opportunity with the publication of this final volume in the Series, to thank three sets of person, for their cooperation, hard work, tolerance and persistence. First, the volume editors, who have been skilful in cajoling their authors into sticking to deadlines, restricting their contributions to required length, and integrating the material they offer in a coherent and stimulating fashion. While, as series editor, I have recruited the volume editors, it is the volume editors who have selected, trained and mastered their distinguished authors. Anyone reading this Series will appreciate that effort and the high level of quality of material which has been sustained. Secondly, I must thank Michael Coombs of John Wiley and Sons, who first commissioned the Series, and Wendy Hudlass, who for several years has sustained courtesy, kindness and thoughtful support with what must have seemed to be a rabble of disorganized academics, overwhelmed by an overdose of commitments. Finally, my wife, Liz, whose courage in living with me and my work for so many years defies understanding. A tremendously busy professional person herself, she has always found time to smoothe the troubled brow, and to remind me that life and work are always superior to idleness and slow death.

ANTHONY GALE
University of Southampton, November 1991

REFERENCES

Cacioppo, J.T. and Tassinary, L.G. (eds) (1990) *Principles of Psychophysiology: Physical, Social, and Inferential Elements.* Cambridge: Cambridge University Press.

Gale, A. and Edwards, J.A. (1986) Individual differences. In M.G.H. Coles, E. Donchin and S.W. Porges (eds), *Psychophysiology: Systems, Processes, and Applications.* New York: Guilford Press, pp. 431–507.

Chapter 1

Psychophysiology: A Programme for Individual Differences Research?

Anthony Gale
Department of Psychology, University of Southampton, Highfield, Southampton, England SO9 5NH

and

Michael W. Eysenck
Department of Psychology, Royal Holloway and Bedford New College, University of London, Egham Hill, Egham, Surrey, England TW20 0EX

INTRODUCTION

Psychophysiology, is still emerging as a systematic and coherent discipline, although its key journal *Psychophysiology*, published by the Society for Psychophysiological Research, is now over twenty-five years of age. Other important journals in the field include *Biological Psychology*, the *Journal of Psychophysiology*, and the *International Journal of Psychophysiology*. These journals are published by learned societies in North America and Europe and the ability to sustain such a set of relatively specialist journals reflects the vigour and continuing level of scientific activity in the field.

Handbook of Individual Differences: Biological Perspectives
Edited by Anthony Gale and Michael W. Eysenck

The study of individual differences has a much longer track record, going back to early human medicine, and drawing upon both clinical and psychometric traditions, the latter being stimulated by the need for widespread testing in two world wars and by the development of universal education in western societies. Individual differences research has been integrated within mainstream psychology and in areas as disparate as cognitive psychology (Eysenck, 1977), social psychology (see Hampson in this volume) and health psychology (Strube, 1991). There are distinguished journals like the *Journal of Personality and Social Psychology* (American Psychological Association) and more recently *Personality and Individual Differences* (International Society for the Study of Individual Differences).

Theory building and empirical research in the fields of personality and intelligence have a long and distinguished history; thus, while the majority of academic undergraduate courses in psychology include extended consideration of these topics, in recognition of their importance within general psychology, psychophysiology, in contrast, is still likely to be only an option.

Psychometrics has achieved very much more by way of reliable description of individual differences than has psychophysiology; and so far, paper-and-pencil tests, based on self-report, appear to offer more stable data that can be achieved through physiological monitoring. Some areas of psychometrics, for example, in the measurement of intelligence, have achieved good levels of predictive validity for psychologically and socially important human behaviours. Psychometric tests are in constant use in a variety of applied contexts, in education, employment counselling and personnel selection. In contrast, psychophysiological measurement (including ambulatory monitoring) is still deployed largely in basic research rather than applied contexts (Gale, 1987b; Turpin, 1983; 1990). Part of the reason for the rare use of psychophysiological measures in applied settings is the high cost in terms of equipment, personnel and data analysis, although as with the general trend in electronics, computing, equipment and software costs are gradually diminishing.

The aim of researchers in the psychophysiology of individual differences has typically been to draw the two approaches together, in order to identify the biological variables which correlate with or are causally related to, psychometrically derived indices of individual variation. However, there is much more agreement about key methods, measurement theory, and fundamental principles in psychometrics than there is in psychophysiology. Only recently have psychophysiologists recognized the need to incorporate principles from psychometric test theory into measurement frameworks within psychophysiology (see Strube, 1990) and while some psychophysiological journals refuse to accept scientific papers which do not follow prescribed measurement principles in relation to certain physiological measures (for example, electrodermal activity and heart rate) many papers are still published using measures idiosyncratic to particular laboratories (see Gale and Edwards, 1983a for a discussion of the undisciplined variety of measures used, for example, in electroencephalographic studies of personality).

Psychophysiology seeks to integrate data along a bio-social continuum, recognizing that physiological data reflect both inherent properties of the nervous system and the impact of extended adaptation to the environment. The ideal psychophysiological study combines physiological measurement with aspects of behaviour, performance and experiential report (Cacioppo and Tassinary, 1990). Inherent biological characteristics and the results of adaptation are both seen as expressed in the electrophysiology and biochemistry of the nervous system and its functional organization.

As with psychometrics, measurement *per se* has been a major focus of attention in psychophysiology. Earlier work on the capture of signals derived from the central and automatic nervous system was concerned with transduction, data processing and the exclusion of measurement artefact. Many of the earlier problems have been solved. The development of the minicomputer and then the microcomputer and the extension of computer memory have opened the way to major experiments, employing large participant samples, in a way reminiscent of the early exploitation of mainframe systems by psychometricians. Thus there is no longer any justification for the very small participant populations typically used in the past in psychophysiological studies of individual differences and multivariate, multi-level studies should now become the norm (see Fahrenberg in this volume, and Royce and Powell, 1985). While psychophysiological instrumentation will continue to be relatively expensive (as compared with psychometric tests) the unit cost and manageability of data should no longer be a problem. Earlier limitations on the interpretation of research findings which were constrained by limited sampling of participant methods combined with univariate approaches may no longer apply.

Major handbooks and specialist texts on psychophysiological measurement problems and techniques and including chapters describing psychophysiological achievements in substantive areas of psychology continue to appear, reflecting continuing growth in both basic understanding and application (Andreassi, 1980; Cacioppo and Petty, 1982; 1983; Cacioppo and Tassinary, 1990; Coles, Donchin and Porges, 1986; Gale and Edwards, 1983b; Greenfield and Sternbach, 1972; Jennings and Coles, 1991; Martin and Venables, 1980; Venables and Martin, 1967; Wagner, 1988; Wagner and Manstead, 1989).

A number of fundamental conceptual issues remain to be resolved within psychophysiology. For example, the number of possible relations between identified units of behaviour and units of physiological response (one-to-one, one-to-many, many-to-many and so on) has yet to be explored (Cacioppo and Tassinary, 1990). When physiological, behavioural and cognitive data are seen as elements within an interactive *system* it is no longer acceptable to talk of physiological data as mere *correlates*, since causal modelling is not compatible with the notion of parallel domains of description. Just as in psychometrics there is concern as to the referential data upon which subjects draw in responding to questions about their own behaviour and experience, so the relationship in psychophysiology between verbal report, awareness, and physiological response remains a major puzzle (Levey and Martin, 1991). Such conceptual difficulties should not be under-estimated, for they influence theory construction, causal modelling and indeed, the black art of imaginative experimentation.

DRAWING TOGETHER THE TWO TRADITIONS OF PSYCHOPHYSIOLOGY AND INDIVIDUAL DIFFERENCES

Eysenck and Eysenck (1985), Gale (1987a), Gale and Edwards (1983c; 1986) and Gale, Strelau and Farley (1985) have derived the common characteristics shared by biological approaches to the study of human temperament, personality and intelligence. The following discussion sets out these key themes, which are reflected in the majority of the chapters in this volume. Together, these themes constitute the rationale for the book.

Loss of Theoretical Power

Eysenck (e.g. 1967) has frequently argued that general theories of behaviour or discrete models of performance in particular contexts, lose theoretical power if they do not recognize that some of the error term can be systematically accounted for in terms of individual differences. Differences in the ways in which particular subject groups respond systematically to stimulation or task demands can themselves provide insights into the general psychological mechanisms or processes in question. Thus neglect of individual differences leads to a wasteful enhancement of the error term and reduces explanatory power and the potential for theoretical advance. If such a view is accepted then any account of human behaviour is incomplete if it focuses on general mechanisms at the expense of individual differences. Psychophysiological research is no exception to this principle and indeed, between-subject variations in both tonic and phasic levels of electro-physiological activity are themselves a major source of difficulty in psychophysiological research, where repeated measures designs, with their inherent problems of inflated variance and asymmetrical transfer effects, call for considerable guile in experimental design and data analysis. The possibility that some of the between-subject variance is itself a function of persistent and invariant traits helps both to gain more control of the data and increase the power of prediction.

Genetic Transmission

Biological factors, genetically transmitted, account for a significant proportion of the variation attributable to individual differences (see Eaves, Eysenck and Martin, 1989). One of the key aims of biological theories of individual differences is to identify genetically transmitted factors by psychometric means and then explore their functioning by a combination of physiological, behavioural and cognitive/experiential measures. However, genetically transmitted characteristics may appear at different *levels* of functional expression. This important issue is considered further below because different authorities have different expectations concerning the point or points in the causal chains of behaviour at which we might expect to identify biologically determined factors.

Phenotypical Expression

That which is transmitted is expressed in a variety of ways in the structure and anatomy of the nervous system, in neurophysiological functioning, biochemical processes, and other aspects of the hardwiring of the nervous system and the functional relationships between structures and processes. Psychophysiological studies have sought to identify correlates of such phenotypical expression. Thus, for example, researchers have sought to identify aspects of electrocortical activity which parallel psychometrically estimated differences in extraversion–introversion (e.g. Gale, 1981); it has been assumed that both extraversion–introversion and associated electrocortical characteristics reflect fundamental biogenetic differences in brain function, in this case the excitatory/inhibitory balance between the neocortex and the brainstem reticular activation system.

Biological Universals

A working hypothesis is that such genetically transmitted characteristics, when viewed across populations, are biologically adaptive for the species. Thus, it is a reasonable expectation that such properties can be identified across cultures, within different traditions of psychological reasearch, and within cultures across time. For example, coherence among key personality factors and their biological correlates identified in both Western and Eastern European research laboratories is seen as evidence of the existence of biological universals (Strelau, 1987). As Kline demonstrates in this volume, a handful of traits appear with remarkable consistency across laboratories and across cultures; Hampson also shows how psycholexical studies (Digman, 1990) derived from actual language in everyday use to describe personality characteristics have also yielded almost identical factors. Thus there is a prima-facie case that the necessary condition of cross-cultural invariance has been satisfied by such work, although it does not constitute a sufficient condition for the claim of biological universals. Some authors (e.g. Zuckerman, 1979) have argued that gender-related differences in psychobiological variables also indicate a species-specific genetically transmitted adaptive function. However, as Manstead indicates in the present volume, the establishment of physiological differences between the sexes does not necessarily imply functional differences of any significance.

General Adaptive Processes

If genetically transmitted characteristics have adaptive properties, it is possible that they are not solely species-specific to man but reflect general and evolutionary adaptive processes. Authorities who draw a distinction between temperament and personality (Strelau, 1987) suggest that certain characteristics might be properties of nervous systems as such (temperamental traits) and not necessarily the preserve of human nervous systems (temperamental traits *plus* acquired personality characteristics). For example, Strelau (1983; 1987) sees information-processing capacity (broadly defined) as a general characteristic of nervous systems. Such a claim makes possible the comparative study of individual differences in nervous system characteristics (Gray, 1982; Matysiak, 1986). Much of Gray's work on anxiety (critically evaluated by M. W. Eysenck in this volume) is based on rat preparations. According to Strelau (1983), following the Pavlovian and neo-Pavlovian approach to personality, temperamental differences reflect basic properties of nervous systems *per se*. They thus reflect genetic transmission at the most primary level of nervous system functioning.

Energy Transmission

In the following section we discuss the status of the concept of arousal, which has played a prominent role in psychophysiological research into individual differences. Several authorities have drawn distinctions between the energetic or activational principles governing behaviour, and the directional aspects; thus for Duffy (e.g. 1972) arousal or activation provides the means whereby the organism can direct attention and action towards the stimulus. Energy transmission is of course a property of all organisms and living systems. Energy is absorbed, stored, provides system maintenance, and is discharged in a variety of ways, including action. It is not unreasonable to expect that such biological characteristics are reflected in individual variations in behaviour.

Brener (1980; 1987) has argued for a *rapprochement* between bioenergetics, information processing and psychological concepts in general. Within the psychophysiology of individual differences, there is both an explicit and implicit reference by many theorists, to temperamental or personality differences couched in terms of differences in energy transmission (Eysenck, 1967; Strelau, 1983). For example, Gale (1987a) proposed a conceptual framework in which extraversion–introversion, neuroticism–stability, anxiety, depression and schizophrenia, could be understood in terms of differences in energy intake, energy release, and stability in energy storage. Individual differences in energic factors might refer to tonic state or readiness to respond, degree of responsiveness, persistence and/or resilience in the face of continuing information gain, and/or speed of recovery of psychological processes, following intensive stimulation. Arousal may or may not be subjectively related to epiphenomenal correlates of energy exchange (e.g. Thayer, 1985). We discuss the concept of arousal in the following section; in spite of continued dissatisfaction with the concept and its power as an aid to the explanation of behaviour, it still maintains a tenacious hold on individual differences theory.

Self-regulation

Adaptive properties of biological organisms have evolved in the context of the evolution of a parallel environment; thus adaptive traits cannot be seen as passive, but as functionally related to environmental demands. Such demands include both physical characteristics of the environment and other organisms, and in the case of the human species, other human beings. Active regulatory strategies evolve to ensure maximal adaptation between biological dispositions and environmental demands. Such strategies involve the regulation of behaviour, through feedback and as a result of experience. Thus the relationship between dispositional traits and environmental factors will not be a simple one-to-one relationship, nor will dispositional traits necessarily be reflected in a straightforward way within the physiological domain. If temperamental characteristics represent the primary level of genetic transmission, regulatory strategies represent learned means of adapting temperament to environmental demands, the modes of adaptation themselves being dictated in part at least by temperamental constraints. In this volume, M. W. Eysenck describes research studies which show differences in attentional allocation between high- and low-anxious subjects; attentional allocation strategies may thus be conceived of as second-level coping mechanisms.

Coping Styles

It is possible that coping strategies, as a second-order patterning of response, will themselves be reducible to a taxonomy of response styles (Strube, 1991). The outcomes of particular coping strategies will themselves feed back upon biological mechanisms. Such strategies might then mask relationships between traits and physiological indices; for example, Weinberger, Schwartz and

Davidson (1979) showed that expected relationships between anxiety and physiological indices only appeared once the effects of a repressive coping style were partialled out. A repressive coping style, expressed in terms of socially desirable responses to questions concerning anxiety responses, may serve to mask psychometric indices of anxiety. The Weinberger, Schwartz and Davidson (1979) study is therefore of heuristic value as well as offering a technique for enhancing personality–physiology correlations.

Cultural Norms

Anxiety was for Freud (1936) the principal source of human motivation, and moral anxiety arises through fear of transgression of social norms. The ego ideal offers a standard of perfection to the individual so that pride or guilt is experienced when social norms are followed or breached. While the story of psychoanalysis might not be accepted, the notion that cultural norms, acquired and introjected during personal development, influence our behaviour and our experience of positive and negative affect, is clearly compatible with some accounts of individual differences (Gale, 1987a). For example, Gray (1983) demonstrates differences between extraverted and introverted individuals in terms of differential responsiveness to reward and punishment. Since the signals for reward and punishment are culturally defined, the learning of cultural norms will interact with biologically determined dispositions and self-regulatory strategies.

A key problem for the authors in this volume is to tease out the evidence for the validity of the themes set out above. Several authors refer to genetic evidence and Van Toller in particular reviews evidence for the effects of nutritional and other basic bodily processes on individual variations. He suggests that nutritional factors might both affect the individual's behaviour and the social reaction of others to the individual, in turn affecting the style of the individual's social skills. Kline shows that the ubiquity of certain measures of intelligence and personality offers a prime facie case for biological universals; nor is it hard to argue for the functional significance of such factors as intelligence, extraversion, and anxiety. Psychophysiological measurement is justified in terms of its capacity to monitor in real time the operation of both basic primary biogenetic processes and secondary acquired adaptive strategies. Stelmack and Geen, Barrett and H. J. Eysenck, and Raine and Venables, examine the evidence for psychophysiological correlates of extraversion–introversion, intelligence, and antisocial behaviour respectively. Apter and Svebak introduce new data on psychophysiological correlates of telic and paratelic states; their emphasis is on processes and the description of dynamic changes in state. At the same time such complex interactions create demands for appropriate methods of measurement and research design (see chapters by O'Connor; and Revelle and Anderson); there are serious challenges to the validity of contemporary research designs and the limitations of univariate modelling. Hampson, in exploring social psychological perspectives on personality, while recognizing genetic influences, nevertheless underlines the notion of personality as a social construction, and identifies the capacity to monitor the self and personal action as a source of individual differences in its own right. Among the authors in this volume, Hampson is perhaps the most critical of an exclusively biological approach to individual differences; she reminds us of the dangers of working in isolation from other theoretical and empirical developments in individual differences research. Fahrenberg, in providing a review of more than two decades of research, concludes that our understanding of physiological correlates of psychometrically measured anxiety is still very limited, while M. W. Eysenck offers a more optimistic view, based on his detailed studies of attentional mechanisms in anxious and non-anxious subjects. Finally, Manstead offers a subtle analysis of theory and research in the field of sex differences, showing that claims that males and females differ in emotional expression are not easy to justify; there is further difficulty in tracing the causal origins of such differences, even where their existence can be demonstrated.

The contributors to this volume, while clearly recognizing the substance of the key themes within the psychophysiology of individual differences are nevertheless sharply critical of unquestioned acceptance of their assumptions. One major issue is whether the concept of arousal is alive or dead or indeed in constant threat of resurrection.

THE STATUS OF AROUSAL AS A PSYCHOLOGICAL CONCEPT

As Claridge (1987) put it: "I have often felt that as an explanatory concept in psychology 'arousal' has many of the qualities of a difficult but persuasive lover, whom reason tells one to abandon yet who continues to satisfy an inescapable need" (p. 134). So far as the psychophysiology of individual differences is concerned, the concept of arousal has been and continues to be a vital part of theory building, even though for psychophysiology in general it has come into disrepute. It seems that at its present stage of development the psychophysiology of individual differences continues to need the concept of arousal as a source of conceptual or theoretical coherence and as a means of generating testable empirical hypotheses. Several of the authors in this volume deploy the term arousal as an explanatory concept. From a radical behaviourist perspective, concepts like arousal or intelligence are misleading intervening variables, unnecessary verbal baggage, which add little to our understanding of behaviour; functional analyses of the relation between stimulus and response do not need to call upon organismic variables which resist systematic operationalization. A question to be addressed in this section, therefore, is whether the concept of arousal can survive and in what form?

Johnson and Anderson (1990) trace the history of the concept of arousal and its association with the concept of stress, as a general body state or reaction to aversive stimulation. Key landmarks in the development of the concept are Cannon's (1914; 1929) emphasis on homeostatic mechanisms and global responses to aversive stimulation, Selye's (1936) General Adaptation Syndrome as a general response to stress, the discoveries about the Ascending Reticular Activating System by Moruzzi and Magoun (1949) and others, Hull's (1943) notion of a general drive state, and the elaboration into a specifically human psychological characteristic by Malmo (1959) and Duffy (e.g. 1972). The classic paper of Lindsley (1952) (focusing on electrocortical measurement) proposed a continuum of arousal from deep coma to extreme agitation, and part of this continuum was elaborated upon in the sleep research of the 1960s. What had evolved was the notion of a graded bodily response, tied to the release of energy, reflecting both reaction to the external environment and the stimulation and release of internal bodily processes. This continuum or gradient of energy could be deployed to support the directional properties of behaviour (Duffy, 1951). M. W. Eysenck (1982) reviews the application of arousal to a broad range of cognitive and behavioural contexts.

In the field of individual differences, Eysenck's (1967) theory of the neurophysiological basis of extraversion–introversion and neuroticism–stability, drew upon these ideas and specifically identified brain mechanisms associated with arousal (extraversion–introversion) and activation (neuroticism–stability). This powerful synthesis of psychometric and neurophysiological and allied concepts was responsible for a major growth of research in individual differences, and Eysenck's ideas are still extant in contemporary studies. Stelmack (in this volume) reviews the present state of play with regard to Eysenck's theory of extraversion–introversion and shows that systematic manipulation of task demands and the direct manipulation of tonic arousal can produce consistency in results obtained with some physiological measures. In contrast Fahrenberg (in this volume), working with the concept of anxiety, has failed after many years of attempts to identify any clear physiological correlates. He also demonstrates that other researchers have similarly reported very few links between psychometric and psychophysiological measures of anxiety, in spite of its status as a clearly pervasive human characteristic.

The arguments set out in Lacey's (1967) classic attack on the concept of arousal still hold, and in the Festschrift to the Laceys, Venables (1974) reviewed the problems which Lacey identified. Gale (1987a) reviews the case against the concept of arousal as argued by Venables and many others, and we reproduce some of those arguments here.

Lacey (1967) produced empirical evidence to demonstrate four critical points (a) that behavioural and physiological arousal are dissociable, (b) that different physiological indicators of arousal are dissociable, (c) that particular situations reliably produce particular patterns of physiological responding, and (d) that feedback or buffering mechanisms operate between physiological systems. Such evidence makes it difficult to persist in the view that arousal is a unitary phenomenon and indeed few theorists continue to subscribe to a unitary viewpoint.

Arousal might seem to operate both within and between individuals as intelligence appears to operate between individuals, namely as a construct which relates to performance in a continuous fashion. However, while factor-analytic studies provide evidence of a general intelligence factor, no such correlational framework has been produced to support arousal as a unitary framework, the intercorrelations between the physiological measures purported to measure arousal being both low in magnitude and inconsistent in direction. Lacey (1967) demonstrated that electrodermal activity and heart rate change can move in opposite directions, depending on the task and the instructions to subjects. Indeed, the notion that heart rate can increase or decrease as a function of attentional mechanisms (intake-rejection) and the respondent's interpretation of the stimulus, has itself been deployed as a means of distinguishing between pathological groups (Hare, 1978). In contrast to physiological measures, there is evidence that subjective measures of mood can be factored to yield two bipolar arousal clusters, one relating to alertness/arousal (sleep/wakefulness) and the other to affect/stress (positive/negative hedonic tone) (Mackay, 1987). However, reports of systematic relationships between physiological response systems and subjective measures of mood are few and far between (but see Mackay, 1980); and a key feature of the Hodgson and Rachman (1974) theory of anxiety is the *decoupling* of physiological, behavioural and subjective components.

One of the difficulties with the arousal concept is its ubiquitous use in a variety of contexts in which it plays differing roles, while retaining a proportion of its original meaning; thus it has acquired the status of a Wittgensteinian family resemblance, where each context of use bears some similarity to one or more other contexts, in the absence of a common core of meaning which straddles all contexts. Thus the face validity of the concept is high, but its reliability, construct validity and predictive validity are low.

If, for example, we return to the basic notion of energetics, we can find different examples of use, namely, rate of energy intake, rate of storage, efficiency of energy storage, and aspects of energy utilization, such as intensity, patterning of release, and temporal distribution (Gale and Edwards, 1986; Gale, 1987a). Thus temperamental or personality typologies may refer to differences in tonic arousal, phasic response, recovery from stimulation or self-regulation and individuals may differ in any or all of these (Strelau, 1987).

The explanatory power of the arousal concept is clearly undermined and devalued by inflationary use in too many contexts. Gale and Edwards (1986) list the following:

> in individual differences, extraversion–introversion, acute versus chronic schizophrenia, psychopathy, depression, autism, hyperactivity, primary–secondary function, field dependence–independence, anxiety, sensation seeking, stimulus hunger, locus of control, sex differences, and so on; in stress research, noise, loss of sleep, heat, cold, incentives, knowledge of results, and pacing; in circadian studies and biological rhythm research, time of day, menstrual cycle, sexual stimulation, hunger and post-prandial states, and so forth; in social-psychological and organizational theory, social facilitation, social intimacy, personal space, evaluation apprehension, organizational climate, and so on; in experimental studies, vigilance, memory, RT, stimulus complexity, and the like; and in drug and addiction research, stimulants, depressants, alcohol, caffeine, nicotine and so forth. . . . Thus arousal is used by different voices as a source of stimulation, as a trait or state threshold for response, as a response to stimulation, as endogenous variation, as experienced drowsiness or alertness, as a correlate or consequence of action, as a measure of intensity of action, or as a drive or motivator of action (pp. 491–492).

In spite of these very substantial problems with the arousal concept, it does serve the useful function of providing some explanations for several otherwise puzzling interactions of factors. For example, the fact that noise interacts with time of day in determining performance, and the fact that loss of sleep interacts with incentive, suggests that these factors have something in common. It is difficult to think of any commonality other than their effects on a hypothetical level of arousal. One way of attempting to preserve the arousal concept while at the same time providing a more realistic account was suggested by M. W. Eysenck (1982). He developed Broadbent's (1971) proposal that there are two arousal systems. He argued that arousal has a relatively passive effect on performance due to the appropriateness or otherwise of the state of arousal for performance; in addition, there is a more active and effortful response which is designed to compensate for the adverse effects of arousal on performance. Arousal as measured psychophysiologically stems from an amalgam of these passive and active effects and so such measures often provide rather unclear information about internal processes.

A clear inference from M. W. Eysenck's extension of Broadbent's theory is that researchers into the psychophysiology of individual differences need to recognize a taxonomy of tasks and experimental situations which reflects the degree of passivity-effort required of subjects.

A SYSTEMS APPROACH TO THE PSYCHOPHYSIOLOGY OF INDIVIDUAL DIFFERENCES

While the concept of arousal is an explicit or implicit element within psychophysiological approaches to individual differences, it cannot be claimed that there is any evidence of a unitary arousal process; an alternative approach to the problem is called for. In his review of the failings of the arousal construct,

Venables (1974), following Lacey (1967) invites us to consider psychophysiological response systems as interrelated, within the overall framework of control theory.

Systems consist of units (with their attributes) and the relationships between units. Such relationships require communication systems and information exchange between sub-systems or units, and units may be more or less open to information. Much of the information which passes is concerned with the state of particular units, so that comparison may be made with appropriate set points, showing the extent to which the unit state is deviating from a blueprint state. Systems are organized hierarchically, so that some units (those higher in the hierarchy) have more latitude, variance and control than other units. Homeostasis, and the related concept of dynamic equilibrium, are processes which maintain the system in a constant state. Some bodily systems must have homeostatic mechanisms which are inviolate; otherwise, survival is at risk. Such general principles have long been recognized by physiologists, who have borrowed systems concepts from control engineering (see Johnson and Anderson, 1990). Higher organisms are much more open to external sources of information than are lower organisms or engineered systems, and there may be limits to the extent to which new information can be processed or reconciled with existing relationships between sub-system units. The notion of emergence refers to new properties which a system might acquire as a result of interaction with novel environments.

This means that it is feasible to talk not of arousal in global terms, but of the arousal or activation of particular sub-system units, which may or may not have mutually excitatory or inhibitory effects. At the macro level, biologically determined primary traits may be modulated by acquired regulatory strategies, which have been shaped by feedback from both cognitive and emotional subsystems. Gale (1987a) applies system concepts to the modelling of key personality variables, with a particular emphasis on energic systems, showing that temperamental and personality traits may vary in terms of setpoints, states, or feedback mechanisms. As Johnson and Anderson (1990) indicate, some progress has been made in psychophysiology in the understanding of the operation of systems properties in relation to particular structures (e.g. cardiovascular systems) and their relationships with other structures (e.g. neural control mechanisms, and muscular activity). Such problems will need to be solved within psychophysiology before we can apply the theoretical approach to the study of individual differences. A particular problem is that most psychophysiological laboratories develop expertise in only one or two psychophysiological measures, while individual differences researchers would benefit from combinations of measures and an understanding of their interrelationships.

M. W. Eysenck (in this volume) shows that subjects high and low on anxiety vary the style in which attention is allocated to tasks, thus maximizing certain sorts of incoming information, which in turn will interact with and feedback on, information about bodily state and the present level of operation of cognitive functions. This offers a paradigm for psychophysiological study of cognitive processes in relation to psychometrically measured and clinically assessed differences in an anxiety. O'Connor in his chapter argues that the analysis of processes of this nature, and the understanding of the interaction between bodily process, cognitive state and observable behaviour, require a different style of research and statistical analysis.

CONCLUSION

There is often a dynamic tension between a relatively precise but narrow approach and a much less precise, broadly-based approach. This is certainly the case so far as the study of individual differences is concerned. For example, several researchers have investigated individual differences in personality largely from the psychometric perspective, but it is difficult to gain much understanding of relevant biological factors from that perspective. One of the central themes running through this book is the value of multidisciplinary research. Such research is more difficult and more time-consuming than more narrowly based research, but it is ultimately likely to be more rewarding. More specifically, there is increasing evidence that the disciplines of individual differences and psychophysiology can usefully be linked. Furthermore, bridge-building between these two disciplines and cognitive and social psychology can serve to further our understanding of individual differences.

We anticipate that in future research, there will be more recognition of task demands and social context in the design of psychophysiological studies of individual differences. Early critics (e.g. Gale, 1973) warned that the laboratory itself provides a social context, provoking responses and differential coping strategies on the part of different personality groups which then are confounds for the variables being studied; similarly Averill (1973) demonstrated that aversive stimuli vary in their degree of threat, depending on the subject's own perception of them and prior experience of threatening situations. The development of ambulatory monitoring (Turpin, 1990) combined with the use of self-report techniques in real-life situations, might serve to increase the face validity of psychophysiological studies, particularly where repeated sampling over time and events is possible.

This volume offers a state-of-the-art account of progress made so far in understanding biological aspects of individual differences. It would be a fair judgement that in spite of several decades of research, our understanding of the psychophysiology of individual differences is still limited; however, we have begun to appreciate the errors in research strategy that have been committed in the past and can identify growthpoints for the future. Gale and

Edwards (1986) refer to Seven Deadly Sins in this field of endeavour: theoretical simplemindedness, obsession with correlation not process, poor psychometrics, poor physiology, the trivial experiment, procedural insensitivity, and low-level data handling and interpretation. The chapters in this volume reveal that such criticisms are more applicable to the work of the 1970s and early 1980s than to contemporary research. Nevertheless, there is a danger that some developments in new technology (for example, brain mapping) might lead researchers to replicate once again the mistakes in research strategy and execution that were redolent of earlier work (see Garber *et al.*, 1989). Hopefully, the questions raised in this volume will serve to redirect future research in the psychophysiology of individual differences.

REFERENCES

Andreassi, J.L. (1980) *Psychophysiology: Human Behavior and Physiological Response.* New York: Oxford University Press.

Averill, J.R. (1973) Personal control over aversive stimuli and its relationship to stress. *Psychological Bulletin*, **80**, 286–303.

Brener, J.M. (1980) Energy, information and man. In A.J. Chapman and D.M. Jones (eds), *Models of Man.* Leicester: British Psychological Society.

Brener, J.M. (1987) Behavioural energetics: effects of uncertainty on the mobilization and distribution of energy. *Psychophysiology*, **24**, 499–512.

Broadbent, D.E. (1971) *Decision and Stress.* London: Academic Press.

Cacioppo, J.T. and Petty, R.E. (eds) (1982) *Perspectives in Cardiovascular Psychophysiology.* New York: Guilford.

Cacioppo, J.T. and Petty, R.E. (eds) (1983) *Social Psychophysiology: A Sourcebook.* New York: Guilford Press.

Cacioppo, J.T. and Tassinary, L.G. (1990) Psychophysiology and psychophysiological inference. In J.T. Cacioppo and L.G. Tassinary (eds), *Principles of Psychophysiology: Physical, Social and Inferential Elements.* New York: Cambridge University Press.

Cannon, W.B. (1914) The interrelations of emotions as suggested by recent physiological researches. *American Journal of Psychology*, **25**, 256–282.

Cannon, W.B. (1929) *Bodily Changes in Pain, Hunger, Fear and Rage.* Boston: Charles T. Brandford.

Claridge, G. (1987) Psychoticism and arousal. In J. Strelau and H.J. Eysenck (eds), *Personality Dimensions and Arousal.* New York: Plenum.

Coles, M.G.H., Donchin, E. and Porges, S.W. (1986) *Psychophysiology: Systems, Processes and Applications.* New York: Guilford Press.

Digman, J.M. (1990) Personality structure: emergence of the five-factor model. *Annual Review of Psychology*, **41**, 417–440.

Duffy, E. (1951) The concept of energy mobilization. *Psychological Review*, **58**, 30–40.

Duffy, E. (1972) Activation. In N.S. Greenfield and R.A. Sternbach (eds), *Handbook of Psychophysiology.* New York: Holt, Rinehart & Winston.

Eaves, L.J., Eysenck, H.J. and Martin, N.G. (1989) *Genes, Culture and Personality: An Empirical Approach.* London: Academic Press.

Eysenck, H.J. (1967) *The Biological Basis of Personality.* Springfield, Illinois: Charles C. Thomas.

Eysenck, H.J. and Eysenck, M.W. (1985) *Personality and Individual Differences.* New York: Plenum Press.

Eysenck, M.W. (1977) *Human Memory: Theory, Research and Individual Differences.* Oxford: Pergamon Press.

Eysenck, M.W. (1982) *Attention and Arousal: Cognition and Performance.* New York: Springer.

Freud, S. (1936) *The Ego and the Mechanisms of Defence.* London: Hogarth Press.

Gale, A. (1973) The psychophysiology of individual differences: studies of extraversion–introversion and the EEG. In P. Kline (ed.), *New Approaches in Psychological Measurement.* Chichester: John Wiley & Sons.

Gale, A. (1981) EEG studies of extraversion–introversion: What's the next step? In R. Lynn (ed.), *Dimensions of Personality: Essays in Honour of H.J. Eysenck.* Oxford: Pergamon Press.

Gale, A. (1987a) Arousal, control, energetics and values: An attempt at review and appraisal. In J. Strelau and H.J. Eysenck (eds), *Personality Dimensions and Arousal.* New York: Plenum.

Gale, A. (1987b) The psychophysiological context. In A. Gale and B. Christie (eds), *Psychophysiology and the Electronic Workplace.* Chichester: John Wiley & Sons.

Gale, A. and Edwards, J.A. (1983a) EEG and human behaviour. In A. Gale and J.A. Edwards (eds), *Physiological Correlates of Human Behaviour. Volume 2. Attention and Performance.* New York: Academic Press.

Gale, A. and Edwards, J.A. (1983b) *Physiological Correlates of Human Behavior.* Volumes 1, 2 and 3. New York: Academic Press.

Gale, A. and Edwards, J.A. (1983c) A short critique of the psychophysiology of individual differences. *Personality and Individual Differences,* **4**, 429–435.

Gale, A. and Edwards, J.A. (1986) Individual differences. In M.G.H. Coles, E. Donchin and S.W. Porges (eds), *Psychophysiology: Systems, Processes and Applications.* New York: Guilford Press.

Gale, A., Strelau, S. and Farley, F.H. (1985) Introduction, overview and critique. In J. Strelau, F.H. Farley and A. Gale (eds), *The Biological Bases of Personality and Behavior: Theories, Measurement Techniques and Development.* New York: Hemisphere Press.

Garber, H.J., Weilburg, J.B., Duffy, F.H. and Manschreck, T.C. (1989) Clinical use of topographic brain electrical activity mapping in psychiatry. *Journal of Clinical Psychiatry,* **50**, 205–211.

Gray, J.A. (1982) *The Neuropsychology of Anxiety: An Enquiry into the Functions of the Septo-hippocampal System.* Oxford: Oxford University Press.

Gray, J.A. (1983) Anxiety, personality and the brain. In A. Gale and J.A. Edwards (eds), *Physiological Correlates of Human Behavior. Volume 3. Individual Differences and Psychopathology.* New York: Academic Press.

Greenfield, N.S. and Sternbach, R.A. (eds) (1972) *Handbook of Psychophysiology.* New York: Holt, Rinehart & Winston.

Hare, R.D. (1978) Electrodermal and cardiovascular correlates of psychopathy. In R.D. Hare and D. Schalling (eds), *Psychopathic Behaviour: Approaches to Research.* Chichester: John Wiley & Sons.

Hodgson, R. and Rachman, S. (1974) Desynchrony in measures of fear. *Behaviour Research and Therapy,* **12**, 319–326.

Hull, C.L. (1943) *Principles of Behavior.* New York: Appleton-Century-Crofts.

Jennings, J.R. and Coles, M.G.H. (1991) *Handbook of Cognitive Psychophysiology: Central and Autonomic Nervous System Approaches.* Chichester: John Wiley & Sons.

Johnson, A. and Anderson, E. (1990) Stress and arousal. In J.T. Cacioppo and L.G. Tassinary (eds), *Principles of Psychophysiology: Physical, Social and Inferential Elements.* Cambridge: Cambridge University Press.

Lacey, J.I. (1967) Somatic response patterning and stress: Some revisions of activation theory. In M.H. Appley and R. Trumbull (eds), *Psychological Stress: Issues in Research.* New York: Appleton-Century-Crofts.

Levey, A.B. and Martin, I. (1991) Psychophysiology and the inner world. *Journal of Psychophysiology*, **5**, 1–3.

Lindsley, D.B. (1952) Psychological phenomena and the electroencephalogram. *Electroencephalography and Clinical Neurophysiology*, **4**, 443–456.

Mackay, C.J. (1980) The measurement of mood and psychophysiological activity using self-report techniques. In I. Martin and P.H. Venables (eds), *Techniques in Psychophysiology.* Chichester: John Wiley & Sons.

Mackay, C.J. (1987) Self-report techniques. In A. Gale and B. Christie (eds) *Psychophysiology and the Electronic Workplace.* Chichester: John Wiley & Sons.

Malmo, R.B. (1959) Activation: a neurophysiological dimension. *Psychological Review*, **66**, 367–386.

Martin, I. and Venables, P.H. (1980) *Techniques in Psychophysiology.* Chichester: John Wiley & Sons.

Matysiak, J. (1986) Self-exposure to sensory stimuli in rats as activity motivated by the sensory drive. In J. Strelau, F.H. Farley and A. Gale (eds), *The Biological Bases of Personality and Behavior: Psychophysiology, Performance and Application.* New York: Hemisphere Press.

Moruzzi, G. and Magoun, H.W. (1949) Brain stem reticular formation and activation of the EEG. *Electroencephalography and Clinical Neurophysiology*, **1**, 455–473.

Royce, J.R. and Powell, A. (1985) An overview of Multifactor System Theory. In J. Strelau, F.H. Farley and A. Gale (eds), *The Biological Bases of Personality and Behavior: Theories, Measurement Techniques and Development.* New York: Hemisphere Press.

Selye, H. (1936) A syndrome produced by diverse noxious agents. *Nature*, **138**, 32.

Strelau, J. (1983) *Temperament — Personality — Activity.* London: Academic Press.

Strelau, J. (1987) Personality dimensions based on arousal theories: Search for integration. In J. Strelau and H.J. Eysenck (eds), *Personality Dimensions and Arousal.* New York: Plenum.

Strube, M.J. (1990) Psychometric principles: from physiological data to psychological constructs. In J.T. Cacioppo and L.G. Tassinary (eds), *Principles of Psychophysiology: Physical, Social and Inferential Elements.* Cambridge: Cambridge University Press.

Strube, M.J. (ed.) (1991) *Type A Behavior.* Newbury Park, Cal.: Sage.

Thayer, R.E. (1985) Activation (arousal): the shift from a single to a multidimensional perspective. In J. Strelau, F.H. Farley and A. Gale (eds), *The Biological Bases of Personality and Behavior: Theories, Measurement Techniques and Development.* New York: Hemisphere Press.

Turpin, G. (1983) Psychopathology and the social environment. In A. Gale and J.A. Edwards (eds), *Physiological Correlates of Human Behavior. Volume 3. Individual Differences and Psychopathology.* New York: Academic Press.

Turpin, G. (1990) Ambulatory clinical psychophysiology: an introduction to techniques and methodological issues. *Journal of Psychophysiology*, **4**, 299–304.

Venables, P.H. (1974) Arousal: an examination of its status as a concept. In M.G.H. Coles, J.R. Jennings and J.P. Stern (eds), *Psychophysiological Perspectives.* New York: Van Nostrand.

Venables, P.H. and Martin, I. (1967) *A Manual of Psychophysiology.* Amsterdam: North-Holland.

Wagner, H.L. (ed.) (1988) *Social Psychophysiology and Emotion: Theory and Clinical Applications.* Chichester: John Wiley & Sons.
Wagner, H.L. and Manstead, A. (1989) *Handbook of Social Psychophysiology*. Chichester: John Wiley & Sons.
Weinberger, D.A., Schwartz, G.E. and Davidson, R.J. (1979) Low-anxious, high-anxious and repressive coping styles: psychometric patterns and behavioral and physiological responses to stress. *Journal of Abnormal Psychology*, **88**, 369–380.
Zuckerman, M. (1979) *Sensation-seeking: Beyond the Optimum Level of Arousal.* Hillsdale, NJ: Erlbaum.

Chapter 2

Biochemistry:
Individual Differences and Psychonutrition

Steve Van Toller

Warwick Human Chemoreception Research Group, Department of Psychology, University of Warwick, Coventry, Warwickshire, UK CU4 7AL

ABSTRACT

With notable exceptions psychology has tended to overlook variations in the various measures it has used, electing instead to operate in terms of group data and averages; tending to discard outliers in data sets as irrelevant or unexplainable. In the early years of this century most researchers in experimental psychology firmly placed their trust in a concept related to the "normal"; however, fortunately this trend is slowly reversing and interest is reviving in the individual case. This chapter is concerned to raise questions about the value of the concept "normal" and to draw attention to the range of individual variations and to consider some of the factors, particularly biochemical, that might produce or exacerbate variation. Over a period of some eighty years Roger Williams, doyen of the study of individual differences, collected data showing the wide ranges of both bodily sizes and activity. Williams concluded that his findings made the case for a refinement in the concept of "normality". After an initial discussion considering the literature on bodily types and anatomical variations the chapter goes on to look at the interaction between genetics and biochemistry before considering the role of metabolic errors and the variations they produce in behaviour. Biochemical reactions are also sensitive to a wide range of external factors such as psychoecological

Handbook of Individual Differences: Biological Perspectives
Edited by Anthony Gale and Michael W. Eysenck

disorders which include diet-induced behavioural problems. These factors are examined for the evidence that they cause behavioural difficulties. The concept of "normal" owes more to a convenience or statistical concept than it does to reality and we should realize the limitations imposed by its use.

INTRODUCTION

In an article on insanity published in the ninth edition of the *Encyclopaedia Britannica* (1881) the author stated:

> It is generally accepted that the brain is the organ through which mental phenomena are manifested, and therefore that it is impossible to conceive of the existence of an insane mind in a healthy brain.

This presents a black-and-white case and clearly the author was not concerned with subtle differences. Yet shortly after this statement was published, Thudichum (1884) put forward the idea that differences in the fatty tissues of the brain were correlated with abnormal behaviours. Thudichum's book presaged the beginnings of scientific investigation into the processes of the brain and individual differences but progress in this area was slow and over one hundred years later we still have a limited understanding of how metabolic activity affects behaviour. The average human brain is approximately 3% of the total body weight but in a resting body state it accounts for 20% of the heat production from that body. This heat is generated from the metabolic processes occurring in the brain. However, despite the fact that many of the quantifiable electrical signals used by psychophysiologists are based on underlying metabolic reactions a limited amount of attention has been paid to biochemical concepts. Only slowly are we beginning to reach a position where we are concerned to examine the extent by which behavioural differences might be due to underlying biochemical reactions. Van Toller (1983) has written an introductory account of the biochemistry for psychologists and interested readers should consult one of the many introductions to biochemistry (Conn *et al.*, 1987; Lehninger, 1982; Newsholme and Leech, 1983). A useful biochemistry book based on a case-orientated approach has been published by Montgomery *et al.* (1980).

There have been a number of attempts to categorize humans—what we might call type theories—with most involving relatively rigid classifications, ignoring variabilities. The first was made by Hippocrates who separated men into just two categories: short, heavy and strong; tall, slight and weak. The two types were held to be susceptible to different diseases. Hippocrates also argued that there were four basic types of temperament associated with four bodily fluids. Kretschmer (1921) used 4000 photographs and divided bodily types into four categories: the compact pyknic types; strong athletic types;

fragile asthenic types; mixed dysplastic types. Sheldon, Stevens and Tucker (1940) and Sheldon and Stevens (1942) using factor analysis produced a theory of temperaments based on bodily types relating to various embryonic tissues. These were: the comfort loving viscerotonics who derived from the endomorphic tissues; the assertive, competitive somatotonics who derived from the mesomorphic or muscular tissues of the embryo; the temperamental types, who were the emotionally restrained cerebrotonics who derived from the outer layers or ectomorphic tissues of the embryo. Sheldon's types were broad classifications which failed to take fully into account the intermediate or mixed types and we may presume that pure physical types, both in physique and temperament, are the exception rather than the rule. Indeed, subsequent workers have failed to confirm Sheldon's original findings. For example, Rees and Eysenck (1945) in a factorial follow-up study concluded that the exclusive categories they had created needed to be abandoned in favour of continuous variation. Rees (1973) has reviewed this literature and totally rejected Sheldon's position of discrete categories for one involving variation.

ANATOMICAL VARIATIONS

Anatomical variability is another aspect that has escaped the attention it deserves. Despite familiarity with the normal curve with its suggestion of underlying variability lying along the percentile points of the abcissa, few psychological models take account of the underlying variability. On 20 February 1988, Roger Williams, the doyen of the study of individual differences, died at the age of 94 years. Williams spent much of his life discovering reports relating to individual variations and in doing so pointed to the need to refine the accepted concept of "normality". His collected wisdom is published in two books (Williams, 1956, 1967) in which he is concerned to show that the concept of "the standard" body with its "standard" internal biochemical reactions is far from reality. He points out that too often we forget that the concept of normality is statistical; for example, the mythical average family with 2.54 children. It is probable that the age of mass production with its critical reliance upon standardization has led us to make tacit assumptions that the human body is similarly standardized. This is far from the case and Williams claimed that individuals have four or five metabolic defects in their bodies.

Data relating to variation has been available; for example, Anson (1951) in an atlas of human anatomy produces evidence of marked variations in human organs. The oesophagus can show a fourfold variation in width and this will obviously have a profound effect on swallowing behaviour and eating speed is, in part, related to the width of the oesophagus. The human stomach may show a six- to eight-fold variation in size. This is perhaps not too surprising as the stomach is very elastic and it can be considerably enlarged as we observe in the expanded shape of the habitual beer drinker. However, stomach sizes and shapes show marked differences at birth. The human heart is not built to a standard size and pattern. Similarly the brain shows marked variations in size and activity. To illustrate this bodily variation Anson devotes two full pages to showing the differences found in the extensor muscles of the index finger. The small muscles of the fingers like other muscles in the body are far from assembly-line-look-alikes. It is indeed likely that, given the necessary and critical opportunities, the skilled hands of the concert hall pianist are to a large degree born.

Despite these facts we tend to assume that the internal physiological organs are all more or less of a standard size and shape. In part, the problem probably relates to the human propensity for egocentricity. Tengenev, the Russian novelist, made this point succinctly when he stated:

> a man is capable of understanding anything—how the ether vibrates and what's going on in the sun—but how any man can blow his nose differently from him, that he is incapable of understanding.

Williams in his two books is at pains to point out that to overlook variation in structure and function by subsuming it into an average value is to restrict comprehension of what it is we seek to understand. Lashley (1947) was one of the very few psychologists to have considered and have written about the problem of variation in the nervous system. In his conclusion about the rat's brain he stated his considered view with the following words:

> The brain is extremely variable in every character that has been subjected to measurement . . . some of the structural variations have been shown to correlate with functional disturbances. . . . From what is known of the variations in other systems, it may be concluded that the variants which produce pathological symptoms are not discontinuous characters but are the extremes of a normal distribution. Lesser deviations in the same direction, resulting in behaviour which is not classified as pathological, are to be expected. . . . The heredity of the smaller variants has not been studied and we can only argue their probable genetic determination by analogy with variations in more readily observed strucures. . . . Even the limited evidence at hand, however, shows that individuals start life with brains differing enormously in structure. . . . The correlation of variations with behaviour presents much greater difficulties. Yet I believe that the results of such studies will repay the labour.

Cannon (1932) wrote a book that became very influential in the later developing areas of cybernetics, in which he described the inbuilt mechanisms that regulate the vital functions of the autonomic nervous system. This particular concept tended to convey the idea of standardization but Cannon was aware of the idiosyncratic and variable nature of the autonomic nervous system (Cannon and Rosenblueth, 1949). Unfortunately he failed to consider how these vagaries of the autonomic nervous system might relate to behaviour. In addition, Cannon indicated that differences he described were peculiar to the autonomic nervous system rather than a general fact or concerning the nervous system (Van Toller, 1978). Ader, Felten and Cohen (1990) have drawn attention to the interaction between the immunological system and the brain; clearly this is an important area relating to individual variations to stress immunity.

GENETICS

Basic biochemical processes are laid down by the genetic processes (a genetic disease is, by definition, a biochemical disease) and we need briefly to consider this aspect. Genetics as a topic is either ignored or used as a tautological explanation, usually expressed as a correlation (Thompson, 1988) but such correlations indicate genetic predisposition rather than causation. In any event, inheritance is polygenetic and profoundly influenced by inputs from the environment (Hahn *et al.*, 1990). This input is not a passive inert one-way process because organisms will seek out aspects of the environment that are required or found attractive. As suggested previously, the skilled muscles of the concert pianist require genetic endowment plus an appropriate environment for the ability to express itself.

Mendel (1822–1884), by fertilizing and growing varieties of peas with pronounced physical differences, demonstrated that the differences in the peas were under the control of genes (he called them particulates). He demonstrated that each physical characteristic was controlled by a pair of genes (phenotypes) created by equal contributions from each parent. The genes existed in two or more alternate forms now called alleles (e.g. AA, Aa, aA, aa). Identical copies (AA) of the same gene are called homozygous and different copies (Aa) are called heterozygous. One of the pair of an allele may be dominant, while the other is a recessive gene. The dominant gene controls the nature of the phenotype. Whilst only one copy of the inherited genotype will be used by an individual, the alternative or recessive forms will be copied and passed on to any offspring where they may or may not be expressed. The total collection of genes within an individual is called the genotype.

Although the basics of genetics was demonstrated almost in its entirety by Gregor Mendel the detailed biochemical cellular mechanisms have only been worked out in considerable detail during the last three decades. The basic unit of genetic information is deoxyribonucleic acid (DNA); complex strings of DNA form the genes which are the basis of the genetic code. Genes are organized into chromosomes and all cells in the human body contain a certain number of paired chromosomes which represent the information inherited by each individual. Each species has a characteristic number of chromosomes: for example, in humans the number of chromosomes is 46 in 23 pairs; in the rat the number is 42 in 21 pairs. The number of chromosomes inherited is critical; in Down's syndrome (Mongolism) the defects arise from an additional 47th chromosome.

On 22 of the chromosomes, the genes are arranged so that the gene for a given trait is found on the corresponding segment of the pair. Genes on the 23rd chromosome are sex-linked with the female X and/or the male Y chromosome. The DNA in cells about to reproduce duplicates itself in a process called mitosis, and the developing new cells receive identical copies of the DNA genetic information. In reproductive cells, division involves a more complex process called meiosis. During meiosis, which occurs shortly before cellular division, genes are randomly exchanged between the pairs of chromosomes through a random breaking of the chromosomes as the pairs separate. Four new cells are produced with each twin cell containing one set of about 50% of the original genetic information. The process of fertilization or conception brings these 23 chromosomes together with another randomly assorted 23 chromosomes from the sexual partner. What particular genotypical traits are found in the offspring depends upon a number of factors. Some of these relate to the dominant and recessive genes but it is known that individuals can display a mixture of genes called intermediate heterozygosity. Of particular interest to this chapter are the genes that are dormant unless triggered by the environment. An example of this would be an allergy produced by exposure to specific environmental substances or toxins. The point is that genetic interactions show considerable levels of plasticity. One is reminded of the story of a well-known beauty queen who wrote to the critic and famous writer George Bernard Shaw saying that with her body and his brain the two of them should get together to produce the perfect child. Shaw, who was a tall skinny man is reported to have replied, "But what madam if the child has my body and your brain?"

Most genetic diseases are inherited as homozygotic recessive abnormalities with the affected person receiving defective genes from both parents. A homozygotic gene will affect one in four of the siblings from a common union. The more complex heterozygous genetic diseases arise because of a defective allele from one of the two parents. A further genetic related problem may arise because a patient inherits two different alleles which result in enzyme deficiencies via an interaction called compound heterozygosity. In general, a simple heterozygote carrying a single abnormal gene will be revealed by a partial deficiency of an enzyme system causing a minor metabolic disturbance. For example, parents of phenylketonuric children often have blood phenylalanine levels that are above the average population level suggesting a partial deficiency of the enzyme phenylalanine hydroxylase in the livers of the parents. The level of the parents will be in the range of one to one-and-a-half times above the average population value whereas a phenylketonuric child will show elevated levels of thirty times or more. We will return to this concept of differential sensitivity when we come to consider food intake.

Thus the genetic predisposition of an individual will determine his/her bodily metabolic activity and these reactions will, in turn, influence the formation and functional levels of the nervous system which affect behavioural characteristics. Genetically identical twins could provide a fascinating insight into biochemical genetics and many of the incredible coincidences reported about identical twins can probably be attributed to biochemical and nervous system similarities. With their shared genetic similarities twins are likely to develop similar dispositions that may be expressed at critical maturational points in their life cycles. For example, if two male identical twins, separated from birth, wear a hat because genetically determined thinning hair causes them to have cold heads and both twins have a genetic perceptual predisposition that results in the aesthetic favouring of tartan patterns, it should not be too surprising to find them both having selected tartan caps to solve their body temperature problem. Identical twins will differ in the degree of genetic identicality they share but their communality will be greater than that found in fraternal twins or non-twin siblings. As such they are an especially valuable source when considering individual differences and it is to be hoped that researchers will consider this aspect in future investigations. Wilson (1972) has reported similar biochemical activity in terms of spurts and plateaux in identical twins.

Children adopted shortly after birth and raised away from their biological parents provide interesting cases because in this situation we have the genetic predisposition modified by the adopting parents who provide the learning experiences and act as role models. Mednick and Hutchings (1978), carried out a study in Denmark examining the effect of criminal tendencies in either the biological or the adopting fathers. Where neither of the fathers had criminal records about 10% of the sons acquired criminal records. At the other extreme, where both fathers had criminal records, the incidence in the sons rose to about 36%. Where the biological father but not the adopting father had a criminal record the incidence was 21%. In the reverse situation where the adopting but not the biological father had a criminal record, the incidence was about the same level as where neither father had a criminal record. However, even in the extreme case where both fathers had criminal records, the majority of the boys studied did not acquire criminal records. Crowe (1975) has shown a similar pattern of genetic influence in children with mothers having criminal records. This study involved children of both sexes who were adopted at a mean age of four months.

INBORN ERRORS OF METABOLISM AND VARIABILITY

The term ''inborn errors of metabolism'' was coined by Garrod (1909) in a book of that name. This insight arose from study of a condition known as alkaptonuria which is characterized by urinary excretion of homogentisic acid. This substance is not normally found in urine but alkaptonurics excrete several grams each day. It is a dramatic condition because although the sufferer's urine is the normal colour when excreted, oxidation of the homogentisic acid rapidly causes it to turn black; hence, the disorder is readily recognized in babies. Alkaptonurics are usually quite healthy although in later life they are prone to develop arthritis. Garrod noticed that if he fed homogentisic acid to non-sufferers they were able to metabolize it readily and none was excreted in their urine. However, if he fed homogentisic acid to alkaptonuric patients they excreted increased urinary levels. In addition he showed that excreted levels were increased by augmented feeding with proteins and that the effect was due to the aromatic amino acids, phenylalanine and tyrosine. Garrod inferred that homogentisic acid was an intermediate enzyme in the phenylalanine and tyrosine metabolic pathway. His assumptions were correct but it was not until 50 years later that the enzymatic process was finally demonstrated by taking liver biopsies from alkaptonurics. Garrod also drew attention to the familial distribution of this condition, concluding that the condition arose from a congenital deficiency of a particular enzyme due to a recessive Mendelian gene. The importance of the concept advanced by Garrod was that the normal allele of this particular gene must be necessary for the formation of a particular enzyme in a normal person.

Williams discusses what he calls the genotropic concept of biochemical individuality. By this term he means an interplay of genetic, biochemical, physiological and other factors that influence the complex myriad of chemical processes found in the body. In a chapter on biochemical individuality Williams lists a whole range of values in different physiological organs, muscles and bones. These show marked differences from average values for both chemical and biochemical substances with characteristic values differing considerably in individuals from accepted normal values. In addition, Williams discovered differences of 10- to 50-fold reported in the literature denoting marked variations in metabolic processes between individuals. Endocrines show similar variations and Williams concludes that the idea of normal hormonal levels with freaks departing from the normal state, is clearly untenable.

Williams, Brown and Shideler (1955) offer graphic examples of biochemical variability in an experiment carried out involving male subjects giving five or six samples of blood at weekly intervals under basal conditions. Samples were analysed for sugar, lactic acid, urea, creatinine, uric acid, inorganic phosphates, amylase, lipase, acid phosphatase, alkaline phosphatase and acetylcholinesterase. For some of the biochemical tests the obtained values were within the average population range but this was not the case for all the values obtained. One individual showed a consistently low blood sugar level on every reading. Another showed a high uric acid count, with all values above the normal range. A third exhibited serum amylase values below what would normally be considered acceptable. A fourth had consistently high alkaline phosphatase values. Finally, a fifth person exhibited acetylcholinesterase levels well above average. In addition to high or low values shown by some subjects, large intersubjective variations were found. One subject showed a two-fold spread in his blood creatinine values whilst another gave six identical readings.

Genetic abnormalities in child development have been reviewed by Horowitz (1975), and patterns of inheritance, calculation of genetic risk, as well as many examples are given in his volume. Horowitz points out that many of the 2000 or so known genetic diseases have multisystem effects. Some may affect a child immediately; others, like Huntington's chorea, may not manifest themselves until the third or fourth decade of life. A recent example in a multiauthored paper suggested that a mutation in the amyloid percursor protein has an effect on the development of Alzheimer's disease (Goate *et al.*, 1991). There are also ethnic genetic differences and these can be quite marked. For example, most Chinese shun milk products; in part, this is due to their digestive biology and they tend to lack or show deficiencies in the enzyme required to digest the milk sugar, galactose. Chinese also tend to show very low thresholds for alcohol and, accordingly, they drink little alcohol. One behavioural consequence of this is that drunkenness does not present the same severe problems for the Chinese as it does for the Western societies. Environments also favour certain genetic predispositions; for example, it is known that many Asiatic peoples experience calcium levels that would be considered inadequate in the Western world. Clearly this type of environment would genetically favour people with low demands for calcium. Those with higher bodily demands for calcium would be handicapped by their deficiency and probably eventually be eliminated from the genetic pool making up that particular population. Consideration of this aspect in relation to child development can be found in Scarr and McCartney (1983).

Probably the most well-known biochemical disease found in babies is phenylketonuria. This genetic disease is caused by an autosomal recessive gene carried by approximately 2% of the population. It occurs in 1/10 000 births and is the most common of the amino acidurias and a number of abnormal phenylalanine metabolites are found in the urine of sufferers. Because of lack of pigmentation these babies have blond hair, with blue eyes and fair skin. However, if untreated they suffer mental retardation; losses of one IQ point for each week the biochemical abnormality remains undetected have been quoted. The condition is treated by placing the infant on an unpleasant tasting diet low in phenylalanine. It has not yet been finally established if the diet needs to be given permanently or if there is a critical period of development, which, once passed, means that these children can revert to a normal diet. The exact cause of mental retardation in these sufferers has not been established but high levels of phenylalanine are known to interfere with synthesis of the important biogenic amine serotonin which is found in low levels in phenylketonuric infants.

Another genetic disease involving a defect in an autosomal recessive gene is galactosaemia. Galactosaemic babies have very fair hair and display the attractive physical features that were noted for phenylketonurics. In galactosaemia the biochemical problem arises from an inability to utilize D-galactose to D-glucose. The disaccharide lactose is the main carbohydrate in milk. Treatment is to exclude milk from the diets of these infants. It is thought that some capacity to metabolize ingested D-galactose occurs in later life. At the other extreme of the life cycle is Huntington's chorea which does not manifest itself unless the person lives until middle age. This has meant that in the past the defective genotype has been passed on to offspring without awareness. Huntington's chorea is a progressive degenerative disease of the nervous tissue involving a spasmodic movement disorder and dementia. The involuntary movements can become extremely violent and require immobilization of the patient during the terminal stages of the illness.

At a more specific level, Harris (1966) demonstrated that if red blood cell acid phosphatases levels were measured in a randomly selected sample of individuals, an apparently continuous unimodel distribution was obtained. However, this apparently smooth distribution is a summation of a series of separate but overlapping distributions, each corresponding to a discrete phenotype. Furthermore, most of the variance in the distribution can be attributed to three alleles. This finding suggests that many, if not all, examples of quantitative enzyme variation may have a similar genetic variation. The distribution of red cell phosphatase found by Harris is shown in Figure 2.1.

Most of the examples given so far involve proteins but in addition there are classes of genetic error involving carbohydrate metabolism. Glycogen is composed of very complex macromolecules with many branches giving a high potential for metabolic defects. In addition, within individual cells there are stored large numbers of hydrolytic enzymes and to keep them isolated from the cellular metabolism processes until required they are kept in lysomes. There are a number of known diseases related to defects in this particular cellular storage system. Returning to the point where this chapter started, namely, Thudichum, a well-known class of genetic error is the sphingolipidoses (these are long chains of base lipids or fats) where different members of the sphingolipids are accumulated. Examples of this class of genetic defect are Tay–Sachs disease and Sandhoff's disease in which the accumulation of a ganglioside called GM2 is found in the brain. This biochemical defect arises from an inability to cleave a terminal residue from

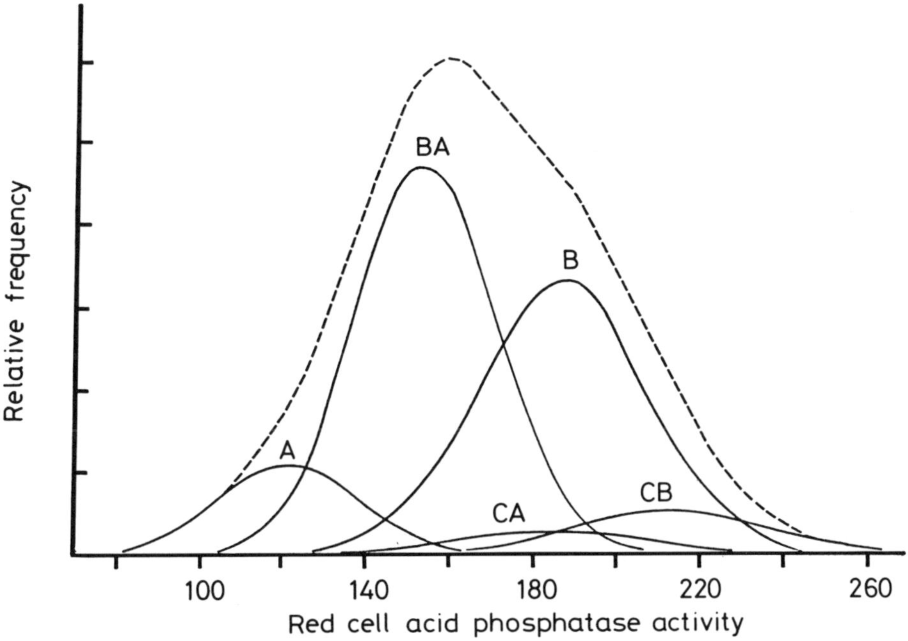

Figure 2.1. Drawings of the four discrete distributions (A, BA, B, CA) that make up the apparently smooth total distribution shown under the dotted line. Most of the variance shown in this figure can be attributed to three alleles. (Reproduced from Harris (1966) by permission of Elsevier Science Publishers.)

carbohydrate chains. Previously it was thought that this class of genetic defect was homogeneous but systematic investigation has revealed a considerable degree of unsuspected genetic heterogeneity (Harris, 1980).

Acute porphyria is an example of a disease due to a genetically caused partial enzyme deficiency. Porphyrins are natural pigments that occur in bile and haem and they have the ability to combine with metal ions and nitrogenous substances. There are at least four known conditions relating to this disorder. Another class of biochemical defect is found within the receptors on cellular membranes with receptors failing to respond to signals from molecules in the extracellular fluid. Failure to react to these external signals can produce biochemical defects within the cell. Alternatively, receptors may not form properly, be produced in limited numbers or distorted. All of these defects can affect metabolic processing and rate. Thus, there are a number of cellular membrane defects that can give rise to metabolic disturbances. There is also a condition resulting in high cholesterol levels arising from defects in the active transport system of fats within the body. This type of secondary metabolic disorders will, in general, be more difficult to identify than the classic single defective enzyme, but can be just as profound in their effects.

A further class of malfunction involves consideration of biochemical errors affecting drug metabolism. Tolerance levels of individuals to drugs would be a simple example. It has long been axiomatic in psychopharmacology that individual reactions to drugs are very variable with people showing marked idiosyncratic responses (Kruk and Pycock, 1979) and more recently Holaday (1985) has discussed this point in relation to endogenous opioids. Finally, there are the converse examples where increased enzymatic activity can lead to disease by causing increased metabolic rates. Harris (1980) contains two excellent review chapters concerning inborn errors of metabolism and their related biochemistry and he gives a number of specific examples.

SMELL AND BIOCHEMICAL DISORDERS

Mace *et al.* (1976) and Smith, Smith and Levinson (1982) have drawn attention to the lost skills of physicians who formerly made use of their sense of smell in diagnosing patients' ailments. This skill related to the ability to detect odours on the patient's breath denoting underlying metabolic disorders. For example, the smell of acetone on the breath of a child would lead to suspicion of a condition of diabetic keto-acidosis. Phenylketonuria is associated with a mousy, musty or horse-like odour. The smell of maple syrup would indicate a urinary disease, which, unless identified and treated promptly, leads to seizures and eventual coma. Dietary restriction to treat this sweet-smelling disease involves reduction of branch-chained amino acids to minimal daily requirements. Infants who are not diagnosed early enough tend to show motor rather than the mental disturbances found in phenylketonuric children. The aromatic, diagnostic table presented by Mace and his colleagues is reproduced in Table 2.1. Al-Waiz *et al.* (1988) have identified a "fish-odour syndrome" in certain patients that is caused by a biochemical inability to break down the chemical trimethylamine that is responsible for "fishy" smells. Not surprisingly, sufferers are reported as tending to lead lonely lives. The authors of this paper estimate that there are about 250 000 carriers in the UK of the gene responsible for the fish-odour syndrome and between two to three thousand sufferers. Clearly this is one biochemical defect that can have profound behavioural effects. Smells and their effects on behaviour is a much neglected area of sensory psychology (Van Toller, 1988; Van Toller and Dodd, 1988).

GROUP DIFFERENCES AND BIOCHEMISTRY

Rosenzweig, Kretch and Bennett (1960) examined the relationship between groups of rats selected for their ability to solve problems and cerebral cholinesterase. Cholinesterase (ChE) is the enzyme that deactivates the

Table 2.1. Metabolic disorders reported to be associated with unusual odours of the breath. (Table taken from Mace *et al.*, 1976, with permission of the Editor of *Clinical Pediatrics.*)

Disease	Enzyme defect	Odour	Clinical features	Treatment
Diabetes mellitus	Lack of insulin or insulin activity	Acetone on breath	Polyuria, polyphagia, polydipsia, weight loss, acidosis, coma	Insulin administration
Phenylketonuria	Phenylalanine hydroxylase	Musty, "mousy," "horsey"	Progressive mental retardation, eczema, decreased pigmentation, seizures, spasticity	Diet low in phenylalanine
Maple syrup urine disease	Branched chain decarboxylase	Maple syrup	Marked acidosis, seizures, coma leading to death in first year or two of life or mental subnormality without acidosis or intermittent acidosis without mental retardation	Diet low in branched chain amino acids. Protein restriction and/or thiamine in large doses
Oasthouse urine disease	Defective transport of methionine, branched chain amino acids, tyrosine, and phenylalanine	Yeast-like dried-celery-like	Mental retardation, spasticity, hyperpnoea, fever, oedema	Restrict methionine in diet
Odour of sweaty feet. Syndrome I	Isovaleryl CoA dehydrogenase	Sweaty feet	Recurrent bouts of acidosis, vomiting, dehydration, coma, aversion to protein foods	Restrict leucine in diet
Odour of Sweaty* feet. Syndrome II	Green acyl dehydrogenase	Sweaty feet	Onset of symptoms in first week of life with acidosis, dehydration, seizures and death	High CHO diet? Low fat diet?
Odour of cat's syndrome	Beta-methylcrotonyl-CoA carboxylase	Cat's urine	Neurologic disorder resembling Werdnig–Hoffmann's disease. Ketoacidosis, failure to thrive	Leucine restriction? Biotin administration
Fish odour syndrome	Unknown	Like dead fish	Stigmata of Turner's syndrome, neutropenia, recurrent infections, anaemia, splenomegaly	Unknown
Odour of rancid butter syndrome	Unknown	Rancid butter	Poor feeding, irritability, progressive neurologic deterioration with seizures and death. Hepatic dysfunction. Possible same as acute tyrosinosis	Response to decreased phenylalanine and tyrosine intake?

*There is evidence to suggest the subjects reported with this disorder actually had isovalericacidaemia.

transmitter substance acetylcholine (ACh) and it was argued that there should be a one-to-one relationship between the two substances. Rats in the group with greater ability on the selected tasks would have an overall greater cerebral synaptic activity and this would be reflected by increased levels of acetylcholinesterase. After failing to demonstrate a reliable correlation between acetylcholine levels in the brain and intelligence in rats, David Kretch in a mood of pessimism wrote:

> The first law of psychopharmacology is that no generalizations can be made about the biochemical control of the complex human mind. The second law is that there are many exceptions to the first law. The third law is that the first and second laws hold only for extreme cases, except where they do not hold.

This surely misses the point and merely states a case for the complexity of the biochemical processes in the brain. Biochemical and behavioural relationships are unlikely to be discovered by looking at overall levels of the most common transmitter substance found in the brain. In addition, the authors were placing their data into group averages and this would not give any indication of individual differences. The need surely is for qualitative investigations within specific and circumscribed regions of the brain within individual animals. Indeed, what we might well be looking for is an overall patterning of activity rather than total levels (Skarda and Freeman, 1987).

NUTRITION

Apart from genetics the greatest influence on the biochemistry of the body is via nutritional intake because to a large extent metabolism depends upon precursors which, in turn, depend upon dietary intake. In Western societies during the course of 24 hours the average intake of substances is about 1 kg of dry weight food, 3 kg of water and 15 kg of air. As individuals we have specific biochemical predispositions which lead us to seek out or avoid certain foods. Through experience individuals learn to avoid foods which do not agree with them. Pauling (1968) coined the term orthomolecular medicine to refer to the treatment of disease by varying the intake of molecules. The term means, "pertaining to the right molecule" and practitioners believe that treatment of illness should be a matter of varying and achieving the correct concentration of vitamins, trace elements, amino acids, enzymes and hormones etc. Philpott and Kalita (1980) have published a book dealing with brain allergies and treatments by orthomolecular means. Their book gives examples of the treatment and cites a number of cases and gives examples of regimens to be followed when testing for food allergies.

The discipline of biochemistry was founded during the second decade of this century and within another two decades some quite dramatic biochemical/behavioural breakthroughs had been achieved. Perhaps the most dramatic was the cure of pellagral psychosis. This psychosis (Carpenter, 1981) arises from a nutritional skin disease and at one time it was estimated that 400 000 Americans, mainly in the Mid-Western or corn-belt areas, suffered from this complaint. The problem arises from an inability adequately to synthesize niacin; this may be due to either infection or a poor diet. At that time a typical Mid-Western diet consisted of corn, which has a very low tryptophan content and it is this amino acid that serves as the substrate for much of the body's niacin requirements. The simple and dramatic cure, proposed by Spies in 1930, involved giving the sufferers a vitamin of the B complex. The disease was last seen in large numbers in the Japanese prisoner-of-war camps where the prisoners were fed a diet of polished rice. It is now a rarely observed illness found only in alcoholics or similar groups who characteristically have an unbalanced nutritional diet.

A second dramatic biochemical breakthrough came in 1947 when Gjessing demonstrated the relationship between bodily nitrogen metabolism and periodic catatonia. Periodic catatonia was said to account for 2% of schizophrenics. By careful measurements Gjessing was able to show that during periods of catatonia, body nitrogen levels were low, but during the patient's excitatory phases excessive excretion of urine nitrogen was observed. Gjessing showed that treatment with thyroxin combined with a low protein diet produced stable levels of bodily nitrogen and he was able to abolish the periodic swings of the psychosis in his patients. Sourkes (1962) has discussed the history of biochemistry and mental disease.

PSYCHO-ECOLOGICAL DISORDERS

Rippere (Rippere and Adams, 1982; Rippere, 1983; 1985) has been concerned to examine the effects of nutrition and diet on the behavioural problems of her patients. Rippere and Adams (1982) have stated that, although psychological disorders are heterogeneous, both in nature and causation, there are clear-cut classes of disorder caused by non-psychological agents which include organic, toxic, infectious, hormonal, nutritional (Fredericks, 1976), metabolic or immunological factors. The authors claim that all of these factors have been shown to play aetiological roles in mental dysfunctions and that, in some cases, treatment of mental disturbance by psychological treatments are inappropriate and ineffective. They feel that there is a demonstrated need to differentiate classes of ecological patients from classes of psychological patients. The latter patients respond to behavioural, and cognitive therapies but these traditional methods are inappropriate for ecological patients. As a result many ecological patients have been subjected to long periods of irrelevant treatment.

According to Rippere and Adams, ecological patients complain predominantly about episodic or chronic symptoms which are not directly related to psychological or social situations. These patients also tend to present a portmanteau of somatic complaints that previously in their case history would have been labelled as anxiety induced. The authors are at pains to state that they are not recommending replacement of traditional psychological methods but that their ecological methods should supplement those used by clinical psychologists. The short introductory article by Rippere and Adams (1982) provoked a negative correspondence in the *Bulletin of the British Psychological Society*. The substance of these follow-up letters appeared to be that an ecological approach was not felt to be appropriate and few, if any, clinical psychologists would have received training in the ecological approach. The letters were indicative of a hostile and unreceptive attitude towards ideas about biochemical and nutrient causes for behaviour problems.

On reading this review by Rippere and Adams I recalled the time during a teaching year in the late 1970s that I spent in America. We held a children's birthday party and to our surprise most of the young guests turned up clutching pieces of paper which contained detailed instructions about the amount of sugar they were allowed to eat and prescriptions about certain food colours they were not allowed to ingest (Conners, 1980). The experience was one of those unexpected cultural shocks you often experience when living for short periods in the USA. However, it caused me to peruse and think about the small body of scientific literature relating to allergies and behavioural problems caused by food intake. In addition to food, Urbach (1941) pointed out that smells could cause allergic responses to low concentrations. It should be pointed out that an air pollution concentration of 1 part per million (p.p.m.) amounts to an intake of pollutant of 10 mg per day or 3.65 gm each year. Urbach confined his remarks to natural smells but did include allergic responses to the smell of animals. He also noted that in certain cases he had shown an allergic response to a smell in the absence of hypersensitivity to pollen from trees and flowers. This extended his observations into non-biological causes.

Randolph (1970) demonstrated that odours of man-made materials could, indeed, produce allergic responses. He felt that, in particular, exposure to hydrocarbons could give rise to a variety of illnesses ranging from physical fatigue to depression. He presented a graphic example of the temper tantrums of an eight-year-old child whose behaviour was sufficient for him to be banned from school. By chance the child was moved for a period into his sister's bedroom and it was noted that his symptoms stopped but when he was put back into his own bedroom his symptoms reappeared. Investigations revealed that the symptoms had started the previous year and coincided with the installation of a gas-fire in the child's bedroom. A cure was effected by changing the heating system in his bedroom. Randolph also drew attention to the idea that many winter illnesses might be due to odours rather than infections. For example, patients had been shown to be allergic to the hydrocarbons released from Christmas fir trees. Berglund and Lindvall (1983) have also drawn attention to the fact that in considering the symptoms caused by a "sick building" attention should include detailed consideration of both the taste and smell sense. What remains to be clearly demonstrated is whether or not the observed reactions were simply the result of learned or conditioned emotional reactions. Urbach quoted earlier workers who had reported a case of extreme sensitivity to egg albumen. The patient suffered an attack in a room where, unknown to the patient, an egg had been cracked. Randolph pointed out that a patient's eating habits should be considered before arriving at a diagnosis. In common with drug users patients seek to alleviate withdrawal symptoms by eating the offending food which will then produce the allergic symptoms.

An overview of clinical ecology has been edited by Seely *et al.* (1985) and this book should be read by anyone with an interest in this developing area of research which has profound psychological implications. The various authors deal with aspects of a problem found mainly in affluent societies. In Western societies the prolongation of life as a consequence of an adequate diet is to a large degree countered by diseases that arise as a consequence of an over-rich diet. For example, diseases of the circulatory systems are virtually unknown in the poorer countries of the world, whereas in the prosperous countries, mortality from coronary disease begins by the third or fourth decade of life.

The most seemingly innocuous foods can produce problems in certain people. For example, coeliac disease is caused by bread. With the exception of certain parts of Ireland, where the incidence is about one in 300, the overall incidence is low, being about one in several thousand births. The problem for these sufferers arises from wheat which contains proteins called gliadins. Gliadins are toxic to intestinal tissues but in normal individuals the dose required to produce toxicity is very large. Although the exact physiological mechanisms causing coeliac disease are not known, sufferers show unusual sensitivity to the action of gliadin and treatment is provided by the patients eating a gluten-free diet. However, in a small proportion of patients it has been claimed that the symptoms are not alleviated by the removal of gluten (Freed and Seely, 1985). An analogous problem is found in cigarettes where the process of burning the tobacco produces the toxic material, cyanide. The threshold for the average person is high and the toxic threshold is not exceeded because the breakdown of cyanide is too rapid. However, in a very small proportion of extremely sensitive people cyanide levels produced from smoking a cigarette could be fatal.

FOOD RELATED PSYCHOLOGICAL DISORDERS

Freed (1985) quotes an incidence in the general population covering a range of 0.4 to 40% for food intolerances. The range is large because many sufferers have such obvious symptoms that they do not need to seek advice and produce their own cure by avoiding the offending foods. There is also a level of food intolerance where only slight symptoms are produced and these are undetected or tolerated by the sufferer. Symptoms which are attributed to other causes may be malaise, tiredness or transient depression. As Freed suggests, the few patients who do seek treatment may be the tip of a very large iceberg in that they represent only extreme cases.

Many plants produce poisonous alkaloids as a natural defence mechanism against attack by insects and herbivores and these can produce difficulties when ingested as foods, especially if the person eating the food has a low sensitivity to the alkaloid being ingested. Throughout recorded human history there have occurred massive outbreaks as a result of plant toxicity; an example was the outbreak of epidemics that came to be called the sacred flame disease. Sporadic outbreaks of this epidemic occurred for over a thousand years before the disease was finally shown to be caused by the rye fungus ergot, *Claviceps purpurea.* This plant grows alongside rye and if ground up with the rye grain produces a toxic flour containing fatal alkaloids. As most are aware, humans increasingly interfere with natural growth by using plant hormones and pest control agents and these can produce problems. These and other relevant points are discussed in detail by Silverstone (1985). It should be realized that often food allergies or individual intolerances will only occur when several factors present themselves. This is illustrated in a case where a patient with an allergy to shellfish showed symptoms only on days when he had been jogging (Maulitz, Pratt and Shocket, 1979). Strangely in many cases of food allergy the food causing the problem is a favourite of the patient. As mentioned earlier, patients with a food allergy experience withdrawal symptoms and eat the offending food in order to alleviate withdrawal symptoms. Freed (1985) has listed the most common problems encountered when attempting to diagnose and treat cases of food intolerance.

Food intolerance appears to be on the increase and one reason is almost certainly increased awareness resulting in people being knowledgeable about this type of problem. This means that they are more likely to report potential food intolerances to their doctors. It is difficult today to pick up a magazine and not find articles relating to the dangers of food and legislation is attempting to keep pace with the ever-growing list of revelations. The 1984 Food Labelling Regulations produce for the first time a list of the European-code (E-code) preservatives etc. being added to food products. United Kingdom food additives and their E-code numbers are listed and, in many cases, their physiological and behavioural effects summarized (Hanssen, 1984 and Hanssen and Marsden, 1987).

Rippere (1983) has produced a personal and informed account of her own considerable food intolerances and her related growing interest in clinical ecology. Apart from the personal and insightful aspects, the book gives examples of her questionnaires used to diagnose patients suffering from mental and behavioural disorders due to food intolerances. In a review Rippere (1984) has listed food intolerances in psychiatric patients under seven broad headings: cerebral allergy; food addiction; hypoglycaemias; caffeinism; hypersensitivity to chemical food additives; reactions to vasoactive amines in food; reactions to neuropeptides formed from food constituents.

Cerebral Allergy

The basic premise attributed to this heading is that antibodies can be evoked by food materials. Philpott and Kalita (1980) state that one third of cerebral allergic reactions are mediated by histamine which is released in response to the presence of antibodies produced to food peptides. The other two thirds of the allergic reactions are produced by inflammatory responses provoked by the presence of partially digested peptides derived from food.

Food Addiction

Rippere claims a high level of specific food addictions have been identified in routine screening of patients. She states that addicts to foods are recognized by the multiplicity of their symptoms with some reporting 30 or more. This multiplicity of symptoms often results in such food addicts being labelled as hypochondriacs. Treatment begins by getting patients to fill in a food diary to identify the foods which are most likely causing them problems. As pointed out, food addiction produces alternating stimulation and withdrawal symptoms (Randolf, 1976).

Hypoglycaemias

Psychological symptoms are associated with low blood sugar or hypoglycaemia and often include depression. The neuroglucopenic syndrome is often associated with patients who do not eat a breakfast and who may not eat very well during the rest of the day. In such people the blood sugar level is low and may dip below fasting levels. The adrenergic syndrome induced by low blood sugar levels is often diagnosed as a functional anxiety state. Rippere states that she has treated several agoraphobics who on examination were found to be suffering from reactive hypoglycaemia.

Caffeinism

Caffeine intoxication is now recognized as a psychiatric syndrome and classified as such in the *APA Diagnostic and Statistical Manual of Mental Disorders.* Two syndromes are listed. The first is acute intoxication which arises from excessive consumption of caffeine. Symptoms of this extreme state relate to sympathetic and central nervous system overarousal. They include restlessness, nervousness, excitement, insomnia, muscle twitching, as well as rambling thoughts and speech. Patients are normally shown to have had a recent consumption of caffeine in excess of 250 mg. Certain individuals with low thresholds of tolerance will exhibit symptoms at lower levels of caffeine consumption. The second caffeine syndrome concerns chronic addiction which arises from prolonged consumption. As with all addictions, attempts to alleviate the caffeine withdrawal symptoms will produce increasing consumption of the caffeine. It has also been found that overconsumption of caffeine can exacerbate existing pyschopathologies.

Hypersensitivity to Chemical Food Additives

Two classes of chemicals that have received detailed investigation are monosodium glutamate (MSG), a taste enhancer, and artificial dyes used in food colouring. MSG is associated with the Chinese Restaurant Syndrome or Kwok's disease, which is caused by the excessive use of MSG in certain types of Chinese cooking. Most sufferers experience a tightening around the top of the head but others may suffer from a headache. However, in extreme cases panic attacks may occur with feelings of depersonalization. The original hypothesis about the possible psychotoxicity of food dyes has not been fully confirmed (Harley *et al.*, 1978) but Rippere states that workers reporting treatments using individualized studies, report adverse behavioural effects in a large proportion of treated children. As emphasized at several points in this chapter we would expect a wide range of sensitivity in terms of response to chemical additives and certain children might be found to be extremely sensitive. As suggested in Hanssen (1984) caution is probably the best policy when dealing with children and we need to be aware of potential problems and to take action should they occur. A recent review of this area has been provided by Conners (1989).

Reactions to Vasoactive Amines in Food

Interest in certain foods, containing vasoactive amines, was aroused in the 1960s when monoamine oxidase inhibitor drugs were developed as antidepressants. Patients prescribed these drugs, often developed very high blood pressures which were traced to foods high in tyramines and other vasoactive amines. Typically these would be cheese, chocolate and pickled foods. Vasoactive amines can also precipitate headaches in migraine sufferers. The actual causes are not known but they appear to be related to immunological factors.

Reactions to Neuropeptides Formed from Food Constituents

Dohan (1980) reported a positive correlation between hospital admission for schizophrenia and the consumption of wheat in Scandinavia during the Second World War. Three explanations have been put forward to explain this correlation. The first is that wheat gluten impedes the absorption of neural active drugs. The second is that schizophrenics are allergic to cereal grains; some schizophrenics have been shown to produce serum antibodies to cereals. The third hypothesis is that schizophrenics are reactive to certain neuroactive peptides formed from food substances, in particular, the glutens in wheat. Dohan argues for the causal agent being a gliadin peptide which is the one mentioned earlier as causing digestive problems in coeliacs. Cross-species evidence for this position comes from Hemmings (1978) who found that rats fed with radioactively labelled gliadins showed that significant amounts of the labelled peptide had penetrated to the rats' brains. This indicates that these large peptides are probably able to penetrate the blood-brain barrier and reach critical central nervous system tissues.

What conclusions can be drawn from consideration of the developing area of clinical ecology? Clearly, responses to ingested food will vary over a wide continuum. However, it seems reasonable to suppose that certain individuals will show either defective metabolic mechanisms or have low levels of sensitivity or tolerance that will make them particularly vulnerable to certain foods. The exact percentage who are vulnerable to a degree to produce marked psychological impairment, is not known. However, there will be variations in these biochemical tolerances and these can be expected to have behavioural effects which will also range over a wide continuum from being virtually negligible to profound.

PERSONALITY AND BIOCHEMISTRY

In addition to biochemical effects on behaviour there are a number of psychological models which are based upon hypothetical physiological conceptions; examples can be found in the chapters by Eysenck (1983) and Gray (1983). The limited value of such models lies in the restricted and often hypothetical physiology postulated; also, they usually classify into exclusive categories rather than using a continuum which is found in normal physiological states. For example, Eysenck and Eysenck (1976) argued the case for a biological hypothesis for a P (psychoticism or tough-mindedness) dimension for their three dimension classificatory personality model on the grounds that males showed higher P scores. Furthermore, as aggressiveness was a component trait it was suggested that the hormone testosterone might play a role as the biological basis for the trait.

Zuckerman (1987) in a Presidential address to the Society for the Study of Individual Differences attempted to define Eysenck's P dimension under four headings: personality in terms of its constituent traits; biological correlates; genetic bases; relation to forms of psychopathy. He pointed out that most studies looking for neurochemical correlates with behaviour had tended to look at a single biological variable. Yet as he observed, single factors tend to interact with many other biological variables and it might be of value to run a factor analysis on a number of the relevant variables. For the P trait and a group of biological factors Zuckerman reported that subjects showing high P scores were characterized by a lack of behavioural control and tended to show poor conditioning and augmenting of cortical evoked potentials to high levels of stimulation. These subjects showed low levels of the enzymes, dopamine-B-hydroxylase (DBH) and monoamine oxidase (MAO), which regulate the monoamines. In addition, they showed low levels of serotonin and cortisol and high levels of testosterone and oestradiol. More than half the variance in P psychological traits and more than 80% of the variance in the correlated enzymes MOA and DBH was said to be determined by heredity. It must be remembered that the evidence relies heavily on correlations and cross-species comparisons, but evidence is accumulating which suggests the genetic/environment interaction is critical in the sense that individuals actively select certain aspects of the environment rather than being passively shaped by the environment in which they are placed. However, the environment is likely to have an overall influence on individuals who are intermediate in terms of genetic predisposition (Zuckerman, 1987). How physiological and psychological traits interact with the environment is still a problem that remains to be resolved by research workers in the areas of biopsychology (Eaves, Eysenck and Martin, 1989). The final answer is likely to be multidimensional in nature and will inevitably include detailed knowledge about the biosocial systems of human behaviour. In seeking this knowledge we will need to pay attention to the differences as well as the similarities of humans.

CONCLUSIONS

Pure psychological research is largely concerned with generalizations and tends to ignore variations, but in applied psychological studies the individual is of paramount concern and you ignore the individual at your peril. The range of the normal distribution in terms of biochemistry and many psychological variables ranges from extreme sensitivity to extreme insensitivity. The major problem using traditional psychological experimental techniques to examine individual differences lies in achieving sufficient numbers. The use of a central measure avoids the low numbers associated with the extremes of any distribution. For example, in toxicity there will be wide variation in the dose response reaction and to overcome this it is usual to select the LD_{50} response where half of the animals will die. But at this halfway point there will be a number of animals who would have died at much lower concentrations and survivors who would have survived dosages at the LD_{80} or the LD_{90} levels. The point is, they will be few in number but they exist and should be accounted for in a complete statement.

We are becoming sufficiently familiar with the idea of genetic fingerprinting to accept the idea that there is a unique genetic/biochemical pattern in individuals. This unique biochemical patterning will produce a unique metabolic pattern which will have behavioural effects. It is to be hoped that psychologists will eventually be able to incorporate such biochemical concepts into their understanding of behaviour and its abnormalities. Apart from the examples already given, there are many areas that remain to be explored by the scientific community. For example, what contribution do biochemical factors make to handedness? What major differences are there in terms of biochemistry between the left and right hemispheres? What is the role of metabolic activity in the brain for intelligence? Such questions raise problems relating to cause and effect; a chicken and egg problem of what came first. The answer is likely to be in terms of subtle genetic and environmental interactions.

The intelligent but absent-minded professor can be explained by preoccupation, but how can we explain an idiot savant, an extreme autistic, unable to comprehend the most elementary rules of social behaviour, yet capable of isolated prodigious mental feats? At the extremes the differences are very obvious but in between there are all types of other variations, some of which will be very subtle and probably overlooked. One person will be able to hold an accurate cognitive spatial map in his or her mind while another will lack this ability completely. Certain people have an easy facility with numbers while others are seemingly doomed consistently to make elementary arithmetical errors. How can we explain these differences? On what could they be based? Clearly, learning is involved and its effects can be very influential. A relevant and stimulating introduction will be positively rewarding whereas the converse may have served to produce fear and anxiety. Beneath the software influences lie genetic differences that involve basic biochemical reactions. One can only conclude by saying, happy are those who work in areas of their genetic strengths.

ACKNOWLEDGEMENTS

I should like to thank my colleague Dr G.H. Dodd for some observations and some suggested reference sources relating to this fascinating area.

REFERENCES

Ader, R., Felten, D. and Cohen, N. (1990) Interactions between the brain and the immune system. *Annual Review of Pharmacology and Toxicology*, **30**, 561–602.

Anson, B.J. (1951) *Atlas of Human Anatomy*. Philadelphia: W.B. Saunders.

Al-Waiz, M., Ayesh, R., Mitchell, S.C., Idle, J.R. and Smith, R.L. (1988) Trimethylaminuria (''fish-odour syndrome''): a study of an affected family. *Clinical Science*, **74**, 231–236.

Berglund, B. and Lindvall, T. (1983) Sensory reactions to ''sick buildings''. Report No. 60. Dept. of Psychology, University of Stockholm.

Carpenter, K.J. (ed.) (1981) *Pellagra*. Stroudsberg, PA.: Hutching Ross.

Cannon, W.B. (1932) *The Wisdom of the Body*. New York: Appleton.

Cannon, W.B. and Rosenblueth, A. (1949) *The Supersensitivity of Denervated Structures*. New York: Macmillan.

Conn, E.E., Stumpf, P.K., Bruening, G. and Doi, R.H. (1987) *Outlines of Biochemistry*. New York: John Wiley & Sons.

Conners, C.K. (1980) *Food Additives and Hyperactive Children*. New York: Plenum Press.

Conners, C.K. (1989) *Feeding the Brain: how Foods affect Children*. New York: Plenum Press.

Crowe, R.R. (1975) An adoptive study of psychopathy: preliminary results from arrest records and psychiatric hospital records. In R.R. Fieve, D. Rosenthal and H. Brill (eds), *Genetic Research in Psychiatry*. Baltimore: Johns Hopkins Press.

Dohan, F.C. (1980) Hypothesis: genes and neuroactive peptides from food as causes of schizophrenia. In E. Costa and M. Trabucchi (eds), *Neural Peptides and Neuronal Communication*. New York: Raven Press.

Eaves, L.J., Eysenck, H.J. and Martin, N.G. (1989) *Genes, Culture and Personality: an Empirical Approach*. London: Academic Press.

Eysenck, H.J. (1983) Psychophysiology and personality: extraversion, neuroticism and psychoticism. In A. Gale and J.A. Edwards (eds), *Physiological Correlates of Human Behaviour. Volume III: Individual Differences and Psychopathology*. London: Academic Press.

Eysenck, H.J. and Eysenck, S.B.G. (1976) *Psychotism as a Dimension of Personality*. London: Hodder & Stoughton.

Fredericks, C. (1976) *Psychonutrition*. New York: Grosset & Dunlap.

Freed, D.L.J. (1985) Food allergy and food intolerance. In S. Seely, D.L.J. Freed, G.A. Silverstone and V. Rippere (eds), *Diet-related Diseases: the Modern Epidemic*. Beckenham, UK: Croom Helm.

Freed, D.L.J. and Seely, S. (1985) Diseases known to be caused by the diet. In S. Seely, D.L.J. Freed, G.A. Silverstone and V. Rippere (eds), *Diet-related Diseases: the Modern Epidemic*. Beckenham, UK: Croom Helm.

Goate, A., and 20 other authors (1991) Segregation of a missense mutation in the amyloid precursor protein gene with familial Alzheimer's disease. *Nature*, **349**, 704–706.

Garrod, A.E. (1909) *Inborn Errors of Metabolism*. Oxford: Oxford University Press.

Gray, J.A. (1983) Anxiety, personality and the brain. In A. Gale and J.A. Edwards (eds), *Physiological Correlates of Human Behaviour. Volume III: Individual Differences and Psychopathology*. London: Academic Press.

Hahn, M.G., Hewitt, J.K., Henderson, N.D. and Benno, R. (eds) (1990) *Developmental Behaviour Genetics: Neural Biomedical and Evolutionary Approaches*. Oxford: Oxford University Press.

Hanssen, M. (1984) *E for Additives*. Wellingborough, UK: Thorsons.

Hanssen, M. and Marsden, J. (1987) *The New E for Additives*. Wellingborough, UK: Thorsons.

Harley, J.P., Ray, R.S., Tomasi, L., Eichman, P.L., Matthews, C.G., Chun, R., Cleeland, C.S. and Traysman, E. (1978) Hyperkinesis and food additives: testing the Feingold hypothesis. *Pediatrics*, **61**, 818–828.

Harris, H. (1986) Enzyme polymorphisms in man. *Proceedings of the Royal Society, London* **B.174**, 1.

Harris, H. (1980) *The Principles of Human Biochemical Genetics*. 3rd edition. Amsterdam: Elsevier/North-Holland.

Hemmings, W.A. (1978) The entry into the brain of large molecules derived from dietary protein. *Proceedings of the Royal Society, London* **B., 200**, 175–192.

Holaday, J.W. (1985) *Endogenous Opioids and their Receptors*. New York: John Updike.

Horowitz, F.D. (ed.) (1975) *Review of Child Development, Volume 4*. Chicago: University of Chicago Press.

Kretschmer, E. (1921, 1936) *Physique and Character*. New York: Harcourt. Originally pub. in German, 1921.

Kretch, D. (1968) Brain chemistry and anatomy: Implications for behavioral therapy. In C. Rupp (ed.), *Mind as Tissue*. New York: Harper & Row.

Kruk, Z.L. and Pycock, C.J. (1979) *Neurotransmitters and Drugs*. London: Croom Helm.

Lashley, K.S. (1947) Structural variation in the nervous system in relation to behaviour. *Psychological Review*, **54**, 325–334.

Lehinger, A.L. (1982) *Principles of Biochemistry*. New York: Worth Publishers.

Mace, J., Goodman, S.I., Centerwall, W.R. and Chinnock, R.F. (1976) The child with the unusual odour. *Clinical Pediatrics*, **15**, 57–62.

Maulitz, R.M., Pratt, D.S. and Shocket, A.L. (1979) Exercise-induced anaphylatic reaction to shellfish. *Journal of Allergy and Immunology*, **63**, 433–434.

Mednick, S.A. and Hutchings, B. (1978) Genetic and psychophysiological factors in asocial behaviour. In R.D. Hare and D. Schalling (eds), *Psychopathic Behavior: Approaches to Behavior*. New York: John Wiley & Sons.

Montgomery, R., Dryer, R.L., Conway, T.W. and Spector, A.A. (1980) *Biochemistry: a Case-orientated Approach*. St Louis: Mosby.

Newsholme, E.A. and Leech, A.R. (1983) *Biochemistry for the Medical Sciences*. Chichester, UK: John Wiley & Sons.

Pauling, L. (1968) Orthomolecular psychiatry. *Scientific Journal*, **160**, 265–271.

Philpott, W.H. and Kalita, D.K. (1980) *Brain Allergies: the Psychonutrient Connection*. New Canaan, Conn. USA: New Keats.

Randolph, T.G. (1970) Domiciliary chemical air pollution in the etiology of ecological mental illness. *International Journal of Social Psychiatry*, **16**, 243–265.

Randolph, T.G. (1976) Stimulatory and withdrawal levels and the alternations of allergic manifestations. In L.D. Dickey (ed.) *Clinical Ecology*. Springfield, Ill: Thomas.

Rees, L. (1973) Constitutional factors and abnormal behaviour. In H.J. Eysenck (ed.), *Handbook of Abnormal Psychology* (2nd edn). London: Pitman.

Rees, L. and Eysenck, H.J. (1945) A factorial study of some morphological and psychological aspects of human constitution. *Journal of Mental Science*, **19**, 8–24.

Rippere, V. (1983) *The Allergy Problem: Why People should Suffer and What Should be Done.* Wellingborough: Thorsons.

Rippere, V. (1984) Some varieties of food intolerance in psychiatric patients: an overview. *Nutrition and Health*, **3**, 125–126.

Rippere, V. (1985) Diet and mental illness. In S. Seely, D.L.J. Freed, G.A. Silverstone and V. Rippere (eds), *Diet-related Diseases: the Modern Epidemic.* Beckenham, UK: Croom Helm.

Rippere, V. and Adams, N. (1982) Clinical ecology and why clinical psychology needs it. *Bulletin of the British Psychological Society*, **35**, 151–152.

Rosenzweig, M.R., Kretch, D. and Bennett, E.L. (1960) A search for the relations between brain chemistry and behaviour. *Psychological Bulletin*, **57**, 476–492.

Scarr, S. and McCartney, K. (1983) How people make their own environment: a theory of genotype-environment effects. *Child Development*, **54**, 424–435.

Seely, S., Freed, D.L.J., Silverstone, G.A. and Rippere, V. (1985) (eds), *Diet-related Diseases: the Modern Epidemic.* Beckenham, UK: Croom Helm.

Sheldon, W.H., Stevens, S.S. and Tucker, W.B. (1940) *The Varieties of Human Physique.* New York: Harper & Row.

Sheldon, W.H. and Stevens, S.S. (1942) *The Varieties of Temperament.* New York: Harper.

Silverstone, G.A. (1985) Possible sources of food toxicants: plants, some foods of animal origin, micro-organisms and food additives. In F. Seely, D.L.J. Freed, G.A. Silverstone and V. Rippere (eds), *Diet-related Diseases: the Modern Epidemic.* Beckenham, UK: Croom Helm.

Skarda, C.A. and Freeman, W.J. (1987) How brains make chaos in order to make sense of the world. *Behavioural & Brain Sciences*, **10**, 161–195.

Smith, M., Smith, L.G. and Levinson, B. (1982) The use of smell in differential diagnosis. *The Lancet*, December, 1452–1453.

Sourkes, T.L. (1962) *Biochemistry of Mental Disease.* New York: Harper & Row.

Thompson, J.G. (1988) *The Psychobiology of Emotions.* New York: Plenum Press.

Thudichum, J.L.W. (1884) *A Treatise on the Chemical Constitution of the Brain.* Hamden, Conn: Archon Books (1962).

Urbach, E. (1941) Odors (osmyls) as allergenic agents. *Journal of Allergy*, **13**, 387–396.

Van Toller, S. (1978) *The Nervous Body: an Introduction to the Autonomic Nervous System and Behaviour.* Chichester: John Wiley & Sons.

Van Toller, S. (1983) Biochemistry of the nervous system. In A. Gale and J.A. Edwards (eds), *Physiological Correlates of Human Behaviour, Vol. 1: Basic Issues.* London: Academic Press.

Van Toller, S. (1988) Odours, emotion and psychophysiology. *International Journal of Cosmetic Science*, **10**, 171–197.

Van Toller, S. and Dodd, G.H. (eds) (1988) *Perfumery: the Psychology and Biology of Fragrance.* London: Chapman & Hall.

Williams, R.J. (1956) *Biochemical Individuality: the Basis for the Genetotropic Concept.* New York: John Wiley & Sons.

Williams, R.J. (1967) *You are Extraordinary.* New York: Random House.

Williams, R.J., Brown, W.D. and Shideler, R.W. (1955) Metabolic peculiarities in normal young men as revealed by repeated blood analysis. *Proceedings of the National Academy of Science, U.S.*, **41**, 615–620.

Wilson, R.S. (1972) Twins: early development. *Science*, **175**, 914–917.

Zuckerman, M. (1987) Personality in the third dimension: a psychobiological approach. Presidential address at the third meeting of the International Society for the Study of Individual Differences. Toronto, Canada. 18–22nd June.

Chapter 3

Design and Analysis in Individual Difference Research

K. O'Connor
Centre de Recherche, Hôpital Louis-H. Lafontaine, 7401 rue Hochelaga, Université de Montréal, Quebec, Canada H1N 3M5

ABSTRACT

Traditional variance-based designs may not be optimal for the requirements of the individual difference experimental psychophysiologist (IDEP). Analysis of variance (ANOVA) notions of probability, construct validity and theory testing are compared with an individual difference approach emphasizing personal statistics, the contextual nature of inference, and person-centred process design. Bayesian, likelihood, and possibilistic designs offer ways of adequately accounting for the subject × situation focus of the IDEP and for the dimensional nature of the models of variation used in individual difference research. An onion-skin approach to programmatic research is preferred whereby constructs and theory are developed bottom-up by observation of individual differences over related contexts so that design is experience rather than theory-led.

INTRODUCTION

This chapter addresses methodological issues in the experimental psychophysiology of individual differences. These issues are discussed in the light of concerns about the appropriateness of popular conventional probabilistic statistics for psychophysiological data.

Handbook of Individual Differences: Biological Perspectives
Edited by Anthony Gale and Michael W. Eysenck

There have always been technical concerns as to whether psychophysiological data conform to stochastic and other requirements of conventional designs and whether analysis of variance (ANOVA) does justice to the group × situations × state interactions of interest to individual difference researchers. But there are the wider questions of concern to both philosophers (and psychologists) of science, as to the validity of any method seeking discrete, factual knowledge of events or accepting the existence of objective probability. These questions partly depend on whether the person's response and the world are best seen as connected and interactive rather than as constituting independent realms. Indeed, on whether we apply an individual difference paradigm to scientific behaviour. Such debates may all seem distant to the practically minded psychophysiologist, glueing on electrodes and detecting peak responses. After all if you can detect a peak, it must be there. So what is there to talk about? But if there is no knowledge except partial personal knowledge and if the only probability is subjective probability as De Finetti (1974) argues, then most of the experimental design assumptions aimed at controlling error, choosing hypotheses, selecting number of subjects, repeating stimulus presentations, and treating responses as "variables" collapse like a house of cards. So I make no apologies for devoting the first few pages of this chapter to a cursory discussion of epistemological questions. What is perhaps most ironic here is that much of the impetus for "personal" statistics has come from active agency models of information processing and "action" models of knowledge, emotion and behaviour, derived from the research of both experimental psychologists and psychophysiologists. Lang (1979), for example, proposes that subjects make sense of stimulus and response information by generating a conceptual structure and embedding data in personal semantic networks. But such models are rarely extended by these investigators themselves to the processing of psychophysiological data. It seems, however, certain we are entering a period of flexibility in accepted inferential procedures, one that will be guided more by empirical considerations of data than the rule by faith and fiat characteristics of the null-hypothesis era. Assessing significance and constructing contexts for measurement will depend more on the questions asked than on conformity to rigid expectations.

Feyerabend (1975) in his "against method" argued that there must be no accepted method in science, that all forms of inference have equal status. I suggest that individual difference psychophysiologists (IDEP), as relative newcomers to the scientific scene who, as it were, had to "make do" with what was available, might benefit from this "epistemological anarchy" to reassert their methodological rights, and devise an inferential method that deals with their units of interest in psychophysiology.

As Lewin (1951) observed "The first prerequisite of a successful observation in any science is a definite understanding about what size of unit one is going to observe" (p. 157). It seems to me for the IDEP this unit must be the person. Whereas social psychologists may choose as units group, family or cultures. The IDEP must always place measurements on the skin of the individual person, rather than on say the walls of a group therapy room or the roof of the family house. The person of course may be viewed in a social, interpersonal, familial, cultural or individual context, but the unit remains the person. In the later section of this chapter I discuss a method that allows the significance and the comparative context of psychophysiological measures to be assessed primarily on a personal basis. This is not a case-study approach but rather an approach that replaces the conventional hypothetical probability distribution with a possibility distribution. The latter is derived empirically from the range of possible "personal" processes of the individual. This "measure of the man" provides the same information as the probability distribution but as I argue helps overcome some inferential ambivalences. I end by focusing on debates central to future IDEP programmatic research: combining qualitative and quantitative information, matching process and effect, and complementing idiopathic and nomothetic approaches to individual differences.

SOURCE OF THE ERROR: OVERVIEW

Individuals and single events are not respected as sources of information in experimental psychology. Why so?

First, there are the technical considerations. Computer handling storage and retrieval of vast amounts of individual data has only recently become available. Though since the availability there has hardly been a rush amongst researchers to explore descriptive statistics which respect ordering of individual data. Rather the increased computing facilities have generally been used to produce more extensive representative statistics of the multivariate type as shown in computer package updates (e.g. Norusis, 1983).

Secondly, there is the "artefact" argument. As McGuire (1969) has stated any artefact in behavioural research goes through three stages—ignorance, coping and exploitation. A new phenomenon starts its scientific life as being unusual, unknown and a bit of a nuisance. Science then learns to cope with this intrusion and also in the process learns more about it. Finally, the phenomenon becomes a source of speculation, theorizing and experimental exploitation in its own right. It could be argued that only recently has a coherent conceptual framework been given to classifying and explaining individual types as experimental units (e.g. Eysenck's promotion of the individual difference paradigm).

A third argument and the most parsimonious I think is the ideological one; that there is a firm cognitive undercurrent in methodology against considering individual differences. Unfortunately it is not a simple "political" matter, with a few hard-core "dirigistes" determined not to let individual differences upset their grand theories of group ensemble function. The relegation of individual differences to secondary consideration is endemic to conventional statistical units, current concepts in method, current paradigms and to the current consensus about what constitutes sufficient knowledge of personal behaviour and how one should seek it. Behavioural science has become encumbered with a highly formalized deductive system of statistical theorizing which interferes with the empirical business of treating individual observations as information. The main instrument by which the individual datum is sanitized of idiosyncrasy is variance and by implication the random sampling with replacement probability model on which most variance models are based.

VARIANCE

There are sociological connotations to the notion of mean and variance; a searching for an "ideal type" to which individual expression can only ever be an approximation. Weber (1947), Cicourel (1964), Douglas (1971) and other social theorists have pointed to the role of the "ideal type" in legitimating collective goal seeking at the expense of the individual and in going beyond what is personal to some higher truth.

The individual datum can only be recognized if its contribution can be justified in a context greater (and better) than itself. This has led Weimer (1979) and others to term objective science "justificationist". "In all sciences," wrote P. B. Medawar (1987) (p. 114), "we are being progressively relieved of the burden of singular instances, the tyranny of the particular." The thesis of this chapter is that individual difference research is essentially incompatible with probabilistic-variance assumptions about data.

But with what do we replace formal deductive procedures? Do we simply return to what Berkson termed intraocular traumatic significance tests (Edwards, Lindman and Savage, 1962): the findings are significant because they hit us between the eyes. Of course, the whole point of current statistical methodology is to escape from such unbridled empiricism. It is an escape from the subjectivity of the observer, the incomparability of qualitatively different conditions and the unreliability of data. In short an escape from individual differences to the robustness of group similarity. So is it statistically impossible to quantify individual experience without losing its unique quality? The answer here is that it is possible, only by placing all measurements within a personalized context. But first it is necessary to challenge current assumptions about knowledge and observation.

As Clark (1983) states all measurement and analysis is an attempt to give a phenomenon a context. The variance method views events in the context of a population of random events separate and uncontrolled by the observer, but it is a naïve realistic view. The observer's behaviour and the observed world are not independent. So should not observed events be understood in the first instance in a behavioural rather than a mathematical context? If this behavioural contextualization of statistical decision making is pursued, traditionally separate areas of subjective and objective statistics collapse into personal statistics. All knowledge is considered more or less personal and the individual rather than the group becomes the basic statistical unit.

OBSERVATION: A SENSE OR AN ACT?

Use of the hypothetico-deductive method and its associated statistics requires belief in objective knowledge. This in turn requires that observation be considered a sense. A sense is an interface between the person and the world through which information passes in the form of signals. A sensor does not create signals or information, it simply records and registers. These are basically the characteristics the behavioural scientist would like to ascribe to him/herself.

But observation is not a "sense" it is an "act". Whereas a sense tends to leave the person out as a passive receiver, the notion of an "act" includes the person as a performer. The justification for viewing knowledge as part of a personal act comes from agency theories of information processing.

Sensory data are input through a matrix of personal meaning. This meaning derives from what the person is doing at the time. Scientists have always appreciated the influence of personal bias on perception and tried to screen it out. The link between knowledge and meaning is less disturbing than the link between knowing and being, since this implies that personal bias is not simply a worrisome addition to "pure" sensory perception. It seems rather that no perception is possible which does *not* emerge from a background of personal knowledge, to give it direction and acuity whether one views the knowledge cognitively in terms of expectation and selection, or ecologically in terms of environmental "affordances". An apt analogy of observation as an act is as a form of decision-making whose options have been specified in advance of the choice of stimuli being observed. If knowledge is personal not by error but because it cannot be otherwise, then the question should be not how do we eliminate bias but how do we make sure we have defined the knowledge in question personalistically enough? Seeking objective facts and objective knowledge in the traditional sense becomes undesirable simply because it is impossible. Indeed, it has always been impossible.

Recent studies of the scientific method (Kulkani and Simons's (1988) study of Hanskreb's idiosyncratic reasoning about the urea cycle, or Gresemer and Wade's (1988) study of the role of personal preference in selecting causal factors in laboratory models) show how it must and always will incorporate personalistic elements in practice in order to progress. There have always been positive empirical benefits to admitting beliefs and prior opinion into scientific thinking though this has not been officially recognized.

PERSONAL ELEMENTS IN SCIENTIFIC THINKING

At a macro-sociological level both Feyerabend (1978) and Weimer (1979) have recently offered versions of the philosophy of science which do not so much propose grand ideal inferential schemes but rather look empirically at what scientists say they do and what they actually do. Feyerabend's (1978) conclusion is that all major advances in science were irrational. Rational rules were violated, for example, and perceptive scientists were aware of this because such rules had to be violated. He suggests that since all methodologies have their limits, strict dogmatic rules are the wrong solution for science and should be replaced by "epistemological anarchism".

Polanyi (1958) and Cohen (1981) at a more micro-level have emphasized the inevitable role of intuition and irrationality in what is considered an objective method. Polanyi (1958) has detailed the role of what he terms tacit knowledge in scientific discovery. Tacit, personal or intuitive knowledge accounts for (a) valid knowledge of a problem, (b) the scientist's capacity to pursue it, and (c) valid anticipation of the as yet indeterminate implications.

Cohen points out that even rational systems of deduction such as formal logic appeal ultimately to common intuition, that is "immediate and untutored intuition without evidence or inclination" (Cohen, 1981, p. 318). If science can admit individual bias as a basis for theory why must it exclude individual bias as a unit in analysis? We return to the point that knowledge worth having must go beyond the personal.

IMPERSONAL PROBABILITY AND PERSONAL CERTAINTY

The probabilistic model rejects the only knowledge we can be certain of, namely personal knowledge, in favour of impersonal knowledge. But reality is not an immutable state it is a volatile consensus, something that must be agreed upon. The constituents of sensory reality often change from time to time and certainly from culture to culture (see Feyerabend, 1988). Reality is what might be termed "collectively personal" rather than purely impersonal. It was the insight that "truth" could never be achieved independent of common agreement that led Popper (1963) to opt for falsification as a better bet in science than verification. In general it is easier to agree on what is not there than what is there. There are more degrees of freedom for negative agreement. Hence the "impersonal" appearance of a probability distribution masks the arbitrary and personal nature of decisions made for example about choice of significance level, interpretation of significance and status of alternative hypotheses.

PERSONAL KNOWLEDGE AND ITS BEHAVIOURAL CONTEXT

Considering all knowledge as personal places observations in a precise and certain behavioural context rather than a probabilistic context. Every description of an objective attribute in the world implies an action context. I might describe this table as 5 ft wide. But 5 ft wide to whom? To anyone with a tape-measure and more specifically to anyone who wants to measure it with a tape measure. In other words, implied in the "fact" that the table is 5 ft wide is a behavioural context that forms the basis for describing the attribute. But the apparent invariance of the "fact" is, in fact, an invariance in the behavioural context not in the table.

In an individual context this relativity is recognized, so that I may say with legitimate fallibility that in this light I saw the table as red, or that from my position the face looked like John's. By openly reporting my behaviour along with the fact perceived, I recognize the personal nature of my observation and the role of my intentions in observing. But when the context is culturally shared it is forgotten. The result is that objective methods rarely mention context as a limiting factor. The tendency is to argue that the "fact" is independent of context and generalizable across people and time. As mentioned earlier, the scientific observation is assumed to be impersonal when it is rather collectively personal.

Response invariance amongst concepts in experimental psychology is more often attributable to a shared cultural consensus rather than scientific consensus. This point has been made well by Shawver (1977) who noted that as soon as we move away from taken for granted common language concepts in science, convergence of findings decreases. Invariant concepts like "sex" appeal to a cultural identity beyond their experimental context.

So if I wish to give knowledge meaning I must include the action context in which it is observed. Every observation only emerges because it is part of an implicit context of culturally and personally legitimate action. In everyday life this behavioural context is implicit. But in scientific investigation this must be made explicit, otherwise we cannot begin to understand the nature of the phenomenon being reported. More importantly it is change in the behavioural context of the observer that allows new "facts" to be discovered. In recognizing the personal context against which observation takes place we can begin to place our expectations in *certain* empirical terms, rather than in the uncertain abstract context of probability.

A good case example here is the classic probability paradigm of coin throwing. To the conventional statistician coin tossing is the paradigm *par excellence* of a random (binomial) distribution. With a perfect coin pure chance determines outcome. But coin throwing is also an act. Only if I choose to abstract the coin toss from the behavioural context in which it is thrown can I pretend that it represents some passive chance phenomenon. Within an act framework it is quite clear that active behavioural measures like intention, habit or skill will a priori affect the a posteriori outcome (Mead, 1910; Cohen, 1981) and its interpretation.

If I am to take account of the behavioural context surrounding my observation then there is no reason not to include intuitive observations as well as rational deductive ones since they have the same status as personal *behaviour.* If we consider that the significance of any event arises within an appropriate behavioural context, the distinction between personal and objective knowledge disappears.

There is a difference here between what is conventionally termed subjective and what I am calling personalistic. Personalistic means describing a context *including* the person's beliefs, expectations about an event, not one *springing* from these beliefs. The best way to think of the personalized approach is as a behaviouralization of statistics. Viewing both intuitive and deductive reasoning in the context of the same behavioural act, helps control rather than confound the role of belief in statistical decision making.

IMPLICATIONS FOR IDEP

The general implication of this "act" epistemology for psychophysiologists is that all experimental results can only be understood within the behavioural context of both experimenter and subject at the time of the experiment. This unique context is person-centred and can involve all aspects of behaviour from whatever source and motivation. Contextualizing knowledge is the only way to give it meaning. Hence the relativity of results is not an impediment to impartial knowledge but an aspect to be precisely explored and described as a part of knowledge. This reconceptualization of knowledge should be good news for the IDEP since it gives prominence to the interactive aspects of person and context as a primary qualifier of effects. But ANOVA and its associated probability models do not cope well with the contextual view of knowlege.

WHAT'S WRONG WITH ANOVA?

Most useful research in psychophysiology in the past 40 years has derived from ANOVA designs and even when data do not meet the assumptions of ANOVA, the techniques are often robust enough to give valid results (Winer, 1971). The question is not whether they are useful but whether they are the most useful or appropriate. The challenge to ANOVA falls into two parts. First are we extracting as much as possible from the data? In other words is it a cost effective procedure? Secondly are the inferences derived from ANOVA the most appropriate?

ANOVA designs arose in the thirties through Fisher (1959) in response to agriculture concerns of comparing "yields" of differently arranged plots of land. The farming terminology still persists in textbooks (e.g. split-plot design). The yields (cell contents) were easily observable, the processes involved in producing the yield (growth) were obvious so that results were interpretable and even if an efficient cause to explain the effect was not identifiable the influences responsible for the effect could be controlled.

It is not clear (at least to me) how psychophysiological "responses" correspond to yields in the Fisherian terminology. Perhaps if psychophysiologists were measuring toe-nail clippings or designer stubble these might qualify as "yields". Responses are not yields but events, and it is on this dynamic basis that they are identifiable. Often the responses represent physiological or psychological events distant from the recording site. In practice physiological measures bear very different relationships to the processes underlying them. The EMG probably within a certain range varies linearly with underlying muscle activity. Conversely the form of ongoing scalp recorded EEG varies very little with specific underlying neuronal activity. Why then are single amplitude or peak measures identified as EEG response units? The problem for the psychophysiologist is that *something* has to play the role of a "yield"—a constant throughout the study—*if* the ANOVA is to report on a constant effect. But without knowledge of the processes producing the response how do we know that the response measured on trial 2 is the same phenomenon as that measured on trial 1 or 3? How do we know that experimentally induced differences can be accounted for by changes in the same process? If there is no reliable process context in which to relate a significant effect, the effect does not bring us any closer to understanding function since several functions may produce the same effect.

One solution I have proposed to identifying process context is to consider all recorded activity as relevant activity in the first instance, and describe it as a process prior to parcelling it up into components and testing effects (O'Connor, 1990). This avoids making assumptions about relevant and irrelevant responses. This approach does mean identifying activity as a process, but psychophysiological activity appears as a process not a discrete event. It is constantly in transition, and it never repeats itself. In my experience I have found it impossible to affect one component of an activity without also affecting the relationship between components. These secondary effects may be dismissed as of lesser degree and less systematic than the effect on the major component, but they emphasize that from a functional viewpoint recorded activity is a *Gestalt* of interacting process not a series of discrete events. In practice researchers accommodate considerable variation in the "yield" by granting indulgent criteria for identifying latency and amplitude of the "response". So, for example, positive going evoked-response peaks identifiable as the P300 may occur between 300–600 msec latency with no set amplitude requirement. Interestingly it is implicitly recognized that the sequence or order of appearance of a peak response, not its timing, identifies it (in relation to other peaks). But it is difficult to operationalize this relational aspect without losing credibility for a "stand alone" discrete response.

I question the validity of identifying credible components on the basis of isolating their functional significance. For example, successive components of evoked responses are identified as they correspond to independent stages of information, sensory registration, match–mismatch, orienting, etc. Rather than adopting this homunculus idea of waveform activity, it seems to me less presumptive to consider the recorded process as continuous and recursive, and that any part of the process is conditioned by its relationship with other future or past parts of the process. This process represents an intentional flow of activity on the part of the processor which may or may not correspond to a serial succession of stages (O'Connor, 1989). The boundary of the process context is defined as the unit considered by the person to be *their* meaningful unit of activity in this context regardless of whether this unit includes, from a functional point of view, independent cortical components. If the subject is in the process of scanning an array of lights in order to detect a mismatch and then press a button, then this is the unique process context (unit) for all activity recorded and this process taken as a whole conditions the relations of each component to the other as they appear in the activity.

As well as locating the response in the context of ongoing activity this process approach also emphasizes Aristotle's formal causation (Altman, 1988) of identifying patterns and forms of relationships and accepting that the same principle may not account for all phenomena in all circumstances. Whereas the conventional ANOVA viewpoint tends to seek a limited number of explanations, the contextual approach emphasizes that a variety of explanations may be needed for similar events. The ANOVA procedure cannot accept that the same "responsible variable" might represent a qualitatively different process at the beginning and at the end of an experiment. Hence the tendency to reify "activity" as singular responses. Likewise ANOVA cannot accept a complex sequence of variables serving as "the response".

In short, the first problem for the IDEP is that ANOVA cannot accept psychophysiological activity as it is—a process. But what are the valid inferences that can be drawn from the classical ANOVA procedure?

THEORY TESTING IN ANOVA

The major inferential claim to fame of ANOVA is that its deductive procedures are theory led and are really the only way in which theory can develop systematically. Walmpold, Davis and Good (1990) note "Research hypotheses are derived from theory and can be characterized as statements about presumed relations amongst constructs" (p. 361). The crucial word here, in my opinion, is "construct". The construct is the vital link between theory and practice. Walmpold, Davis and Good (1990) continue:

> The design of experiments involves deriving research hypotheses from theory matching statistical hypotheses to research hypotheses and creating the experiment in order to obtain the results. . . . Inference proceeds in the opposite direction, the results are used to make decisions about statistical hypotheses (e.g. reject the null hypothesis) and these decisions indicate whether the theory is corroborated. Examining crucial hypotheses leads to the extension of knowledge, the winnowing of theories, the clarification of discrepancies, the identification of active ingredients and so on.

These authors proceed to list several problems that may beset a good procedure, such as: inconsequential hypotheses, a non-specific null hypothesis, the problems of adjusting p-values for effect sizes, the dangers of data mining with omnibus tests, and hypothesis procedures that may favour either type I and II errors.

Both these and previous authors (e.g. Chow, 1988) have concluded that the key to inferential success is a precise, crucial, binary hypothesis at the outset which makes the inferences straightforward. *I disagree.* Despite ANOVA buzz-words like sharp hypothesis, robust effect, strong inference, the inferences derived from ANOVA are arbitrary and often chaotic, and though ANOVA may encourage binary hypothesis testing, this often ends in vague theorizing because hypothesis validity is pursued at the expense of construct validity. I shall discuss these two points about *hypotheses* and *constructs* separately.

BELIEF AND ASSUMPTION IN HYPOTHESIS TESTING

The shortcomings of the use of null hypotheses and significance testing are well documented elsewhere (Bakan, 1967; Morrison and Hankel, 1970; Phillips, 1973; Rozeboum, 1960; Steger, 1971). A more recent review is given in a tutorial paper by Rosnow and Rosenthal (1989). It is worth emphasizing the part that belief and personal intuition play in conventional inference. The whole business of taking a sample from a population is based on a probability model that is never tested. The sample mean is assumed to be one of an infinite number of means and that therefore its value is unlikely to fall into the extremes of the distribution. But such a distribution remains hypothetical.

The binary hypothesis testing procedure which apparently gives sharp precision to the aims of the experiment depends for its validity on the null hypothesis notion. In practice the null hypothesis is very vague, often inaccurate and arbitrarily biased, because everyone knows it is false from the start. The null hypothesis (usually of the variety that there is no difference between means) is almost certainly in error from the true situation. This leads to an asymmetry in favour of H_1, such that the more subjects run the more likely will the error of H_0 depart from the true situation and the more likely will it be rejected. This also means that the significance of the "significance" level or rejection region chosen will also vary arbitrarily from study to study, as a function of null hypothesis error.

Ironically, as Edwards (1972) has pointed out, the traditional decisions to use the cut-off around the 5% confidence interval are established on the basis of the personal experience of its general utility rather than for other logical reasons. Strictly speaking the p-value should be chosen in advance of the results, but in practice the choice between significance levels in general is left up to the personal integrity of the experimenter or editor. Acceptable significance levels can differ not only between disciplines but amongst different areas within a discipline (Rosnow and Rosenthal, 1989).

The status of both the hypothesis and the datum post-significance test remains ambivalent because the conclusions are couched in purely negative terms (the null hypothesis was not supported). Also there is no viable parameter space (empirical context) available in which to interpret results (Steger, 1971). In practice, most experimenters do not confine themselves to purely negative and binary conclusions, hence personal speculations often make up the bulk of discussion sections.

Statistical control is also patchy, experimenters frequently sample subjects and measures in a strict random fashion to ensure representativeness, but, as Brendan Maher (1978) has pointed out, they do not usually sample stimuli, environments or experimenters in the same way. The marriage of fixed and random effects in mixed model ANOVA is often one of convenience. Experimental control procedures can take on the air of a classical obsessional case where rigid control over a small aspect of life masks chaos elsewhere. What is one to control in a multi-factor environment? Experimenters will often control stimulus activity and presentation whilst paying little attention to subjects' peripheral activity, which may be a crucial variable (Gale and Baker, 1981).

Amongst exponents of variance statistics there seems confusion over what is belief, hypotheses and intuitive knowledge. To believe is to hold something as certain that cannot or will not be proved. To hypothesize is to proposition in advance of proof. To intuit is to gain knowledge other than by reason or trial and error. The hypothetico-deductive method assumes that the probability models it constructs are hypothetical (i.e. awaiting proof) whereas in fact they are belief systems. Hence any certainties drawn from them are largely intuitive.

CONSTRUCT VALIDITY

The problem for the deductive method and ANOVA is its context-independence. The theory admits no empirical context to the significance of effects. All effects are referred to an absolute hypothetical probability model for validation. As a consequence construct validity is weak. The role of the construct in hypothesis testing is to operationalize the theory. The theory is inevitably an explanatory theory (of the type A does B because they are in state X) so the construct is also explanatory. The problem is that whereas a theory can be illogical and impractical, a construct cannot. A construct must be highly specific to conform to the practical requirements of its measurement. A strong construct reflects the idiosyncrasies of the data rather than the theory. If for example I have a theory-led experiment which examines the hypothesis that group A is more aroused than group B, I must operationalize my measure of arousal. If as usual, the construct is imposed top-down then whatever measure I choose must always reflect my definition of arousal otherwise the construct validity is weakened. So all findings with this measure must be convergent and none divergent. This encourages both theory and construct to be vague. If I am too specific in my definition of construct (say as a change in skin conductance of a definite value), I risk my construct being invalidated, but if I am overgeneral—say any change in skin conductance represents arousal—I am on a safer bet. So a vague construct confirms a vague theory, and if it disconfirms it, the theory is likely to become more complex but not less vague to accommodate the findings. As Feyerabend (1988, p. 170) notes: "The battle cry 'we need a new theory' is heard whenever a researcher or a discipline does not know what to do." In practice the hypothetico-deductive method encourages vague dichotomous statements at the expense of coherent stories. But precise theory develops from particular observations, hunches, connections, and toying with numerous possibilities at once. It drifts from the particular to the abstract, from the multiple to the binary hypothesis. The theory is clarified and winnowed by a certain sequence of discovered convergences and divergences which may eventually culminate in a strong binary hypothesis. But this binary choice arrives by induction and is not fabricated at the outset in terms of a null hypothesis.

If, however, constructs originate in observation they are inevitably empirically strong, follow logic and lead to a bottom-up theory development. Let us suppose I notice that a number of individuals (group A) adopt a fast strategy in a performance task and a number of others (group B) a slow strategy. Here I have a construct "speed-strategy" with two divergent groups, A and B. Now supposing I examine this construct over a number of other contexts and I find that distraction diminishes the differences and task complexity makes no difference. I notice that EEG frequency changes in the fast group A but autonomic measures do not change. I now have the beginning of bottom-up theory, namely that the speed strategy involves central rather than autonomic actions, and may be directed by cognitive rather than sensory factors. Divergent, discrepant findings do not knock validity since at root my construct remains grounded in a particular observable context and has empirical validity. It is this ability to accommodate both divergent and convergent findings in winnowing down the theory which according to Shawver (1977) is the mark of a strong construct. In the case of a top-down construct such as arousal I cannot go from the particular to the general since I have already started at the most general level possible.

The above distinction has nothing to do with the quite valid notion that some constructs address molar and others molecular behaviour, so the former must necessarily be more general than the latter (Coles, Gratton and Gehring, 1987), nor to the Brinberg and McGrath (1985) idea that some constructs relate to a conceptual others to a substantive domain. The issue is about the way the theory is constructed. As Springer (1990) notes there seems a fear amongst practitioners that unless their theories are abstract they will be redundant on observation to the extent they are situation specific. But generality comes from diversity and to do this theories must be able to lay down principles that apply to a variety of particular and diverse instances. Non-redundancy on specific instances then follows as a by-product: in fact though knowledge acquisition requires a conceptual structure, it does not require a ready-made parallel theory, and as Feyerabend (1988) notes discoveries frequently precede theories to explain them. So there are strong empirical objections to the attempt to use constructs undefined by an empirical context.

There are also strong *logical* objections to the top-down approach of imposing theory-led constructs. In order to possess internal coherence a construct must correspond to the variation in its measurement. But this internal coherence must be established independent of these measurements.

If construct A relates to a set of measures O^{ai-j} then there must be a set of measures O^{bi-j} to which it does not relate. Otherwise the construct has no specificity. Also the same set of measures O^{ai-j} that index A must also in a different state index its complement $\bar{A}$. With an empirical construct, I already know to what behaviour the construct applies and to what it does not. This logical coherence provides a framework for deciding what measures are specific to the construct and what others will be non-pertinent. But in the case of arousal, the question is what are the independent criteria for when the person is aroused and when are they not? If HR is my measure of arousal what physiological measures are irrelevant to arousal? In what situations is "being aroused" an exclusive preoccupation, independent of other constructs, say, attention or memory? The illogical nature of a psychophysiological construct could produce as much theoretical turmoil in psychophysiology as a fuzzy hypothesis.

In summary the ANOVA model attempts in theory to be context-independent and to relate findings to an absolute parameter space. The result in practice is to leave significant and non-significant effects without any viable empirical parameter space by which to interpret findings. This impedes the build-up of strong constructs and theories from a bottom-up approach. Also, because so much theory is vague, in practice "objective" decisions end up containing a large arbitrary and personal element. Construct validity is as important as hypothesis validity for the IDEP who is frequently interested in a biased sample of individuals selected along a dimensional construct. The interpretability of IDEP findings depends on the validity of the construct rather than on hypothetical theory. The IDEP is also more likely to be interested in seeing to what extent a strong construct diverges in terms of person × context interactions over occasions rather than how findings converge to demonstrate a general uniform effect.

A final point on cost effectiveness for the IDEP relates to number of subjects required to produce a robust significant effect. The "cast of thousands" spirit is well represented in a recent review (of smoking outcome research) by Lando (1989, p. 206), who says there may be no alternative to spending millions of dollars to enlist thousands of subjects in order to show valid intervention effects. The report that a study has not enough subjects is a certain damnation of its credibility. But when is enough, enough or not enough?

As with other ANOVA procedures the limit is rule of thumb. In fact, as Morrisson and Hankel (1970) point out a study with too many subjects is likely to be counter-productive since it increases type II error. There are certainly mathematical reasons why for example the ratio of subjects/variables > 1 when determinants of matrices are involved. But the rationale for large number of subjects is that the ANOVA sample reflects the entire population and a general effect, whilst the IDEP is more likely to be interested in the behaviour of a smaller number of subjects from a precisely defined population over several repetitions.

Of course much fruitful IDEP research has been accomplished through ANOVA designs but these often involve stretching the assumptions. Individual differences and context-dependent interactions can be explored using longitudinal repeated measures designs (O'Connor, 1986). The problems to be overcome here are testing overall model acceptability on a range of subgroups and individuals (Rouanet, Lepine and Holender, 1978), investigating individual change in process variables (Collins, Cliff and Dent, 1988), balancing repeated time series requirements of multiple repetitions to smallish numbers of subjects (Iacobucci and Wasserman, 1988), interpreting second and third order interactions, and interpreting change in these subject × condition interactions over occasions (Benassi and Belli, 1989).

However, even so ANOVA cannot accommodate other IDEP requirements such as multiple and complex predictions on the same measures, and taking the individual and the context as the basic unit of analysis. But there are alternatives to the variance approach.

I discuss here three alternative attempts to systematize information gathering within a personalistic context. These are the *Bayesian* approach, the *likelihood* approach and the *possibilistic* approach. All these approaches are similar in their adoption of behavioural statistics though they differ in the kind of contexts they advocate and the extent to which they reject probability models.

Table 3.1. Key differences in experimental characteristics between objective-impersonal design and contextual personal design.

Objective (impersonal)	Contextual (personal)
Context-free significance level defined by absolute probability space	Context-dependent parameter space defines subjective probability
Binary hypotheses	Multiple alternative predictions
Fixed uniform processes	Variable processes
Top-down causal theory and constructs	Bottom-up descriptive empirically specific constructs
Main effects	Complex interactive processes
Large number of subjects	Small numbers of highly selective subjects
Must employ probabilistic methods	Can employ non-probabilistic methods

BAYESIAN APPROACH

The Bayesian position is the oldest and best established alternative and has been the most thorough in its critique of traditional probability and espousal of ''subjective'' probability. The most comprehensive exposition of the Bayesian position has been given by Savage (1962), Lindley (1965), Barnard (1969), and Edwards (1972).

The premise of the Bayesian position is that all probability is subjective, and that it is tied to personal experience. The word Bayesian originates from the Reverend Bayes an English clergyman who was the first to articulate the query of how to reconcile prior experience of a die with a random model that excludes prior experience in calculating the outcome of the next throw (Bayes, 1763). He was introducing in a vague way the importance of personal context as we discussed it earlier.

The hallmark of Bayesian statistics is the personal involvement of the person in estimating the probability of an event and it is formalized in terms of Bayes' theorem. The theorem proposes that the a posteriori probability of a hypothesis given the data ($P(H/D)$ is a function of the probability of the hypothesis weighted by the probability of the data but conditioned by the probability of the data given the hypothesis ($P(D/H)$).

$$\text{Bayes' theorem:} \quad P(H/D): \frac{P(D/H) \times P(H)}{P(D)}$$

It is only in terms of a behavioural model that the notions of a priori and a posteriori probability make sense. The Bayesian position has moved from the passive observation of the coin toss with only one probability, to the active modification of probability as a function of personal involvement and commitment to outcome. The decision about probability of an event is made on the basis of evidence. *But* the significance of the evidence is related to the person since s/he constructs alternative decisions in terms of their relative (ratio of) utility functions to him/herself. The probability of an outcome depends on the choice of decisions available to the person and their personal investment in the outcome. Hence the a posteriori probability therefore reflects outcome plus prior experience and personal utility.

The point of specifying, through previous knowledge, the decisions required from the data is to give some behavioural perspective or context to the observation in order to be certain that the evidence will have implications for further action. Hence the data are significant to the Bayesian whatever the outcome. The question is simply which of a number of several hypotheses are best supported by the data. The more hypotheses to which I can attach prior probabilities the better, since greater precision can then be attached to the final decision.

Conventional statistics limits itself to a binary hypothesis since only one significant effect is to be yielded from the otherwise chance behaviour of variables. As mentioned earlier this significance can only be interpreted in a probabilistic not a personalistic context, and data are fitted into the null hypothesis format. In contrast the Bayesian is said to fit the models to the data. This is sometimes termed "inverse probability".

The fact that the Bayesian starts from a relativist position whilst the conventional statistician begins from an objective position leads to crucial differences in the conception of sample populations and what they and the measures taken on them represent.

SPECIFYING POPULATIONS

The conventional researcher must infer from the sample to the population. The sample statistics therefore must be representative of a larger population. Variables considered are hence dependent on their conformity to a population norm. A personality measure for example must be representative of the population of such personality measures. A reaction time measure similarly is one of a population of RT measures. So all the elements of the experiment already owe their allegiance to a population outside of the experiment. This population is of course hypothetical and has already been determined in advance of measurement.

The variables in an experiment are like delegates at a conference whose affiliation is crucial to their identity. Any interaction with other variables within an experiment means a loss or blending of independent identity and suggests they are untypical. Hence the reasons for statistical constraints on independence of observations and interactive confounding of main effects.

But for the Bayesian the only context is the context of the experiment. The Bayesian is not concerned with *representing* a population but with *creating* one, so that s/he deals with aggregates not samples. The Bayesian asks how many of these types of situations show these characteristics? Rather than how representative is my measure of the population that must somewhere exist? In the Bayesian case the population is determined empirically by what is observed, not hypothetically tied to an assumed population distribution.

There are key differences in design that spring from this difference in inference. Principally, the Bayesian is not bound by formal statistical constraints: in dealing with independence of observations; interaction of measures; in comparing/combining separate measures; in defining sample space; and in generalizing findings.

SPECIFYING SAMPLE SPACE

In conventional experimentation the tendency is to make descriptions of populations as bare and essential as possible. All else is supposedly controlled, though in practice confounding interactions may continue unreported. In the behavioural case, as far as possible everything relevant to the experimental set-up is described in detail at the outset. Since the attributes we describe are the whole independent population they can take as many levels and interactions as required. The question of interaction and confounding of experimental variables is not a headache for the Bayesian.

In conventional analysis an interaction is a conditional qualifier to main factors of the experiment. But in Bayesian analysis one cannot conceive of knowledge that is not in some way conditional, since in order to achieve any kind of certain knowledge, as we have said, we must recognize context. So to describe an experimental context as the recording of reaction time (RT) in extraverts who score high on impulsivity, whilst smoking, after ingestion of caffeine and with one foot in a bucket of water provides no greater difficulty for the Bayesian than defining the context as recording RT within a group of extraverts—period. In both cases any specific interactions or subdivisions of personality are welcome as marking the particular idiosyncrasy of this context and hence giving decisions on outcome a more precise and relative (hence personally meaningful) applicability.

The Bayesian analysis allows the bottom-up approach to begin from detail and become more general whereas the conventional designer starts from the general and is forced to be more specific and/or to qualify general statements by the evidence. A classic case in personality research is where a difference is reported between two personality groups in say the effect of caffeine. The finding is replicated but this time no overall personality effect is found. However, subsequent comparison of the studies reveals one of the following: subjects were tested on different times of day; the groups differed on some sub-scale of personality (e.g. sociability or impulsiveness in the case of extraversion); some other demand characteristic differed in the experiments. Such a qualification frustrates the researchers' desire to be as general as possible in inference. Subsequent experiments might even qualify the findings further (relative to apparatus, temperature, sex). Either the experimenter must control for these effects or incorporate them into some grand multivariate matrix. Such a multivariate analysis, however, becomes very weak with respect to the main effect of personality. It also involves the experimenter in all sorts of problems with range, homogeneity and sphericity of variance assumptions. The power of such an analysis is low and the procedure expensive. The more variables the greater likelihood of a spurious chance finding.

The researcher faced with a complicated n^{th}-order interaction is likely to abandon the thesis about personality as a factor on performance, ironically in the face of too much evidence rather than too little. In contrast the Bayesian begins by describing as specifically as possible the conditional aspects of the personality group under study. Such conditional qualifiers are not a nuisance. The more specific we can be about these at the beginning the better, since we are describing our *entire reference population.*

SPECIFYING QUESTIONS

The Bayesian use of a priori knowledge means that decisions about the type of effect one is expecting can be specified more precisely than in conventional methods.

A Bayesian question would be likely to take the form: which is the RT more typical of a population of extraverts who have just ingested caffeine, an RT of 150 msec or one of 200 msec? The hypothesis and its alternatives would be decided solely on the degree of specific knowledge about an attribute and consequently how high or low a probability could be attached to each alternative outcome. My knowledge might allow me to quote these alternative RT outcomes within 10 msec of each other or only within 100 msec of each other. I may for example be able to attribute a higher probability to the person's RT being between 100–200 msec than between 200–400 msec if I know they are extravert. But if I know also they are high on impulsivity and disinhibition scales the probability may become higher. Further knowledge may make the outcome predicted become more precise, say, between 100–150 msec. The aim is to achieve as much precision as possible. One moves away from general classifications like "personality" to the specific attributes this classification entails.

SPECIFYING ALTERNATIVES

In the Bayesian case one must not only be able to specify the alternative hypotheses but accord them a probability relative to each other and summing to unity. If one cannot specify alternative probabilities one is not in a position to say what is and is not relevant information and so define the experimental context.

A situation where one has absolutely no preference amongst alternatives is the case known variously as a "state of ignorance" or a "uniform prior" and where one would accord two very general alternatives equal prior probability. This case, which is a very special case, most closely approximates the classical null hypothesis type experiment, where binary hypotheses of the kind, "this general event will/will not happen" are all that can be specified. But this is a special case of ignorance. It is clear that one must have some form of prior knowledge in order to do any experiment. In the absence of more precise knowledge one could simply summarize a priori knowledge, and hence the context for decision making, as "more likely to find out about personality, by doing this experiment than by sitting in the pub". A state of complete and genuine ignorance would preclude any experiment since no prior could be strengthened or weakened and so any outcome would be uninformative.

SUMMARY

The general procedure in the experimental design of a Bayesian is as follows:

(1) Current and prior knowledge and experience leads to a general question being formulated about behaviour (or its parameters). This is not necessarily associated with a coherent theory of the behaviour but is associated with strong construct validity.
(2) The question is formulated as specifically as possible and couched in terms of alternative outcomes expected after observing the behaviour.
(3) Alternative outcome is quantified as alternative probabilities in favour of a decision about behaviour.
(4) The context of the experiment (the one which will best permit prior knowledge to be updated) is described as an independent variable.
(5) All behaviour, attributes, levels of factors relevant to the context are described as fully and specifically as possible. Irrelevant ones are not described.
(6) Sufficient relevant behaviour is recorded during experimental performance to evaluate a posteriori probabilities of prior predictions.
(7) Prior probabilities about outcomes are updated on the basis of evidence.
(8) Depending on decisions required from the data and the strength of prior knowledge the experiment may be repeated. Either the alternative probabilities or the descriptions of behaviour may be revised in the interests of more accurate future predictions of outcome.

ADVANTAGES AND DISADVANTAGES OF THE BAYESIAN APPROACH

The Bayesian approach then has advantages for the IDEP. It enables interactive effects to be established as primary factors. One can deal both with individuals and with individual measures as independent units. Attributes of individuals can be specified precisely at the outset. We can for example qualify the concept of personality at various levels experimentally without fear of confounding its integrity.

A major Bayesian contribution is in clarifying the interpretation of interaction terms. Rouanet and co-workers (1978, 1983), for example, replace interaction "effects" with upper and lower "fiducial limits" of the actual variable of interest. This gives a more practical guide as to the actual values of the variables of interest, and whether findings are "notable" in terms of what we already know about the limits of the variable as well as significant in experimenter terms.

As mentioned the Bayesian operationalizes alternative personal decisions as alternative probabilities. So if I have for example 2, 3, 4, etc. hypotheses about the type of response I might expect, I must, to be logically coherent, express them as mutually exclusive probabilities which sum to unity. (Since unity is the upper limit on probability.) This means assuming the alternatives come from a uniform set and that they are always mutually exclusive and can be enumerated to add up to one. Now it is easy enough to compare the probabilities of heads or tails or the fall of a die where outcome is constrained to be mutually exclusive. In everyday life events tend to come from qualitatively different "sets" or classes and quantitative comparison is very difficult. How for example do I enumerate the probability that on a rainy day someone might eat an ice-cream, go to the library or stay in bed all day? The evaluation of a behavioural event requires its behavioural context to be known since this, not a probability model, will decide the events with which association and comparison is more meaningful. The advantages of a personalized comparative unit are addressed in the possibilistic section.

The Bayesian having issued a devastating critique of the objectivist position is practically speaking, still left on shaky ground. Whereas the objectivist has a permanent model in the binomial distribution (based admittedly on the erroneous assumption of the symmetry of H_1 and H_0 hypotheses), the Bayesian subjectivist has to construct probability distributions anew out of a subjective guess on events. This is particularly difficult where parameters may have many qualitatively different subjective alternatives or levels since multinomial distributions can often take strange forms. A criticism raised by Kaplan (1989) is that in fact people do not generally quantitatively assess alternatives in decision making and that this Bayesian procedure is prescriptive not descriptive.

THE LIKELIHOOD DISTRIBUTION

The likelihood approach and its sister concept "information" overcome some of the practical problems of the Bayesian approach. Firstly they are concerned from the beginning with likelihood ratios, which describe the relative context of a probability rather than an absolute probability. In other words, the basic unit is the probability of event A compared with event B rather than just the probability of event A—period. This makes it easier to ascribe probability to qualitative events. Likelihoods transcend the constraints of probability by dealing with a second moment, which Edwards (1972) terms "support".

In deciding on the prior support for one hypothesis, I support the one against another to the same degree as if I had conducted an experiment leading to experimental support in a situation in which I had no prior preferences. Prior support is thus defined in terms of an imaginary experiment. It has the same properties as experimental support and is not as in the Bayesian case a qualitatively different expression of subjective ignorance.

$$\text{Posterior support} = \text{prior support} + \text{experimental support.}$$

All the information which the data provide concerning the relative merits of two hypotheses is contained in the likelihood ratio of those two hypotheses on the data. The posterior likelihood is centred around the actual relative accuracy of each hypothesis given the data. This value is termed the maximum likelihood. Given this actual observed ratio of two hypotheses the question to be answered is how likely are other likelihood ratios observed in other data to support the assertions made about this data? The answer to this question is inferred from the likelihood distribution which is constructed around the maximum value in accordance with statistical limits on how far observed values may differ from the maximum likelihood and still be considered equivalent. So the likelihood or support curve would tell the experimenter that a certain observed proportion and other proportions within so many units of this maximum, support the relative assertion A over relative assertion B. But if values outside of these limits are observed the support dwindles away. O'Connor (1985) discusses in more detail the application of likelihood inference to psychophysiology.

The main points of likelihood or "support" theory are summarized below:

(1) The likelihood ratio of two hypotheses on some data is the ratio of their likelihoods on that data.
(2) The likelihood ratios of two hypotheses on independent sets of data may be multiplied together to form the likelihood ratio on the combined data.
(3) The likelihood can be quoted for a family of hypotheses for each value versus the value at which it is maximum.
(4) This continuous function may be termed the likelihood function or curve.
(5) The term "supports" is used for the natural log of likelihood.
(6) A particular set of data supports one statistical hypothesis better than another if the likelihood of the first hypothesis, on the data, exceeds the likelihood of the second hypothesis.

The disadvantages of the likelihood approach is that it must still make some assumptions about uniformities and continuities in the data. The "support" function depends crucially on the exact nature of alternative hypothetical models put forward. When it is impossible to be precise about the exact form of these models or when they are complicated or irregular (as often is the case in everyday events) the support function, though robust, loses precision.

THE POSSIBILISTIC APPROACH

I think some of these statistical problems in Bayesian and likelihood approaches arise because the experimenter is forced to deal with a probability space, and I suggest one solution is to limit the parameter space to an empirical possibility space centred around possible relevant processes of the individual. Chihara (1987, p. 559) makes the point that the degrees of belief one has in a proposition is a function of what one sees as the possibilities. Defining possibilities defines the alternatives being considered. This avoids some of the problems encountered in rationalizing subjective probability estimates and resulting in uneven support functions.

It will be recalled that in the Bayesian and likelihood approach, we attribute alternative probabilities or likelihoods to hypotheses. One is most likely, another is least likely, and the others in between form a distribution about the most likely. In the possibilistic approach the distribution is of alternative *events* surrounding the actual event that occurred rather than of alternative *probabilities.* The possibility distribution is constructed with the aid of the assumption that any event that occurs is already the centre of its own distribution of alternative possible events, otherwise it would not have occurred. In the possibilistic approach the presenting context of an event is respected. A context does not have to be ascribed to it or statistically invented. It does not have to be accorded a significance; it is already significant by virtue of its appearance.

In other words any event that occurs is by definition the most possible (because it occurred) but either side of this maximum possibility there are alternative comparative events which did not occur and hence by definition are less possible. The alternative events which did not occur obviously differ slightly in some empirical observable manner. This difference if it can be found and unitized then forms an empirical dimension along which alternative behavioural acts to the one that occurred can be ranked according to their possibility value.

CONSTRUCTING A POSSIBILISTIC CONTEXT

We observe for example an EMG profile of a certain shape and magnitude. According to the possibilistic approach, this profile is the most possible to occur under the unique circumstances of the present observation. But its significance is defined by the context of a distribution of less possible forms of the EMG which could have occurred but did not. These less possible forms might take a different but related shape. The experimenter's job is to order these alternative events according to a process dimension. This dimension then gives us an empirical context which can be said to guarantee the first EMG event's emergence. It guarantees the event's emergence in the sense that given this particular context of possible EMG events ordered according to this particular behavioural dimension the profile we first observed will *certainly* occur. We discover this alternative distribution first by postulating potential comparative units to the reference unit. The size and nature of these units are decided by how I classified the original reference unit. The construction of the possibility space is further aided by describing all actions or events logically in terms of a bipolar process dimension (O'Connor, 1987; 1990). The example in Figure 3.1 shows a raw root mean square (RMS) EMG recorded from the biceps during the process of throwing a dart at a target. This process of dart throwing is carefully described in the caption. The person throwing is of intermediate skill level, and we are varying accuracy by asking the person to throw the dart towards a smaller and smaller target area. So there are two dimensional constructs here, one is the intended accuracy of the throw, the other is the skill of the thrower.

So much, for the moment, for the behavioural context of the person, what now about *my* (E^s) personalistic context. My observation, like the subject's behaviour, did not arrive in a vacuum. It is itself, one of a number of possible observations I could have made. This context gives background and meaning to my own observation, and I may construct it possibilistically in the same way that I constructed the subject's behavioural context. This experimental

Table 3.2. The proportion of each EMG waveform given in Figure 3.1 above the (overall) median value of 7.5 microvolts.

	Figure 3.1(a) (inaccurate)	Figure 3.1(b) (accurate)	Figure 3.1(c) (inaccurate)
>7.5 μV	0.12	0.42	0.17

The likelihood ratio of Figure 3.1(c) belonging to inaccurate rather accurate throwing process

$= L(Pa \backslash Pc)/L(Pb \backslash Pc)$
$= Pa^{Pc}(1-Pa)^{(1-Pc)}/Pb^{Pc}(1-Pb)^{(1-Pc)} = 2.56$

The odds in favour of 3.1(a) are 2.56 times greater than 3.1(b). These odds can now act as prior odds to weight process classification of subsequent EMG recordings using this amplitude parameter.

Higher odds sharpen the experimenter's distribution of most-least possible differences between processes and lead to more comprehensive theory development as shown in Figure 3.2 and Figure 3.3.

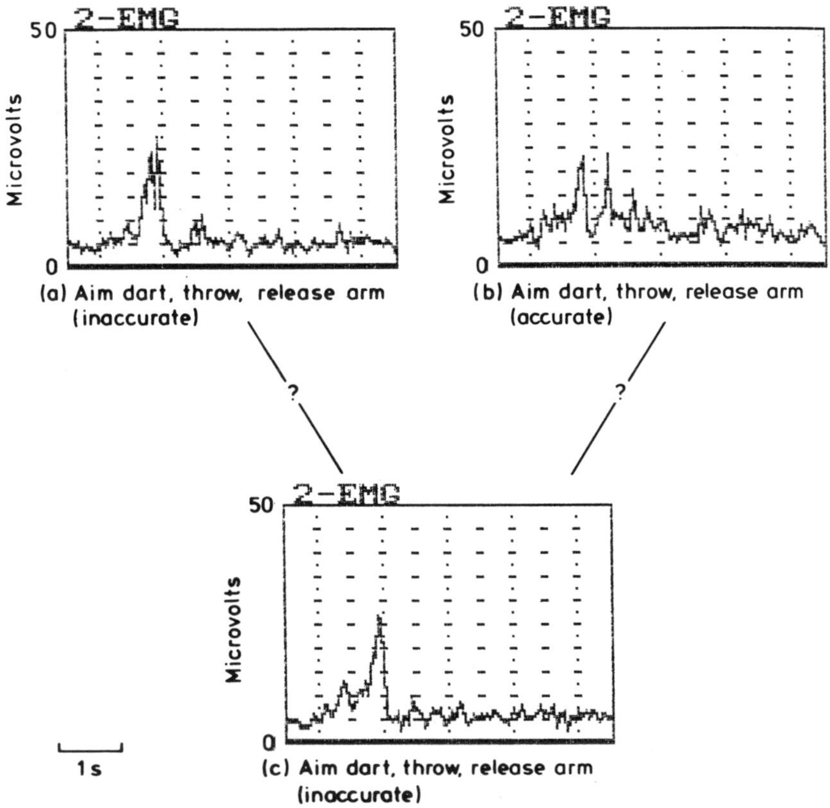

Figure 3.1. Raw RMS biceps EMG activity recorded during accurate–inaccurate dart-throwing processes. Figure 3.1 illustrates the principle of quantifying psychophysiological activity as a process episode, in this case throwing a dart, and of ordering individual differences along one dimension of this process (accurate–inaccurate throw). This dimension is my possibility space for this process. In order to quantify the process I consider a parameter that takes into account the whole process not just isolated peaks, since the whole waveform is relevant activity. The most straightforward measure is to consider the EMG as a distribution of amplitude values which are either above or below a median value (for this person) of 7.5 μV. The proportions above 7.5 μV for an inaccurate (a) and accurate throw (b) are given in Table 3.1 together with the proportion for Figure 3.1(c), which is another inaccurate throw. The likelihood of (c) belonging to the process (a) is stronger than the likelihood of it belonging with (b). These odds strengthen my own (E^s) possibility distribution concerning differences in processes (as measured by my amplitude measure) between accurate/inaccurate throws and lead me to form a sharper possibility distribution (Fig. 3.2). By systematizing variation of the waveform along an individual difference dimension of process I have allowed more to be said about the data than would be possible with point measures and variance statistics.

observation was obviously considered by me to be the most likely to yield informative results. Why did I choose this? What were the alternatives? In the same way that I considered only relevant context in defining the EMG possibility space, I do the same with my hypothesis space. There is obvously a fairly large behavioural context behind my deciding to do the experiment that could involve various professional, financial or biographical details. In fact I have chosen this paradigm rather than a dual task methodology or distraction task, because I am interested in dartitis. This is a psychomotor problem affecting experienced darts players and involves difficulty in releasing the dart during the throw (Bender, Cooper and Hallam, 1985). In this example I am at mid-theory stage. On the basis of other experience I have developed a theory that at a high skill level certain independent actions of the thrower overlap and act as antagonists to one another so creating a cramp. This cramp is worse when the person is intending to throw accurately than when not. I therefore have two independent dimensions: skill (novice-experienced) of the thrower and intended focus of throw. So I have systematized both individual differences of the thrower and of the action, and now in systematizing my hypotheses' context, I am allowing for individual differences amongst experimenters as well.

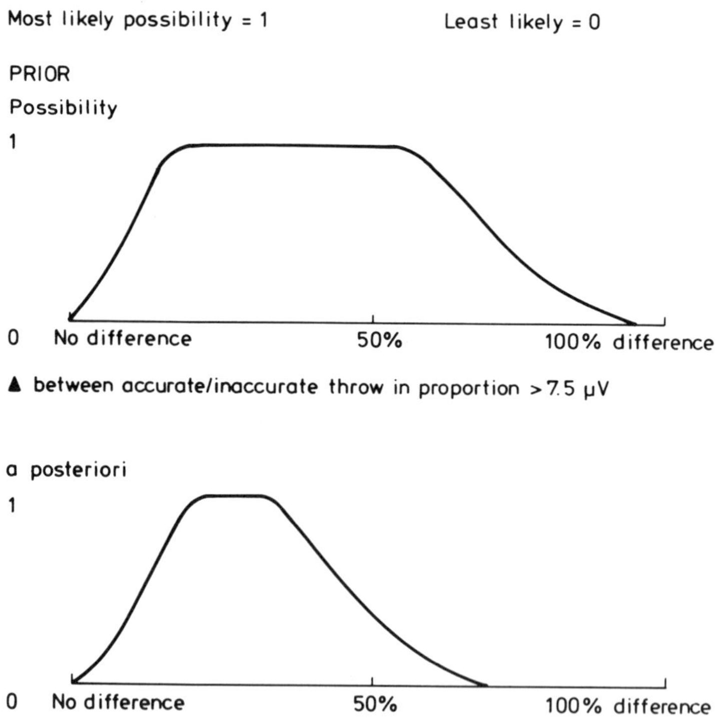

Figure 3.2. Experimenter's possibility distribution regarding EMG difference (▲) between accurate–inaccurate throw prior to and post the experiment.

I have several complex predictions about the outcome based on my own hunches and experience and the degree to which the predictions will be informative depends both on their specificity and on my confidence in them. First I am predicting that there will be less variation in the skilled thrower's than in novice's EMG since the more skilled will have developed a more automated style of throwing *but* none the less I expect there will be a less equivalence in process between focused and non-focused throw in the skilled than novice's. The development of a throw pattern does arise fairly early on in skill development (Jaegers and coworkers, 1989) so I expect a process pattern to emerge in intermediate skill levels but not in novice levels. I am taking percentage amplitude as my measurement so I expect a difference in the process to be reflected by a change in proportional presence or absence of amplitude values.

The above is my core prediction but it is not my only one since according to my possibility distribution some outcomes I can consider more possible than others depending on how close they are to my core prediction. If I found no EMG process difference at all between novice and skilled player, this would clearly lead to a complete shift in my possibility distribution. If, on the other hand, my prediction was generally correct but the degree of change in process is not as predicted, then some aspects will have to be revised but the essential distribution remains intact.

SHARPENING THEORY ACROSS PERSONAL CONTEXTS

These and subsequent predictions are nested within a related context. The largest context is the possibility distribution centred around a difference between skilled and unskilled throwers. The next context specifies alternative types of difference. Then there are further subsequent predictions of the magnitude of this type of a difference. This is a kind of onion-skin approach where one peels away a context at a time to refine the relevant dimension of behaviour but without losing the relatedness of each context (see Figure 3.3). This refining feeds back to my overall aim to winnow down a theory related to the occurrence of dartitis in skilled players. The next experimental context to follow here will be to look at a competitive/non-competitive dimension within skilled players only. These future findings would be related back to the present experiment to permit a coherent development of my theory over different contexts.

The way this research strategy compares with the usual hierarchic hypothetico-deductive procedure is given in Figure 3.3. In the traditional top-down approach the theory has four options: it can be strengthened, weakened, abandoned, or rationalized, but it cannot really be changed directly by the data. In the current approach the theory develops from narrow to comprehensive propositions as the experiments travel across related contexts. This is not quite the programmatic research of Lakatos (1978) but conducting

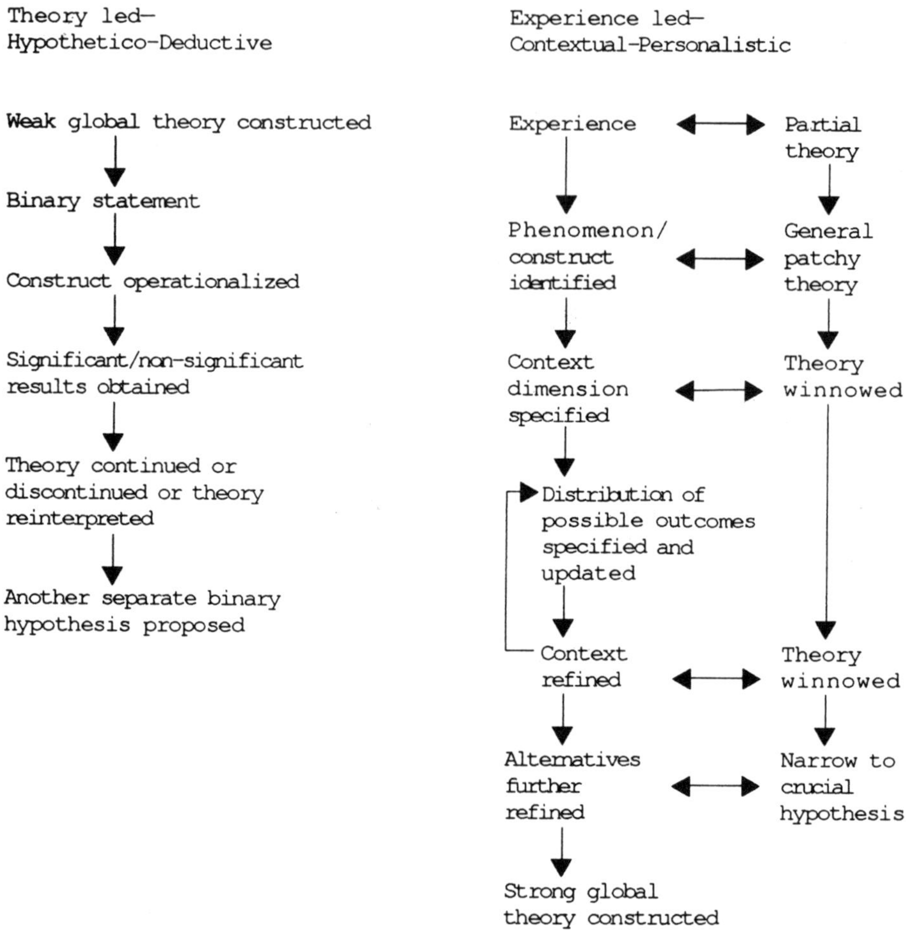

Figure 3.3. Comparison of theory development in conventional theory led hypothetico-deductive and in experience led contextual-personalistic approaches to method.

experiments in the context of a series of related studies reduces considerably the risk of type I and II errors.

This onion-skin approach integrates experience and theory. In traditional research the two are divorced and despite what the researcher may know or feel by experience, s/he is required to consider the theory as an absolute statement disconnected from prior or past immediate experience. But in practice it is sharp experience which dictates adequate experimentation and discovery; sharp theory can come later. Inductive development of knowledge involves the integration of learning by experience rather than probabilistic inference (Eells, 1988).

ECONOMY OF DESIGN FOR THE IDEP

There is also a gain here in the cost effectiveness of number of subjects used. As well as repeating behavioural episodes along a dimension to give variance a contextual meaning, my individual subjects are likewise patterned along a dimension. The subjects I am using in my darts example are highly selected from a highly selective population. This is necessary for my highly selective predictions, I do not wish to sample from a random population. But more especially I do not wish to sample randomly from my selected population, since I have ordered this variation dimensionally according to degree of skill. In fact, given the present specificity of my theory, I can draw some conclusion about the credibility of distribution of possible outcomes from one person (assuming I know their skill level). If I use another person it is more informative to choose someone from another part of the dimension, and subsequently a third person from another part rather than just repeat subjects at random, since this adds individual difference information.

The need for replication does depend on the confidence I have in my predictions. If my theory is at an initial very general stage, I might wish to run a number of subjects just to gain information for more specific predictions. If, for example, I really have no idea of the actual limits of my EMG measure during a particular process I might improve my confidence through repetition. But when, for example, after two or three repetitions of the same category of skilled thrower I have settled on EMG limits dividing the high-low accuracy category there is nothing to be gained by simply finding out more of the same. It is more informative to look at a different category along the dimension or refine the context further and test out a more refined prediction. As I have said, theory develops at the same pace as experience develops, so the research is experience led not theory led. But theory is never totally absent since there must be some general purpose behind the programme of studies or one would not be doing the experiment in the first place. The telic basis of the experimenter's behaviour would be lacking. There must be some intentional behavioural context surrounding glueing on electrodes no matter how vague and even personal the theory. Personalistic context can include rational and irrational elements. In fact, admitting such a personalistic behavioural context to a study might aid comparison of studies. Knowing that the design of an experiment about imagery and somatic activity was partly related to laboratory availability and that the department only had enough money for one EMG channel could help contextualize the possibilities available to the experimenter. All these minor factors bear on the possibilistic context—the alternative possibilities—open to the experimenter along her or his personal dimension of most possible to least possible choice of experiment.

SUMMARY

In summary the "possibilist" proceeds as follows:

(1) Prior experience identifies a psychophysiological behaviour as a construct.
(2) The limits of the psychophysiological process in question are defined and described very specifically as in the example of aiming, throwing and releasing a dart.
(3) This process is considered as an active dimension (e.g. accurate versus inaccurate throwing). A possibility space and distribution is constructed by recording the form of other possible processes along this dimension. Several dimensions of process can be considered at the same time and the person themselves ordered along an individual difference dimension.
(4) Non-probabilistic statistics can establish whether these possible processes are separate or equivalent (see O'Connor (1990) on process limits).
(5) The experimenter considers his/her observation as a process and constructs a distribution of least and most possible observations in order to allow outcome to update prior experience. Outcomes falling outside of limits of the maximum possibility lead to a change in observer's possibility space.
(6) When the experimenter is confident that his/her current possibility distribution is the best supported above comparable ones, the psychophysiological construct is refined along another related process dimension and other experimental context is considered.
(7) As experience of the construct is gained over different dimensions and contexts, theory is developed until a comprehensive theory can be supported by a very sharp experimenter possibility distribution. This theory is preferred over others as a consequence of combined maximum possibilities developed over successive process contexts.

CONCLUDING REMARKS

The possibilistic approach incorporates elements of the other personalistic approaches but avoids some of the statistical problems by replacing probability with a person centred possibility distribution. The approach also helps connect theory and description, process with outcome and deductive with inductive inference.

Starting with complex qualitative behaviour as a unit links process and effect approaches. Arranging subjects along an ordered dimension rather than sampling at random, means the sanctity of individual information is retained in a group context by making the dimensional construct *the* context.

This has recently been of much concern to psychotherapy research where discrepancies of individual differences in process and group effects are a major problem. For example, Werbart (1989) suggests process and outcome research are at opposite poles. Effect research investigates whether psychotherapy has any impact at all and process research examines what, for whom and in what manner it is effective in psychotherapy. Werbart (1989) ties in the process—outcome conflict with another contradiction—that between measurement and description or between quantitative and qualitative methods. He suggests qualitative aspects may perform a crucial function at the beginning of clinical investigation. He proposes a methodological norm postulating that research methods need to take into account essential aspects of what is being investigated in the study of psychotherapy outcome. The gap between psychotherapy research and clinical practice can be reduced by identifying processes such as the patient's perception of change and their perception of the therapeutic relationship—crucial variables that may not be accessible to quantitative methods.

Shahom-Salomon (1990) notes that the traditional idea that therapeutic processes have unique and fixed meanings cannot be taken for granted in light of the possibility that their meanings are context bound. Different processes can serve a similar outcome and a particular process can serve different outcomes in different contexts. He suggests this upsets correlational studies which imply a uniformity of process amongst the change in variables they are correlating. Shahom-Salomon (1990) illustrates the pitfalls of ignoring process with the example that change in process within a context and the change over sessions may well be in opposite directions. So for example increased compliance during a therapy session could be accompanied by decreased compliance across sessions, indicating context is important to understanding the process of compliance. In a therapeutic context the complex nature of processes requires the analysis of patterns, looking at a more focused inquiry of the differential contribution of that process within different contexts.

Greenberg (1986) is of the view that processes can be viewed in a hierarchy of contexts. According to Greenberg, speech acts are embedded in therapeutic episodes that in turn are embedded in other social relationships, and it is this pattern of variables that reveal therapeutic significance not the presence of any single variable. The approach I am advocating here for IDEP also suggests that experiments should progress across embedded process contexts in order to elaborate theory.

But a key point in qualitative inference is centring observation on the individual. This issue touches on the importance of causal versus telic accounts of experimental behaviour. Howard, Youngs and Siatczynski (1989) make the point that in behavioural terms telic and causal accounts are rivals. "Did you jump or were you pushed?" are incompatible accounts of agency. The authors suggest personal agency involves primarily plans for future action, and suggest that much of what is seen in explanatory theories as causal is really telic behaviour. So personal activity becomes the central observation point for deciphering both internal and external events (O'Connor, 1987; 1989). Considering activity of the person as the defining context for psychophysiological effects, involves in my opinion the least possible theoretical assumptions about what is being observed.

A principal objection to this personal process unit approach in psychophysiology is that constructs taken from what is observable may not be relevant to underlying process that is unobservable. This argument, for example, has been put forward by Coles, Gratton and Gehring (1987) who made the point that "correlation" is distinct from "manifestation" and that identifying antecedent or consequent behaviour accompanying an evoked potential peak, say, is not the same as identifying activity manifested in the peak. This argument assumes that the only relation between mind and body is one of causal isomorphism; that a brain state causes a behavioural state and vice versa. But rather I am suggesting a descriptive isomorphism; that what the person is doing is relevant to what is being measured. The assumption, one well supported currently, is that what goes on in my brain and nervous system at the moment is in some way relevant to my behavioural activity at the moment and the observer's job is to find the right sized window to describe the relevant process. The question of core-relevance is tackled through the successive narrowing of contexts, but the construct remains through all contexts identified as an active attribute of the person's behaviour. If this assumption of isomorphism is incorrect, and current brain activity turns out to be more related to my activity yesterday or in 2 months' time, then at the moment, I think mine will not be the only red face in the research community.

Finally, considering behaviour as an independent attribute in design aids negotiations between the two psychologies: nomothetic and idiopathic. The personalistic approach allows a mating of the two schools of psychology so important to personality and individual differences, namely, the nomothetic and idiopathic, exactly because of the method's descriptive nature. Both experimental and associational type studies become interchangeable since the experimental construct has initially been identified as an attribute. This is an attempt that Eysenck made in 1954 with his criterion analysis. Eysenck's idea was to provide a criterion by which to identify attributes from factor analysis as potential variables in research experiments. But the attempt to be both descriptive and manipulative is extremely difficult within the explanatory variance framework. Where all items in a sample space are considered independent attributes (whether behavioural, or characterological) they can be ordered dimensionally according to whether they represent presence or absence of a factor. Then higher-order trait association studies can link directly to corresponding molecular level attributes used in experimental settings.

REFERENCES

Altman, I. (1988) Process, transaction/contextual and outcome research: an alternative to the traditional distinction between basic and applied research. *Social Behaviour*, **3**, 259–280.

Bakan, D. (1967) *On Method.* San Francisco: Jossey-Bass.

Barnard, G.A. (1969) Statistical inference. *Journal of the Royal Statistical Society*, **11(B)**, 115–149.

Bayes, T. (1763) An essay towards solving a problem in the doctrine of chances. *Philosophical Transactions of the Royal Society*, **53**, 370–418.

Benassi, V. and Belli, R. (1989) Statistics and replication experiments: comparing interaction effects. *Cognitive Therapy and Research*, **13**(3), 283–293.

Bender, M., Cooper, A. and Hallam, R. (1985) What is dartitis: a review. *Darts World*, June, 12–13.

Brinberg, P. and McGrath, J.E. (1985) *Validity and the Research Process.* Beverly Hills, CA: Sage.

Chow, S.L. (1988) Significance test or effect size? *Psychological Bulletin*, **103**, 105–110.

Chihara, C.S. (1987) Some problems for Bayesian confirmation theory? *British Journal of Philosophy of Science*, **38**, 551–560.

Cicourel, A.V. (1964) *Method and Measurement in Sociology*. New York: Free Press.

Clark, D. (1983) *Action Systems.* Oxford: Oxford University Press.

Cohen, L.S. (1981) Can human irrationality be experimentally demonstrated? *Behavioural and Brain Science*, **4**, 317–370.

Coles, M., Gratton, G. and Gehring, W. (1987) Theory in cognitive psychophysiology. *Journal of Psychophysiology*, **1**, 13–16.

Collins, L.M., Cliff, N. and Dent, C.W. (1988) The longitudinal quitman simplex: a new methodology for measurement of dynamic constructs in longitudinal panel studies. *Applied Psychological Measurement*, **12**(3), 217–230.

De Finetti, B. (1974) *Theory of Probability.* New York: Wiley.

Douglas, J.D. (1971) *Understanding Everyday Life.* London: Routledge & Kegan Paul.

Edwards, A.W.F. (1972) *Likelihood.* Cambridge: Cambridge University Press.

Edwards, W., Lindman, M. and Savage, L.J. (1962) Bayesian statistical inference for psychological research. *Psychological Review*, **70**, 193–242.

Eells, E. (1988) On the alleged impossibility of inductive probability. *British Journal of Philosophy of Science*, **39**, 111–116.

Eysenck, H.J. (1954) Criterion analysis. *Psychological Review*, **61**(1), 59–74.

Feyerabend, P. (1975) *Against Method.* London: New Left Books.

Feyerabend, P. (1978) *Science in a Free Society.* London: New Left Books.

Feyerabend, P.K. (1988) Knowledge of the role of theories. *Philosophy of the Social Sciences*, **18**, 157–178.

Fisher, R.A. (1959) *Statistical Methods and Scientific Inference, 2nd edn.* Edinburgh: Oliver Boyd.

Gale, A. and Baker, S. (1981) In vivo or in vitro? Some effects of laboratory environments with particular reference to the psychophysiology experiment. In M.J. Christie and P.G. Mellett (eds), *Foundation of Psychosomatics.* London: John Wiley & Sons.

Greenberg, L.S. (1986) Change process research. *Journal of Consulting and Clinical Psychology*, **54**, 4–9.

Gresemer, J.R. and Wade, M.J. (1988) Laboratory models, causal explanations and group selection. *Biology and Philosophy*, **3**, 67–96.

Howard, G.S., Youngs, W.H. and Siatczynski, A. (1989) A research strategy for studying telic human behavior. *Journal of Mind and Behavior*, **10**(4), 393–410.

Iacobucci, D. and Wasserman, S. (1988) A general framework for the statistical analysis of sequential dyadic interaction data. *Psychological Bulletin*, **103**(3), 379–390.

Jaegers, S., Peterson, R., Dantuma, R., Millen, B., Geuze, R. and Schellekens, J. (1989) Kinesiologic aspects of motor learning in dart throwing. *Journal of Movement Studies*, **16**, 161–171.

Kaplan, M. (1989) Bayesianism without the Black box. *Philosophy of Science*, **56**, 48–69.

Kulkani, D. and Simons, M.A. (1988) The processes of scientific discovery, the strategy of experimentation. *Cognitive Science*, **12**, 139–175.

Lakatos, I. (1978) Methodology of scientific research programs. In J. Worrall and G. Currie (eds), *Philosophical Papers, Vol. 1.* Cambridge: Cambridge University Press.

Lando, M. (1989) Treatment outcome evaluation methodology in smoking cessation strengths and key issues. *Advances in Behavior, Research and Therapy*, **11**, 201–214.

Lang, P.J. (1979) A bio-informational theory of emotional imagery. *Psychophysiology*, **16**, 495–512.

Lewin, K. (1951) *Field Theory in Social Science.* New York: Harper.

Lindley, P.V. (1965) *Introduction to Probability and Statistics From a Bayesian View Point.* Cambridge: Cambridge University Press.

Maher, B. (1978) Stimulus sampling in clinical research: representative design reviewed. *Journal of Consulting and Clinical Psychology*, **46**(4), 643–647.

McGuire, R.D. (1969) The life of an artefact. In R. Rosenthal and R.L. Rosnow (eds), *Artefact in Behaviour Research.* London: Academic Press.

Mead, G.M. (1910) *The Philosophy of the Act.* Chicago: University of Chicago Press.

Medawar, P.B. (1967) *The Art of the Soluble.* London: London University Press.

Morrisson, D.E. and Hankel, R.E. (eds) (1970) *The Significance Test Controversy.* Chicago: Aldine.

Norusis, M.J. (1983) *SPSS-X.* New York: McGraw-Hill.

O'Connor, K. (1985) The Bayesian-inferential approach to defining response processes in psychophysiology. *Psychophysiology*, **22**(4), 464–483.

O'Connor, K. (1986) The effects of smoking and personality on slow cortical potentials recorded within a signal detection paradigm. *Physiological Psychology*, **14**(1), 49–62.

O'Connor, K. (1987) A response process model of behavior. In H.J. Eysenck and I. Martin (eds), *Theoretical Foundations of Behavior Therapy.* New York: Plenum.

O'Connor, K. (1989) Psychophysiology and skilled behaviour: a theoretical revision. *Journal of Psychophysiology*, **3**, 219–223.

O'Connor, K. (1990) Towards a process paradigm in psychophysiology. *International Journal of Psychophysiology*, **9**, 209–223.

Phillips, L.D. (1973) *Bayesian Statistics for Social Scientists.* London: Nelson.

Polanyi, M. (1958) *Personal Knowledge: Towards a Post-Critical Philosophy.* Chicago: University of Chicago Press.

Popper, K. (1963) *Conjectures and Refutations.* London: Routledge & Kegan Paul.

Rosnow, R.L. and Rosenthal, R. (1989) Statistical procedures and the justification of knowledge in psychological science. *American Psychologist*, **44**(10), 1276–1284.

Rouanet, H. and Lecoutre, B. (1983) Specific reference in ANOVA: From significance tests to Bayesian procedures. *British Journal of Statistical and Mathematical Psychology*, **36**, 252–268.

Rouanet, H., Lepine, D. and Holender, D. (1978) Model acceptability and the use of Bayes-fiducial methods for validating models. In J. Requin (ed.), *Attention and Performance VII.* Hillsdale: Lawrence Erlbaum.

Rozeboum, W.W. (1960) The fallacy of the null hypothesis significance test. *Psychological Bulletin*, **57**, 416–428.
Savage, L.J. (1962) *The Foundations of Statistical Inference*. London: Methuen.
Shawver, L. (1977) Research variables in psychology and the logic of their creation. *Psychiatry*, **40**, 1–16.
Shahom-Salomon, V. (1990) Interrelating research processes of process research. *Journal of Consulting and Clinical Psychology*, **58**(3), 295–303.
Springer, K. (1990) In defense of theories. *Cognition*, **35**, 293–298.
Steger, J.A. (ed.) (1971) *Readings in Statistics for the Behavioral Scientist*. New York: Holt, Rinehart & Winston.
Walmpold, B.E., Davis, B. and Good, R. (1990) Hypothesis validity of clinical research. *Journal of Consulting and Clinical Psychology*, **58**(3), 360–367.
Weber, M. (1947) *The Theory of Social and Economic Organization*. New York: Oxford University Press.
Weimer, W.R. (1979) *Notes on the Methodology of Scientific Research*. Hillsdale, NJ: Lawrence Erlbaum.
Werbart, A. (1989) Psychotherapy research between process and effect: the need of new methodological approaches. *Acta Psychiatrica Scandinavica*, **79**, 511–522.
Winer, B.J. (1971) *Statistical Principles in Experimental Design (Section 7.6)*. Tokyo: McGraw-Hill Kogakosha.

Chapter 4

Models for the Testing of Theory

William Revelle

and

Kristen Joan Anderson

Department of Psychology, Northwestern University, Evanston, IL 60208, USA

ABSTRACT

A variety of methods for testing theories linking arousal, personality, and motivation to behavior are reviewed. Stress is placed on construct validity, boundary conditions, selection and interpretation of dependent measures, and levels of analysis. Illustrations from research relating impulsivity and stress to cognitive performance are used to clarify our arguments.

INTRODUCTION

In this chapter, we discuss a variety of methodologies for examining the relationship of individual differences to the motivational constructs of effort and arousal. While many approaches are profitable, we concentrate on several central design considerations and the advantages and disadvantages of specific techniques that are particularly well suited to such research. Specifically,

Handbook of Individual Differences: Biological Perspectives
Edited by Anthony Gale and Michael W. Eysenck

we address (a) the construct validity of causes presumed to underlie personality and motivational effects, (b) the boundaries that limit or mediate these influences, (c) the choice and interpretation of dependent measures, and (d) the level of analysis appropriate to tests of various personality- or motivation-related hypotheses. We will discuss these issues within the framework of an individual differences (trait) perspective, drawing heavily from our research, which has addressed the impact of introversion–extraversion (I-E) and its lower-order component of impulsivity on cognitive performance.

Our aim is to use illustrations from the study of I-E to suggest useful strategies for experimental personality and motivation research. We will not discuss purely correlational or other non-experimental research strategies, even though they are traditional within the field of personality, as the difficulties of drawing causal inferences from such approaches are well known. (See, however, Cook and Campbell, 1979, for a discussion of non-experimental designs that do permit causal interpretation.) Although it has been argued (e.g. Carlson, 1971) that no personality research can be truly experimental, some individual difference dimensions are linked to constructs such as effort or arousal that can be experimentally manipulated. Within such a framework, attention to the logic of construct validation allows experimental research.

CONSTRUCT VALIDITY OF PRESUMED UNDERLYING CAUSES

We agree with many psychologists that construct validity is one of the most fundamental issues confronting researchers. That is, given that theoretical constructs can never be directly observed, as all measurement reflects the influence of both relevant and irrelevant sources of variation to some extent, progressive development within a program of research requires the use of techniques designed to justify theoretical interpretation of imperfect empirical observation. Thus, we argue that the most meaningful research on personality, effort, or arousal takes place within a theoretical framework (a nomological network) and that every effort must be made to counter plausible alternative accounts of observed phenomena. Many of the pertinent design issues have been discussed at length elsewhere (e.g. Campbell and Stanley, 1963; Cook and Campbell, 1979; Cronbach and Meehl, 1955); we stress the importance of multiple operational definitions of constructs and experimental designs that foster complex predictions (Anderson, 1990).

Of all the dimensions of individual differences, I-E is perhaps that with the best defined nomological net (H. J. Eysenck, 1991). Furthermore, I-E is linked to the construct of arousal, thus allowing experimental manipulation. Specifically, it has long been suggested that I-E is related to individual differences in physiological arousal or to the neo-Pavlovian dimension of strength of the nervous system (Claridge, 1967; H.J. Eysenck, 1967; Gray, 1964). Hans Eysenck's theory of I-E as it relates to cognitive performance may be summarized in terms of two postulates: (a) Introverts are more aroused physiologically than extraverts and (b) performance is an inverted-U function of arousal. Evidence for the first of these postulates was put forward by Claridge (1967) and H. J. Eysenck (1967) and has been recently reviewed by H. J. Eysenck and M. W. Eysenck (1985) and Stelmack (1981, 1990). Eysenck's second postulate is based on the Yerkes–Dodson law, which has received substantial empirical support (e.g. Anderson, 1988; Broadhurst, 1959; Duffy, 1962; Hebb, 1955; Yerkes and Dodson, 1908), although it is not unequivocally accepted.

In combination with the assumption that increases in stimulation lead to increases in arousal, these two postulates suggest that on tasks of moderate difficulty, introverts will perform better than extraverts in non-stimulating situations, as well as extraverts in moderately stimulating situations, and less well under high stimulation or stress. This model predicts, then, that there should be a consistent (although complex) pattern of differences in cognitive performance as a function of individual differences in I-E in combination with variations in situationally induced stress.

Revelle, Amaral, and Turriff (1976) tested these predictions by manipulating the arousal of introverts and extraverts before asking them to complete a difficult task involving verbal ability items similar to those of the Graduate Record Examination (GRE). Three conditions—(a) relaxed, (b) time pressure, and (c) time pressure with caffeine—were used in a within-subjects design. The results were quite clear-cut: The scores of introverts fell by about 0.6 standard deviations from the relaxed to the most stressed condition, while those of extraverts rose by about the same amount. Although these results do not provide direct evidence for the curvilinearity postulate, they are compatible with that generalization, assuming that introverts were at their optimal arousal in the relaxed condition and were over-aroused in the time pressure and time pressure plus caffeine conditions, while extraverts were under-aroused in the relaxed condition and were brought up to their optimal level with increasing stress.

This study illustrates the use of an important technique in personality research: Not only were multiple operational definitions of arousal employed (I-E, caffeine, and time stress), but moreover, these definitions varied in ways that minimized the extent to which their non-arousal-related aspects overlapped. For example, while experimental manipulations of arousal (e.g. caffeine or time stress) may produce information that requires cognitive processing (e.g. physiological changes or worry), arousal-related personality variables are less plausibly linked to preemption of information processing resources, as they involve habitual or highly familiar and predictable states. As Campbell and Fiske (1959) and Cook and Campbell (1979) have noted, the argument for construct validity is strengthened when results from different methods of operationalization converge because such data reduce the plausibility of attributing observed effects to the irrelevancies associated with any particular operational definition.

Several different types of experimental designs allow inclusion of multiple operational definitions and can thus be effectively employed to examine personality-behavior relationships. Each has advantages and disadvantages, and in practice, most studies (including our own) employ too few levels of the relevant construct or require too many assumptions to be conclusive. We will consider three main designs—factorial, additive, and multiple levels—in some detail. The examples we use are drawn primarily from our own research, which has involved a variety of different designs. Our experiences have afforded us familiarity with the strengths, and particularly the weaknesses, of these strategies.

FACTORIAL DESIGNS

The standard factorial design in research addressing causal models of personality compares the behavior of people who differ along a trait dimension across conditions assumed to vary in terms of the construct believed to underlie that individual differences variable. Thus, rather than using several levels of one variable, the experimental conditions are combinations of several different operational definitions that are usually defined dichotomously. For example, Davies and Hockey (1966) assumed noisy conditions to be more arousing than quiet conditions, a high signal frequency to be more arousing than a low signal frequency, and introverts to be more aroused than extraverts. When they combined these variables in a $2 \times 2 \times 2$ factorial design, they found that scores on a visual cancellation test could be arranged in a manner compatible with their assumptions and with the additional assumption of an inverted-U performance–arousal function.

Unfortunately, the experimental conditions resulting from factorial combination of variables presumed to index the same construct cannot be uniquely ordered. That is, it is not possible to order all eight cells in such a $2 \times 2 \times 2$ design unambiguously, although it is possible to form six different "partial orders", each of four cells. (See Figure 4.1.) For example, extraverts in quiet with a low signal frequency are less aroused than introverts in the same condition, who are less aroused than introverts with a high signal frequency, who are in turn less aroused than introverts with a high signal frequency tested with noise. Some comparisons cannot be made, however (e.g. between introverts in quiet and extraverts in noise). If the assumption that each independent variable is related to the same construct is correct, then each of these partial orders should be related to behavior in a predictable way. But this analysis is complicated by the hypothesis that links the construct to

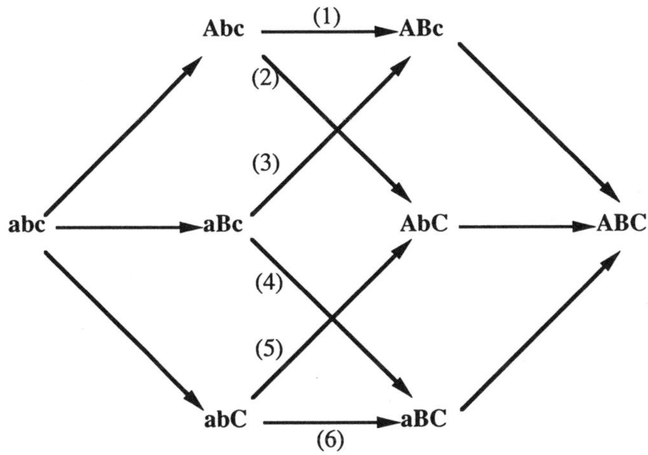

Figure 4.1. Partial orders formed by the factorial combination of three dichotomously defined variables (represented by different letters of the alphabet). Upper-case letters indicate the high level of the variable (e.g. high arousal); lower-case letters, the low level. Thus, for partial order (1), the four conditions in order of increasing level of the presumed underlying construct are: abc, Abc, ABc, and ABC.

behavior: In this case, the assumption of a single-peaked relationship between arousal and performance allows for simple increases in performance with arousal, inverted-U relationships, or simple decreases. Even so, the model can be tested by examining each partial order.

While Davies and Hockey admit that their ordering of the eight cells is *post hoc*, they suggest that such an ordering is necessary to understand their results. But a factorial design is more appropriate for demonstrating that different variables do not have similar effects on behavior than it is to show that they do. Thus, this type of design is particularly appropriate for testing whether different manipulations affect the same underlying construct (e.g. arousal).

In the context of the arousal–performance relationship, factorial designs with dichotomously defined variables have a further disadvantage, as such designs are unable to produce compelling evidence for curvilinearity *per se*: With random data, of the 40 320 (i.e. 8!) ways to order the eight cells derived from a 2 × 2 × 2 design, 2880 ways (i.e. 7%) are compatible with the assumption of an inverted-U relationship between arousal and performance. The number of variables included in a factorial design is of obvious importance in this sense. For example, a 2 × 2 design is much weaker than a 2 × 2 × 2 design: of the 24 possible orderings of the four cells, one half will allow for both partial orders of length three to be satisfied by chance (Table 4.1).

A useful variation on this factorial approach is to include a variable that should influence the effect under investigation but that is not itself an operational definition of the presumed causal construct. For example, since the

Table 4.1. Probability of observing at least *N* partial orders that fit a monotonically increasing or curvilinear (single peaked) hypothesis for different experimental designs.

Design	Length of partial orders	Probability of satisfying at least *N* partial orders 0	1	2	3	4	5	6
Factorial								
2 × 2	3	1.000	0.833	0.500				
2 × 2 × 2	4	1.000	0.710	0.533	0.346	0.241	0.099	0.071
Multi-level								
2 × 3	4	1.000	0.556	0.300	0.144			
2 × 4	5	1.000	0.294	0.147	0.065	0.027		
2 × 5	6	1.000	0.127	0.058	0.024	0.010	0.003	
3 × 3	5	1.000	0.360	0.210	0.121	0.057	0.037	0.015

Adapted and extended from Revelle, 1973.

original formulation of the Yerkes–Dodson law (1908) was in terms of task difficulty as well as stress, a task variable can be factorially crossed with two or more operational definitions of arousal. Thus, it is possible to cross I-E with an arousal manipulation (e.g. caffeine versus placebo), and to examine the effects on performance at two levels of task difficulty (e.g. Anderson and Revelle, 1982; 1983). The pattern of results may then be compared with the partial orders predicted by theory. (The simpler design in which a task variable is crossed with only an individual difference variable is much less satisfactory, as results could simply reflect individual differences in the abilities pertinent to the tasks.)

Our primary concern in addressing task variables has been to clarify the aspects of task difficulty relevant to the relationship between arousal, effort, and performance. Two different theories suggest which tasks should be facilitated and which hurt by high arousal. One of these models suggests that curvilinearity results from a single monotonic relationship. Easterbrook (1959) proposed that the range of cue utilization narrows with increasing arousal. Thus, tasks with fewer requirements for simultaneous information processing should generally be helped by increases in arousal while tasks with greater information processing demands should be hurt. An alternative model focuses on two components of cognitive processing that are presumed to be affected in opposite ways by arousal. Specifically, it is argued that arousal facilitates sustained information transfer (SIT) or the rapid throughput of information, but reduces the likelihood of information being available after a short period of time. This latter effect can be thought of as arousal hindering short-term memory (STM) or the retrieval of information (Folkard, 1975; Hamilton, Hockey, and Rejman, 1977; Hockey, 1979; Humphreys and Revelle, 1984, Humphreys *et al.*, 1980, Revelle, 1989). (As a simplistic construct, STM is likely to yield to more sophisticated models such as a mutlicomponent working-memory system as data accumulate, but it is used here to avoid some of the restricting assumptions associated with more specific models of short-term storage or retrieval. For example, the Baddeley and Hitch, 1974, concept of working memory assumes capacity limitations; while STM can be interpreted in capacity terms, it does not require it.) We have completed two experiments with results compatible with both of these theories (Anderson and Revelle, 1982; 1983). The first examined the effect of impulsivity and caffeine on proofreading; the second examined visual scanning.

The proofreading task, which was previously used by Weinstein (1974, 1977) in research on noise, assessed the detection of two types of errors. The detection of intraword errors, such as misspellings, was assumed to require fewer processing resources than that of interword errors, such as faulty grammar. We used a factorial design that crossed impulsivity (low or high), experimentally manipulated arousal (caffeine or placebo), and task difficulty (intra- or interword errors). (As discussed below, research suggests that impulsivity mediates the association between arousal and I-E.) To control for diurnal effects, all subjects were run at 9:00 a.m. The results indicated a significant triple interaction between impulsivity, drug, and type of error. For the interword errors, caffeine reduced the sensitivity of the less impulsive subjects but had a slight facilitative effect for the more impulsive subjects. For the intraword errors, on the other hand, caffeine had a detrimental effect for both high and low impulsives. In addition, caffeine reduced the number of words read by the low impulsive subjects and increased it for the high impulsives.

These results suggest that increases in arousal lead to decrements in performance on tasks that require a broad range of cue utilization. Alternatively, the results suggest that tasks with a higher STM load are more sensitive to arousal-induced decrements than tasks with a lower STM load. The problematic decrease in sensitivity with caffeine for the high impulsives on the intraword task is impossible to interpret, since these subjects also read more lines. Thus, their decrease in sensitivity could have been due to a speed–accuracy trade-off.

A second experiment (Anderson and Revelle, 1983) employed a task with a more obvious STM component: a visual scanning task sensitive to diurnal variations in arousal (Folkard, *et al.*, 1976). This task involves searching through strings of letters looking for those strings that contain all of a set of target stimuli. The target set consisted of either 2 letters (low memory load) or 6 letters (high memory load). Folkard and his colleagues have shown that performance on the 2-letter task improves when subjects' body temperature increases and decreases when body temperature decreases. Performance on the 6-letter task, in contrast, has an inverse relationship to arousal as indexed by body temperature.

We conceptually replicated that study using caffeine and impulsivity as indexes of arousal; subjects were run at 9:00 a.m. As expected, there was a reliable interaction between drug and target size. This cross-over interaction indicated that caffeine was associated with greater accuracy on the 2-letter task and decreased accuracy on the 6-letter task. Caffeine also led to a greater increase in the number of lines read in the 2-letter than in the 6-letter condition, although this interaction was not reliable.

The assumption that caffeine and impulsivity involves a similiar activational state (arousal) implies that there should have been a similar interaction between impulsivity and task. This interaction did not occur. Instead there was a reliable interaction between impulsivity, target size, and task sequence. (Target size had been counterbalanced using two different task sequences.) As discussed elsewhere (Anderson and Revelle, 1983), this interaction suggested strategic differences between high and low impulsive subjects.

What is clear from both of these experiments is that the impact of arousal on performance can be moderated by task variables. Factorial designs that include a task factor can thus allow an exploration of the basis of the task-difficulty parameter of the Yerkes–Dodson law: by showing that systematic arousal effects are dependent on task parameters, these results support the interpretation that arousal affects some central aspect or aspects of information processing. That is, the effects of arousal on performance do not appear to be simply generalized stress reactions. Not surprisingly, it is also apparent that high and low impulsives differ from each other in more than just their arousal. This observation highlights the need for careful consideration of the impact of the irrelevancies included in any single operational definition of a construct (Matthews, 1989; Matthews, Jones and Chamberlain, 1989).

ADDITIVE DESIGNS

In contrast to factorial designs, additive designs do (or at least should) allow unambiguous ordering of conditions presumed to index a single underlying construct. With this design, several different operational definitions of a construct (e.g. several different stressors) are combined through successive addition rather than factorial combination. One example of this approach has already been described—the study of Revelle, Amaral, and Turriff (1976) that examined the effects of I-E, time stress, and caffeine on GRE performance.

Additive designs have been used successfully by a number of researchers (e.g. Geen, 1985), but as our second example, we describe an experiment that illustrates its chief disadvantage. Revelle (1973) studied the effects of group size, incentives, and noise on a variety of simple cognitive tasks by successively increasing one variable at a time. Six conditions, in presumed order of increasing arousal, were:

(a) working alone without incentives or noise;
(b) working with another person without incentives or noise;
(c) working in a two person group with competitive instructions;
(d) competing in a two person group with monetary incentives for good performance;
(e) competing in an eight person group with monetary incentives;
(f) competing in an eight person group with monetary incentives and 80 db(A) noise.

Unfortunately for the hypothesis, this ordering was not as unambiguous as desired: a physiological index of arousal (skin conductance) suggested that increases in group size led to decreases in arousal. A *post hoc* explanation for this unexpected (cf. Zajonc, 1965) decrease in arousal was that subjects were more frightened by the experimental apparatus (e.g., the skin conductance electrodes) when alone than when in the safety of a large group. Furthermore, contrary to a simple arousal hypothesis, it was found that while skin conductance and I-E were related to performance within conditions, the addition of social incentives eliminated this relationship. That is, when social incentives did not vary, performance was a negative monotonic function of skin conductance for introverts, but an inverted-U function for extraverts. When social incentives were varied (i.e. across conditions), this interaction did not occur. Thus, although the six conditions seemed to be unambiguously ordered a priori, the results suggested that the separate manipulations were not affecting the same underlying dimension. Instead, the results suggested that at least two motivational dimensions, effort and arousal, were involved (cf. Humphreys and Revelle, 1984; Revelle, 1989).

MULTIPLE-LEVELS DESIGNS

In the final experimental strategy we will discuss, three or more levels of the same operational definition are included. In its simplest version, only one independent variable is examined. Although such a procedure generally ensures unequivocal ordering of experimental conditions, evidence for construct validity in such a design is relatively weak, relying on confirmatory manipulation checks or extrapolation from earlier research.

A much stronger design combines this simple multiple-levels approach with the factorial approach: two or more operational definitions are crossed, with three or more levels of at least one of these indexes being included. For example, Gilliland (1976) studied the effects of three levels of caffeine (0, 2, and 4 mg/kg of body weight) on the performance of introverts, ambiverts and extraverts using the same verbal performance task (a practice Graduate Record Exam or GRE) used by Revelle, Amaral and Turriff (1976). Gilliland found that while there was an inverted-U relationship between caffeine and performance for introverts, there was a flat relationship for ambiverts and a monotonically increasing one for extraverts. The overall interaction of personality × caffeine was statistically reliable, and more importantly, the pattern of five of the six partial orders fits those predicted by the curvilinear hypothesis (from Table 4.1 this has a non-parametric probability < 0.04). Gupta (1977) found that performance on an IQ test decreased for introverts with increasing doses of amphetamine while the performance of extraverts showed an inverted-U relationship; peak performance for extraverts was with 10 mg of amphetamine, with lower performance at 0, 5 and 15 mg. Thus, both of these between-subjects studies showed reliable group-level evidence for curvilinearity as well as demonstrating that introverts are more susceptible to performance deficits than extraverts.

Anderson (1988) employed an even more complex design, crossing impulsivity (low or high) with five levels of caffeine (0, 1, 2, 3, and 4 mg/kg body weight) and two levels of task difficulty (easy, a letter cancellation task, or difficult, GRE items). Each subject completed both tasks in each dose condition at 9:00 a.m. Results for the GRE task largely replicated Gilliland's findings: The performance of the high impulsive subjects generally improved with increasing dosage levels, while the performance of low impulsive subjects first improved and then deteriorated as dose increased. In contrast, performance on the easy task reflected a reliable linear (increasing) component of the dose effect regardless of personality, again demonstrating that the arousal–performance relationship is mediated by task difficulty.

COMPARISON OF METHODS

We can summarize this brief review of strategies for experimental personality research by noting the most salient advantages and disadvantages of each design. In terms of weaknesses, (a) the factorial design suffers from problems in assessing the degree of the presumed underlying construct reflected by different combinations of operational definitions; (b) the additive design suffers from the necessity of assuming that different operational definitions are associated with the same underlying dimension; and (c) the multiple-levels design suffers from the difficulty of finding indexes of the construct that are quantifiable enough to use in distinguishably different amounts.

But each of these methods also has some advantages, most notably: (a) the factorial design tests whether different operational definitions in fact affect behavior in similar ways; (b) the additive design allows for efficient allocation of subjects across a presumed range of the underlying dimension; and (c) multiple levels of a single operational definition can provide relatively strong evidence regarding hypotheses that specify particular personality–behavior functions (e.g. curvilinear ones).

Finally, each of these approaches allows tests of causal hypotheses that are relatively high in construct validity. We have already explicitly noted the importance of multiple operational definitions of the presumed underlying construct. We have also pointed to a second important design consideration—the complexity of the experimental hypothesis. In a purely probabilistic sense, more complex designs (i.e. those with more variables in a factorial design, more combinations in an additive design, or more levels in a multiple-levels design) are capable of yielding more compelling evidence than simpler designs because a smaller proportion of the possible outcomes can be construed as compatible with the experimental hypothesis. Our comparison of the 2×2 and $2 \times 2 \times 2$ factorial designs highlighted this issue. But complex designs, or more precisely, complex hypotheses, have a further advantage: as noted by Cronbach and Meehl (1955), evidence that is consistent with a complex set of predictions that represent different aspects of a nomological network (e.g. predictions that involve different operational definitions or that compare expected mediators of causal effects) is generally less open to alternative interpretation than evidence compatible with simpler predictions. Thus, construct validity is generally strengthened by tests of complex hypotheses.

BOUNDARIES OF THE EFFECT UNDER INVESTIGATION

Most of the relationships that are of concern to psychologists, whether associative or causal, can be said to hold only within certain boundary conditions. While such a comment may seem trite, failures to consider such boundaries are not uncommon and could lead (and have led) to misconceptions. We will address two such issues, one of general concern to the study of stable personality characteristics, the other more specific to the arousal–performance relationship.

STABILITY OF BEHAVIOR ACROSS SITUATIONS

Guided by a belief in the stability of at least some aspects of personality, many psychologists (quite reasonably) sought evidence for behavioral consistencies across situations. Not surprisingly, the evidence has not always indicated stability. What is surprising is the extent to which that evidence has been seen as incompatible with a trait perspective. It has become increasingly popular to respond to this evidence by claiming that individual differences in personality are not very important sources of variation in human behavior: It has been suggested that the search for consistent dimensions of personality has not proved to be very useful and should therefore be abandoned. Furthermore, it has been suggested that any non-cognitive traits that can be identified show very little consistency across situations.

Several alternative approaches have been offered to replace the trait perspective on personality. One of these has been termed "interactionism"; it argues that the interaction between situations and traits accounts for more variance than simple main effects (Endler and Magnusson, 1976). Unfortunately, as noted by Epstein (1977), examination of the proportion of variance explained by personality, situations, or their interaction may be misleading, as these proportions will depend on such issues as the range of behaviors sampled. Furthermore, there is a serious weakness in this type of interactive approach in that it does not specify when the interactions should occur. We believe that an individual differences perspective, when guided by an appropriate theory, can answer the question of what personality variables should interact with what situational variables. That is, trait theories of personality are inherently interactive: behavior can rarely be predicted solely on the basis of traits; rather the theoretical definition of a trait allows identification of relevant situational variables with which the trait has interactive (non-additive) effects. Strong trait theories do not predict consistency across all situations, but rather predict differences in responses across situations that may be organized and expressed in terms of individual differences in traits. Strong theories define the boundary conditions and the situational manipulations which modify or otherwise limit cross-situational correlations. It is only those with a naive and simple-minded understanding of trait theory who predict either constancy (i.e. no situational effect) or consistency (i.e., perfect correlation from situation to situation) across situations. Interactions are a fundamental component of adequate trait theories.

Our research illustrates the use of a theory of stable individual differences to predict what may appear to be behavioral instability: introverts and extraverts do not consistently differ in a simple way in their cognitive performance. Rather, whether they differ and, if so, in what direction, can be shown to depend on theoretically relevant aspects of the situation (e.g. the level of stress and the difficulty of the task). What is important in this interactive pattern is that these differences are predictable from an arousal interpretation of I-E. In fact, evidence of such superficial behavioral inconsistency is necessary to support the present interpretation of the stable trait of I-E. Similar arguments can be made for other personality traits (see, for example, the discussion of achievement motivation by Atkinson, 1974, 1977).

Models of personality and motivation that incorporate time as a parameter offer a more refined elaboration of this general position by suggesting that traits determine the rate of change in response to situations (e.g. Atkinson and Birch, 1970; 1978; Revelle, 1983; 1986; 1989; Spielberger, Gorsuch, and Lushene, 1970). The dimension of impulsivity, for example, may reflect individual differences in the rate of change in activation in response to the environment; we will discuss this possibility more fully below.

In short, the search for behavioral invariance is misguided. There are many reasons for behavioral inconsistency (e.g. Block, 1968). The question for personality researchers is not whether behavior is invariant across situations or whether people with different levels of some trait always behave differently, but whether individual personality differences are associated with predictable behavioral differences within those contexts in which such differences should occur according to an appropriate theoretical framework. The prediction of behavioral differences as a function of personality must reflect consideration of the boundaries of the personality–behavior relationship, including both trait-related determinants of the response to a particular situation and situational modifiers of the expression of underlying dispositions.

IMPULSIVITY AND TIME OF DAY

These general concerns regarding the boundaries within which prediction can meaningfully occur can be illustrated by some of the contingent variables that we currently believe to be important in mediating the relationship between personality, arousal, and cognition.

In a series of studies following the initial demonstration that cognitive performance is an interactive function of I-E, time pressure, and caffeine (Revelle, Amaral, and Turriff, 1976), Revelle *et al.* (1980) found that although the relationship between personality, caffeine, and performance was very consistent, it was not as compatible with Eysenck's theory as originally believed. Instead, the most consistent relationships were with a subscale of I-E, impulsivity, and these relationships were moderated by time of day.

The first follow-up study was Gilliland's, which has already been briefly described. Gilliland (1976) reports that I-E as assessed by the Eysenck Personality Inventory (EPI, H. J. Eysenck and S. B. G. Eysenck, 1964) had the expected interactive relationship with caffeine in terms of its effect on performance, but when I-E was measured by the Eysenck Personality Questionnaire (EPQ, S. B. G. Eysenck and H. J. Eysenck, 1975), it did not have the expected effects. The primary difference between these two measures of I-E is in the saturation of impulsivity (Rocklin and Revelle, 1981): The EPI I-E scale has two subscales, impulsivity and sociability, while the EPQ I-E scale has only sociability content. Closer examination of Gilliland's results showed that the expected interaction of I-E with caffeine was due to the impulsivity subscale.

The remaining studies reported by Revelle *et al.* (1980) examined these impulsivity findings more closely. A similar paradigm was used in each study: subjects who differed in impulsivity were given either placebo or caffeine and then asked to complete a difficult task (usually practice GRE items). In several studies, subjects came for several sessions on different days, but we will discuss only the first-day results.

In each of five studies run in the morning, the same pattern was found: Under placebo conditions, low impulsive subjects (introverts) outscored high impulsives (extraverts) by an average (median) of 0.45 standard deviations. With the administration of caffeine, however, this result was reversed: With caffeine, high impulsives did better than low impulsives by 0.36 standard deviations. In fact, in every study done in the morning, caffeine hindered the performance of low impulsives and facilitated that of high impulsives.

These results stood in contrast to the results for the other component of I-E, sociability, which did not show such a consistent pattern of results. I-E, which is a combination of impulsivity and sociability, showed slightly more consistent interactions, as expected given the impulsivity results.

Evidence that the changes in performance in response to caffeine were not due to idiosyncratic or impulsivity-related sensitivity to caffeine but instead involved a more central process came from the results of four studies conducted in the evening. In striking contrast to the results from morning sessions, in each of the evening studies the performance of high impulsives was hindered by caffeine. The performance of low impulsives was actually helped by caffeine in three of four studies; in the fourth, there was a slight decrease from placebo to caffeine for the low impulsives and a very large decrease from placebo to caffeine for the high impulsives. The median improvement for low impulsives was 0.18 standard deviations; the median loss for high impulsives, 0.15 standard deviations.

In summary, these results indicate that in the morning, caffeine helped the performance of high impulsives and hindered that of low impulsives, but in the evening these effects were reversed. Caffeine hindered the performance of high impulsives and helped that of low impulsives. Thus, two subjects who performed equally well in the morning without caffeine could be made to differ by 0.8 standard deviations by the administration of caffeine or by 0.6 standard deviations by having them take the test in the evening.

The significance of these findings is twofold: First, they are consistent with data presented by Blake (1967; 1971) that introverts differ from extraverts in the phase of their diurnal body temperature rhythm. Taken together, these data suggest that I-E (or at least the impulsivity component of I-E) involves a phase shift in diurnal arousal rhythm rather than a difference in basal arousal level, with extraverts being less aroused than introverts during the morning, but more aroused than introverts during the evening (but see Wilson, 1990 for contradictory evidence). Second, they show that impulsivity is probably responsible for the previously reported relationships between I-E and arousal. This finding is congruent with other studies that have shown that many findings attributed to I-E are actually impulsivity effects (Anderson, 1988; Campbell, 1983; H. J. Eysenck and Levey, 1972; M. W. Eysenck and Folkard, 1980; Frcka and Martin, 1987; Gray, 1972; Loo, 1980; O'Gorman and Lloyd, 1987).

The interaction of impulsivity, caffeine, and time of day requires a reconsideration of the concept of stable (trait) differences in basal arousal. As Gray (1981) aptly noted, much of Eysenck's theory of I-E hinges upon the assumption of stable arousal differences between introverts and extraverts. But if these differences reverse by the evening, then why are not introverts extraverts at night? We suspect that differences between people in the extraverted behavior called impulsivity are mediated by a stable individual difference dimension, one that does not vary as a consequence of diurnal changes in arousal. We believe that there is some characteristic that leads to both impulsivity and a later diurnal arousal rhythm, and that this underlying process involves rate of change in reaction to stimuli over time. Such a characteristic could be the speed of build-up of arousal, or, alternatively, the speed of decay of arousal (habituation). If so, then non-impulsives would become aroused more quickly than impulsives during the morning. After several hours, high and low impulsives would reach similar arousal levels, but high impulsives would have to seek new stimulation constantly to maintain their arousal. By the evening, non-impulsives, who have been aroused for much of the day, would be fatigued and cease seeking arousal. Arousal would decay and the non-impulsive would retire for the evening. But impulsives, who would not have been as aroused for as long, would not yet be fatigued. Instead, they would still want to maintain a high arousal level and would continue to seek stimulation. Eventually, fatigue would set in and even impulsives would call it a night. Although this interpretation incorporates additional concepts into an already complex theory, it avoids the nonsensical prediction that introverts should prefer lively parties late in the evening while extraverts should seek out sex orgies in the morning. (See Revelle, Anderson, and Humphreys (1987) for a more complete discussion of this hypothesis and the implications of diurnal arousal variations for Eysenck's theory.)

In pointing to the mediating role that time of day exerts on the personality-performance relationship, these results underscore the importance of careful attention to the boundaries of empirical phenomena (cf. H. J. Eysenck, 1981). We suspect that other factors probably influence the relationships we have studied. For example, in considering the various tasks that we have employed in our research, a comparison of those that yielded the predicted impulsivity effects with those that did not suggests that impulsivity by caffeine interactions may be most likely to occur when the task involves a long-term-memory component (Revelle, Anderson, and Humphreys, 1987). Finally, the distinction between impulsivity and I-E illustrates the importance of detailed examination of the pattern of evidence obtained with different measures to the effort to identify operative causal constructs. Our data indicating that performance varies as a function of impulsivity, but not sociability, as predicted by an arousal model suggests that specification of the arousal-personality link in terms of I-E is too broad. Conversely, this effort to delineate underlying causal constructs has implications for choice of operational definitions: for example, although there are a variety of measures of impulsivity, use of the EPI subscale allows progressive development within a well-established and productive nomological network.

CHOICE AND INTERPRETATION OF DEPENDENT MEASURES

Selection and interpretation of dependent measures are obviously of crucial importance. In the context of performance, tasks clearly differ from one another in a great many ways (cf. Fleishman, 1975; Sanders, 1986); thus, choice of a theoretically appropriate task or set of tasks is as central to experimental design as choice of operational definitions of the presumed causal constructs. Our arguments regarding the construct validity of causes also apply to that of effects. Rather than review the full array of issues of concern, we focus on two aspects of dependent variable measurement that we believe are important but that appear to have received less detailed consideration than is warranted. Specifically, we stress issues related to the selection of operational definitions for potentially multifaceted dependent constructs and issues related to scaling effects and consequent data interpretation.

SELECTION OF DEPENDENT MEASURES

To clarify our arguments regarding dependent measures, we continue with examples from our work on the determinants of performance. Even when an appropriate task or set of tasks has been selected, it is important to realize that measures of performance efficiency typically reflect a combination of effects at several levels, and these component influences need not parallel one another. Instead, trade-offs can occur between cognitive processes (e.g. between information transfer and short-term memory), between task strategies (e.g between rapid and accurate performance, Dickman and Meyer, 1988), or between tasks themselves (e.g. between one defined by the experimenter and one defined by the subject). (For a fuller discussion of these points, see Revelle, 1987, 1989.) Furthermore, the extent to which such trade-offs occur, the direction of such exchanges, and the type or types of trade-offs that are involved are likely to be differentially affected by particular operational definitions of arousal or effort.

For example, our research suggests that experimental manipulations of arousal are likely to affect trade-offs between cognitive processes, with arousal facilitating SIT and hindering STM, but our data do not indicate a consistent influence of manipulated arousal on speed-accuracy trade-offs. In contrast, our research suggests that impulsivity affects the SIT/STM trade-off and is also associated with speed-accuracy trade-offs, with high impulsives favoring speed and low impulsives favoring accuracy. Similarly, Cooper and Brebner (1987) have offered data suggesting that in comparison to extraverts, introverts are more strongly oriented towards the stimulus-analysis demands of a task but less strongly oriented towards response-organization demands. Finally, the vigilance decrement typically observed in extraverts could suggest a link between impulsivity and task choices (experimenter- or subject-defined). A more striking example of a trade-off between tasks derives from work indicating that highly test anxious subjects are more prone to worry (a self-relevant "task") than their non-test-anxious counterparts (e.g. Sarason, 1975; Wine, 1971).

Several different strategies permit investigation of efficiency at these component levels. Task selection is an obvious method, and one that affords several possibilities. In general, this strategy assumes subject participation in the experimenter-defined task; task selection is thus most effective for examining or controlling potentially traded components of on-task activity. First, a task can be selected because it renders a particular trade-off implausible. For example, if one is concerned specifically with the effects of arousal on speed of performance, then a task that guarantees high accuracy rates can be selected.

We adopted this strategy in one of our studies (Anderson, Revelle, and Lynch, 1989) aimed at exploring the basis of the arousal-performance relationship. We employed a modified Sternberg (1966) paradigm similar to that used by Burrows and Okada (1976) and M. W. Eysenck and M. C. Eysenck (1979). Accuracy rates are typically quite high on such tasks; the response characteristic of concern is thus reaction time for correct answers. Using our standard impulsivity by caffeine paradigm, we presented subjects with a memory set followed by a single probe word that either did or did not come from the memory set. Each subject worked under three instructional conditions at 9:00 a.m.: to determine if the probe (a) exactly matched an item from the memory set, (b) exemplified a category named in the memory set, or (c) either (a dual-task condition).

Both the Easterbrook and the Humphreys–Revelle accounts of the impact of arousal on cognitive processing imply that rates of access to information should be affected: Easterbrook's hypothesis suggests that arousal interferes with simultaneous information processing. Thus when there are extensive demands on the system, as when the subject is performing a dual task, high arousal should force sequential rather than parallel processing. Arousal should therefore be associated with longer latencies to response in such contexts. Specifically, the slope of the regression of reaction time on memory-set size should be steeper for the dual-task search than for the single-task searches under high arousal conditions. In contrast, Humphreys and Revelle suggest that arousal facilitates SIT but interferes with STM. This hypothesis thus predicts that high arousal should be associated with steeper slopes across all tasks (because arousal decreases the rate at which STM is accessed) but with lower zero-intercepts (because arousal increases the rate of information transfer).

Our results indicated support for Humphreys and Revelle's position: Caffeine reduced the time needed to prepare to respond (the intercept) but increased the time needed to scan STM for each additional item (the slope). Impulsivity did not have a parallel effect on slopes or intercepts, again suggesting the influence of non-arousal-related aspects of that individual difference dimension. Neither caffeine nor impulsivity interacted with type of instructions (single or dual) in determining slopes, as had been predicted by Easterbrook's position.

A second task-selection strategy for examining or controlling potential trade-offs between various aspects of performance efficiency is to provide multiple versions of a task that vary in only one component. The visual scanning task that we previously described (Anderson and Revelle, 1983) exemplifies this strategy: by using two versions of this task that differed only in the size of the set of target stimuli, we were able to manipulate STM load while recognizing that both SIT and STM were potentially involved in performance on both task versions (cf. Folkard *et al.*, 1976).

In a more complicated version of this technique, tasks can be constructed to reflect factorial combinations of several relevant components. For example, Revelle and Benzuly (1985) presented subjects with geometric analogies that differed in difficulty along two dimensions: the number of elements in each term of the analogy and the number of transformations applied to each element. Following Mulholland, Pellegrino, and Glaser (1980), the number of elements was thought to reflect information transfer load; number of transformations was assumed to be related to memory load. Subjects were given either 0 or 4 mg/kg of caffeine at 10:00 a.m. Potential differences in speed-accuracy trade-offs were controlled by presenting each item for a fixed period of time before it was removed and the response requested. Caffeine interacted significantly with the number of transformations, facilitating performance on analogies with one transformation (independent of the number of elements) but hindering performance on those with three transformations.

Finally, a task can be selected because it affords indexes of each of several relevant components of performance, for example, of speed and accuracy or of sensitivity and response bias. In this case, effects on each of the components can be examined, but trade-offs remain possible and can render certain results uninterpretable. We encountered this difficulty in our proofreading study (Anderson and Revelle, 1982), described earlier. Thus, this strategy is probably the least adequate for resolving questions regarding the impact of arousal on specific components of performance, although it does allow investigation of tasks that subjects are likely to encounter in non-laboratory contexts.

Each of these techniques of task selection offers the advantage of permitting examination of the effects of arousal variables on particular aspects of performance efficiency. Unfortunately, however, these strategies tend to ignore other potential trade-offs (e.g. on- versus off-task activity).

Experimental manipulations can also be employed to examine components of performance that may be traded for one another. Varying task instructions provides the clearest example of this approach, and typically involves emphasizing the primacy of one or another aspect of performance. Because such instructions again require the cooperation of the subjects, they are most effective in addressing aspects of performance efficiency that are under strategic control. Geen and Kaiser (1985) used a variation of this technique that is particularly well-suited to the exploration of individual differences: subjects who differ along a personality dimension that might be associated with a particular type of trade-off (e.g. between speed and accuracy) can be asked to work on a task without giving them specific instructions regarding which aspect is to be considered more important. Their performance can then be compared with that obtained under instructions that specifically direct subjects to work (a) as rapidly and (b) as accurately as they can. (See also the analysis of impulsivity and speed-accuracy trade-offs by Dickman and Meyer, 1988.)

The aim of each of these techniques is to foster a clearer understanding of the locus of performance efficiency effects. The importance of distinguishing between these various determinants of efficiency is highlighted by the differences we have observed between the effects of particular operational definitions of arousal on specific components of performance: We believe that some trade-offs are directly affected by arousal (e.g. between SIT and STM), but that others are mediated by personality but not by arousal (e.g. between speed and accuracy). More generally, we suspect that individual differences are often associated with stylistic or strategic patterns that may be irrelevant to the presumed underlying cause of personality-behavior relationships. That is, while we believe that traits are important determinants of behavior and furthermore, that their theoretical interest is magnified by link to a presumed underlying construct (e.g. the link of impulsivity to arousal), we also argue that the patterns of behavior associated with particular traits need not all be traceable to that underlying construct (e.g. impulsivity-related speed-accuracy patterns are not likely to be a direct result of arousal but may instead reflect a greater sensitivity to cues for reward on the part of high impulsives, Gray, 1982; Zinbarg and Revelle, 1989). Thus selection and interpretation of dependent measures must reflect sensitivity to the distinction between effects that are central to the causal construct under investigation and those that are tangential. (See also the distinction made by Strelau (1985) between dimensions of temperament and dimensions of personality.)

Finally, note that our arguments regarding dependent measures are not restricted to research on cognitive performance. Many dependent constructs are multifaceted; the selection and interpretation of dependent measures should thus reflect careful analysis of the potential differences between various aspects of behavior. In their analysis of the dynamics of action, for example, Atkinson and Birch (1970) point to the differences between choice, intensity, frequency, and duration measures of motivation. The strength of a motive to talk (for instance) can be assessed by the probability of talking in a group, by the intensity of speech, by the latency of starting to talk when in a new group, by the persistence of talking rather than listening, the frequency of initiating an utterance, and the total amount of time spent talking. Although all are measures of motivation, these separate indices will yield different patterns of results depending upon the experimental design and the manner in which the behavioral data are analyzed. For instance, in a two-person group the number of times that a person takes over the lead in the conversation will yield a completely different result from the total time spent talking.

SCALING EFFECTS AND INTERPRETATION OF RESULTS

Our concerns regarding the construct validity of presumed effects have further implications for the interpretation of data. When statistics are reported on observed scores (e.g. the number of problems solved correctly or the average reaction time to make a response), inferences are usually made about constructs thought to underlie these observed scores. These constructs, variously called "true scores" or "latent scores", are not themselves immediately observable. Thus a basic concept of test theory is that any observed score is made up of some (unspecified) amount of true score and some amount of random error. Procedures used to estimate reliability are meant to find the relative amounts of error and true score variance in any particular measure. Unreliability of measurement causes the relationship between observed variables to be attenuated from the true relationship between latent variables (Lord and Novick, 1968). Thus, differences in reliabilities can lead to incorrect inferences about the strength of relationships. Corrections for such attenuation are basic to algorithms used to test various causal models (Bentler, 1980).

A somewhat less appreciated problem with the distinction between latent and observed scores is that although the relationship is generally assumed to be monotonic, it is in many cases definitely nonlinear. Such nonlinearity can lead to serious inferential problems. A simple reason for nonlinearity is that observed scores are typically bounded by 0 and 1 (e.g. the probability of a correct response on an ability test), while the underlying attribute (e.g. ability) is thought of as unbounded. It is clearly impossible to map a continuous and unbounded latent variable into a continuous but bounded observed variable with a linear mapping rule. (Total scores do not get around this problem: a 100 item ability test is bounded by 0 and 100 and is merely 100 times the average probability.) A typical transformation in the ability domain that matches empirical data quite well is the Rasch (1960/1980) transformation $(P_{c/a} > d) = e^{(a-d)}/(1 + e^{(a-d)})$, where $P_{c/a} > d$ is the probability of a correct response on an item given that one's ability (a) is greater than the item's difficulty (d) and e is the base of the natural logarithms. Figure 4.2 shows the probability of a correct response as a function of increasing levels of ability for three levels of item difficulty using a Rasch model.

The significance of such a nonlinear relationship between latent and observed scores is at least two-fold: it makes comparisons between means difficult if variances are unequal, and more importantly, makes the interpretation of non-crossover interactions problematic if not impossible (Maxwell and Delaney, 1985). In the first case, if two groups have equal means but unequal variances on the latent variable, then the group with the larger variance will have a lesser, equal, or greater mean on the observed score, depending upon whether an easy, moderate, or difficult test is used. To clarify this statement,

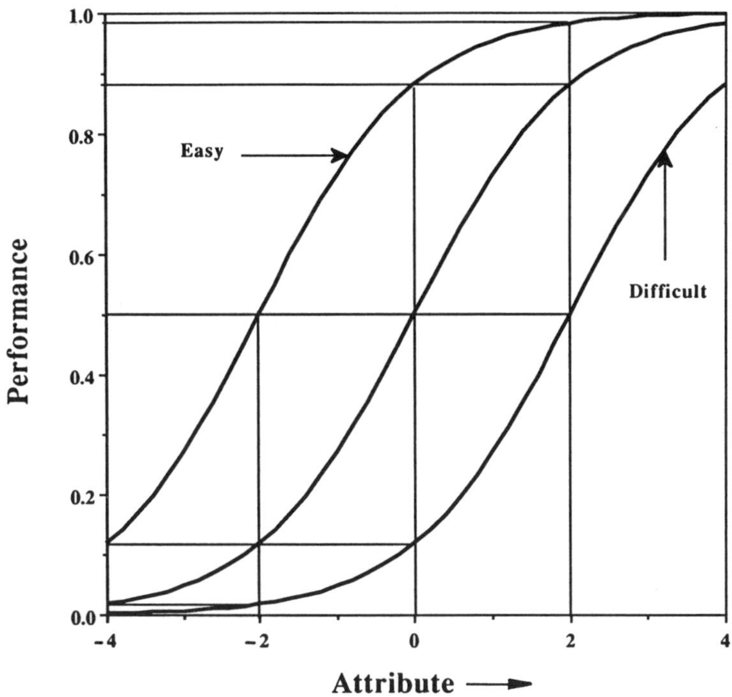

Figure 4.2. Predictions for observed scores as a function of latent attribute for three performance tasks differing in difficulty if a Rasch transformation applies.

consider two groups of subjects taking exams with trace lines similar to those in Figure 4.2. Group A has scores of –1, 0, and 1 on the latent variable; group B has scores of –2, 0, and 2 on the same latent variable. Obviously, the mean latent score for both groups is equal and is 0. Group A, however, has a higher mean on the easy test than does group B (0.87 versus 0.83), an equal mean on the moderate test (0.5), and a lower mean on the difficult test (0.13 versus 0.17)!

In addition to the problem of making inferences about latent means, the interpretation of interactions also depends upon scaling properties. Consider a typical experiment with two groups of subjects differentiated by some personality dimension (e.g. high and low impulsives) and two levels of an experimental manipulation that provides an alternative operational definition of the construct presumed to underlie the individual differences variable (e.g. 0 and 4 mg caffeine/kg body weight). The performance measures are obtained from three tasks that differ in difficulty, with performance being positively related to the latent variable (in this case, arousal) for each version. For the purposes of demonstration, assume that high impulsives have a mean latent score of –2 and low impulsives have a mean latent score of 0. Further, assume that caffeine leads to a 2 unit increase in the latent variable. With these assumptions, caffeine and impulsivity have equally important additive effects on the latent variable. Their effects on the observed outcome variable, however, depend on the difficulty of the performance measure. Using the relationships shown in Figure 4.2, on an easy task caffeine would facilitate performance 0.38 units for the high impulsives (from 0.50 to 0.88) but only facilitate the performance of low impulsives 0.10 units (from 0.88 to 0.98). On a difficult task, however, this seeming greater benefit of caffeine for high impulsives is reversed, with high impulsives going up to 0.10 units (from 0.02 to 0.12) and low impulsives improving 0.38 units (from 0.12 to 0.50). On a moderately difficulty task, both groups improve 0.38 units with high impulsives going from 0.12 to 0.50 and low impulsives from 0.50 to 0.88. Thus, an interaction between impulsivity and caffeine at the observed score level does not necessarily imply an interaction at the latent level.

As with any inferential problem, consistency of results across multiple operationalizations of the construct allows greater confidence that results do not reflect measurement problems. Investigators should, however, routinely consider scaling interpretations of their results as competing hypotheses to control for, just as other potential confounds need to be considered and addressed either experimentally or through conceptual replication.

Even when measurement issues have been addressed appropriately, the interpretation of interactions is not necessarily straightforward. A typical assumption in stage analyses of cognitive processing (e.g. Sanders, 1983; Sternberg, 1969) is that interactions imply effects at the same stage while additive effects in the absence of interaction imply effects at different stages. Broadbent's (1982) reservoir example, which can be demonstrated by considering a hypothetical stage analysis of time spent washing dishes, shows the weakness in this argument. Logically, dish washing involves three stages: filling the sink, washing the dishes, and then emptying the sink. Some variables have additive effects at only certain stages (e.g. water pressure affects only the time necessary to fill the sink; drain size, only the time spent emptying the sink). But other variables that ''should'' affect only one stage actually affect all stages. For example, the number of dishes might at first glance appear to affect only stage 2, but if there are more dishes, then more water may be needed, leading to more time at stages 1 and 3. Furthermore, variables that ''should'' affect only one stage can have interactive effects with some (but not necessarily all) variables associated with a different stage. Continuing with our example, the number of dishes will interact with some variables that affect stage 1, such as sink size or water pressure (doubling the number of dishes and doubling the sink size leads to four times the amount of time spent filling the sink, although it only doubles the amount of time spent in stage 2) but the number of dishes does not interact with other stage 1 variables, such as amount of water previously in the sink.

This example illustrates some of the difficulties of interpreting interactions, and together with arguments based on the possibility of nonlinear latent-observed variable associations, points to the potential hazards of viewing interactive effects as necessarily conceptually distinct from additive ones. The fundamental issue is not whether a variable has an additive or interactive effect with other variables, but how the evidence relates to the hypotheses under investigation and the extent to which alternative explanations (including scaling interpretations) are rendered implausible.

LEVEL OF ANALYSIS

All of the designs that we have discussed so far focus on effects evident at the level of aggregated data. That is, the type of results we have described all involve comparisons of group means. Although most models of arousal, effort, and behavior can be phrased in terms of aggregated data, many hypotheses actually describe intra-individual phenomena (Venables, 1984). In this context, while each of the strategies that we have discussed has important advantages, they all suffer from a common flaw: analyses at the group level do not necessarily provide an accurate description of the behavior of specific individuals even when a repeated-measures design is used (cf. Estes, 1956; Sidman, 1952).

Indeed, parallel explorations of a set of data using differing units of analyses need not yield convergent results. Bickel, Hammel, and O'Connell (1975) provided a striking example of this phenomenon in their correlational analysis of sex discrimination in graduate admissions at Berkeley: When the unit of analysis was the university as a whole, results suggested a significant bias against women, but when individual departments were examined, more appeared to discriminate against men than against women. (The overall effect was due to the fact that more women applied to the more stringent departments.) Similarly, in the context of research on arousal and information processing, patterns of group means reflect a combination of the arousal-performance curves of specific individuals, but it is possible that none of the individual subjects who were tested displayed the pattern evident at the group level. For example, an inverted-U pattern of means could result if the performance of some subjects is a monotonically increasing but negatively accelerated function of arousal while the performance of other subjects is a monotonically decreasing but positively accelerated function of arousal.

We have already described some of the results of Anderson's (1988) multi-level study in which subjects who differed in impulsivity were each given five different doses of caffeine and then tested on both an easy and a difficult task (letter cancellation and GRE items). We noted that the group-level analysis of overall performance efficiency provided support for the Yerkes–Dodson law, with the performance of the low impulsive subjects on the difficult task being hindered by the highest dose of caffeine, but with caffeine otherwise tending to facilitate performance efficiency. The performance of individual subjects was also examined in that study, and the results illustrate some of the distinctions between individual- and group-level comparisons.

Although a detailed description of the techniques employed to examine the behavior of specific individuals is beyond the scope of this chapter, some aspects of that process warrant attention. As noted above, any single data point reflects an unspecifiable combination of random and systematic influences. Tukey (1977) has compellingly demonstrated that unrefined analysis of non-aggregated data often fails to reveal even marked patterns. Tukey's "smoothing" technique was therefore used to minimize the impact of extraneous forces. That is, instead of examining performance on each task for each dose of caffeine, scores across consecutive pairs of doses were averaged, yielding four scores for each task for each subject. Scores were also adjusted to remove the influence of irrelevant but reliable influences (e.g. trial effects).

Primary analysis at the individual level confirmed the group-level observations regarding overall performance efficiency: more subjects than expected on the basis of chance conformed to the Yerkes–Dodson law. That is, (a) both the number of correctly identified targets on the letter cancellation task and the number of correctly answered GRE questions changed with dose of caffeine in a manner compatible with a single-peaked function (i.e., indicating a monotonically increasing, inverted-U, or monotonically decreasing function of dose of caffeine) and (b) the dose of caffeine associated with the subject's best performance on the easier letter task was higher than that associated with optimal efficiency on the more difficult GRE task.

Given our concern with the component determinants of performance efficiency, secondary analyses addressed speed and accuracy. Again, when the individual provided the unit of analysis, results supported the Yerkes–Dodson law. In contrast, analysis of aggregated speed and accuracy data failed to support this generalization. The difference between the two levels of analysis when performance speed was examined are particularly interesting, as the results of the two were in some ways contradictory. At the group level, performance speed was an interactive function of task, caffeine, and impulsivity. This interaction suggested that higher doses were generally associated with more rapid performance, but that on the GRE task, the speed with which high impulsive subjects worked was a U-function of dose, a result that is incompatible with the Yerkes–Dodson law (assuming that these subjects were engaged in the experimenter-defined task). But as already noted, examination of the speed of individual subjects across doses and across tasks supported a task-mediated single-peaked arousal–performance relationship. Moreover, the number of high impulsive subjects for whom speed on the GRE task first declined but then increased with increasing dose of caffeine did not differ reliably from that expected on the basis of chance.

We believe that the differences between these individual and group-level analyses illustrate the potential hazards of data aggregation. While the pattern of group means can be said to summarize the average behavior of a group of subjects, it does not necessarily reflect the behavior of particular individual subjects, nor even the behavior of the "average" subject. Only analyses that preserve the individual as the unit of examination can directly address hypotheses that concern intra-individual effects.

We are thus advocates of research designs that permit investigation of the behavior of individuals. There are, however, some important disadvantages to these approaches. An obvious drawback is that such projects require complicated designs that are inefficient in terms of allocation of subjects across conditions. Moreover, depending on the particular experimental design, results can be confounded with situational or order effects; our data (e.g. Anderson, 1988; Revelle *et al.*, 1980) indicate that order effects are likely. Such designs also require acceptance of many assumptions (e.g. about the appropriate adjustment procedures and the criteria to be used in judging compatibility with prediction). Perhaps more importantly, techniques for examining individual subjects are not necessarily well suited to investigating between-subject differences, an issue of considerable importance to those of us interested in individual differences. The debate between advocates of idiographic and nomothetic research is an old one, but as previously noted, evidence for construct validity increases when hypotheses involving different empirical approaches converge. We thus strongly argue for the incorporation of several types of experimental designs in a program of research: Data from individual subjects should be examined to explore those hypotheses that are stated at the intra-individual level; these analyses should supplement comparisons between subjects at the level of aggregated data.

GENERAL METHODOLOGICAL CONSIDERATIONS

Throughout our discussion, we have emphasized the importance of a theoretical framework and of careful attention to appropriate translation of hypotheses to experimental contexts. But it is important to remember that the linkage between theory and data is often quite complex. Consider, for example, the assumptions that were necessary to relate Easterbrook's (1959) theory to the results of our proofreading study (Anderson and Revelle, 1982):

(a) Easterbrook assumed that (1) arousal reduces the range of cue utilization and (2) irrelevant cues are excluded from processing before task relevant cues.
(b) From previous research, we assumed that (3) in the morning, low impulsives are more aroused than high impulsives and (4) caffeine increases arousal.
(c) For this particular experiment, we assumed that (5) the detection of interword errors requires processing of more cues than the detection of intraword errors, (6) our index of sensitivity provided a valid index of performance accuracy, (7) our results were not the product of scaling artifacts, and (8) we had taken all relevant boundary conditions into account.
(d) To fit the particular pattern of obtained results, we assumed that (9) high impulsives given placebo had too broad a range of cue utilization, (10) low impulsives given placebo had the optimal range of cue utilization, and (11) the drop in sensitivity to intraword errors for the high impulsives given caffeine was due to a trade-off between speed and accuracy.
(e) To argue that these results supported Easterbrook's positions—an intraindividual hypothesis—we assumed that (12) these aggregated-data comparisons accurately reflected the impact of arousal on individual subjects.

With these assumptions, we are able to claim that the results support Easterbrook's hypothesis. But while some of our assumptions are quite reasonable, others are more difficult to justify. For example, to argue that a broader range of cues must be processed to detect interword errors than intraword errors, we accepted a certain model of text processing. In other words, implicit in our arguments are additional assumptions about the nature of the task. Thus, because our personality constructs and our task constructs are necessarily embedded in the same nomological network, a direct way of testing both a theory of motivational effects and a theory of tasks is not possible. Justification for our interpretation relies on the extent to which we can defend the construct validity of our measures and the extent to which we can refute alternative explanations of the results.

This particular study illustrates the latter problem, as the results are interpretable from both the Easterbrook and the Humphreys–Revelle models, and similar problems exist when we try to understand the results in terms of the Humphreys–Revelle hypothesis: We assume that arousal facilitates SIT and hinders STM, but are unable to specify exactly how either process is related to performance. This inability is partly due to an incomplete understanding of the determinants of task performance and partly due to the ambiguity of the terms SIT and STM.

What do we mean when we say that sustained information transfer processes are facilitated by arousal? We have shown (Bowyer, Humphreys, and Revelle, 1983) that on a recognition memory test, high impulsives experienced a vigilance-like decrement over blocks of trials, and that this effect was reduced by caffeine. The similarity of this result to earlier studies of vigilance suggests that a common explanation should be applied to tasks that require staying prepared to process incoming stimuli, transmit information, or to execute rapid responses, but the precise nature of this SIT process has yet to be delineated.

Similarly, there are several different theories (e.g. capacity, strength) of the processes involved in short-term memory. Without a specification of how these processes are affected by arousal, we are unable to make more than very general predictions about the presumed detrimental effect of arousal on STM (cf. Humphreys *et al.*, 1983). Does arousal reduce the size of a memory buffer or does arousal cause the strength of memory codes to decay faster? Are detrimental effects of arousal on STM due to an inability to recover appropriate memory codes because of their weakness or due to increased strength of competing codes?

Again, our nomological net incorporates both a theory of tasks and a theory of performance-related individual differences. Stated more generally, serious consideration of the logic of construct validation underscores the complexity of the relationship between theory and data: all aspects of the translation of hypotheses and their constructs to empirically observable events are liable to alternative interpretation. Therefore, in a progam of research, each assumption requires empirical or conceptual attention. (See Gale and Edwards, 1986, for a further discussion of the complexities of incorporating psychophysiological hypotheses into theories of individual differences.)

SUMMARY AND CONCLUSIONS

In this chapter, we have reviewed some of the evidence relating the personality dimension of introversion–extraversion and its lower-order factor of impulsivity to cognitive performance, stressing methodological strategies for examining such effects. We have discussed the importance of multiple operational definitions and of complex predictions, reviewing several types of research design that incorporate these principles and hence allow a relatively strong case for construct validity. We have stressed the importance of the boundaries that mediate or restrict the application of hypotheses, arguing that with attention to such conditions and with an appropriate theory, seeming inconsistencies in behavior may be understood. We have addressed dependent variable measurement, noting some of the implications of the potential trade-offs between sub-components of behavioral constructs and some of the interpretative difficulties associated with scaling effects. We have also pointed to differences between analyses of aggregated data and of the behavior of individual subjects, arguing for the use of a combination of research designs that highlight different aspects of the effect under investigation. All of these arguments stress the complexity of the translation of theory to data. We hope that we have suggested strategies for experimental research that will allow meaningful tests of issues of theoretical importance regarding such personality and motivational constructs as effort and arousal. And finally, we hope that we have shown that an individual differences perspective can provide a viable framework for understanding behavior.

ACKNOWLEDGEMENTS

The research reported in this chapter was supported in part by Grant MH 29209 (01-04) from the National Institutes of Mental Health to William Revelle and Michael Humphreys, by Grant MH 29209 (05-07) to William Revelle, and by faculty research grants from Colgate University and Haverford College to Kristen Joan Anderson. Preparation of this manuscript was partly supported by contract MDA903-90-C-0108 from the US Army Research Institute to William Revelle and Kristen Anderson. The views, opinions, and findings contained in this report are those of the authors and should not be construed as an official Department of the Army position, policy, or decision, unless so designated by other official documentation.

REFERENCES

Anderson, K.J. (1988) Impulsivity, caffeine, and task difficulty: a within-subjects test of the Yerkes–Dodson law. Unpublished manuscript, Colgate University.

Anderson, K.J. (1990) Arousal and the inverted-u hypothesis—a critique of Neiss's reconceptualizing arousal. *Psychological Bulletin*, **107**, 96–100.

Anderson, K.J. and Revelle, W. (1982) Impulsivity, caffeine, and proofreading: a test of the Easterbrook hypothesis. *Journal of Experimental Psychology: Human Perception and Performance*, **8**, 614–624.
Anderson, K.J. and Revelle, W. (1983) The interactive effects of caffeine, impulsivity and task demands on a visual search task. *Personality and Individual Differences*, **4**, 127–134.
Anderson, K.J., Revelle, W. and Lynch, M.J. (1989) Caffeine, impulsivity, and memory scanning—a comparison of 2 explanations for the Yerkes–Dodson effect. *Motivation and Emotion*, **13**(1), 1–20.
Atkinson, J.W. (1974) Strength of motivation and efficiency of performance. In J.W. Atkinson and J.O. Raynor (eds), *Motivation and Achievement* (pp. 117–142). New York: Winston (Halsted Press/Wiley).
Atkinson, J.W. (1977) Motivation for achievement. In T. Blass (ed.), *Personality Variables in Social Behavior.* New York: Wiley.
Atkinson, J.W. and Birch, D. (1970) *The Dynamics of Action.* New York: Wiley.
Atkinson, J.W. and Birch, D. (1978) *Introduction to Motivation.* New York: Van Nostrand.
Baddeley, A.D. and Hitch, G. (1974) Working memory. In G. Bower (ed.), *Advances in Learning and Motivation (Vol. 8).* New York: Academic Press.
Bentler, P.M. (1980) Multivariate analysis with latent variables: Causal modeling. *Annual Review of Psychology*, **31**, 419–456.
Bickel, P.J., Hammel, E.A. and O'Connell, J.W. (1975) Sex bias in graduate admissions: data from Berkeley. *Science*, **187**, 398–404.
Blake, M.J.F. (1967) Relationship between circadian rhythm of body temperature and introversion–extraversion. *Nature*, **215**, 896–897.
Blake, M.J.F. (1971) Temperament and time of day. In W.P. Colquhoun (ed.), *Biological Rhythms and Human Performance.* London: Academic Press.
Block, J. (1968) Some reasons for the apparent inconsistency of personality. *Psychological Bulletin*, **70**, 210–212.
Bowyer, P.A., Humphreys, M.S. and Revelle, W. (1983) Arousal and recognition memory: the effects of impulsivity, caffeine, and time on task. *Personality and Individual Differences*, **4**, 41–49.
Broadbent, D.E. (1982) Task combination and selective intake of information. *Acta Psychologica*, **50**, 253–290.
Broadhurst, P.L. (1959) The interaction of task difficulty and motivation: The Yerkes–Dodson Law revived. *Acta Psychologica*, **16**, 321–338.
Burrows, D. and Okada, R. (1976) Parallel scanning of physical and category information. *Memory and Cognition*, **4**, 31–35.
Campbell, D.T. and Fiske, D.W. (1959) Convergent and discriminant validation by the multitrait-multimethod matrix. *Psychological Bulletin*, **56**, 81–105.
Campbell, D.T. and Stanley, J.C. (1963) *Experimental and Quasi-Experimental Designs for Research.* Chicago: Rand McNally.
Campbell, J.B. (1983) Differential relationships of extraversion, impulsivity, and sociability to study habits. *Journal of Research in Personality*, **17**, 308–314.
Carlson, R. (1971) Where is the person in personality research? *Psychological Bulletin*, **75**, 203–219.
Claridge, G. (1967) *Personality and Arousal.* Oxford: Pergamon.
Cook, T.D. and Campbell, D.T. (1979) *Quasi-Experimentation: Design and Analysis Issues for Field Settings.* Chicago: Rand McNally.
Cooper, C. and Brebner, J. (1987) Excitation–inhibition and arousal as explanatory concepts for extraversion. In J. Strelau and H.J. Eysenck (eds), *Personality Dimensions and Arousal.* New York: Plenum.

Craig, M.J., Humphreys, M.S., Rocklin, T. and Revelle, W. (1979) Impulsivity, neuroticism, and caffeine: do they have additive effects on arousal? *Journal of Research in Personality*, **13**, 404–419.

Cronbach, L.J. and Meehl, P.E. (1955) Construct validity in psychological tests. *Psychological Bulletin*, **52**, 281–302.

Davies, D.R. and Hockey, G.R.J. (1966) The effects of noise and doubling the signal frequency on individual differences in visual vigilance performance. *British Journal of Psychology*, **57**, 381–389.

Dickman, S.J. and Meyer, D.E. (1988) Impulsivity and speed-accuracy tradeoffs in information processing. *Journal of Personality and Social Psychology*, **54**, 274–290.

Duffy, E. (1962) *Activation and Behavior*. New York: John Wiley & Sons.

Easterbrook, J.A. (1959) The effect of emotion on cue utilization and the organization of behavior. *Psychological Review*, **66**, 183–201.

Endler, N. and Magnusson, D. (eds) (1976) *Interactional Psychology and Personality*. New York: John Wiley & Sons.

Epstein, S. (1977) Traits are alive and well. In D. Magnusson and N.S. Endler (eds), *Personality at the Crossroads*. New York: John Wiley & Sons.

Estes, W.K. (1956) The problem of inference from curves based on group data. *Psychological Bulletin*, **53**, 134–140.

Eysenck, H.J. (1967) *The Biological Basis of Personality*. Springfield, IL: Charles C Thomas.

Eysenck, H.J. (1981) General features of the model. In H.J. Eysenck (ed.), *A Model for Personality*. Berlin: Springer.

Eysenck, H.J. (1991) Dimensions of personality: 16: 5 or 3? criteria for a taxonomic paradigm. *Personality and Individual Differences*, **12**, 773–790.

Eysenck, H.J. and Eysenck, M.W. (1985) *Personality and Individual Differences: A Natural Science Approach*. New York: Plenum.

Eysenck, H.J. and Eysenck, S.B.G. (1964) *Eysenck Personality Inventory*. San Diego, CA: Educational and Industrial Testing Service.

Eysenck, H.J. and Levey, A. (1972) Conditioning, introversion–extraversion and the strength of the nervous system. In V.D. Nebylitsyn and J.A. Gray (eds), *Biological Bases of Individual Behavior*. New York: Academic Press.

Eysenck, M.W. and Eysenck, M.C. (1979) Memory scanning, introversion–extraversion, and levels of processing. *Journal of Research in Personality*, **13**, 305–315.

Eysenck, M.W. and Folkard, S. (1980) Personality, time of day, and caffeine: some theoretical and conceptual problems. In Revelle *et al. Journal of Experimental Psychology: General*, **109**, 32–41.

Eysenck, S.B.G. and Eysenck, H.J. (1975) *Manual of the EPQ (Personality Questionnaire)*. London: Hodder & Stoughton.

Fleishman, E.A. (1975) Toward a taxonomy of human performance. *American Psychologist*, **30**, 1127–1149.

Folkard, S. (1975) Diurnal variation in logical reasoning. *British Journal of Psychology*, **66**, 1–8.

Folkard, S., Knauth, P., Monk, T.H. and Rutenfranz, J. (1976) The effect of memory load on the circadian variation in performance efficiency under a rapidly rotating shift system. *Ergonomics*, **19**, 479–488.

Frcka, G. and Martin, I. (1987) Is there—or is there not—an influence of impulsiveness on classical eyelid conditioning? *Personality and Individual Differences*, **8**, 241–252.

Gale, A. and Edwards, J.A. (1986) Individual differences. In M.G.H. Coles, E. Donchin, and S.W. Porges (eds), *Psychophysiology: Systems, Processes, and Applications* (pp. 431–507). New York: Guilford.

Geen, R.G. (1985) Evaluation apprehension and response withholding in solving anagrams. *Personality and Individual Differences*, **6**, 293–298.

Geen, R.G. and Kaiser, M. (1985) Test anxiety and performance on the Stroop color-word task. Unpublished manuscript, University of Missouri.

Gilliland, K. (1976) The interactive effect of introversion–extraversion with caffeine induced arousal on verbal performance. Unpublished doctoral dissertation, Northwestern University.

Gray, J.A. (ed.) (1964) *Pavlov's Typology*. Oxford: Pergamon.

Gray, J.A. (1972) The psychophysiological basis of introversion–extraversion: A modification of Eysenck's theory. In V.D. Nebylitsyn and J.A. Gray (eds), *The Biological Basis of Individual Behavior*. New York: Academic Press.

Gray, J.A. (1981) A critique of Eysenck's theory of personality. In H.J. Eysenck (ed.), *A Model for Personality*. Berlin: Springer.

Gray, J.A. (1982) *Neuropsychological Theory of Anxiety: An Investigation of the Septal-Hippocampal System*. Cambridge: Cambridge University Press.

Gupta, B.S. (1977) Dextroamphetamine and measures of intelligence. *Intelligence*, **1**, 274–280.

Hamilton, P., Hockey, G.R.J. and Rejman, M. (1977) The place of the concept of activation in human information processing theory. In S. Dornic (ed.), *Attention and Performance*, 6. New York: Academic Press.

Hebb, D.O. (1955) Drives and the C.N.S. (conceptual nervous system). *Psychological Review*, **62**, 243–254.

Hockey, R. (1979) Stress and cognitive components of skilled performance. In V. Hamilton and D.M. Warburton (eds), *Human Stress and Cognition*. Chichester: Wiley.

Humphreys, M.S., Lynch, M.J., Revelle, W. and Hall, J.W. (1983) Individual differences in short-term memory. In R.F. Dillon and R.R. Schmeck (eds), *Individual Differences in Cognition (vol. 1)*. New York: Academic Press.

Humphreys, M.S. and Revelle, W. (1984) Personality, motivation, and performance: a theory of the relationship between individual differences and information processing. *Psychological Review*, **91**, 153–184.

Humphreys, M.S., Revelle, W., Simon, L. and Gilliland, K. (1980) Individual differences in diurnal rhythms and multiple activation states: a reply to M.W. Eysenck and S. Folkard. *Journal of Experiment Psychology: General*, **109**, 42–48.

Loo, R. (1980) Role of primary personality factors in the perception of traffic signs and driver violations and accidents. *Accident Analysis and Prevention*, **11**, 125–127.

Lord, F.M. and Novick, M.R. (1968) *Statistical Theories of Mental Test Scores*. Reading, Ma: Addison-Wesley.

Matthews, G. (1989) Extraversion and levels of control of sustained attention. *Acta Psychologica*, **70**, 129–146.

Matthews, G., Jones, D.M. and Chamberlain, A.G. (1989) Interactive effects of extraversion and arousal on attentional task-performance — multiple resources or encoding processes. *Journal of Personality and Social Psychology*, **56**(4), 629–639.

Maxwell, S.E., and Delaney, H.D. (1985) Measurement and statistics: an examination of construct validity. *Psychological Bulletin*, **97**, 85–93.

Mulholland, T.M., Pellegrino, J.W. and Glaser, R. (1980) Components of geometric analogy solution. *Cognitive Psychology*, **12**, 252–284.

O'Gorman, J.G. and Lloyd, J.E.M. (1987) Extraversion, impulsiveness, and EEG alpha activity. *Personality and Individual Differences*, **8**, 169–174.
Rasch, G. (1960/1980) *Probabilistic Models for Some Intelligence and Attainment Tests*. Chicago: University of Chicago Press.
Revelle, W. (1973) Introversion/extraversion, skin conductance and performance under stress. Unpublished doctoral dissertation, University of Michigan.
Revelle, W. (1983) Factors are fictions, and other comments on individuality theory. *Journal of Personality*, **51**, 707–714.
Revelle, W. (1986) Motivation and efficiency of cognitive performance. In D.R. Brown and J. Veroff (eds), *Frontiers of Motivational Psychology: Essays in Honor of John W. Atkinson*. Berlin: Springer.
Revelle, W. (1987) Personality and motivation: sources of inefficiency in cognitive performance. *Journal of Research in Personality*, **21**, 436–452.
Revelle, W. (1989) Personality, motivation, and cognitive performance. In P. Ackerman, R. Kanfer and R. Cudeck (eds), *Learning and Individual Differences: Abilities, Motivation, and Methodology* (pp. 297–341). Hillsdale: Erlbaum.
Revelle, W., Amaral, P. and Turriff, S. (1976) Introversion/extroversion, time stress, and caffeine: effect on verbal performance. *Science*, **192**, 149–150.
Revelle, W., Anderson, K.J. and Humphreys, M.S. (1987) Empirical tests and theoretical extensions of arousal-based theories of personality. In J. Strelau and H.J. Eysenck (eds), *Personality Dimensions and Arousal*. London: Plenum.
Revelle, W. and Benzuly, M. (1985) Caffeine and memory load: Their effect on analogical reasoning. Unpublished manuscript, Northwestern University.
Revelle, W., Humphreys, M.S., Simon, L. and Gilliland, K. (1980) The interactive effect of personality, time of day and caffeine: A test of the arousal model. *Journal of Experimental Psychology: General*, **109**, 1–31.
Rocklin, T. and Revelle, W. (1981) The measurement of extraversion: A comparison of the Eysenck Personality Inventory and the Eysenck Personality Questionnaire. *British Journal of Social Psychology*, **20**, 279–284.
Sanders, A.F. (1983) Towards a model of stress and human performance. *Acta Psychologica*, **53**, 61–97.
Sanders, A.F. (1986) Energetical states underlying task performance. In G.R.J. Hockey, A.W.K. Gaillard and M.G.H. Coles (eds), *Energetics and Human Information Processing* (pp. 139–154). Dordrecht: Martinus Nijhoff.
Sarason, I.G. (1975) Anxiety and self-preoccupation. In I.G. Sarason and C.D. Spielberger (eds), *Stress and Anxiety (vol. 2)*. Washington, DC: Hemisphere.
Sidman, M. (1952) A note on functional relations obtained from group data. *Psychological Bulletin*, **49**, 263–269.
Spielberger, C.D., Gorsuch, R.L. and Lushene, R.E. (1970) *STAI Manual for the State-Trait Anxiety Inventory ("Self-Evaluation Questionnaire")*. Palo Alto, CA: Consulting Psychologists Press.
Stelmack, R.M. (1981) The psychophysiology of extraversion and neuroticism. In H.J. Eysenck (ed.), *A Model for Personality*. Berlin: Springer.
Stelmack, R.M. (1990) Biological bases of extraversion—psychophysiological evidence. *Journal of Personality*, **58**, 293–311.
Sternberg, S. (1966) High-speed scanning in human memory. *Science*, **153**, 652–654.
Sternberg, S. (1969) The discovery of processing stages: extensions of Donders' method. In W.G. Koster (ed.), Attention and Performance II. *Acta Psychologica*, **30**, 276–315.
Strelau, J. (1985) Temperament and personality: Pavlov and beyond. In J. Strelau, F.H. Farley and A. Gale (eds), *The Biological Bases of Personality and Behavior: Psychophy-*

siology, Performance, and Application (Volume 1) (pp. 25–43). Washington, DC: Hemisphere Publishing. pp. 25–43.

Tukey, J.W. (1977) *Exploratory Data Analysis.* Reading, MA: Addison-Wesley.

Venables, P.H. (1984) Arousal: an examination of its status as a concept. In M.G.H. Coles, J.R. Jennings and J.P. Stern (eds), *Psychophysiological Perspectives: Festschrift for Beatrice and John Lacey* (pp. 134–142). New York: Van Nostrand.

Weinstein, N.D. (1974) Effect of noise on intellectual performance. *Journal of Applied Psychology*, **59**, 548–554.

Weinstein, N.D. (1977) Noise and intellectual performance: a confirmation and extension. *Journal of Applied Psychology*, **62**, 104–107.

Wilson, G.D. (1990) Personality, time of day and arousal. *Personality and Individual Differences*, **11**, 153–168.

Wine, J. (1971) Test anxiety and direction of attention. *Psychological Bulletin*, **76**, 92–104.

Yerkes, R.M. and Dodson, J.D. (1908) The relation of strength of stimuli to rapidity of habit-formation. *Journal of Comparative Neurology and Psychology*, **18**, 459–482.

Zajonc, R. (1965) Social facilitation. *Science*, **149**, 269–274.

Zinbarg, R. and Revelle, W. (1989) Personality and conditioning—a test of 4 models. *Journal of Personality and Social Psychology*, **57**, 301–314.

Chapter 5

The Emergence of Personality: a Broader Context for Biological Perspectives

Sarah E. Hampson
Oregon Research Institute, 1899 Willamette Street, Eugene, OR 97401, USA

ABSTRACT

Personality is shaped, in part, by the proximal effects of consciousness and culture, so biological perspectives are limited by their emphasis on distal causes of behavior and the physical level of analysis. The constructivist approach to personality is a non-biological perspective that views personality as a product of the interaction between an actor and an observer. However, biology influences the behaviors and inference processes involved in personality construction. Intersections between constructivist and biological approaches are identified to demonstrate how a fuller understanding of personality can be achieved by considering both perspectives.

INTRODUCTION

In a collection devoted to biological perspectives on individual differences, the aim of this chapter is to represent another point of view. Specifically, I explore the role of biology in what is probably the least biologically oriented approach to personality—the constructivist position. In so doing, biological

Handbook of Individual Differences: Biological Perspectives
Edited by Anthony Gale and Michael W. Eysenck

perspectives are placed in a broader context, with the intention being to demonstrate that individual differences in the realm of personality cannot be understood by biology alone.

There is a sense in which any approach to individual differences is biological, given that all such differences can, in theory, be described at one or more biological level. All human thought and behavior has some physical substrate, and all environmental influences must operate through biological mechanisms that constitute the human organism. Thus, the distinction between biological and non-biological is superficial, given that any phenomenon can be translated into a different level of analysis. However, the phenomenon may lose something in translation, and this is the heart of the critique of biological perspectives.

Although the distinction between biological and non-biological is only superficial, it implies deep differences in the approach to the study of individual differences. Rushton (1988; 1990) observed that psychological explanations range along a distal-proximal continuum with evolutionary explanations at one extreme and phenomenological experience at the other. Biological perspectives may be broadly divided into three kinds: evolutionary, behavioral genetic, and psychophysiological (Buss, 1990). The biological evolutionary and behavioral genetic approaches are primarily concerned with distal causes of behavior, whereas non-biological approaches, such as social constructivism, emphasize the proximal contingencies that shape behaviors. Psychophysiology represents a biological approach that can be applied at various points on the distal–proximal continuum.

In the first part of this chapter, I discuss some limitations of adopting a biological bias in the study of personality. More consideration is given to evolutionary and behavioral genetic approaches because they receive less coverage in this book than does psychophysiology. In the main part of this chapter I present a social-psychological and cognitive view of personality, one in which personality is seen as a property that *emerges* in the course of interpersonal behavior. This approach lies near the proximal extreme of the distal-proximal continuum of explanation, and contrasts sharply with biological approaches. Nevertheless, intersections between biological and constructivist approaches are identified as promising directions for further research.

THE LIMITATIONS OF BIOLOGY

Psychology is an extraordinary discipline because it encompasses such a wide range of approaches. The same phenomenon can be studied in numerous different ways. Several of the subdisciplines of psychology are biological in perspective. That is, they adopt a level of description and explanation that is grounded in the physical, as opposed to psychological, reality of the human organism. Biological approaches satisfy the needs of some to view psychology as a physical science. By fixing every psychological phenomenon to an aspect of human physiology, biological approaches to psychology are only a step away from medical science, the other major discipline devoted to the study of humans. Apparently, it is easier to convince oneself and others that one is studying something important if it has a demonstrable physical reality.

However, whatever approach one adopts, psychology is the study of human thoughts, feelings, and behaviors. Biological psychologists select their subject matter from thoughts, feelings, and behaviors, and proceed to uncover its biological bases and origins. But their work is only significant for psychology in so far as it can be related back to thoughts, feelings, and behaviors. The danger with biological perspectives is that one may wrongly assume that everything of psychological importance can be captured at the various levels of physical inquiry. In fact, humans are unique because of consciousness and culture, and these are eminently non-physical phenomena. The limitations of a biological bias are illustrated in the following discussion of evolutionary and behavioral genetic perspectives.

EVOLUTION AND PERSONALITY

The evolutionary perspective on individual differences forms a part of human sociobiology. Sociobiological theories explain the origin and maintenance of specific behaviors in terms of their adaptive significance (Wilson, 1978). It is somewhat paradoxical to apply sociobiology to the understanding of personality. Sociobiology is concerned with the genetic basis of the universals of human nature, whereas personality psychology emphasizes the ways in which individuals differ. Indeed, following the logic of the evolutionary approach to its extreme, one would predict that the principles of natural selection would favor the most adaptive personalities to the point that there are few if any individual differences.

Proponents of the evolutionary perspective have two counter-arguments (Buss, 1990). First, personality psychology includes theories about universals as well as variation. In particular, when studying individual differences, one must first agree on the set of traits upon which individuals vary. There are many ways to approach this basic question about personality, but the evolutionary bias would argue that such fundamentals of human nature are adaptive characteristics shaped by ancestral environments. Such an argument assumes that the traits constituting personality are each equally biologically based. In other words, it does not allow for some aspects of human nature to be the product of nurture.

Starting from a different perspective, the psycholexical approach to personality looks for the fundamentals of human nature in another kind of evolution. The natural language is viewed as the repository of all the individual differences deemed of sufficient significance to warrant a label. Language is sensitive to cultural changes, and trait adjectives can change in meaning or even disappear from common usage. This process of evolution renders today's dictionary an excellent guide to the individual differences deemed of significance to a given language community (Goldberg, 1981). Starting from the dictionary, personality researchers have established what is now a widely adopted taxonomy consisting of five broad dimensions subsuming many specific traits (Digman, 1990; John, 1990). These dimensions are (I) Extraversion (e.g. bold, sociable, energetic versus unassured, submissive, timid), (II) Agreeableness (e.g. warm, kind, cooperative versus cold, rude, unfair), (III) Conscientiousness (e.g. responsible, efficient, organized versus frivolous, careless, lazy), (IV) Emotional stability (e.g. calm, relaxed, good-natured versus nervous, emotional, insecure), and (V) Intellect (e.g. intelligent, creative, sophisticated versus boorish, unimaginative, stupid).

Researchers are converging upon a description of the nature of the broad dimensions of personality, but what still remains to be developed is a theoretical basis for these fundamental individual differences. Sociobiology may be useful, but only for those characteristics that are relatively biologically driven. For example, (I) Extraversion and (IV) Emotional stability seem good candidates for biological inquiry, whereas (II) Agreeableness and (III) Conscientiousness seem more culturally based. In short, both biological evolution and cultural evolution have determined human nature.

The second counter-argument from evolutionary psychologists to the view that evolution is about universals is that natural selection may have favored several different adaptive strategies for the same problem. For example, Gangestad and Simpson (1990) proposed that women vary in the degree of attachment and length of acquaintance necessary before entering into a sexual relationship. They argue that the two extremes of this dimension, restricted versus unrestricted sociosexuality, constitute two adaptive strategies that have evolved via frequency-dependent selection. The value of each strategy decreases as its frequency increases thus permitting both strategies to be maintained. The result of frequency-dependent selection in our past is the observed variation in female sociosexuality today.

Evolutionary accounts provide a distal explanation of human behavior. That is, they are concerned with the environmental factors that impinged upon our ancestors and resulted in the biological mechanisms with which we are now equipped. Evolutionary accounts pay no heed to the proximal causes of behavior arising from contemporary conditions, which include all-important cultural factors unique to human behavior (Archer, 1988; Cantor, 1990). Current environmental factors complicate evolutionary accounts, as can be illustrated by Gangestad and Simpson's (1990) two sociosexual strategies. During the 1960s, the birth control pill and the availability of cures for known sexually transmitted diseases created an environment conducive to the unrestricted strategy. In the 1990s, the threat of HIV infection is a compelling reason for adopting a restricted strategy. Sexual mores have changed in the space of one generation, demonstrating the rapid and powerful effects of culture. There are both distal and proximate causes for human behavior, and ignoring proximal ones can be seriously misleading.

BEHAVIORAL GENETICS AND PERSONALITY

Behavioral genetics has made tremendous advances in recent years. As a result of several large-scale twin, adoption, and family studies, and the application of more sophisticated statistical techniques such as structural equation modelling, it is now widely concluded that about 50% of the variance in self-report personality measures may be accounted for by heredity (Loehlin, Willerman, and Horn, 1988). This finding is consistent across a range of personality measures, including broadband ones such as the Eysenck Personality Questionnaire (Eaves, Eysenck, and Martin, 1989), the Minnesota Multiphasic Personality Inventory (Pogue-Geile and Rose, 1985), the California Personality Inventory (Loehlin and Nichols, 1976), and the Multidimensional Personality Questionnaire (Tellegen *et al.*, 1988), as well as measures of more specific aspects of personality such as self-reported delinquency (e.g. Rowe, 1983).

Having established the magnitude of the genetic contribution to individual differences in personality, investigators are now proceeding to more complex questions (Loehlin, Horn, and Willerman, 1990; Plomin and Nesselroade, 1990; Rowe, 1987). With as much variance left to be explained by environmental factors (and error) as is explained by genetics, attention has been focused on the relative importance of shared and non-shared environmental influences. Intuitively, one would expect that the shared environmental experience of children reared together in the same family would result in similarities in personality. However, there is substantial evidence that such common experience has little effect if any on personality variance (Rowe and Plomin, 1981). For example, zero correlations on personality measures have been found for genetically unrelated adopted siblings raised together (Loehlin, Willerman and Horn, 1988). The work of Rose (e.g. Rose, 1988; Rose and Kaprio, 1988) represents a dissenting voice on this issue. His twin data provide evidence for the effects of shared experience on some aspects of personality, including an effect on extraversion. Given the apparent lack of importance of the shared environment on personality, investigators have turned to the non-shared environment. Siblings' experiences while being raised in the same family are not identical, and these non-shared influences do appear to have some effect on personality (Baker and Daniels, 1990).

Behavioral geneticists are also examining the question of personality development and change in more complex ways by taking multiple observations over situations and occasions instead of single snapshots (Plomin and Nesselroade, 1990). For example, do the relative contributions of heredity and environment to personality differ over the life course? What is the role of heredity in age changes in personality? Do genetics play a part in the short-term, even moment-by-moment, changes in a person's states (as opposed to more enduring traits)? Definitive answers to questions such as these are not yet forthcoming but are being actively pursued, and it seems likely that genetics will be found to play a significant part in personality change.

The findings from behavioral genetic research serve to confirm the significance of both heredity and environment for understanding personality. From an applied perspective, behavioral genetics has made important contributions by taking us closer to understanding familial risk factors for undesirable behaviors such as alcoholism and delinquency. However, the danger of applying a genetic perspective to a behavioral problem is to focus on its immutable aspects. For example, knowing the genetic marker for alcoholism would not in itself lead to a reduction in the number of alcoholics. Behavioral interventions to prevent and remedy alcoholism would still be necessary to counteract the genetic tendency. Humans are less controlled by genetic blueprints than any other animal, so complex human behavior will never be adequately explained by genetics.

CONCLUSIONS

Because human behavior is also strongly influenced by the proximal effects of consciousness and culture, evolutionary and behavioral genetic perspectives are limited by their focus on distal causes. Psychophysiological perspectives reduce human behavior to its physical counterparts and consequently are unable to study constructs that are not amenable to such reduction. Many important influences on human behavior, particularly those deriving from the interpersonal nature of our construction of reality, are too abstract to be translated meaningfully into the physical realm. Accordingly, biological perspectives need to be set in a wider context to make up for their deficiencies. In the remainder of the chapter, I will present a constructivist approach to personality that emphasizes proximal causes such as phenomenological experience and interpersonal behavior, and develop some ideas about how biology could augment such an approach to individual differences.

THE CONSTRUCTION OF PERSONALITY

The constructivist approach to personality is one example of the broader social-constructivist movement in psychology (Gergen, 1985; Landman and Manis, 1983). Socially constructed concepts (e.g. madness, childhood, and ageing) are composed of objective features in the real world and the social significance attached to them (Gergen, 1985). As such, they do not have significance in the absence of cultural recognition. Similarly, personality is also a social creation (Hampson, 1984; 1988a). Personality concepts combine features of the world (such as behavioral and situational attributes) with social knowledge (the social meaning of those attributes).

The constructivist approach to personality emphasizes the role of interpersonal behavior for the creation and maintenance of personality. It is influenced by the dramaturgical model (e.g. Goffman, 1959; Harré, 1979, 1983), and symbolic interactionism (Cooley, 1902; Mead, 1934), both of which stress the importance of the audience for personality. Individuals are viewed as being concerned about the impressions they are making on real or imagined audiences (e.g. Baumeister, 1982; Schlenker, 1980; Tedeschi, 1981). Personality construction involves an actor (who is the target of the personality construction process) and an observer. Instead of locating personality exclusively *within* individuals, constructivism assumes that personality is created in the context of interpersonal encounters. The actor brings certain biological and learned characteristics that interact with environmental variables to result in behaviors. These are the observable components in the construction of personality. These behaviors are comprehended by the observer in terms of personality constructs or categories. Therefore, personality cannot be equated with either the actor's behavior or the observer's inferences. They are mutually dependent components which together constitute the actor's personality.

Personality may be regarded as a compound or *Gestalt* possessing properties not present in its separate constituents. Water is an excellent example of the *Gestalt* concept of the whole being different from the sum of its parts. The liquid, thirst-quenching properties of water—its essential *wateriness*—bear no resemblance to its gaseous constituents. Indeed, they may be said to be emergent since "They inhere in no single part but emerge when the parts constitute the whole" (Boring, 1950, p. 588). By viewing personality as emergent, the constructivist approach emphasizes the study of the whole, not the isolated parts.

An essential factor in personality construction is the capacity for actors and observers to be self-aware. Actors can monitor their behaviors and their impact on the observer. Furthermore, observers can monitor their observations and their impact on the actor. Therefore, both actors and observers can also be self-observers. These self-observations may then become significant inputs in determining subsequent actions and inferences. Participants in an interaction will vary in the extent to which they "step outside themselves" and consider the impact of their actions and inferences on the other person. Self-observation operates in both a state-like and trait-like manner. Whereas the actor may be self-observing while "performing" a behavior (i.e. be conscious of its impact on an audience), the observer may not be self-consciously making personality inferences about the actor's behavior. Alternatively, the actor may not be self-observing, whereas the observer may be self-consciously using certain categories with which to infer the actor's personality. Thus being in self-observer mode is independent of the role of actor or observer. Self-observation is trait-like because both the actor and the observer may be chronically predisposed to be either low or high on the self-observer dimension.

The actor and the observer are interpersonal roles that are exchanged at each turn in the interaction. At the same time, both participants will also, to varying degrees, be self-observing. The constructivist approach emphasizes the role of constructive inference. Personality inference is grounded in reality, beginning with "raw behavior". This behavior, along with information about the circumstances in which it occurred, is interpreted by the observer in the light of the observer's conceptual knowledge, and a personality inference is made. That inference, in turn, may have implications for the behavior of the observer in the next turn of the interaction, when the observer becomes the actor. The actor is also making personality inferences on the basis of his or her behavior, and these inferences may result in subsequent modifications to the actor's performance.

The above account describes the simplest interpersonal encounter, one in which only two people are involved. Reality is often far more complex, with multiple participants involved. Moreover, observers need not be physically present but can form an imagined audience that influences the way the actor behaves. The actor can construct as many different personalities as there are audiences. Even in the simplest case of the two-person encounter, both individuals are not only involved in the construction of the other's personality but also in their own personality construction.

In the following three sections, I will discuss the contributions to personality construction of the modes of actor, observer, and self-observer. In each section, I will emphasize points of intersection between biological and constructivist approaches.

BIOLOGY AND THE ACTOR

At any point in time, the actor is the end product of all his or her preceding personality-construction experiences. Consequently, the actor brings characteristics to the situation such as values, goals, and traits. The actor is the most extensively researched component of constructed personality. The non-interpersonal determinants of many aspects of the actor's behavior are discussed in the other chapters. Here, I will limit myself to a consideration of the variables affecting the actor's choice of situations, and the role of constructive processes in situation choice.

CHOICE OF SITUATIONS

Until recently, investigators have paid little attention to two important facts of life: People exert considerable control over the situations in which they choose to place themselves, and once in those situations people will exert an influence over them. Where a person chooses to be is of crucial importance for personality construction. In addition to constraining the actor's behavior, the situation determines who the observer or observers will be in the construction process. Therefore, it is necessary to understand the causes of situational choice, from both biological and non-biological perspectives.

The major basis for distinguishing among situations is behavioral appropriateness (Van Heck, 1984). Consequently, we can be confident that people are able to discriminate among situations in terms of their potential for personality construction. However, situation taxonomies ignore individual differences in situation perception. Presumably, although there is a common culture of the semantics of situations, there are also individual differences in the perception and exploitation of a situation's potential for personality expression.

Dworkin and Goldfinger (1985) explored the role of individual differences in determining how women perceived social situations. Following Gibson's (1979) theory of perceptual affordance, they examined women's perceptions of a range of situations varying in potential (or affordance) for sociability. Women who regarded the trait of sociability as important for understanding their own behavior generated more sociable attributes for situations and recalled more of the social content of a conversation than did other women. Women who scored either at the high or the low poles of a sociability scale were found to anticipate more social than non-social characteristics of situations relative to moderate scorers, and they also showed higher recall for events that they associated with "friendly feelings". For Gibson (1979), affordances are species-specific and biologically determined. As a result of the way an organism is "hard-wired", it is attuned to species-specific affordances in the environment. Possibly, some elements of humans' situation perception is affected in a similar way, creating intra-species differences as a result of biological and non-biological factors.

The idea that individuals will choose to spend time in situations that offer them the chance to express their personalities has been proposed by several authors (e.g. Magnusson and Endler, 1977), but it has not been extensively tested. Snyder and Ickes (1985) reviewed several studies apparently supporting this position. For each personality variable examined (extraversion, sensation-seeking, authoritarianism, locus of control, self-monitoring), individuals reported actively choosing to spend time in situations which allowed the behavioral expression of these characteristics. In these studies, willingness to enter the situation was assessed by questionnaire rather than by actual behavioral choices.

However, Diener, Larsen, and Emmons (1984) related extraversion to real-life situational choices, and found some support for compatible situation choice. Subjects (undergraduates) made on-line reports of their moods and activities at random intervals over a six-week period. High extraverts recreated more often in social situations than alone, and persons high in need for order spent less time in novel situations. However, several predicted trait-situation choice correlations were near zero, and the authors concluded that they had obtained only moderate support for the situation-choice hypothesis. Given that situation choice in real-life is often constrained, particularly for students attending college, moderate support was probably all that could be expected.

It follows from the situational-choice hypothesis that particular social and occupational groups that occupy well-defined "niches" in society should attract individuals with similar personality characteristics. Support for this is to be found in the literature on occupational choice. Borden (1984) reviewed the evidence that personality variables discriminate among students specializing in different fields of study and among adults in different occupations. Holland's (1973) influential theory of occupation choice, in which both persons and jobs are characterized by the same typology, is based on the assumption that people will be most satisfied, productive, and stable in work environments congruent with their personalities.

DETERMINANTS OF SITUATION CHOICE

What causes situational choice? Some personality theorists have offered biological explanations for personality-situation congruence. For example, according to Eysenck's (1967) theory of extraversion, extraverts are driven to seek high levels of stimulation because of their chronic levels of cortical under-arousal. Swann (1984) argued that we tend to seek out *familiar* places and people and that this tendency may be rooted in a biological drive. Presumably familiarity is safer and promotes survival.

Recently, Buss (1984a; 1985) has applied principles from evolutionary biology to personality psychology. In his examination of human assortative mating, Buss (1984b) assumed that married couples provide a valuable test of person-environment correspondence, on the grounds that the spouse is a major environmental factor. Not only is one on the receiving end of one's spouse's actions, but one enters into many joint activities initiated by one's spouse. In his study of the personalities of husbands and wives, Buss found behavioral correlations on some but not all traits. Spouses' extraversion, dominance, quarrelsomeness, and ingenuousness were moderately positively correlated. For example, extraverted women tend to marry extraverted men. In addition, because extraverts reportedly spend time in environments offering opportunities for extraverted behavior (Furnham, 1981), the extraverted couple will gravitate towards extraverted "niches," thus perpetuating this aspect of their personalities.

Scarr and McCartney (1983) argued that some situational choices can be traced to the genotype. They proposed that the child's environment is influenced directly by the child's genotype as well as indirectly through the child's phenotype. Moreover, they proposed three kinds of effects of the genotype on the environment: (1) *Passive* effects are the result of parents providing the child's early environment; (2) *evocative* effects refer to the responses in the environment evoked by the child's genotype, and (3) *active* effects refer to the influence of the child's genotype in the process of seeking out and influencing situations. The relative importance of these three effects changes over time. For the young child, passive and evocative effects are important, whereas in adults the passive effects decline and the active effects increase in importance. Although Scarr and McCartney (1983) are not claiming that *all* environmental effects can be traced to the genotype, they none the less argue that differences in experience are not the major factor in determining individual differences.

From a non-biological perspective, constructivist reasoning assumes that when one makes a considered situational choice, one reviews the behaviors afforded by the situation and decides whether these behaviors are compatible with the personality one has constructed in the past or with the impression one now wishes to create. Consequently, the constructivist approach provides an explanation for the observed relations between person and situation variables in situation choice. The perspective is particularly helpful in explaining those cases where an individual chooses an incongruent situation. For example, a shy person may choose to attend the office happy hour in order to become more sociable and make friends. Therapists will give their clients assignments involving new behaviors and new situations in order to bring about changes in self-perceptions. Change entails new situations, and one way to bring about personality change is to place oneself in novel situations.

CONCLUSIONS

Actors exert some control over the situations in which they find themselves. The research indicates that actors typically choose situations congruent with their personality characteristics, although occasionally they will deviate from this pattern and deliberately select an incongruent situation. Understanding situational choice is important because situations constrain the actor's behavior and provide the observer component of personality construction. The actor's role in the perception of situations and in determining situation choice needs further investigation. Biology can contribute to the explanation of congruent situation choices, but constructivism can also account for incongruent choices.

BIOLOGY AND THE OBSERVER

The investigation of the observer component in personality construction involves the study of the lay use of personality concepts. Personality-descriptive nouns and adjectives are the vehicles for personality construction. They are used for the categorization of behaviors and of the people performing them. The observer bases the categorization on the attributes of the behavioral event, which include not only the actor's physical movements but information about the context in which the behavior is performed and the inferred intentions of the actor. Thus, the actor's handshake at the conclusion of a transaction may be categorized by the observer as ''businesslike'', whereas the actor's handshake on being introduced to the president of the company might be categorized as ''polite'' or possibly ''obsequious''. The same behavior is perceived differently depending upon the sourrounding context. For example, a handshake can have many meanings. It is only when the behavior has been categorized (e.g. as businesslike or polite) by the observer (or self-observer) that it takes on significance for the personality of the actor.

Once the behavior has been categorized, the observer gains all the advantages of categorization in any domain: the categorization provides an explanation of the behavior, and it may help predict subsequent behavior. Specifically, personality traits serve a dual purpose: they can be used to categorize both behaviors and people (Wyer and Gordon, 1984). The actor's handshake may be categorized as businesslike and so may the actor. However, the rules used by the observer in making these two kinds of categorizations are different. In categorizing behavior, the observer is concerned with matching the attributes of the specific behavioral instance to a personality category. In categorizing a person, the observer attributes the personality category to the actor on the basis of attribution rules (Heider, 1958; Jones and Davis, 1965; Kelley, 1967, 1971). The two kinds of categorization provide different explanations (Hampson, 1988b). Behavior categorization may not involve causal explanation, whereas categorization of the actor typically does. The actor's handshake may be businesslike in one instance, not because he or she is a businesslike person but because it is the expected thing to do. The observer will probably require more evidence before inferring that the actor is businesslike. However, in order to attribute a trait to the actor, the actor's behavior must first be categorized in personality terms.

The distinction between behavior categorization and trait attribution is consistent with the view of the social perceiver as a cognitive miser conserving resources by expending no more than necessary to meet current needs (Fiske and Taylor, 1984). Trait attribution is a complex form of information processing that provides a more powerful (causal) explanation than behavior categorization, but at some cost in terms of processing commitment. The form of categorization used will depend upon the observer's goals. If the observer's goal is to form an impression of the actor, then trait attributions may be made, whereas if the actor is tangential to the observer's goals, then categorizing the actor's behavior may suffice.

Personality construction does not take place in all encounters. It may be sufficient for the observer's comprehension goals to categorize the behavior in non-personality terms (e.g. simply as a "handshake"). However, when personality construction does take place, it involves the application of personality categories to the actor's behaviors, and in some cases to the actor. In discussing the observer component of personality construction, I will consider factors that affect both forms of categorization. There are two classes of variables that affect the observer's contribution to personality construction. By long-term characteristics, I refer to the relatively stable patterns of availability of personality constructs (e.g. an individual's implicit personality theory), whereas short-term characteristics refer to temporarily induced changes to that stable pattern of availability brought about by situational factors.

LONG-TERM OBSERVER CHARACTERISTICS

These refer to the categories that the observer typically uses to construct personality. Kelly (1955) called them personal constructs, and proposed that every individual possesses a unique set for interpreting the social world. According to Kelly, the observer's categories for constructing the actor's personality constitute the observer's personality. (Similarly, the actor's personality is constituted by the actor's personal construct system.) However, investigations into people's beliefs about the meanings of personality constructs and their interrelations suggest that there is considerable agreement among individuals' implicit personality theories (Schneider, 1973).

Although we may have a common understanding of personal constructs, we may each be more prone to interpret the behaviors of ourselves and others in terms of a particular subset of traits. Evidence for this proposition was provided by Higgins, King, and Mavin (1982). They investigated the role of construct accessibility in impression formation and recall by first having subjects describe themselves and others in trait terms. Two measures of trait accessibility were used. Traits that were used in more than one description or traits that appeared first in the description were defined as accessible. Each subject was then given a target description that consisted of behaviors related either to the subject's accessible or inaccessible traits. Subjects' written impressions of the target and recall of the target information showed greater omission of behaviors related to inaccessible traits than to accessible ones. These findings suggest that observers are characterized by their own subset of accessible personality categories which they apply in personality construction.

What determines the categories that are likely to be chronically accessible to the observer? To the extent that self-descriptive or self-relevant categories are more likely to be applied to others (Hirschberg and Jennings, 1980), then the observer's self-perceptions will also determine the observer's perceptions of others. A situational factor that can influence the observer's long-term category accessibility is the individual's cultural milieu. Social categories that are prevalent within a particular subgroup (Forgas, 1983) or prevail in the culture as a whole (Church, 1987) will be more accessible than those that are less familiar.

Another factor affecting long-term category accessibility is the purpose served by trait categorization. Categorization permits explanation and prediction, and some traits may be more powerful at explaining and predicting than others. John, Hampson, and Goldberg (1991) examined the observer's preference in personality description for broad traits (which refer to a wide range of behaviors) versus narrow traits (which refer to a more limited range of behaviors). They found a reliable preference for broad traits, one that was immune to several manipulations. Moreover, broad traits (e.g. extraverted, irresponsible, talented) are perceived as having greater explanatory power than narrow traits (e.g. talkative, unpunctual, musical) (John, 1986). Broad traits, therefore, appear to be more useful for observers than narrow traits, particularly when the observer not only wishes to categorize the actor's behavior but also to make personality attributions about the actor.

SHORT-TERM OBSERVER CHARACTERISTICS

The observer's long-term pattern of category accessibility can be temporarily altered by contextual factors and the observer's goals. Temporary changes can be brought about indirectly by recent experiences that activate particular categories (e.g. priming effects), and directly by the framing of the actor-observer encounter.

Recent Experience

Several studies have demonstrated that the recent use of trait categories can drastically alter the way that personality information is processed (Wyer and Gordon, 1984). Subjects first engage in a priming task, in which they encounter several trait constructs. The effects of these primed traits on the processing of ambiguous target descriptions are then observed. Higgins, Rholes, and Jones (1977) demonstrated that a target's evaluatively ambiguous behaviors (e.g. rowing the Atlantic) were encoded in the same evaluative direction as the priming traits. Those subjects primed with desirable terms described the target as "adventurous", whereas those primed with undesirable terms described the target as "reckless". Subsequently, Srull and Wyer (1979) demonstrated priming effects that extended not only to descriptively similar traits but also to traits that were descriptively different but evaluatively similar.

Other temporary changes in category accessibility can be brought about more explicitly by altering subjects' expectations. For example, Berman, Read, and Kenny (1983) demonstrated that subjects made more accurate judgements when judging traits consistent with previous trait information about the target than when judging inconsistent traits. In addition, the observer's motivational state may also temporarily influence category accessibility. For example, Stephan, Berscheid, and Walster (1971) found that males in a state of sexual arousal perceived their potential dates as being more sexually receptive than did unaroused males.

Framing the Actor-Observer Encounter

It is to be expected that observers will process information differently depending on the purpose of their encounter with the actor. When future interaction is expected, people appear to concentrate more on forming impressions than when no future interaction is anticipated. For example, Monson *et al.* (1982) observed that subjects made more extreme and more valid trait attributions about the target when expecting future interaction than when not. Jeffery and Mischel (1979) found that subjects expecting to describe the target or to predict the target's subsequent behavior used trait categories to sort the target information, whereas subjects expecting to have to recall target information used situational categories. Recall based on situational categories proved superior to recall based on trait categories. In a subsequent study, Hoffman, Mischel, and Mazze (1981) compared subjects' preferences for either trait-based or goal-based organization in their sorting of behavioral episodes. Both kinds of organization were available in the descriptions of the episodes. Subjects expecting to write impressions used trait-based categories to sort the episodes, whereas subjects expecting to recall the information used goal-based categories. Hoffman, Mischel and Mazze (1981) speculated that goals serve to interpret a wide range of behaviors and situations, thus making them easier to recall.

THE ACTOR'S BEHAVIOR

So far the observer's role in personality construction has been viewed in terms of the observer's cognitive activity—how the observer operates on the information provided by the actor. However, the observer's contribution will be affected by the nature of the information with which he or she has to work, namely the actor's behavior. There are several ways in which the actor's behavior will affect the observer's categorization. The observer will have difficulty constructing the less visible aspects of the actor's personality. Part of the actor's behavioral expression of his or her personality will be covert, such as worrying and experiencing headaches. If an actor chooses not to indicate to the observer that he or she is worrying or having a headache, then the observer may not have the behavioral basis for a personality categorization (Funder and Dobroth, 1987). More visible traits generate higher agreements among self, peer, and parental ratings (Kenrick and Stringfield, 1980). Moreover, there may be individual differences in trait visibility. For example, some people probably express anxiety and neuroticism more overtly than do others.

Traits may differ in the amount or variety of behavior necessary from the actor. For example, undesirable traits require fewer behavioral manifestations in order for them to be ascribed than do desirable traits. A person once caught stealing is labelled ''dishonest'' more readily than a person once observed talking is labelled ''talkative'' (Rothbart and Park, 1986). Other qualities of the behavior also may be important, such as its intensity.

It is interesting to speculate how biological factors may affect those characteristics of the actor's behavior that affect the observer's categorizations. It seems reasonable to assume that some traits are more biologically based than others (Schaie and Parham, 1976)—although the identification of such traits is not proving straightforward (Rowe, 1987). Are more biologically based traits expressed differently than less biologically based traits, and is this difference detected by observers and used in trait categorization?

Some indirect support for this idea comes from attribution theory. People are more likely to perceive a person's actions as determined by the person's personality characteristics than by situational factors when the actions are socially undesirable (Jones and Davis, 1965). Such behaviors are more diagnostic of the actor's personality because they are perceived as being less controllable by the actor. Observers are aware of impression management (they engage in it themselves); therefore, they may be on the alert for more or less managed behavior. When a behavior is undesirable or counternormative, the observer may take this as an indication that it is relatively biologically determined.

Studies of lay theories of delinquency (Furnham and Henderson, 1983) indicate that people's explanations for criminal behavior are biological (e.g. mental instability) as well as sociological (e.g. unemployment). If undesirable behavior is perceived as diagnostic of biologically determined personality variables, then more shocking crimes should be explained biologically, whereas relatively mundane crimes should be explained sociologically. Hollin and Howells (1987) found that sexual assault and rape were attributed to mental instability, whereas burglary and robbery were attributed to poor education and parenting.

Lay theories can provide valuable insights for the scientist (Sternberg, 1985). Lay beliefs about the degree of biological determination underlying a personality trait would be useful both for understanding the observer's categorization process and for the identification of more versus less biologically based personality variables.

CONCLUSIONS

In this section I emphasized the factors affecting the observer's choice of traits in categorizing the actor's behavior and in attributing traits to the actor. The observer's category use is influenced by both long-term and short-term personal factors, as well as by characteristics of the actor's performance. One question singled out as promising for further research is the lay perception of biologically based traits and behaviors. Traits that are more biologically than culturally based are probably less open to impression management, but this does not mean they are not socially constructed. The underlying biology is expressed in behavior, and it is this behavior that the observer uses when making a trait categorization. Behavior reflects cultural and learned factors as well as biology. Particularly in constructing adults' personalities, observers base their trait categorizations of relatively biological traits on the "content-saturated" behavior of the actor (Strelau, 1987). For example, Buss and Plomin (1984) identify emotionality, activity, and sociability as temperament traits. These traits cannot be expressed in a content-free manner in the adult. Instead, adults engage in specific forms of socially regulated emotional, active, or sociable behaviors. Observers' knowledge of the social meanings of the behaviors results in the application of these temperament-trait categories to these behaviors. One problem faced by temperament researchers is the design of equivalent measures of temperament traits across the life-span, ones that permit the increase in content-saturation with age and yet remain valid measures of the same temperament. By studying the behaviors that observers use to categorize behavior with temperament traits, scientists may gain some valuable guidelines for the development of their measures.

BIOLOGY AND THE SELF-OBSERVER VARIABLE

The human capacity for self-awareness produces an added dimension of complexity to the process of personality construction. Humans are aware of their self-presentations and can use this knowledge to control the impression they believe they are making on others.

The capacity for self-awareness allows the actor to try to assess the impact he or she is having on the observer. The actor knows that the observer is forming an impression of him or her, and the actor forms an impression of the observer's impression. The actor may then wish to modify his or her behavior in order to affect the impression the observer is forming. Why should the actor be concerned about the observer's impression? For theorists in the symbolic-interactionist and impression-management traditions, the impression of the actor negotiated by the actor and the observer in the course of interaction *is* the actor's personality. Consequently, the actor is concerned that the observer's impression corresponds to the actor's self-perceptions.

There is some debate over whether people aim to produce an impression that is consistent with their *actual* self-concept (self-verification) or with their *ideal* self-concept (self-presentation) (Deaux and Major, 1987). According to self-verification, people may even present themselves in an undesirable way in order to be consistent with their negative self-concept (Swann, 1983), whereas in self-presentation people are striving to maintain a public image of a positive nature. In most cases, however, both self-verification and self-presentation result in a concern to make a favorable impression.

People vary in the extent to which they are concerned with the personality construction process. A skillful self-presentation not only depends on having the necessary repertoire of social behaviors but also on an appreciation of the effect of one's self-presentation on the observer. It seems intuitively reasonable that people vary in the extent to which they think about and try to influence the impression they make on others. These intuitions are reflected in constructs measuring two different aspects of this form of self-awareness, public and private self-consciousness (Fenigstein, Scheier, and Buss, 1975). Public self-consciousness refers to the tendency to rely on other people as sources of information about oneself, whereas private self-consciousness refers to the tendency to focus on private thoughts and feelings and self-observations of behavior. Differences in self-presentational behavior between people high versus low on public self-consciousness have been found for various behaviors both inside and outside the laboratory (Scheier and Carver, 1983).

The extent to which self-observations influence behavior may depend on factors other than public and private self-consciousness. Buss and Briggs (1984) criticized the dramaturgical model for neglecting individual differences. People differ in the extent to which self-presentational demands win out over individual propensities. Buss and Briggs proposed three factors that influence self-presentation. Some individuals are not as good at *pretending* as others (Christie and Geis, 1970). Individuals vary in their preferred degree of *formality*. A formal person placed in an informal situation may have difficulty adapting to the unscripted nature of the causal setting. Finally, self-presentation is affected by a person's *shyness*. For some people, their social roles amount to their personalities, whereas for others their individuality dominates their personality, and social roles are temporary or never deeply entered into. Buss and Briggs's model seems a sensible counterweight to the purely self-presentational view of personality.

In sum, self-awareness enables people to play an active part in the construction of their personalities. However, people probably differ in their degree of involvement in the construction process. These individual differences (e.g. high versus low public self-consciousness) include both biological and non-biological factors. Even if an individual is highly sensitive to personality construction, he or she may be restricted by another factor, such as shyness. Our understanding of the variables that facilitate or inhibit personality construction is still limited and warrants further study.

THE DYNAMIC NATURE OF PERSONALITY CONSTRUCTION

So far, I have examined the separate modes of actor, observer, and self-observer in the process of personality construction. However, the dynamic nature of the interaction among these three components is central to the constructivist view. Observers are also actors, and actors are also observers. Both parties are concerned with the construction of their personalities as well as that of the other. Both parties are, to varying degrees, self-observers. Although Harré (1979) proposed that social life developed for the purpose of personality construction, not all interactions are undertaken with the goal of personality construction in mind. Whatever the goal, the participants will modify their self-presentation in such a way as to enhance the likelihood of attaining that goal. Both actors and observers play an active part in the construction process.

One way of demonstrating the process of personality construction is to observe personality change that comes about as the result of social interactions (Darley and Fazio, 1980). For example, Miller and Turnbull (1986) discuss the changes to the actor's self-concept that occur as a result of the observer's expectancies. There are two steps to this process. First, observers expecting to interact with a certain kind of person ask questions that will confirm their initial beliefs. Second, the actors induced to behave in such a confirmatory manner come to see themselves as this kind of person. Evidence for the first step is exemplified by Snyder and Swann's (1978) study of behavioral confirmation. Interviewers demonstrated a confirmatory bias in selecting questions to determine whether interviewees were extraverted or introverted. Interviewees responded to these questions in ways that confirmed the interviewers' expectations. Fazio, Effrein, and Falender (1981) investigated the second step. They induced confirmatory extraverted or introverted behavior in their subjects by asking them either extraverted or introverted questions in an interview. Immediately after the interview, the subjects who responded to the extravert questions described themselves as more extraverted and were rated as more extraverted than the subjects who had responded to the introverted questions.

However, as noted by Pennington (1987), none of the research on behavioral confirmation has used naturalistic face-to-face interactions nor have the subjects' personalities been taken into account. Consequently, the passive role of the actor in personality construction may have been exaggerated. In Pennington's own study, in which interaction was face-to-face and the personalities of the interviewees were measured, interviewers did not use confirmatory strategies, and their impressions of the interviewees were determined by the interviewees' personalities. These findings confirm that personality construction depends upon the active parts played by actor and the observer, and they highlight the danger of attempting to understand the process by focusing too exclusively on one or the other.

CONCLUSIONS

In considering the dynamics of personality construction, proximal causes of behavior were emphasized. The notion that personality is constructed from moment to moment in response to interpersonal dynamics is a far cry from biological perspectives. Interestingly, as discussed earlier, behavioral geneticists are beginning to investigate the process of personality change. The issue of personality change and stability, in both the long and short term, is central to personality psychology. It will be fascinating to see how biological and non-biological approaches can be integrated in the effort to understand personality change. Biology may be able to demonstrate limits to possible change, and even attribute a portion of change to genetic as opposed to environmental factors. Nevertheless, the importance of social and cognitive factors for personality development and change will not be diminished by a better understanding of distal variables.

FINAL REMARKS

Recently, Deaux and Major (1987) have developed a model of gender-related behavior that incorporates both the expectations of perceivers (observers) and the self-systems of the target (actors). Gender-related behavior is seen as being the product of negotiated social interaction. The parallels between that model and the process of personality construction can readily be drawn. Indeed, the negotiation of the actor's gender identity through the display of gender-related behavior is one part of the broader personality-construction enterprise in which all aspects of the actor's identity are under negotiation. Deaux and Major's model is intended to supplement but not replace other models of gender. For example, biological approaches account for sex differences in genetic, hormonal, and other physical terms. Deaux and Major (1987) propose that their model accounts for the *display* of sex-differences but not the *acquisition* of sex differences. However, in making the distinction between display and acquisition they do not exploit the power of their model to provide a means of bringing these various approaches closer together. The process of personality construction (or the negotiation of identity) takes place throughout the life-span, building layer upon layer of socially significant actions, which are repeatedly displayed and modified producing a series of changing forms. Consequently, display and acquisition are part of the same process.

My aim in this chapter has been to describe the factors involved in just one cycle of the complicated display and acquisition process of personality construction. As a counterweight to biological perspectives, I have presented a view of personality that stresses social and cognitive proximal variables. However, I have also considered how biology could be incorporated in and benefit from such a contrasting perspective. The goal has been not to argue for the superiority of any one perspective, but rather to indicate that a biological bias will result in an incomplete understanding of personality.

ACKNOWLEDGEMENTS

The preparation of this chapter was supported by Grant MH-39077 from the National Institute of Mental Health. The following colleagues' insightful comments on an earlier version are gratefully acknowledged: Chris Brand, Patricia A. Casselden, William F. Chaplin, Gerald L. Clore, Russell E. Glasgow, Lewis R. Goldberg, Oliver P. John, and Mary K. Rothbart.

REFERENCES

Archer, J. (1988) The sociobiology of bereavement: A reply to Littlefield and Rushton. *Journal of Personality and Social Psychology*, **55**, 272–278.

Baker, L.A. and Daniels, D. (1990) Nonshared environmental influences and personality differences in adult twins. *Journal of Personality and Social Psychology*, **58**, 103–110.

Baumeister, R. (1982) A self-presentational view of social phenomena. *Psychological Bulletin*, **91**, 3–26.

Berman, J.S., Read, S.J. and Kenny, D.A. (1983) Processing inconsistent social information. *Journal of Personality and Social Psychology*, **45**, 1211–1224.

Borden, E.S. (1984) Psychodynamic model of career choice and satisfaction. In D. Brown and L. Brooks (eds), *Career Choice and Development*. San Francisco: Jossey-Bass.

Boring, E.G. (1950) *A History of Experimental Psychology* (2nd edn). New York: Appleton-Century-Crofts.

Buss, A.H. and Briggs, S.R. (1984) Drama and the self in social interaction. *Journal of Personality and Social Psychology*, **47**, 1310–1324.

Buss, A.H. and Plomin, R. (1984) *Temperament: Early Developing Personality Traits*. Hillsdale, NJ: Lawrence Erlbaum.

Buss, D.M. (1984a) Evolutionary biology and personality psychology: Toward a conception of human nature and individual differences. *American Psychologist*, **39**, 1135–1147.

Buss, D.M. (1984b) Toward a psychology of person-environment (PE) correlation: The role of spouse selection. *Journal of Personality and Social Psychology*, **42**, 361–377.

Buss, D.M. (1985) The act frequency approach to the interpersonal environment. In R. Hogan and W.H. Jones (eds), *Perspectives in Personality* (Vol. 1). Greenwich, CT: Jai Press.

Buss, D.M. (1990) Toward a biologically informed psychology of personality. *Journal of Personality*, **58**, 1–16.

Cantor, N. (1990, October) Social psychology and sociobiology: What can we leave to evolution? Paper presented at the meeting of the Society of Experimental Social Psychology, Buffalo, NY.

Christie, F. and Geis, F.L. (eds) (1970) *Studies in Machiavellianism.* New York: Academic Press.

Church, A.T. (1987) Personality research in a non-western culture: The Philippines. *Psychological Bulletin*, **102**, 272–292.

Cooley, C.H. (1902) *Human Nature and the Social Order.* New York: Scribner.

Darley, J.M. and Fazio, R.H. (1980) Expectancy confirmation processes arising in the social interaction sequence. *American Psychologist*, **35**, 867–881.

Deaux, K. and Major, B. (1987) Putting gender into context: an interactive model of gender-related behavior. *Psychological Review*, **94**, 369–389.

Diener, E.D., Larson, R.J. and Emmons, R.A. (1984) Person × situation interactions: choice of situations and congruence response models. *Journal of Personality and Social Psychology*, **47**, 580–592.

Digman, J.M. (1990) Personality structure: Emergence of the Five-Factor model. *Annual Review of Psychology*, **41**, 417–440.

Dworkin, R.H. and Goldfinger, S.H. (1985) Processing bias: Individual differences in the cognition of situations. *Journal of Personality*, **53**, 480–501.

Eaves, L.J., Eysenck, H.J. and Martin, N.G. (1989) *Genes, Culture and Personality: An Empirical Approach.* New York: Academic Press.

Eysenck, H.J. (1967). *The Biological Basis of Personality.* Springfield, IL: C.C. Thomas.

Fazio, R.H., Effrein, E.A. and Falender, V.J. (1981) Self-perceptions following social interaction. *Journal of Personality and Social Psychology*, **41**, 232–242.

Fenigstein, A., Scheier, M.F. and Buss, A.H. (1975) Public and private self-consciousness: Assessment and theory. *Journal of Consulting and Clinical Psychology*, **43**, 522–527.

Fiske, S.T. and Taylor, S.E. (1984) *Social Cognition.* Reading: Addison-Wesley.

Forgas, J.P. (1983) The effects of prototypicality and cultural salience on perceptions of people. *Journal of Research in Personality*, **17**, 153–173.

Funder, D.C. and Dobroth, K.M. (1987) Differences between traits: properties associated with interjudge agreement. *Journal of Personality and Social Psychology*, **52**, 409–418.

Furnham, A. (1981) Personality and activity preference. *British Journal of Social and Clinical Psychology*, **20**, 57–68.

Furnham, A. and Henderson, M. (1983) Lay theories of delinquency. *European Journal of Social Psychology*, **13**, 107–120.

Gangestad, S.W. and Simpson, J.A. (1990) Toward an evolutionary history of female sociosexual variation. *Journal of Personality*, **58**, 69–96.

Gergen, K.J. (1985) The social constructionist movement in modern psychology. *American Psychologist*, **40**, 266–275.

Gibson, J.J. (1979) *The Ecological Approach to Visual Perception.* Boston: Houghton Mifflin.

Goffman, E. (1959) *The Presentation of Self in Everyday Life.* New York: Doubleday.

Goldberg, L.R. (1981) Language and individual differences: The search for universals in personality lexicons. In L. Wheeler (ed.), *Review of Personality and Social Psychology* (Vol. 2). Beverly Hills, CA: Sage Publications.

Hampson, S.E. (1984) The social construction of personality. In H. Bonarius, G. Van Heck and N. Smid (eds), *Personality Psychology in Europe: Theoretical and Empirical Developments.* Lisse: Swets & Zeitlinger.

Hampson, S.E. (1988a) *The Construction of Personality: An Introduction* (2nd edn). London: Routledge.

Hampson, S.E. (1988b) The dynamics of categorization and impression formation. In R.S. Wyer and T.K. Srull (eds), *Advances in Social Cognition Volume I: A Dual Process Model of Impression Formation.* Hillsdale, NJ: Lawrence Erlbaum.

Harré, R. (1979) *Social Being.* Oxford: Blackwell.

Harré, R. (1983) *Personal Being.* Oxford: Blackwell.

Heider, F. (1958) *The Psychology of Interpersonal Relations.* New York: Wiley.

Higgins, E.T., King, G.A. and Mavin, G.H. (1982) Individual construct accessibility and subjective impressions and recall. *Journal of Personality and Social Psychology,* **43**, 35–47.

Higgins, E.T., Rholes, W.S. and Jones, C.R. (1977) Category accessibility and impression formation. *Journal of Experimental Social Psychology,* **13**, 141–154.

Hirschberg, N. and Jennings, S.J. (1980) Beliefs, personality, and person perception: A theory of individual differences. *Journal of Research in Personality,* **14**, 235–249.

Hoffman, C., Mischel, W. and Mazze, K. (1981) The role of purpose in the organization of information about behavior: Trait-based versus goal-based categories in person cognition. *Journal of Personality and Social Psychology,* **40**, 211–225.

Holland, J.L. (1973) *Making Vocational Choices: A Theory of Careers.* Englewood Cliffs, NJ: Prentice-Hall.

Hollin, C.R. and Howells, K. (1987) Lay explanations of delinquency: global or specific? *British Journal of Social Psychology,* **26**, 203–210.

Jeffery, K.M. and Mischel, W. (1979) Effects of purpose on the organization and recall of information in person perception. *Journal of Personality,* **47**, 397–419.

John, O.P. (1986) Direction and type of causal explanations in trait hierarchies. Unpublished manuscript, Oregon Research Institute, Eugene, OR.

John, O.P. (1990) The "Big Five" factor taxonomy: Dimensions of personality in the natural language and in questionnaires. In L.A. Pervin (ed.), *Handbook of Personality: Theory and Research.* New York: Guilford.

John, O.P., Hampson, S.E. and Goldberg, L.R. (1991) The basic level in personality-trait hierarchies: Studies of trait and accessibility in different contexts. *Journal of Personality and Social Psychology,* **60**, 348–361.

Jones, E.E. and Davis, R.E. (1965) From acts to dispositions: the attribution process in person perception. In L. Berkowitz (ed.), *Advances in Experimental Social Psychology* (Vol. 2). New York: Academic Press.

Kelley, H.H. (1967) Attribution theory in social psychology. In D.D. LeVine (ed.), *Nebraska Symposium on Motivation* (Vol. 15). Lincoln: University of Nebraska Press.

Kelley, H.H. (1971) Attribution in social interaction. In E.E. Jones (ed.), *Attribution: Perceiving the Causes of Behavior.* Morristown, NJ: General Learning Press.

Kelly, G.A. (1955) *The Psychology of Personal Constructs.* New York: Norton.

Kenrick, D.T. and Stringfield, D.O. (1980) Personality traits and the eye of the beholder: Crossing some traditional philosophical boundaries in the search for consistency in all of the people. *Psychological Review,* **87**, 88–104.

Landman, J. and Manis, M. (1983) Social cognition: some historical and theoretical perspectives. In L. Berkowitz (ed.), *Advances in Experimental Social Psychology* (Vol. 16). New York: Academic Press.

Loehlin, J.C. and Nichols, R.C. (1976) *Heredity, Environment and Personality: A Study of 850 Sets of Twins*. Austin: University of Texas Press.

Loehlin, J.C., Horn, J.M. and Willerman, L. (1990) Heredity, environment, and personality change: Evidence from the Texas Adoption Project. *Journal of Personality*, **58**, 221–243.

Loehlin, J.C., Willerman, L. and Horn, J.M. (1988) Human behavior genetics. *Annual Review of Psychology*, **39**, 101–133.

Magnusson, D. and Endler, N.S. (eds) (1977) *Personality at the Crossroads: Current Issues in Interactional Psychology*. Hillsdale, NJ: Lawrence Erlbaum.

Mead, G.H. (1934) *Mind, Self and Society*. Chicago: University of Chicago Press.

Miller, D.T. and Turnbull, W. (1986) Expectancies and interpersonal processes. *Annual Review of Psychology*, **37**, 233–256.

Monson, T.C., Keel, R., Stephens, D. and Genung, V. (1982) Trait attributions: Relative validity, covariation with behavior, and prospect of future interaction. *Journal of Personality and Social Psychology*, **42**, 1014–1024.

Pennington, D.C. (1987) Confirmatory hypothesis testing in face-to-face interaction: an empirical refutation. *British Journal of Social Psychology*, **26**, 225–235.

Pogue-Geile, M.F. and Rose, R.J. (1985) Developmental genetic studies of adult personality. *Development Psychology*, **21**, 547–557.

Plomin, R. and Nesselroade, J.R. (1990) Behavioral genetics and personality change. *Journal of Personality*, **58**, 191–220.

Rose, R.J. (1988) Genetic and environmental variance in content dimensions of the MMPI. *Journal of Personality and Social Psychology*, **55**, 302–311.

Rose, R.J. and Kaprio, J. (1988) Frequency of social contact and intra-pair resemblance of adult MZ co-twins: Does shared experience influence personality after all? *Behavior Genetics*, **18**, 309–328.

Rothbart, M. and Park, B. (1986) On the confirmability and disconfirmability of trait concepts. *Journal of Personality and Social Psychology*, **50**, 131–142.

Rowe, D.C. (1983) Biometrical genetic models of self-reported delinquent behavior: A twin study. *Behavior Genetics*, **13**, 473–489.

Rowe, D.C. (1987) Resolving the person-situation debate: Invitation to an interdisciplinary dialogue. *American Psychologist*, **42**, 218–227.

Rowe, D.C. and Plomin, R. (1981) The importance of nonshared (E1) environmental influences in behavioral development. *Developmental Psychology*, **17**, 517–531.

Rushton, J.P. (1988) Epigenetic rules in moral development: Distal-proximal approaches to altruism and aggression. *Aggressive Behavior*, **14**, 35–50.

Rushton, J.P. (1990) Sir Francis Galton, epigenetic rules, genetic similarity theory, and human life-history analysis. *Journal of Personality*, **58**, 117–140.

Scarr, S. and McCartney, K. (1983) How people make their own environments: A theory of genotype environments effects. *Child Development*, **54**, 424–435.

Schaie, K.W. and Parham, A. (1976) Stability of adult personality traits: Fact or fable? *Journal of Personality and Social Psychology*, **34**, 146–158.

Scheier, M.F. and Carver, C.S. (1983) Two sides of the self: One for you and one for me. In J. Suls and A.G. Greenwald (eds), *Psychological Perspectives on the Self* (Vol. 2). Hillsdale, NJ: Erlbaum.

Schlenker, B.R. (1980) *Impression Management: The Self-Concept, Social Identity, and Interpersonal Relations*. Monterey, CA: Brooks/Cole.

Schneider, D.J. (1973) Implicit personality theory: A review. *Psychological Bulletin*, **79**, 294–309.

Snyder, M. and Swann, W.B., Jr. (1978) Hypothesis-testing processes in social interaction. *Journal of Personality and Social Psychology*, **36**, 1202–1212.

Snyder, M. and Ickes, W. (1985) Personality and social behavior. In G. Lindzey and E. Aronson (eds), *Handbook of Social Psychology* (Vol. II). New York: Random House.

Srull, T.K. and Wyer, R.S., Jr. (1979) The role of category accessibility in the interpretations of information about persons: Some determinants and implications. *Journal of Personality and Social Psychology*, **37**, 1660–1672.

Stephan, W., Berscheid, E. and Walster, E. (1971) Sexual arousal and heterosexual perception. *Journal of Personality and Social Psychology*, **20**, 93–101.

Sternberg, R.J. (1985) Implicit theories of intelligence, creativity, and wisdom. *Journal of Personality and Social Psychology*, **49**, 607–627.

Strelau, J. (1987) The concept of temperament in personality research. *European Journal of Personality*, **1**, 107–117.

Swann, W.B., Jr. (1983) Self-verification: bringing social reality into harmony with the self. In J. Suls and A. Greenwald (eds), *Psychological Perspectives on the Self* (Vol. 2). Hillsdale, NJ: Erlbaum.

Swann, W.B., Jr. (1984) Quest for accuracy in person perception: a matter of pragmatics. *Psychological Review*, **91**, 457–477.

Tedeschi, J.T. (ed.) (1981) *Impression Management Theory and Social Psychological Research*. New York: Academic Press.

Tellegen, A., Lykken, D.T., Bouchard, T.J. Jr., Wilcox, K.J., Segal, N.L. and Rich, S. (1988) Personality similarity in twins reared apart and together. *Journal of Personality and Social Psychology*, **54**, 1031–1039.

Van Heck, G. (1984) The construction of general taxonomy of situations. In H. Bonarius, G. Van Heck and N. Smid (eds), *Personality Psychology in Europe*. Lisse: Swets & Zeitlinger.

Wilson, E.O. (1978) *On Human Nature*. Cambridge MA: Harvard University Press.

Wyer, R.S. and Gordon, S.E. (1984) The cognitive representation of social information. In R.S. Wyer and T.K. Srull (eds), *Handbook of Social Cognition*. Hillsdale, NJ: Erlbaum.

Chapter 6

The Factor Structure in the Fields of Personality and Ability

Paul Kline
Department of Psychology, Washington Singer Laboratories,
University of Exeter, The Queen's Drive,
Exeter, EX4 4QG Devon, UK

ABSTRACT

In this chapter I argue that the main dimensions of ability and personality, as they have emerged from factor analysis, should be incorporated into experimental designs, thus accounting for individual differences. Factor analytic methodology was discussed in order to resolve the problem that different methods of analysis and different factor analysts tend to produce different results. However, it was shown that rotation to simple structure after the correct number of factors had been selected led to meaningful and replicable findings. The most important factors in the fields of ability and personality were briefly described, including the two intelligence factors, crystallized and fluid ability, and the personality factors of extraversion and anxiety. If individual differences are important, it is these factors which should be measured.

INTRODUCTION

Since the time of Spearman, psychologists have been trying to account for individual differences in terms of underlying factors or dimensions. Since that time too, there have been numerous factorial accounts of individual

Handbook of Individual Differences: Biological Perspectives
Edited by Anthony Gale and Michael W. Eysenck

differences, not all by any means the same, such that sceptics of factor analysis (e.g. Heim, 1975) have eschewed the method as valueless for obtaining a firm foundation of knowledge.

However, modern computing facilities have rendered that view quite untenable. There is now considerable agreement among factorists as to how stable, replicable factor analyses, whose factors actually refer to dimensions that can be recognized through other methods of investigation, can be carried out. Cattell (1973, 1978), Carroll (1981) and Kline (1979) have advocated highly similar approaches to the problem and Hashemi (1981) has provided some much needed empirical support with psychological data for this methodology.

SOME GUIDELINES FOR TECHNICALLY SOUND FACTOR ANALYSES

Cattell (e.g. 1978) has argued that many of the differences between different factor analytic results were due to the technical deficiencies of the factor-analytic methods employed. Hence he suggested a number of rules for conducting technically competent analysis. These rules are not all equally important but the most critical are set out.

(a) There must be adequate sampling of subjects. This refers both to the number (factor analyses are inherently unreliable with Ns less than 100) and the heterogeneity of the sample. In studies of students, for example, intelligence may be a relatively trivial factor because, in the UK at least, students are homogeneous for intelligence.

(b) There must be adequate sampling of variables. If the aim of the analysis is essentially exploratory, to map out the most important variables, then sampling of variables must be good. Here the old adage, that you get out (in factor analyses) what you put in must be true. If no tests of say, numerical ability are included, there can be no numerical factor. Generally three variables are required to compose a factor.

(c) It is imperative that there be more subjects than variables. This, of course, is well known. However, the ratio of subjects to variables has been the subject of much debate. Nunnally (1978) is the most conservative, advocating 10 to 1. Guilford (1956) the least at 2 to 1. Few writers, however, offer any rationale for their favoured ratio other than experience. Barrett and Kline (1981) put this matter to the test with some item data from the Eysenck Personality Questionnaire, the EPQ. They found that a clear factor structure was successfully reproduced with a 2 to 1 ratio. Where factors were less clear the smallest ones were not always found. However, at 3 to 1 there seemed little difficulty. Nevertheless the more subjects the better.

(d) Principal factors rather than components: Principal components utilizes all the variance in the matrix and produces as many components as variables. Principal factors or axes attempts to exclude the error variance by inserting into the diagonals of the correlation matrix, test reliabilities or some other estimate of the commonality. Carroll (1981) strongly argues for factors rather than components, on the grounds that error variance is thereby excluded from the analysis. While this is true, it must be remembered that with large matrices (20 variables), Harman (1976) has shown that components and factors are identical.

(e) The importance of simple structure: Cattell and most factorists of any note all follow Thurstone (1947) and aim to reach simple structure. The rationale for this is clear-cut. Since there is an infinity of mathematically equivalent factorial solutions, a method has to be found to choose between them. If each solution is regarded as an hypothesis to account for the observed correlations between variables, then by the law of parsomony the simplest solution is best. Simple structure gives us the simplest solution which Thurstone essentially defined as the solution which yielded factors each with a few high loadings and their other loadings zero. Thus, the basic aim of the method suggested here is to maximize simple structure.

(f) Number of factors to rotate: It is generally agreed that this is a crucial variable in the search for simple structure. Rotate too many factors and there is a loss of clarity with factors splitting. Rotate too few and second-orders tend to appear at the first order.

There are a variety of different methods of factor extraction. Barrett and Kline (1982a) studied some of these methods with real rather than artificial data and found no real agreement. Generally it seemed safest to use more than one method and to try out different solutions. One point, however, did emerge. The Kaiser–Guttman criterion of rotating all factors with eigenvalues (which indicate the size of the factors) greater than unity certainly with large matrices leads to over-factorization. As Mulaik (1972) pointed out, the Kaiser–Guttman criterion was never intended for choosing significant factors. Two useful selection procedures appear to be Cattell's (1966) Scree test and Velicer's (1976) method using partial correlations. Generally it seems sensible, if these give different solutions to try both and see which provides better simple structure, often by examining the hyperplane count (the number of zero loadings).

(g) Oblique or orthogonal rotation? Orthogonal rotation, yielding uncorrelated factors, is claimed by some (e.g. Guilford, 1959) as better than oblique because they are *per se* more simple. However, Cattell favours the oblique solution because by allowing factors to take up the best possible position relative to simple structure each factor becomes more simple. In addition, to demand orthogonality is a restraint unlikely to be in accord with psychological reality. In the end this becomes a matter of taste. I think especially in the field of personality, that orthogonality is a priori unlikely and hence prefer oblique solutions. This is especially true if factors are regarded as corresponding to underlying (even causal) influences.

(h) Which rotation method? Hakstian (1971) studied the efficiency of a number of different rotational methods at reaching simple structure. Carroll (1981) advocates Direct Oblimin (Jennrich and Sampson, 1966) and certainly Barrett and Kline (1980) in their study of the EPQ found it highly efficient. However, in practical terms, in respect of the interpretation of factors, differences in results between methods were not as large as suggested by Cattell (1978). Each method can be caught out by local maxima which affect its particular computation procedures, so a check with another rotation can be useful.

However, two facts do stand out. If an orthogonal rotation is preferred, Varimax is agreed by all to be the most efficient procedure. The second point that is now established is that Procrustes rotations are not to be trusted. As the work of Horn and Knapp (1973) showed, Procrustes is so powerful that it can fit almost any set of results to a target even when the results are actually antithetical to the target. Procrustes should be used (if at all) only when a very precise set of factor loadings can be hypothesized. It is this problem which has rendered Guilford's Structure of Intellect model of dubious value.

(i) Second and higher-order factoring. A good check on a factor structure but obviously only in oblique rotations, is to carry out higher order factoring. If this is done it seems best to "ground" the secondaries against the original variables rather than the lower-order factors for this makes easier accurate location. Grounding secondaries is a technique by which the loadings of the original variables (tests), rather than the first-order factors, on the second-order factors, are computed. There is a variety of methods to do this but the Hendrickson and White (1966) procedure is effective.

If these guidelines are followed, simple structure can usually be obtained. In my experience in factoring over the last few years replicable factors and factor structures clearly emerge. These factors in the field of personality have also been psychologically meaningful.

(j) Objection to the method. There is a powerful statistical objection to the factor-analytic approach which I have described above: there is no significance test for the factors. The rotational procedures are no more than convenient algorithms, not, therefore, a suitable basis for scientific analysis. In my view this is an exaggerated claim. The work of Cattell, Thurstone and Eysenck, just to name three factorists, over the years, and experimental studies of well-known factors such as extraversion or g (e.g. the work of Sternberg, 1988), indicates that replicated, simple-structure factors are not the artefacts of algorithms.

However, this statistical objection has been answered by the development of confirmatory analysis by Joreskog (1969), which attempts to fit a hypothesized factor structure, and allows a statistical test of the fit. However, although this now gives factor analysis a reputable statistical basis, there are a number of arguments which make its use, in psychology, at least, far from obligatory. The first concerns its chi-square test of fit. When the sample size is large this is so powerful that it is difficult to reject any hypothesis. This, of course, is so severe an objection that the others are somewhat otiose. Suffice it to say that in many cases, especially where studies are exploratory, it is difficult to define a target matrix. The less well defined the target, the easier it is to fit. There is a final empirical point. Whereas factor analysis has revealed, as we shall argue, some factors important in the real world, so far little has come from confirmatory analysis.

Thus, in brief, I argue that when simple-structure factor analyses are conducted replicable factors emerge which despite the differences of nomenclature reveal themselves on examination as essentially similar. This list which we have fully discussed in Kline (1979) and Kline and Barrett (1983) constitutes the main constructs relating to individual differences and it is these which we must take into account in psychological research. They are the traits of trait psychology, the elements of a psychometric model of man (cf. Kline, 1980).

I shall now list the main factors which have emerged from such technically adequate studies.

ABILITIES

In the field of abilities, the work of Cattell (e.g. 1971) stands out as being comprehensive and technically sound. Five second-order factors account for much of the primary ability variance. These are:

gf Fluid intelligence. This is the basic reasoning ability, common to much problem solving. The multivariate biometric analyses of human abilities suggest that this is a largely hereditarily determined factor.

gc Crystallized intelligence. This is a general ability as it is evinced in a particular culture, where it loads on the skills valued in that culture, in the West for example, verbal, numerical and mechanical ability. It reflects the investment of fluid intelligence in the culture. It is the factor of traditional verbal intelligence tests.

gv Visualization. This is the factor underlying all those skills in which visualization is helpful.

gr Retrieval capacity or general fluency. This is the ability to search through and locate information quickly in long-term memory. It is, therefore, the factor underlying Guilford's work on creativity. The fluent effortless talker, is high on gr. Peter Ustinov, actor, playwright and raconteur, readily comes to mind.

gs Cognitive speed. This factor affects speed in a wide range of tasks such as writing and numerical computation. It is, however, not related to speed of problem solving, which is a function of gf.

These are clearly the most important cognitive factors and should be included in any study where abilities need to be measured. These second-orders account for the variance in first-order factors. Cattell and his colleagues have identified 27, but this primary list is inevitably somewhat arbitrary because many skills, e.g. cheese tasting, understanding horses (indubitably an individual difference among jockeys and between jockeys and the lay public), have never been tested. Many of the best known primaries were isolated by Thurstone. These include: verbal ability, numerical ability, spatial ability, perceptual speed, speed of closure, inductive reasoning, flexibility of closure, three memory factors, ideational flexibility, ideational fluency and word fluency.

Actually a list of the 23 largest primary ability factors together with marker tests has been produced by Ekstrom *et al.* (1976). See Table 6.1.

The list given in Table 6.1 certainly includes all the most important ability factors which have so far been identified.

The work of Cattell and his colleagues is often regarded as technically brilliant but idiosyncratic. Cattell is really in the tradition of the brilliant amateur scientist, typified by Darwin and Galton. Carroll (1986), however, is careful and scrupulous in his scientific judgements and recently he has reanalysed all extant data sets relevant to the factorization of abilities using factorial methods which are virtually identical to those advocated in this chapter. His results are strikingly similar to those of Cattell and as set out in Table 6.2 indicate the relation of the primary factors to these second orders.

The only real difference between Carroll's list and that of Cattell is the name given to the fluency factor, "retrieval" in the one case and "idea production" in the other. Cattell did have a memory factor (which I did not include) and he used no auditory tests in the battery which he gave—hence there was no auditory factor in the list. This agreement on the most important factors is an impressive illustration of the replicability of factor analysis when these are carried out to technically adequate standards and when simple structure is attained. It should be noted that the most recent studies of the third-order ability factors by Gustaffson (1988) support this work of Carroll.

Table 6.1.

CF Closure, Flexibility of
1. Hidden figures test
2. Hidden patterns test
3. Copying test

CS Closure, Speed of
1. *Gestalt* completion test
2. Concealed words test
3. Snowy pictures

CV Closure, Verbal
1. Scrambled words
2. Hidden words
3. Incomplete words

FA Fluency, Associational
1. Controlled associations test
2. Opposites test
3. Figures of speech

FE Fluency, Expressional
1. Making sentences
2. Arranging words
3. Rewriting

FF Fluency, Figural
1. Ornamentation test
2. Elaboration test
3. Symbols test

FI Fluency, Ideational
1. Topics test
2. Theme test
3. Thing categories test

FW Fluency, word
1. Word endings test
2. Word beginnings test
3. Word beginnings and endings test

I Induction
1. Letter sets test
2. Locations test
3. Figure classification

IP Integrative Processes
1. Calendar test
2. Following directions

MA Memory, Associative
1. Picture–number test
2. Object–number test
3. First and last names test

MS Memory Span
1. Auditory number span test
2. Visual number span test
3. Auditory letter span test

MV Memory, Visual
1. Shape memory test
2. Building memory
3. Map memory

N Number
1. Addition test
2. Division test
3. Subtraction and multiplication test
4. Addition and subtraction correction

P Perceptual speed
1. Finding A's test
2. Number comparison test
3. Identical pictures test

RG Reasoning, General
1. Arithmetical aptitude test
2. Mathematics aptitude test
3. Necessary arithmetic operations test

RL Reasoning, Logical
1. Nonsense syllogisms test
2. Diagramming relationships
3. Inference test
4. Deciphering languages

S Spatial Orientation
1. Card rotations test
2. Cube comparisons test

SS Spatial Scanning
1. Maze tracing speed test
2. Choosing a path
3. Map planning test

V Verbal Comprehension
1. Vocabulary test I
2. Vocabulary test II
3. Extended vocabulary test I
4. Advanced vocabulary test I
5. Advanced vocabulary test II

VZ Visualization
1. Form board test
2. Paper folding test
3. Surface development test

XF Flexibility, Figural
1. Toothpicks test
2. Planning patterns
3. Storage test

XU Flexibility of Use
1. Combining objects
2. Substitute uses
3. Making groups
4. Different uses

Table 6.2.

"g"	(3rd-order)	General intelligence
Gf	(2nd-order)	(possibly identical to g) fluid ability
	I	Induction
	RG	General reasoning (mainly deductive)
	RL	Logical reasoning
	IPA	Information-processing accuracy
	IPSA	Accuracy of semantic information processing
Gc	(2nd order)	Crystallized intelligence
	V	Verbal comprehension
	LX	Lexical knowledge
	WS	Word sense (knowledge of properties of words)
	PC	Phonetic coding
	GS	Grammatical sensitivity
Gv	(2nd-order)	General visual perception
	SR	Spatial relations
	VZ	Visualization
	CF	Flexibility of closure
	CS	Speed of closure
GA	(2nd-order)	General Auditory Perception
	TT	Temporal tracking
	DSP	Discrimination among sound patterns (pitch sense)
	SPD	Speech perception under distraction
	MJR	Maintaining and judging rhythm
Gs	(2nd-order)	General Speed
	P	Perceptual speed
	NA	Naming speed
	RT	Reaction time
Gi	(2nd-order)	General Idea Production (fluency)
	FA	Associative fluency
	FE	Fluency of expression
	FF	Figural fluency
	FW	Word fluency
	FP	Practical ideational fluency (sensitivity to problems, conceptual foresight)
	O	Originality
Gm	(2nd-order)	General Memory Capacity
	MA	Associative memory
	ME	Episodic memory
	MS	Memory span
	MV	Visual memory

The conclusions from the scrutiny of these findings are clear. There can be little doubt how abilities should be tested in any psychological experiment. If there is only time for a few tests then the second-order factors should be measured. If more time is available and more detailed coverage is required the primary factors should be sampled, as relevant. If the whole sphere of abilities needs to be tested, the second-order factors which by definition cover a broad range of variance should be used.

Some readers may be surprised because reference to the works of Guilford on human intelligence (Guilford, 1967) has so far been restricted to a mention that the Procrustes rotations which he used resulted in unreliable factors. In fact, this work by Horn and Knapp (1973) is so damning that it is not possible any longer, in my view, to take seriously the factorial claims of Guilford concerning the number of ability factors.

As was discussed above, Procrustes rotations allow any target matrics to be reached. Thus his structure of intellect model cannot be regarded as having factor analytic support.

Thus simple structure rotations must be relied on, the basis of the factorial lists in this chapter. However, this is not to deny the utility of the structure of intellect model for designing interesting tests and covering a large range of possible materials. For this it is useful but the factorial nature of the resulting tests is clearly not as Guilford described.

PERSONALITY

There is far less agreement in the field of personality than in the ability sphere. I have previously examined this field at some length (Kline, 1979) and recently in even greater detail (Kline and Barrett, 1983) for it is a complex field with its myriad of apparently dissimilar factors, each set claimed by its authors as the most comprehensive. Comrey, Guilford, Cattell, Eysenck and Howarth have all produced factors and test batteries.

PERSONALITY QUESTIONNAIRES

The rationale for the selection of the personality factors in this chapter has been fully described, as was indicated above, by Kline and Barrett (1983). However, in essence the criteria were simple. The factors had to be replicated, to be derived from technically adequate factor analyses (and thus derived from simple structure analyses) and to be identified both by marker variables and by external criteria.

Since there is considerable disagreement concerning the number and nature of personality factors (unlike the field of abilities) it is necessary to say a word about factor identification. This is best done by relating the factor to some external criterion beyond the confines of the test and items loading on the factor. Thus in the case of neuroticism, for example, we would expect psychiatric patients to score more highly than controls on this factor. Another method of factor identification is to locate factors in factor space which involves rotating them together with a set of known factors to mark out the space. This method quickly demonstrates identical factors albeit with different names and different factors with the same name—both sources of considerable error in the field of personality.

Among normal subjects judged by the criteria which have been discussed, Kline and Barrett (1983) were able to find few reliable and replicable factors. For approximately fifty years of factor-analytic searching the haul was meagre in the extreme.

At the second-order level three factors regularly stand out almost regardless of the test used: extraversion (exvia in the Cattell system), neuroticism (anxiety in the Cattell system) and psychoticism. The first two hardly need description and psychoticism is characterized by cruelty and lack of empathy. These are higher-order factors which were identified with startling clarity in a sample of 1200 adults analysed by Barrett and Kline (1980). What is noteworthy, however, is that in some recent studies (e.g. Eysenck and Eysenck, 1978) these higher-order factors are breaking down into primaries. Thus primaries of sociability and impulsivity have been found together with sensation seeking and empathy. Another second-order factor which stands up well is that of obsessional traits. In a recent study of authoritarianism Kline and Cooper (1984a) found a clear obsessional factor. There was also at the second-order a Machiavellianism factor-loading mainly on the Christie and Geis (1970) scales. However, although further investigation is here required, it seems possible that this Machiavellian factor loads highly on P, psychoticism. This certainly makes sound psychological sense.

At the primary factor level, reliable factors are indeed hard to find. Kline and Barrrett (1983) have examined these factors in great detail and were forced to conclude that there was little stability. Certainly the factors in the Cattell Sixteen Personality Factor Test (16PF) do not stand empirical scrutiny (see Barrett and Kline, 1982b).

Nor do the factors in the Guilford scales (Guilford, Zimmerman and Guilford, 1976) which when rotated to oblique simple structure are similar to the primaries in the Cattell system and at the higher-order level are little different from the factors in the Cattell and Eysenck tests. The same strictures apply to the tests devised by Comrey (1970), the Howarth Scales (Howarth, 1980) and to the Personality Research Form (Jackson, 1974) which has almost no evidence for the external validity of its scales. Indeed, the only other factors at the primary level which seem to be relatively reliable are two masculine and feminine attitudes. These are clearly a set of culture bound behaviours.

Nevertheless the four factors that are clear, extraversion, neuroticism, psychoticism and obsessional traits are important and well-known variables established beyond the confines of psychometrics and factor analysis. It is these without doubt which should form the basis of studies of individual differences in personality among normal subjects in psychology as in other branches of psychology.

RATING SCALES

McCrae and Costa (1985) accept the rather pessimistic conclusions concerning questionnaire factors in normal subjects but argue that it would be useful to consider adjective checklists and ratings which generally yield five factors (e.g. Norman, 1963; Goldberg, 1980): extraversion, neuroticism, conscientiousness, agreeableness and openness to experience.

McCrae and Costa (1985) linked measures of these five factors to the Eysenck factors and although the five-factor questionnaire is not extensively validated the results were not unexpected. Extraversion and neuroticism were similar to the questionnaire factors which I have described and psychoticism was the low pole of agreeableness and conscientiousness. Thus these ratings have yielded only one possible new factor— openness to experience—and for this external validity studies are badly needed. It should also be pointed out that the obsessional factor, which was not measured on their study, is obviously related to conscientiousness. Thus at best rating scales among normal subjects might add to one new factor—openness to experience which, as the authors point out, may be a variant of Zuckerman's sensation-seeking scale (Zuckerman, 1974). Recently this five-factor analysis of ratings has been supported by the development of a new questionnaire, the Professional Personality Questionnaire (PPQ) which measures these variables with some evidence of validity (Kline and Lapham, 1990).

ABNORMAL SUBJECTS

Among normal subjects different factors may be found simply because there may be more variance in traits on which normal subjects always score low, even though such factors can be seen as dimensions common to both normal and abnormal subjects.

Recently Johnson *et al.* (1984) factored the whole MMPI item pool using two samples of more than 5000 subjects. Twenty-one orthogonal factors were extracted and sent to experts for naming. There was remarkable consensus among these judges and it can be said that with so large a sample and with replicated factors, the results must be taken seriously. However, it must be noted that factors were identified from their item loadings (which is little more than face validity) and that the rotation was orthogonal not oblique and thus unlikely to have reached simple structure.

It is noteworthy that the two largest factors were neuroticism and psychoticism both, of course, implicated in abnormal behaviour. Social extraversion was the fifth of the 21 factors to emerge—smaller here than usual because the sample was abnormal. Femininity and masculinity also appeared while many of the other factors were clearly symptom clusters rather than traits and are irrelevant to the purpose of this chapter. It can be concluded, therefore, that this study of the factors in the MMPI supports the previous results with normal subjects.

OTHER FIELDS

Other fields than ability and personality have been subjected to factor analysis in order to elucidate underlying structure. Moods and states, being transient, are not of general interest unless such states are a particular target of research. What has been found here is that personality trait factors often have a state or change factor associated with them which accounts for the well-known feeling that one does, in fact, vary over time on what appear to be relatively fixed traits (Cattell, 1973).

Two other fields deserve mention although the routine use of tests or scales, as shall be seen, cannot be recommended at present. There are the areas of motivation and the objective testing of personality—both aspects of factor analysis which have been pioneered, and to some extent albeit not fully enough, developed by Cattell. Objective tests are defined by Cattell (e.g. Cattell and Kline, 1977) as tests which are objectively scored and of which the purport cannot be guessed by subjects, thus making them particularly useful for selection where deliberate distortion is all too easy with questionnaires. A full description of these can be found in Cattell and Johnson (1986) and a number of objective test factors has been isolated by Cattell (Cattell and Warburton, 1967). However, a detailed study of these tests by Kline and Cooper (1984b) showed that they were not valid but measured a mixture of ability and personality factors. Far more research with these measures is required before they can be used as substantive tests.

The field of motivation (Cattell and Child, 1975) has also yielded a number of motivational factors, ergs and sentiments, fear, mating, career sentiment for example. However, a detailed study of the factor structure of the ergs and sentiments was disappointing and they should be used only for research into their own nature rather than as variables in their own right.

CONCLUSIONS

From this discussion the conclusions are simple. If individual differences are important in the field of abilities it is wise to study the main second-order factors—crystallized ability, fluid ability, fluency and visualization. If more time is possible the smaller ability factors should have priority.

In the field of personality four questionnaire factors stand out: extraversion, neuroticism, psychoticism and obsessional traits. If all the factors of ability and personality are included in experimental studies it is certain that the main factors among individual differences will have been embraced.

SUMMARY

Various factor-analytic procedures aimed at obtaining replicable simple-structure factors were examined. The application of the methods in the field of ability and personality was scrutinized. It was concluded that among the best established factors were fluid ability, fluency, visualization, extraversion, neuroticism, psychoticism and obsessionality.

REFERENCES

Barrett, P. and Kline, P. (1980) Personality factors in the Eysenck personality questionnaire. *Personality and Individual Differences*, **1**, 317–333.

Barrett, P. and Kline, P. (1981) The observation to variable ratio in factor analyses. *Personality Study and Group Behavior*, **2**, 23–33.

Barrett, P. and Kline, P. (1982a) Factor extraction: an examination of three methods. *Personality Study and Group Behaviour*, **2**, 84–98.

Barrett, P. and Kline, P. (1982b) An item and radial parcel analysis of the 16PF questionnaire. *Personality and Individual Differences*, **3**, 259–270.

Carroll, J.B. (1981) Ability factors and processes. Paper at the NATO Conference on Cross-Cultural Psychology, Kingston, Ontario.

Carroll, J.B. (1986) Factor analytic investigations of cognitive abilities. In S.E. Newstead, S.H. Irvine and P.L. Dan (eds), *Human Assessment: Cognition and Motivation*, pp. 3–8. Dordrecht: Nijhoff.

Cattell, R.B. (1966) The Scree Test for the number of factors. *Multivariate Behavioural Research*, **1**, 140–161.

Cattell, R.B. (1971) *Abilities: Their Structure, Growth and Action*. Boston: Houghton Mifflin.

Cattell, R.B. (1973) *Personality and Mood by Questionnaire*. New York: Jossey-Bass.

Cattell, R.B. (1978) *The Scientific Use of Factor Analysis in Behavioral and Life Sciences*. New York: Plenum.

Cattell, R.B. and Child, D. (1975) *Motivation and Dynamic Structure*. New York: Halstead.

Cattell, R.B. and Johnson, R.C. (eds) (1986) *Functional Psychological Testing*. New York: Bruner Mazel.

Cattell, R.B. and Kline, P. (1977) *The Scientific Study of Personality and Motivation*. London: Academic Press.

Cattell, R.B. and Warburton, F.W. (1967) *Objective Personality and Motivation Tests: A Theoretical Introduction and Practical Compendium*. Champaign, Illinois: Illinois University Press.

Christie, R. and Geis, F.L. (1970) *Studies in Machiavellianism.* New York: Academic Press.

Comrey, A.L. (1970) *The Comrey Personality Scales.* San Diego, California: Educational and Industrial Testing Service.

Ekstrom, R.B., French, J.W., Harman, H.H. and Dermen, D. (1976) *Manual for Kit of Factor-Referenced Cognitive Tests.* Princeton: Educational Testing Service.

Eysenck, S.B.G. and Eysenck, H.J. (1978) Impulsiveness and venturesomeness: their position in a dimensional system of personality description. *Psychological Reports,* **43**, 1247–1255.

Goldberg, L.R. (1980) Some ruminations about the structure of individual differences: developing a common lexicon for the major characteristics of human personality. Paper at Western Psychological Association Convention, Honolulu, Hawaii.

Guilford, J.P. (1956) *Psychometric Methods.* New York: McGraw-Hill.

Guilford, J.P. (1959) *Personality.* New York: McGraw-Hill.

Guilford, J.P. (1967) *The Nature of Human Intelligence.* New York: McGraw-Hill.

Guilford, J.S., Zimmerman, W.S. and Guilford, J.P. (eds) (1976) *The Guilford Zimmerman Temperament Survey Handbook.* San Diego: Sheridan.

Gustaffson, J.E. (1988) Hierarchical models of individual differences in cognitive abilities. Chapter 2 in Sternberg, R.J. (ed.), *Advances in the Psychology of Human Intelligence,* Vol. IV. Hillsdale, NJ: Erlbaum.

Hakstian, A.R. (1971) A comparative evaluation of several prominent methods of oblique factor transformation. *Psychometrika,* **36**, 175–193.

Harman, H.H. (1976) *Modern Factor Analysis,* Second edition. Chicago: University of Chicago Press.

Hashemi, K. (1981) The factor structure of the EPQ and 16PF tests. Unpublished PhD Thesis, University of Exeter, England.

Heim, A. (1975) *Psychological Testing.* London: Oxford University Press.

Hendrickson, A.E. and White, P.O. (1966) A method for the rotation of higher-order factors. *British Journal of Mathematical and Statistical Psychology,* **18**, 97–103.

Horn, J. and Knapp, J.R. (1973) On the subjective character of the empirical base of Guilford's structure of intellect model. *Psychological Bulletin,* **80**, 33–43.

Howarth, E. (1980) *Howarth Personality Questionnaire.* Alberta: University of Alberta Press.

Jackson, D.N. (1974) *Personality Research Form.* New York: Research Psychology Press.

Jennrich, R.I. and Sampson, P.F. (1966) Rotation for simple loadings. *Psychometrika,* **31**, 313–323.

Johnson, J.H., Butcher, J.N., Niell, C. and Johnson, K.N. (1984) Replicated item level factor analysis of the full M.M.P.I. *Journal of Personality and Social Psychology,* **47**, 105–114.

Joreskog, K.G. (1969) A general approach to confirmatory maximum likelihood factor analysis. *Psychometrika,* **34**, 183–202.

Kline, P. (1979) *Psychometrics and Psychology.* London: Academic Press.

Kline, P. (1980) Models of man: the psychometric model. In A.J. Chapman, and D.M. Jones (eds), *Models of Man.* Leicester: British Psychological Society.

Kline, P. and Barrett, P. (1983) *Factors in Personality Questionnaires.* Oxford: Pergamon Press.

Kline, P. and Cooper, C. (1984a) A factor analytic study of authoritarianism. *British Journal of Psychology,* **75**, 171–176.

Kline, P. and Cooper, C. (1984b) The construct validity of Cattell's objective analytic battery. *Personality and Individual Differences,* **5**, 323–347.

Kline, P. and Lapham, L. (1990) *The Professional Personality Questionnaire.* London: Psychometric Systems (UK) Ltd.
McCrae, R.R. and Costa, P.T. (1985) Comparison of EPI and psychoticism scales with measures of the five-factor model of personality. *Personality and Individual Differences,* **6**, 587–597.
Mulaik, S.A. (1972) *The Foundations of Factor Analysis.* New York: McGraw-Hill.
Norman, W.T. (1963) Towards an adequate taxonomy of personality attributes: replicated factor structure in peer nomination personality ratings. *Journal of Abnormal and Social Psychology,* **66**, 574–583.
Nunnally, J. (1978) *Psychometric Theory.* New York: McGraw-Hill.
Sternberg, R.J. (1979) The nature of human abilities. *American Psychologist,* **34**, 214–230.
Sternberg, R.J. (ed.) (1988) *Advances in the Psychology of Human Intelligence,* Vol. IV. Hillsdale, NJ: Erlbaum.
Thurstone, L.L. (1947) *Multiple Factor Analysis.* Chicago: University of Chicago Press.
Velicer, W.F. (1976) Determining the number of components from the matrix of partial correlations. *Psychometrika,* **41**, 321–327.
Zuckerman, M. (1974) The sensation-seeking motive. In B. Maher (ed.), *Progress in Experimental Personality Research,* Vol. 7. Academic Press: New York, pp. 79–148.

Chapter 7

The Nature of Anxiety

Michael W. Eysenck
Department of Psychology, Royal Holloway and Bedford New College, University of London, Egham Hill, Egham, Surrey TW20 0EX, England

ABSTRACT

There have been various different attempts to provide theoretical accounts of the nature of anxiety. In view of the relative failure of psychophysiologically-based accounts, it appears useful to consider cognitive factors. Gray has proposed an influential theory which integrates physiological and cognitive factors, and which has proved successful. However, there are grounds for arguing that his views on cognitive factors in anxiety are only partially correct, and that there is a major involvement of the pre-attentive and attentional systems in anxiety.

INTRODUCTION

Those theorists (e.g. Eysenck, 1967; Gray, 1982a) who have been interested in individual differences in anxiety from the biological perspective have typically started by identifying a personality dimension of trait anxiety or neuroticism. There are several relevant questionnaires, including the Manifest Anxiety Scale (Taylor, 1953), the State-Trait Anxiety Inventory (Spielberger, Gorsuch and Lushene, 1970), and the Eysenck Personality Questionnaire (Eysenck and Eysenck, 1975). There are substantial inter-correlations among these various measures of trait anxiety and neuroticism, as has been demonstrated

Handbook of Individual Differences: Biological Perspectives
Edited by Anthony Gale and Michael W. Eysenck

convincingly by Watson and Clark (1984) in their review of the literature. For example, the neuroticism scale of the Eysenck Personality Questionnaire correlates on average approximately +0.70 with standard scales of trait anxiety, and the inter-correlations of trait-anxiety scales typically exceed +0.80. In view of these data, it will be assumed that all of these tests can be used to assess individual differences in proneness to anxiety.

If this personality dimension possesses biological reality, then there are various kinds of prediction which can be made. First, if the level of trait anxiety forms part of one's physical constitution, then it seems reasonable to anticipate that individual differences in trait anxiety would be determined at least in part by genetic factors. Secondly, it should be possible to identify the part or parts of the brain most involved in affecting an individual's level of trait anxiety. Thirdly, there should be systematic differences in physiological functioning between those high and low in trait anxiety. Fourthly, if trait anxiety is indeed grounded in a constitutional factor of biological importance, then it is likely that there are major similarities in the structures and processes involved across several species.

The evidence relating to all of these predictions will be considered in detail in this chapter. However, there are other predictions which can be made. For example, it would be expected from the biological perspective that trait anxiety would exhibit reasonable longitudinal consistency. This issue was discussed at lengthy by Conley (1984). He reviewed longitudinal studies in which a variety of different measures of trait anxiety or neuroticism had been used, including Bell's scale of Emotional Maladjustment, the neuroticism scale of the Eysenck Personality Inventory, the Hypochondriasis scale of the Minnesota Multiphasic Personality Inventory, and the 0 scale of Cattell's 16 Personality Factor test. While the test-retest reliability over long periods of time was sometimes relatively low, this is due in large measure to the poor internal consistency or period-free reliability of some of the personality measures. When Conley (1984) took account of this, he discovered that the annual stability of trait anxiety or neuroticism was approximately 0.98. This is slightly less than is the case for most measures of intelligence, but is nevertheless indicative of reasonably high longitudinal consistency. It is possible, of course, that some of this consistency reflects stable environmental conditions rather than genetic factors. However, the changing circumstances of most people's lives indicate that no more than a small proportion of the observed longitudinal consistency can be explained in environmental terms.

HEREDITY

There has been a certain amount of theoretical controversy concerning the issue of whether individual differences in trait anxiety or neuroticism are due primarily to heredity or to environment. Eysenck (1967) and Gray (1982a) have both emphasized the importance of heredity, whereas Spielberger (1972) argued that early childhood experiences play a major role in determining individual differences in trait anxiety.

Much of the relevant evidence has been reviewed by Eysenck and Eysenck (1985). The most convincing findings have emerged from twin studies, and it is clear from these studies that heredity is of major significance. For example, Shields (1962) assessed the personalities of 42 pairs of separated monozygotic twins, as well as groups of monozygotic and dizygotic twins brought up together. The intra-class correlation coefficient for neuroticism on an early version of the Maudsley Personality Inventory was +0.53 for the monozygotic twins brought up apart, +0.38 for the monozygotic twins brought up together, and only +0.11 for the dizygotic twins brought up together. These data provide strong evidence for the involvement of heredity, since monozygotic twins brought up apart were on average much more similar in neuroticism level than dizygotic twins brought up together in spite of the virtual certainty that there was greater environmental similarity for the dizygotic twins than for the monozygotic twins.

The finding from the Shields (1962) study that monozygotic twins brought up together were on average more similar with respect to neuroticism than were dizygotic twins brought up together has been replicated by other researchers (e.g. Loehlin and Nichols, 1976). This finding is open to various interpretations, since it has often been argued that monozygotic twins tend to be treated more alike than dizygotic twins. Confirmatory evidence was reported by Loehlin and Nichols (1976). However, they also discovered that the similarity of treatment correlated only modestly with degree of similarity in terms of personality and ability. This led Loehlin and Nichols (1976) to conclude: "It is clear that the greater similarity of our identical twins' experience in terms of dress, playing together, and so forth cannot plausibly account for more than a very small fraction of their greater observed similarity on the personality and ability variables of our study" (p. 52).

The largest twin study investigating personality was conducted by Floderus-Myrrhed, Pedersen, and Rasmusson (1980). They administered a short form of the Eysenck Personality Inventory to 12898 pairs of twins in Sweden. Their data produced an estimated heritability of 0.58 for neuroticism in females; the corresponding figure for males was 0.50.

This is not the place to enter into a detailed discussion of the complex ways in which twin-study data have been analysed in order to clarify their interpretation; the interested reader is referred to Fulker (1981). However, an impression of what has been discovered through the use of biometrical genetics as the method of analysis can be gleaned from Fulker's (1981) conclusions concerning the personality traits of neuroticism, extraversion, and psychoticism:

> The main finding both from the older literature employing related tests and from the more recent literature employing the Eysenck scales overwhelmingly supports the view that the bulk of variation for these traits is controlled by the simplest of all possible genetic and environmental systems, involving only additive genetic variation specific to the individual. . . . The high heritability, once unreliability is removed, the absence of common family environment and the similarity of genetic and environmental covariance suggests a high, if not total, degree of constitutional determination of reliable individual variation and provides strong support for a biological theory of the origin of these traits (p. 120).

EYSENCK'S (1967) THEORY

Eysenck (1967) attempted to identify the physiological basis of individual differences in neuroticism. His specific suggestion was that an individual's level of neuroticism depends on the functioning of the visceral brain, which consists of "the hippocampus, amygdala, cingulum, septum, and hypothalamus" (p. 230). Eysenck (1967) claimed that differences between those high and low in neuroticism can be accounted for "in terms of differential thresholds for hypothalamic activity" (p. 237), and in terms of individual differences in responsivity of the sympathetic nervous system, "with high neuroticism scores associated with greater responsivity" (p. 237).

In other words, Eysenck (1967) argued that individuals high and low in neuroticism differed in emotional responsiveness, which is reflected in autonomic activation. Since his emphasis was on individual differences in physiological *responsiveness*, it would be expected that large systematic differences in autonomic activation between those high and low in neuroticism would be more readily obtainable under stressful than non-stressful conditions. It is, therefore, rather unfortunate that practically all the research on psychophysiological differences between high and low neuroticism scorers has utilized relatively non-stressful conditions. As a consequence, it could be argued with some justice that many of the studies discussed below are of no more than partial relevance to Eysenck's (1967) theory. However, Plouffe and Stelmack (1979) manipulated stress and failed to obtain any evidence of an interaction between the degree of stress and the level of neuroticism. They discovered that stress in the form of the cold pressor test reduced pupillary constriction to light stimulation, but there were negligible effects of neuroticism on the pupillary response under either stress or non-stress conditions.

Several studies have investigated the effects of neuroticism on the rate at which the orienting reaction habituates to repeated stimuli. O'Gorman (1977) reviewed eleven studies, in five of which there was a significant effect of neuroticism on habituation rate. However, the significant findings could hardly present a more confused picture. High neuroticism slowed down the rate of habituation in two studies, speeded it up in a third, and both directions of relationship were reported in the other two significant studies! However, it is worth mentioning that two of the best studies from the point of view of technical merit (those of Coles, Gale and Kline (1971), and of Nielsen and Petersen (1976)) reported that habituation rate was slower among high scorers on neuroticism than among low scorers.

O'Gorman (1977) also reviewed twelve studies which examined the effects of trait anxiety on habituation rate. There were non-significant effects of trait anxiety on habituation rate in nine of these studies, but high trait anxiety significantly reduced habituation rate in the three remaining studies. Some sense can be made of the data if account is taken of the psychophysiological measures recorded. Trait anxiety did not affect the speed of habituation when electrodermal responses were obtained, but there were significant effects of trait anxiety in all three studies in which finger-volume responses were measured.

Inconsistent findings have been obtained when EEG indices of cortical arousal have been obtained. Coles, Gale and Kline (1971) reported a negative relationship between neuroticism and cortical arousal, but a positive relationship was reported by Winter, Broadhurst and Glass (1972). It is possible that this difference in results is due, at least in part, to the degree of stress in the experimental situation.

The most thorough investigation of psychophysiological differences between those high and low in trait anxiety or neuroticism was carried out by Fahrenberg (1987). In essence, he has failed to uncover any consistent psychophysiological differences. This led him to the following pessimistic conclusion:

> Psychophysiological research on physiological correlates of the established *emotionality (neuroticism)* trait dimension has come to a standstill. Findings of questionnaire studies generally support the postulated psychophysiological relationship, but research that employs objectively measured physiological parameters in large-scale methodologically well-controlled and replicated investigations has not substantiated these hypotheses (p. 117).

However, there is other research which suggests that this conclusion may be premature. It has been suggested that conventional questionnaire measures of neuroticism and trait anxiety may provide a rather inadequate assessment of individual differences in susceptibility to anxiety. More specifically, there is increasing evidence that low scorers on trait anxiety actually constitute a rather heterogeneous group. Some of these low scorers are genuinely relatively untroubled by anxiety, whereas others are much affected by stress but attempt to handle it in a defensive fashion.

How can these two sub-groups of low trait-anxiety scorers be distinguished? A relatively straightforward method which has been used a number of times (e.g. Schwartz, 1983; Weinberger, Schwartz and Davidson, 1979) is to administer the Marlowe–Crowne Social Desirability Scale (Crowne and Marlowe, 1964). Despite its name, this questionnaire is basically a measure of defensiveness, affect inhibition, and protection of self-esteem. It is usually assumed that those who have low scores on trait-anxiety questionnaires and on the Marlowe–Crowne Social Desirability Scale are genuinely low-anxious individuals, whereas those who have low scores on trait anxiety but high scores on the Marlowe–Crowne are defensive repressors.

Powerful evidence that these two groups are very different from each other was reported by Weinberger, Schwartz and Davidson (1979). They obtained three physiological measures (heart rate, spontaneous skin resistance responses, and forehead muscle tension) and three performance measures from low-anxious subjects, defensive repressors, and high-anxiety subjects who were required to perform a moderately stressful task. The crucial result was that the defensive repressors appeared to be more stressed or anxious than the low-anxious subjects on all of the physiological and performance measures. More strikingly, the defensive repressors seemed to be more stressed than subjects high in trait anxiety on most of the measures.

This is not an isolated finding. Schwartz and Ahern (reported in Schwartz, 1983) measured arousal under resting conditions by alpha EEG activity. They discovered that defensive repressors were more aroused than those high in trait anxiety, who in turn were more aroused than genuinely low-anxious subjects.

The implications of these findings for Eysenck's (1967) theory are obvious. If a substantial number of those who score low on tests of neuroticism or trait anxiety are actually very susceptible to stress, then it is simply not the case that individual differences in autonomic responsiveness are predictable on the basis of trait-anxiety scores alone. However, the findings reported by Weinberger, Schwartz and Davidson (1979) and by Schwartz (1983) suggest that partial support for Eysenck's (1967) theory might be obtained if high-anxiety subjects were compared physiologically with genuinely low-anxious subjects.

GRAY'S (1982a) THEORY

THEORETICAL ASSUMPTIONS

Since, by their very nature, psychophysiological measures can provide no more than indirect reflections of the functioning of brain structures, it is perhaps not surprising that progress has been slow. As a consequence, other research strategies have been used, notably by Gray (1982a). In essence, the research strategy he has adopted in an attempt to understand anxiety has made use of two interrelated stages. The first stage involved assessing the behavioural consequences of administering anti-anxiety drugs to animals belonging to various species. The second stage involved looking for interventions in the brain which produced similar behavioural effects to those resulting from the administration of anti-anxiety drugs. The basic rationale was that combining information from these two stages could prove extremely useful in identifying the neural substrate of anxiety.

The effects of various anti-anxiety drugs on performance have been assessed. The drugs which have been used include benzodiazepines such as Librium and Valium, barbiturates (e.g. sodium amylobarbitone), and alcohol. Of course, each of these drugs is likely to have idiosyncratic effects in addition to those effects specifically related to reducing anxiety. As a consequence, what is of interest are those behavioural effects which are common to all three classes of drugs. These shared behavioural effects should reflect fairly directly the impaired functioning of the system mediating anxiety, which Gray (1982a) called the "behavioural inhibition system".

Several hundred studies with anti-anxiety drugs have been carried out on several different species ranging from goldfish to chimpanzees. According to Gray (1982a, b; 1985), there are only minor differences from one species to another in the effects of anti-anxiety drugs. This means that the system impaired by anti-anxiety drugs (i.e. the behavioural inhibition system) functions in an approximately equivalent fashion across species. The behavioural inhibition system was described in detail by Gray (1982a), and so only a short description will be presented here.

The first theoretical assumption is that there are four types of stimuli which can activate the behavioural inhibition system: signals of punishment, signals of non-reward, novel stimuli, and innate fear stimuli. It has been argued by others that signals of punishment produce fear, whereas signals of non-reward produce conditioned frustration, but Gray (1982a) argued that both types of signal are functionally equivalent in that they both elicit anxiety. Novel stimuli produce anxiety because they produce a discrepancy or mismatch between what is presented and what was expected. Innate fear stimuli include stimuli which are associated with specific dangers (e.g. snakes) and stimuli which occur during the course of social interaction (e.g. angry or threatening facial expressions).

While it is reasonable to assume that all these types of stimuli affect the behavioural inhibition system, it perhaps seems strange that unconditioned punishing stimuli are not included among those classes of stimuli acting on the behavioural inhibition system. The reason for this omission is that the behavioural effects of unconditioned and conditioned punishing stimuli are quite different, which indicates that they probably affect different internal mechanisms. According to Gray (1982a), it is the "fight-flight" system which is affected by unconditioned punishment and non-reward.

The behavioural inhibition system possesses a number of functions. These were described in the following terms by Gray (1975):

> (a) to inhibit all ongoing behaviour, whether instrumental or classically conditioned or innate; and (b) to perform the maximum possible analysis of current environmental stimuli, especially novel ones. The orienting responses would then be one consequence of activity in this system. The other major outputs are an initial inhibition of all previously operative behaviour patterns; coupled with an increment in arousal level, i.e., an increment in the intensity of whatever behaviour finally does occur (p. 354).

There is, of course, a large gap between observing the effects of anti-anxiety drugs on goldfish (or even chimpanzees) and understanding human anxiety at the neuropsychological level. However, Gray (1982a; 1985) argued that the issue of extrapolation is less problematical than one might initially assume. Indeed Gray (1985) was prepared to state unequivocally that, ''Anxiety in man and anxiety in the rat must have the same basic neurology, because the two respond to the same drugs. It follows that I can go into the animal's brain to ask what brain systems mediate anxiety'' (p. 103). The fact that several different species all appear to possess comparable behavioural inhibition systems suggests that the neural basis of anxiety is likely to involve brain structures which are found in all of these species, which rules out the neocortex.

Before moving on to a discussion of the brain structures mediating anxiety, it is worth considering the relevance of the behavioural inhibition system to individual differences in trait anxiety. According to Gray (1982a), the link is a very simple one: individuals who are high in trait anxiety have a much more active behavioural inhibition system than those who are low in trait anxiety. This is due, at least in part, to the fact that high-anxiety individuals are more sensitive than low-anxiety individuals to signals of punishment, signals of non-reward, and novelty. Individuals who are low in trait anxiety may have a predisposition towards primary psychopathy; alternatively, they may have a high susceptibility to psychotic depression.

Research with rats has indicated that lesions to the septo-hippocampal system produce effects which are extremely similar to those produced by the administration of anti-anxiety drugs. Indeed, of the 19 performance measures for which the relevant data are available, 18 indicate similar effects of septo-hippocampal lesions and anti-anxiety drugs (Gray, 1985). The only exception is social aggression. This is reduced by septo-hippocampal lesions but tends, if anything, to be increased by anti-anxiety drugs. The substantial overlap between the effects of the drugs and the lesions suggests that anti-anxiety drugs affect behaviour by impairing the functioning of the septo-hippocampal system. Additional research supports the more specific hypothesis that anti-anxiety drugs reduce the noradrenergic input to the septo-hippocampal system.

There is some interesting recent research which has suggested the involvement of the septo-hippocampal system in anxiety at the human level. Reiman *et al.* (1984) compared anxious patients with panic attacks with normal controls. Analysis by means of positron emission tomography revealed that the two groups of subjects differed only in the entorhinal cortex (which contains the main input to the septo-hippocampal system) and in the subicular area (which contains the main output from the same system).

If it can be accepted that anxiety is mediated by activity in the septo-hippocampal system, then the next step is to consider the functions of this system in more detail. Gray (1982a; 1985) argued that the hippocampus is part of a system which acts as a comparator. This comparator receives information about the current state of the world together with a prediction as to what that state should be. Armed with this information, the comparator must decide whether there is a match or a mismatch between the predicted and actual events. If there is a match, then the comparator simply checks the next actual event to decide whether or not it accords with prediction. Matters are quite different if the comparator detects a mismatch, in the sense either of a discrepancy between actual and expected events or a stimulus warning of an event (punishment or non-reward) which could disrupt planned behaviour. In other words, those stimuli which produce a mismatch in the comparator are precisely those which act on the behavioural inhibition system. Accordingly, the detection of a mismatch by the comparator leads to the outputs of the behavioural inhibition system (e.g. behavioural inhibition) which have already been described.

The part of Gray's (1982a) theory which deals with the comparator can be extended to link up with clinical anxiety. Excessive anxiety can occur if the comparator's checking system is over-active, and this appears to resemble the major symptom of obsessive-compulsive neurosis. Excessive anxiety can also occur if the comparator detects too many mismatches, which produces the behavioural inhibition characteristic of phobic patients.

Gray's (1982a) neuropsychological theory emphasizes strongly the similarities that exist between anxiety in man and anxiety in other species. However, he did not claim that there are no important differences. For example, Gray (1982a) admitted that the brain structures mediating anxiety in man can be affected by neocortical influences, in particular those which originate in the prefrontal and cingulate regions. This is suggested by the fact that destruction of these areas has proved successful in the treatment of anxiety (Powell, 1979).

EVALUATION

Gray's (1982a; 1985) neuropsychological theory of anxiety is a major achievement. Indeed, it probably represents the most impressive attempt yet to identify the brain structures mediating anxiety and to describe their functions. However, while the theory may provide an excellent animal model of anxiety, it is not altogether clear that it is adequate to account for individual differences in trait anxiety at the human level. Gray (1982a; 1985) may well be right that there are important similarities between rat and man in terms of the brain structures which mediate anxiety, but it is much less likely that the cognitive processes associated with anxiety are the same in the two species. This point was made rather well by Hallam (1985):

> Even if the layman or clinician were to accept that perceiving events as, say, signals of punishment or non-reward called forth biological responses that we have in common with other species, they might still argue that the cause of complaints of anxiety was in perceiving events in this way, and not in possessing the biological mechanism of these responses (p. 218).

Gray (1985) claimed that his theoretical approach had a very broad scope: "I want to show you how one can go from a behaviourist starting point to a cognitive end, and how in doing this one has to go through the brain" (p. 100). Despite this claim, the theory is actually quite limited in a number of ways. More specifically, the theory is inadequate in terms of the assumptions which are made concerning the involvement of the cognitive system, and in particular the proposed functioning of the comparator. These inadequacies are much more apparent at the human level than with other species. The relatively primitive cognitive system described by Gray (1982a) may be accurate so far as rats are concerned, but it does not match up to the complexity of human cognitive functioning in stressful situations.

Gray (1982a) assumed that the comparator decides whether there is a match or a mismatch between actual and expected events, with activation of the behavioural inhibition system, and thus anxiety, occurring if there is a mismatch. In order to evaluate these theoretical assumptions, it is obviously important to know precisely how information about actual and predicted events is processed by the cognitive system. According to Gray (1982b), prediction typically depends, "on the conjunctions of the present state of the world, stored past environmental regularities, the next intended step in the motor programme, and stored past relationships between such steps and changes in the environment" (p. 476). Information about actual events is selected, according to Gray (1982b),

> in the light of what is predicted. Such selection can in principle be accomplished in one of two ways. The subject's motor behaviour can be left under the control of other systems, with selection accomplished by choosing among the sensory events occurring anyway as a result of that motor behaviour, or the selection mechanism can take active control over motor behaviour and command exploratory action (p. 476).

In other words, the particular information about actual events which is attended to and processed, and the specific prediction which is formed, are both determined in large measure by the relevant information which is stored in long-term memory. Since we usually do not know exactly *what* information is stored in long-term memory, nor *how* that information is used, it will be difficult to submit this part of Gray's theory to empirical test.

At this point, it is worth considering the issue of why it is that a neurotic introvert (i.e. someone high in trait anxiety) "is an individual with a highly sensitive or reactive behavioural system" (Gray, 1982a, p. 453). Unfortunately, this part of Gray's (1982a) theory is less developed than most of the others, but presumably what he has in mind is that individuals vary genetically in the responsiveness of the brain structures associated with the behavioural inhibition system. This is in all probability part of the answer, but our earlier discussion suggests that individual differences in the contents of long-term memory could have implications for the amount of anxiety which is experienced.

The above issue has been addressed by Eysenck and Mathews (1987), who argued that there are strong theoretical reasons for assuming that individuals high and low in trait anxiety differ in predictable ways in the information which they have stored in long-term memory. For example, consider the phenomenon of mood-congruent learning (Bower, Gilligan and Monteiro, 1981), in which emotionally-toned material is learned best when its affective value matches the learner's current mood. Since individuals high and low in trait anxiety differ considerably in their characteristic mood states (Watson and Clark, 1984), it follows that the contents of long-term memory should vary systematically as a function of trait anxiety. As a consequence, predictions about events may well vary as a function of trait anxiety; indeed, it is well known that the predictions and expectations of high-anxiety individuals are generally more pessimistic than those of low-anxiety individuals (Eysenck, 1982). Thus, a complete understanding of trait anxiety will require detailed analysis of individual differences in cognitive processes preceding activation of the behavioural inhibition system.

If we present individuals high and low in trait anxiety with a stimulus signalling punishment, what would we expect on Gray's (1982a) theory? The natural prediction is that high-anxiety subjects should react with greater activity of the behavioural inhibition system, because of genetic factors and because they are more likely on the basis of stored information to interpret the stimulus as threatening. However, a little ingenuity will enable us to generate the opposite prediction! If high-anxiety individuals tend to produce pessimistic predictions whereas low-anxiety subjects tend to produce optimistic predictions, then the novelty value or extent of the mismatch between predicted and actual events will be less for the high-anxiety subjects. This would, of course, lead to less activity in the behavioural inhibition system for high-anxiety subjects.

There are other, more general, problems with Gray's (1982a) views, concerning the functioning of the comparator. For example, while it is easy to see that the presentation of a novel stimulus will produce a mismatch, it is much more difficult to accept that this will invariably lead to activity in the behavioural inhibition system and thus to anxiety. In fact, it seems likely, as Lyons (1982) pointed out, that the presentation of a novel stimulus might elicit various emotional states other than that of anxiety (e.g. surprise, joy, excitement). In reply, Gray (1982c) argued quite correctly that, while there is an enormous variety of terms used to describe emotional states, there are only a limited number of biologically fundamental emotions. As a consequence, one and the same physiological state may be labelled in several different ways depending on the context in which it is experienced. However, this does not appear to be a complete answer. There is surely a fundamental distinction between mismatches where the actual event is preferable to what has been predicted and mismatches where the opposite is the case. It may make sense to argue that mismatches of the former type all lead to anxiety or some cognate emotional state, but it seems totally implausible that mismatches of the latter type produce anxiety.

There is another problem with the comparator system as postulated by Gray (1982a) in his neuropsychological theory. According to the theory, the cognitive evaluation of stimuli which determines whether or not the behavioural inhibition system is activated is rather limited. Stimuli are assessed in terms of whether they are anticipated or unanticipated and in terms of whether they are aversive or non-aversive, and that is all. Compare this account against the one offered by Lazarus (e.g. Lazarus and Averill, 1972). He has consistently claimed that there are three different kinds of cognitive processes which are of fundamental importance in accounting for emotional states. Primary appraisal processes involve evaluating environmental stimuli against relevant information in long-term memory in order to make an assessment of the danger or distress involved. Secondary appraisal processes involve considering the threat in relation to one's own action alternatives (e.g. deciding whether one's coping skills will enable the threatening situation to be controlled). Reappraisal processes are activated when actions have been initiated and are starting to have effects on the threatening situation.

It is obvious that Gray's (1982a) account of the role of cognitive processes in anxiety is much less rich than the one offered by Lazarus. If one were to compare the two theoretical accounts directly, then it is approximately the case that Gray (1982a) focused largely on primary appraisal, but had relatively little to say about either secondary appraisal or about reappraisal. These theoretical differences may stem, at least in part, from the fact that Gray (1982a) has studied rats whereas Lazarus has investigated only human anxiety. While virtually all species presumably engage in primary appraisal, it seems likely that the processes of secondary appraisal and of reappraisal are much more common in the human species than in any other.

In sum, the main thrust of this evaluation has been that Gray's (1982a) theory is much more successful at identifying the brain structures and processes mediating anxiety than it is at specifying the cognitive processes which determine whether or not those brain structures and processes are activated. A much more specifically cognitive approach to anxiety, and to the issue of individual differences in trait anxiety, is presented in the next section.

THE COGNITIVE SYSTEM

BASIC ASSUMPTIONS

A theoretical account of individual differences in trait anxiety from the cognitive perspective has been developed in recent years (Eysenck, 1986; 1987; 1988; Eysenck, MacLeod and Mathews, 1987; Eysenck and Mathews, 1987). While parts of this theoretical approach are entirely consistent with the neuropsychological theory proposed by Gray (1982a), it is most unlikely that he would endorse all of it. Despite the differences, both theories address the key question of why it is that some individuals are characteristically much more anxious than others. However, the two theories differ crucially in their answer to that question. Gray (1982a) argued that differences in responsiveness of the behavioural inhibition system explain individual differences in trait anxiety. Eysenck (e.g. 1987) and Eysenck and Mathews (1987) accepted that there are major differences between those high and low in trait anxiety in physiological functioning, but argued that differences in the functioning of the cognitive system are also important.

One of the basic assumptions of the theoretical approach favoured by Eysenck (1987) is that individuals high and low in trait anxiety differ substantially in the information which they have stored in long-term memory. As was discussed earlier in this chapter, the phenomenon of mood-congruent learning provides strong support for this assumption. Further supporting evidence comes from the phenomenon of mood-state-dependent retrieval (Bower, 1981), i.e. information which is learned in one mood state has a greater probability of being recalled later when the mood state at the time of recall is similar to that at the time of learning. There have been various failures to demonstrate mood-state-dependent retrieval (e.g. Bower and Mayer, 1985), but it can be reliably obtained provided that the learner perceives a causal link between the information which must be learned and his or her current mood state (Bower, 1985). This would typically be the case in everyday life. Mood-state-dependent retrieval occurs because information about the mood state at the time of learning is stored in long-term memory. Individuals high and low in trait anxiety differ systematically in their mood states, and this then produces differences in the information stored in the long-term memory.

The focus so far has been on individual differences in the contents of long-term memory. However, it is assumed that high- and low-anxiety individuals also differ in terms of cognitive processes. As a consequence, a complete cognitive account of trait anxiety will necessarily involve consideration of both the *structure* of the cognitive system (e.g. the precise organization of long-term memory) and the *processes* involved in cognition (e.g. pre-attentive and attentional processes).

There is a final basic assumption underlying the theoretical approach adopted by Eysenck (1987) and Eysenck and Mathews (1987), namely, that anxiety involves a number of conceptually distinct systems which are nevertheless usually highly inter-dependent in their functioning. For example, Lang (1971) argued for a distinction among behavioural, physiological, and verbal response systems. Such a theoretical approach is supported by the fact that these various response systems frequently respond discordantly (e.g. Craske and Craig, 1984; Weinberger, Schwartz and Davidson, 1979).

It could, of course, be argued that discordant patterns of responses are due to measurement limitations, and are thus of little or no theoretical significance. However, it is assumed here that some of these discordant patterns are predictable and of great theoretical interest. For example we have already referred to the experimental studies reported by Schwartz (1983) and by Weinberger, Schwartz and Davidson (1979), in which certain individuals (defensive repressors) were non-anxious in terms of their verbal repsonse systems but highly anxious in terms of their physiological response systems. According to Schwartz's (1983) disregulation theory, these individuals have developed a strategy of ignoring distress signals from the physiological system. This strategy is unhealthy, because it prevents the different systems from regulating each other to produce order and stability. This discordance between the physiological and the verbal response systems leads to a failure of self-regulation which Schwartz (1983) terms "disregulation", and which can in turn lead to psychological disorder.

The research which is discussed below deals almost exclusively with the cognitive system. However, an analysis of the functioning of the cognitive system is seen as a prelude to the important task of investigating the ways in which the various systems involved in anxiety interact.

RECENT RESEARCH

The starting point for much recent research on cognitive functioning in high- and low-anxiety individuals is a theory proposed by Byrne (1964). He argued that sensitizers approach threatening stimuli, whereas repressors tend to avoid threatening stimuli. This is highly relevant here, because Byrne's Repression-Sensitization Scale correlates approximately +0.80 with questionnaire measures of trait anxiety such as Taylor's Manifest Anxiety Scale

(Watson and Clark, 1984). This correlation is so high that the Repression-Sensitization Scale can reasonably be regarded as a measure of trait anxiety. It will thus be assumed that sensitizers are equivalent to high-anxiety individuals, whereas repressors are equivalent to low-anxiety individuals.

Early tests of Byrne's (1964) hypothesis have been discussed at length by Eysenck (1989). In essence, according to Watson and Clark (1984), the results have been "overwhelmingly negative" (p. 481). In many of the studies a paradigm was used in which the minimal presentation times to recognize neutral and taboo or emotionally threatening words were recorded. Perceptual defence is said to occur when the recognition thresholds are higher for the threatening stimuli than for the neutral ones. The obvious prediction from Byrne's (1964) hypothesis is that repressors (i.e. those low in trait anxiety) should show a greater perceptual defence effect than sensitizers (i.e. those high in trait anxiety). In fact, no significant differences in perceptual defence between repressors and sensitizers were obtained in the great majority of the studies.

Why have these studies of perceptual defence produced predominantly negative findings? The theory which we have investigated assumes that there are individual differences in a selective mechanism which is used when at least one threatening and one neutral stimulus are presented concurrently. More specifically, it is predicted under these circumstances that sensitizers or those high in trait anxiety will allocate processing resources to the threatening stimulus rather than to the neutral one, whereas repressors or those low in trait anxiety will demonstrate the opposite tendency. The selective mechanism cannot be used in situations (such as the typical perceptual defence study) in which only one stimulus is presented at a time.

This selective processing hypothesis was first tested by a student of mine, Christos Halkiopoulos, and is reported in Eysenck, MacLeod and Mathews (1987). In essence, pairs of words were presented together, one to each ear. Either both words were neutral or one word was threat-related (e.g. grave, fail) and the other was neutral. The allocation of processing resources was inferred from the speed with which subjects responded to an occasional tone which was presented to one ear only very shortly after a pair of words had been presented. Subjects were allocated to personality groups on the basis of the Facilitation-Inhibition Scale (Ullmann, 1962), which is a reasonable measure of trait anxiety. As predicted, facilitators (that is, individuals high in trait anxiety) preferentially allocated processing resources to the ear where a threat-related word had just been presented. In contrast, inhibitors (that is, individuals low in trait anxiety) appeared to be avoiding allocating processing resources to the ear where a threat-related word has just been presented.

A visual analogue of the above task has been used in studies by MacLeod, Mathews and Tata (1986) and Broadbent and Broadbent (1988). The study by MacLeod, Mathews and Tata (1986) compared patients with generalized anxiety disorder against normal controls, whereas the other studies compared high-anxiety and low-anxiety normals. In all cases, the same basic pattern as that reported by Eysenck, MacLeod and Mathews (1987) was obtained.

The evidence to date seems to accord well with the selective processing hypothesis. When selective processing is not possible, no differences between individuals high and low in trait anxiety are discovered. In contrast, when selective processing is possible, high-anxiety subjects show the approach strategies and low-anxiety subjects the avoidance strategies with threatening stimuli which are predicted by Byrne (1964).

It may seem likely that these selective biases would depend in important ways on the nature of the threatening words used. However, no evidence for this was found by MacLeod, Mathews and Tata (1986) when they compared the results from words referring to physical health concerns (e.g. injury, agony) and those referring to social concerns (e.g. criticized, ashamed). The reason for this may be that the selective biases operate at a pre-attentive level (cf. Mathews and MacLeod, 1986) before detailed information about the specific nature of the threatening stimulus is available.

How important are these selective biases? In everyday life, we are usually bombarded with numerous stimuli at the same time, so that the basic conditions for selective biases to operate are usually present. In terms of Gray's (1982a) theory, it is probable that the excessive processing of minor threat-related stimuli characteristic of high-anxiety compared with low-anxiety individuals would produce greater activity of the behavioural inhibition system, and so more anxiety. However, a note of caution is advisable at this point. The evidence which is available so far is essentially correlational in nature. It is, therefore, somewhat dangerous to assume that it is the functioning of the cognitive system which is affecting the amount of anxiety experienced rather than vice versa.

Various cognitive differences (other than in pre-attentive selective biases) between high- and low-anxiety individuals have been demonstrated, but only one will be considered here. A number of studies have considered the interpretation of ambiguous stimuli as a function of individual differences in trait anxiety or repression-sensitization. The obvious prediction from Byrne's (1964) hypothesis is that sensitizers (or those high in trait anxiety) should be more likely than repressors (or those low in trait anxiety) to interpret ambiguous stimuli and situations in a threatening fashion. As predicted, when ambiguous stimuli are presented which can be interpreted in either a threatening or a neutral fashion, those high in trait anxiety typically produce a greater number of threatening interpretations than those low in trait anxiety (Blaylock, 1963; Eysenck, MacLeod and Mathews, 1987; Haney, 1973). These findings do not necessarily mean that those high and low in trait anxiety actually differ in their interpretative mechanisms, since the reported interpretations of ambiguous stimuli can clearly be affected by various response biases. However, if the findings with ambiguous stimuli can be taken at face value, they may help to explain why it is that the environment seems subjectively more threatening to those high in trait anxiety, and also why they experience more anxiety.

In sum, there is increasing evidence that those high and low in trait anxiety differ both in terms of *what* stimuli are processed and *how* stimuli are processed. If that is the case, then it is impossible that an adequate account of individual differences in trait anxiety can be provided unless the functioning of the cognitive system is considered in some detail. In essence, those high and low in trait anxiety differ in at least two important ways; (1) in the responsiveness of the behavioural inhibition system or some related system; (2) in the amount of processing accorded to threatening stimuli and in the interpretation of ambiguous stimuli and situations.

THE BIOLOGICAL APPROACH

The basic assumption which has been made in this chapter is that the biological approach to individual differences in trait anxiety is a valuable one in many ways, but that it needs to be supplemented by a more cognitively-oriented approach. We have already considered some of the deficiencies of the biological approach favoured by Eysenck (1967) and by Gray (1982a), but there are other problems with this approach which might potentially be remedied by a cognitive orientation. Perhaps the most obvious deficiency of the biological approach is that it emphasizes the importance of heredity, but fails to provide a satisfactory account of the role played by environmental factors in affecting an individual's level of trait anxiety. Precisely this point was conceded by Gray (1982a):

> Studies . . . of the personality traits of neuroticism and extroversion . . . estimate the contribution of heredity to these conditions at about 50 per cent of the variance. But that means, of course, that another 50 per cent of the variance remains to be accounted for; and it is likely that learning (of as yet unknown kinds) plays a determining role in this respect (p. 438).

It is probable that many (or even most) of the environmental events which affect an individual's level of trait anxiety do so by modifying the cognitive system, especially the long-term memory store. Obviously, the cognitive system is highly modifiable, and direct evidence of this modifiability with respect to the interpretation of ambiguity has recently been obtained by Eysenck *et al.* (1991). The starting point for their work was the finding by Eysenck, MacLeod and Mathews (1987) that normals high in trait anxiety produced threatening interpretations of more ambiguous words than normals low in trait anxiety.

Eysenck *et al.* (1991) discovered that patients suffering from generalized anxiety disorder were significantly more likely than subjects who had recovered from the same disorder to interpret ambiguous sentences in a threatening fashion.

A theoretical issue which is of relevance to an evaluation of the biological approach is whether trait anxiety should be regarded as a uni-dimensional or a multi-dimensional construct. The most natural expectation from the perspective of the biological approach is that trait anxiety should be uni-dimensional. If, as Gray (1982a) assumed, there are consistent individual differences in the responsiveness of the behavioural inhibition system, then it seems likely that those with a very responsive behavioural inhibition system would tend to be highly anxious in all kinds of stressful situations, whereas those with an unresponsive behavioural inhibition would be relatively free from anxiety in all situations.

A reasonably comprehensive review of the evidence concerning the uni-dimensional versus multi-dimensional nature of trait anxiety was provided by Endler (1983). According to Endler (1983), it is possible to identify at least five different dimensions or domains of trait anxiety: social evaluation; interpersonal; physical danger; ambiguous situations; and daily routines. That theoretical view has been tested by assuming that the amount by which a threatening situation increases state anxiety will be greater among high-anxiety than low-anxiety individuals only when there is congruence between the dimension of trait anxiety and the nature of the threatening situation. While Endler (1983) claimed that research supports the notion that there are five different dimensions of trait anxiety, there is, in fact, convincing evidence only so far as the dimensions of social evaluation and physical danger are concerned.

A multi-dimensional view of trait anxiety is potentially consistent with a schema-based cognitive theory, with a schema being regarded as a broad memory structure consisting of packets of interrelated information. For example, Butler and Mathews (1983) argued that anxious patients possess "danger schemata". The evidence for this was that the anxious patients believed that they were much more at risk from several potential environmental dangers than were other people, whereas a group of normals did not show this self–other discrepancy. If there are separate schemata for the major areas of stress in everyday life (e.g. situations involving social evaluation, situations involving physical danger), then it is entirely reasonable that someone might have a strong schema relating to social evaluation but only a weak schema relating to physical danger.

At the risk of over-simplification, it is possible to describe the essence of the biological and cognitive approaches to trait anxiety in the following way. The biological approach emphasizes the importance of heredity, it focuses on the physiological system, and it involves a rather static conceptualization in which consistency of trait anxiety over time is stressed. In contrast, the cognitive approach emphasizes the importance of environment and of learning experiences, it naturally focuses on the processes and structures (e.g. long-term memory store) of the cognitive system, and it involves a dynamic conceptualization in which anxiety level is systematically affected by experience.

At first sight, it would seem impossible to provide a synthesis of two such contrasting approaches to trait anxiety. However, synthesis may be easier to achieve than it looks. First, since individual differences in trait anxiety depend approximately equally on heredity and environment, it is obviously necessary to have a theory which can account for the influence of both factors. A synthesis of the biological and cognitive approaches could achieve this. Secondly, there is strong evidence that the physiological and cognitive systems both differ in important ways between individuals high and low in trait anxiety. As a consequence, an adequate theory of trait anxiety must incorporate the physiological and cognitive systems, and their interdependent modes of functioning. Thirdly, the evidence from longitudinal studies indicates that levels of trait anxiety do remain reasonably constant over time, but that at least some people do show systematic changes in trait anxiety. It is thus necessary to identify those factors tending to produce consistent levels of trait anxiety and those producing change. An inherited behavioural inhibition system might help to account for consistency, whereas alterations to schemata may lead to changed levels of trait anxiety.

CONCLUSIONS

The theoretical notions put forward in this chapter are severely limited in a number of ways. The focus has been on the initial processing by the cognitive system of ambiguous or threat-related stimuli, and on the possible implications of this processing on activity within the behavioural inhibition system. While there is a paucity of evidence, it must be the case that matters are actually much more complex than this. For example, activity of the behavioural inhibition system may in turn lead to attention being directed at it, and so the physiological system can affect the cognitive system as well as vice versa. When an individual responds to an ambiguous or threatening situation, then the success or otherwise of the coping behaviour displayed will usually be evaluated by the cognitive system. The process of cognitive evaluation may then lead to either increased or decreased activity of the behavioural inhibition system. In other words, a realistic model of anxiety, and of individual differences in trait anxiety, would need to consider the complex, interdependent functioning of the cognitive, physiological, and behavioural systems. All of this, however, forms an agenda for the future.

REFERENCES

Blaylock, B.A.H. (1963) Repression-Sensitization, Word Association Responses and Incidental Recall. Unpublished Master's thesis. University of Texas, Austin.

Bower, G.H. (1981) Mood and memory. *American Psychologist*, **36**, 129–148.

Bower, G.H. (1985) Discussant at Mood and Cognition Symposium, Cognitive Psychology Section, British Psychological Society, Oxford.

Bower, G.H. and Mayer, J.D. (1985) Failure to replicate mood-dependent retrieval. *Bulletin of the Psychonomic Society*, **23**, 39–42.

Bower, G.H., Gilligan, S.G. and Monteiro, K.P. (1981) Selectivity of learning caused by affective states. *Journal of Experimental Psychology: General*, **110**, 451–473.

Broadbent, D.E. and Broadbent, M. (1988) Anxiety and attentional bias: state and trait. *Cognition and Emotion*, **2**, 165–183.

Butler, G. and Mathews, A. (1983) Cognitive processes in anxiety. *Advances in Behaviour Research & Therapy*, **5**, 51–62.

Byrne, D. (1964) Repression-sensitization as a dimension of personality. In B.A. Maher (ed.), *Progress in Experimental Personality Research*. New York: Academic Press.

Coles, M.G.H., Gale, A. and Kline, P. (1971) Personality and habituation of the orienting reaction: tonic and response measures of electrodermal activity. *Psychophysiology*, **8**, 54–63.

Conley, J.J. (1984) The hierarchy of consistency: a review and model of longitudinal findings on adult individual differences in intelligence, personality and self-opinion. *Personality and Individual Differences*, **5**, 11–25.

Craske, M.G. and Craig, K.D. (1984) Musical performance anxiety: the three-systems model and self-efficacy theory. *Behaviour Research and Therapy*, **22**, 267–280.

Crowne, D. and Marlowe, D. (1964) *The Approval Motive*. New York: Wiley.

Endler, N.S. (1983) Interactionism: a personality model, but not yet a theory. In M.M. Page (ed.), *Nebraska Symposium on Motivation: Personality—Current Theory and Research*. Lincoln: University of Nebraska Press.

Eysenck, H.J. (1967) *The Biological Basis of Personality*. Springfield, Ill: C.C. Thomas.

Eysenck, H.J. and Eysenck, M.W. (1985) *Personality and Individual Differences*. New York: Plenum.

Eysenck, H.J. and Eysenck, S.B.G. (1975) *Manual of the Eysenck Personality Questionnaire*. London: Hodder & Stoughton.

Eysenck, M.W. (1982) *Attention and Arousal: Cognition and Performance*. Berlin: Springer-Verlag.

Eysenck, M.W. (1986) Individual differences in anxiety, cognition and coping. In G.R.J. Hockey, A.W.K. Gaillard and M.G.H. Coles (eds), *Energetics and Human Information Processing*. Dordrecht: Martinus Nijhoff.

Eysenck, M.W. (1987) Trait anxiety. In J. Strelau and H.J. Eysenck (eds), *Personality Dimensions and Arousal*. New York: Plenum.

Eysenck, M.W. (1988) Trait anxiety and stress. In S. Fisher and J. Reason (eds), *Handbook of Life Stress, Cognition, and Health*. Chichester: Wiley.

Eysenck, M.W. (1989) Personality, stress arousal, and cognitive processes in stress transactions. In R.W.J. Neufeld (ed.), *Advances in the Investigation of Psychological Stress*. New York: Wiley.

Eysenck, M.W., MacLeod, C. and Mathews, A. (1987) Cognitive functioning and anxiety. *Psychological Research*, **49**, 189–195.

Eysenck, M.W. and Mathews, A. (1987) Trait anxiety and cognition. In H.J. Eysenck and I. Martin (eds), *Theoretical Foundations of Behavior Therapy*. New York: Plenum.

Eysenck, M.W., Mogg, K., May, J., Richards, A. and Mathews, A. (1991) Bias in interpretation of ambiguous sentences related to threat in anxiety. *Journal of Abnormal Psychology*, **100**, 144–150.

Fahrenberg, J. (1987) Concepts of activation and arousal in the theory of excitability (neuroticism). In J. Strelau and H.J. Eysenck (eds), *Personality Dimensions and Arousal.* London: Plenum.

Floderus-Myrrhed, B., Pedersen, N. and Rasmusson, I. (1980) Assessment of heritability for personality based on a short form of the Eysenck Personality Inventory. *Behavior Genetics*, **10**, 153–162.

Fulker, D.W. (1981) The genetic and environmental architecture of psychoticism, extraversion and neuroticism. In H.J. Eysenck (ed.), *A Model for Personality.* Berlin: Springer-Verlag.

Gray, J.A. (1975) *Elements of a Two-process Theory of Learning.* London: Academic Press.

Gray, J.A. (1982a) *The Neuropsychology of Anxiety: An Enquiry into the Functions of the Septo-hippocampal System.* Oxford: Oxford University Press.

Gray, J.A. (1982b) Precis of 'The Neuropsychological of Anxiety: An enquiry into the Functions of the Septo-hippocampal System'. *The Behavioral and Brain Sciences*, **5**, 469–534.

Gray, J.A. (1982c) On mapping anxiety. *The Behavioral and Brain Sciences*, **5**, 506–525.

Gray, J.A. (1985) A whole and its parts. Behaviour, the brain, cognition and emotion. *Bulletin of the British Psychological Society*, **38**, 99–112.

Hallam, R.S. (1985) Anxiety and the brain: A reply to Gray. *Bulletin of the British Psychological Society*, **38**, 217–219.

Haney, J.N. (1973) Approach-avoidance reactions by repressors and sensitizers to ambiguity in a structured free-association. *Psychological Reports*, **33**, 97–98.

Lang, P. (1971) The application of psychophysiological methods to the study of psychotherapy and behaviour modification. In A. Bergin and S. Garfield (eds), *Handbook of Psychotherapy and Behaviour Change.* London: Wiley.

Lazarus, R.S. and Averill, J.R. (1972) Emotion and cognition: With special reference to anxiety. In C.D. Spielberger (ed.), *Anxiety Current Trends in Theory and Research*, Vol. 2. New York: Academic Press.

Loehlin, J.C. and Nichols, R.C. (1976) *Heredity, Environment and Personality.* Austin: University of Texas Press.

Lyons, W. (1982) Some questions of strategy in neuropsychological research on anxiety. *The Behavioral and Brain Sciences*, **5**, 490–491.

MacLeod, C., Mathews, A. and Tata, P. (1986) Attentional bias in emotional disorders. *Journal of Abnormal Psychology*, **95**, 15–20.

Mathews, A. and MacLeod, C. (1986) Discrimination of threat cues without awareness in anxiety state. *Journal of Abnormal Psychology*, **95**, 131–138.

Nielsen, T.C. and Petersen, K.E. (1976) Electrodermal correlates of extraversion, trait anxiety and schizophrenia. *Scandianvian Journal of Psychology*, **17**, 73–80.

O'Gorman, J.G. (1977) Individual differences in habituation of human physiological responses: a review of theory, method, and findings in the study of personality correlates in non-clinical populations. *Biological Psychology*, **5**, 257–318.

Plouffe, L. and Stelmack, R.M. (1979) Neuroticism and the effect of stress on the pupillary light reflex. *Perceptual and Motor Skills*, **49**, 635–642.

Powell, G.E. (1979) *Brain and Personality.* London: Saxon.

Reiman, E.M., Raichle, M.E., Butter, F.K., Hersovitch, P. and Robins, E. (1984) A focal brain abnormality in panic disorders, a severe form of anxiety. *Nature*, **310**, 683.

Schwartz, G.E. (1983) Disregulation theory and disease. Applications to the repression/cerebral disconnection/cardiovascular disorder hypothesis. *International Review of Applied Psychology*, **32**, 95–118.
Shields, J. (1962) *Monozygotic Twins.* Oxford: Oxford University Press.
Spielberger, C.D. (1972) Anxiety as an emotional state. In C.D. Spielberger (ed.), *Anxiety: Current Trends in Theory and Research*, Vol. 1. London: Academic Press.
Spielberger, C.D., Gorsuch, R., and Lushene, R. (1970) *The State–Trait Anxiety Inventory (STAI) Test Manual Form X.* Palo Alto, Calif.: Consulting Psychologists Press.
Taylor, J.A. (1953) Personality scale of manifest anxiety. *Journal of Abnormal and Social Psychology*, **48**, 285–290.
Ullmann, L.P. (1962) An empirically derived MMPI scale which measures facilitation-inhibition of recognition of threatening stimuli. *Journal of Clinical Psychology*, **18**, 127–132.
Watson, D. and Clark, L.A. (1984) Negative affectivity: the disposition to experience aversive emotional states. *Psychological Bulletin*, **96**, 465–490.
Weinberger, D.A., Schwartz, G.E. and Davidson, R.J. (1979) Low-anxious, high-anxious, and repressive coping styles: psychometric patterns and behavioural, and physiological responses to stress. *Journal of Abnormal Psychology*, **88**, 369–380.
Winter, K., Broadhurst, A. and Glass, A. (1972) Neuroticism, extraversion and EEG amplitude. *Journal of Experimental Research in Personality*, **6**, 44–51.

Chapter 8

Psychophysiology of Neuroticism and Anxiety

Jochen Fahrenberg

Forschungsgruppe Psychophysiologie, Psychologisches Institut, Universität Freiburg i.Br., Belforstrasse 20, D-7800 Freiburg, Germany

ABSTRACT

The psychophysiology of neuroticism (emotionality) and anxiety is basic to biologically oriented personality research. Eysenck's postulate that relates emotionality and physiological responsiveness and recent multimodal research on anxiety disorders are evaluated. The psychophysiology of neuroticism (emotionality) and anxiety, despite intense and extensive research activities, has not yet attained a consistent factual basis or a theoretical foundation of general acceptance. A re-orientation of research is mandatory. The discussion refers to advances in differential psychophysiology, and such issues as response fractionation and patterning, triple response measurement, multimodal assessment, and complementary laboratory-field studies.

1 INTRODUCTION

In his treatise on "those disorders, which are called nervous", more than two hundred years ago, Whytt (1765) observed that individuals who complain about mood fluctuations and irritability also tend to report many somatic

Handbook of Individual Differences: Biological Perspectives
Edited by Anthony Gale and Michael W. Eysenck

dysfunctions and symptoms. This nervousness syndrome later was substantiated in empirical personality research with standardized questionnaires. A systematic relationship exists in which an individual's score on a trait scale assessing emotionality (neuroticism, trait anxiety) significantly predicts the reported frequency and intensity of somatic complaints, for example headaches, cardiovascular and gastrointestinal complaints, muscular tension, pain, tiredness and exhaustion, and intense visceral perceptions during conditions of emotion and stress.

A correspondence between emotionality and autonomic-somatic responsiveness which eventually might be reduced to a common substrate in the hypothalamic-limbic regulatory mechanisms would be of particular relevance to biologically oriented personality research. If this observation were to hold true, the traditional constitutional research could finally claim an essential step in clarifying the biological basis of temperament. Implications for clinical work have always been apparent. A psychophysiological theory of personality that introduces neuroticism and anxiety as theoretically bridging psychophysiological concepts would be fundamental to the aetiology of neurotic and psychosomatic disorders, for clinical diagnosis, for allocation of patients to therapy, and for prediction of outcome. The valid definition and reliable assessment of such biologically rooted personality traits could provide many insights relevant for clinical and other practical applications.

Decades of research, however, have failed to substantiate nervousness as a consistent psychophysiological personality trait. Multimodal assessments of subjective, physiological and behavioural aspects instead have accumulated evidence against this initially plausible trait concept. Basic discrepancies between the different modes of assessment exist, and because response fractionation is highly evident, anxiety research has focused on such discrepancies and desynchronies as a phenomenon in its own right. Attempts to advance multiple operationalizations of neuroticism and anxiety as psychophysiological personality traits generally have not achieved convergent validity. The obvious inconsistencies among research findings and contradictions between various investigators seem to have brought research to a standstill.

The psychophysiology of neuroticism and anxiety is in need of a critical re-evaluation of traditional research questions and research methodology. In this process, global concepts eventually have to be abandoned and replaced by a multivariate conceptualization and multicomponent models derived from reliably replicated empirical findings. Thus, much more demanding methodology in differential psychophysiology would convey a less assuming theorizing based on more precise construct-operation units and bottom-up analyses.

The present chapter does not intend to give another review of the many scattered research publications pertaining to the psychophysiology of neuroticism and anxiety. Such summaries already exist (Bellack and Lombardo,

1984; Bernstein, Borkovec and Coles, 1986; Eysenck and Eysenck, 1985; Gale and Edwards, 1986; Hobbs, 1990; Hodges, 1976; Lader, 1975; Lang, 1977; Myrtek, 1984; Stelmack, 1981; Taylor and Agras, 1981). O'Gorman's (1977) review on individual differences in habituation of the orienting response in non-clinical populations may serve as an illustrative example for the ambiguous nature of findings. Six studies failed to observe a relationship between N-scale and speed of habituation. Five studies reported significant effects; however, the observed correlations happened to be in both directions. The analogous count with respect to anxiety is nine to three although there are some indications that studies assigning pulse volume amplitude as the dependent variable come out better than those with electrodermal activity. Although internal validity and effect size of such experiments should be taken into account the contradictions are appalling. The review by Naveteur and Freixa i Baqué (1987) on relationships between electrodermal activity and anxiety provides another characteristic example for the confused state of affairs. "In conclusion, it seems that the question of the relationship between electrodermal activity and anxiety is far from being solved, even if some experiments have obtained significant results" (p. 619). These authors report findings of their own but their data, actually, indicate lower electrodermal activity in highly anxious subjects.

Many of these investigations are rather small-scale studies with respect to sample size, selection of variables and conditions of measurement. Multivariate investigations are rare and attempts at exact cross-laboratory replications are the exception. Most of the reviews point out serious inconsistencies in the research literature, offer rather speculative interpretations, for example concerning deficiencies in experimental design and data analysis, possible moderator effects, and suggest *ad-hoc* hypotheses to account for this confusing state of affairs. After decades of persistent research, the psychophysiology of the nervousness concept is in need of a critical analysis of the many fallacies and of the gradual progress in research methodology which have resulted in concurrent decline and dissection of a once plausible and seemingly well-substantiated theoretical construct.

Neuroticism and anxiety include many biological aspects that are not in the scope of this chapter but are addressed in other contributions to this *Handbook*: genetics, neuroendocrinology, neuropsychology and psychopharmacology. The present chapter follows a multivariate perspective that is essential to differential psychophysiology. Basic research questions and persisting dilemmas are evaluated with reference to findings from a 20-year research programme conducted at the Psychologisches Institut, Universität Freiburg i.Br. and some perspectives derived from this work.

In a first section some relevant concepts of neuroticism and anxiety and corresponding assessment strategies are delineated with special attention to multimodal assessment. In a condensed form, substantial evidence from the questionnaire mode in favour of the psychophysiological nature of individual differences in emotionality (neuroticism and anxiety) is presented. Subsequently the contradictory findings from multimodal assessments are discussed with special attention to so-called triple response measurement strategies in agoraphobia and panic attacks.

2 RELEVANT CONCEPTS OF NEUROTICISM AND ANXIETY

2.1 THE DIMENSIONAL PERSPECTIVE

The general nervousness syndrome has had many labels attached to it, thus reminiscent of the chameleon (Whytt, 1765) description of its nervous symptoms: neurosis, hypochondriasis, neurasthenia, déséquilibré, unstable constitution, emotional-autonomic lability, neurotic disposition, neuroticism, emotionality, anxiousness, characterological or trait anxiety etc. (for a review, cf. Fahrenberg, 1967).

Neuroticism and anxiety, understood as personality dimensions covering the normal range as well as clinical expressions in one continuum, are related trait concepts. Controversies about psychometric issues, common variance of personality scales to assess emotionality and anxiety, valid differentiation of emotionality, neuroticism and trait anxiety (these concepts are often used interchangeably) are suspended at times and are revived by further theoretical speculation or by introducing another assessment instrument.

Cattell and Scheier (1961) attempted to clarify the conceptual confusion by proposing a multifactor theory of neuroticism and anxiety. Furthermore, they developed the distinction of trait and state aspects by conducting P- and R-technique analyses on multimodal assessments. Cattell and Scheier insisted that the theory of neuroticism and anxiety could be clarified by multivariate methodology and structured measurement of relevant components on the level of primary factors. They consider the primary factors (IPAT Anxiety Scale) C emotionally unstable, L suspicious, O worried, Q3 uncontrolled, and Q4 tense to be essential characteristics of trait anxiety. Although there is considerable agreement between anxiety and neurotic disposition, neurotics differ from normals on more factors (E weak and submissive, F inhibited, G low super ego strength, H overacting to threat) (Cattell and Kline, 1977; Krug, 1977).

However, the factor analytic work by Cattell and associates and the demanding techniques of multimodal personality assessment for several reasons have not become a standard reference for personality description. The majority of personality researchers, instead, still appear to be content with mostly univariate research methodology and a few measures that provide a rather narrow assessment of individual differences in this domain. A notable exception are Royce and Powell (1983).

After reviewing the evidence for alternative resolutions of the personality structure, Eysenck and S. B. Eysenck (1969), Eysenck and M. W. Eysenck (1985) and M. W. Eysenck (1987) retained the notion of emotionality as a second-order dimension in questionnaire data orthogonal to extraversion–introversion. These authors are rather sceptical concerning personality dimensions at the primary level which, from their point of view, are not invariant across sex, age, and education and represent "half arbitrary, half accidental conglomerations of items" (Eysenck and Eysenck, 1969, p. 331).

This conclusion was confirmed by independent statistical analyses carried out with the items from the Freiburger Persönlichkeitsinventar FPI, a multidimensional personality inventory widely used in Germany (Fahrenberg, Hampel and Selg, 1989). Attempts at decomposing the Emotionality Scale FPI–R–N (an equivalent to Eysenck's EPI–N) did not yield psychometrically satisfying primary factors although a comparatively large item pool and a representative subject sample were used. The task of structuring personality inventory items from the neuroticism domain to obtain consistent primary factors thus appears to be unresolved and probably should be restricted to subpopulations that are less heterogeneous.

A multidimensional view of trait anxiety was proposed by Endler (1983) who claimed that there are at least five different facets: physical danger, social evaluation, interpersonal relations, ambiguous situations and daily routines. The individual's manifest level of anxiety would depend on the interaction between the specific trait dimension and the particular type of situation. Clinical psychologists likewise have depicted many specific manifestations of anxiety and phobic behaviours.

Spielberger, Lushene and McAdoo (1977) on the other hand, advocate factorially complex concepts of trait anxiety and state anxiety. Gray (1981) also adheres to the assumption of a consistent trait dimension at a secondary level although he prefers a rotation by 45 degrees from Eysenck's factor solution. The two new resulting dimensions are anxiety (neurotic introvert to stable extravert) and impulsivity (neurotic extravert to stable introvert). Gray appears to be convinced that this reformulation more easily could result in a matching of personality traits and neuropsychological systems.

Although Cattell's multifactor approach was not generally adopted by other researchers, his strategic use of R-technique and P-technique in factor analytic personality research became influential in the development of the State-Trait Anxiety Inventory STAI (Spielberger, Gorsuch and Lushene, 1970). The same latent personality factor is assumed to underlie both the trait and state variables. Only recently, Majcen, Steyer and Schwenkmezger (1988) employed analyses of linear structural relationships on data from the German version of the STAI to support the state-trait distinction by identification of consistency, specificity and reliability as proportions of variance determined by latent variables occurring in the model.

2.2 THE CLINICAL PERSPECTIVE

When neuroticism and anxiety are considered from a psychometric and factor analytic viewpoint, the interindividual variability in these phenomena is reduced to the notion of a universal personality trait that provides a continuum for rank ordering healthy as well as clinical subjects. However, clinical aspects of anxiety (as well as the relationship between, and partial overlapping of, anxiety and depression, cf. Helmchen and Linden, 1986) might not be adequately represented by this dimensional perspective. Various syndromes of pathological anxiety as well as specific assessments through interviews, questionnaires, experience sampling method, and behaviour ratings are extensively described in the literature (cf. Barlow, 1988; Dijkman and de Vries, 1987; Hallam, 1985; McReynolds, 1968; Mavissakalian and Barlow, 1981; Noyes, Roth and Burrows, 1988; Roberts *et al.*, 1983; Shaw *et al.*, 1986; Tuma and Maser, 1985; Turner, 1984).

Actually, the psychophysiological research on anxiety has been considerably stimulated by two relatively specific clinical research interests: the multimodal assessment (subjective, behavioural, physiological) and ambulatory monitoring of agoraphobics and patients suffering from panic attacks. Both clinical fields (cf. Section 5.2) are extremely relevant for theoretical development and methodology in anxiety research.

Interindividual differences in manifest anxiety, so far, have been conceived of as indicating individual differences in an underlying personality dimension or a set of dimensions and syndromes. It is supposed explicitly or implicitly that such relatively permanent (trait) or momentary (state) dispositions are expressions of rather distinct neurobiological structures or processes that can be pinpointed and explained.

2.3 IS ANXIETY MERELY A LAY CONSTRUCT?

The assumption that anxiety is an actual entity existing in the central nervous system is basically challenged by those theorists who prefer information processing ("cognitive") approaches. Emotions are interpreted as being cognitive systems that serve communication and transaction in a social system. Psychological processes in internalization of such social constructs, in self-attribution and in the labelling of emotions should therefore have more bearing on emotion research than the unspecific and variably organized biological systems (Averill, 1976).

Hallam (1985), recently, has proposed a psychological theory of anxiety by further developing this perspective. He suggests that we look at anxiety as a multireferential lay construct. Among the referents are conceptual schemata representing beliefs and attributions of causality, contextual environmental events, internal sensory feedback from somatic processes, overt and covert behaviour, etc. This conceptualization does not deny that a number of antecedents as well as internal and external consequences are functionally related to self-reports of anxiety. But the individual's information processing would be extremely complex and to some extent idiosyncratic, thus demanding idiographic approaches. The notion of anxiety—and nervousness—as multireferential, often metaphorical lay constructs would assist understanding basic inconsistencies and discrepancies in anxiety research as well as individuality of verbal reports.

The validity assumptions in using verbal data to assess individual differences in emotionality (anxiety) are obviously challenged by Hallam's theoretical considerations. His information processing approach appears to be in accordance with the methodological criticism of questionnaire data that is referred to in Section 3.1.

2.4 ANXIETY: A CONFUSING AND SUPERFLUOUS CONCEPT?

In the present context it is necessary to refer to both orientations in anxiety research: psychophysiological research which postulates a neurobiological basis to anxiety and the antithesis assuming but a multireferential lay construct.

Neither the multitude of more specific theories of anxiety nor the broad spectrum in self-report and behavioural assessment strategies will be reviewed here (the reader is referred instead to the literature: Barlow, 1988; Bernstein, Borkovec and Coles, 1986; M. W. Eysenck, 1987; Fowles, 1982; Haynes and Wilson, 1979; McReynolds, 1968; Mavissakalian and Barlow, 1981; Tuma and Maser, 1985; Turner, 1984; Zuckerman, 1976). It is evident from the literature that the multifaceted (multidimensional, multireferential) nature of anxiety is generally recognized. The consequences for a concise theory and valid assessment of anxiety or treatment strategies are equivocal. Delprato and McGlynn (1984) offer a radical, however in this respect, not entirely novel solution:

> Acceptance of the multidimensional nature of anxiety leads directly to its abandonment as an explanatory entity. The subjective, physiologic, and motoric vocabularies that would be brought to bear in elucidating the multiform construct would be the same as the vocabularies used in detailing the to-be-explained anxiety events. Hence explanatory anxiety constructs are (at least) superfluous (p. 35).

Indeed, the conclusion to abandon anxiety as a theoretical term in psychology is hardly novel. From a different perspective, for example Krasner and

Ullmann (1973) argued that the concept of anxiety is superfluous because it does little to provide specific information about the stimulus conditions and the resulting components of behaviour; its reification and use as an explanatory concept are inappropriate and would hinder precise functional analysis.

It is not likely that a majority of psychologists and psychophysiologists at present or in the near future will come up with such radical conclusions to abandon anxiety as a superfluous concept or to accept the reductionism of either a purely biological or purely phenomenological view. Therefore it is strongly argued that the many facets of anxiety should be more adequately assessed in multimodal investigations employing multivariate and pattern analytic procedures. The persistent confusion caused by the vague meaning of "anxiety" can be at least partially counteracted by explicitly stating the specific construct-operation units and by elaborating more precise operationalizations.

3 ASSESSMENT STRATEGIES

3.1 ASSESSMENT BY QUESTIONNAIRES

In standardized personality scales for assessing neuroticism and trait anxiety the investigator has a rather limited choice. Among them are Eysenck's inventories, the EPI and EPQ, Spielberger's STAI, Cattell's IPAT Anxiety Scales, Taylor's MAS, Endler's S-R Anxiousness Scales, and the NEO by Costa and McCrae. A closer look reveals that these scales have many themes and even particular items concerning irritability, tenseness, fatigue, moods, perception of autonomic responses, etc. in common. A considerable number of self-rating scales are available including scales for general anxiety and specific aspects of anxiety (cf. Bellack and Lombardo, 1984; Bernstein, Borkovec and Coles, 1986; Eysenck and Eysenck, 1985; Haynes and Wilson, 1979; Roberts *et al.*, 1983). Relatively few instruments are of psychometrically sound construction, continuously refined or standardized with large representative samples.

In the questionnaire domain, from a psychometric viewpoint, there is hardly a more satisfactory alternative than Eysenck's inventory for assessing the postulated personality dimension underlying neuroticism and general anxiety, although the dysthymic characteristics (emotional and introverted) may be more in agreement with conventional notions of general anxiety. Substantial correlations between EPI–N (EPQ–N) and scores from the STAI, IPAT, MAS will be observed, and psychoneurotic and psychosomatic patients as well as various categories of anxiety disorders usually will attain higher than average scores on the N-scale.

There is little doubt that personality assessment by questionnaire, for example the dimensions E and N, contributes substantial variance to predicting important psychological aspects of an individual's adaptation or maladaptation to the psychosocial environment and, eventually, to diagnosing neurotic disorders. Thus it seems justified to focus on research that investigates the physiological basis of emotionality (neuroticism) as a personality dimension that is operationally defined by N-scales from Eysenck's EPI or EPQ, and equivalent scales in foreign languages, respectively. It is conceivable, however, that such personality assessments may be less valid with respect to biologically oriented research in temperament.

The research question expressed in these terms implies that questionnaires actually provide operational definitions of personality traits for substantive psychophysiological theories. This assumption has been questioned repeatedly for various reasons by some psychologists and recently research has advanced to more thorough exploration of the processes people use to produce their verbal responses: strategies in questionnaire taking, implicit personality theories and inferences from everyday usage of trait labels, understanding questionnaire items, role of semantic bias and linguistic variables, and decision making in responding (see Angleitner and Wiggins, 1986). Using verbal reports as data demands at least a rudimentary theory of how subjects produce such responses. It seems to be still unclear, whether the information processing approach and other current theoretical considerations will lead to technical refinements and thus to more advanced operationalizations of relevant trait concepts (Fiske, 1978; 1986).

Personality questionnaires usually will be the first choice when reliability and economy of assessments are essential criteria. The handicaps are also known: individual scores result from internal non-transparent information processing which probably is distorted by implicit concepts specific to the individual and confounded with general stereotypes in naive person perception.

Behavioural assessment by behaviour ratings and objective behaviour measures is desirable but much more demanding, especially when a differentiation between situations and a systematic aggregation across time intervals and across equivalent situations are intended. The relative scarcity of truly behavioural analyses in evaluating Eysenck's theory was pointed out for example by Gray (1981) and Gale and Edwards (1983).

The laboratory setting in psychophysiological research is not particularly favourable to eliciting a valid spectrum of individual behaviours because subjects usually are instructed to perform specific tasks and to otherwise restrict their movements to reduce recording artefacts. Especially the laboratory studies of emotion like anxiety may raise criticisms on several grounds (cf. Levenson, 1988; Ney and Gale, 1988; Stemmler, 1984; 1989). Developments in ambulatory monitoring and multimodal investigations of anxiety states are promising to achieve more representative designs that overcome the still predominant use of questionnaires however reliable and stable these scores may be.

3.2 MULTIMODAL ASSESSMENT

Cattell's Research Strategy and Critical Multiplism

A demanding research programme was developed by Cattell and collaborators (e.g. Cattell, 1966; 1988) to systematically assess personality factors: (1) by combination of data from the three observation media L, Q, and T (life and behaviour data, questionnaires, and objective tests) and (2) by definition of the data box that comprises the different modes (individuals, variables, situations, replications etc.). In Eysenck's research multimethod strategies and a multivariate perspective were more apparent in the initial stages than in the later work. The basic intention was that multiple operationalizations should complement each other to confirm factor identification (factor matching across different media of observation) although specific variances and possible method factors are acknowledged. The rationale of the multiple operationalization strategy has been put forward in an influential paper by Campbell and Fiske (1959) on convergent and discriminant validity in multitrait–multimethod designs.

The critical multiplism as stated by Cook (1985) appears to be a theoretical development from this multimodal and multimethod assessment approach (Cattell, 1966; Fiske, 1978). Observed inconsistencies present a challenge for reformulation of the basic relationships between hypothetical constructs, intervening variables and observed empirical data (cf. Messick, 1981; Kozak and Miller, 1982).

Response Fractionation

Response fractionation is an essential concept in psychophysiology. This term depicts the conclusion derived from a large number of empirical investigations. The many attempts at defining basic constructs like activation, arousal, anxiety, and stress through multiple operationalizations generally did not result in assessments of convergent validity between methods. In their critical review of the literature on psychophysiological assessment Haynes and Wilson (1979) define response fractionation as the general concept for "lack of significant covariation, nonsignificant common variance, or dyssynchrony among overt behavioral, cognitive, subjective, and physiological measures" (p. 343).

Some aspects of the fractionation phenomenon in physiological responses have been articulated in Lacey's work (1962, 1967) on directional fractionation and particularly in his earlier work on individual response stereotypes. "I think the experiments show that electroencephalographic, autonomic, motor, and other behavioral systems are imperfectly coupled, complexly interacting systems'' (Lacey, 1967, p. 15).

The concepts of response fractionation, response patterning, and idiosyncratic reactions of course have many historical antecedents that date back to the very beginning of multi-channel recordings, for example in Wundt's laboratory. Still much older is the classical aetiological theory of *locus minoris resistentiae sive majoris irritationis*, i.e. a site of lowered resistance and heightened irritation, and the constitutional research on physiological, biochemical and adaptive individuality (Fahrenberg, 1986).

Recent multivariate investigations covering a comparatively large subject sample size, broad sampling of variables and advanced methods in data analysis have confirmed response fractionation as a general phenomenon in psychophysiological activation processes. Although an individual's score on a certain activation variable may characterize the functioning of the particular response system, there is no sufficient empirical support for reliably assuming a corresponding proportional score in another autonomic-somatic system of that individual. Generally, it seems to be impossible to reliably predict an individual's state or state change on one activation variable based on the score from another variable. This result not only holds for the often reported low or even insignificant correlation between self-report and physiological measures but also among the important marker variables for different autonomic-somatic subsystems (for a review, cf. Fahrenberg, 1988).

Triple Response Measurement

The notion ''triple response measurement'' is a common concept in the psychophysiological literature on anxiety and phobia and related fields of psychophysiology, for example in the words of Lang, Rice and Sternbach (1972, p. 624), ''In human subjects, emotional behavior includes responses in three expressive systems: verbal, gross motor and physiological (autonomic, cortical, neuromuscular). The responses of no single system seem to define or encompass an 'emotion' completely, thus demanding for a triple response measurement.''

The triple response measurement (TRM) concept is often attributed to Lang, but the notion of multimodal assessment, of course, is much older and TRM appears to be a rather simplified version thereof. TRM specifies three response systems, i.e. the verbal, motor and physiological mode. Other authors prefer to distinguish four or five principal aspects in the description of emotions: subjective feeling, cognition, gross behaviour, expressive behaviour (facial expression, voice etc.), physiology (CNS, ANS, neuromuscular, endocrine, etc.). In practical assessment, obviously many more sources of psychological and neurobiological data can be distinguished. A more thorough perspective from system theory would provide further differentiation of many hierarchical levels of functioning and a manifold of systems and essential subsystems. Assuming an epistemological perspective of fundamental differences in categories, however, would lead to recognizing but two basically different systems—the introspective and the biobehavioural frame of reference.

Speaking of physiology as one of three systems could too easily pass over how many systems and subsystems should be accounted for on this level: cortical, limbic-hypothalamic, medullary, neuromuscular, autonomic, neuroendocrine, immunological, etc. By haemodynamic analyses in a psychophysiological context it can be easily demonstrated that the multiple regulatory mechanisms cannot be reduced to a single indicator that validly represents an individual's cardiovascular responses. A particular hormonal measure would equally insufficiently depict the neuroendocrine function of the hypothalamic–hypophyseal–adrenocortical axis.

The TRM is a prominent concept but it suggests selecting one indicator for each system. Many investigators seem to justify their assessment strategy by referring to the TRM concept, but this does not come up to the present standard of psychophysiological methodology. The TRM concept is detrimental if it hinders the insight that response fractionation and patterning exist not only between but likewise within these principal levels of description.

Response Patterns and Synergisms

The generally small amount of common variance in psychophysiological measures and its consequences for methodology and applied psychophysiology constitute one of the most important issues for differential psychophysiology. For decades the phenomenon of response fractionation has troubled investigators interested in individual differences and prediction. In fact, a considerable proportion of the methodological discussion in psychophysiology is a consequence of this covariation problem and the motive to eventually find a sufficient explanation in the particular and perhaps inadequate research methodology (for a review, cf. Fahrenberg, 1988; Stemmler and Fahrenberg, 1989; Stemmler, 1992).

Traditional theories of emotion, on the other hand, have pointed out that basic emotions are not uniform activation processes but exhibit distinct patterns. Pioneers such as Lange, Weber, Lehmann, Wundt and later researchers such as Wittkower and Ax were convinced that, associated with emotional states, specific physiological patterns occur in peripheral functions. This view has been challenged by other researchers and the controversy is still unsettled empirically (cf. Section 5.1).

Specificity in this context means that particular emotional states are associated with different central nervous, autonomic, and muscular patterns.

Likewise, physiologial patterns in responding to qualitatively different stimuli or experimental tasks can be investigated. There are, however, other fundamental aspects of response patterning besides stimulus specific response behaviour. Patterning of activation arises from the constitutional (genetic or acquired) characteristics of the individual, as well as from the momentary or habitual interaction between a subject and a particular situation. Threefold patterning has been defined as stimulus specific response (SSR) pattern, individual specific response (ISR) pattern, and motivation specific (MSR) pattern. These concepts have been developed by the work of researchers such as Lacey, Malmo and Shagass, Ax, Wenger, Davis, Engel (for a review and a summary of multivariate investigations on SSR, ISR and MSR, cf. Fahrenberg, 1986). Schwartz (1977) and Davidson (1978) in tentative terms discussed differential response topography and patterning in biobehavioural systems concerning possible implications for biofeedback and behaviour change.

Many reviewers of psychophysiological research, for example, in the context of behavioural assessment of anxiety and phobia refer to earlier research on response patterns and seem to acknowledge the theoretical as well as practical relevance of this issue. However, more recent developments and comprehensive statistical analyses of the threefold patterning SSR, ISR and MSR are overlooked and in general, pattern analysis does not appear to be of particular interest to present day psychophysiology although research methodology is much more advanced than at the time of those pioneers.

The response fractionation phenomenon in psychophysiological data may be partially accounted for by response specificities. There is accumulating evidence from recent studies that about one third of all subjects in psychophysiological experiments exhibit a significant individual response specificity. Altogether the three-fold patterning SSR, ISR and MSR accounts for a substantial percentage of the total variance (for a review, cf. Fahrenberg, 1986; Foerster, 1985).

The concept of stimuli-specific response patterns corresponds to the notion of synergisms in physiology. According to Hess (1924) synergism denotes the interaction between higher physiological systems in their effects on the peripheral system (endorgans). During physical exercise, for example, some organs show sympathetic effects, and other organs show parasympathetic effects (Hess, 1924; Gellhorn, 1970). In particular, a functional polarity, the ergotropic state, and the trophotropic state was specified by these researchers. In the language of recent psychophysiology this concept is represented by the assumptions of diverse activation systems that are variably coupled depending on the momentary situational demands, thus exhibiting a variety of biologically programmed synergistic patterns (Myrtek, Stemmler and Fahrenberg, 1987).

There are a number of known adaptive physiological mechanisms which determine rather uniform response patterns, for example during exposure to heat and cold, atmospheric pressure, and anoxia. In cardiovascular physiology several relevant patterns like the defense reaction, withdrawal response, the dive pattern, and other regulatory processes have been delineated. An extension of such functional and pattern analyses, as advocated by Wenger and Davis for psychophysiological research, eventually could provide standards of reference and perhaps a taxonomy of the principal SSR-pattern. Such standards would be particularly useful in evaluating certain tasks in the psychophysiological laboratory that are supposed to elicit distinct physiological patterns with respect to "alpha-adrenergic", "beta-adrenergic", and "vagal" effects (for a discussion, cf. Steptoe, 1985).

In a sophisticated treatise on methodological issues in differential psychophysiology, Stemmler (1992) developed a framework of assessment models that relates theoretical assumptions, relevant data acquisition and basic data-analytic procedures. As a special case of an assessment model that incorporates the conceptualization of activation as a multicomponent process, the Model of Autonomic Cardiovascular Activation Components was developed and thoroughly examined. Stemmler employed pharmacological autonomic receptor blockades (indoramin, propranolol and atropine) in 48 male subjects to estimate alpha adrenergic, beta-adrenergic, and cholinergic cardiovascular activation components. In a cross-over design, 22 cardiovascular measures were derived from multi-channel recordings of physiological changes under seven laboratory tasks (easy and difficult versions). These data were used in component descriptions, discriminant analyses and multistage linear estimation procedures to estimate variable coefficients and scores of subjects on putative cardiovascular components as well. Furthermore, task profiles and task difficulty effects were studied. Obviously, such empirically derived multicomponential descriptions provide a more advanced frame of reference as compared with univariate measurement. Stemmler's research is an excellent example how pharmacological agents, adequate experimental designs, modelling and multivariate statistical procedures can be combined to advance psychophysiological assessment and validity.

Activation and Arousal

The postulate of distinct patterns in peripheral autonomic responses that are specific to basic emotions had been challenged by other investigators, for example by Cannon with his concept of a uniform emergency function, by the proponents of activation theory, Duffy and Lindsley, by Selye in his theory of the General Adaptation Syndrome and, implicitly by Schachter and by Lazarus in cognitive theories of emotion and stress (cf. Plutchik and Kellermann, 1980).

Many investigations have indeed demonstrated the well-known activation reaction, i.e. the ergotropic pattern of increased experience of tension, decreased synchronization of the EEG, increase in heart rate, blood pressure, respiratory minute volume, electrodermal activity, muscular tension, output of adrenaline, cortisol, and so forth. This frequently observed average response profile formerly has been conceived of as an indication of a unitary dimension of activation or deactivation shown in a systemic, unidirectional, homogeneous increase/decrease of many parameters. An evaluation of such data from a *differential perspective*, however, has failed to establish an empirical basis for uni-dimensional activation theory. Instead, response fractionation and patterning of responses have been recognized.

Concepts of uni-dimensional activation and arousal therefore have been questioned and rejected by several authors (for more recent theoretical discussions of this issue, cf. Brocke, 1985; Brocke and Battmann, 1985; Fahrenberg, 1987; Gale, 1987; Neiss, 1990; Stelmack, 1990; Stemmler, 1991; Stemmler and Meinhardt, 1990; Thayer, 1985; Venables, 1984; Zuckerman, 1983; 1991). While there is no support from differential psychophysiology for a uni-dimensional continuum of activation, this theoretical construct still is widely used in present day research. Many contributors refer explicitly, or at least implicitly, to such concepts as activation (or arousal or stress–strain reaction) and many experimenters still suggest that, for instance, a single parameter of electrodermal activity, of EEG, or of heart rate change could be viewed as an adequate indicator of this theoretical construct (see for example TRM assessment strategies).

In the literature there are obvious discrepancies between the theoretical understanding of activation as a patterned (multi-component) process and the actual assessment of activation processes generally based on a single measure or on a few indices. The surplus meaning in the term "activation parameter", if unsubstantiated in principle, may lead to confusion rather than serve to advance heuristic purposes.

Activation and arousal define an area of research, rather than a set of coherent theoretical constructs at present. Theoretical statements about activation (arousal, stress reaction) should be more explicit with respect to the assumed data basis or functional system, and should acknowledge response fractionation and response patterning.

4 FINDINGS FROM QUESTIONNAIRE STUDIES

The nervousness syndrome as observed by Whytt (1765) emerges also from the findings in Eysenck's Maudsley Medical Questionnaire (MMQ) and subsequent inventories—MPI, EPI, and EPQ (Eysenck and Eysenck, 1969, 1976). Emotionality is a second-order personality dimension including such components as mood fluctuations, sleeplessness, irritability, sensitivity, inferiority feelings, and absentmindedness. However, somatic complaints were gradually omitted during test development and scale revisions so that the EPQ–N-scale now retains only a few items of this kind: sleeplessness, tiredness and fidgetiness.

The Freiburger Persönlichkeitsinventar FPI, a personality inventory that is widely used in Germany (Fahrenberg and Selg, 1970), contains a considerably higher proportion of somatic complaint items than the EPI and EPQ. The FPI-1 Nervousness scale represents a broad spectrum of such complaints about autonomic, motor, and sensory dysfunctions. An even more extended item pool was used in factor analyses to develop the 10 scales, 6 to 10 items each, of the Freiburger Beschwerdenliste (FBL) (Questionnaire for Somatic Complaints, Fahrenberg, 1975): General State of Health, Emotional Reactivity, Cardiovascular, Gastrointestinal, Nose and Throat, Tension, Sensory, Pain, Motoric, Skin, and Somatic Complaint Total Score (FBL-11).

The FPI consists of 10 first-order scales and, additionally, two second-order scales FPI-E and FPI-N were derived during this test construction to match Eysenck's concepts. At that stage FPI-N did not contain any somatic complaint items in order to investigate the relationship between Emotionality and FPI-1 Nervousness. Although the item content did not overlap, a substantial correlation exists between FPI-N and FPI-1, namely $r = 0.64$ ($N = 3318$ normal subjects, male and female, with an age range from 15 to 84 years). With respect to particular dimensions of somatic complaints subsequent investigations revealed consistent relationships between Emotionality (FPI-N) and all of the 10 FBL-scales with a correlation between N and FBL-11 (total score) in the order of $r = 0.55$ (Fahrenberg, 1975).

The recently revised FPI-R now reunites emotionality items and somatic complaint items to give an integrated FPI-R-N second-order dimension (Fahrenberg, Hampel and Selg, 1989). Based on a sample of $N = 2035$ adults 16 years and older (representative of population of the Federal Republic of Germany) it may be concluded that Emotionality (FPI-R-N) is substantially related to first-order factors Life satisfaction ($r = -0.64$), Strain (0.61), Irritability (0.58), and Somatic complaints (0.55). Consequently, it can be predicted reliably that individuals who report mood fluctuations, irritability, worry and inferiority feelings will also report more frequently and more intensely various autonomic, motor and sensory complaints.

The substantial correlation between Emotionality (FPI-N) and Somatic complaints (FBL 11) has been repeatedly observed in our research, with samples from the general population as well as with cardiac patients, students, and many other samples (e.g. Fahrenberg, 1975; Myrtek, 1984). These findings are in agreement with many other investigations in Germany, Britain, and the USA that used equivalent scales to assess individual differences in Emotionality and Somatic Complaints (e.g. Costa and McCrae, 1987).

Derived by statistical methods, a generalized and rather stable trait of psychosomatic disturbance is evident, thus giving an empirical and psychometrically consistent basis to Whytt's original notion of nervousness. Although an extremely broad concept, it proves to be a highly reproducible trait that represents a relatively large proportion of interindividual variance in personality inventory data.

Such evidence derived from questionnaires continues to be a strong motive to seek for a biological basis of emotionality. One of the major research questions within the context of biologically oriented personality research would be to investigate whether psychophysiological correlates exist that could explain nervousness (emotionality) as a constitutional pattern or trait. Are individual differences in emotionality assessed by questionnaire indeed systematically related to objectively measured differences in physiological responsiveness, for example in autonomic lability?

5 FINDINGS FROM MULTIMODAL INVESTIGATIONS

5.1 RESEARCH ON ANXIETY AS AN EMOTION

In subjects who report intense feelings of acute anxiety, avoidance behaviour as well as prominent physiological changes can generally be observed. There can be little doubt that such response profiles averaged across subjects exhibit a multimodal state change. Anxiety probably is the primary emotion that has received most attention in research with respect to theories of emotion, personality and clinical psychology.

Physiological responses during anxiety were reported by many investigators and from various fields, i.e. observations of patients with anxiety disorders, *in vivo* exposure therapy for phobia, psychophysiological studies in healthy subjects and animal experimentation (for reviews, cf. Barlow, 1988; Beidel, 1989; Bernstein, Borkovec and Coles, 1986; Hobbs, 1990; Le Doux, 1987; Lader, 1975; Nesse *et al.*, 1985; Roth, Noyes and Burrows, 1988; Shaw *et al.*, 1986; Tuma and Maser, 1985). Among the findings that are most often reported are increases in heart rate and blood pressure, peripheral vasoconstriction, increases in sweating and in electrodermal activity, muscular tension and finger tremor, increases in norepinephrine, epinephrine and cortisol. This response profile depicts a massive sympathetic-adrenergic arousal in anxiety. This notion originated from Cannon's formulation of fear as a somatic emergency reaction preparing for fight or flight. But autonomic perceptions and psychophysiological recordings indicate that response systems are not always affected in a direction consistent with sympathetic arousal. For example, a reduced cardiac output causing syncope and increased intestinal activity, eventually causing diarrhoea, may be observed during anxiety, thus suggesting increased parasympathetic tone also.

Psychophysiological work for decades has focused on examining the traditional issue of response specificity in emotions. The controversy whether anxiety is characterized by a specific physiological response pattern as compared, for example, with anger and joy, is not satisfactorily settled (for reviews, cf. Barlow, 1988; Henry, 1986; Plutchik and Kellermann, 1986; Popp and Baum, 1989; Stemmler, 1984, 1989; Sternbach, 1966; Wagner, 1989, for reviews concerning facial expressions, cf. Fridlund and Izard, 1983; Manstead, 1988; Scherer, 1988).

Henry (1986) for example appears to be convinced that fear and anger can be reliably differentiated by measures of peripheral physiological functions and neuroendocrine functions. He refers to animal experiments and cites psychophysiological studies in man in which professional actors or histrionically gifted students were able to experience emotional states. However, Henry's (1986) overview on cardiovascular and neuroendocrine responses in anger and fear depicts differences in magnitude but not in patterning, with the exception of cortisol, that is supposed to increase in fear but is unaffected by anger. Wagner (1989) in his recent review concluded, however, that fear is primarily associated with excretion of epinephrine and anger with excretion of epinephrine and norepinephrine.

Most reviewers in this field agree that little evidence exists to reliably assume distinct emotional pattern in measures of peripheral autonomic nervous system functions although seemingly positive results are occasionally published (for example, Levenson, Ekman and Friesen, 1990; and a recent EEG study, cf. Machleidt, Gutjahr and Mügge, 1989). Stemmler's (1984) critical review of the research literature and his own multivariate investigation on the differentiation of fear, anger, and joy indicate that the retention of the null-hypothesis is more appropriate. This conclusion, of course, is based on research that attempted directly inducing emotions in the laboratory and considers autonomic, motor and EEG parameters but excludes neuroendocrine measures and facial expression.

Thus, the focus of research on the physiological differentiation of basic emotions has shifted to the hormonal measures (catecholamines and their metabolites, corticosteroids), to the adrenocorticotropic hormone (ACTH) and the corticotropin releasing hormone (CRH). A newer area of inquiry includes sophisticated studies of neurotransmitters and neuropharmacologic systems involved in anxiety, especially the benzodiazepine-gamma-aminobutyric acid (BZD-GABA) receptor complex (Bohus, 1988; Cameron and Nesse, 1988; Insel, 1986; Tyrer, 1989). There is strong evidence that distinct neurotransmitter systems play an essential role in modulation of anxiety phenomena, but the specificity of such mechanisms is as yet unknown. Almost any change in stimulation seems to increase catecholamine excretion; much of the observed changes in neurotransmitters and receptor systems likewise may prove to be a rather unspecific aspect of generalized activation.

Much of the recent work seems to repeat the methodological deficiencies that are characteristic of earlier research on the specificity issue in peripheral ANS functioning: univariate assessment (single emotion, single parameter design), disregarding basic issues of internal validity instead of examining response profiles in multi-emotion designs (Levenson, 1988; Ney and Gale, 1988; Stemmler, 1984; 1992). Stemmler (1989) proposes to differentiate various meanings of physiological "emotion specificity" that would lead to different hypotheses and research strategies. More precise data from multi-emotion experiments in humans are still lacking that account for differences in overall intensity of effects and employ adequate statistical concepts in examining multiparameter profiles.

A valid answer as to whether anxiety comprises a specific physiology separate from that of "anger" or "joy", will, in the end, depend on neurobiological research. For example, what are the biologically distinctive characteristics in corticolimbic interactions, in noradrenergic and serotonergic connections etc.? (for reviews, cf. Graeff, 1990; Gray, 1983; Joseph, 1990; Plutchik and Kellerman, 1986; Strian and Ploog, 1988). After reviewing neuroanatomical and neurofunctional aspects, Strian and Ploog (1988, p. 462) conclude that "human anxiety is based on specific neural mechanisms just as are other neuropsychological functions". At present, however, these complex structures and functional interactions need further elucidation.

Such investigations were mostly not directed at individual differences, although it continues to be a relevant issue in clinical psychology whether self-report data, behavioural, and physiological measures can be used interchangeably to assess the degree of anxiety and to predict the course of an individual's anxiety state, for example in the process of psychotherapy.

To examine the correspondence between various indicators of anxiety a multiple assessment study was conducted by van Heck (1988) in which self-rated anxiety, overt expressive reactions, and physiological changes were recorded in eight situations like public speaking, accusation, injection, unsolvable word-completion task, and threat of shock. Although only 28 psychology students participated in this study, an exceptionally broad spectrum of variables was selected. The assessment included 15 self-report items, 19 behavioural observation measures (e.g., tense mouth region, restless eye movements, tension of gross movements, tense laughing), and three physiological measures, i.e. heart rate, skin conductance level and forehead temperature.

The author concluded that there was no evidence of substantial convergence between the various modes.

> Neither high positive correlations, pointing to simple convergence, nor high negative correlations, indicating some sort of compensatory role of the various components were obtained. Instead zero correlations were found. The fact that such findings are obtained frequently seems to warrant the conclusion that the

reported findings reflect more the state of nature than the noise of measurement (van Heck, 1988, p. 211).

The absence of substantial multimethod correlations is in accordance with previous research (cf. Section 3.2) and inclusion of further variables, e.g. multiple hormonal measures would probably emphasize the basic response fractionation. Critical multiplism, thus, fails to establish anxiety as a unitary phenomenon.

5.2 RESEARCH ON EMOTIONALITY (NEUROTICISM)

Theoretical Assumptions

A basic relationship between emotionality (emotional lability, neuroticism) and physiological responsiveness (autonomic lability, autonomic imbalance) was postulated by Eysenck (1953, 1967) who re-interpreted some findings by Wenger (1948) on physiological correlates of personality questionnaire data. It seemed plausible that in a global sense emotional lability and autonomic lability could be functionally related. The limbic system of the brain is thought to be the neuroanatomical basis of this temperament trait because it appears to be largely involved in the regulation of emotions.

The somewhat more detailed postulate says "some people are innately predisposed to respond more strongly, more lastingly and more quickly with their autonomic nervous system to strong, painful or sudden stimuli impinging upon the sense organs" (Eysenck and Rachmann, 1965, p. 31). "On the whole the studies reported so far give a definite impression that neurotic and anxious subjects as a whole respond more strongly to stimuli, show greater variability of response, and in particular take much longer to return to their prestimulus baselines" (Eysenck, 1967, p. 68).

The first research question derived from this postulate would be: Are high emotionality (neuroticism) scores in fact associated with greater responsivity especially under stressful conditions? (Eysenck, 1967, p. 237). The second research question is derived from the theoretically postulated interactions of cortical arousal and autonomic activation. It is supposed that the distinction between these systems tends to break down when highly emotional individuals are involved. Individuals who have experienced powerful emotions over long periods of time would emotionally react to "quite mild stimuli" (Eysenck, 1967, p. 233). Are patients with chronic emotional states actually more physiologically responsive than normal control subjects?

More precise hypotheses or operational definitions of essential methodological issues in testing these hypotheses are not available (cf. Eysenck and Eysenck, 1985; Stelmack, 1981; 1990). The general expectation would be that a substantial relationship exists between physiological responsiveness and high questionnaire scores in emotionality (high-N) or chronic emotional state (neurosis). This correlation would not be evident in relaxed conditions but should emerge in normals with higher (stressful) stimulus intensities and in neurotic-anxious patients with mild stimulus intensities.

Physiological Responsiveness

Physiological responsiveness as an enduring characteristic or constitutional personality trait traditionally has been evaluated in relation to a few rather general concepts like sympatheticotonia-vagotonia, autonomic imbalance, and autonomic lability (for reviews, cf. Fahrenberg, 1977; Myrtek, 1984; Wenger and Cullen, 1972). Very few investigators, among them Myrtek (1984), extended the notion of autonomic lability to consider a wider spectrum of data that comprises autonomic functions and neuromuscular and biochemical parameters as well.

The overwhelming research evidence is that such global terms like autonomic lability and physiological reactivity are not tenable on empirical grounds. Myrtek (1984) in his exceptionally thorough series of studies on several samples of male students, conducted haemodynamic and respiratory analyses under various physical and psychological challenges (functional tests), various medical ratings, and collected biochemical data. He concludes, ''If such a global dimension of autonomic lability were to exist, the reaction scores of various variables, as measured by various functional tests, should correlate at a high level with each other, which is definitely not the case here'' (p. 183). Myrtek observed three kinds of correlational results:

> (a) medium-high correlations between the same variables as measured by various functional tests; (b) low and frequently insignificant correlations between various variables according to the same functional test; and (c) very low and primarily insignificant correlations between various variables as measured by various functional tests (p. 183).

Advanced studies and more precise operationalization, thus, did not result in defining a unitary second-order dimension to parallel the emotionality dimension that is consistently assessed by questionnaire.

By a series of factor analyses that were conducted separately for rest values, strain values, and change scores of physiological data from different experimental conditions, Myrtek (1984) obtained a number of primary factors, for example, circulatory volume reactivity, heart rate reactivity, blood pressure reactivity, respiratory volume reactivity, respiratory economy, etc. More specific aspects of physiological reactivity also were suggested by other investigators, for example, spontaneous electrodermal fluctuations, differences in the response characteristics of the pupillary reflex, differential output of urinary catecholamines and other stress hormones. However, attempts to provide multiple operational definitions across physiological systems generally have failed to achieve convergent validity. A well-known example is the inconsistency of various indices of the speed of habituation as measured by EDA, heart rate, finger-pulse volume, desynchronization of the EEG (e.g. Bernstein *et al.*, 1982; Koriat, Averill and Malmstrom, 1973; O'Gorman, 1977).

Since Eysenck's postulate gives no specifications of which primary factors or particular variables are especially suited, distinct preferences cannot be given on theoretical grounds. A multifactor approach as followed by Myrtek (1984) or, at least, a design that employs multiple recordings would be more appropriate in simultaneously testing several indices (various variables, various testing conditions, different scoring methods). Critical issues in operational definitions of arousal and arousability with respect to Eysenck's theory were also reviewed by Stemmler and Meinhardt (1990).

The conclusion is: physiological responsiveness as a consistent trait is not tenable on empirical grounds. The generally low and often insignificant intersystem correlations are not compatible with the notion of a second-order dimension in differential physiology. There are many good reasons why it is much more advantageous to the organism to possess many relatively independent regulatory mechanisms and patterned responses.

Examination of Psychophysiological Correlation

For examining the postulated psychophysiological correlation, Myrtek (1984) used the Emotional Lability Scale from the FPI (Fahrenberg and Selg, 1970) which is conceptually and psychometrically equivalent to the N-scales published by Eysenck. The findings of this work are especially relevant since Myrtek's series of investigations in male students and cardiac patients is more valid than earlier research with respect to scope of variables, variety of tasks used, subject sample size, refinement in univariate and multivariate statistical analyses and replication of studies.

Correlations were tested on different levels of data reduction. First, rest and change scores from physiological variables were correlated with emotional lability and extraversion (FPI-N, FPI-E) across 100 student subjects and examined again in an independent sample equal in size. Second, for each sample a common factor analysis in 45 physiological and psychological variables was computed. Third, personality questionnaire scores were correlated with factor scores derived within the 13 domains consisting of a total of 172 variables.

These analyses produced concurrent negative results, and Myrtek strongly argues for the retention of the null-hypothesis with respect to global psychophysiological relationships as suggested by Eysenck. There is increasing evidence for an alternative explanation: interindividual differences in somatic complaints largely depend on subjective attitude, implicit beliefs and neuroticism-related styles of perceiving and reporting physiological experiences (Costa and McCrae, 1987; Myrtek, 1984; Pennebaker and Epstein, 1983). Is it conceivable that the notion of emotional-autonomic lability as a psychophysiological personality trait is merely based on subjectively consistent complaints of nervousness?

It would be equally constructive to examine the second research question that pertains to the assumed hyper-reactivity of anxiety-neurotic patients. However, the serious difficulties of obtaining control groups that actually are equivalent in other aspects relevant to the investigation are obvious. Besides the many obstacles in matching patients and controls there is some evidence that some categories of patients may be under-reactive and others may be over-reactive. Patients may also differ in their pre-experimental resting levels due to specific interaction and anticipatory effects that determine initial values (for a review, cf. Barlow, 1988; Lader, 1975; Zuckerman, 1991). The validity of the psychophysiological trait postulate, therefore, can be more reliably examined in the normal population range.

In two independent investigations the predictive validity of scores in the FPI-N with respect to individual differences in physiological activation processes was subsequently tested. A gradual clarification requires large-scale multivariate studies, utilizing a variety of tasks and stressors with a large subject sample and a broad spectrum of dependent variables. Such an approach permits the utilization of adequate statistics and additional strategies to avoid capitalizing on chance, which may have occurred in previous work. It should also uncover relationships between dispositional characteristics and activation processes, defining the relevant parameters, if they indeed exist; alternatively, if no such relationships emerge, the sample size and the breadth of the experimental attack will permit a confident acceptance of the null hypotheses.

Male student volunteer subjects ($N = 125$), none from psychology courses, took part in a study consisting of (1) personality assessment by paper-and-pencil tests, (2) cardiovascular assessment, and (3) a typical activation experiment, in which polygraph recordings were obtained in 10 channels under conditions of rest, mental arithmetic, interview, anticipation of taking a blood sample and actual blood taking. In this investigation a set of seven physiological criterion variables were selected according to biometric aspects from a considerably larger pool consisting of 161 parameters. A partitioning of covariance, factor analyses, item analyses, and scale construction procedures as well as models engaging an increasing number of components were used to study the covariation and consistency of these activation parameters. The marker variables that were finally selected to represent certain physiological systems were: heart rate, finger pulse volume amplitude, electrodermal activity (frequency of SCR), EEG relative power in 8–13 Hz band, respiratory irregularity index, eye blink activity, and EMG (forehead and extensor

Table 8.1. Correlation analysis between nine criterion variables and two predictor variables for activation state and activation reaction ($N = 125$).

	Self-report "tense"	Heart rate	Pulse volume amplitude	EDA (SCR-Freq.)	EEG α (Rel. power)	Respiratory irregularity	Eye-blink activity	EMG	Composite PHYS
Predictor variables									
			Activation state initial rest						
FPI–N	0.16	0.08	–0.15	0.04	–0.11	0.00	–0.01	0.06	0.05
FBL–11	0.11	0.09	–0.06	0.07	0.02	0.03	–0.12	0.06	0.01
			Activation reaction mental arithmetic (ALS)						
FPI–N	0.05	–0.13	–0.09	–0.06	–0.09	0.16	–0.11	–0.11	–0.05
FBL–11	–0.10	–0.24†	–0.13	–0.01	–0.12	0.00	–0.03	–0.17	–0.04
			Activation reaction four conditions combined						
FPI–N	0.16	–0.01	–0.03	0.08	0.00	0.19*	–0.11	–0.09	0.08
FBL–11	–0.03	–0.18*	–0.10	0.10	–0.09	0.01	0.10	–0.13	0.11

Note: Predictor variables are emotional lability (FPI–N) and total score of somatic complaints (FBL–11).
PHYS is a composite derived from the seven physiological variables after standardization. The four conditions were mental arithmetic, interview, anticipation of taking a blood sample, blood taking.

* $p < 0.05$ † $p < 0.01$.

digitorum). Additionally a composite index of physiological activity being the sum of the standardized scores of the seven physiological variables was computed. Among the predictor variables that were examined are the individual's Emotional Lability score FPI-N (Freiburger Persönlichkeitsinventar, Fahrenberg and Selg, 1970) and the total score of Somatic Complaints FBL-11 (Freiburger Beschwerdenliste, Fahrenberg, 1975).

A more extended report on the general research strategy and methods may be found in Fahrenberg *et al.* (1983) and Fahrenberg and Foerster (1982). Table 8.1 gives but a small segment of the findings, which is, however, central to the present research question.

The conclusion is evident. Both hypothetical predictor variables, emotional lability and somatic complaint scores, fail to reliably predict individual differences in state and reaction parameters of activation processes. The null-hypothesis is likewise retained (1) for single physiological variables, (2) for the composite score based on seven variables, and (3) for a composite score at a higher level of aggregation that combines change scores in seven variables from four stressor conditions. Multiple regressions, controlled by jack-knife techniques, confirmed these negative results.

As to the generalizability of results appropriate reservations should be offered. This investigation did, however, take special precautions as to subject sample size, broad sampling of variables, intensity of stimulation, reliability estimates, different scoring methods and selection of criterion variables according to specified biometric standards. Several biometric problems that are generally thought to complicate the evaluation of such data (i.e. non-linear relations, the problem of initial values, differing sensibility curves of physiological systems, individual response specificities) were considered and tested empirically.

A replication of this investigation appeared to be the most adequate strategy to examine whether the null-hypothesis can be accepted reliably as suggested by the preceding work. Data from a subsequent experiment that primarily was concerned with the issue of laboratory-field comparison in psychophysiological assessments were used to further test the predictive validity of FPI-N and FBL-11 scores because of the relevance of this research question in differential psychophysiology and psychosomatic theory (Fahrenberg *et al.*, 1986).

In this investigation recordings were taken from 58 male students of physical education under conditions of rest, mental arithmetic, reaction time test, anticipation of free speech, and cold pressor test. Financial rewards were given to increase the challenge imposed by performance tests and the painful cold pressor test. This multi-situational study was repeated after three weeks, three months, and one year. The same general strategy with respect to assessing individual differences, response scaling, and statistical data analysis was adopted; however, besides heart rate, EDA, index of respiratory irregulatory, and eye-blink activity, in this study systolic blood pressure and an index of cardiac output (from impedance cardiography) were used to examine the predictive validity. Again, composite scores were computed for a cardiovascular, respiratory, electrodermal, and electrooculogram component in physiological activation processes, and an aggregate composed of the whole set of marker variables as well.

The findings are quite clear and it would be superfluous to give a table of results since there would be no significant entries for relationships between predictors FPI-N and FBL-11 and physiological criterion variables. With respect to mental arithmetic task, for example, change scores for the six physiological marker variables and five composite scores were not significantly correlated with questionnaire scores; an exception was the significant relationship between FBL-11 and respiratory irregularity, but this finding was not confirmed by the data from the second assessment three weeks later. The supposed predictive validity of emotional lability scores was not confirmed.

The negative results of both multivariable and multi-situational investigations are in full agreement with Myrtek's research that took a somewhat different approach to test Eysenck's hypothesis. The retention of the null hypothesis of psychophysiological correlation with respect to emotionality is the essential conclusion from this research programme and from recent research by Stemmler and Meinhardt (1990) and Stemmler (1992) conducted in this laboratory. Further use of emotionality (neuroticism) assuming a consistent pyschophysiological basis would be misleading as this theoretical construct has not been sufficiently substantiated by empirical data in independent investigations.

Methodological Considerations

Many psychologists who are interested in the biological basis of personality probably will not abandon emotionality as a psychological concept at present since now and then positive results have been reported and the general nervousness dimension is quite evident in questionnaire data. Thus the discussion on methodological issues of how to adequately test the postulates will continue.

According to Eysenck (1981), the basic assumptions of this hypothesis are valid only if certain parameters of testing are adequately selected. With respect to negative results Eysenck tends to answer that the low or moderate challenges applied in most of these studies are insufficiently stressful to provide a proper test for his theory. Since operational definitions of appropriate stimulus parameters and experimental settings were not given by Eysenck a fundamental methodological issue exists. Precisely under what conditions is an adequate test of Eysenck's hypothesis linking emotionality and physiological responsiveness, especially autonomic activation, to be conducted?

In earlier research low to moderate stimulus intensities were thought to be sufficient to provoke differential physiological responses. The use of habituation paradigms or of particular variables like electrodermal activity or finger pulse volume otherwise would be meaningless because these methods generally are not practicable with high stimulus intensities. If it is now argued that the theoretically predicted differences will emerge only under highly stressful conditions, we have to consider whether the empirical validity of Eysenck's theory actually can be adequately tested in the laboratory. For both ethical and practical reasons there are prohibitions against presenting high stimulus intensities and truly stressful challenges in the laboratory, so that an extension from the laboratory to daily life assessment based on ambulatory monitoring appears to be an essential step.

Other methodological aspects that are relevant to the evaluation of Eysenck's theory were discussed by Gale and Edwards (1983; 1986), Stelmack (1981; 1990), Amelang and Ullwer (1991), and Fahrenberg (1987) who also refers to Eysenck's comments on investigations that report negative results. Gale (1981) reviewed the many sources of error that could threaten the internal validity of such experiments especially with respect to EEG studies of extraversion–introversion, but many of the basic issues are identical in examining autonomic lability and emotional lability. An essential contribution to conceptual clarification was made by Brocke (1985) in a semantic analysis of Eysenck's arousal-activation theory. He concludes that more precise hypotheses and specifications of the essential parameters of testing are crucial for theory testing (cf. Fahrenberg, 1987).

In their evaluation of research on physiological correlates of emotionality, Eysenck and Eysenck (1985) cite only a few experiments, and they do not refer explicitly to methodological developments in psychophysiological assessment. A number of relevant multivariate investigations that deal with the empirical test of the theory were not mentioned. Their general conclusions are still based on a few univariate experiments although other sources are available that give a multivariate reconceptualization and provide strong evidence for retention of the null hypothesis.

The attempts at testing Eysenck's postulate probably will continue but there seems to be little chance of making sense of existing contradictory findings. Such univariate explorations employing unstandardized assessment methods and a variety of experimental designs are hardly promising. An empirical clarification, for example of inconsistent results concerning speed of habituation or spontaneous electrodermal fluctuations, would require a panel of experts to precisely define parameters of testing, standardization of measurement and analysis, and to establish criteria that would allow conclusions to whether empirical findings, in fact, are replicated and whether the hypothesis can be reliably accepted or not.

It could be further questioned whether basic psychological deficiencies exist that preclude more positive results in psychophysiological experiments relating to Eysenck's hypotheses. The possible role of extraversion–introversion, although orthogonal to emotionality in questionnaire data, may be considered, but interestingly, Eysenck and Eysenck (1985) did not specify particular predictions or restrictions relevant to examining the emotionality–physiological responsiveness postulate.

Some psychologists have raised the issue of coping dispositions and coping processes that may have moderating effects on physiological responses. There is an extended literature about stress and coping (cf. Goldberger and Breznitz, 1982). Many aspects of the individual's information processing and subjective evaluation may be brought up to ''explain'' insignificant or contradictory results. Generally, questionnaires of some kind are used to assess individual differences in coping but the preceding and fundamental question of how a subject can identify what processes he/she has undergone remains unanswered. Such mechanisms are often regarded as complex interactions or psychodynamic, partly unconscious processes. Extended research, so far, has not come up with reliable operational definitions or standardized assessment instruments. Findings that are reproducible in cross-laboratory comparison are not conspicuous.

Attempts at defining defensive styles by using discrepancies between self-report and physiological indices of stress (Weinstein *et al.*, 1968) were not generally accepted, largely for biometric reasons (Walschburger, 1981). Differentiation of low-anxious and high-anxious subjects according to repressive coping styles was suggested by Weinberger, Schwartz and Davidson (1979), but again, Q-data definitions of such minitypologies in coping styles lack confirmatory empirical evidence.

Strelau (1987) reviewed the possible interrelations between biologically based personality (temperament) dimensions concerning several domains: psychometric (inventory) data, sensory thresholds, the amplitude of auditory evoked potentials to stimuli of different modality, the efficiency of conditioning, and general behavioural activity including the stimulatory value of activity. He seems to suggest that psychometric scores are more valid for the assessment of such temperament traits than psychophysiological measures. However, the notion of temperament basically includes a biological basis of individual differences, and the validity of such theoretical propositions has to be examined referring to neuro-psycho-physiological measures. Negative results, of course, are detrimental to temperament theories and, acknowledging the basic deficiencies of questionnaire data (cf. Section 3.1), would necessarily mean a serious devaluation of such assessments that initially were thought to bridge psychological and physiological levels in personality description and research.

It is desirable that future empirical research relating to the postulated physiological correlates of emotionality should focus on the central issues and should adhere to an advanced methodology. Research reports that often appear to be mere by-products in correlating questionnaire scores with arbitrary physiological data in small-scale studies are no longer meaningful. The theory is not tenable in the original global formulation and thus demands a basic attempt at semantically and operationally structuring and revising it (as proposed by Brocke) for a subsequent specification of fields of validity in differential psychophysiology. At present, such fields are not evident.

5.3 RESEARCH ON ANXIETY DISORDERS

Triple Response Measurement in Agoraphobia

In research on behaviour modification in anxiety disorders a research orientation has more recently emerged that appears to be largely independent of traditional work concerning the specificity issue or psychophysiological concepts of patterning but, nevertheless, turns out to be especially pertinent to this field. Agoraphobia and panic attacks are recognized as productive models to evaluate multimodal (triple response measurement) assessment strategies and to challenge traditional theoretical concepts.

The wave of TRM investigations in anxiety disorders was initiated by Hodgson and Rachman (1974). They examined the behaviour therapy literature concerning covariation of fear and avoidance and concluded:

> There is no doubt that during the next decade psychologists will be concerned with the differential changes of various response systems and need to consider the factors which tend to reduce correlations between measures at a particular point in time (i.e. discordance) and between change scores from one point in time to another (i.e. desynchrony) (p. 319).

Thus, the phenomenon familiar to personality researchers of disappointingly low convergent validities in multimethod designs and the analogous phenomenon of response fractionation and response patterning familiar to psychophysiologists were rediscovered in this domain. The basic correspondence to these traditional issues was only gradually acknowledged (cf. Himadi, Boice and Barlow, 1985; Hugdahl, 1981).

Hodgson and Rachman (1974) offered some theoretical speculations about the dissociation of fear and avoidance and about desynchrony in measures of fear. They suggested that desynchrony is dependent on the intensity of arousal, level of demand, therapeutic technique, length of follow-up and choice of physiological measure. Since these issues raised by Hodgson and Rachman also are of practical relevance to evaluating the process and outcome of behaviour therapy in anxiety disorders a considerable number of papers have been published as predicted.

Case studies and small sample studies served to substantiate the view that discordance and desynchrony in measures of fear clearly exist (e..g Holden and Barlow, 1986; Leitenberg *et al.*, 1971; Mavissakalian and Barlow, 1981; Mavissakalian and Michelson, 1982). Agoraphobia in this respect is an especially instructive example because self-reported discomfort, achieved distance in a behavioural test walk, and heart rate seem to be comparatively plausible indices of the basic anxiety and many behaviour therapists as well as other psychologists would expect such measures to covary.

The general assumption that discordance and desynchrony in measures of fear are related to the outcome of therapy subsequently was examined by several authors. The findings are inconsistent and tend to contradict Hodgson and Rachman (1974) and it became clear that their considerations initially were not sufficiently specified to allow for precise tests (Barlow, 1988; Craske, Sanderson and Barlow, 1987; Grey, Sartory and Rachman, 1979; Haynes, Falkin and Sexton-Radek, 1989; Matias and Turner, 1986; Mavissakalian and Barlow, 1981; Michelson, Mavissakalian and Merchione, 1988; Vermilyea, Boice and Barlow, 1984).

In the present context it will be more relevant to pay attention to the conceptual development of assessment strategies with particular reference to the psychophysiological perspective. In their review on triple response measurement concerning agoraphobia Himadi, Boice and Barlow (1985), after commenting on the rationale for TRM and Lang's popularization of TRM, conclude that three stages may be distinguished: "an initial exploratory phase dominated by expectancies of convergent measures, a second phase of confusing results and disillusionment and a third phase where more subtle and idiosyncratic patterns emerge that may prove useful as prognostics" (p. 315).

Response fractionation as a general phenomenon in the assessment of anxiety was further substantiated by Sallis, Lichstein and McGlynn (1980) based on a meta-analysis of 95 published studies on clinical and analogue populations. The percentages of "synchronous" change differed widely, depending on which two modalities were compared and whether the subjects were actual clinical cases or normal subjects. Sallis, Lichstein and McGlynn (1980) report synchrony across all three modalities in 20% of the time in the analogue studies and in 58% of the time in clinical case reports. Behaviour–verbal, behaviour–physiological and verbal–physiological synchrony or desynchrony appear to be roughly of the same order, but in laboratory analogue studies behaviour–verbal correspondence is considerably higher than behaviour–physiological or verbal–physiological correspondence.

In evaluating this review and possible conclusions concerning selective use of measures to assess anxiety states it should be noted that studies where TRM has been employed in a more sophisticated fashion are scarce. A variety of self-report measures often are set against a single behavioural measure and a one-channel recording of heart rate or electrodermal activity. Although Lang,

Rice and Sternbach (1972) had pointed out some of the many reservations with respect to the complexity of recording and interpretation of physiological measures most investigators in this field adhere to a one-channel–one-indicator methodology. The simple TRM-typology (e.g. Jerremalm, Jansson and Öst, 1986) that distinguishes between cognitive, behavioural and physiological "reactors", in the latter respect based on a single physiological variable, namely heart rate, illustrates the detrimental effects of TRM concepts to adequately recognizing individuality and patterning of responses.

Himadi, Boice and Barlow (1986) specifically discussed the limitations of physiological measurement for treatment and outcome purposes. They recommend a standardized assessment package to measure clinical change containing five measures each for the deterimination of outcome and endstate functioning in agoraphobic patients who respond to treatment. A particular physiological index for treatment outcome is not recommended. Correspondingly, Williams (1985) seems to have reached the same conclusion.

The readiness to dispense with psychophysiological assessment of anxiety indicates a fundamental theoretical revision in this field in favour of self-report data. Since the empirical work concerning multimodal assessments in agoraphobia still is scare the rationale of such reductive strategies should be questioned. Is, in fact, insufficient validity of psychophysiological assessment established or is the cognitive trend in behaviour therapy here a simple way of coping with often discrepant and perhaps irritating findings that do not fit into pseudo-parsimonious concepts of anxiety? What happened to the once attractive idea that self-report data, behavioural analysis and physiological recordings should complement each other in delineating the specific functional sequences in acquisition and treatment of anxiety disorders? The significance of subjective experience in labelling a particular state of discomfort as "anxious" is evident but this perspective should not preclude assessing the magnitude and regulatory characteristics of autonomic-somatic processes and the behavioural outcome criteria in therapy as well.

It should be noted, on the other hand, that the conclusions indicated so far are not unanimous (e.g. Agras and Jacob, 1981; Bellack and Lombardo, 1984). Bernstein, Borkovec and Coles (1986) point out that "research statements about anxiety are now routinely based upon at least one measurement in each of the three main assessment channels" (p. 355), and Michelson, Mavissakalian and Merchione (1988, p. 96) state that "Consequently, the effects of behaviour therapy should always be evaluated through measurement of multiple response modalities."

Hodgson and Rachman (1974) made their assumptions largely independent of conceptual and methodological developments in differential psychophysiology and the more recent discussion in multimodal personality research. This may explain why they avoided operational definitions and used rather general terms to describe response fractionation. Despite the complex validity assumptions and the many moderator variables and psychometric issues involved, only insufficient reliabilities that possibly reduce covariation are discussed to any extent. But the majority of the subsequent studies in this field also lack an adequate methodology, especially with respect to assessment and statistical analyses. The research question obviously demands correlational analyses, cross-correlation techniques, multiple regressions, partitioning of covariance and pattern analyses instead of simple ANOVA designs that preclude adequate recognition of individual differences, response patterning, and differences in temporal characteristics. There are no attempts to utilize either composite scores derived from multiple physiological recordings or to regard the maximally responding physiological system as the optimal (idiosyncratic) indicator. The reason for this lack of transfer between related research domains remains unclear. As Bellack and Lombardo (1984) earlier remarked it is disconcerting to find that the methodological approach to examining discordance and desynchrony is not substantially different today from what it was a decade ago.

Panic Disorder

Recently panic disorder has become an essential model in anxiety research. Panic disorder appears to be especially suited for confronting biological and psychological explanations in the classification and aetiology of anxiety disorders and therefore calls for multimodal assessment (for reviews, cf. Baker, 1989; Hand and Wittchen, 1986; Klein, 1980; Margraf and Ehlers, 1989).

According to the *Diagnostic and Statistical Manual DSM-III-R* published by the American Psychiatric Association panic disorder is diagnosed when at least four panic attacks within a four-week period are registered provided that at least four from altogether 13 characteristic symptoms are present during each attack. Ten of these items refer to somatic complaints like dyspnoea, palpitations, sweating, and faintness. Differential diagnostic problems exist with respect to hyperventilation syndrome, postprandial hypoglycaemia, and vestibular abnormalities.

Biological models in explaining panic attacks consider spontaneity of attacks, panic induction by biochemical substances such as sodium lactate, drug specificity in treatment of symptoms, and family data. Ehlers and associates (1986) conducted a thoroughly controlled experiment that examined biological as well as psychological hypotheses. They concluded that anxiety stimulated by lactate infusion is not specific to panic patients because subjective and objective responses were approximately equal in normal controls. Panic attacks seem to be superimposed on generally elevated levels of anxiety and cardiovascular functions. Anxiety reactions to perceived physiological changes could be one factor that contributes to onset and course of panic attacks (Ehlers *et al.*, 1986; Ehlers *et al.*, 1988).

Margraf and Ehlers (1989), in reviewing the evidence for biological models of panic disorder, state that presently a purely biological model appears to be inadequate while alternative approaches that account for the role of cognition and learning would be more capable of integrating the relevant findings. A more comprehensive model should include the interaction of perceived physiological changes, situational cues, and the subjective appraisal of this information as dangerous. The panic attack could represent an autonomic discharge that is independent of psychological information processing. In contrast to the notion of a biological dysfunction the psychological view would assume internal cues immediately triggering individual panic attacks. The two approaches are not necessarily mutually exclusive but both would require a multimodal assessment of panic attacks and relevant conditions of onset. Since such investigations in laboratory settings are limited with respect to spontaneity and ecological validity of panic attacks, ambulatory monitoring would be the method of choice.

Actually, a few studies on ambulatory monitoring of agoraphobic patients exist (e.g. Barlow, Mavissakalian and Schofield, 1980; Holden and Barlow, 1986; Woods *et al.*, 1987; for a review, cf. Öst, 1990) and recently ambulatory monitoring of panic disorders has been reported (Anastasiades *et al.*, 1990; Freedman *et al.*, 1985; Taylor, Telch and Havvik, 1983; for a review, cf. Margraf, 1990). Such assessment will be useful in the diagnosis of panic disorder and in the evaluation of treatment outcome but the findings are also fundamental to theoretical consideration of anxiety.

Margraf (1990) concludes:

> these studies suggest that a fair number of panic attacks occur with measurable changes in heart rate that are not caused by differences in physical workload. However, these changes are typically of moderate intensity and the variability between attacks is pronounced. A large subgroup of attacks occur without heart rate increases (p. 324).

Such discrepancies are well known from psychophysiological assessments in various fields but the lack of systematic correlation is particularly impressive with panic attacks.

Several reviewers have raised the question as to whether there are qualitative differences between panic (spontaneous attacks) and other types of anxiety (cf. Barlow, 1988; Hallam, 1985; Margraf and Ehlers, 1989). The findings on response fractionation in ambulatory monitoring suggest a further differentiation. Is it conceivable that with respect to subjective and physiological symptoms concordant and discordant states of naturally occurring panic attacks exist that can be distinguished by referring to antecedent and consequent conditions or specific behavioural aspects? Panic attack appears to be a promising research paradigm for evaluating such speculations by examining systematic effects and individual patterning in onset and course of these processes, thus gradually clarifying basic issues in anxiety research and fundamental questions in psychophysiology as well.

In concluding it is imperative that more precise assessments be planned to adequately diagnose such patients. Such assessments have to be multimodal and should employ available techniques of ambulatory monitoring complementary to laboratory recordings in order to attain external (ecological) validity.

6 CONCLUSIONS AND PERSPECTIVES

6.1 RELEVANCE OF TRAIT CONCEPTS OF EMOTIONALITY AND ANXIETY (Q-DATA)

Emotionality (neuroticism) and anxiety as assessed by questionnaire scales are consistent personality dimensions and individual scores indicate a rather stable disposition. Multifaceted concepts originated from subjective feelings of nervousness and emotional experience of recurrent or chronic states of anxiety; however, these fuzzy sets were psychometrically refined and now constitute important theoretical constructs in personality research. Emotionality and anxiety still can be seen as representing multi-referential lay constructs, none the less they are empirically valid with respect to many essential aspects of the self-concept and social relationships, for example the individual's adaptation and global well-being or discomfort. These traits have personal meaning and theoretical relevance, and it would therefore be unnecessary and unrealistic to suggest radically abandoning such concepts. The task, however, is to dispense with unwarranted surplus meanings that are still prominent in the literature and in clinical applications.

6.2 RETENTION OF THE PSYCHOPHYSIOLOGICAL NULL-HYPOTHESIS

The psychological validity and practical utility of emotionality and trait anxiety (Q-data) does not imply that such constructs derived from self-report data are automatically the appropriate theoretical constructs for investigating the biological basis of personality. Such second-order factors that represent substantial variance in self-report data would be an economical strategy to begin with, but specific items, habits, or other behavioural measures would have obvious advantages.

Over many decades research has failed to substantiate the physiological correlates that are assumed for emotionality and trait anxiety. There is virtually no distinct experimental finding that has been reliably replicated across studies and laboratories. No more successful than earlier research are the more recent multivariate investigations that controlled for many sources of variance as well as for experimental and statistical artefacts.

There is strong empirical evidence against Eysenck's theoretical postulate that emotionality and anxiety (Q-data) are substantially correlated with higher physiological responsiveness. In previous sections of this chapter several theoretical issues and experimental findings were discussed, and the postulate was found untenable on empirical grounds. This conclusion, in principle, does not exclude the vague possibility that even more refined methodology eventually could shift the evidence. But at present, the retention of the null-hypothesis is much more appropriate. The conclusion thus is to dispense with this, once plausible notion of an unitary psychophysiological personality dimension emotionality (anxiety).

Biologically oriented personality researchers by recognizing this state of affairs would profit from critical re-evaluation of traditional research questions and research methodology in this domain. A step in this direction would be to acknowledge advances in differential psychophysiology. The discussion in this chapter largely attends to a consideration of such developments.

6.3 ADVANCES IN DIFFERENTIAL PSYCHOPHYSIOLOGY

Recent research in differential psychophysiology confirmed the phenomenon of response fractionation in psychophysiological recordings thus contradicting concepts of uni-dimensional activation and arousal that, despite much criticism, at least implicitly seem viable to many investigators. The notion of general activation, global sympathetic-adrenergic arousal, general stress–strain syndrome, etc., now at best is limited to response profiles for particular conditions that are averaged across subjects. Correlating individual change scores in various physiological measures would exhibit response fractionation.

Multivariate methodology served to substantiate the position that physiological responses are patterned especially to situational demands, individual characteristics and interactions. It is a major challenge to present-day psychophysiology to advance more precise definitions of such patterns and corresponding standard assessment procedures eventually validated against pharmacologically induced reference patterns. There is a notable trend to further differentiate global concepts by employing multiple recordings of autonomic and somatic functions, more specific parametrization, and increased sampling rates (e.g. beat-to-beat analysis) to aid functional analysis of system dynamics. Assessing neuroendocrine functions to obtain multihormonal profiles with higher sampling rates will further assist this development.

6.4 COMMENSURABLE CONCEPT LEVELS

More specific physiological-neuroendocrine assessments, further differentiation of regulatory pattern and development of multi-component models of activation processes raise the essential issue of how psychological concepts could be specified to adequately meet this differentiation concerning systemic level and type of aggregation, i.e. averaging across time intervals, classes of situations or areas of content.

Attempts at decomposing second order (Q-data) trait concepts, emotionality and anxiety, appear to have failed so far for psychometric reasons. Multifactor approaches probably would end in analogous difficulties just one level below and could not overcome the basic limitations of self-report data. The failure to obtain reliable correlations between emotionality (Q-data) and rather subtle and specific physiological measures like spontaneous electrodermal fluctuations or speed of habituation may be a consequence of incommensurable concept levels.

Bottom-up strategies could take questionnaire items or single self-report adjective scales as counterparts of the physiological measures in examining psychophysiological relationships (cf. Fahrenberg, 1987). However, such items usually ask the individual to aggregate his/her experience averaged across various intervals, situations etc., and, thus, self-reports remain multireferential, basically vague data.

A few authors, therefore, have advocated renewing the behavioural measurement tradition in the field of emotionality and anxiety that once seemed to be a promising approach to biological personality research. It is only fair to say that methods of behavioural measurement have attracted relatively little interest in recent personality research. Continuing research programmes are scarce and technical developments that provide new instruments for behaviour recordings and ambulant monitoring are hardly used. The explicit use of multimodal assessment strategies in research on anxiety disorders, however, could serve as a model.

6.5 MULTIMODAL ASSESSMENT AND THE TRM CONCEPT

For theoretical and methodological reasons there is a strong case for advancing multimodal assessments wherever appropriate and achievable in practice. The term multimodal here refers to the broad notion that was developed in Cattell's (1966; 1988) conceptualization which is still basic to the methodology in differential psychological research. This includes the different modes of data and the particular modes of the data box (covariation chart). Wittmann (1988) recognized that this scheme is fundamental to advanced formulations of multivariate reliability theory and generalizability issues. Furthermore, it provides an adequate frame of reference for structuring the possible ways to aggregate data as discussed in recent contributions to the state-trait controversy.

Overwhelming evidence exists in many fields of personality and clinical research that multiple operational definitions do not lead to satisfactory convergent-discriminant validities in multitrait-multimethod designs. To dispense with discordant or even contradictory data, for example in diagnosis and treatment of anxiety disorders, would mean taking a high risk in decision making and prediction as a consequence of biased selection of predictors. Thus Seidenstücker and Baumann (1987) recommended multimodal assessment to be the standard in relevant clinical research and practice.

On the other hand, researchers are strongly advised to dispense with the popular TRM concept in its simple version of assessing one self-report, one behavioural and one physiological measure or deriving a simple TRM typology. This misleading simplification precludes adequate recognition of general and individual response patterning.

The scope of this multimodal approach (critical multiplism, cf. Cook, 1985; principles of symmetry and representative designs, cf. Wittmann, 1988) will provoke criticism concerning its feasibility and practical application. The search for more valid assessments may strain many laboratories and thus could hinder practical applications of psychophysiological concepts and methods. However, conventional single-channel physiological measurements, certainly, are obsolete in most psychophysiological research orientations.

6.6 COMPLEMENTARY ASSESSMENT IN LABORATORY AND FIELD

The strategic combination of laboratory and field assessments can be seen as an extension of the multimodal approach. The utility of such complementary assessments is evident, for example in diagnosis and treatment evaluation of anxiety disorders. The issues of internal and external validity and the demand for more ecological validity in psychological work are well known. Several authors have, for example, pointed out the importance of combined laboratory-field studies in stress research, but only recently psychophysiologists have begun to actually test the predictabilty and generalizability of individual differences in activation processes (Anastasiades *et al.*, 1990; Dimsdale, 1984; Fahrenberg, 1991; Fahrenberg *et al.*, 1986; Turner and Carroll, 1985). The selection of suitable situations is the crucial issue. Such a laboratory-field comparison inevitably will evoke the basic criticism of whether corresponding conditions can be considered functionally equivalent in their demand characteristics and specific synergisms of the activation process.

Field studies (ambulatory monitoring) in psychophysiology usually are designed to search for naturally occurring behaviour episodes that may qualitatively (type of behaviour, spontaneity) and quantitatively (range of obtained measures) differ. Ambulatory 24-hour monitoring of the ECG or blood pressure is now a common practice with patients. Several other research questions and clinical perspectives would profit immediately from complementary laboratory and field assessments. Psychophysiologists who are concerned with individual differences should direct more reseach activities to assessment and prediction of real-life criterion situations for their healthy subjects or patients. In the future, probably more effort will be devoted to defining complementary strategies of basic laboratory and applied field research. Such investigations are increasingly aided by advanced microprocessor-based systems for multichannel recordings of physiological, behavioural, and verbal data outside the laboratory (Fahrenberg *et al.*, 1991; Heger, 1990; Turpin, 1990).

Again, the cost–benefit relation can be questioned, for example in personality research. Of course, it would be more convenient if just a few measures taken in the laboratory (or clinic) would suffice to provide relevant predictions. It would be even more convenient and economical if scores from a personality inventory could reliably predict individual differences in physiological responsiveness and stress–strain. Since the present empirical evidence is against both propositions there appears to be no alternative to multimodal assessment despite the difficulties involved.

6.7 RE-ORIENTATION OF RESEARCH

The psychophysiology of neuroticism (emotionality) and anxiety, despite intense and extended research activities, has not yet attained a consistent factual basis or a theoretical foundation of general acceptance. A re-orientation of research is mandatory.

Investigation of acute states of anxiety, especially *in vivo* studies of agoraphobics and panic attack patients, is one promising area of research that could provide a model for understanding the development of individual differences in emotionality. Acknowledging that anxiety is a multireferential lay concept and, likewise, a multireferential psychological construct should, consequently, guide us to more precise scientific terms. Global terms have to be replaced by distinct empirical descriptions however demanding this multiplistic approach. Drawing our attention away from highly speculative theories of anxiety might aid us in our re-orientation to a descriptive (bottom-up) approach which is thoroughly executed and explicitly states the multiplicity of construct-operation units.

The explanation of individual differences in anxiety states will depend on our understanding of how synergistic coupling and dynamic uncoupling of the many essential organismic subsystems is processed. Among the perspectives and subsystems to be emphasized are the following:

— emotional experience (feeling);
— interoceptive experience of visceral changes;
— individual information processing, evaluation and attribution of internal and external cues;
— verbal reports on feeling states and physical symptoms (and assumed interactions as well) in subjective terms but relating to acquired schemata and lay concepts.
— facial and vocal expression, muscular tone and gross body movement;
— EEG topography, corticolimbic regulation of peripheral functioning, and distinct receptor system activity in modulation of the hormonal axes;
— peripheral autonomic and neuroendocrine measures.

Such conceptualization of the necessary descriptions will require more sophisticated designs than those that simply correlate between-subjects indices of physiological activation with self-report questionnaire data. Namely, adequate formulation will require emphasis on systems theory and within subject designs. More precise functional analysis referring to multilevel processing of emotion obviously demands not only multimethod strategies but higher sampling rates of essential measures than usually employed; otherwise neither the time course (rise and recovery, latencies and sensibility curves of subsystems) nor the enhancement and dampening of subsystems in coupling and uncoupling can be observed.

The scope of this task and the basic methodological issues appear to be prohibitive. However, in order to resolve the confusing state of psychophysiological research on anxiety, there is no alternative. An essential step, here, would be the integration of research orientations that previously have developed rather independently, i.e. behaviour therapy research, ambulatory monitoring methodology, and differential psychophysiology.

ACKNOWLEDGEMENTS

The author would like to thank A. Ehlers, A. Gale, J. Margraf, T.W. Roth and G. Stemmler for their valuable comments on a former draft of this chapter, and J. Whittaker-Stemmler for polishing up the English.

REFERENCES

Agras, W.S. and Jacob, R.G. (1981) Phobia: nature and measurement. In M. Mavissakalian and D.H. Barlow (eds), *Phobia. Psychological and Pharmacological Treatment* (pp. 35–62). New York: Guilford Press.

Amelang, M. and Ullwer, U. (1991) Correlations between psychometric measures and psychophysiological as well as experimental variables in studies of extraversion and neuroticism. In J. Strelau and A. Angleitner (eds), *Explorations in Temperament* (pp. 287–315). New York: Plenum Press.

Anastasiades, P., Clark, D.M., Salkovskis, P.M., Middleton, H., Hackman, A., Gelder, M.G. and Johnston, D.W. (1990) Psychophysiological responses in panic and stress. *Journal of Psychophysiology*, **4**, 331–338.

Angleitner, A. and Wiggins, J.S. (eds) (1986) *Personality Assessment via Questionnaire. Current Issues in Theory and Measurement.* Berlin: Springer.

Averill, J.R. (1976) Emotion and anxiety: sociocultural, biological, and psychological determinants. In M. Zuckerman and C.D. Spielberger (eds), *Emotions and Anxiety* (pp. 87–130). New York: John Wiley & Sons.

Baker, R. (ed.) (1989) *Panic Disorder: Theory, Research, and Therapy.* New York: John Wiley & Sons.

Barlow, D.H. (1988) *Anxiety and its Disorders. The Nature and Treatment of Anxiety and Panic.* New York: Guilford Press.

Barlow, D.H., Mavissakalian, M.R. and Schofield, L.D. (1980) Patterns of desynchrony in agoraphobia: a preliminary report. *Behaviour Research and Therapy*, **18**, 441–448.

Beidel, D.C. (1989) Assessing anxious emotion: a review of psychophysiological assessment in children. *Clinical Psychology Review*, **9**, 717–736.

Bellack, A.S. and Lombardo, T.W. (1984) Measurement of anxiety. In S.M. Turner (ed.), *Behavioral Theories and Treatment of Anxiety* (pp. 51–89). New York: Plenum Press.

Bernstein, A.S., Frith, C., Gruzelier, J., Patterson, P., Straube, E.,Venables, P. and Zahn, T. (1982) An analysis of the skin conductance orienting response in samples of American, British, and German schizophrenics. *Biological Psychology*, **14**, 155–211.

Bernstein, D.A., Borkovec, T.D. and Coles, M.G.H. (1986) Assessment of anxiety. In A.R. Climinero, K.S. Calhoun and H.E. Adams (eds), *Handbook of Behavioral Assessment* (2nd edn.) (pp. 353–403). New York: John Wiley & Sons.

Bohus, B. (1988) Limbic-midbrain mechanisms and behavioral physiology of interaction with CRF, ACTH and adrenal hormones. In D. Hellhammer, I. Florin, and H. Weiner (eds), *Neurobiological Approaches to Human Disease* (pp. 267–285). Lewiston: Huber.

Brocke, B. (1985) The structure of the arousal/activation theory of personality. An analysis in view of the standard representation mode for psychological theories. *The 2nd Conference of the International Society for the Study of Individual Differences.* St. Feliu, Spain.

Brocke, B. and Battmann, W. (1985) Die Aktivierungstheorie der Persönlichkeit. Eine systematische Darstellung und partielle Rekonstruktion. *Zeitschrift für Differentielle und Diagnostische Psychologie*, **6**, 189–213.

Cameron, O.G. and Nesse, R.M. (1988) Systemic hormonal and physiological abnormalities in anxiety disorders. *Psychoneuroendocrinology*, **13**, 287–307.

Campbell, D.T. and Fiske, D.W. (1959) Convergent and discriminant validation by the multitrait-multimethod matrix. *Psychological Bulletin*, **56**, 81–105.

Cattell, R.B. (1966) The data box: its ordering of total resources in terms of possible relational systems. In R.B. Cattell (ed.), *Handbook of Multivariate Experimental Psychology* (pp. 67–128). Chicago: Rand McNally.

Cattell, R.B. (1988) The data box: its ordering of total resources in terms of possible relational systems. In J.R. Nesselroade and R.B. Cattell (eds) *Handbook of Multivariate Experimental Psychology* (2nd edn) (pp. 69–130). New York: Plenum Press.

Cattell, R.B. and Kline, P. (1977) *The Scientific Analysis of Personality and Motivation.* New York: Academic Press.

Cattell, R.B. and Scheier, I.H. (1961) *The Meaning and Measurement of Neuroticism and Anxiety.* New York: Ronald.

Cook, T.D. (1985) Postpositivist critical multiplism. In R.L. Shotland and M.M. Mark (eds), *Social Science and Social Policy* (pp. 21–62). Beverly Hills, Ca.: Sage.

Costa, P.T. and McCrae, R.R. (1987) Neuroticism, somatic complaints, and disease: Is the bark worse than the bite? *Journal of Personality,* **55**, 299–316.

Craske, M.G., Sanderson, W.C. and Barlow, D.H. (1987) How do desynchronous response systems relate to the treatment of agoraphobia: a follow-up evaluation. *Behaviour Research and Therapy,* **25**, 117–122.

Davidson, R.J. (1978) Specificity and patterning in biobehavioral systems. Implications for behavior change. *American Psychologist,* **33**, 430–436.

Delprato, D.J. and McGlynn, F.D. (1984) Behavioral theories of anxiety disorders. In S.M. Turner (ed.), *Behavioral Theories and Treatment of Anxiety* (pp. 1–49). New York: Plenum Press.

Dijkman, C.I.M. and de Vries, M.W. (1987) The social ecology of anxiety. Theoretical and quantitative perspectives. *The Journal of Nervous and Mental Disease,* **175**, 550–557.

Dimsdale, J.E. (1984) Generalizing from laboratory studies to field studies of human stress physiology. *Psychosomatic Medicine,* **46**, 463–469.

Ehlers, A., Margraf, J., Roth, W.T., Taylor, C.B. and Birbaumer, N. (1988) Anxiety induced by false heart rate feedback in patients with panic disorder. *Behaviour Research and Therapy,* **26**, 1–11.

Ehlers, A., Margraf, J., Roth, W.T., Taylor, C.B., Maddock, R.J., Sheikh, J., Kopell, M.L., Gossard, D., Agras, W.S. and Kopell, B.S. (1986) Lactate infusions and panic attacks: do patients and controls respond differently? *Psychiatry Research,* **17**, 295–308.

Endler, N.S. (1983) Interactionism: a personality model, but not yet a theory. In M.M. Page (ed.), *Nebraska Symposium on Motivation: Personality—Current Theory and Research* (pp. 155–200). Lincoln: University of Nebraska Press.

Eysenck, H.J. (1953) *The Structure of Human Personality.* London: Methuen.

Eysenck, H.J. (1967) *The Biological Basis of Personality.* Springfield, Ill.: Thomas.

Eysenck, H.J. (1981) General features of the model. In H.J. Eysenck (ed.), *A Model for Personality* (pp. 1–37). Berlin: Springer.

Eysenck, H.J. and Eysenck, M.W. (1985) *Personality and Individual Differences.* New York: Plenum Press.

Eysenck, H.J. and Eysenck, S.B.G. (1969) *Personality Structure & Measurement.* London: Routledge & Kegan Paul.

Eysenck, H.J. and Eysenck, S.B.G. (1976) *Psychoticism as a Dimension of Personality.* London: Hodder & Stoughton.

Eysenck, H.J. and Rachman, S. (1965) *The Causes and Cures of Neurosis.* London: Routledge & Kegan Paul.

Eysenck, M.W. (1987) Trait theories of anxiety. In J. Strelau and H.J. Eysenck (eds), *Personality Dimensions and Arousal* (pp. 79–97). New York: Plenum Press.

Fahrenberg, J. (1967) *Psychophysiologische Persönlichkeitsforschung.* Göttingen: Hogrefe.

Fahrenberg, J. (1975) Die Freiburger Beschwerdenliste FBL. *Zeitschrift für Klinische Psychologie,* **4**, 79–100.

Fahrenberg, J. (1977) Physiological concepts in personality research. In R.B. Cattell and R.M. Dreger (eds), *Handbook of Modern Personality Theory* (pp. 585–611). Washington, DC: Hemisphere.

Fahrenberg, J. (1986) Psychophysiological individuality: a pattern analytic approach to personality research and psychosomatic medicine. In S. Rachman and T. Wilson (eds), *Advances in Behaviour Research and Therapy*, **8**, 43–100.

Fahrenberg, J. (1987) Concepts of activation and arousal in the theory of emotionality (neuroticism). A multivariate conceptualization. In J. Strelau and H.J. Eysenck (eds), *Personality Dimensions and Arousal* (pp. 99–120). New York: Plenum Press.

Fahrenberg, J. (1988) Psychophysiological processes. In J.R. Nesselroade and R.B. Cattell (eds), *Handbook of Multivariate Experimental Psychology* (2nd edn) (pp. 867–914). New York: Plenum Press.

Fahrenberg, J. (1991) Differential psychophysiology and the diagnosis of temperament. In J. Strelau and A. Angleitner (eds), *Explorations in Temperament* (pp. 317–333). New York: Plenum Press.

Fahrenberg, J. and Foerster, F. (1982) Covariation and consistency of activation parameters. *Biological Psychology*, **15**, 151–169.

Fahrenberg, J., Foerster, F., Schneider, H.J., Müller, W. and Myrtek, M. (1986) Predictability of individual differences in activation processes in a field setting based on laboratory measures. *Psychophysiology*, **23**, 323–333.

Fahrenberg, J., Hampel, R. and Selg, H. (1989) *Das Freiburger Persönlichkeitsinventar FPI-R* (5. Aufl.). Göttingen: Hogrefe.

Fahrenberg, J., Heger, R., Foerster, F. and Müller, W. (1991) Differentielle Psychophysiologie von Befinden, Blutdruck und Herzfrequenz im Labor-Feld-Vergleich. *Zeitschrift für Differentielle und Diagnostische Psychologie*, **12**, 1–25.

Fahrenberg, J. and Selg, H. (1970) *Das Freiburger Persönlichkeitsinventar FPI.* Göttingen: Hogrefe.

Fahrenberg, J., Walschburger, P., Foerster, F., Myrtek, M. and Müller, W. (1983) An evaluation of trait, state, and reaction aspects of activation processes. *Psychophysiology*, **20**, 188–195.

Fiske, D.W. (1978) *Strategies for Personality Research.* San Francisco: Jossey-Bass.

Fiske, D.W. (1986) The trait concept and the personality questionnaire. In A. Angleitner and J.S. Wiggins (eds), *Personality Assessment via Questionnaires. Current Issues in Theory and Measurement* (pp. 35–46). Berlin: Springer.

Foerster, F. (1985) Psychophysiological response specificities: a replication over a 12-month period. *Biological Psychology*, **21**, 169–182.

Fowles, D.C. (1982) Heart rate as an index of anxiety: failure of a hypothesis. In J.T. Cacioppo and R.E. Petty (eds), *Perspectives in Cardiovascular Psychophysiology* (pp. 93–126). New York: Guilford Press.

Freedman, R.B., Ianni, P., Ettedgui, E. and Puthezhath, N. (1985) Ambulatory monitoring of panic disorder. *Archives of General Psychiatry*, **42**, 244–248.

Fridlund, A.J. and Izard, C.E. (1983) Electromyographic studies of facial expressions of emotions and patterns of emotions. In J.T. Cacioppo and R.E. Petty (eds), *Social Psychophysiology. A Sourcebook* (pp. 243–286). New York: Guilford Press.

Gale, A. (1981) EEG studies of extraversion–introversion: what's the next step? In R. Lynn (ed.), *Dimensions of Personality. Papers in Honour of H.J. Eysenck* (pp. 181–207). Oxford: Pergamon Press.

Gale, A. (1987) Arousal, control, energetics, and values. An attempt at review and appraisal. In J. Strelau and H.J. Eysenck (eds), *Personality Dimensions and Arousal* (pp. 287–316). New York: Plenum Press.

Gale, A. and Edwards, J.A. (1983) Psychophysiology and individual differences: theory, research procedures, and the interpretation of data. *Australian Journal of Psychology*, **35**, 361–379.

Gale, A. and Edwards, J.A. (1986) Individual differences. In M.G.H. Coles, E. Donchin and S.W. Porges (eds), *Psychophysiology: Systems, Processes and Applications.* New York: Guilford Press.

Gellhorn, E. (1970) The emotions and the ergotropic and trophotropic systems. *Psychologische Forschung*, **34**, 48–94.

Goldberger, L. and Breznitz, S. (eds) (1982) *Handbook of Stress. Theoretical and Clinical Aspects.* London: Free Press.

Graeff, F.G. (1990) Brain defense systems and anxiety. In G.D. Burrows, M. Roth and R. Noyes (eds), Handbook of Anxiety, Vol. 3. *The Neurobiology of Anxiety* (pp. 307–354). Amsterdam: Elsevier.

Gray, J.A. (1981) A critique of Eysenck's theory of personality. In H.J. Eysenck (ed.), *A Model for Personality* (pp. 246–276). New York: Springer.

Gray, J.A. (1983) Anxiety, personality, and the brain. In A. Gale and J.A. Edwards (eds), *Physiological Correlates of Human Behaviour* (pp. 31–44). London: Academic Press.

Grey, S., Sartory, G. and Rachman, S. (1979) Synchronous and desynchronous changes during fear reduction. *Behaviour Research and Therapy*, **17**, 137–147.

Hallam, R.S. (1985) *Anxiety: Psychological Perspectives on Panic and Agoraphobia.* London: Academic Press.

Hand, I. and Wittchen, H.U. (eds) (1986) *Panic and Phobias.* Berlin: Springer.

Haynes, S.N., Falkin, S. and Sexton-Radek, K. (1989) Psychophysiological assessment in behaviour therapy. In G. Turpin (ed.), *Handbook of Clinical Psychophysiology* (pp. 175–214). Chichester: John Wiley & Sons.

Haynes, S.N. and Wilson, C.L. (1979) *Behavioural Assessment.* San Francisco: Jossey-Bass.

van Heck, G.L. (1988) Modes and models in anxiety. *Anxiety Research*, **1**, 199–214.

Heger, R. (1990) Apparative Datenerfassung in Feldstudien. *Diagnostica*, **36**, 60–80.

Helmchen, H. and Linden, M. (eds) (1986) *Die Differenzierung von Angst und Depression.* Berlin: Springer.

Henry, J.P. (1986) Neuroendocrine patterns of emotional response. In R. Plutchik and H. Kellerman (eds), *Emotion, Theory, Research, and Experience.* Vol. 3: *Biological Foundations of Emotion* (pp. 37–60). Orlando: Academic Press.

Hess, W.R. (1924) Über die Wechselbeziehungen zwischen psychischen und vegetativen Funktionen. *Archiv für Neurologie und Psychiatrie*, **15**, 260–277.

Himadi, W.G., Boice, R. and Barlow, D.H. (1985) Assessment of agoraphobia: triple response measurement. *Behaviour Research and Therapy*, **23**, 311–323.

Himadi, W.G., Boice, R. and Barlow, D.H. (1986) Assessment of agoraphobia—II. Measurement of clinical change. *Behaviour Research and Therapy*, **24**, 321–332.

Hobbs, W.R. (1990) The physiology of anxiety states. In G.D. Burrows, M. Roth and R. Noyes (eds), Handbook of Anxiety, Vol. 3. *The Neurobiology of Anxiety* (pp. 135–157). Amsterdam: Elsevier.

Hodges, W.F. (1976) The psychophysiology of anxiety. In M. Zuckerman and C.D. Spielberger (eds), *Emotions and Anxiety* (pp. 175–194). Hillsdale, NJ: Erlbaum.

Hodgson, R. and Rachman, S. (1974) Desynchrony in measures of fear. *Behaviour Research and Therapy*, **12**, 319–326.

Holden, A.E. and Barlow, D.H. (1986) Heart rate and heart rate variability recorded in vivo in agoraphobics and nonphobics. *Behavior Therapy*, **17**, 26–42.

Hugdahl, K. (1981) The three-systems-model of fear and emotion: a critical analysis. *Behaviour Research and Therapy*, **19**, 75–85.

Insel, T.R. (1986) The neurobiology of anxiety: a tale of two systems. In B.F. Shaw, Z.V. Segal, T.M. Vallis and F.E. Cashman (eds), *Anxiety Disorders: Psychological and Biological Perspectives.* New York: Plenum Press.

Jerremalm, A., Jansson, L. and Öst, L.-G. (1986) Cognitive and physiological reactivity and the effects of different behavioral methods in the treatment of social phobic. *Behaviour Research and Therapy*, **24**, 171–180.

Joseph, R. (1990) *Neuropsychology, Neuropsychiatry, and Behavioural Neurology*. New York: Plenum Press.

Klein, D.F. (1980) Anxiety reconceptualized. *Comprehensive Psychiatry*, **21**, 411–427.

Koriat, A., Averill, J.R. and Malmstrom, E. (1973) Individual differences in habituation: some methodological and conceptual issues. *Journal of Research in Personality*, **7**, 88–101.

Kozak, M.J. and Miller, G.A. (1982) Hypothetical constructs versus intervening variables: a re-appraisal of the three-systems model of anxiety assessment. *Behavioral Assessment*, **4**, 347–358.

Krasner, L. and Ullmann, L.P. (1973) *Behavior Influence and Personality*. New York: Holt, Rinehart & Winston.

Krug, S.E. (1977) *Psychological Assessment in Medicine*. Champaign, Ill.: IPAT.

Lacey, J.I. (1962) Psychophysiological approaches to the evaluation of psychotherapeutic process and outcome. In E. Rubinstein and M.B. Parloff (eds), *Research in Psychotherapy* (pp. 160–208). Washington, DC: APA.

Lacey, J.I. (1967) Somatic response patterning and stress: some revision of activation theory. In M.H. Appley and R. Trumbull (eds), *Psychological Stress: Issues in Research* (pp. 14–37). New York: Appleton-Century-Crofts.

Lader, M.H. (1975) *The Psychophysiology of Mental Illness*. London: Routledge & Kegan Paul.

Lang, P.J. (1977) Physiological assessment of anxiety and fear. In J. Cone and R. Hawkins (eds), *Behavioral Assessment* (pp. 178–195). New York: Brunner & Mazel.

Lang, P., Rice, D.G. and Sternbach, R.A. (1972) The psychophysiology of emotion. In N.S. Greenfield and R.A. Sternbach (eds), *Handbook of Psychophysiology* (pp. 623–643). New York: Holt.

Le Doux, J.E. (1987) Emotion. In V.B. Mountcastle, R. Plum and S.R. Geiger (eds), *Handbook of Physiology Sec. 1. The Nervous System (Vol. 5). Higher Functions of the Brain. Part I* (pp. 419–459). Bethesda, MD: American Physiological Society.

Leitenberg, H., Agras, S., Butz, R. and Wincze, J. (1971) Relationship between heart rate and behavioral change during the treatment of phobias. *Journal of Abnormal Psychology*, **78**, 59–68.

Levenson, R.W. (1988) Emotion and the autonomic nervous system: a prospectus for research on autonomic specificity. In H.L. Wagner (ed.), *Social Psychophysiology and Emotion: Theory and Clinical Applications* (pp. 17–42). New York: John Wiley & Sons.

Levenson, R.W., Ekman, P. and Friesen, W.V. (1990) Voluntary facial action generates emotion-specific autonomic nervous system activity. *Psychophysiology*, **27**, 363–384.

Machleidt, W., Gutjahr, L. and Mügge, A. (1989) *Grundgefühle. Phänomenologie, Psychodynamik, EEG-Spektralanalytik*. Berlin: Springer.

Majcen, A.M., Steyer, R. and Schwenkmezger, P. (1988) Konsistenz und Spezifität bei Eigenschafts- und Zustandsangst. *Zeitschrift für Differentielle und Diagnostische Psychologie*, **9**, 105–120.

Manstead, A.S.R. (1988) The role of facial movement in emotion. In H.L. Wagner (ed.), *Social Psychophysiology and Emotion: Theory and Clinical Applications* (pp. 105–129). New York: John Wiley & Sons.

Margraf, J. (1990) Ambulatory psychophysiological monitoring of panic attacks. *Journal of Psychophysiology*, **4**, 321–330.

Margraf, J. and Ehlers, A. (1989) Etiological models of panic — medical and biological aspects. In R. Baker (ed.), *Panic Disorder: Theory, Research and Therapy* (pp. 145–203). London: John Wiley & Sons.

Matias, R. and Turner, S.M. (1986) Concordance and discordance in speech anxiety assessment: the effects of demand characteristics on the tripartite assessment method. *Behaviour Research and Therapy*, **24**, 537–545.

Mavissakalian, M. and Barlow, D.H. (eds) (1981) *Phobia, Psychological and Pharmacological Treatment.* New York: Guilford Press.

Mavissakalian, M. and Michelson, L. (1982) Patterns of psychophysiological change in the treatment of agoraphobia. *Behaviour Research and Therapy*, **20**, 347–356.

McReynolds, P. (1968) The assessment of anxiety: a survey of available techniques. In P. McReynolds (ed.), *Advances in Psychological Assessment* (pp. 244–264). Palo Alto: Science & Behavior Books.

Messick, S. (1981) Constructs and their vicissitudes in education and psychological measurement. *Psychological Bulletin*, **89**, 575–588.

Michelson, L., Mavissakalian, M. and Merchione, K. (1988) Cognitive, behavioral, and psychophysiological treatment of agoraphobia: a comparative outcome investigation. *Behavior Therapy*, **19**, 97–120.

Myrtek, M. (1984) *Constitutional Psychophysiology.* New York: Academic Press.

Myrtek, M., Stemmler, G. and Fahrenberg, J. (1987) Rejoinder to Perkins' 'Use of terms to describe results: additive versus synergistic', *Psychophysiology*, **24**, 720–721.

Naveteur, J. and Freixa i Baqué, E. (1987) Individual differences in electrodermal activity as a function of subjects' anxiety. *Personality and Individual Differences*, **5**, 615–626.

Neiss, R. (1990) Ending arousal's reign of error: a reply to Anderson. *Psychological Bulletin*, **107**, 101–105.

Nesse, R.M., Curtis, G.C., Thyer, B.A., McCann, D.S., Huber-Smith, M.J. and Knopf, R.F. (1985) Endocrine and cardiovascular responses during phobic anxiety. *Psychosomatic Medicine*, **47**, 320–332.

Ney, T. and Gale, A. (1988) A critique of laboratory studies of emotion with particular reference to psychophysiological aspects. In H.L. Wagner (ed.), *Social Psychophysiology and Emotion: Theory and Clinical Applications* (pp. 65–83). Chichester: John Wiley & Sons.

Noyes, R., Roth, M. and Burrows, G.D. (eds) (1988) *Handbook of Anxiety. Vol. 2 Classifications, Etiological Factors and Associated Disturbances.* Amsterdam: Elsevier.

Öst, L.-G. (1990) Psychophysiological assessment of agoraphobia. *Journal of Psychophysiology*, **4**, 315–319.

O'Gorman, J.G. (1977) Individual differences in habituation of human physiological responses: a review of theory, method, and findings in the study of personality correlates in non-clinical populations. *Biological Psychology*, **5**, 257–318.

Pennebaker, J.W., and Epstein, D. (1983) Implicit psychophysiology: effects of common beliefs and idiosyncratic physiological responses on symptom reporting. *Journal of Personality*, **51**, 468–496.

Plutchik, R. and Kellerman, H. (eds) (1980) *Emotion: Theory, Research, and Experience. Vol. 1. Theories of Emotion.* New York: Academic Press.

Plutchik, R. and Kellerman, H. (eds) (1986) *Emotion, Theory, Research, and Experience. Vol. 3. Biological Foundations of Emotion.* Orlando: Academic Press.

Popp, K. and Baum, A. (1989) Hormones and emotions: affective correlates of endocrine activity. In H.L. Wagner and A. Manstead (eds), *Handbook of Social Psychophysiology* (pp. 99–120). New York: John Wiley & Sons.

Roberts, S., Aronoff, J., Jensen, J. and Lambert, M.J. (1983) Measurement of outcome in anxiety disorders. In M.J. Lambert, E.R. Christensen and S.S. Dejulio (eds), *The Assessment of Psychotherapy Outcome* (pp. 304–365). New York: John Wiley & Sons.
Roth, M., Noyes, R. and Burrows, G.D. (eds) (1988) *Handbook of Anxiety* (3 vols). Amsterdam: Elsevier.
Royce, J.R. and Powell, S. (1983) *Theory of Personality and Individual Differences: Factors, Systems, and Processes.* Englewood Cliffs, NJ: Prentice-Hall.
Sallis, J.F., Lichstein, K.L. and McGlynn, F.D. (1980) Anxiety response patterns: a comparison of clinical and analogue populations. *Journal of Behavior Therapy and Experimental Psychiatry*, **11**, 179–183.
Scherer, K.R. (ed.) (1988) *Facets of Emotion. Recent Research.* Hillsdale, NJ: Lawrence Erlbaum.
Schwartz, G.E. (1977) Biofeedback and patterning of autonomic and central processes: CNS-cardiovascular interactions. In G.E. Schwartz and J. Beatty (eds), *Biofeedback. Theory and Research* (pp. 138–219). New York: Academic Press.
Seidenstücker, G. and Baumann, U. (1987) Multimodale Diagnostik als Standard in der Klinischen Psychologie, *Diagnostica*, **33**, 243–258.
Shaw, B.F., Segal, Z.V., Vallis, T.M. and Cashman, F.E. (eds) (1986) *Anxiety Disorders: Psychological and Biological Perspectives.* New York: Plenum Press.
Spielberger, C.D., Gorsuch, R.L. and Lushene, R. (1970) *Manual for the State-Trait Anxiety Inventory.* Palo Alto, CA: Consulting Psychologists Press.
Spielberger, C.D., Lushene, R.E. and McAdoo, W.G. (1977) Theory and measurement of anxiety states. In R.B. Cattell and R.M. Dreger (eds), *Handbook of Modern Personality Theory* (pp. 239–253). New York: Hemisphere.
Stelmack, R.M. (1981) The psychophysiology of extraversion and neuroticism. In H.J. Eysenck (ed.), *A Model for Personality* (pp. 38–64). Berlin: Springer.
Stelmack, R.M. (1990) Biological bases of extraversion: psychophysiological evidence. *Journal of Personality*, **58**, 293–311.
Stemmler, G. (1984) *Psychophysiologische Emotionsmuster. Ein empirischer und methodologischer Ansatz zur inter- und intraindividuellen Begründbarkeit spezifischer Profile bei Angst, Ärger und Freude.* Frankfurt: Lang.
Stemmler, G. (1989) The autonomic differentiation of emotions revisited: convergent and discriminant validation. *Psychophysiology*, **26**, 617–632.
Stemmler, G. (1992) *Differential Psychophysiology: Persons in Situations.* Heidelberg: Springer.
Stemmler, G. and Fahrenberg, J. (1989) Psychophysiological assessment: conceptual, psychometric, and statistical issues. In G. Turpin (ed.), *Handbook of Clinical Psychophysiology* (pp. 71–104). Chichester: John Wiley & Sons.
Stemmler, G. and Meinhardt, E. (1990) Personality, situation and arousability. *Personality and Individual Differences*, **11**, 293–308.
Steptoe, A. (1985) Theoretical bases for task selection in cardiovascular psychophysiology. In A. Steptoe, H. Rüddel and H. Neus (eds), *Clinical and Methodological Issues in Cardiovascular Psychophysiology* (pp. 6–15). Berlin: Springer.
Sternbach, R.A. (1966) *Principles of Psychophysiology.* New York: Academic Press.
Strelau, J. (1987) Personality dimensions based on arousal theories. Search for integration. In J. Strelau and H.J. Eysenck (eds), *Personality Dimensions and Arousal* (pp. 269–286). New York: Plenum Press.
Strian, F. and Ploog, D. (1988) Anxiety related to central nervous system dysfunction. In R. Noyes, M. Roth and G.D. Burrows (eds), *Handbook of Anxiety. Vol. 2. Classification, Etiological Factors and Associated Disturbances* (pp. 431–475). Amsterdam: Elsevier.

Taylor, C.B. and Agras, S. (1981) Assessment of phobia. In D.H. Barlow (ed.), *Behavioral Assessment in Adult Disorders* (pp. 181–208). New York: Guilford Press.

Taylor, C.B., Telch, M.J. and Havvik, D. (1983) Ambulatory heart rate changes during panic attacks. *Journal of Psychiatric Research*, **17**, 261–266.

Thayer, R.E. (1985) Activation (arousal): the shift from a single to a multi-dimensional perspective. In J. Strelau, F.H. Farley and A. Gale (eds), *The Biological Bases of Personality and Behavior. Vol. 1 Theories, Measurement Techniques, and Development* (pp. 115–127). Washington: Hemisphere.

Tuma, A.H. and Maser, J.D. (1985) *Anxiety and the Anxiety Disorders.* New Jersey: Erlbaum.

Turner, J.R. and Carroll, D. (1985) The relationship between laboratory and 'real world' heart rate reactivity: an exploratory study. In J.F. Orlebeke, G. Mulder and L.J.P. van Doornen (eds), *Psychophysiology of Cardiovascular Control: Models, Methods, and Data* (pp. 895–907). New York: Plenum Press.

Turner, S.M. (ed.) (1984) *Behavioral Theories and Treatment of Anxiety.* New York: Plenum Press.

Turpin, G. (1990) Ambulatory clinical psychophysiology: an introduction to techniques and methodological issues. *Journal of Psychophysiology*, **4**, 299–304.

Tyrer, P. (1989) *Psychopharmacology of Anxiety.* Oxford: Oxford University Press.

Venables, P.H. (1984) Arousal: an examination of its status as a concept. In M.G.H. Coles, J.R. Jennings and J.A. Stern (eds), *Psychophysiological Perspectives. Festschrift for Beatrice and John Lacey* (pp. 134–142). New York: Van Nostrand.

Vermilyea, J.A., Boice, R. and Barlow, D.H. (1984) Rachman and Hodgson (1974) a decade later. *Behaviour Research and Therapy*, **22**, 615–621.

Wagner, H. (1989) The peripheral physiological differentiation of emotions. In H. Wagner and A. Manstead (eds), *Handbook of Social Psychophysiology* (pp. 77–87). New York: John Wiley & Sons.

Walschburger, P. (1981) Die Diskrepanz zwischen subjektiven und physiologischen Belastungsreaktionen: ein informativer Indikator des individuellen Bewältigungsstils? *Schweizerische Zeitschrift für Psychologie und ihre Anwendungen*, **40**, 55–67.

Weinberger, D.A., Schwartz, G.E. and Davidson, R.J. (1979) Low-anxious, high-anxious, and repressive coping styles: psychometric patterns and behavioral and physiological responses to stress. *Journal of Abnormal Psychology*, **88**, 369–380.

Weinstein, J., Averill, J.R., Opton, E.M. and Lazarus, R.S. (1968) Defensive style and discrepancy between self-report and physiological indexes of stress. *Journal of Personality and Social Psychology*, **10**, 406–413.

Wenger, M.A. (1948) Studies of autonomic balance in Army Air Forces personnel. *Comparative Psychology Monographs*, **19**, Whole No 101.

Wenger, M.A. and Cullen, T.D. (1972) Studies of autonomic balance in children and adults. In N.S. Sternbach and R.A. Greenfield (eds), *Handbook of Psychophysiology* (pp. 535–576). New York: Holt.

Whytt, R. (1765) *Observations on the Nature, Causes and Cure of those Disorders which are Called Nervous* (2nd edn). Edinburgh.

Williams, S.L. (1985) On the nature and measurement of agoraphobia. In M. Hersen, R.M. Eisler and P.M. Miller (eds), *Progress in Behavior Modification*, **19**, 109–144.

Wittmann, W.W. (1988) Multivariate reliability theory: principles of symmetry and successful validation strategies. In J.R. Nesselroade and R.B. Cattell (eds), *Handbook of Multivariate Experimental Psychology* (2nd edn) (pp. 505–560). New York: Plenum.

Woods, S.W., Charney, D.S., McPherson, C.A., Gradman, A.H. and Heninger, G.R. (1987) Situational panic attacks. Behavioral, physiological, and biochemical characterization. *Archives of General Psychiatry*, **44**, 365–375.

Zuckerman, M. (1976) General and situation-specific traits and states: new approaches to assessment of anxiety and other constructs. In M. Zuckerman and C.D. Spielberger (eds), *Emotions and Anxiety* (pp. 133–174). New York: John Wiley & Sons.

Zuckerman, M. (1983) *Biological Bases of Sensation Seeking, Impulsivity and Anxiety.* London: Erlbaum.

Zuckerman, M. (1991) *Psychobiology of Personality.* Cambrige: Cambridge University Press.

Chapter 9

The Psychophysiology of Extraversion

Robert M. Stelmack
University of Ottawa, School of Psychology, 408B Monpetit Hall, Ottawa, Ontario, Canada K1N 6N5

and

Russell G. Geen
University of Missouri-Columbia, Department of Psychology, 209 McAlester Hall, Columbia, Missouri 65211, USA

ABSTRACT

This chapter reviews the current status of research that explores the biological basis of personality, notably extraversion and sensation seeking, using psychophysiological recording techniques. The review emphasizes electrodermal and event-related potential methods, although other techniques are briefly noted. Overall, there is a good deal of evidence that introverts are more sensitive to physical stimulation than extraverts. This effect was observed under different conditions with various modes of stimulation and methods of response recording. The data endorse the view that introverts are characterized by enhanced arousability, or physiological response to stimulation, compared with extraverts. Although the neurological mechanisms that mediate these effects are not certain, there is continued progress towards that objective.

Handbook of Individual Differences: Biological Perspectives
Edited by Anthony Gale and Michael W. Eysenck

INTRODUCTION

Contemporary psychophysiological methods are composed of a family of bioelectric recording techniques. Electroencephalographic and evoked potential averaging measures are employed to monitor electrocortical activity; electrodermal, cardiac, and vasomotor methods are non-invasive procedures that record autonomic nervous system activity. During the past twenty years, there was an intensive effort to establish the functional significance of the bioelectric signals derived from these techniques and to localize the neurological generators of the bioelectric activity. On both counts, this enterprise has met with varying degrees of success. Overall, however, this work continues to advance our understanding of fundamental psychological processes such as sensation, perception, attention, and learning, as well as individual differences in those processes (Martin and Venables, 1980).

Psychophysiological measures were applied with some success to the elaboration of the biological bases of personality dimensions, notably extraversion and sensation seeking. Explicit hypotheses of the biological bases of individual differences were formally stated for both extraversion (Eysenck, 1967) and sensation seeking (Zuckerman, 1979). The present chapter presents an overview of the current status of research that examined these personality dimensions with psychophysiological procedures.

The view that these personality dimensions are influenced by biological or constitutional predispositions is endorsed by biometric analyses that examined the heritability of extraversion and sensation seeking (Fulker, Eysenck and Zuckerman, 1980) and by pharmacological assays that link differences in personality to variation in neurohormonal and catecholamine activity (Zuckerman, 1984). Psychophysiological methods provide an important means of focusing the physiological systems and mechanisms that are thought to mediate the personality differences. This chapter begins with a brief outline of the biological hypotheses that guided the psychophysiological research on extraversion and sensation seeking. For each of the psychophysiological measurement techniques considered, prominence is given to effects that are reported with some consistency and to observations that provide new insights into the problem. The theoretical implications of this work are also considered.

THE PHYSIOLOGICAL BASIS OF PERSONALITY

Much of the impetus for research on the psychophysiology extraversion stemmed from Eysenck's (1967) theory of personality. He proposed that introverts are characterized by lower thresholds of arousal in the ascending reticular activating system (ARAS) than are extraverts. The increased cortical arousal that develops with ARAS activity was known to play an important role in attention and learning. The excitatory and inhibitory influence that the ARAS exercised on cortical and muscular activity made this system an appropriate choice as a biological basis for the individual differences in attention and conditioning which were thought to be important determinants of extraversion. Although the physiological mechanisms were only broadly outlined, the hypothesis proved to have a strong heuristic appeal. It was successful in generating hundreds of research initiatives that examined individual differences in extraversion with psychophysiological measures of cortical and autonomic activity that were consistent with differential activity in reticulocortical brain systems. This hypothesis was challenged only relatively recently by the proposal of an alternative view of the physiological basis of extraversion (Gray, 1973). In Gray's schema, individual differences in anxiety, that is introverted neuroticism in Eysenck's typology, are linked with variation in a behavioral inhibition system. In this view, highly anxious individuals are thought to be more sensitive to signals of punishment and frustrative non-reward, behaviors that are influenced by activity in the septo-hippocampal system. Gray also argues that individual differences in impulsiveness, extraverted neuroticism in Eysenck's typology, may be characterized by a heightened sensitivity to signals of reward. A tentative physiological substrate for this appetitive system was outlined that focused on central nervous system catecholamines that are implicated in reward mechanisms.

In the main, the biological determinants that were proposed for the sensation seeking trait were similar to those sketched by Eysenck and Gray (Zuckerman, 1979). In early work, it was proposed that sensation-seeking, like extraversion, was determined in part by differences in optimal levels of arousal in the ARAS (Zuckerman, 1969). In the most recent statement of the sensation-seeking model, Zuckerman (1979, 1984) suggests that arousing, intrinsically rewarding experience is sought by high sensation seekers in order to elevate brain catecholamines from initially low levels that are evident in the absence of such stimulation.

It must be clear that a direct assessment of the biological bases of personality that were proposed cannot be achieved by the methods of psychophysiological analysis that are currently available. Variation in psychophysiological measures can only provide indirect evidence of differences in reticulocortical activity and for the most part, the neural generators of electrocortical activity are only broadly understood. Despite these limitations, research has provided information that can shape and focus our understanding of the biological determinants of personality.

EXTRAVERSION AND ELECTRODERMAL ACTIVITY

The extent of electrodermal activity recorded from electrodes placed on the fingers or palmar surface is a direct function of the amount of sweat gland activity at those sites. The neural innervation of the sweat glands is by the sympathetic branch of the autonomic nervous system. However, the postganglionic synapse is cholinergic rather than noradrenergic, with acetylcholine as the neurotransmitter. Central nervous system mechanisms which play a role in the elicitation of the electrodermal response include the descending activity of the ventro-medial reticular formation, the ARAS, and, of course, the cortex which has an important role in the control of all lower brain centres (cf. Venables and Christie, 1973). Consistent with the modulatory effects of reticulocortical activity that are thought to mediate individual differences in extraversion, it was expected that:

(1) Introverts would display higher tonic levels of arousal than extraverts, as expressed in higher skin conductance levels or in more frequent spontaneous skin conductance responses.
(2) Introverts would display greater electrodermal response amplitude to moderate intensity stimulation.
(3) Under conditions intended to increase tonic arousal level, there would be interactive effects with intensity of stimulation such that introverts would reach asymptotic electrodermal response amplitudes at lower levels of stimulus intensity than extraverts.

EXTRAVERSION AND SKIN CONDUCTANCE LEVEL

In the main, comparisons between introverts and extraverts in tonic or base level of arousal are indexed by measures of skin conductance level (SCL) that are recorded during periods prior to stimulation. When conditions of the experiment involve simple sensory stimulation and subjects are not challenged or threatened by task demands, differences between personality groups are seldom reported (e.g. Coles, Gale and Kline, 1971; Neilsen and Petersen, 1976; Davis and Cowles, 1988). However, there is some evidence of higher skin conductance levels for introverts that is observed when they are confronted with challenging task demands, such as performing arithmetic problems (Fowles, Roberts and Nagel, 1977) or performing a task that requires sustained attention (Smith, Rockwell-Tischer and Davidson, 1986). Frequency of non-specific skin conductance responses, that is responses which spontaneously occur in the absence of punctate stimulation, is also considered as a good index of tonic arousal state (Raskin, 1973). Although null effects have been most often reported (e.g. Hastrup and Katkin, 1976;

Hastrup, 1979; Sostak, 1978), a higher frequency of non-specific responses among introverts has been sometimes observed (Coles, Gale and Kline, 1971; Crider and Lunn, 1971; Gange, Geen and Harkins, 1979; Mangan and O'Gorman, 1969). Nevertheless, only four of about forty studies report these differences in spontaneous fluctuations. Overall, under neutral or low stress conditions, there is little compelling evidence from measures of SCL or non-specific electrodermal fluctuations to suggest that introverts are characterized by enhanced levels of tonic or basal levels of arousal.

EXTRAVERSION AND SKIN CONDUCTANCE RESPONSE

Although electrodermal measures of tonic arousal level do not reliably distinguish introverts and extraverts, there is considerable success with measures of skin conductance response (SCR). Differences between introverts and extraverts in arousability, or in response to specific stimulation, were explored almost exclusively within the framework of the orienting response habituation paradigm (Sokolov, 1963). The procedure typically involved the recording of skin conductance responses to the repetitive presentation of simple auditory or visual stimuli. The elicitation of the OR is relevant to excitatory processes that are associated with sensory facilitation, attention, and learning, while the habituation, or decrease in skin conductance response amplitude that accrues with repeated presentations of the stimulus is relevant to inhibitory processes associated with extinction. More generally, enhanced skin conductance responses can be regarded as indicative of greater arousability.

Thorough reviews of the research that examined differences in SCR between introverts and extraverts reveal a good deal of information that is relevant to the evaluation of the hypothesis of enhanced arousability for introverts (Stelmack, 1981; Geen, 1983; Smith, 1983). It is important to recognize that these studies are characterized by significant variations in recording, scoring, subject selection, and stimulation procedures. In fact, it is clear that no study is an exact replication of any other. Accordingly, it is not surprising that specific effects observed in one study do not invariably emerge in another. Nevertheless, there is sufficient consistency in the effects that have been reported to make the following observations. First, studies that have employed low intensity stimuli, for example auditory stimuli of 60 dB or lower intensity, typically fail to yield significant effects (Mangan and O'Gorman, 1969; Coles, Gale and Kline, 1971; Siddle, 1971; Sadler, Mefferd and Houck, 1971; Koriat, Averill and Malmstrom, 1973; Hastrup, 1979). However, the greater SCR of introverts than extraverts is reported with some consistency when auditory stimuli of moderate intensity (75 to 90 dB) are used, and when visual stimuli are applied. The enhanced SCR of introverts to stimuli of moderate arousal value was observed in greater initial response amplitude, slower habituation rate, more frequent number of responses, or greater response amplitude to test stimuli following the habituation series (Mangan and O'Gorman, 1969; Crider and Lunn, 1971; Wigglesworth and Smith, 1976; Nielsen and Petersen, 1976; Smith and Wigglesworth, 1978; Stelmack *et al.*, 1979; Gange, Geen and Harkins, 1979; Smith, Rypma and Wilson, 1981; Stelmack, Plouffe and Falkenberg, 1983). These results are in general agreement with Eysenck's hypothesis that introverts are characterized by higher levels of arousal than extraverts.

With high intensity auditory stimuli (above 90 dB), it was observed that extraverts show greater electrodermal activity than introverts with both tonic SCL (Fowles, Roberts and Nagel, 1977; Smith, Wilson and Jones, 1983) and phasic SCR measures (Wigglesworth and Smith, 1976; Smith, Rypma and Wilson, 1981; Smith, Wilson and Jones, 1983; Smith, Wilson and Davidson, 1984). These authors speculate that this reversal at high intensities may implicate mechanisms that protect the individual from the painful effects of high intensity stimulation and that these mechanisms are invoked at lower intensities for introverts than extraverts. Such an interpretation is consistent with the lower pain thresholds observed for introverts (cf. Kohn, 1987). It can also be inferred that introverts may prefer stimuli of lower intensity than extraverts. Insight into the significance of these differential effects of stimulation has been achieved in a number of interesting experiments.

Geen (1984) examined differences in electrodermal activity among extraverts and introverts in a study that was designed to investigate arousal, preferred level of stimulation, and performance on a learning task. In the first phase of the experiment, subjects were asked to adjust the intensity of bursts of noise stimuli to a level that they would prefer to receive during a subsequent paired associate learning task. Introverts chose a noise level (55 dB) that, on average, was 17 dB lower than the level of intensity preferred by extraverts (72 dB). During the subsequent learning task, three groups of introverts were stimulated with 1 s bursts of noise, either at the level that they had preferred, at the level chosen by the introvert group, or at the higher intensity level preferred by the extravert group. In a similar fashion, three groups of extraverts were composed with one of the groups receiving stimuli at the lower intensity level preferred by the introvert group. The number of conductance responses occurring in a 4-minute period just before and during the first trial of the learning task was employed as the index of level of arousability. Introverts, who received noise at the intensity chosen by extraverts, displayed a greater number of SCRs, that is, were more aroused, than all other groups. Extraverts who were assigned the noise level chosen by the introverts were the least aroused. Extraverts and introverts exhibited the same number of conductance responses when stimulated at their preferred noise level, as did introverts and extraverts who were assigned the noise level preferred by their comparable personality group. Table 9.1 shows these findings.

Table 9.1. Mean trials to criterion (Experiment 1).

Personality	Choice	Noise treatment: Assigned introvert choice*	Noise treatment: Assigned extravert choice†
Extraverts	5.5†	7.3*†	5.4†
Introverts	5.7†	5.8†	9.1*

Note: Cells having common superscripts are not significantly different at the 0.05 level by the Duncan multiple-range test.

* Subjects assigned noise at intensity chosen by introverts.

† Subjects assigned noise at intensity chosen by extraverts.

It should also be noted that the introverts who were stimulated at the higher intensity level displayed a performance decrement on the learning task. Overall, the results of this study support the notion that both introverts and extraverts choose, when possible, a level of stimulation that induces a level of arousal that may be conducive to optimum performance on cognitive tasks.

EXTRAVERSION AND THE INVERTED-U

The differential effects of high and low intensity stimulation for introverts and extraverts prompted several experiments that examined the response to stimulation under conditions that were designed to manipulate tonic or base level of arousal. In general, it was expected that introverts, if they are indeed characterized by higher levels of arousal than extraverts, would show response decrements to high intensity stimulation under conditions that were designed to induce high levels of arousal (Gray, 1967). Again, this decrease in response amplitude to high intensity stimulation may be indicative of a protective mechanism. Moreover, such effects are broadly consistent with a curvilinear or inverted-U relationship between preferred level of stimulation and level of arousal. Remarkably consistent personality effects were reported with procedures that manipulated arousal level with task demands and with caffeine administration.

Fowles, Roberts and Nagel (1977) conducted several studies that compared SCL for introverts and extraverts with a series of high or moderate intensity tones. The stimuli were preceded by easy or difficult paired-associate learning tasks that were intended to induce high or low arousal states. When a difficult task preceded the tones, extraverts exhibited a greater increase in SCL to the high (103 dB) intensity tone than introverts. When the tones were preceded by a rest period, SCL was higher for introverts than extraverts, in particular for the moderate intensity tones. These results clearly demonstrated that introverts display a skin conductance decrement to high intensity stimulation while extraverts displayed a skin conductance increase.

Extraversion and the interactive effects of stimulation and base level of arousal was also examined by using caffeine to increase base level of arousal and a preparatory signal to reduce response amplitude (Smith, Wilson and Davidson, 1984). Groups of introverts and extraverts were administered either a low, medium, or high dosage of caffeine, or a placebo. Subjects were then stimulated with a series of tones of different intensities (60, 70, 80, 90, 100, and 110 dB). Half of the tones were preceded by a warning signal and half were not. Caffeine had the effect of increasing SCL, particularly for the introverted subjects. The most salient effect was the greater amplitude SCRs of introverted subjects to lower intensity tones (60–80 dB) during the placebo condition. Increasing caffeine dosage also had the effect of increasing SCR monotonically for the extraverted subjects. The preparatory signal had no effect on SCR amplitude for the extraverts. For the introverts, however, increasing caffeine dosage had the opposite effect of decreasing response amplitude, an effect that was attenuated when the tones were preceded by a warning signal. Overall, this study presents compelling evidence of the interactive effects of personality and response to stimulation under different conditions of tonic arousal level. The response to stimulation of introverts is seen to vary systematically, and in a manner that is consistent with their enhanced arousal or response to sensory stimulation.

SENSATION-SEEKING AND SKIN CONDUCTANCE RESPONSE

An interesting and paradoxical relationship among E–I, psychoticism (P), and sensation seeking has been noted by Stelmack, Plouffe and Falkenberg (1983). They pointed out that there is consistent evidence of a negative relationship between extraversion and electrodermal response to moderate intensity stimulation. It can also be argued that psychoticism, a scale of tough-mindedness, risk-taking and impulsiveness in Eysenck's typology, relates to electrodermal activity in a negative way. Paradoxically, sensation-seeking scales, which correlate positively with extraversion and psychoticism, have shown a positive relation to electrodermal response amplitude (Neary and Zuckerman, 1976). This paradox was examined in a study of habituation of the electrodermal response to two types of visual stimuli: simple words and pictures. Negative relationships between electrodermal response amplitude and extraversion and psychoticism to both pictures and words were observed. Sensation seeking was also negatively correlated with electrodermal response amplitude to the pictures. However, sensation seeking was positively correlated with the electrodermal response to words. When pre-experimental conductance levels were partialled out, the magnitude of both correlations was attenuated. This paradox led Stelmack and his associates to suggest the systematic manipulation of skin conductance levels, pharmacologically or through task demands, and to recommend the structuring of conditions to exploit such dispositions as need for novel stimulation and sensitivity to reward that were proposed as determinants of sensation seeking.

In a more recent experiment, the differential effects of relevant, novel stimulation on electrodermal activity were examined for groups of high and low sensation seekers (Smith *et al.*, 1986). Auditory and visual stimuli were selected that were relevant to items on the sensation-seeking scales, such as hang-gliding, marijuana smoking, mountain climbing and the like. The procedure also involved the presentation of neutral slides and audio-tape segments, words, and moderate intensity tones. High sensation seekers displayed larger initial response amplitudes than the low sensation seekers to all types of stimuli except the neutral stimulus items. The high sensation seekers also displayed higher skin conductance levels than low sensation seekers in the word condition, an observation that replicates the effect reported by Stelmack *et al.* (1983). As Smith, Rockwell-Tischer and Davidson (1986) suggest, these differences in electrodermal response between high and low sensation seekers "may be observable only under limited conditions involving novel stimulation having direct bearing on the sensation-seeking dimension".

EXTRAVERSION AND CARDIOVASCULAR ACTIVITY

A small number of studies address the question of whether introverts and extraverts differ in cardiovascular activity. The overall results are mixed and inconclusive. Whereas they found evidence of E–I differences in skin conductance and vasomotor activity, Stelmack *et al.* (1979) found no comparable differences in heart rate. On the other hand, Gange, Geen and Harkins (1979) observed higher heart rates in introverts than in extraverts in all conditions of an experiment on vigilance, including one in which no task was performed. Gange, Geen and Harkins found no E–I differences in heart rate during a baseline measurement period; their findings may indicate, therefore, that E–I differences reflect to some extent a reaction on the part of subjects to any sort of experimental procedures.

Others have proposed that heart rate change is associated with the nature of the stimulation given to the subject. Orlebeke and Feij (1979) argue that phasic deceleration is the cardiac component of the orienting response and that phasic acceleration is the cardiac component of the defensive response (Graham and Clifton, 1966). If a stimulus of high intensity is more stimulating for introverts than for extraverts, it should follow that introverts are more likely to react to such a stimulus with defensive heart rate acceleration than are extraverts. On the other hand, extraverts should be more likely than introverts to manifest heart rate deceleration to a stimulus of low intensity. Data reported by Orlebeke and Feij (1979) indicate that introverts responded to a tone of 60 dB intensity with a greater rate of cardiac acceleration than did extraverts. This finding is difficult to evaluate, however, in the absence of comparative data related to tones of greater or lesser intensity than the single one used in the study.

An experiment by Hirschman and Favaro (1980) sheds some additional light on the issue raised by Orlebeke and Feij. They presented subjects with photographs of persons who had died violently; earlier research had established that these pictures were highly aversive to viewers and, hence, likely to elicit defensive reactions. Hirschman and Favaro (1980) analysed differences between the average heart rate for the five beats that preceded each stimulus and each of the fifteen beats that followed it. They found that extraverts showed no change in rate over the first eight post-photograph beats, and continuous deceleration thereafter. Introverts showed an initial cardiac acceleration, followed by deceleration. Thus, the overall reactions of introverts and extraverts to the stimuli were consistent with the assumptions made by Orlebeke and Feij (1979).

In a study referred to earlier, Geen (1984) obtained findings suggesting that at high levels of stimulus aversiveness the usual extravert–introvert difference may not be found. Geen measured pulse rates of introverts and extraverts in response to four intensities of noise stimulation in the context of a learning experiment. The four intensities were derived from choices of noise level made by introverts and extraverts. Two intermediate intensities represented those chosen by Es and Is, respectively, as background noise during the task. The lowest intensity was that chosen by introverts as the lowest tolerable one (provided that it was greater than zero). The highest intensity was that chosen by extraverts as the highest tolerable one. By means of a yoked control design, equal numbers of Is and Es were exposed to the four noise intensity levels. The mean pulse rates of the two personality groups, shown in Figure 9.1, indicate that Is had higher rates than Es only when stimuli of the two intermediate intensities were given. These data are consistent with the view that arousal is related to stimulation in the form of an inverted U, with introverts showing maximum response rate at lower stimulation levels than extraverts.

OTHER PHYSIOLOGICAL CORRELATES OF EXTRAVERSION

Studies that attempt to show a relationship between extraversion–introversion and physiological variables other than those already discussed are few and

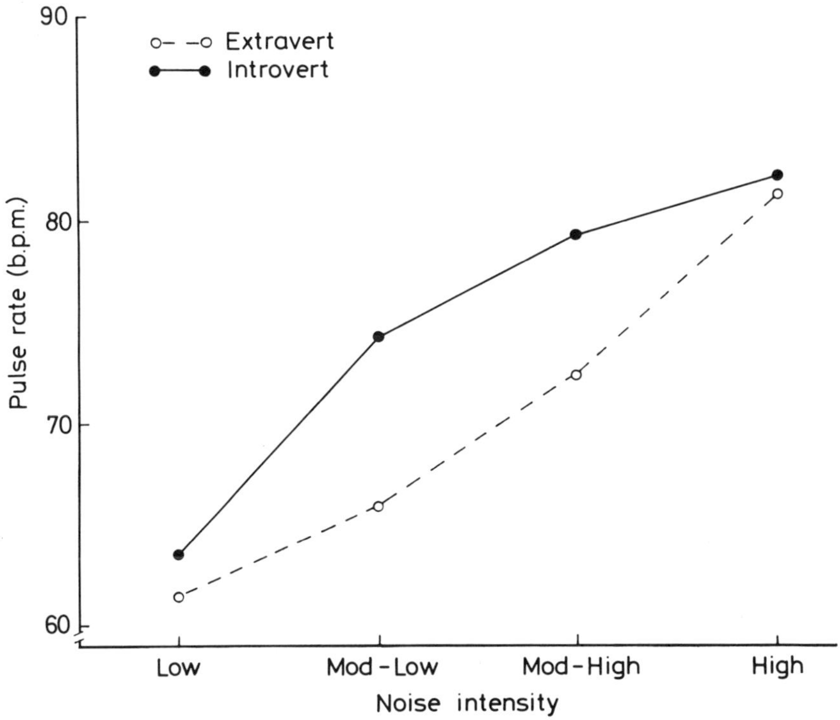

Figure 9.1. Mean pulse rates for introverts and extraverts during noise of four different intensity levels.

inconclusive. Faria and Drummond (1982) tested resting levels of systolic blood pressure in 30 males and found through a discriminant analysis that among several personality variables the one that discriminated best between hypertensives and normotensives was extraversion–introversion. In addition, the best combination of discriminator variables was E–I, social desirability, and the Type A behavior pattern. In two studies of E–I differences in pupillary activity, extraversion was found to be related to constriction (Holmes, 1967) and introversion to dilation (Stelmack and Mandelzys, 1975). In an investigation of personality variables involved in muscle potentials during task performance, Hinton and Craske (1976) found no differences related to extraversion–introversion.

A few attempts have been made to link extraversion–introversion to biochemical activity. Early investigations failed to find such links (Fine and Sweeney, 1968; Seagraves, 1970), but more recent studies indicate that a relationship may exist. Ballenger *et al.* (1983) examined the levels of neurotransmitters and their metabolites within the cerebrospinal fluid of

43 patients and found no relationship between E–I and either norepinephrine, its principal metabolite MHPG, or the enzyme DBH, which is involved in NE synthesis. They did find, however, that levels of calcium in the cerebrospinal fluid (which have been shown to be inversely related to arousal) were positively correlated with extraversion. CSF calcium was also negatively correlated with scores on the Social Introversion scale of the MMPI (a measure of neurotic introversion) and with scores on the neuroticism scale of the EPQ. Ballenger and his associates concluded that CSF Ca is positively related to stable extraversion. Finally, a study by Demisch *et al.* (1982) showed that levels of platelet monoamine oxidase (MAO) were correlated negatively with both extraversion and spontaneous aggressiveness in a sample of men. This evidence suggests that low platelet MAO activity is a characteristic of a disinhibited and impulsive personality and marks a promising beginning for establishing the biochemical bases of personality.

EXTRAVERSION AND THE ELECTROENCEPHALOGRAPH

The development of the electroencephalograph (EEG) was an important technological advance that offered researchers an objective method of recording bioelectric brain signals from scalp electrodes. EEG measures not only provided reliable indices of brain pathology but they proved to be valuable tools in the investigation of the physiological mechanisms that influence sleep, wakefulness, attention and arousal. The EEG was extensively employed to investigate individual differences in arousal between introverts and extraverts. Indeed, this psychophysiological technique was used for this purpose more than any other measure. The interest in the application of this method was consistent with a large body of research that examined the relationship between EEG measures and learning during the 1950s (Thompson, Patterson and Teyler, 1972). In particular, EEG desynchronization, that is the transition from low frequency, high amplitude activity to high frequency, low amplitude activity, was linked to attention and to response acquisition. The association between EEG desynchronization and activity in the ARAS was also well established. Enthusiasm for exploring learning processes with EEG measures has diminished considerably because of difficulties in establishing response specificity in the measures. Nevertheless, these lines of enquiry did enjoy considerable popularity for a time and the EEG methods were employed quite extensively to explore the basis for proposed differences in conditioning and socialization between introverts and extraverts.

The copious literature that addressed the arousal hypothesis with EEG techniques was periodically reviewed by Gale (1981; 1983). These reviews offer a detailed, technical assessment of research on extraversion and the EEG that will not be repeated in this review. Overall, it may be said that this body of work is disappointing because of pervasive weaknesses in methodology and design that characterize the research. There does seem to be a trend for more technically adequate and more recent work to conclude that extraverts are characterized by lower levels of arousal than introverts (e.g. Rösler, 1975; Golding and Richards, 1985). However, none of the effects reported are very impressive. For example, the lower level of cortical arousal for extraverts reported by Rösler was obtained with a high frequency EEG factor derived from a factor analysis of EEG data from only 32 subjects. The effect was apparent across a series of seven situations but was prominent in a stressful task in interaction with neuroticism. None of these effects have been replicated. In the Golding and Richards experiment, which also had considerable technical merit, the lower cortical arousal for extraverts was apparent for only one of nine EEG indices. In this case, more efficient photic driving at a lower frequency (16 Hz) rate of stimulation. In general, the conclusion drawn in a previous review of the EEG literature can be maintained (Stelmack, 1981). That is, the general direction of the results of these inquiries is towards higher levels of cortical activity for introverts under conditions intermediate between semi-somnolence and stressful. It may be noteworthy too that there is a conspicuous absence of differences between introverts and extraverts when they are compared on EEG measures recorded during sleep (cf. Thompson and Mueller, 1984). At this low end of the arousal continuum, at least, there is no evidence of differences in cortical arousal between introverts and extraverts.

EXTRAVERSION AND EVENT-RELATED POTENTIALS

Event-related potentials (ERP) are indices of electrocortical activity that develop in response to physical stimulation, and in the course of processing cognitive events such as attending to or remembering items. By averaging the electrocortical activity that is contingent on the repeated occurrence of an event, a consistent or characteristic ERP waveform for the event is extracted from the spontaneous EEG. This method allows the examination of event related activity that is often difficult to discern in the ongoing EEG activity. ERPs can be recorded for all sensory modalities, with each modality having a characteristic waveform under specific conditions. In general, the earlier in the waveform that a peak emerges, the more likely that the peak is determined by physical stimulus characteristics. Later peaks, such as positive going waves between 300 ms to 600 ms, are sensitive indices of selective attention and decision-making activity and thus they can be referred to endogenous cognitive processes. Several ERP paradigms were used to examine cortical activity that, on the basis of the arousal hypothesis, would be expected to differentiate introverts and extraverts.

EXTRAVERSION AND AUDITORY EVENT-RELATED POTENTIALS

Consistent with the arousal hypothesis, introverts are more sensitive than extraverts to auditory stimulation, as evidenced, for example, by psychophysical procedures (Stelmack and Campbell, 1974). Since the auditory ERP augments in amplitude with increasing stimulus intensity, it was reasonable to predict that the enhanced auditory sensitivity of introverts would be reflected in enhanced ERP responses. Although the research on this point is not univocal, there is good evidence showing that introverts display an enhanced response to moderate intensity tones. This effect, which develops about 200 ms after stimulation, may appear more clearly in some conditions than others. Low frequency tones, that show greater individual variability in ERP amplitude than high frequency tones, may be more effective than high frequency tones in differentiating introverts and extraverts (Stelmack, Achorn and Michaud, 1977). The greater amplitude response of introverts than extraverts to low frequency tones is illustrated in Figure 9.2. Stimulus presentations in which physical stimulus characteristics are varied within a series, either by alternating high and low tonal frequency or by varying intensity levels (Bruneau *et al.*, 1984) are more effective in demonstrating differences than when tones are presented in a simple repetitive series. When the interstimulus interval is short, the enhanced response of introverts is only observed in response to the first stimulus in a repetitive series (Stelmack and Michaud-Achorn, 1985). In this case response amplitude is greatly reduced after the first stimulus presentation, an effect which suggests that neural response recovery is incomplete. Varying stimulus characteristics such as intensity, frequency or duration within the series, procedures that facilitate response recovery or delay response habituation, may be necessary to promote effective comparisons between introverted and extraverted groups.

Notwithstanding these considerations, the greater auditory ERPs of introverts than extraverts that are cited in these reports endorse the arousal hypothesis. The effects were observed from electrodes at the vertex placement; potentials from this site are often regarded as non-specific since waveforms derived from auditory, visual, and somatosensory stimulation display a similar morphology. It is also clear, however, that this ERP wave receives input from specific sensory projection areas and therefore the effects may also refer to differences in sensory reactivity between introverts and extraverts (Näätänen and Picton, 1987).

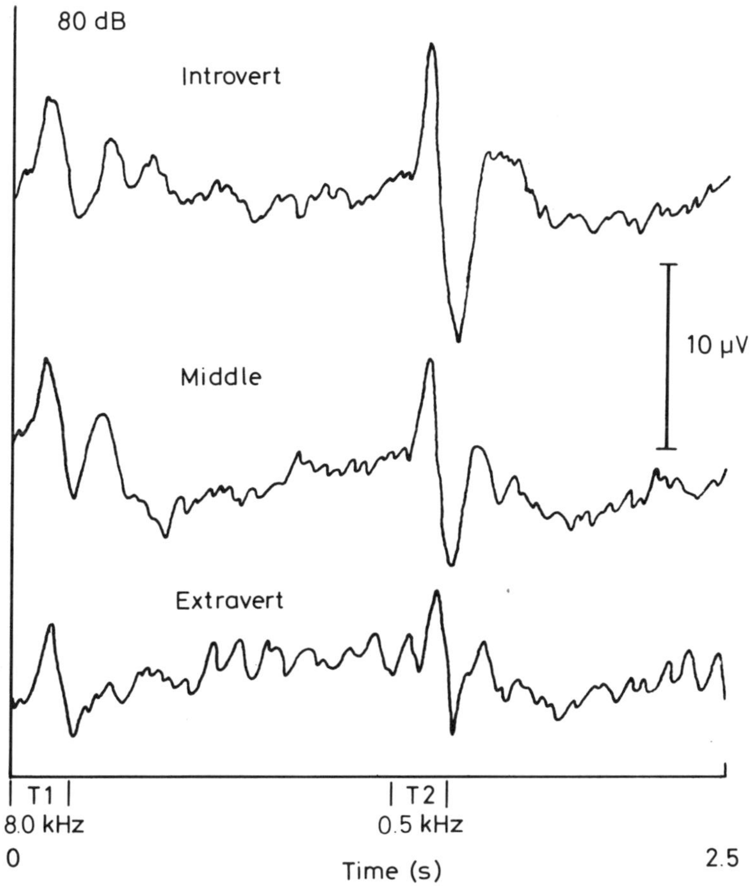

Figure 9.2. Amplitude of the auditory evoked response (N1P2) to high (8.0 kHz) and low (0.5 kHz) frequency 80 dB tones for introverts and extraverts.

EXTRAVERSION, ATTENTION, AND EVENT-RELATED POTENTIALS

As previously noted, activity in the ARAS is known to play an important role in attention as well as stimulus reception. There is some behavioral evidence indicating that introverts detect more infrequent signals in vigilance tasks than extraverts (cf. Geen, McCown and Broyles, 1985). The elaboration of attentional mechanisms with ERP methods has been approached in two ways, specifically, by manipulating attentional set and by manipulating frequency of stimulus occurrence. Attentional set was varied in the study by Stelmack and Michaud-Achorn (1985) by requiring subjects to either ignore or attend to a series of low frequency tones. In both conditions, introverts displayed larger amplitude of the N1P2 response complex, notably the positive wave of 200 ms, that was recorded from a central (Cz) electrode site. In the absence of any clear differences between the attend or ignore condition for either group, the effects could not be attributed to attentional mechanisms.

Differences between introverts and extraverts were also examined using a selective attention paradigm (Daruna, Karrer and Rosen, 1985). In this case, extreme groups of introverts and extraverts were instructed to predict the occurrence of high or low frequency tones. Responses were averaged for frequently occurring tones (80%), infrequently occurring tones (20%), and for the frequent tones which occurred prior to the rare tones. The amplitude of a positive wave at 350 ms (P3) was larger for the rare tones than the infrequent tones and showed maximum amplitude at a posterior (Pz) electrode site, a characteristic selective attention effect. As shown in Figure 9.3, introverts displayed larger amplitude ERPs for this positive wave at frontal, central and parietal sites and some differences were evident for all three tone conditions. The enhanced P3 response for introverts that was observed for the infrequent tone would seem to implicate differences in strength of response of attentional mechanisms. However, it is noteworthy that the enhanced response of introverts was also evident for the frequent tone conditions as well. Thus, the novelty or attentional demand of the stimulation cannot be solely responsible for the effects.

Overall, it seems clear that the enhanced response of introverts is apparent in attention paradigms that manipulate attentional set and frequency of stimulus occurrence. Whether these effects that were demonstrated are determined by general arousal mechanisms that pervade both the attention and control conditions or whether the effects refer to mechanisms which mediate the greater sensory sensitivity of introverts is not clear.

EXTRAVERSION AND SOMATOSENSORY EVOKED RESPONSES

A number of authors examined individual differences in extraversion using somatosensory ERPs that develop in response to repetitive electrical stimulation of the finger. Overall, the outcomes of these studies are not impressive. In the first study to report significant effects, introverts displayed larger amplitude responses than extaverts for an older sample of subjects but the reverse effect was observed with a group of younger subjects (Shagass and Schwartz, 1965). No significant effects were observed in several subsequent reports (Haseth, Shagass and Straumanis (1969); Maushammer, Ehmer and Eckel, 1981; Ashton *et al.*, 1985). In the most recent study, extraversion, psychoticism, and sensation seeking were associated with smaller somatosensory ERPs (Golding *et al.*, 1986). The technical and statistical merit of this report was superior to previous work. It should be noted that only a perimeter

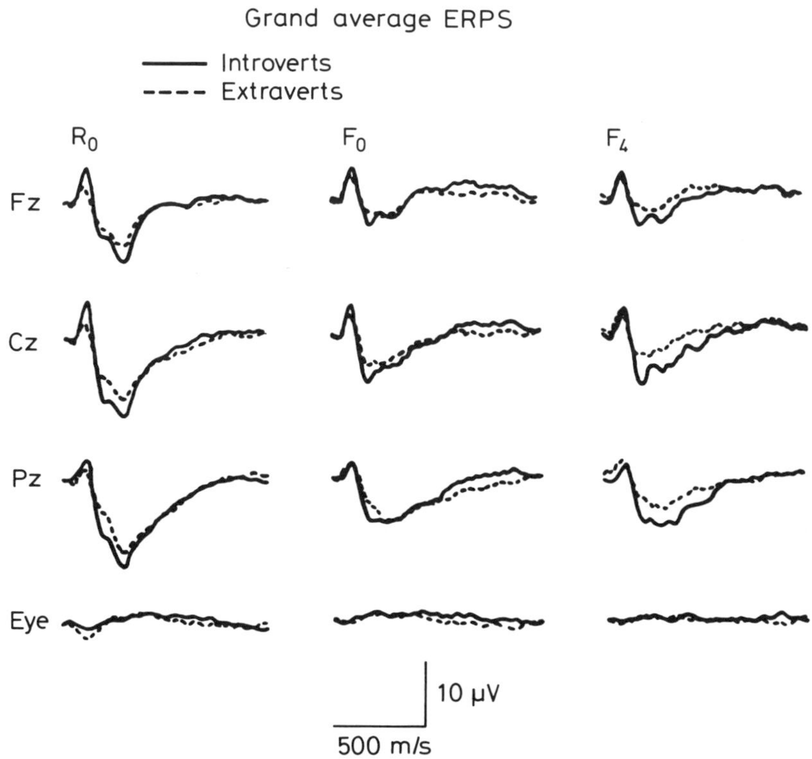

Figure 9.3. Amplitude of the auditory evoked response to rare (Ro) low frequency tones (0.6 kHz; 65 dB), frequent (Fo) high frequency tones (2.4 kHz, 65 dB) occurring immediately following a rare tone, and frequent (F4) tones occurring immediately before a rare tone.

amplitude measure revealed the effect but area and peak amplitude measures did not. Further, the effects tended to be stronger for psychoticism than for extraversion. Confidence in all of these reports is tempered by the unselected, and relatively small, samples from which the data were collected. Nevertheless, the direction of the effects, showing enhanced responses for introverts, is congruent with the effects observed with auditory ERPs and is indicative of the introvert's enhanced response to somatosensory stimulation.

SENSATION SEEKING AND AUGMENTING–REDUCING OF VISUAL EVOKED RESPONSES

Following the pioneering work of Buchsbaum and Silverman (1968), a number of authors have investigated individual differences in amplitude changes of visual ERPs to increases in the intensity of light flashes. Individuals who displayed an increase in amplitude with increasing intensity, as indicated by a positive slope, were termed stimulus augmenters; those who displayed a negative slope, showing a decrease in ERP amplitude with increasing stimulus intensity, were termed stimulus reducers. The procedure was heralded as a useful means of examining individual differences in stimulus modulation. There is general agreement that visual ERP amplitudes do not increase monotonically in all subjects; there is also some agreement that a reduction in amplitude occurs in some subjects when stimulus intensity is increased. The component which has been the principal focus of interest is a wave (P1N1) that develops at about 100 ms when recorded from a central vertex electrode. There are a number of studies which report that high sensation seekers, or more specifically, those who have higher scores on the disinhibition subscale, display visual ERP augmenting for this wave (Buchsbaum, 1971; Zuckerman, Murtaugh and Siegal, 1974; von Knorring, 1981; Lukas, 1987). There is also a fascinating demonstration that cats that display the augmenting phenomenon tend to be more active and inquisitive, similar to high sensation seekers, than cats who display the reducing effect (Lukas and Siegel, 1977).

The association of ERP augmenting and high sensation seeking was adduced in support of the view that sensation seeking is characterized by a need for novel stimulation to elevate the low arousal levels that prevail in the absence of such stimulation (Zuckerman, Buchsbaum and Murphy, 1980). In this regard, ERP augmenting is assumed to reflect the amplification of stimulation that is required to elevate the low arousal levels, while ERP reducing is indicative of a protective mechanism. There is some evidence that subjects who are characterized by lower arousal levels, as indexed by skin conductance measures, tend to display ERP augmenting, while higher skin conductance levels are associated with ERP reducing (Birchall and Claridge, 1979). This evidence is consistent with the sensory modulation function that is attributed to the augmenting–reducing effect. However, there does not seem to be a strong case to support the notion that sensation seekers amplify stimulation or experience simple physical stimulation more intensely than low sensation seekers. Indeed, what little evidence there is on this point would seem to indicate the contrary. Correlative studies show that high sensation seeking is associated with greater pain tolerance, greater extraversion, and less hypochondriasis (cf. Kohn, Hunt and Hoffman, 1982). Moreover, high sensation seekers have higher absolute sensory thresholds (Goldman, Kohn and Hunt, 1983), indicative of a relative insensitivity to stimulation and consistent with their greater pain tolerance as previously noted. From this perspective, it may be that sensation seekers expose themselves to more intense stimulating situations and activities, not because of a need for stimulation to increase arousal levels, but simply because of a relative insensitivity to strong stimulation.

It should also be noted that the association of ERP augmenting with sensation seeking is tempered by several considerations. First, there has been one large-scale project that reported that ERP reducers are high sensation seekers (Haier *et al.*, 1984). The only notable departure in procedure from previous work was that extreme ERP augmenting and reducing was used as the classification criterion and personality scores as the dependent measure rather than the reverse. Secondly, the relevance of the augmenting–reducing procedure has been challenged on the grounds that different methods of deriving intensity–ERP amplitude slopes yield different measures and in some circumstances, contradictory results. It is also the case that ERP augmenting observed at the central vertex electrode placement site may be accompanied by ERP reducing at the posterior occipital electrode placement (Connolly and Gruzelier, 1982). Finally, there is a recent study by Lukas (1987) that is exemplary for the control exercised over the stimulus presentation. In this case, augmenting was observed at both the vertex and occipital placements. As shown in Figure 9.4, both high and low disinhibition groups displayed similar augmenting slopes at the occiput, although the low disinhibition group appeared to display larger amplitude responses across all intensity levels. At the vertex placement, the high disinhibition group also augmented but the low disinhibition group produced the largest ERP amplitude to the next to lowest intensity level and did not display the augmenting effect.

Overall, the weight of the evidence associates sensation seeking or more

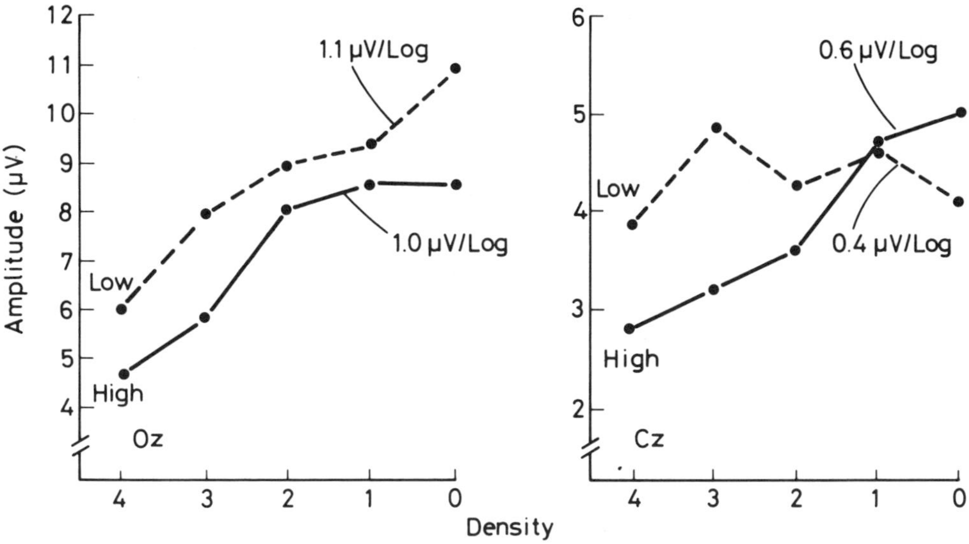

Figure 9.4. Amplitude of the visual evoked response (P1N1) to light flashes of increasing intensity (indexed by lower neutral density filter number) recorded from the vertex (Cz) and occipital (Oz) electrode placements for high and low disinhibition subjects on Zuckerman's Sensation Seeking Scale.

specifically, high disinhibition, with ERP augmenting. This effect has been observed with some consistency for the P1N1 wave recorded from the vertex placement despite rather marked differences in the method of scoring that component. The range of intensity levels employed to describe the extent and direction of ERP amplitude changes with increases in intensity also requires careful consideration, since there is some consensus that ERP reducing, when it occurs, is likely to develop at the highest intensity levels. Whether the ERP augmenting for the high disinhibition group refers to a disposition to amplify stimulation, in the service of enhanced sensory experience as Zuckerman claims, is an issue that has not been resolved. However, a number of behavioral effects can be seen to contradict this view.

EXTRAVERSION AND AUDITORY BRAINSTEM EVOKED RESPONSES

Auditory brainstem evoked responses (BER) develop within the first 10 ms of stimulation (Jewett and Williston, 1971). The neural generators of this waveform are better understood than the more commonly recorded waves that develop within 100 to 500 ms of stimulation. Wave I and Wave II of the BER emanate from the auditory nerve and cochlear nucleus respectively, while Wave V is determined primarily from activity at the inferior colliculus (Buchwald and Huang, 1977). Unlike the later waves, auditory BERs are remarkably invariant during different stages of sleep and arousal (Campbell and Bartoli, 1986) and even metabolic coma (Achor and Starr, 1980). The demonstration of differences between introverts and extraverts in their auditory BER, particularly in Waves I and II, would refer the differences to peripheral nervous system mechanisms that are relatively independent of the cortical arousal systems that were proposed to mediate differences in degree of extraversion (Eysenck, 1967; Gray *et al.*, 1983). That is, such effects could not be predicted from the activity of cortical arousal systems.

Introverts and extraverts were compared in their auditory BER to brief click stimuli that varied in intensity from 55 to 90 dB (Stelmack and Wilson, 1982). The most salient effects observed were positive correlations between extraversion and Wave I latency at the 75, 80 and 85 dB intensity levels. Thus, introversion is associated with faster response latencies. Similar effects have been observed by Andress and Church (1981) and by Szelenberger (1983) though null effects have been reported by Campbell, Baribeau-Braun, and Braun (1981). Since Wave I latency decreases with increasing stimulus intensity, the faster response latencies of introverts are congruent with their greater auditory sensitivity observed with psychophysical methods. However, a clear correspondence between intensity-loudness functions and intensity-BER latency functions has not been demonstrated (Wilson and

Stelmack, 1982); therefore, the convergence of BER latency and auditory sensitivity is uncertain. Nevertheless, the association of extraversion and Wave I latency refers differences between extraverts and introverts to the level of the auditory nerve and these effects are of potential significance to the neurological bases of extraversion that have been proposed. As previously noted, auditory BERs are largely unaffected by changes in sleep, attention, or arousal and thus the BER effects cannot be directly accounted for in terms of reticulo-cortical arousal mechanisms as described in Eysenck's (1967) theory of extraversion nor from the more complex system of limbic structures described in Gray's modification of Eysenck's theory. Although the olivocochlear bundle exercises an inhibitory influence on the auditory nerve, the inhibitory influence is reduced for intensities above the 75 dB range where extraversion differences are evident (Desmedt, 1975). Such inhibitory effects would, in any event, be independent of the reticular system. The auditory BER effects observed may require the elaboration of the neurological basis of extraversion, which currently focuses on individual differences in the brainstem reticular formation and mechanisms of the limbic system, to accommodate differences in axonal or synaptic transmission that are present in peripheral nervous system processes.

SENSATION SEEKING, EXTRAVERSION, AND MOTONEURONAL EXCITABILITY

Sensation seeking and extraversion are characterized by variation in a wide range of motor activities that are evident in both social and experimental settings. For example, both high sensation seekers and extraverts tend to be more impulsive, more physically active, more involved in contact sports (Zuckerman, 1983; Eysenck, Nias and Cox, 1982) and more restless in restricted environments (Zuckerman *et al.*, 1966; Gale, 1969) than subjects who obtain low scores on those scales. Introverts tend to perform more effectively than extraverts on tasks that demand refined motor control, such as pursuit-rotor tracking tasks (Frith, 1971), and they commit fewer false positive errors in reaction time tasks (Brebner and Flavell, 1978). Consideration of differences in the expression of motor behavior and control along the sensation seeking and extraversion dimensions has prompted the analysis of individual differences in spinal motoneuronal excitability.

In a recent experiment (Pivik, Stelmack and Bylsma, 1988), the response characteristics of compound muscle action potentials, the H-reflex, and associated motor responses were examined for a relatively large sample of subjects who were classified on the basis of their scores on the *Sensation Seeking Scales* and the *Eysenck Personality Questionnaire.* A paired stimulus method was employed to assess the extent of individual differences in reflex

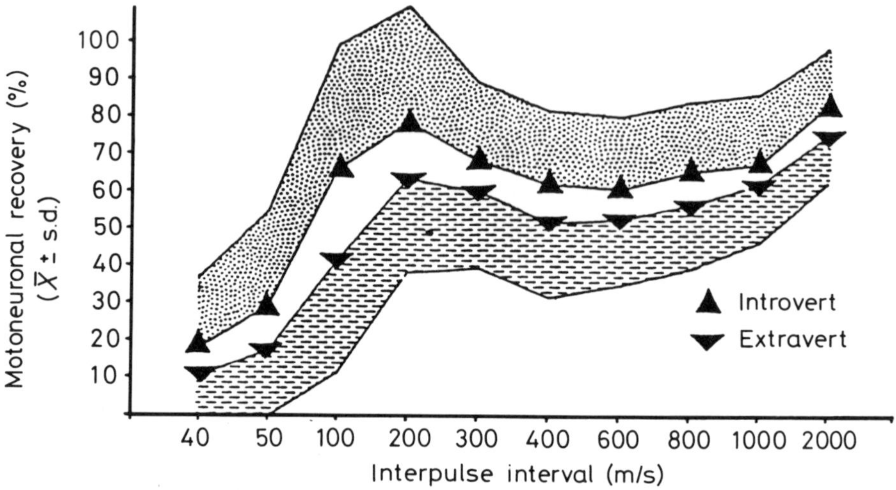

Figure 9.5. Percent motoneuronal recovery for introverts and extraverts at increasing interpulse intervals.

amplitude recovery by determining reflex response ratios for pairs of equal intensity electrical pulses. The pairs of stimuli were delivered every 10 s with the interpulse interval of the pairs ranging from 40 to 2000 ms. With increasing interpulse intervals, the reflex response amplitude of the second pulse increases, or recovers, relative to the first pulse. As shown in Figure 9.5, both high disinhibition and high extraversion groups displayed reduced motoneuronal excitability as determined by analysis of reflex recovery functions. These results demonstrate that differences in extraversion and disinhibition can be referred to discrete levels of CNS motor system activity.

Since the extraversion and disinhibition groups did not differ with respect to either the intensity of stimulation required to elicit muscle action potentials or the nerve conduction velocities of those potentials, the effects cannot be explained in terms of differences in initial hypoexcitability, or need for stimulation. Rather, the effects reflect reduced motor excitability that becomes evident once motoneuronal activity is initiated. It is also interesting to note that decreased motoneuronal excitability, as indexed by reflex recovery function measures, has been linked to increased dopaminergic activity. Both the high disinhibition and extravert groups have been found to exhibit low levels of monoamine oxidase and dopamine-beta-hydroxylase in the noradrenergic system (Umberkoman-Witta, Vogel and Wiita, 1981; Zuckerman *et al.*, 1983). These neuro-regulators can be associated with increased dopaminergic activity. Overall, the results of this study invite one to focus on the seeking, that is, the motor aspect of sensation-seeking and extraverted behavior, rather than sensation or the need for stimulation.

CONCLUSIONS

The past ten years define a period of deliberate progress in the exploration of the biological bases of personality, notably extraversion and sensation seeking, using psychophysiological methods. Both the successes and the failures of this research serve to enlighten our view of the neurological basis of personality. First, there has been a failure to demonstrate consistent differences between introverts and extraverts with either EEG measures or measures of skin conductance level under relaxed, resting conditions. Notwithstanding the difficulty in determining a truly resting, stimulation free condition, the exception being a sleep state, there is little evidence to indicate that introverts and extraverts differ in tonic or basal levels of physiological activity. There has been considerable success in demonstrating the enhanced response to stimulation of introverts with various modes of stimulation and methods of response recording. As suggested by Claridge some time ago (1967), it is useful to distinguish between arousal level and arousability with the latter being notably relevant to personality differences.

There is good evidence from both electrodermal and evoked potential recording methods that introverts display greater response to moderate intensity auditory stimulation. The electrodermal research that has manipulated tonic skin conductance level with stimulant agents such as caffeine is particularly impressive. This work demonstrates predictable interactive effects of arousal level and response to stimulation and, in general, endorses the view that introverts are more sensitive to stimulation than extraverts. Whether this enhanced sensitivity to stimulation refers the differences to central or peripheral nervous system mechanisms, or both, is uncertain. However, auditory brainstem evoked potential effects that were described would implicate differences at the level of the auditory nerve.

There is some consensus that sensation seeking is associated with visual ERP augmenting. There may be some argument regarding the interpretation of this effect. However, in our view, the increase in ERP amplitude maintained by high disinhibition subjects with increasing stimulus intensity converges with evidence associating sensation seeking with greater tolerance of intense or painful stimulation. That is, high disinhibition subjects are less sensitive or reactive to stimulation than low disinhibition subjects. Recent evidence shows that the enhanced electrodermal response of high sensation seekers may be observable with specific stimuli that are relevant to preferences and activities that define sensation seeking. These data may be helpful in resolving paradoxical electrodermal effects that have been reported. The demonstration of individual differences in motoneuronal excitability introduces a new direction in research that is relevant to both extraversion and sensation seeking. The method of determining motor reflex recovery may provide an interesting means of exploring motoneuronal mechanisms that influence the expression of individual differences in activity level and impulsiveness.

REFERENCES

Achor, J.L. and Starr, A. (1980) Auditory brainstem response in the cat. I. Intracranial and extracranial recordings. *Electroencephalography and Clinical Neurophysiology*, **48**, 154–173.

Andress, D.L. and Church, M.W. (1981) Differences in brainstem auditory evoked responses between introverts and extraverts as a function of stimulus intensity. *Psychophysiology*, **18**, 156 (Abstract).

Ashton, C.H., Golding, JF., Marsh, V.R. and Thompson, J.W. (1985) Somatosensory evoked potentials and personality. *Personality and Individual Differences*, **6**, 141–143.

Ballenger, J.C., Post, R.M., Jimerson, D.C., Lake, C.R., Murphy, D.L., Zuckerman, M. and Cronin, C. (1983) Biochemical correlates of personality traits in normals: an exploratory study. *Personality and Individual Differences*, **4**, 615–625.

Birchall, P.M.A. and Claridge, G.S. (1979) Augmenting-reducing of the visual evoked potential as a function of changes in skin conductance level. *Psychophysiology*, **16**, 482–490.

Brebner, J. and Flavell, R. (1978) The effect of catch-trials on speed and accuracy among introverts and extraverts in a simple RT task. *British Journal of Psychology*, **69**, 9–15.

Bruneau, W., Roux, S., Perse, J. and Lelord, G. (1984) Frontal evoked responses, stimulus intensity control, and the extraversion dimension. In R. Karrer, J. Cohen and P. Teuting (eds), Brain and information: event-related potentials. *Annals of the New York Academy of Sciences*, **425**, 546–550.

Buchsbaum, M. and Silverman, J. (1968) Stimulus intensity control and the cortical evoked response. *Psychosomatic Medicine*, **30**, 12–22.

Buchsbaum, M. (1971) Neural events and the psychophysical law. *Science*, **172**, 502.

Buchwald, J.S. and Huang, C.M. (1977) Interpretation of the vertex short-latency acoustic response: a study of single neurons in the brainstem. *Brain Research*, **137**, 291–303.

Campbell, K.B., Baribeau-Braun, J. and Braun, C. (1981) Neuroanatomical and physiological foundations of extraversion. *Psychophysiology*, **18**, 263–267.

Campbell, K.B. and Bartoli, E.A. (1986) Human auditory evoked potentials during natural sleep: the early components. *Electroencephalography and Clinical Neurophysiology*, **65**, 142–149.

Claridge, G.S. (1967) *Personality and Arousal.* London: Pergamon.

Coles, M.G.H., Gale, A. and Kline, P. (1971) Personality and habituation of the orienting reaction: tonic and response measures of electrodermal activity. *Psychophysiology*, **8**, 54–63.

Connolly, J.F. and Gruzelier, J.H. (1982) Amplitude and latency changes in the visual evoked potential to different stimulus intensities. *Psychophysiology*, **19**, 599–608.

Crider, A. and Lunn, R. (1971) Electrodermal lability as a personality dimension. *Journal of Experimental Research in Personality*, **5**, 145–150.

Daruna, J.H., Karrer, R. and Rosen, A.J. (1985) Introversion, attention and the late positive component of event-related potentials. *Biological Psychology*, **20**, 249–259.

Davis, C. and Cowles, M. (1988) A laboratory study of temperament and arousal: a test of Gale's hypothesis. *Journal of Research in Personality*, **22**, 101–116.

Demisch, L., Georgi, K., Patzke, B., Demisch, K. and Bochnik, J. (1982) Correlation of blood platelet MAO activity with introversion: a study on a German rural population. *Psychiatry Research*, **6**, 303–311.

Desmedt, J.E. (1975) Physiological studies of the efferent recurrent auditory system. In W.D. Keidel and W.D. Neff (eds), *Handbook of Sensory Physiology, Vol. 5*. Berlin: Springer.

Eysenck, H.J. (1967) *The Biological Basis of Personality*. Springfield, Ill.: Thomas.

Eysenck, H.J., Nias, D.K.B. and Cox, D.N. (1982) Sport and personality. *Advances in Behavior Research and Therapy*, **4**, 1–56.

Faria, I.E. and Drummond, B.J. (1982) Circadian changes in resting heart rate and body temperature, maximal oxygen consumption and perceived exertion. *Ergonomics*, **25**, 381–386.

Fine, B.J. and Sweeney, D.R. (1968) Personality traits, situational factors, and catecholamine excretion. *Journal of Experimental Research in Personality*, **3**, 15–27.

Fowles, D.C., Roberts, R. and Nagel, K. (1977) The influence of introversion/extraversion on the skin conductance response to stress and stimulus intensity. *Journal of Research in Personality*, **11**, 129–146.

Frith, C.D. (1971) Strategies in rotary pursuit tracking. *British Journal of Psychology*, **62**, 187–197.

Fulker, D.W., Eysenck, S.B.G. and Zuckerman, M. (1980) The genetics of sensation seeking. *Journal of Personality*, **14**, 261–281.

Gale, A. (1969) "Stimulus hunger": individual differences in operant strategy in a button-pressing task. *Behaviour Research and Therapy*, **7**, 263–274.

Gale, A. (1981) EEG studies of extraversion–introversion: what's the next step? In R. Lynn (ed.), *Dimensions of Personality: Papers in Honour of H.J. Eysenck*. Oxford: Pergamon.

Gale, A. (1983) Electroencephalographic studies of extraversion–introversion: a case study in the psychophysiology of individual differences. *Personality and Individual Differences*, **4**, 371–380.

Gange, J.J., Geen, R.G. and Harkins, S.G. (1979) Autonomic differences between extraverts and introverts during vigilance. *Psychophysiology*, **16**, 392–397.

Geen, R.G. (1983) The psychophysiology of extraversion–introversion. In J. Cacioppo and R. Petty (eds), *Social Psychophysiology: A Sourcebook*. New York: Guilford Press.

Geen, R.G. (1984) Preferred stimulation levels in introverts and extraverts: effects on arousal and performance. *Journal of Personality and Social Psychology*, **46**, 1303–1312.

Geen, R.G., McCown, E.J. and Broyles, J.W. (1985) Effects of noise on sensitivity of introverts and extraverts to signals in a vigilance task. *Personality and Individual Differences*, **6**, 237–241.

Golding, J.F. and Richards, M. (1985) EEG spectral analysis, visual evoked potential and photic driving correlates of personality and memory. *Personality and Individual Differences*, **6**, 67–76.

Golding, J.F., Ashton, C.H., Marsh, V.R. and Thompson, J.W. (1986) Early and late SEPs—the later the potential the greater the relevance to personality. *Personality and Individual Differences*, **7**, 787–794.

Goldman, D., Kohn, P.M. and Hunt, R.W. (1983) Sensation seeking, augmenting-reducing, and absolute auditory threshold: a strength of the nervous system perspective. *Journal of Personality and Social Psychology*, **45**, 405–411.

Graham, F.K. and Clifton, R.K. (1966) Heart rate change as a component of the orienting response. *Psychological Bulletin*, **65**, 305–320.

Gray, J.A. (1967) Strength of the nervous system, introversion–extraversion, conditionability and arousal. *Behaviour Research and Therapy*, **5**, 151–169.

Gray, J.A. (1973) Causal theories and how to test them. In J.R. Royce (ed.), *Multivariate analysis and Psychological Theory*. New York: Academic Press.

Gray, J.A., Owen, S., Davis, N. and Eleftheria, T. (1983) Psychological and physiological relations between anxiety and impulsivity. In M. Zuckerman (ed.), *Biological Bases of Sensation-seeking, Impulsivity and Anxiety*. Hillsdale, NJ: Erlbaum.

Haier, R.J., Robinson, D.L., Braden, W. and Williams, D. (1984) Evoked potential augmenting-reducing and personality differences. *Personality and Individual Differences*, **5**, 293–301.

Haseth, K., Shagass, C. and Straumanis, J.J. (1969) Perceptual and personality correlates of EEG and evoked response measures. *Biological Psychiatry*, **1**, 49–69.

Hastrup, J.L. and Katkin, E.S. (1976) Electrodermal lability: an attempt to measure its psychophysiological correlates. *Psychophysiology*, **13**, 296–301.

Hastrup, J.L. (1979) Effects of electrodermal lability and introversion on vigilance decrement. *Psychophysiology*, **16**, 302–310.

Hinton, J. and Craske, B. (1976) A relationship between Eysenck's P scale and change in muscle action potentials with attention to perceptual tasks. *British Journal of Psychology*, **67**, 461–466.

Hirschman, R. and Favaro, L. (1980) Individual differences in imagery vividness and voluntary heart rate control. *Personality and Individual Differences*, **1**, 129–133.

Holmes, D.S. (1967) Pupillary response, conditioning and personality. *Journal of Personality and Social Psychology*, **5**, 98–103.

Jewett, D.L. and Williston, J.S. (1971) Auditory-evoked far fields averaged from the scalp of humans. *Brain*, **94**, 681–696.

Kohn, P.M., Hunt, R.W. and Hoffman, F.M. (1982) Aspects of experience seeking. *Canadian Journal of Behavioral Science*, **14**, 13–23.

Kohn, P.M. (1987) Issues in the measurement of arousability. In J. Strelau and H.J. Eysenck (eds), *Personality Dimensions and Arousal*. New York: Plenum.

Koriat, A., Averill, J.R. and Malmstrom, E.J. (1973) Individual differences in habituation: some methodological and conceptual issues. *Journal of Research in Personality*, **7**, 88–101.

von Knorring, L. (1981) Visual averaged evoked responses and platelet monoamine oxidase in patients suffering from alcoholism. In H. Begleiter (ed.), *The Biological Effects of Alcohol*. New York: Plenum.

Lukas, J.H. (1987) Visual evoked potential augmenting–reducing and personality: the vertex augmenter is a sensation seeker. *Personality and Individual Differences*, **8**, 385–395.

Lukas, J.H. and Siegal, J. (1977) Cortical mechanisms that augment or reduce evoked potentials in cats. *Science*, **198**, 73–75.

Mangan, G.L. and O'Gorman, J.G. (1969) Initial amplitude and rate of habituation of orienting reaction in relation to extraversion and neuroticism. *Journal of Experimental Research in Personality*, **3**, 275–282.

Martin, I. and Venables, P.H. (eds) (1980) *Techniques in Psychophysiology*. New York: Wiley.

Maushammer, C., Ehmer, G. and Eckel, K. (1981) Pain, personality and individual differences in sensory evoked potentials. *Personality and Individual Differences*, **2**, 335–336.

Näätänen, R. and Picton, T.W. (1987) The N1 wave of the human electric and magnetic response to sound: a review and an analysis of the component of structure. *Psychophysiology*, **24**, 375–425.

Neary, R.S. and Zuckerman, M. (1976) Sensation seeking, trait and state anxiety and the electrodermal orienting reflex. *Psychophysiology*, **13**, 205–211.

Nielson, T.C. and Petersen, K.E. (1976) Electrodermal correlates of extraversion, trait anxiety, and schizophrenism. *Scandinavian Journal of Psychology*, **17**, 73–80.

Orlebeke, J.F. and Feij, J.A. (1979) The orienting reflex as a personality correlate. In H.D. Kimmel, E.H. van Olst, and J.F. Orlebeke (eds), *The Orienting Reflex in Humans*. Hillsdale, NJ: Erlbaum, pp. 567–585.

Pivik, R.T., Stelmack, R.M. and Bylsma, F.W. (1988) Personality and individual differences in spinal motoneuronal excitability. *Psychophysiology*, **25**, 16–24.

Raskin, D.C. (1973) Attention and arousal. In W.F. Prokasy and D.C. Raskin (eds), *Electrodermal Activity in Psychological Research*. New York: Academic Press.

Rösler, F. (1975) Die abhangigkeit des electroenzephalogramms von den person lichkeitsdimentionen E und N sensu Eysenck und unterschiedlich aktivierdenden situationen. *Z. exp. angew. Psychol.*, **12**, 630–667.

Sadler, T.G., Mefferd, R.B. and Houck, R.L. (1971) The interaction of extraversion and neuroticism in orienting response habituation. *Psychophysiology*, **8**, 312–318.

Seagraves, R.T. (1970) Personality, body-build, and adrenocortical activity. *British Journal of Psychiatry*, **117**, 405–411.

Siddle, D.A.T. (1971) The orienting response and distraction. *Australian Journal of Psychology*, **23**, 261–265.

Shagass, C. and Schwartz, M. (1965) Age, personality and somatosensory evoked responses. *Science*, **148**, 1359–1361.

Smith, B.D. and Wigglesworth, M.J. (1978) Extraversion and neuroticism in orienting reflex dishabituation. *Journal of Research in Personality*, **12**, 284–296.

Smith, B.D., Rypma, C.B. and Wilson, R.J. (1981) The electrodermal OR: effects of caffeine, extraversion and impulsivity on dishabituation and spontaneous recovery. *Journal of Research in Personality*, **15**, 233–240.

Smith, B.D., Wilson, R.J. and Jones, B.E. (1983) Extraversion and multiple levels of caffeine-induced arousal: effects of overhabituation and dishabituation. *Psychophysiology*, **15**, 29–34.

Smith, B.D. (1983) Extraversion and electrodermal activity: arousability and the inverted-U. *Personality and Individual Differences*, **4**, 411–420.

Smith, B.D., Wilson, R.J. and Davidson, R.A. (1984) Electrodermal activity and extraversion: caffeine, preparatory signal and stimulus intensity effects. *Personality and Individual Differences*, **5**, 59–65.

Smith, B.D., Rockwell-Tischer, S. and Davidson, R. (1986) Extraversion and arousal: effects of attentional conditions on electrodermal activity. *Personality and Individual Differences*, **7**, 293–303.

Smith, B.D., Perlstein, W.M., Davidson, R.A. and Michael, K. (1986) Sensation seeking: differential effects of relevant, novel stimulation on electrodermal activity. *Personality and Individual Differences*, **7**, 445–452.

Sokolov, E.N. (1963) *Perception and the Conditioned Reflex*. London: Pergamon Press.

Sostek, A.J. (1978) Effect of electrodermal lability and payoff instructions on vigilance performance. *Psychophysiology*, **15**, 561–568.

Stelmack, R.M. and Campbell, K.B. (1974) Extraversion and auditory sensitivity to high and low frequency tones. *Perceptual and Motor Skills*, **38**, 875–879.

Stelmack, R.M. and Mandelzys, N. (1975) Extraversion and pupillary response to affective and taboo words. *Psychophysiology*, **12**, 536–540.

Stelmack, R.M., Achorn, E. and Michaud, A. (1977) Extraversion and individual differences in auditory evoked response. *Psychophysiology*, **14**, 368–374.

Stelmack, R.M., Bourgeois, R.P., Chain, J. and Pickard, C.W. (1979) Extraversion and the orienting reaction habituation rate to visual stimuli. *Journal of Research in Personality*, **13**, 49–58.

Stelmack, R.M. (1981) The psychophysiology of extraversion and neuroticism. In H.J. Eysenck (ed.), *A Model for Personality*. Heidelberg: Springer-Verlag.

Stelmack, R.M. and Wilson, K.G. (1982) Extraversion and the effects of frequency and intensity on the auditory brainstem evoked response. *Personality and Individual Differences*, **3**, 373–380.

Stelmack, R.M., Plouffe, L. and Falkenberg, W. (1983) Extraversion, sensation seeking, and electrodermal response: probing a paradox. *Personality and Individual Differences*, **4**, 607–614.

Stelmack, R.M. and Michaud-Achorn, A. (1985) Extraversion, attention, and habituation of the auditory evoked response. *Journal of Research in Personality*, **19**, 416–428.

Szelenberger, W. (1983) Brain stem auditory evoked potentials and personality. *Biological Psychiatry*, **18**, 157–174.

Thompson, R.F., Patterson, M.M. and Tyler, P.J. (1972) Neurophysiology of learning. *Annual Review of Psychology*, **23**, 73–104.

Thompson, W.B. and Mueller, J.H. (1984) Extraversion and sleep: a psychophysiological study of the arousal hypothesis. *Personality and Individual Differences*, **5**, 345–564.

Umberkoman-Wiita, B., Vogel, W.H. and Wiita, P.J. (1981) Some biochemical and behavioral (sensation seeking) correlates in healthy adults. *Research Communications in Psychology, Psychiatry and Behavior*, **6**, 303–316.

Venables, P.H. and Christie, M.J. (1973) Mechanisms, instrumentation, recording techniques, and quantification of responses. In W.F. Prokasy and D.C. Raskin (eds), *Electrodermal Activity in Psychological Research*. New York: Academic Press.

Wigglesworth, M.J. and Smith, B.D. (1976) Habituation and dishabituation of the electrodermal orienting reflex in relation to extraversion and neuroticism. *Journal of Research in Personality*, **10**, 437–445.

Wilson, K.G. and Stelmack, R.M. (1982) Power functions of loudness magnitude estimations and auditory brainstem evoked responses. *Perception and Psychophysics*, **31**, 561–564.

Zuckerman, M. (1969) Theoretical foundations I. In J.P. Zubek (ed.), *Sensory Deprivation: Fifteen Years of Research*. New York: Appleton-Century.

Zuckerman, M. (1979) *Sensation Seeking: Beyond the Optimum Level of Arousal*. Hillsdale, NJ: Erlbaum.

Zuckerman, M. (1983) Sensation seeking and sports. *Personality and Individual Differences*, **4**, 285–292.

Zuckerman, M. (1984) Sensation seeking: a comparative approach to a human trait. *Behavioral and Brain Sciences*, **7**, 413–471.

Zuckerman, M., Persky, H., Hopkins, T.R., Murtaugh, T., Basu, G.K. and Schilling, M. (1966) Comparison of stress effects of perceptual and social isolation. *Archives of General Psychiatry*, **14**, 356–365.

Zuckerman, M., Murtagh, T.M. and Siegel, J. (1974) Sensation seeking and cortical augmenting-reducing. *Psychophysiology*, **11**, 535–542.

Zuckerman, M., Buchsbaum, M.S. and Murphy, D.L. (1980) Sensation seeking and its biological correlates. *Psychological Bulletin*, **88**, 187–214.

Zuckerman, M., Ballenger, J.C., Jimerson, D.C., Murphy, D.L. and Post, R.M. (1983) A correlational test in humans of the biological models of sensation seeking, impulsivity and anxiety. In M. Zuckerman (ed.), *Biological Bases of Sensation Seeking, Impulsivity and Anxiety*. Hillsdale, NJ: Erlbaum.

Chapter 10

Brain Electrical Potentials and Intelligence

P.T. Barrett

Luton College of Higher Education, Faculty of Business, Fairview House, Park Square, Luton, Bedfordshire, LU1 3JU, UK

and

H.J. Eysenck

Institute of Psychiatry, Department of Psychology, University of London, De Crespigny Park, Denmark Hill, London, SE5 8AF, UK

ABSTRACT

The relationship between spontaneous EEG, AEP parameters, and psychometric test intelligence is examined. The weight of evidence indicates that these variables are related to some extent, although with so many non-replications of key AEP parameter relationships, it is open to question whether the current EEG/AEP experiment paradigms are adequate to allow the construct of *biological intelligence* to be assessed in any psychometrically valid form. In addition to the general review, Robinson's neuropsychological model and its predictions are also examined in depth using empirical data. It is concluded that Robinson's results, on which the bulk of his model depends, remain unreplicated. Finally, three recommendations are made concerning the methodological procedures to be used by investigators in this area. These recommendations address the problems of sample size and the psychometrics used in computing both the psychological and psychometric variables.

Handbook of Individual Differences: Biological Perspectives
Edited by Anthony Gale and Michael W. Eysenck

INTRODUCTION

The term "intelligence" is used in many different ways. In the Sternberg and Detterman (1986) book, up to 25 definitions are proposed by a variety of psychologists active in the field. From these definitions, it is apparent that intelligence can be viewed from three facets of understanding, the biological, psychometric, and social. Depending upon the reader's viewpoint or attribution of causality of intelligent behaviour, any number of explanations, models, or theories can be proposed at differing levels of specification and generality. While social intelligence may be comfortable to deal with as it appears the most equitable and least divisive of the facets (as in the current vogue for assessing individual differences in supermarket shopping "ability"), it is also the least well defined and lacks little or no measurement structure or empirical conceptual validity. Psychometric intelligence, the most empirically precise of the facets, is the concept addressed by problem solving/reasoning tests of both verbal and non-verbal form. The term *biological intelligence* has been coined recently as some structural precursor to the other two facets of intelligence, psychometric and social. Measures taken from various biological systems (mainly the brain or sensory nerve fibres) and correlated with psychometric intelligence test scores have suggested patterns of relationships between the two facets. This has, in recent years, spawned a variety of elegant and not so elegant explanations, models, and grand theories, culminating in Robinson's neuropsychological model of personality and individual differences.

While social intelligence may be viewed as the most practical and day-to-day attempted expression of intelligent behaviour, it has to date proved useless as a measurement construct against which to compare other facets of behaviour. Only psychometric intelligence has the measurement definition, structure, and validity that enable comparisons between it and any other facet of behaviour or any biological measure. Behavioural genetics provides further embellishment for the construct in that individual differences in psychometric test scores do have a proven sizeable genetic component of about 70% heritability with monozygotic twins (Bouchard *et al.*, 1990). Finally, psychometric test scores do have predictive validity across a wide range of economic, social, and educational variables. So, although psychometric test items appear to have little in common with day-to-day behaviours, the test scores based upon these items are powerful indicators of certain major real-world variables (Eysenck, 1979). Hence, correlating biological measures with these psychometric measures is a procedure pregnant with implications beyond the novelty of observing such relationships. Of course, the first step is to demonstrate consistent, sizeable, and replicable relationships between the biological and psychometric facets. As will be seen below, this is easier said than done!

The study of brain electrical potentials has generally followed two methodologies: spontaneous EEG and evoked potential EEG. The first has concentrated on electrical activity recorded over periods of time generally greater than about 1 min. Parameters extracted from analysis of this activity are basically descriptive of electrical power and waveform frequency. The second methodology has concentrated on activity recorded over very short periods of time, generally from 0.25 to 2 s. This activity is evoked from an individual by presentation of well-defined stimuli or by requiring cognitive performance or motor actions from the individual.

The naive reader might assume that in an area as socially sensitive and psychologically fundamental as this, the methodology and technical awareness of the investigators would be beyond question. Unfortunately this is all too often not the case at all. Brain electrical potentials are very small (down to 1 or 2 μV) and of low frequency (between 1–100 Hz). Noise (electrical mains, computer bus transients and harmonics, earth loops, and electrode instability) can easily surpass EEG power at particular frequencies. Transient spikes due to local device current switching, fluorescent light use, and high voltage transformer supplies can play havoc with spontaneous EEG recording. Worst of all is the insidious low frequency harmonics from badly screened computer hard disc drives, processors, and colour screen driver boards. These can be seen (using appropriate digital signal processing analysis) down in the 20–40 Hz EEG bands at the same power as one might expect from an individual's brain activity. Assuming the investigators can conquer these difficulties, the next hurdle in the measurement process is collecting data, identifying "bad spots", and finally producing parameters with which to correlate the psychometric test scores. It is here that investigators' enthusiasm for results sometimes curtails their objectivity of analysis! Therefore, in the discourse below, we shall attempt to provide some expert guidance and critical appraisal for the reader with regard to certain key studies in the area. Two more general reviews of the area are Eysenck and Barrett (1985), and a particularly outstanding and comprehensive review by Deary and Caryl (1991).

SPONTANEOUS EEG

The ongoing electrical activity of the brain is an obvious source of data for the psychophysiological recording of events possibly related to IQ, but a careful survey by Lindsley (1961) showed quite early on that there is no clear-cut relation in normal adults, although in early childhood (when slower gamma and delta waves give way to faster and prevalent alpha) and in brain-injured persons (Ostow, 1954) some relationships are found. Among younger children and mental defectives, or deteriorated adults with a mental age of between 6 and 10, the correlations range from 0.3 to 0.6 between mental age and more rapid, developed alpha rhythm. Netchine and Netchine (1962) have suggested that correlations with mental age are high if one takes a compound index of alpha frequency with amplitude and certain patterns of the EEG, but the suggestion has not been followed up.

Ellingson (1966), in his review, stated that there was little he could feel confident about other than the rather obvious fact that the EEG signs of gross brain lesions and epilepsy were more common in retarded individuals. Vogel and Broverman (1964, 1966) objected and put forward evidence that in normal children mental age and alpha frequency are correlated, when age and sex are held constant. With the advent of quantitative EEG analysis, new possibilities arose. A landmark was the developmental Goteborg study (Matousek and Petersen, 1973) using six absolute and six relative broad band spectral parameters. Bosaeus, Matousek and Petersen (1977) reported results from a study using 138 normal children aged between 6 and 16 years, using computerized broad spectral band EEG parameters computed from multichannel EEG recordings. Theta power at the parieto-occipital derivations showed the largest correlations (–0.21) with the WISC IQ test (age was partialled out from all correlations).

Recently, Gasser and co-workers (Gasser *et al.*, 1983b; Gasser, 1983a; Gasser, Bacher and Steinberg, 1985) have reported correlations between spectral power and IQ, averaging about 0.5 in children. All EEG parameters were standardized for age as were the tests of intelligence (the Wechsler Intelligence Scales for Children (WISC) verbal subtest and the Columbia Mental Maturity Scale). A group of mentally retarded children ($N = 25$) also used in the 1983 Gasser *et al.* study were shown to generate higher EEG × IQ correlations (averaging about 0.6) than the normal children group ($N = 31$). Gasser *et al.* (1985) demonstrated that the test–retest reliability for absolute and relative spectral power within the six power bands was mostly in the range of 0.60–0.75 ($N = 26$ subjects). Gasser *et al.* linked this finding with earlier work on developmental indices; thus in a sense their findings are concordant with earlier related investigations rather than simply ad hoc observations.

Giannitrapani (1985) has recently published a monograph detailing extensive investigations into the localization of EEG spectral power and mental abilities as assessed by the WISC and Wechsler Adult Intelligence Scales (WAIS). EEG was acquired under eight conditions ranging from white noise, music, complex visual patterns, to solving arithmetic problems. Sixteen monopolar electrode placements were used encompassing prefrontal to occipital placements. The main results from the analysis indicated that performance on the various subtests of the WISC and WAIS was significantly related to EEG power at specific frequencies within specific brain areas. The monograph represents a benchmark, not only for the results but also as an exposition of the experimental techniques necessary for future research in this area.

Finally, Thatcher *et al.* (1983) and Gasser, Jennen-Steinmetz and Verlager (1987) examined the spectral coherence of the EEG from various scalp regions of children, coherence being defined as the similarity estimate of power generated at a particular frequency across two signal channels over a fixed duration. The function varies between +1 and –1, and can be interpreted (and manipulated) much in the same way as a product moment correlation. A coherence value of +1 would indicate that both signals (say from two regions of the brain) have the same power at a particular frequency within a particular duration. The Gasser *et al.* study reported results from the same children as those used in their previous studies. Thatcher *et al*'s sample consisted of 191 children aged between 5 and 16 years; they partialled out age and sex before examining the coherence measures. Overall, both studies showed that higher coherence values were associated with lower IQ. That is, the higher the IQ, the more differentiated the brain activity between scalp regions. Within Gasser *et al*'s mentally retarded group of children, the coherence values were appreciably higher than observed in the normal control group of children. These two studies are an important indicator that one index of biological intelligence may simply be the amount of brain *used* by an individual in any problem solving task. In the EEG area, *use* is being inferred from the disruption of semi-stable background frequency generation across various scalp locations. Two other ways to assess *use* more directly is to examine cerebral regional blood-flow (see reviews by Risberg, 1980; 1986) or regional metabolism of brain nutrients and neurotransmitter activity via positron emission tomography (PET) or a magnetic resonance imaging (MRI). It is fair to say that with the advent of the PET and MRI methodology, and to a lesser extent, the neuromagnetic field recording techniques, regional blood-flow measures cannot match the latter two techniques in terms of spatial resolution and accuracy of measurement. We shall return to these new technologies and their implications below, especially with regard to the increasing obsolescence of electrical brain activity recording.

EVOKED POTENTIAL EEG

From the late 1960s onwards, a systematic body of evidence has been produced indicating several relationships between parameters computed from specific features of averaged evoked potentials (AEPs) and IQ/intelligence test scores. From the spontaneous EEG work had come indications that greater power at higher waveform frequencies might be associated with higher IQ individuals. In addition, the first laboratory digital computers and fast signal processing algorithms were entering the laboratories, enabling the recording of stimulus responses by the brain, over durations less than 1 second. Thus, investigators could at last begin evoking specific responses from the brain, determined and manipulated by a specific stimulus type. Given the pervasive notion that the mental functions of high IQ individuals may work faster in some way than those in low IQ individuals (the mental speed hypothesis), it was not unreasonable that the first reported study examining AEP parameters and IQ test scores should focus on AEP parameter latencies (Chalke and Ertl, 1965). Short visual AEP component peak latencies were found to correlate with high IQ in a group of 48 subjects. This work was replicated and extended further by Ertl and Schafer (1969), Ertl (1971, 1973), Bennett (1968), Shucard and Horn (1972), Hendrickson (reported in Eysenck, 1973, p. 429), Weinberg (1969), and Gucker (1973). The average correlation found across these various studies was about –0.30. However, several investigators were unable to obtain replication of these results (Rhodes, Dustman and Beck, 1969; Dustman and Beck, 1972; Dustman, Schenkenberg and Beck, 1975; Lewis, Rimland and Callaway, 1976; 1977; Davis, 1971; Rust, 1975), generally finding zero or slightly positive correlations between latencies and IQ. Engel and Henderson's (1973) study of 119 children led them to conclude that no relationship existed between visual evoked response latencies and IQ. This was a significant study in that their methodology was good and the subject numbers large. Eysenck and Barrett (1985) discuss more fully this issue and some reasons for the non-replication of Ertl's initial results. One important issue here was the selection of subject groups. Ertl tended to use polarized IQ groups (high versus low IQ) rather than a normal range, a point made specially by Dustman *et al.* (1975) who concluded that the small latency–IQ relationship could only be demonstrated using extreme subject groups.

In addition to the analysis of the AEPs in terms of component latencies, Ertl (1971; 1973), Osaka and Osaka (1980), and Shucard and Callaway (1973) also computed their power spectra. From these analyses they concluded that the amplitude of the maximum spectral frequency did not correlate significantly with IQ. However, Flinn, Kirsch and Flinn (1977) in a similar analysis found that low IQ subjects had larger low frequency (< 12 Hz) amplitudes than high IQ subjects. In addition, high IQ subjects were found to have significantly larger high frequency (> 30 Hz) components than low IQ subjects. The correlation between IQ and amplitude within the lower frequency power bands was about –0.37. For the higher frequency bands it averaged about 0.36. These correlations were computed over 64 12-year-old girls.

Recently, Hendrickson and Hendrickson (1980), Blinkhorn and Hendrickson (1982), and Hendrickson and Hendrickson (1982) have provided new evidence on the correlation of IQ with AEP parameters. Based upon a novel model of synaptic structure, function, and nerve transmission, the Hendricksons derived two measures that could be extracted from an AEP.

A complexity measure (otherwise known as the *string* measure) was assessed by computing the contour perimeter of the AEP waveform; the larger this value, the higher an individual's IQ. (As Deary and Caryl (1991) noted, Rhodes, Dustman and Beck (1969) had used a map wheel measure of total excursion of an AEP waveform. This measure can be said to have anticipated the Hendrickson string measure by several years!) The second measure, the *variance*, was computed by taking the average variability of each sample point on an AEP over a number of epochs. The greater the variance, the lower an individual's IQ. Essentially they have proposed that the neural transmission characteristics of high IQ individuals is such that fewer propagation/transmission errors are made than is the case with low IQ individuals. Consequently, within the AEP, high IQ individuals will tend to have more complex AEPs, the individual component traces being less variable from trial to trial, thus preserving more of the detail of the single evoked potential response. In contrast, the low IQ individuals will produce a more varied evoked response from trial to trial, yielding (when averaged) a smoother, less complex AEP. Thus, the high IQ AEP should yield a longer string measure than the low IQ AEP, and the variability measure should yield a lower value than that for low IQ AEPs. The Hendricksons maintained that a crucial factor in successfully determining the measures was the use of a constant stimulus with replicable signal characteristics of amplitude, duration, and frequency, i.e. no switching transients and no click stimuli.

The empirical evidence regarding the complexity/variance of the AEP is drawn from two studies. The first, reported by Blinkhorn and Hendrickson (1982), correlated the complexity (string) measure with performance on Raven's Advanced Progressive Matrices (APM) and a variety of verbal ability tests. Specifically, data were collected from 17 male and 16 female students. Auditory AEPs were generated, the stimulus consisting of a 1000-Hz sine wave tone, of 30 m/s duration, switched at the zero-crossing point and presented binaurally through headphones at 85 dB SPL. The interstimulus interval was quasi-random between 1 and 8 s. The recording derivation was bipolar with montage Cz–A1 (10–20 system) and epoch time was 512 m/s with a 0.5 m/s sample speed (1024 sample points for each of the 90 epochs). Various correlations between the string measure (computed from AEPs generated over 90, 64 and 32 epochs) and the APM yielded a mid-range correlation of approximately 0.45. The verbal test scores did not correlate significantly with the string measure. However, because the range of the scores on the APM was restricted, Blinkhorn and Hendrickson corrected this value for a full range of IQ. The correlation was thus boosted to a maximum of 0.84. This value is reasonably close to one obtained by the Hendricksons (1980) in an analysis of some published data of Ertl's for which they obtained a correlation of 0.77 between WISC IQs and the string score from the EPs; only extreme IQs were reported in the Ertl study.

In the second study (Hendrickson and Hendrickson, 1982) a reasonably random sample of 219 schoolchildren (121 boys, 98 girls) was used. The WAIS was used to assess IQ, scores being given for 11 separate subscales, a performance total, a verbal total, and an overall IQ. In addition to the complexity and variance measures defined above, D. E. Hendrickson defined a new composite measure. This measure was given simply as the variance score minus the string score. The stimulus presentation, data acquisition, epoch length, EEG derivation, and montage were the same as those reported in the first study. The correlations among the WAIS IQ and string, variance, and composite AEP measures were 0.72, –0.72, and –0.83, respectively. The correlations between the WAIS performance total and the string, variance, and composite measures were 0.53, –0.53 and –0.60 respectively. The correlations between the WAIS verbal total and the string, variance, and composite measures were 0.68, –0.69 and –0.78, respectively.

An additional sample of 16 court stenographers was also tested by the Hendricksons. The correlations between the string, variance, and composite measures and WAIS IQ were 0.80, –0.66 and –0.83. The mean age of this group was 42 years. Caryl and Fraser (1985) were also able to replicate this work on a small sample of 10 student subjects, obtaining a correlation of 0.78 between the string measure and AH4 IQ test score. However, Caryl (private communication, 1990) has since indicated that a recent second study on another student group failed to replicate the 1985 result. Haier *et al.* (1983), using a visual stimulus, also reported a correlation between Raven's Advanced Progressive Matrices scores and the string measure; the value observed was up to 0.45 for a high intensity stimulus. Other evoked potential parameters showed even higher correlations, up to 0.69. An attempted replication by Shagass *et al.* (1981), however, failed to replicate the string × IQ correlation, possibly because of the use of complex visual stimuli. Such stimulus complexity would be in opposition to the Hendricksons' assertion of the necessity for repetition of identical stimuli. Mackintosh (1986) reported negative correlations between string length and Raven's Advanced Progressive matrices and the Mill Hill Vocabulary test (–0.33 and –0.34 respectively). However, only 18 subjects took part and both correlations were non-significant. Barrett and Eysenck (1992) reporting the results from a detailed replication of the Hendrickson paradigm obtained correlations between the full WAIS IQ and string measure up to –0.44 and between the IQ and variability measure, –0.45 (40 subjects, 2-tail, $P < 0.01$). These correlations do not change with age and sex partialled out, neither do outliers account for the relationships. The stimulus used in this study was a 30 m/s, 85dB, 1000 Hz sine wave, with a rise and fall time of 3 m/s each side of the 24 m/s amplitude plateau. There were no switching transients as this was a synthesized rather than switched, ongoing, sampled stimulus waveform. Also of interest here was that average integrated amplitude of the entire 256 m/s waveform correlated significantly negatively with IQ (–0.42) but only 0.34 with the string measure. This negative correlation runs against the expected body of evidence indicating higher power EEG with higher IQ.

Vetterli and Furedy (1985) in a curious critique of the Hendickson string measure claimed that the string measure (as measured by actual string or a map wheel, versus the 1982 quantitative methodology of interpoint distancing) was erroneous. The size of correlations between this string measure and external criteria could be manipulated by varying the scale used to plot the AEP. However no empirical evidence was ever presented to back up this rather bald assertion and no evidence was presented to categorize just how large a size change could be produced in a correlation function. For all the reader knows they could be talking about a *"sizeable"* increase of up to 0.1 on a correlation! Essentially, Vetterli and Furedy were positing a non-linear transformation of the string variable by changing the "length" ratio of the X and Y graph axes. Frankly the paper is quite useless as a piece of scientific work, we only mention it here because it is often cited as a critique of the Hendrickson work.

Vogel *et al.* (1987) also attempted to replicate the Hendrickson string versus IQ correlation. They collected data on two groups of subjects over two modalities (auditory and visual), and under two conditions of interstimulus intervals—random and fixed (1.5 s). As well as computing parameter latencies and component amplitudes, they also computed an "oscillation" measure, akin to Hendrickson's string measure. Group 1 sample size was 236 university students, Group 2 was 24 mentally retarded in-patients from a local mental institution. From a thorough analysis of the data, Vogel *et al.* concluded that there were no general relationships between amplitude, latency, or their version of the string measure and IQ. In fact, their study is remarkable in that it demonstrated practically no significant correlations at all. This was a very important study in that the methodology was exemplary and the analyses extremely thorough.

Finally, Stough, Nettlebeck and Cooper (1990) have reported a replication of the Hendrickson string measure on a sample of 20 students. Sampling EEG 4 times slower than the Hendricksons recommended, they observed a correlation between WAIS IQ and the string measure of up to 0.71 (0.86 after correcting for test unreliability and restriction of range) over a restricted portion of the AEP epoch (100–200 m/s). Contrary to the Haier *et al.* work reported above, Stough *et al.* failed to replicate a previously significant relationship between an N140–P200 amplitude measure and IQ. Unusually, they also failed to obtain correlations between the Raven's Advanced Progressive Matrices and the string measure, at any epoch segment. The Raven's score correlated 0.54 with WAIS full-scale IQ and 0.45 with Performance IQ. Stough *et al.* note that in their study "the APM has become ineffectual as a measure discriminating individual differences in intelligence". Given the correlations between the WAIS and the same restriction on the WAIS full-scale IQ (a mean of 127.3 and SD of 5.2 vs the APM mean of 26.5 and an SD of 4.3), this is not a convincing explanation at all. Stough *et al.* further conclude that

> there is now abundant evidence from experiments employing AEP procedures, inspection time, and reaction time tasks, that variance in psychometric intel-

> ligence can be accounted for by scores and measures from these relatively simple tasks. Theories of intelligence which cannot account in some way for the results now emanating from these studies should be revised.

From the above review of the evidence concerning the Hendrickson paradigm alone, this statement by the authors appears somewhat optimistic.

A second approach to examining the AEP × IQ relationship has focused on the effects of information processing workload on AEPs (Schafer, 1979; Schafer, Amochaev and Russell, 1981; Squires *et al.*, 1976; Israel *et al.*, 1980). These studies have all demonstrated a cognitive modulation of EEG activity, that is, unexpected stimuli tend to produce higher amplitude AEPs than do expected stimuli. Schafer has extended the scope of this empirical phenomenon by hypothesizing that high IQ individuals would commit less neural effort to processing expected stimuli than would low IQ individuals; this difference in effort (neural adaptability) being observed in reduced amplitude AEPs from high IQ subjects. Schafer and Marcus (1973), and Schafer (1982, 1984) reported correlations averaging about 0.63 between the level of neural adaptability and IQ scores. That is, the greater the amplitude disparity between AEPs computed from epochs generated by expected and unexpected series of auditory stimuli, the higher the individual's IQ score. When corrected for attenuation of range within the IQ test scores, the average correlation was about 0.78. It is of interest to note that Callaway (1975) was unable to obtain a significant correlation using a similar methodology. A detailed review of the theories underlying both the Hendrickson and Schafer paradigms and the experimental evidence noted above is provided by Eysenck and Barrett (1985).

Schafer (1984, 1985) has recently modified his paradigm. In our 1985 review paper (Eysenck and Barrett), we had suggested that Schafer's paradigm was basically assessing habituation in terms of EEG amplitude reduction. Schafer noted this suggestion and subsequently modified the paradigm as described below. Using 19 male and 28 female subjects presented with 50 clicks with a 2 s interstimulus duration, he analysed the data by comparing the AEPs generated from the first and last 25 epochs. The percentage difference in amplitude within the N100–P180 waveform excursion served as his measure of AEP habituation. He subsequently achieved a correlation of 0.59 with Fullscale WAIS IQ; correcting for a restriction of range (98–142) this value became 0.73. Unfortunately, Schafer could not assess the superiority of the new over the old paradigm.

There have been two attempted replications of the Schafer work to date, Vogel *et al.* (1987) and Barrett and Eysenck (1991), both reported above. The Vogel *et al.* data while not strictly following the exact Schafer methodology, did use random versus fixed interstimulus intervals to generate their AEPs. They report no significant difference between the two datasets with regard to their correlations between waveform amplitude measures and IQ. Barrett and Eysenck, in a very tight replication of the Schafer paradigm also report no significant correlations between Schafer's measures and WAIS IQ. However, they were able to replicate the Hendrickson variability correlations. Essentially, both high and low IQ subjects had reduced amplitude AEPs in the fixed stimulus condition.

Rather more complex in nature, and closely related to Pavlov's theorizing, is the Robinson (1982a,b) paradigm, which involves Pavlov's concepts of excitatory and inhibitory processes, the concept of concentration/irradiation, and the concept of mobility (a system of conditioned neural connections that is elaborated in the nervous system by experience). The experimental methodology underlying Robinson's analyses is based upon the observation that since the EEG is an oscillatory phenomenon, the kind of relationship linking an input, system properties, and output, is suggested by reference to other physical systems which oscillate. In general, sinusoidal oscillation tends to occur when a system that is displaced from equilibrium is subject to a restoring force that is proportional to the displacement. This is the prototypical case for many oscillatory phenomena and it is consistent with the reciprocal interaction of excitatory and inhibitory neurones that appears to be an almost universal feature of neural organization. For such a system, the relationship between an excitatory input, system properties and the activity of the system is described by the equation for forced harmonic motion. By imposing an oscillatory signal into a theoretically resonant neurone system, Robinson proposed to examine the brain's resonance characteristics in terms of monitoring the known input sine waves against the brain's output sine waves.

The results from the series of experiments carried out by Robinson confirmed that a steady-state solution for the equation accounted for variation in the amplitude of evoked sinusoidal EEG responses. The visual stimulus used was a diffuse white light source continuously modulated sinusoidally at different frequencies within the alpha frequency band. Instead of the light being "flashed" on and off, it would be seen to gradually decrease and then increase in illuminance in a smooth, continuous, fashion. Specifically, mathematically generated curves describing the input–output transfer function derived from the equation accounted for over 95% of EEG response amplitude variation in all but three subjects (in the worst case, just less than 90% of the variation was accounted for). As a consequence of these findings, the variation of EEG response amplitude with variation in stimulus frequency could be attributed to a number of distinct parameters in the equation, which can be resolved with a high degree of precision. Across subjects these parameters take different values in accordance with shape changes in the frequency response curves obtained for different individuals. Of interest in the context of IQ relationships was the result that two parameters, analogous to the capacatance and inductance of an electrical circuit, were strongly related

Table 10.1. Robinson 4 factor solution compared with Barrett and Eysenck data 4 factor solution.

Variable	R1	B1	R2	B2	R3	B3	R4	B4
Information (Info)	0.88	0.73	0	0	0	0	0	0
Comprehension (Compr)	0.68	0.66	0	0	0	0	0	0
Arithmetic (Arith)	0.51	0.40	0.30	0	0	0.41	0.28	0
Similarities (Simil)	0.69	0.70	0.42	0	0	0	0	0
Digit span (DigSp)	0.32	0	0	0	0	0.81	0.52	0
Vocabulary (Vocab)	0.72	0.78	0	0	0	0	0	0
Digit symbol (DigSy)	0	0	0.35	0.57	0	0.48	0.48	0
Picture completion (PictC)	0	0	0.39	0.57	0	0	0	0
Block design (Block)	0	0	0.66	0.74	0.52	0	0	0
Picture arrangement (PictA)	0	0	0.42	0.84	0.54	0	0	0
Object assembly (Objkt)	0	0	0.64	0.90	0	0	0	0
EPQ—Psychoticism	0	0	0	0	0.47	0	0	0.94
EPQ—Social desirability	0	–0.66	0	0	–0.63	0	0	–0.52
Field independence	0		0.66		0.52		0	
Robinson V derived score	0		0		0		–0.80	

Note: Rn = the Robinson factor ($N = 48$); Bn = the Barrett and Eysenck Equivalent ($N = 149$).

to a proposed attention/concentration factor of the WAIS IQ test. This factor, in Robinson's work, is most heavily loaded by the Digit Span, Digit Symbol, Information and Arithmetic subscales. The manner in which the paramaters relate to this factor is complicated by the fact that superior attention depends upon the values of both parameters; that is, when both parameters take intermediate values. All other combinations of parameter values tend to be associated with less than optimal attention/concentration. Robinson expressed this joint function as a scaler variable V. The joint function measure being the length of the distance vector from the origin of a two-dimensional orthogonal co-ordinate system, the two dimensions being the capacitance and inductance measures. This distance variable correlated 0.80 with the WAIS attention/concentration factor.

Instead of further attempting to describe the full complexity and richness of associations of the model, it is apposite to note that to date, there have been no attempted replications of the Robinson series of experiments and analyses (1982a, 1982b, 1983, 1985, 1986a, 1986b, 1988). Given also, the small number of subjects that form the basis for such grand modelling (generally around 50 per study), it is essential that the more testable propositions of the Robinson work are evaluated before any more credence is given to the model/theory. To that end, since we happen to have some data using much larger subject numbers that would allow some of the Robinson statements to be empirically examined, we have undertaken to do so within the context of this chapter. While none of the hypotheses tested relate to EEG effects, these hypotheses all stem from a neuropsychological model based upon brain electrical activity and functions with respect to inhibitory versus excitatory pathways.

Hypothesis 1: The factor analysis of the WAIS subtests is replicable and the factors correspond to those established in other studies.

This hypothesis is an important one as Robinson's 4 factor solution provides some external evidence of the clustering of certain of the WAIS subtests in a manner suggestive of the Pavlovian concepts and associated personality types. His factor analysis, on 48 subjects, over 15 variables is shown in Table 10.1. Alongside his factors are those found by us in a principal components and swept parameter direct oblimin rotation (Barrett and Kline, 1982) of our 149 subjects reported in Barrett and Eysenck (1992).

We had no values for the variables "Field Independence" and V so our solution was computed over 13 rather than 15 variables. We can be said to roughly replicate Robinson's factors 1, 2, and 4. We find no evidence of a "mobility" factor, the third factor in Robinson's solution. However, the Kaiser-Guttman, and autoscree tests of factor extraction yielded three factors for rotation, with the Velicer and Kaiser-Alpha indicating only one general factor (accounting for 49% of the variance). We subsequently rotated three factors and promptly found that the so-called "concentration factor" (Robinson's factor 4) had disappeared. Rather, we obtained a Verbal and Performance pair, with the third factor being loaded only by EPQ-P and EPQ-L with all other loadings on this factor < 0.13. Since doubt about a third factor is expressed by Frank (1983) in his review of factor analytic studies of the WAIS, and since by the inclusion of other non-WAIS variables in our analyses we might be disturbing a stable factor structure, we refactored just the WAIS subtests alone. Table 10.2 presents the results of this analysis, contrasting a three factor and a two factor solution.

The Kaiser-Guttman, Velicer and autoscree tests of factor extraction quantity suggested two factors. The Kaiser-Alpha just one. As can be seen from Table 10.2, at best it could be proposed that a Verbal and Performance factor might be extracted, but really a general factor is the only solution for this particular WAIS data. All loadings on the unrotated first factor are greater than or equal to 0.6. The cluster pattern of the variables would not even allow a graphical rotation to obtain a better Verbal/Performance split than the analytical direct oblimin. Our data, three times the sample size of the Robinson sample, do not support a third WAIS factor of "attention/concentration". However, when using EPQ-P and EPQ-L personality variables

Table 10.2. Barrett and Eysenck Data 3 and 2 factor solutions (direct oblimin)—WAIS subtests ($N = 149$).

Variable	F1	F2	F3	F1	F2
Information (Info)	0.89	0	0	0.75	0
Comprehension (Compr)	0.76	0	0	0.83	0
Arithmetic (Arith)	0.69	0	0	0.72	0
Similarities (Simil)	0.79	0	0	0.83	0
Digit Span (DigSp)	0.35	0	0.75	0.83	0
Vocabulary (Vocab)	0.93	0	0	0.93	0
Digit symbol (DigSy)	0	0.57	0.59	0.46	0.37
Picture completion (PictC)	0	0.54	0	0.49	0.45
Block design (Block)	0	0.69	0	0.44	0.61
Picture arrangement (PictA)	0	0.83	0	0	0.76
Object Assembly (Objkt)	0	0.86	0	0	0.75

with the WAIS subtests, such a factor can be observed. But, when using the EPQ-P, E, N, and L variables with the WAIS subtests, the factor disappears completely, leaving P and L loading together on an otherwise undefined factor. In short, these factor analyses and rotations are highly unstable. Robinson happened to choose a solution that fitted his theory or at least failed to compute several solutions as above in order to determine the factorial stability of his solution. His factor structure is not replicable except under those particular psychometric conditions given the properties of the variables involved. Probably the only solution to this dilemma is a confirmatory factor analysis on a sizeable group of subjects, proposing a two-, three-, and four-factor restricted model. Our data simply indicate that Robinson's solution is one of many plausible exploratory solutions.

Hypothesis 2: Introverts will score higher than extraverts on verbal subtests of the WAIS, extraverts will score higher than introverts on performance tests.

From Robinson (1985), p. 204:

> it has been proposed that the more intense and irradiating thalamocortical activity of introverts favours the development of greater lateral connectivity. It is suggested that this is the anatomical and neurophysiological basis of association learning that is now thought to underlie classical conditioning. Thus, introverted subjects should do better, for example, on tasks that involve the learning of paired-associates. Where rehearsal is possible they would be better able to learn word lists or series of numbers as in the WAIS Digit Span subtest. For introverts rather than extraverts, any particular stimulus should have a greater number of associations and it should be possible to access these more readily. Thus one would expect higher scores on the WAIS Vocabulary and Information subtests. For the same reasons, one would expect introverts to be better on the Similarities and Comprehension subtests. In fact, introverts would be expected

> to do better than extraverts on most of the WAIS Verbal subtests. . . . It has also been proposed that the greater tonic level of activity sustained by the thalamocortical processes of introverts results in stronger inhibition of brain-stem systems normally involved in the elaboration of automatic motor sequences, or the kind of learning that can be related to the operant conditioning paradigm. This inhibition would impair the introvert's ability to acquire manipulative skill, whether in terms of overt responses or the covert cognitive manipulation required by most of the WAIS Performance subtests. . . . Consequently, although introverts should do better than extraverts on most of the WAIS Verbal subtests, there is reason to suppose that they should perform less well than extraverts on most of the WAIS Performance subtests.

In support of this hypothesis, Robinson (1985) presented data in the form of WAIS "weights" that had been computed from his WAIS profiles. He did not present the actual WAIS score profiles for introverts and extraverts. Figures 10.1 and 10.2 below show Robinson's weights and our data across the same subtests. In addition, our sample (drawn from the 149 total subject sample), is age matched (means of 25 and 24 years for introverts and extraverts respectively) and the group separation on extraversion was at least 1 s.d. from the mean of 14.07 (for extraverts, we only included the individuals who scored 21 and above on the scale; for the introverts, the group mean was 5.5) Robinson's samples were not matched in this way. As can be seen from Figures 10.1 and 10.2, our data do not support Robinson's hypothesis.

Figure 10.3 below shows the profiles of introverts and extraverts computed using data collected on Jackson's Multidimensional Aptitude Battery (MAB, 1984), a group administerable version of the WAIS. There is no Digit Span subtest and the MAB also assesses Spatial Ability (Spatl), a subtest not included directly by name in the WAIS. The subject data presented in Figure 10.3 are taken from a total sample of 268 subjects who took part in another experiment within our laboratory. The subsamples are age matched (means of 19 and 21 years for introverts and extraverts respectively) with almost equal males and females within each group. Once again, introvert and extravert group separation on extraversion was at least 1 s.d. from the overall group mean of 14.88. The mean score for the introvert group on extraversion is 7.9, for extraverts, 21.7. This data is even less supportive of Robinson's propositions.

We have to be slightly cautious here because we have made our comparisons not with WAIS profiles but with derived weights. However, since Robinson has clearly enunciated the hypothesis in terms of WAIS scores, our comparison seems to directly address the issue. In addition, working with such low numbers of subjects in *ad-hoc* (albeit objective) selected subgroups, gives one little confidence in the generality of the results.

Hypothesis 3: Ambiverts (mid-scoring subjects on extraversion) can be distinguished from the other groups in terms of their WAIS profiles. Younger

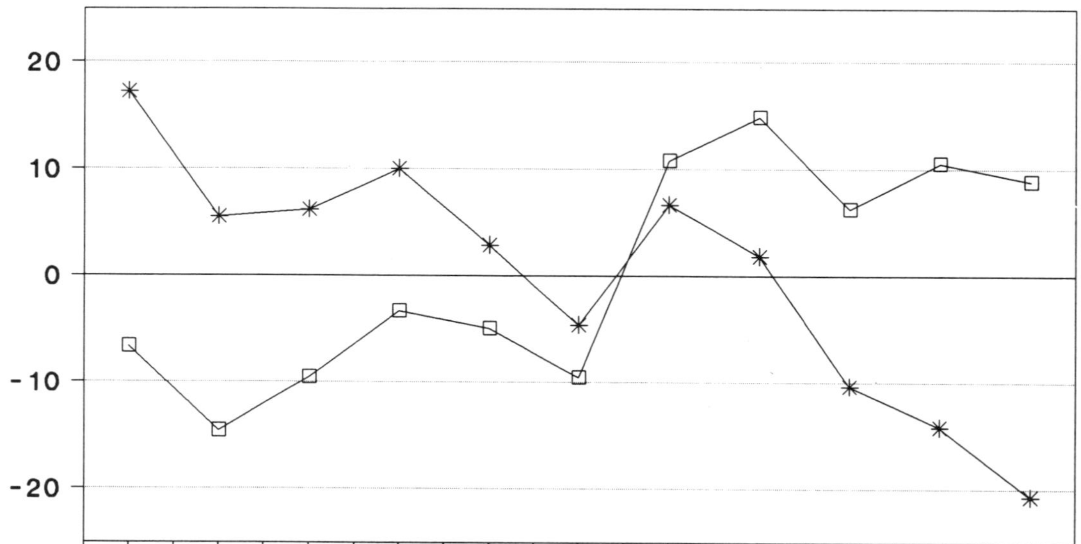

	DigSp	Simil	Info	Vocab	Compr	PictC	DigSy	Objkt	Block	PictA	Arith
Introverts, *N*= 9	17.2	5.44	6.16	9.99	2.8	-4.64	6.63	1.8	-10.4	-14.22	-20.71
Extraverts, *N*= 11	-6.69	-14.58	-9.57	-3.35	-5.01	-9.57	10.78	14.83	6.22	10.53	8.86

Introverts, *N* = 9   Extraverts, *N* = 11

Figure 10.1. Robinson (1985) data. Introvert versus extravert derived weights. DigSp, digit span; Simil, similarities; Info, information; Vocab, vocabulary; Compr, comprehension; PictC, picture completion; DigSy, digit symbol; Objkt, object assembly; Block, block design; PictA, picture arrangement; Arith, arithmetic.

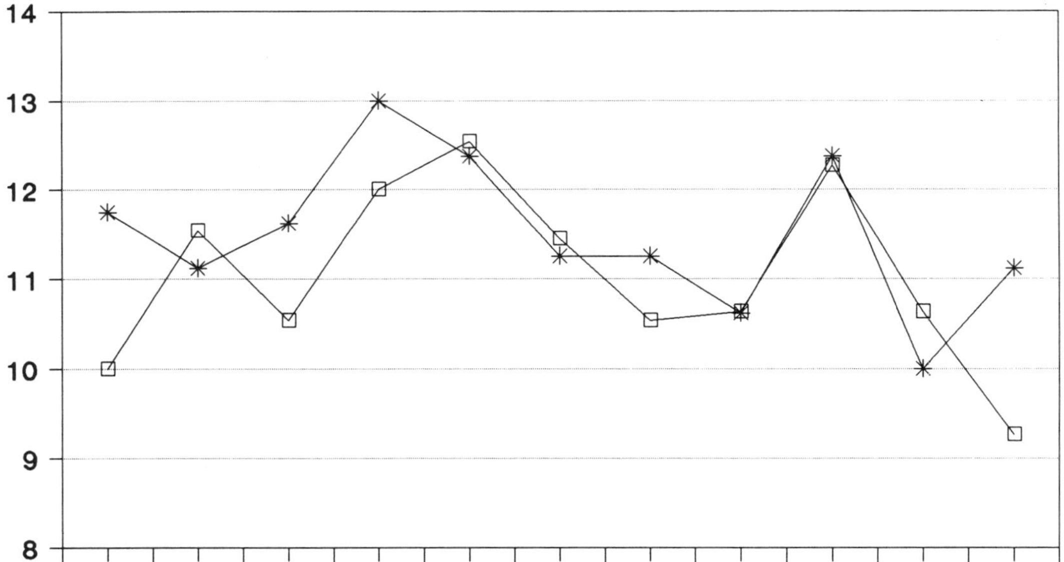

	DigSp	Simil	Info	Vocab	Compr	PictC	DigSy	Objkt	Block	PictA	Arith
Introverts, $N = 8$	11.75	11.12	11.62	13	12.37	11.25	11.25	10.62	12.37	10	11.12
Extraverts, $N = 11$	10	11.54	10.54	12	12.54	11.45	10.54	10.64	12.27	10.64	9.27

Introverts, $N = 8$ — Extraverts, $N = 11$

Figure 10.2. Barrett and Eysenck (1992). Introvert versus extravert WAIS profiles. DigSp, digit span; Simil, similarities; Info, information; Vocab, vocabulary; Compr, comprehension; PictC, picture completion; DigSy, digit symbol; Objkt, object assembly; Block, block design; PictA, picture arrangement; Arith, arithmetic.

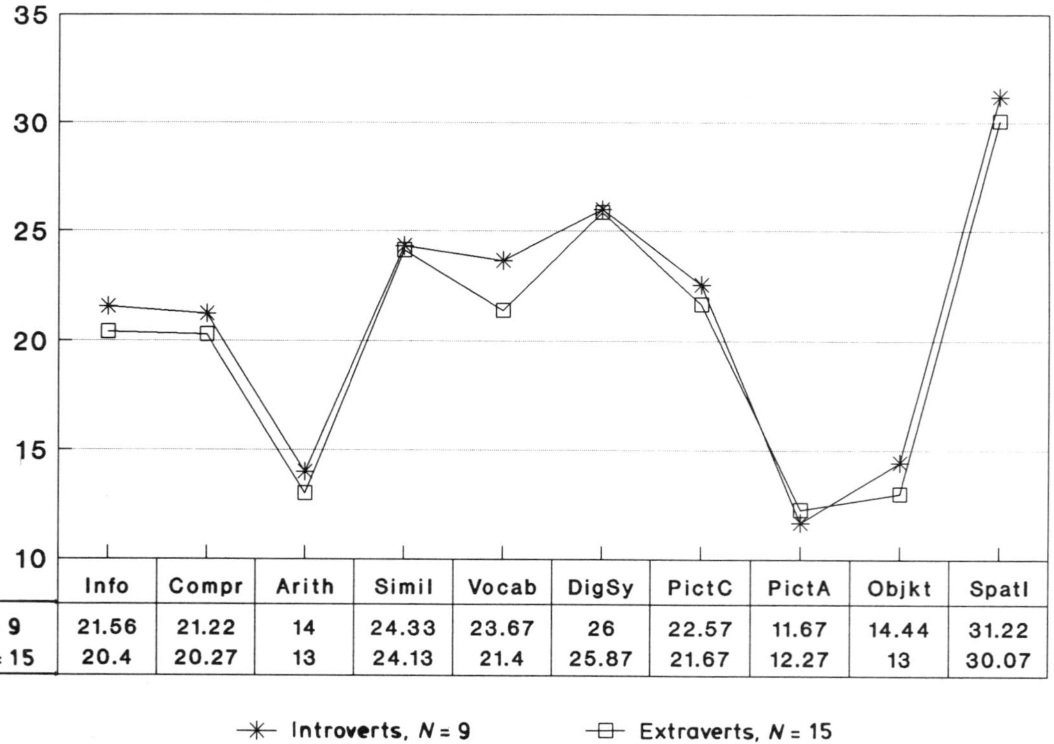

	Info	Compr	Arith	Simil	Vocab	DigSy	PictC	PictA	Objkt	Spatl
Introverts, *N* = 9	21.56	21.22	14	24.33	23.67	26	22.57	11.67	14.44	31.22
Extraverts, *N* = 15	20.4	20.27	13	24.13	21.4	25.87	21.67	12.27	13	30.07

Figure 10.3. Barrett and Eysenck data. Introvert versus extravert raw MAB subtests. Info, information; Compr, comprehension; Arith, arithmetic; Simil, similarities; Vocab, vocabulary; DigSy, digit symbol; PictC, picture completion; PictA, picture arrangement; Objkt, object assembly; Spatl, spatial ability.

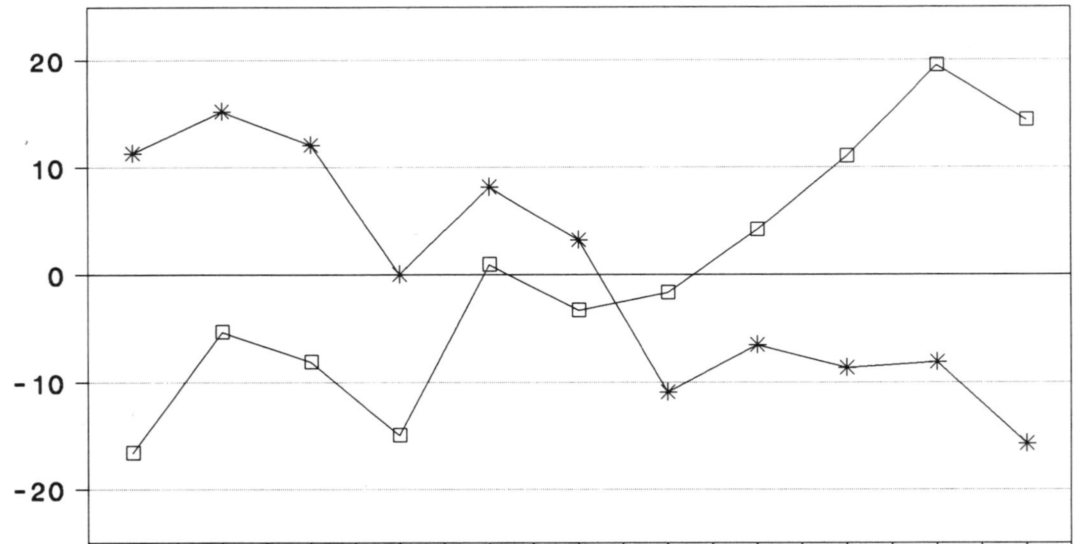

	DigSp	PictA	Block	DigSy	Arith	Info	Vocab	Objkt	Simil	PictC	Compr
Age, < = 26, *N* = 16	11.28	15.26	12.08	0.04	8.18	3.22	-10.94	-6.52	-8.64	-8.11	-15.73
Age, > 26, *N* = 12	-16.59	-5.31	-8.12	-14.98	0.94	-3.3	-1.69	4.15	11.01	19.47	14.43

Age, < = 26, *N* = 16 — Age, > 26, *N* = 12

Figure 10.4. Robinson (1985) data. Ambivert WAIS derived weights. DigSp, digit span; PictA, picture arrangement; Block, block design; DigSy, digit symbol; Arith, arithmetic; Info, information; Vocab, vocabulary; Objkt, object assembly; Simil, similarities; PictC, picture comprehension; Compr, comprehension.

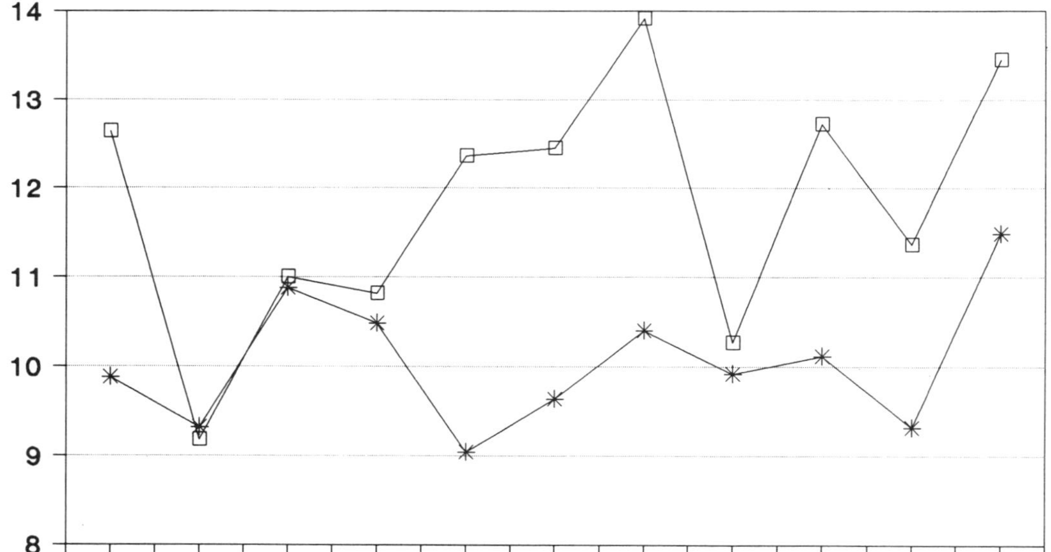

	DigSp	PictA	Block	DigSy	Arith	Info	Vocab	Objkt	Simil	PictC	Compr
Age, < = 26, *N* = 25	9.88	9.32	10.88	10.48	9.04	9.64	10.4	9.92	10.12	9.32	11.48
Age, > 26, *N* = 11	12.64	9.18	11	10.82	12.36	12.45	13.91	10.27	12.72	11.36	13.45

—✳— Age, < = 26, *N* = 25 —□— Age, > 26, *N* = 11

Figure 10.5. Barrett and Eysenck (1992). Ambivert WAIS profiles, DigSp, digit span; PictA, picture arrangement; Block, block design; DigSy, digit symbol; Arith, arithmetic; Info, information; Vocab, vocabulary; Objkt, object assembly; Simil, similarities; PictC, picture comprehension; Comp, comprehension.

(age ≤ 26) and older (age > 26) ambiverts have differing WAIS patterns and substantially different EPQ-P and EPQ-L scores.

Robinson presented the data shown in Figure 10.4 as supporting his overall hypothesis. We present our data in Figure 10.5. Although there are differences, our data do not replicate Robinson's differences. However, in comparison with the data in Figure 10.2, the ambivert data is dissimilar from the introvert and extravert profiles. Our ambiverts were restricted to just ± (about ± ¼ s.d.) score point around the mean extraversion score (within each age group). Robinson included all subjects within ± 1 s.d. around his total sample mean.

With regard to the personality score differences on P and L, we decided to use a third sample of data—the UK reference sample on the EPQ held within the Biosignal laboratory. This sample consists of 1996 males and 2144 females. Subsampling from this for the ambiverts, using the ± 1 score point around each group mean, yielded the results presented in Table 10.3. These results are contrasted with Robinson's (1985) samples which were heavily confounded by sex disparities (in his age ≤ 26 sample, 13 out of his 16 subjects were male, in the age > 26 sample, eight out of the 12 are females). As can be seen from Table 10.3, we replicate the differences demonstrated by Robinson but with far less magnitude.

In summary of these brief attempts to replicate some of Robinson's work, it can be seen that overall, we find little in common between our data and Robinson's. This does not necessarily mean that the neuropsychological model is wrong or inaccurate, simply that to date, most of the empirical data on which it is based remains essentially non-replicated, much in the same way as the Hendrickson model of nerve conduction and brain functions. Like the Hendrickson model, until such empirical confirmation of the variables is obtained, the models are of questionable value to the body of knowledge in this area.

Finally, there is the work by Zhang, Caryl and Deary (1989a; 1989b) on the relationship between visual AEP components, Inspection Time, and IQ (the

Table 10.3. Robinson versus Eysenck ambivert data

	Ambiverts age ≤ 26	Ambiverts age > 26
Robinson EPQ–P	6.8 (*N* = 16)	2.6 (*N* = 12)
Eysenck EPQ–P males	4.3 (*N* = 224)	3.0 (*N* = 160)
Eysenck EPQ–P females	2.8 (*N* = 272)	2.0 (*N* = 149)
Robinson EPQ–L	2.3	7.5
Eysenck EPQ–L males	5.9	8.8
Eysenck EPQ–L females	6.9	10.5

AH5 IQ test). Inspection Time (IT) may be defined as the minimum display time required by an individual to accurately discriminate a difference between two stimuli. The prototypical task emerged from a psychophysical theory developed by Vickers, Nettlebeck and Wilson (1972). Nettlebeck (1987) and Kranzler and Jensen (1989) have reviewed a large body of evidence demonstrating that IT correlates with IQ on average between –0.4 to –0.5. Within the Zhang *et al.* experiments, IT stimuli were presented on a LED display; the task required discrimination of the relative length of pairs of illuminated lines (one twice the length of the other) which were followed by a backward mask. Using an adaptive algorithm, an individual's IT was assessed to 85% accuracy; then another 100 trials were presented at this level. EPs were recorded from the Cz vertex electrode, referred to the left mastoid. Epoch length was 1024 m/s. From the analyses undertaken by Zhang *et al.*, a new AEP component was generated, called the $P200_T$ parameter. This is defined by computing the mean voltage for an AEP, and noting the intersection of this mean value by the upward slope of the waveform from the N140–150 trough, the time is counted until the P200 peak is reached by the waveform. Across two groups of 16 subjects, this parameter correlated from 0.43 to 0.58 with their IT values. From another series of experiments reported in Zhang *et al.* (1989b), the $P200_T$ parameter and AH5 IQ correlated –0.34 across 35 subjects and betweeen $P200_T$ and IT, 0.65 across 37 subjects. As part of this second series of experiments, Zhang *et al.* also included a condition of simple (SRT) and discriminative reaction time (DRT). P300 component amplitude and latency was assessed for each individual and correlated with SRT and DRT values and IQ. None of the correlations between RT and P300 measures was significant. In addition, no P300 measures correlated with IQ. This is in contrast to a recent paper by McGarry-Roberts, Stelmack and Campbell (1992) who recorded P300 potentials during the performance of six simple computer administered cognitive tasks, using 30 subjects. Using the MAB IQ test scores from the subjects, they found that P300 latencies increased with increasing task difficulty and that two canonical variates (for P300 latencies and MAB IQ) correlated inversely with each other (–0.36, $P < 0.05$). There is much more in this paper by McGarry-Roberts, Stelmack and Campbell that is of great interest with regard to longer-term potentials, reaction times, and IQ. P300 amplitude just failed to correlate significantly with IQ and RT (–0.30 and –0.31 respectively), again a result not replicated within the Zhang *et al.* (1989b) paper.

DISCUSSION

From the review of the spontaneous EEG work above, it is the opinion of the first author that there is very little use in continuing with this approach as an attempt to elucidate the causal mechanisms with regard to IQ correlates. The body of work (mostly on children) has shown that differentiated brain activity is related to IQ and that high IQ subjects tend to produce higher frequency EEG under resting or work conditions. However, as Lindsley (1961) concluded in his review of adult spontaneous EEG studies, the relationship between EEG parameters and intelligence in adults is ambiguous. The age patterning of results suggests that the investigators examining the EEG of children are looking at maturational effects which become undifferentiated after about the age of 16 or so. Hence the relationships observed may be those between brain maturation (indirectly assessed by its ongoing electrical activity at certain frequencies) and IQ, rather than EEG frequency patterns irrespective of age.

With reference to the more recent work with children, each investigator has *ad-hoc* explanations or ideas about their results but, because of the crude methodology of the EEG and its relative measurement (all voltages are referred to an arbitrary, assumed electrically ''indifferent'' electrode), it is not really possible to provide explanations in terms of mechanisms or spatial generator dynamics. The cause or structural location of the activity can only ever be inferred, never measured directly. This is in contrast to neuromagnetic recording and PET imaging. Lewis and Sorenson (1989) provide data showing that neuromagnetic recording techniques provide better prediction of job performance than EEG measures. Generally, the magnetic field data were better able to provide spatial localization of activity than were the evoked potential EEG data.

The coherence approach of Thatcher *et al.* (1983) and Gasser, Jennen-Steinmetz and Verleger (1987) reported above is probably the best way forward in terms of mapping discrete changes in brain activity across scalp regions. Gevins and his co-workers at the EEG systems laboratories in San Francisco have taken this approach one step further in quantifying in great detail, the brain activity involved in visuomotor performance tasks (Gevins *et al.*, 1981; Gevins *et al.*, 1983; Gevins *et al.*, 1987; Gevins *et al.*, 1990). However, mapping dynamics of EEG is a field still in its infancy and reliant upon extensive computational resources, not normally found in a typical EEG laboratory. We feel that this area of topographic dynamics (whether via neuromagnetic recording techniques or EEG) will slowly evolve into a joint measurement approach with PET imaging, providing the temporal dynamics of brain activity prior to the PET image scan.

Haier (1990) has gone so far as to suggest that the primary way forward in intelligence research is principally through PET and structural MRI imaging techniques. The basis for such a statement comes from his own (and others') work on cortical glucose metabolic rate in individuals performing cognitive tasks. De Leon *et al.* (1983) in comparing 15 young normal subjects (mean age 26), with 22 elderly normal subjects (mean age 66), and 24 Alzheimer patients (mean age 73), demonstrated significant positive correlations of up to 0.6 between cortical glucose metabolic rate and WAIS-IQ and other tests of cognitive function. These correlations were computed over a combined normal elderly and Alzheimer patient group. Interestingly, there was no significant difference between the young and elderly normal subjects with regard to metabolic rate. Similar results to these were reported by Chase *et al.* (1984) in another study on five normals and 17 Alzheimer patients. Both these studies, however, compared cortical glucose metabolic rates from resting subjects with psychometric test results that had been administered at another time. That is, from the intravenous induction of the tracer material, the subjects sat in a quiet room, isolated from sound and light for 30 min before the PET scanning took place. The study by Haier *et al.* (1988) differed from these earlier investigations by administering Raven's Advanced Progressive Matrices to eight normal subjects during the tracer uptake period. Haier *et al.* found a significant inverse relationship between metabolic rate and Raven's score; the low scoring Raven's subjects showed more cortical activity than did the high scorers. This result is opposite to Chase *et al.*'s positive correlations reported above (however, Haier *et al.* do make the point that Chase *et al.*'s subjects were composed mostly of Alzheimer patients). Haier has proposed a brain efficiency/energy explanation for the results to date. That is, higher IQ subjects use less cortical resources or more efficient resources in cognitive functioning than do lower IQ subjects. Weiss (1986; 1987; 1989) has also been working on an energy model and making some quite testable predictions regarding expected EEG parameter observations. However, this model, couched in quantum mechanics theory is very much like the Robinson model in its grand scope, minimal empirical evidence, and complexity. Unfortunately, Weiss continues to use the studies by De Leon *et al.*, Chase *et al.*, and Riege *et al.* (1985) as indicative of spatial localization of cognitive function, assuming that the cognitive tasks were being done within the tracer uptake period. This is not the case as noted above. All three studies correlated glucose rates assessed during a 30 min "rest" period. The cognitive tests were all given days or weeks before and after the scanning procedures. Therefore, unlike the Haier *et al.* (1988) work, these studies are simply noting relationships between rest-period glucose metabolism and psychometric test results. Haier *et al.* actually looked at glucose uptake "caused" by the cognitive activity involved in subjects answering Raven's problems. An important and potentially crucial difference, especially with regard to the sign reversal of metabolic rate and cognitive functioning correlations.

As indicated above, the challenge is now to marry the EEG or neuromagnetic techniques to the PET work. At present, PET imaging can only show the effects of activity in regions of the brain, not the dynamics. EEG can assist here by obtaining topographic dynamics prior to the PET scan. That is where one likely trend of research is going to be advanced.

With regard to the various studies of AEP correlates of IQ, there is very little that can be said other than that for every study that claims a "significant" result, there is another study that claims the opposite. Perhaps on balance the weight of evidence favours correlation between AEP parameters and IQ but a head count of positive versus negative results is not the way to assess the reality or otherwise of a correlation between AEP parameters and intelligence. Given the somewhat clearer results (although less outstanding than some AEP results) of the spontaneous EEG studies, and the results from the PET scan methodology, it is very likely that there is a correlation between certain evoked brain activity parameters and IQ, including the P300 parameters. However, it appears that no AEP parameter is consistently replicable. This suggests that some other major influence is at work. Perhaps the state of anxiety in a laboratory subject during the experiment recording session has an effect on the output brain activity, in that it introduces non-stimulus related EEG "noise" into the evoked response epochs. While Eysenck and Barrett (1985) sought to explain non-replicability in terms of poor methodology, the results that have appeared since then do not support this argument. Certainly, on close examination and through studies which have replicated the Hendrickson string measure, Barrett and Eysenck (1991) have shown that the Hendrickson "rules for replication" were quite arbitrary with respect to obtaining similar results to their own.

Mackintosh (1986) amongst others has suggested that differences in attention, anticipation, or inability to maintain concentration differentiates high and low IQ individuals. Perhaps, but how can an investigator measure such differences? In addition, these differences could be the biology at work, in neural energy loss, transmission variability, or whatever may underlie the cognitive disparities in IQ. If it were as simple as this, studies would be replicable. The problem is that in some experiments, high and low IQ subjects cannot be differentiated under conditions which previously elicited a differentiation. No, there is probably another major factor at work, something that can affect both high and low IQ individuals or cause one group to produce brain activity indistinguishable from the other. The next generation of experiments is going to have to address this problem, for while it remains, no confidence in correlations between AEP parameters and IQ can be expressed. Certainly, the production of theories, models, and detailed explanations of "biological intelligence" is not warranted by the present state of the empirical evidence to date. It is one matter to have working hypotheses, quite another to produce neuropsychological models such as those by Hendrickson, Robinson and Weiss. It is probable that the next generation of AEP experiments will follow the lead of Zhang *et al.* and McGarry-Roberts *et al.*, both discussed above. By manipulating complex stimulus parameters or tasks that are associated with differential human performance, and recording the brain activity at the same time, a better understanding of the conditions under which certain correlations can be observed may be possible. We say "may" here because the P300 parameters that correlated with the McGarry-Roberts IQ did not correlate within the Zhang *et al.* IQ data. Both studies used a different IQ test and different methods for eliciting the P300. Note, however, that we speak of *A* P300 and of *IQ* as being virtually interchangeable between studies. If the P300 waveform is conceived of as being highly task dependent, then perhaps this may be a reason for non-replication. However, while P300 latencies are known to be related to task difficulty, the underlying principle of the measure should enable the observation of a correlation with IQ, as in the McGarry-Roberts study.

Finally, with regard to future work in the EEG or neuromagnetic field areas, we would like to recommend that investigators:

(1) Use large numbers of subjects—certainly greater than 50, preferably over a hundred. This allows the investigators much more use of their data with respect to multivariate statistics, confidence limit assessment, and room for subsample selections. The argument most often put forward justifying the use of small samples is specious at the current time in this area (the argument states that it is more efficient to carry out small sample research in new areas of inquiry as both time and money are saved if the experiment results show no effects. If a big effect is present, then this is a good indication that it is worth proceeding with more work in the area). The study by Caryl and Fraser (discussed above) replicating a string versus IQ correlation at 0.78 over 10 subjects could not be replicated by Caryl at a later date on a similar student group of subjects. Barrett (1988) has addressed this issue with some empirical data showing clearly how easy it is to obtain spurious results from small numbers of subjects. Efficient experimentation is the key, not cutting down on the work involved!

(2) Ensure a good distribution of IQ or other cognitive or psychometric tests of ability. As Frearson, Barrett and Eysenck (1988) have shown, corrections of correlations for unreliability and attenuation are themselves unreliable unless both bivariate measures are themselves reliable. Given (1) above, (2) may easily follow.

(3) Compute Hendrickson variability versus IQ correlations. In fact, compute every parameter capable and worth being computed from every AEP collected. It is a waste of data to simply compute say a string measure when so many others have been shown as possible predictors of IQ. As with our data (Barrett and Eysenck, 1992), although the string measure correlation was opposite in sign to that reported by the Hendricksons, our variability correlation was in-line with predictions, albeit lower.

In conclusion, Haier (1990) and President Bush of the USA have indicated that this is the decade of the brain. The flurry of work in this area alone in the last five years or so indicates that this field of research is fast becoming one of the most crucial areas of investigation in psychophysiology. We concur with Deary and Caryl's (1991) conclusion to their review that the most successful approach in the short term will now be atheoretical. Given the several more than adequate working hypotheses that are being examined in this area, the production of specific gross models is not yet warranted. The establishment of psychometrically valid psychophysiological parameters will now take precedence. Once these have begun to be established, then the modelling may begin in earnest.

REFERENCES

Barrett, P.T. (1988) Paul's Page: sampling theory, power, and unwise attenuation corrections. *Journal of Psychophysiology*, **2**, 301–305.

Barrett, P.T. and Eysenck, H.J. (1992) Brain evoked potentials and intelligence: The Hendrickson paradigm. *Intelligence* (in press).

Barrett, P.T. and Kline, P. (1982) An item and radial parcel factor analysis of the 16PF questionnaire. *Personality and Individual Differences*, **3**, 269–270.

Bennett, W.F. (1968) Human perception: a network theory approach. *Nature*, **220**, 1147–1148.

Blinkhorn, S.F. and Hendrickson, D.E. (1982) Averaged evoked responses and psychometric intelligence. *Nature*, **295**, 596–597.

Bosaeus, E., Matousek, M. and Petersen, I. (1977) Correlation between paedopsychiatric findings and EEG-variables in well-functioning children of ages 5 to 16 years. *Scandinavian Journal of Psychology*, **18**, 140–147.

Bouchard, T., Lykken, D., McGoo, M., Siegal, N. and Tellegen, A. (1990) Sources of human psychological differences: the Minnesota study of twins reared apart. *Science*, **250**, 223–228.

Callaway, E. (1975) *Brain Electrical Potentials and Individual Psychological Differences.* London: Grune and Stratton.

Caryl, P.G. and Fraser, I.J. (1985) The Hendrickson "string length" measure and intelligence—a replication. *Paper presented at Psychophysiology Society Scottish Conference*, September.

Chalke, F. and Ertl, J. (1965) Evoked potentials and intelligence. *Life Sciences*, **4**, 1319–1322.

Chase, T.N., Fedio, P., Foster, N.L., Brooks, R., Di Chiro, G. and Mansi, L. (1984) Wechsler adult intelligence scale performance: cortical localisation by Fluorodeoxyglucose F18-Positron Emission Tomography. *Archives of Neurology*, **41**, 1244–1247.

Davis, F.B. (1971) The measurement of mental ability through evoked potential recording. *Educational Record Research Bulletin,* No. 1.

De Leon, M.J., Ferris, S.H., George, A.E., Christmas, D.R., Fowler, J.S., Gentes, C., Reisberg, B., Gee, B., Emmerich, M., Yonekura, Y., Brodie, J., Kricheff, I.I. and Wolf, A.P. (1983) Positron emission tomographic studies of aging and Alzheimer disease. *American Journal of Neuroradiology*, **4**, 568–571.

Deary, I. and Caryl, P. (1991) Intelligence, EEG, and evoked potentials. In P.A. Vernon (ed.), *Biological Approaches to Human Intelligence.* New Jersey: Ablex.

Dustman, R.E. and Beck, E.C. (1972) Relationship of intelligence to visually evoked responses. *Electroencephalography and Clinical Neurophysiology*, **33**, 254.

Dustman, R.E., Schenkenberg, T. and Beck, E.C. (1975) The development of the evoked response as a diagnostic and evaluative procedure. In R. Karrer (ed.), *Developmental Psychophysiology in Mental Retardation and Learning Disability*. Springfield, Ill.: Thomas.

Ellingson, R.J. (1966) Relationship between EEG and test intelligence: a commentary. *Psychological Bulletin*, **65**, 91–88.

Engel, R. and Henderson, N.B. (1973) Visual evoked responses and IQ scores at school age. *Developmental Medicine and Child Neurology*, **15**, 136–145.

Ertl, J. (1971) Fourier analysis of evoked potentials and human intelligence. *Nature*, **230**, 525–526.

Ertl, J. (1973) Evoked responses and Fourier analysis. *Nature*, **241**, 209–210.

Ertl, J. and Schafer, E. (1969) Brain response correlates of psychometric intelligence. *Nature*, **223**, 421–422.

Eysenck, H.J. (1973) The biological basis of intelligence. In H.J. Eysenck (ed.), *The Measurement of Intelligence*. Lancaster: Medical and Technical Publishing Co.

Eysenck, H.J. (1979) *The Structure and Measurement of Intelligence*. New York: Springer-Verlag.

Eysenck, H.J. and Barrett, P.T. (1985) Psychophysiology and the measurement of intelligence. In C.R. Reynolds and V.L. Willson (eds), *Methodological and Statistical Advances in the Study of Individual Differences*, New York: Plenum.

Flinn, J.M., Kirsch, A.D. and Flinn, E.A. (1977) Correlations between intelligence and the frequency content of the visual evoked potential. *Physiological Psychology*, **5**, 11–15.

Frank, G. (1983) *The Wechsler Enterprise*. New York: Pergamon Press.

Frearson, W., Barrett, P.T. and Eysenck, H.J. (1988) Intelligence, reaction time, and the effects of smoking. *Personality and Individual Differences*, **9**, 497–517.

Gasser, T., Bacher, P. and Steinberg, H. (1985) The test–retest reliability of spectral parameters of the EEG. *Electroencephalography and Clinical Neurophysiology*, **60**, 312–319.

Gasser, T., Jennen-Steinmetz, C. and Verleger, R. (1987) EEG coherence at rest and during a visual task in two groups of children. *Electroencephalography and Clinical Neurophysiology*, **67**, 151–158.

Gasser, T., Von Lucadou-Muller, I., Verleger, R. and Bacher, P. (1983a) Correlating EEG and IQ: a new look at an old problem using computerized EEG parameters. *Electroencephalography and Clinical Neurophysiology*, **55**, 493–504.

Gasser, T., Mocks, J., Lenard, H.G., Bacher, P. and Verleger, R. (1983b) The EEG of mildly retarded children: developmental, classificatory, and topographic aspects. *Electroencephalography and Clinical Neurophysiology*, **55**, 131–144.

Gevins, A.S., Doyle, J.C., Cutillo, B.A., Schaffer, R.E., Tennehill, R.S., Ghannam, J.H., Gilcrease, V.A. and Yeager, C.L. (1981) Electrical potentials in human brain during cognition: new method reveals dynamic patterns of correlation. *Science*, **213**, 918–922.

Gevins, A.S., Schaffer, R.E., Doyle, J.C., Cutillo, B.A., Tannehill, R.S. and Bressler, S.L. (1983) Shadows of thought: shifting lateralisation of human brain electrical patterns during brief visuomotor task. *Science*, **220**, 97–99.

Gevins, A.S., Morgan, N.H., Bressler, S.L., Cutillo, B.A., White, R.M., Illes, J., Greer, D.S., Doyle, J.C. and Zeitlin, G.M. (1987) Human neuroelectric patterns predict performance accuracy. *Science*, **235**, 580–585.

Gevins, A.S., Bressler, S.L., Cutillo, L., Illes, J.C., Miller, J., Stern, J. and Jex, H.R. (1990) Effects of prolonged mental work on functional brain topography. *Electroencephalography and Clinical Neurophysiology*, **76**, 339–350.

Giannitrapani, D. (1985) *The Electrophysiology of Intellectual Functions.* London: Karger.

Gucker, D.K. (1973) Correlating visual evoked potentials with psychometric intelligence, variation in technique. *Perceptual and Motor Skills*, **37**, 189–190.

Haier, R.J. (1990) The end of intelligence research. *Intelligence*, **14**, 371–374.

Haier, R.J., Robinson, D.L., Braden, W. and Williams, D. (1983) Electrical potentials of the cerebral cortex and psychometric intelligence. *Personality and Individual Differences*, **5**, 293–301.

Haier, R.J., Siegal, B.V., Nuechterlein, K.N., Hazlett, E., Wu, J.C., Paek, J., Browning, H. and Buchsbaum, M.S. (1988) Cortical glucose metabolic rate correlates to abstract reasoning and attention studied with positrin emission tomography. *Intelligence*, **12**, 199–217.

Hendrickson, D.E. and Hendrickson, A.E. (1980) The biological basis of individual differences in intelligence. *Personality and Individual Differences*, **1**, 3–33.

Hendrickson, D.E. and Hendrickson, A.E. (1982) The biological basis of intelligence. In H.J. Eysenck (ed.), *A Model for Intelligence.* New York: Springer-Verlag.

Israel, J.B., Wickens, C.D., Chesney, G.L. and Donchin, E. (1980) The event related potential as an index of display-monitoring workload. *Human Factors*, **22**, 211–224.

Jackson, D.N. (1984) *Manual to the Multidimensional Aptitude Battery.* Research Psychologists Press.

Kranzler, J.H. and Jensen, A.R. (1989) Inspection time and intelligence: a meta analysis. *Intelligence*, **13**, 329–347.

Lewis, G.W. and Sorenson, R.C. (1989) Evoked brain activity and personnel performance. In R.F. Dillon and J.W. Pellegrino (eds), *Testing.* New York: Praeger.

Lewis, G.W., Rimland, B. and Callaway, E. (1976) *Psychobiological predictors of success in a Navy remedial reading program.* NPRDC Report No. 77–13. San Diego: Navy Personnel Research and Development Center.

Lewis, G.W., Rimland, B. and Callaway, E. (1977) *Psychobiological correlates of aptitude among Navy recruits.* NPRDC Note No. 77-7. San Diego: Navy Personnel Research and Development Center.

Lindsley, D.B. (1961) The reticular motivating system and perceptual integration. In D.E. Sheer (ed.), *Electrical Stimulation of the Brain.* Austin: University of Texas Press.

Mackintosh, N.J. (1986) The biology of intelligence? *British Journal of Psychology*, **77**, 1–18.

Matousek, M. and Petersen, I. (1973) Frequency analysis of the EEG in normal children (1–15 yrs) and in normal adolescents (16–21 yrs). In P. Kellaway and I. Petersen (eds), *Automation of Clinical EEG.* New York: Raven Press.

McGarry-Roberts, P.A., Stelmack, R.M. and Campbell, K.B. (1992) Intelligence, reaction time, and event-related potentials. *Intelligence* (in press).

Netchine, G. and Netchine, S. (1962) Organisation psychologique et organisation bioélectrique, cérébrale dans une population d'arriènes mentaux. *Psychologique Française*, **7**, 241–258.

Nettlebeck, T. (1987) Inspection time and intelligence. In P.A. Vernon (ed.), *Speed of Information Processing and Intelligence.* New Jersey: Ablex.

Osaka, M., and Osaka, N. (1980) Human intelligence and power spectral analysis of visual evoked potentials. *Perceptual and Motor Skills*, **50**, 192–194.

Ostow, M. (1954) Psychodynamic disturbances in patients with temporal lobe disorder. *Journal of Man (Sinai Hospital)*, **20**, 293–308.

Riege, W.H., Metter, E.J., Kuhl, D.E. and Phelps, M.E. (1985) Brain glucose metabolism and memory functions: age decrease in factor scores. *Journal of Gerontology*, **40**, 459–467.

Risberg, J. (1980) Regional cerebral bloodflow measurements by ^{133}Xe inhalation: methodology and applications in neuropsychology and psychiatry. *Brain and Language*, **9**, 9–34.

Risberg, J. (1986) Regional cerebral bloodflow in neuropsychology. *Neuropsychologia*, **24**, 135–140.

Rhodes, L.E., Dustman, R.E. and Beck, E.C. (1969) The visual evoked response: a comparison of bright and dull children. *Electroencephalography and Clinical Neurophysiology*, **27**, 364–372.

Robinson, D.L. (1982a) Properties of the diffuse thalamocortical system and human personality: a direct test of Pavlovian/Eysenckian theory. *Personality and Individual Differences*, **3**, 1–16.

Robinson, D.L. (1982b) Properties of the diffuse thalamocortical system, human intelligence, and differentiated vs integrated modes of learning. *Personality and Individual Differences*, **3**, 393–405.

Robinson, D.L. (1983) An analysis of human EEG responses in the alpha range of frequencies. *International Journal of Neuroscience*, **22**, 81–98.

Robinson, D.L. (1985) How personality relates to intelligence test performance: implications for a theory of intelligence, ageing research, and personality assessment. *Personality and Individual Differences*, **6**, 203–216.

Robinson, D.L. (1996a) The Wechsler Adult Intelligence Scale and Personality Assessment: towards a biologically based theory of intelligence and cognition. *Personality and Individual Differences*, **7**, 153–159.

Robinson, D.L. (1986b) On the biological determination of personality structure. *Personality and Individual Differences*, **7**, 435–438.

Robinson, D.L. (1988) A neuropsychological model of personality and individual differences. In J. Strelau and H.J. Eysenck (eds), *Personality Dimensions and Arousal.* New York: Plenum Press.

Rust, J. (1975) Cortical evoked potentials, personality, and intelligence. *Journal of Comparative and Physiological Psychology*, **89**, 1220–1226.

Schafer, E. (1979) Cognitive neural adaptability: a biological basis for individual differences in intelligence. *Psychophysiology*, **16**, 199.

Schafer, E. (1982) Neural adaptability: a biological determinant of behavioural intelligence. *International Journal of Neuroscience*, **17**, 183–191.

Schafer, E. (1984) Habituation of evoked cortical potentials correlates with intelligence. *Psychophysiology*, **5**, 597.

Schafer, E. (1985) Neural adaptability: a biological determinant of g factor intelligence. *Behavioral and Brain Sciences*, **8**, 264–270.

Schafer, E., Amochaev, A. and Russell, M.J. (1981) Knowledge of stimulus timing attenuates human evoked cortical potentials. *Electroencephalography and Clinical Neurophysiology*, **52**, 9–17.

Schafer, E. and Marcus, M.M. (1973) Self-stimulation alters human sensory brain responses. *Science*, **181**, 175–177.

Shagass, C., Roemer, R.A., Straunanis, J.J. and Josiassen, R.C. (1981) Intelligence as a factor in evoked potential studies in psychopathology 1. Comparison of low and high IQ subjects. *Biological Psychiatry*, **11**, 1007–1029.

Shucard, D. and Callaway, E. (1973) Relationship between human intelligence and frequency of analysis of cortical evoked responses. *Perceptual and Motor Skills*, **36**, 147–151.

Shucard, D. and Horn, J.L. (1972) Evoked cortical potentials and measurement of human abilities. *Journal of Comparative Physiological Psychology*, **78**, 59–68.

Squires, K.C., Wickens, C., Squires, N.K. and Donchin, E. (1976) The effect of stimulus sequence on the waveform of the cortical event related potential. *Science*, **193**, 1142–1146.

Sternberg, R.J. and Detterman, D.K. (eds) (1986) *What is Intelligence?* New Jersey: Ablex.

Stough, C.K.K., Nettlebeck, T. and Cooper, C.J. (1990) Evoked brain potentials, string length, and intelligence. *Personality and Individual Differences*, **11**, 401–406.

Thatcher, R.W., McAlaster, R., Lester, M.L., Horst, R.L. and Cantor, D.S. (1983) Hemispheric EEG asymmetries related to cognitive functioning in children. In E. Perecman (ed.), *Cognitive Processing in the Right Hemisphere*. New York: Academic Press.

Vetterli, C.F. and Furedy, J.J. (1985) Evoked potential correlates of intelligence: some problems with Hendrickson's string measure of evoked potential complexity and error theory of intelligence. *International Journal of Psychophysiology*, **3**, 1–3.

Vickers, D., Nettlebeck, T. and Wilson, R.J. (1972) Perceptual indices of performance: the measurement of ''inspection time'' and ''noise'' in the visual system. *Perception*, **1**, 263–295.

Vogel, W. and Broverman, D.M. (1964) Relationship between EEG and test intelligence: a critical review. *Psychological Bulletin*, **62**, 132–144.

Vogel, W. and Broverman, D.M. (1966) A reply to ''Relationship between EEG and test intelligence: a commentary''. *Psychological Bulletin*, **65**, 99–109.

Vogel, F., Kruger, J., Schalt, E., Schnobel, R. and Hassling, L. (1987) No consistent relationships between oscillations and latencies of visual and auditory evoked EEG potentials and measures of mental performance. *Human Neurobiology*, **6**, 173–182.

Weinberg, H. (1969) Correlation of frequency spectra of averaged visual evoked potentials with verbal intelligence. *Nature*, **224**, 813–814.

Weiss, V. (1986) From memory span and mental speed toward the quantum mechanics of intelligence. *Personality and Individual Differences*, **7**, 737–749.

Weiss, V. (1987) The quantum mechanics of EEG-brain dynamics and short term memory. *Biologisches Zentralblatt*, **106**, 401–408.

Weiss, V. (1989) From short term memory capacity toward the EEG resonance code. *Personality and Individual Differences*, **10**, 501–508.

Zhang, Y., Caryl, P.G. and Deary, I.J. (1989a) Evoked potential correlates of inspection time. *Personality and Individual Differences*, **10**, 379–384.

Zhang, Y., Caryl, P.G. and Deary, I.J. (1989b) Evoked potentials, inspection time, and intelligence. *Personality and Individual Differences*, **10**, 1079–1094.

Chapter 11

Antisocial Behaviour: Evolution, Genetics, Neuropsychology, and Psychophysiology

Adrian Raine
Department of Psychology, SGM Building, University of Southern California, University Park, Los Angeles, California 90089-1061, USA

and

Peter H. Venables
Department of Psychology, University of York, Heslington, York YO1 5DD, England

ABSTRACT

Antisocial behaviour, ranging from refractory school behaviour to self-report delinquency, official delinquency, criminality, psychopathy, and schizoid antisociality, is discussed with reference to evolution (anthropological studies and sociobiology), genetics (twin and adoption studies), neuropsychology (frontal lobe dysfunction), and psychophysiology (skin conductance, evoked potentials, smooth-pursuit eye movements). This review indicates that biological factors and their interaction with social factors play a significant role in the development of antisocial behaviour. It is argued that integrated cross-disciplinary research is essential for significant advances to be made in understanding antisocial behaviour.

Handbook of Individual Differences: Biological Perspectives
Edited by Anthony Gale and Michael W. Eysenck

INTRODUCTION

It is increasingly being recognized that the fields of criminology, sociology, forensic psychology, statistics, social psychology, and biological psychology must all be represented in multidisciplinary research ventures if meaningful progress is to be made in our understanding of the complex behavioural process of antisociality (Mednick and Christiansen, 1977; Hinton, 1983). What is less frequently recognized is that subdivisions exist within each of these fields and that research studies within these subdivisions often take place in relative isolation of each other. Biological approaches to antisocial behaviour for example include sub-areas of anthropology and sociobiology, genetics, biochemistry, neuropsychology, and psychophysiology. Even within the one sub-area of psychophysiology there exists a wide range of approaches with a tendency for research studies to concentrate on only one recording technique such as evoked potentials, EEG, skin conductance, or heart rate. A prior requisite to sound multidisciplinary research is sound integrative research within each major field. As such the main purpose of this chapter will be to attempt to integrate four main areas lying within the province of biological research—evolution, genetics, neuropsychology, and psychophysiology—with an emphasis on outlining implications from one sub-area to another. Rather than cover the same ground as previous reviews, more recent research will be emphasized and critically evaluated and an attempt will be made to highlight key issues which have to date received little attention but which have implications for future research. Space limitations preclude a full detailed review of all biologically-related areas and in consequence appropriate reference will be made to detailed, up-to-date reviews.

EVOLUTION

Insights into the evolutionary basis of antisocial behaviour can be gained from two modern-day perspectives: anthropological field studies and sociobiological theory.

ANTHROPOLOGICAL STUDIES

One approach to the understanding of how antisocial behaviour has evolved in man consists of studies carried out by anthropologists. Models of the evolution of antisocial behaviour in humans can be formulated by comparing cultures which differ in their manifest asocial conduct in the context of ecological factors which affect reproductive strategies.

One such model has been developed by Harpending and Draper (1988) in a comparison of the cultures of !Kung Bushmen of the Kalahari desert in

Southern Africa with the Mundurucu villagers in the Amazon Basin. The !Kung Bushmen live in a relatively inhospitable desert environment which favours a social framework based on co-operative hunting, sharing of meat, and a nuclear family unit. Consequently the personal characteristics adapted to this environment and lifestyle consist of good hunting skills, reliable reciprocation of altruistic acts, careful mate choosing and high parental investment in offspring. In contrast the Mundurucu are low-intensity tropical gardeners living in a relatively richer ecological niche which allows the women to carry out most of the food production. This frees males to engage in male–male competitive interactions centred around talking politics, planning raids and warfare, gossiping, fighting, elaborate male ritual ceremonies and occasionally, hunting game which will be traded for sex with the village women. Personal characteristics of the successful male Mundurucu in this competitive society in consequence consist of good verbal skills for political oratory, fearlessness, bluff and bravado, and the ability to manipulate and deceive prospective mates concerning the resources he can offer.

The argument put forward by Harpending and Draper (1988) is that the nature of the Mundurucu's social environment favours the expression of what they term the "antisocial trait". In males this takes the form of sociopathy, characterized by lack of conscience, superficial charm, high verbal skills, promiscuity, and lack of long-term interpersonal bonds. Conversely this antisocial trait is disadvantageous in the milieu of the !Kung Bushmen which demands high male parental effort and reciprocal altruism.

This analysis is of value in so far as it helps to account for the evolution of psychopathic behaviour as a successful reproductive strategy in response to specific environmental conditions which confer a selective advantage to individuals with this trait. The model can, however, be criticized in that there is a major inconsistency between the behaviour of the male Mundurucu and the Western male psychopath. While the Mundurucu engage in long-term interpersonal relationships with members of their own sex and engage in all-male co-operative efforts for the benefit of the whole settlement, psychopaths do not form long-term relationships with either sex and do not co-exist and engage in joint enterprises.

SOCIOBIOLOGY

A similar but more theoretical approach to the understanding of antisocial behaviour in an evolutionary context can be seen in the basic principles adopted by sociobiologists. A detailed elaboration of these principles can be found in Wilson (1975), while seminal discussions of the concepts of kin selection, reciprocal altruism, inclusive fitness, and evolutionary stable strategies may be found in Hamilton (1964), Trivers (1971; 1972), Maynard Smith (1976) and Dawkins (1976).

An individual's genetic fitness is defined in terms of his/her reproductive success or the number of viable offspring produced. This "fitness", measured in terms of the individual's total genetic representation in the next gene pool, can generally be maximized in one of two ways. The individual may either invest a lot of resources in terms of parental effort in just a few offspring, or may maximize number of offspring at the expense of parental effort. A male can successfully adopt this latter reproductive strategy of high offspring–low effort if he "cheats" on female partners by misrepresenting his ability to acquire resources and his long-term parenting intentions.

MacMillan and Kofoed (1984) have evaluated this sociobiological theory of antisocial personality in terms of the success to which theoretical predictions made by the theory are substantiated by the empirical data. These predictions consist of:

(a) a genetic basis to antisocial personality disorder (APD) (cheating is hypothesized to be a genetically-influenced reproductive strategy),
(b) a graded dimension of antisocial personality (reproductive strategies lie on a continuum),
(c) the emergence of antisocial personality at the onset of reproductive age and the "burnout" when potential for future offspring decreases,
(d) a high sex bias towards male antisocial personality disorder (females have a high biological investment in pregnancy and cannot "cheat" as effectively),
(e) a greater genetic predisposition is required in females before manifesting APD (decreased advantage of cheating in females),
(f) greater promiscuity and reduced long-term stable relationships in APD,
(g) an average level of reproductive fitness in APD (predisposition for the disorder is in genetic equilibrium),
(h) low socioeconomic status in APD (no investment of energy in competition within the social dominance hierarchy for female access).

MacMillan and Kofoed (1984) argue that there is a close fit between all of these predictions and the empirical data and that sociobiology has important implications for the understanding and treatment of APD.

EVALUATION OF EVOLUTIONARY PERSPECTIVES

Anthropology and sociobiology while thus providing intriguing accounts of the evolution of antisociality can nevertheless be criticized on a number of counts. A major conceptual problem is that these theories switch inconsistently between usage of the terms "antisocial behaviour" and "sociopathy/antisocial personality disorder". Both perspectives would appear most applicable to the explanation of psychopathy/sociopathy/APD in particular since they hinge on the key psychopathic traits of superficial charm, verbal persuasiveness, deception, lack of remorse and guilt, promiscuous sexual relationships, parasitic lifestyle, irresponsible behaviour as parent and frequent marital relationships (Cleckley, 1976; Hare,1980). Yet most antisocials are not psychopathic and commit criminal offences while maintaining strong affectional bonds to spouse and children. Indeed, the bulk of antisocial conduct is not perpetuated by psychopaths who probably constitute only a third of an incarcerated criminal population (Hare, 1983). As such these sociobiological perspectives do not account for non-psychopathic forms of asociality.

This in turn makes the theoretical-empirical match claimed by MacMillan and Kofoed (1984) much less convincing, since several of the most important predictions (overall genetic basis, higher female genetic predisposition) are tested on genetic studies of antisocial behaviour in general, and not specifically on psychopaths. MacMillan and Kofoed (1984) argue that criminality *per se* is an epiphenomenon of the "psychopathic" reproductive strategy rather than representing an innate tendency in itself, but such a proposition does not mesh with the evidence for a genetic basis to criminality (see below). Sociobiological theory cannot readily explain why general mild forms of antisocial conduct such as theft should have a particularly strong genetic basis (see below) since the notion of a continuum of APD and reproductive strategy should predict a stronger genetic basis to more extreme antisocial conduct. Other predictions are not as well supported as MacMillan and Kofoed suggest. For example, the data for "burn-out" in psychopaths is largely clinical in nature. Quantitative analysis carried out by Hare and Jutai (1983) in contrast indicate that it is non-psychopathic criminals who show a decline in criminal behaviour with increasing age. The prediction of an average level of reproductive fitness in APD made by MacMillan and Kofoed (1984) seems incongruous with both the proposition that APD represents an especially successful reproductive strategy and with the sexual promiscuity of psychopaths. The data cited in support of this prediction are again based on antisocial behaviour in general and not psychopathy in particular (Robins, 1966). The prediction of a higher male:female sex ratio in APD is certainly well supported by the general findings in the clinical literature of a 3–5 to 1 ratio in favour of males (Sigvardsson *et al.*, 1982; Widom, 1978), but it is not completely clear from sociobiological theory why any females should exhibit psychopathic behavioural traits since females in biological reproductive terms are unable to "cheat" in the same way as males.

If sociobiology does provide a valid account of psychopathy, it suggests that powers of verbal persuasion, deception, parasitic lifestyle, frequent sexual relationships, irresponsible behaviour as parent, and nomadic lifestyle represent the key features of psychopathy while other characteristics are more peripheral (see Hare, 1980; Craft, 1966; McCord and McCord, 1964). Sociobiological theory would predict that individuals assessed on these specific characteristics would show stronger evidence for the role of genetic and biological factors underlying their psychopathy than "psychopaths" defined by other criteria.

The anthropological model proposed by Harpending and Draper (1988) suggests a similar proposition. If competitive societies such as the Mundurucu represent a valid model for psychopathy, one could theoretically use such populations for cross-cultural validation of the biological correlates of psychopathy observed in more developed societies. Such cross-cultural consistencies would constitute very strong evidence for the importance of such biological factors in psychopathy, or would conversely provide a unique population of non-institutionalized "psychopaths" free of all the methodological problems associated with prison samples.

GENETICS

The above evolutionary analysis predicts that antisocial behaviour in general and psychopathic behaviour in particular has a genetic basis. To what extent are these predictions supported by twin and adoption studies of antisocial, criminal, and psychopathic behaviour? This section will briefly answer this question, but since several comprehensive reviews already exist in this area the aim here will be to highlight several other issues which stem from twin and adoption studies and which have received little or no discussion in the previous literature. For a more extensive analysis of the evidence for genetic factors in antisocial behaviour the reader is referred to reviews by Eysenck (1977), Christiansen (1977), Mednick and Hutchings (1978), Reid and Bottlinger (1979), Mednick and Finello (1983), Widom and Ames (1988) and Venables and Raine (1987).

THE EVIDENCE—TWIN AND ADOPTION STUDIES

Mednick and Finello (1983) review eight twin studies of criminality carried out since 1929. Studies vary widely in terms of the country of origin, age and sex composition, sample size, determination of zygosity, and definition of asociality. Nevertheless all studies consistently show greater concordance rates for criminality in MZ as opposed to DZ twins, with average concordance of 67.2% (MZ) and 31% (DZ) indicating a substantial role of genetic determination.

A recent study by Rowe (1983) is of interest in that, in contrast to all studies reviewed by Mednick and Finello (1983) which report on official criminality, it reports on anonymous self-report delinquency in 168 MZ and 97 DZ American twin pairs in grades 8 to 12 (approximately 13 to 17 years). The higher concordance rates in MZ relative to DZ twins in both male (MZ = 0.66, DZ =

0.48) and female (MZ = 0.74, DZ = 0.47) twins suggest that evidence for heritability obtained in other studies is not a function of official criminality data which only identify the unsuccessful criminal, and also indicates that even relatively mild forms of antisocial conduct in adolescents show a genetic basis. This latter issue will be returned to later.

In spite of this impressive body of data twin studies possess methodological problems which raise difficulties in making unequivocal statements regarding the genetic basis of antisocial behaviour (Kamin, 1974). In particular, MZ twins may share a more common environment than DZ twins, thereby inflating the concordance rate for MZ twins. Adoption studies are better able to separate out the effects of biological parentage from environmental rearing effects and consequently provide a more sensitive method for estimating heredity and environmental effects. A number of well-executed adoption studies have been carried out into antisocial behaviour in recent years and also without exception support the conclusion drawn from twin studies of a substantial genetic component. Typical of these studies are the findings of a 13% rate of diagnosed antisocial personality in the adoptees of female offenders as compared with 2% in control adoptees of non-offenders (Crowe, 1974), and a 12.1% rate of criminality in adoptees with criminal biological fathers as compared with 2.9% in control adoptees. Essentially similar results have been found in adoption studies undertaken by Schulsinger (1972), Hutchings and Mednick (1975; 1977), Cadoret (1978), Cadoret, Cain and Crowe (1983), Cadoret *et al.* (1985), and Cadoret, Troughton and O'Gorman (1987), while familial studies by Cloninger, Reich and Guze (1975) and Cloninger *et al.* (1978) also support the notion of a significant heredity factor in the genesis of antisocial behaviour. This convergence of results from familial, adoption, and twin studies provides very strong evidence indeed for the role of genetic factors in the aetiology of antisocial conduct. In this light, the question of whether antisocial behaviour has a genetic basis is somewhat trivial. Questions which are less often asked, which are more difficult to answer, will now be posed.

DOES PSYCHOPATHY HAVE A GENETIC BASIS?

It is commonly assumed that psychopathic behaviour has a genetic basis. This assumption would seem very reasonable in so far as psychopathy may be viewed as a very severe form of antisocial behaviour (Eysenck, 1977). If mild antisocial conduct, delinquency, and criminality are in part genetically determined (as the evidence cited above would suggest) then surely more "deviant" forms of antisociality such as psychopathy should have an even greater genetic basis.

With respect to twin data, reviews by Mednick and Hutchings (1978), Eysenck (1977) and Reid and Bottlinger (1979) use terms such as "psychopathy" and "sociopathy", yet all samples consist of criminals on whom no good measure of psychopathy has been taken. This extrapolation from "criminality" to "psychopathy" is even more widespread in adoption and familial studies. At least eight of these studies (Schulsinger, 1972; Crowe, 1974; Cloninger *et al.*, 1975, 1978; Cadoret, 1978; Cadoret *et al.*, 1985, 1987; and Bohman *et al.*, 1982) claim a genetic basis to "sociopathy" or "antisocial personality disorder", yet none of these studies utilizes a convincing or strict diagnosis of psychopathy. Again, the fundamental issue is whether the "psychopathic" behaviour referred to in these studies represents anything over and above criminal behaviour.

The study of Crowe (1974), for example, used DSM-II criteria for the diagnosis of antisocial personality disorder and allocated this diagnosis to six out of 46 adoptees of female offenders as compared with 0 of 46 controls. The difficulty here is that seven probands had arrest and conviction records, and all six of the probands diagnosed as antisocial personality disorder fell into this group. Consequently antisocial personality disorder is virtually synonymous with criminality. Similarly Cadoret (1978) diagnosed antisocial personality disorder in the biological family of adoptees if they were convicted felons, while Cloninger *et al.* (1975) define sociopathy as "a personality disorder characterised by the early onset of repeated antisocial, delinquent, and criminal behaviour" (p. 13). This should be contrasted with other methods for assessing psychopathy such as the Psychopathy Checklist (Hare, 1980) which in addition to the antisocial behaviour features emphasized by DSM-III also contains more clinically-derived personality features such as superficial charm, egocentricity, pathological lying, lack of remorse and guilt, and callousness. This is a strict criterion for psychopathy in that it accepts only about a third of prison inmates as psychopathic (Hare, 1983). It is unfortunate that no adoption or twin study has utilized assessment procedures based on Cleckley's conception of psychopathy (Cleckley, 1976) which closely parallels the "antisocial trait" of Harpending and Draper (1988) and which, from an evolutionary standpoint, would be expected to have a particularly strong genetic basis.

One recent study by Baker (1986) suggests that heritability for "antisocial disorder" is considerably less than that for non-violent property crime. A biometric model-fitting approach was applied to data from 2532 Danish male adoptees and their biological and adoptive parents in order to assess heritability for (a) non-violent property crimes and (b) antisocial disorder, where the latter was based on a composite diagnostic variable based on personality disorder, alcohol use, and drug use (previously found by Moffitt (1984) to be significantly correlated with criminal conviction). Generalized least-squares parameter estimates indicated a relatively small heritability 0.27 for antisocial disorder in comparison with a much higher heritability of 0.45 for property crimes. While these data suggest that psychopathic behaviour does not have a strong genetic basis, "antisocial disorder" is probably only an indirect index of psychopathy in the strict sense of the word.

The implication for research into antisocial behaviour lies in terms of the amount of psychophysiological research carried out into psychopathy as opposed to more general antisocial behavioural processes. The implicit assumption is that psychopathy as an extreme form of antisocial behaviour has a strong genetic basis and thus will evidence a very distinct biological profile. In consequence it has become the focus for extensive psychophysiological research, perhaps at the expense of research into milder forms of antisocial behaviour. As indicated in a review of genetics and antisocial behaviour (Venables and Raine, 1987) it appears that mild forms of criminality (the non-violent "petty" offender committing largely property offences) have a particularly strong genetic basis whereas more severe criminality (crimes of violence, alcohol-related criminality, and possibly psychopathic criminality) does not. At the same time a study which more selectively assesses psychopathy in an adoption sample would be valuable in clarifying the genetic basis to psychopathy and confirming the evolutionary perspective on psychopathy outlined above.

Do females have stronger heritability for criminality?

An extensive review of biology and female crime by Widom and Ames (1988) arrives at the interesting conclusion that the genetic predisposition of a woman has to be greater than that of a man in order for antisocial behaviour to be manifested. Support for this conclusion stems largely from familial studies which show that antisocial females have a higher incidence of familial crime than antisocial males, and from some adoption studies which show a doubling of the rate of criminality in biological parents of criminal females relative to criminal males. Similar conclusions are drawn by Cloninger *et al.* (1975; 1978) and Sigvardsoon *et al.* (1982) who suggest that sex-typing and greater social pressures towards prosocial behaviour in females necessitate a greater genetic predisposition for the manifestation of antisocial behaviour.

As acknowledged by Widom and Ames (1988), however, twin studies do not support the notion of a greater heritability for female crime. Furthermore several recent adoption studies not reported by Widom also fail to support this conclusion. Cadoret (1978) found a slightly higher rate of antisocial personality in the offspring of fathers with antisocial behaviour rather than the offspring of antisocial mothers. Cadoret and Cain (1980) observed no significant sex differences in the genetic predictors of antisocial behaviour in adoptees, while Cadoret *et al.* (1985) found evidence for inheritance of antisocial behaviour in male but not female adoptees. While there is clear evidence from some studies of greater heritability for female crime, the data are by no means unequivocal.

If one was to accept the conclusion of Widom and Ames (1988) that there is greater heritability for criminality in females, then there are potential implications for biologically-oriented research into antisocial behaviour. If female offenders represent in an extreme form those who are genetically predisposed to antisociality, then psychophysiological investigations of such populations could give particularly clear insights into the way in which such a predisposition manifests itself at a psychophysiological level. In practice there has been virtually no psychophysiological research carried out into female offending, possibly because such groups represent a very small percentage of the total criminal population. Nevertheless findings of such investigations would certainly have applicability to understanding the biology of more prevalent male offending and are consequently sorely needed. Psychophysiological studies of antisocial conduct in adolescent female school-children may represent a relatively easily undertaken first step towards the provision of these potentially valuable data.

How important is the H (heredity) × E (environment) interaction?

In recent years there has been a shift in focus towards more biosocially-oriented research into antisocial behaviour (Mednick and Christiansen, 1977; Moffitt and Mednick, 1988; Mednick, Moffitt and Stack, 1989) and a consideration of the interactive effects of social factors in psychophysiology–antisocial relationships (Raine, 1989). This trend is at least partially underpinned by the assumption that environmental factors interact with hereditary factors in the production of antisocial behaviour—the H × E interaction.

Dramatic demonstrations that such is the case have been provided from several sources. Hutchings and Mednick (1977) and Mednick, Gabrielli and Hutchings (1983) report on an important cross-fostering analysis of criminality in 4065 children of either criminal or non-criminal biological parents adopted out to either criminal or non-criminal parents. They found that criminality rates were greatest (24.5%) in children whose biological and adoptive parents were both criminal, that is, where both hereditary and environmental factors were present. Rates for biological parent only criminal, adoptive parent only criminal, and neither parent criminal were 20.0%, 14.7% and 13.5% respectively. A more powerful demonstration of this interaction was reported in an earlier analysis of similar data by Hutchings and Mednick (1977) with corresponding figures of 36.2%, 22%, 11.5% and 10.5%. Even stronger evidence for an H × E interaction, however, is reported by Cloninger *et al.* (1982) in a cross-fostering analysis of "petty" criminality (infrequent minor property offences which are non-alcohol related) similar to Hutchings and Mednick (1977). A total of 862 Swedish adoptees were divided into four groups depending on the presence or absence of (a) a congenital predisposition (i.e., whether biological parents were criminal) and (b) a post-natal predisposition (variables concerned with rearing experiences and adoptive placement). When both predispositional factors were present, 40% of the adoptees were criminal compared with 12.1% with congenital only present, 6.7% for post-natal only, and 2.9% when both factors were absent.

The fact that the 40% rate for criminality when both biological and environmental factors are present is greater than the 18.8% rate given by a combination of "congenital only" and "post-natal only" conditions is indicative of a non-additive interaction between congenital and post-natal factors. Further analyses indicated that occupational status of both biological and adoptive parents were the main post-natal variables involved in this non-additive interaction. Cadoret *et al.* (1983) present data from three adoption studies which again confirm that when both genetic and environmental factors are present, they account for a greater number of antisocial behaviours than a combination of these two factors acting alone.

These data pose a number of questions. One concerns just how much overall variance can genetic factors alone account for, given the seeming importance of the H × E interaction. Buikhuisen (1985) has taken this point further, arguing that no efforts have been made to ascertain the amount of variance explained by genetic factors, and concluding that "there certainly is no reason to see genetics as a primary cause of crime" (p. 105). A second question concerns whether these data really are as strong as they appear. Consideration of less frequently cited studies helps to answer these questions.

Cloninger *et al.* (1978) in their analyses of relatives of 60 probands with felony convictions conclude that their results ". . . raise serious doubt about the importance of nonlinear gene–environment interaction. Our analyses support additive or linear models without major interactions" (p. 949). Cadoret *et al.* (1983) while arguing for the importance of an H × E interaction, report rather small proportions of total variance explained by all factors (H, E, H × E) in two of their three adoption samples (16%, 37% and 12%). Similarly Cloninger *et al.* (1982) report that only 23.6% of the total variance could be explained by main factors and their interaction; while 59.3% of the explained variance could be accounted for by genetic factors alone, only 14.4% of explained variance could be accounted for by an H × E interaction. This result casts doubt on the interpretation of their cross-fostering analysis reported above which suggested a non-additive interaction. Cadoret (1978) while in general arguing for a genetic factor in adoptee antisocial behaviour admits that only 3% of the variance in a multiple regression analysis can be accounted for by biological background, with 3% also accounted for by environmental background. Hutchings (1972) in a multiple regression of criminality in 286 probands reports that 10% of the variance in adoptee criminality can be accounted for by biological background and 3% by adoptive background.

Calculations based on data reported by Baker (1986) for property offending in Danish adoptees indicate that the proportion of phenotypic variance accounted for by additive genetic influences is 20.3%. However, entry of genotype–environment correlations into the biometric genetic model had no effect at all on normal fit indices for the model, indicating a lack of any gene–environment interactions. Biometric models fitted to the self-report delinquency data in twins reported by Rowe (1983) suggest a much higher heritability of 70% than studies of more serious (criminal) antisociality. In this study two models provided equally good fits to the data—one included genetic but not common environmental influences and one which included both factors—suggesting that gene–environmental interactions cannot be entirely ruled out.

These mixed data clearly suggest (a) the proportion of variance accounted by genetic factors is quite modest, (b) the amount of variance accounted for by an H × E interaction is sometimes significant but certainly not as great as other studies indicate. The implications for future research are that interactions between biological and social factors cannot be entirely ignored, but this should not prevent researchers from seeking out direct relationships between both biological and social factors. Biologically-based investigations will not in themselves provide completely adequate explanations of antisocial behaviour. To achieve this goal studies must combine biological and social research strategies in a much more integrated way than hitherto. More specifically, psychophysiological studies rarely, if ever, take into account presence or absence of parental antisocial behaviour, yet a combination of adoption/twin study methodology in conjunction with psychophysiological testing would make for a very potent research strategy.

IS THE GENETIC BASIS TO ANTISOCIALITY AGE-DEPENDENT?

An important question which has not to date received comprehensive analysis is the notion that the genetic basis to antisociality may be stronger in adult rather than child populations. This possibility is hinted at briefly in a number of previous studies.

Eysenck (1977) in his review of twin studies in criminals reports that concordance for juvenile delinquency in MZ twins is 85% versus 75% for DZ twins, and notes in passing that ". . . for juvenile delinquents the evidence in favour of determination by heredity is less impressive" (p. 72). In their review of the genetic basis to female crime, Widom and Ames (1988) point out that the only case of lower concordance in MZ relative to DZ twins occurs in the case of juvenile delinquency. While adoption studies find evidence for a genetic basis to adult crime in adoptees, one study by Bohman (1972) found no association between criminality in biological parents and juvenile delinquency (truancy, lying, stealing) in 10- and 11-year-old adoptees. While Cadoret (1978) found evidence for a genetic factor in adult adoptees, he could find no such evidence for conduct disorders in a sample of child adoptees. Similarly while Cadoret, Cain and Crowe (1983) argued for a significant H × E interaction in three samples of adoptees for adolescent antisocial behaviour, in two of these samples the main effect for heredity (using a multiple regression model) was not significant. West and Farrington (1973) found that criminality in parents is more strongly associated with delinquency in offspring after puberty than before puberty. Pulling these strands of disparate evidence together, it does seem that antisocial behaviour in young samples may not have such a strong genetic basis as in adult samples. Data from a twin study of the inheritance of intelligence by Wilson (1983) provides a useful heuristic parallel. MZ twins became increasingly concordant for IQ from age 3 months to 15 years and in contrast DZ twins regressed to intermediate levels of concordance by age 15 years. Wilson (1983) concludes:

> The effects are most dramatic in early childhood, when the gain is sharpest and the spurts and lags more pronounced. But even during adolescence, as the integrative power of the brain approaches its maximum level, the end phase of this protracted sequence is still subject to maturational processes that are gene-controlled. (p. 312)

Returning to the data on antisocial behaviour, the implication for future biological research is that while studies of young samples are crucial to an understanding of the developmental psychophysiology of antisocial behaviour, such samples may not provide good models for adult antisociality. The question reduces to asking at what age the genetic data from young samples begin to approximate that from adults?

Any answer must be speculative by virtue of the relatively few studies which can be drawn upon, and from the data reviewed above which suggested sex differences in genetic predisposition to antisocial behaviour. Bohman's (1972) data clearly suggest that at 11–12 years there is little genetic basis to antisociality, whereas the data for later adolescence are much more mixed. One clue may be found in a review of studies on heart rate level and antisocial behaviour by Raine and Venables (1984a), where it was argued that the link was non-existent at 7 years, began to emerge at 11 years, and maximized between 13 and 15 years in males. If this psychophysiological measure which itself has a genetic basis (Theorell, de Faire and Fagrell, 1978) can be taken as a manifestation of the genetic basis to antisocial behaviour, it would suggest a cut-off point of about 14 years in males. For females, however, Bohman (1972) found 11–12-year-old antisocial girls had a higher percentage of biological fathers with criminality than antisocial 11–12-year-old boys (56% versus 26%), suggesting that at this age a genetic basis is manifest in females. This sex difference may reflect the key role played by puberty which may in turn index the age at which antisocial behaviour assumes a genetic basis.

A curious paradox, however, is that in childhood there appears to be relatively good evidence for a genetic basis to "behavioural disorders". Eysenck (1977) cites concordance rates of 87% (MZ) and 43% (DZ) in twins with such disorders, while O'Connor *et al.* (1980) cite correlations of 0.72 (MZ) and 0.42 (DZ) for such specific behaviours as "bullying" in 7.6-year-old children. It must also be borne in mind that when one turns to mild forms of self-report delinquency in adolescents, heritability as high as 70% is demonstrated (Rowe, 1983). These discrepancies may indicate that when antisocial behaviour is legally defined heritability is age dependent, but not when antisocial behaviour is more totally encapsulated by self, parent, or teacher observations. This again underlies the potential importance of studying milder, more non-legally defined aspects of antisocial behaviour. One explanation as to why heritability appears to be stronger in children and adults than juveniles is that peer-group pressures are particularly strong in adolescence. As such, these social factors may play a relatively stronger role in determining juvenile delinquency than genetic factors.

ARE ANTISOCIAL BEHAVIOUR AND SCHIZOPHRENIA GENETICALLY RELATED?

Since the pioneering study of Kallman (1938) on the genetics of the schizophrenia and his description of the "schizoid psychopath", a repeated theme in the literature on schizophrenia is the link between this disorder and the childhood antisocial behaviour/adult criminality. The numerous lines of evidence for this link (briefly reviewed in Venables and Raine (1987) and more extensively reviewed by Silverton (1988a)) span retrospective, follow-up, adoption and clinical studies, and make the claimed link difficult to dispute. What may be disputed, however, is the factor which underpins this link. Until recently the most parsimonious explanation was cross-assortative mating (Mednick, 1978), i.e., schizophrenics tend to selectively mate with criminals, with the latter passing on a predisposition to antisociality to the offspring. However, a careful review of the literature (Silverton, 1988a) and new data from three Danish cohort studies (Silverton, 1988b) indicate that the schizophrenia–crime link is genetically mediated.

Silverton (1988a) after a detailed review of the evidence linking crime and schizophrenia examined four main hypotheses which could account for discrepant results in this literature. Two environmental "artefactual" explanations of the proposed genetic link (increased familial stress, cross-assortative mating) were rejected while two explanations consistent with a genetic model (discrepant prevalence rates of disorders in probands and discrepant parent-offspring cross-correlations) were both supported. It was argued that antisocial behaviour is part of the schizophrenia spectrum in that it marks a high-risk genotype in those at risk for schizophrenia.

Silverton (1988b) outlined a model which argues (a) the link between schizophrenia and antisocial behaviour is genetic and (b) specific environmental stressors interact with this genotype to produce either schizophrenia or antisocial behaviour. Four predictions stemming from this model were tested in a large ($N = 6770$) cohort of non-familial male adoptees (examining the relationship between biological parental schizophrenia and adoptee criminality), a separate sample of children of schizophrenics, and a large ($N=$ 9182) Danish birth cohort which assessed children of schizophrenics for antisocial behaviour. All four predictions stemming from a genetic model were supported: schizophrenia in the biological parent related to criminal behaviour in adoptees independent of cross-assortative mating; psychosocial factors associated with crime in high-risk groups were also associated in low-risk groups; variation in phenotypic outcomes in high-risk offspring will be accounted for by psychosocial factors predictive of antisociality of schizophrenia but not predictive of both; there will be a relationship between antisocial behaviour and neurological dysfunction in high but not low risk-for-schizophrenia groups.

The notion that schizophrenia and crime are genetically related may have important implications for research into antisocial behaviour. One such implication would be that psychophysiological investigations into antisocial processes might usefully adopt those psychophysiological variables which have repeatedly been found to characterize schizophrenia and which may act as genetic markers for this illness, for example frequency of skin conductance orienting responses (Bernstein *et al.*, 1982), P3 evoked potentials (Roth *et al.*, 1980) and evoked potential reducing (Buchsbaum, 1975), and smooth-pursuit eye movements (Holzman, Proctor and Hughes, 1973). These variables together with interview or self-report measures of schizoid tendencies may help delineate schizoid antisocials from those who are "purely" antisocial and thus enable the population to be divided into more homogeneous sub-samples. This may help clarify the biological correlates of antisociality *per se*, and would allow separate study of a potentially interesting schizoid antisocial group. The implication for schizophrenia research would again be that antisocial behaviour may prove to be an important moderator variable, producing groups of schizophrenics with and without a history of antisociality which may be more clearly differentiated on biological measures.

NEUROPSYCHOLOGY

One way in which a genetic basis for antisocial conduct may be expressed is by disruption of the normal neural mechanisms which mediate and control behaviour. Criminal and delinquent populations have consequently been investigated using neuropsychological procedures in order to uncover evidence for discrete neurological damage or dysfunction which may account for antisociality. The two most important general propositions to emerge from this area are that antisocials are characterized by (a) left hemisphere damage/dysfunction and (b) frontal lobe damage/dysfunction. Detailed reviews of neuropsychological impairments in general and left hemisphere dysfunction in particular in various antisocial groups may be found in Yeudall and Fromm-

Auch (1979), Yeudall *et al.* (1981), Nachshon (1983) and Moffitt (1988). Rather than reiterate material contained in these reviews, this present section aims to develop and elaborate one contentious theme—that psychopaths and other antisocial groups may suffer from frontal lobe damage.

EVIDENCE FOR FRONTAL LOBE DAMAGE IN ANTISOCIALS

On the basis of data on aggression in temporal lobe epileptics, Flor-Henry (1973) developed an influential theory of psychopathy. As with schizophrenics, Flor-Henry (1973) argued that criminal psychopaths were characterized by left hemisphere damage, and in particular by disruption to frontal and temporal cortical-limbic systems. The notion of dominant hemisphere dysfunction has been supported by repeated findings of Performance > Verbal scores on the WAIS in delinquent and criminal groups (see Nachshon, 1983 for a review), while detailed and extensive testing on neuropsychological test batteries by Yeudall and Fromm-Auch (1979), Yeudall *et al.* (1981), and Yeudall, Fromm-Auch and Davies (1982) revealed evidence for a fronto-temporal locus of dominant hemisphere damage in a wide variety of criminal groups including criminal psychopaths, sexual offenders, male violent criminals, adolescents with conduct disturbances, and behaviour-problem school-children.

While Yeudall's findings are impressive they have been criticized by Hare (1979) and Nachshon (1983), the most important criticism being that subject samples utilized by Yeudall *et al.* are preselected clinical patients suspected of having neuropsychological impairments. It may not be surprising therefore to find a high proportion of these antisocials with neuropsychological impairments. More recent, less frequently cited independent studies have not always supported the findings of Yeudall *et al.* Virkkunen, Nuutila and Huusko (1976) failed to find any increase in criminality in a follow-up of 507 Second World War soldiers with damage to either frontal or temporal lobes. Gornstein (1982) reported psychopaths as showing evidence of frontal lobe dysfunction as assessed by the Wisconsin Card Sorting Test (WCST), Necker Cube reversals, and a sequential matching memory task, but Hare (1984) failed to replicate these findings using a more stringent and reliable procedure for assessing psychopathy. Similarly Sutker, Moan and Allain (1983) failed to find any differences in perseveration between psychopaths and controls in the WCST which would support Gornstein's findings. However, one study by Newman, Pattersen and Kosson (1987) provides very strong support for response perseveration in criminal psychopaths using a card-playing task incorporating monetary rewards.

POSSIBLE MEDIATING FACTORS

While these data cast serious doubt on the frontal lobe hypothesis, a consideration of some of the points made in the previous section suggest that discarding the frontal lobe hypothesis at this stage may be premature. It was suggested earlier that the case for a genetic basis to psychopathy has not yet been clearly demonstrated, whereas there is some reason to believe that there is stronger evidence for a genetic basis to female crime, post-pubertal antisocial behaviour, and petty criminality. It may not therefore be surprising that psychopaths fail to show frontal lobe dysfunction in comparison to control groups made up of non-psychopathic criminals as is the case with studies by Hare (1984) and Sutker, Moan and Allain (1983) which show negative findings. With respect to a possible genetic basis to female and post-pubertal antisociality, a study by Moffitt (1988) is of interest. This study assessed 750 13-year-old normal male and female children in New Zealand on self-report measures of delinquency and a neuropsychological test battery which included several measures of frontal lobe functioning (WCST, Trail Making test, verbal fluency, WISC-R Mazes, Rey-Osterreith Complex Figure Test). Male delinquents did not differ from non-delinquent controls on a composite index of these frontal lobe tasks, but female delinquents were found to have significantly lower frontal lobe scores than female non-delinquents, a result which might be expected if one were to assume greater genetic predisposition to crime in females. A similar finding may be seen in a study on neuropsychological impairment in 13–17-year-old male and female delinquents where Yeudall *et al.* (1982) argued for anterior non-dominant hemisphere dysfunction in delinquency *per se*. However, it is clear from inspection of their Table 2 that this lateralized anterior dysfunction was much more prominent in females (70% non-dominant dysfunction versus 30% dominant) than in males where there was little evidence for a lateralized dysfunction (45% versus 55%).

In both studies evidence for stronger frontal lobe dysfunction, and stronger lateralization of this dysfunction in females, could be a function of a greater genetic predisposition for female antisociality. An equally plausible explanation would be that sex differences in these studies are merely a function of age effects. Girls in Moffitt's (1988) study are more likely to be post-pubertal at 13 relative to boys, and similarly in the 13–17-year-old female delinquents in the study of Yeudall *et al.* (1982) there is a greater likelihood of females having reached full maturity than males.

FRONTAL LOBE DYSFUNCTION IN SCHIZOID ANTISOCIALS

While therefore a frontal lobe hypothesis may not be of great relevance to understanding adult psychopathy, this explanation may be of greater relevance to relatively milder forms of antisocial conduct in either juveniles or young adults. Yet another alternative, based on the view that the link between schizophrenia and antisocial behaviour may be genetically mediated, is the possibility that frontal lobe dysfunction may be of particular relevance to schizoid psychopaths or schizoid antisocials. At a clinical level the region of the frontal lobes which may be of stronger relevance to psychopathy consists of orbitofrontal cortex, whereas damage to dorsolateral regions of frontal cortex may be implicated in schizophrenia. Damage to orbitofrontal regions results in impulsivity, reduced guilt, concern and other emotional feelings, less inhibited sexual behaviour, indifference, emotional outbursts and aggressive behaviour, uninhibited social behaviour, and *Witzelscuht* (puerile jocularity), personality changes which bear some close parallels to the clinical concept of psychopathy (Elliott, 1978). The fact that orbitofrontal lesions produce no clear deficits in intelligence is also consistent with the lack of intellectual/cognitive deficits in psychopaths (Hare *et al.*, 1980). The notion of frontal lobe dysfunction in schizophrenia has received recent support from studies indicating reduced frontal cerebral blood flow during performance of the WCST (Weinberger, Berman and Zec, 1986), MRI scans showing reduced frontal lobe area (Andreasen *et al.*, 1986) and neuropsychological studies of frontal lobe functioning (Taylor and Abrams, 1984). One study (Weinberger, Berman and Zec, 1986) has specifically implicated the dorsolateral prefrontal area of frontal association cortex in schizophrenia using both regional cerebral blood flow and WCST measures of frontal lobe functioning. Damage to this area induces impairments in abstract reasoning and concept formation (such as response perseveration as measured by the WCST), loss of foresight and ability to plan ahead, poor motivation and work capacity, flat affect, social withdrawal, a lack of insight, poor sustained attention, and poor concentration.

There are clear difficulties, however, in attempting to relate psychopathy with orbitofrontal lesions and schizophrenia with dorsolateral lesions. Elliott (1978), for example, has pointed out that patients with prefrontal damage show bad judgment in both their own and other's affairs whereas psychopaths show good judgment in theoretical situations concerning other people and do not display the apathy seen in patients with prefrontal damage. Similarly Levin (1984) discussing one important caveat to a frontal lobe hypothesis of schizophrenia points out that patients with frontal damage often display "an emotional lability and disregard for the consequences of their actions" (p. 66), behaviour which is less consistent with the diagnosis of schizophrenia.

In contrast, the application of a frontal lobe hypothesis to schizoid psychopaths may be less problematic. Hare (1984) in discussing the failure to observe frontal lobe impairments in psychopaths nevertheless suggests that criminals who show some features of psychopathy but who fall short of the complete psychopathic syndrome show greater evidence of neurological impairment and similarly both Elliott (1978) and Damasio (1979) have suggested that frontal lobe patients appear as "partial psychopaths". Raine (1991) found that partial psychopaths (medium scorers on the Psychopathy Checklist) are characterized by higher scores on DSM III Borderline and

Schizotypal Personality Disorder and self-report measures of schizoid personality (e.g. schizophrenism and withdrawn–disturbed relationships) and may correspond to Kallman's (1938) notion of schizoid psychopathy. These individuals are particularly characterized by features of psychopathy relating to an impulsive, unstable, nomadic lifestyle, a lack of life planning, a trivial sex life, and an inability to maintain long-term relationships, features which bear several close parallels to Heston's (1966) description of adopted away criminal sons of schizophrenic mothers. At the same time these individuals possess social withdrawal, isolation, and a degree of perceptual and cognitive disturbances which bear parallels to the more negative features of schizophrenia (Andreasen, 1982). This might be predicted since Levin (1984) has argued on the basis of neurochemical and neuroanatomical evidence that a frontal lobe hypothesis of schizophrenia is particularly relevant to the more chronic negative symptoms of schizophrenia.

It may be that schizoid psychopathy constitutes a syndrome which most clearly represents the genetic relatedness between schizophrenia and psychopathy and which is in part determined by dysfunction of both orbitofrontal and dorsolateral areas of the frontal lobes, with orbitofrontal cortex contributing to the psychopathic-like personality features and dorsolateral prefrontal cortex contributing to the cognitive and social withdrawal features of schizotypal personality. At present there is little evidence to support this speculative proposition. A study by Devonshire, Howard and Sellars (1988), found impulsive and socially withdrawn "secondary psychopathy" to show frontal lobe damage as indicated by more perseveration errors on the WCST, whereas "primary psychopaths" demonstrated no such deficits. To the extent that these secondary psychopaths can be equated with schizoid psychopaths, this finding would provide partial support for the above proposition. A further study which bears on this hypothesis will be discussed in the following section.

Finally, it should be pointed out that failures to observe WCST perseveration errors in psychopaths may not be entirely unexpected if orbitofrontal dysfunction provides the major basis for psychopathic personality since lesions to this area do not produce cognitive deficits. Returning to the notion of dorsolateral dysfunction as a possible basis to schizoid psychopathy, an interesting feature of patients with dorsolateral frontal lesions is that behaviourally they make perseveration errors even though at a verbal level they are fully cognizant of their errors and the appropriate response strategy (Milner, 1963). This bears an interesting parallel to a similar dissociation between the psychopath's verbalizations and his actual behaviour (Cleckley, 1976). Left frontal lobe dysfunction may not account for the full syndrome of schizoid psychopathy or psychopathy, but it may help account for some of the verbal peculiarities of psychopaths. Individual analysis of psychopathic traits (Raine, 1985) may help clarify any relationship between frontal lobe dysfunction and psychopathy.

PSYCHOPHYSIOLOGY

A relatively large number of studies have sought to establish the biological basis of antisocial behaviour through psychophysiological recording techniques, and such research represents that area of biological research most extensively employed with antisocial groups. Reviews of most of the work in this area may be found in Hare and Schalling (1978), Mednick and Christiansen (1977), Mednick, Moffitt and Stack (1989), Moffitt and Mednick (1988), Raine (1988a; 1988b; 1989), Venables and Raine (1987) and Mednick and Volavka (1980). Rather than overlap with this literature, this present section will instead briefly recapitulate on implications for psychophysiological research stemming from points made in earlier sections, and then concentrate on very recent research which has not to date received critical comment.

Consideration of anthropological and sociobiological perspectives suggested that if psychopathy has a psychophysiological basis which reflects a genetic predisposition to psychopathy, one might expect strong psychophysiological relationships with those specific traits of psychopathy which correspond to personality characteristics of the Mundurucu or a "cheating" reproductive strategy. The notion of a stronger genetic basis to female criminality suggests that psychophysiological research into female antisocial behaviour may offer particularly clear insights into antisocial behaviour in general. The fact that petty rather than serious criminal offending may have a stronger genetic basis suggests that more psychophysiological research should be directed towards the "softer" end of the antisociality spectrum. The discussion of H × E interactions suggested that psychophysiological research should be more biosocial in nature and attempt to take into account criminality in the subjects' parents. The genetic link between schizophrenia and crime in turn suggests that established psychophysiological correlates of schizophrenia are worth exploring in antisocial populations. None of these issues have to date been addressed in psychophysiological research into antisocial behaviour, although these lines have the potential to lead to genuine advances in this area of research. Two of the above issues are worth exploring in more detail in relation to relatively recent research findings, while a third area of recent research concerns prospective psychophysiological studies of crime.

MILD LEVELS OF ANTISOCIAL CONDUCT

The first of these concerns the view that psychophysiological research may be usefully directed at mild as opposed to severe levels of antisocial behaviour. Support for this view emerges from recent EEG studies of criminals reported by Volavka *et al.* (1984). A review of EEG research on more severe, psychopathic criminals by Syndulko (1978) concludes that most studies are methodologically unsound and produce conflicting results. However, the two studies reported by Volavka *et al.* (1984) indicate very striking and clear relationships between EEG measures and theft offences. In one study carried out in Denmark (Mednick *et al.*, 1981) males with police registrations for theft at 19 years were characterized by an excess of EEG activity in the 8–10 Hz band when initially tested at age 13 years. A second check on police records three years later when subjects were aged 22 years again confirmed this relationship. In both cases increased alpha activity differentiated thieves from non-offenders, and alpha was also positively related to number of thefts. In a second study in Sweden by Petersen *et al.* (1982) subjects who had committed theft offences were found to have more power in the slow alpha range (7.5–9.5 Hz) relative to the fast alpha range (9.5–12.5 Hz) as assessed twelve years previously at age 1–15 years. Again there was a relationship between extent of slow alpha power and repeated theft. No other study appears to have related EEG measures to specific mild forms of criminality such as thievery, and in the light of previous inconsistent findings in this area these two studies strongly endorse the value of placing milder forms of criminal behaviour under psychophysiological scrutiny.

A second recent study which endorses the value of this orientation towards mild forms of crime consists of an analysis reported by Buikhuisen *et al.* (1984). This study is of interest in that the subject sample consisted of what Buikhuisen *et al.* (1984) called "privileged offender"—Dutch university undergraduates assessed on self-report measures of criminal offences. Since subjects are relatively free of adverse social background factors associated with delinquency (Rutter and Giller, 1983), the social push towards antisociality is minimal and potentially allows for a greater role to be played by biological factors (Mednick *et al.*, 1977; Raine and Venables, 1981). Criminality measures (theft, violence, evasion, traffic and vandalism offences), personality traits, parental home factors, and psychophysiological variables (skin conductance parameters measured to 120 dB stimuli) were subjected to a factor analysis which produced four main factors. Factor 2 (labelled "general propensity to criminal behaviour" as all five offence types gave significant loadings) and Factor 4 ("committing crimes of violence" with loadings from crimes of violence and traffic offences) have low and largely non-significant loadings from psychophysiological parameters. In contrast Factor 3 ("evasion crimes") had large and significant loadings from low skin conductance (SC) levels (–0.88), reduced SC spontaneous fluctuations (–0.72), smaller SC amplitudes (–0.85) and longer SC recovery times (0.43). Evasion crimes consisted of acts such as evading taxes, not declaring goods at customs, and abusing social security.

That such a "classic" under-aroused profile emerges for this category of offence but not for more serious offending may be explained either by (a) the fact that petty criminality rather than violent offending has a genetic basis, (b) the fact that under-arousal and a lack of anxiety is a particularly pertinent psychophysiological state for the commission of acts such as customs evasion, (c) the fact that evasion crimes can be seen as more "white-collar" crimes perpetrated by the middle classes and which are not so closely associated with social predispositional factors and hence are better explained by biological factors. In support of this latter interpretation is the fact that parental home variables (e.g. "father/mother beats son") do not load on this factor. Although these interpretations of the data are not those given by Buikhuisen *et al.* (1984), they are nevertheless feasible and again demonstrate the value of assessing less serious, more "middle class" antisociality free of the methodological problems associated with institutionalized samples in relation to psychophysiological variables.

A third area of research which suggests the value of assessing mild forms of antisocial behaviour consists of psychophysiological studies of relatively normal, non-institutionalized school-children who show refractory behaviour at school. Examples of this approach can be found in studies demonstrating relationships between this type of antisociality and electrodermal non-responding (Raine and Venables, 1984b), skin conductance conditioning (Raine and Venables, 1981), longer skin conductance half-recovery time (Clark, 1982), lower heart rate levels (Davies and Maliphant, 1971; Raine and Venables, 1984a), and larger P3 evoked potentials (Raine and Venables, 1987).

ANTISOCIAL BEHAVIOUR AND SCHIZOPHRENIA

A second issue worthy of more detailed elaboration concerns research aimed at establishing a possible psychophysiological link between antisocial behaviour and schizophrenia. Not surprisingly very little psychophysiological research has explored this avenue. As indicated earlier Hare and colleagues (Hare, 1984, 1985; Hare and Forth, 1985) have speculated that criminals who are partially psychopathic have schizoid personalities and are more likely to be neurologically impaired, but this speculation is only to date supported by neuropsychological data.

Partial support for a psychophysiological link between antisocial behaviour and schizoid-antisocial tendencies is, however, suggested by a number of studies. Raine and Venables (1984b) found antisocial 15-year-old male schoolchildren (defined by self-report and teacher rating measures) to be characterized by SC non-responding to orienting stimuli, a psychophysiological variable which has been consistently associated with schizophrenia (Bernstein *et al.*, 1982). However, when the antisocial group were divided into those with and without schizoid tendencies (anxious, socially withdrawn, psychotic personality) it was found that it was the schizoid antisocials who were particularly characterized by SC non-responding. The authors interpreted this data as indicating that SC non-responding may represent a common biological predisposing factor in antisocial as well as schizophrenic disorders, and may possibly reflect an abnormal allocation of attentional resources to incoming stimuli.

A more recent study by Raine (1987a) confirmed this relationship between schizoid antisocials and SC non-responding in top-security adult male prisoners. Within this criminal group scores on one index of anhedonia—psychoticism (social anhedonia, physical anhedonia, psychoticism, and hallucinatory predisposition) were significantly correlated with frequency of orienting SCRs ($r = -0.43$, $p < 0.05$) in the direction of reduced orienting in schizoid criminals. However, early home environment was found to mediate this effect in that this relationship was moderately large and significant in those from intact homes ($r = -0.51$, $p < 0.05$) but not in those from broken homes ($r = -0.26$, $p > 0.36$), a result which again underlies the importance of taking into account social factors in psychophysiology–antisociality relationships (Raine, 1988a). WAIS subtests dependent on verbal working memory (digit span, arithmetic) were strongly correlated with both schizoid tendencies (–0.62) and SC orienting ($r = 0.70$) in the intact home sample and were in statistical terms found to fully account for the link between these two latter variables. This is of interest in that Nuechterlein and Dawson (1984) in a review of information processing in the development of schizophrenia conclude that deficits in children of schizophrenics on active, effortful, capacity-demanding tasks (which would place heavy loads on working memory) reflect a reduced allocation of available processing capacity to such tasks, a process similar to that ascribed by Bernstein *et al.* (1982) to reduced SC orienting. It may well be that this reduced ability to meet high moment-to-moment processing capacity demands, which is in part assessed by both SC orienting and working memory-related WAIS measures, underlies conjoint antisocial and schizoid tendencies.

A study by Raine (1987b) also bears on the issue of the antisociality–schizophrenia link. This study related three well-replicated psychophysiological characteristics of schizophrenia (deviant smooth-pursuit eye movements, electrodermal non-responding, and reduced P3 evoked potentials) to dimensional measures of "schizoid psychopathy" (psychopathic traits correlated with schizoid measures as described earlier) and "psychopathy" (psychopathic traits unrelated to schizoid features). Schizoid psychopathy was associated with disturbances in smooth-pursuit eye movements and enhanced P3 evoked potentials to target stimuli (elicited using a continuous performance task), whereas psychopathy was unrelated to these measures. These results suggest that schizoid psychopathy is dissociated from psychopathy at an underlying psychophysiological level, and given the surprising finding of enhanced P3 evoked potentials also suggest a dissociation from schizophrenia. They additionally suggest that the dimension of schizoid psychopathy may be a salient psychopathological condition differing somewhat from both psychopathy and schizophrenia, conceivably representing a "half-way house" between these two disorders.

Another recent study suggesting that there is a subgroup of criminals characterized by schizoid tendencies used abnormalities in smooth-pursuit eye movements to divide a group of criminals into high and low subgroups of "schizoid criminals" (Raine and Venables, 1990). Poor eye-tracking is a well-replicated correlate of schizophrenia and has been proposed as a genetic marker for schizophrenia. Subgroups were then tested on the ERP augmenting–reducing paradigm. The schizoid subgroup of criminals were found to show a pattern of cortical reducing (reduced ERP amplitudes to stimuli of increasing intensity), whereas non-schizoid criminals showed the more normal pattern of cortical augmenting (increased ERP amplitudes to stimuli of increasing intensity).

Since schizophrenics are characterized by either cortical reducing or else a failure to augment (Pritchard, 1986), the finding of reducing in criminals with abnormal smooth-pursuit eye movements is consistent with the view that such individuals represent a schizoid subgroup. That this subgroup has affinities to schizophrenia is suggested by the fact that the mean smooth-pursuit signal/noise ratio was 4.27, non-significantly *poorer* than a value of 4.31 reported by Mitchell (1988) for 45 chronic schizophrenics tested using the same procedures. These values lie in contrast to values of 4.85 obtained for a normal control group. These findings indicate that schizoid subgroups can be clearly delineated within criminal populations using psychophysiological markers for schizophrenia. Further research along similar lines holds out the possibility of elucidating our presently poor understanding of the psychophysiological link between crime and schizophrenia-spectrum disorders.

PROSPECTIVE PSYCHOPHYSIOLOGICAL RESEARCH AND CRIME

One of the greatest barriers to a more complete understanding of antisocial and criminal behaviour is the lack of prospective, longitudinal studies. One major problem with many previous psychophysiological studies of antisocial behaviour is that measures of psychophysiology and crime are taken concurrently in time. In the prospective design, however, psychophysiological measures of relevance to crime are measured earlier in life in order to predict later criminal behaviour. A second methodological problem with many psychophysiological investigations is that almost all employ institutionalized samples, and consequently it is possible that differences are a result of differences in length of incarceration and the effects of prison stress and crowding on psychophysiological responses. Again, prospective designs help to overcome this problem. Such designs clearly constitute a more powerful technique by which to explore potential cause–effect relationships.

To date there have only been four prospective psychophysiological studies conducted into crime, and none have recorded from more than one psychophysiological response system (Wadsworth, 1976; Loeb and Mednick, 1977; Mednick *et al.*, 1981; Petersen *et al.*, 1982). However, each of these studies provides individual evidence implicating reduced arousal in the development of criminality in the cardiovascular or electrodermal or cortical response systems.

A recent study by Raine, Venables and Williams (1990a; 1990b) provides some striking evidence for the power of the prospective design in the psychophysiological investigation of criminal behaviour. Between 1978 and 1979, a random sample of 101 male school-children aged 15 years were tested in a series of psychophysiological paradigms. In December 1988 searches were made for all subjects at the computerized central Criminal Records Office in London for the total sample. Subjects found guilty of crimes and sentenced at courts were classified as "criminal". Using this criterion, 17 out of the 101 subjects were found to possess a criminal record. Offences ranged in severity from theft to wounding, with the most common offence being burglary and theft. Five of the 17 had been imprisoned at some point in time following psychophysiological testing. Crimes recorded at the Criminal Records Office are synonymous with "serious" offending and do not include trivial offences such as traffic violations.

In the first psychophysiological paradigm (Raine, Venables and Williams, 1990a), measures of skin conductance, heart rate, and EEG were taken during a resting period in order to provide indices of electrodermal, cardiovascular, and cortical arousal. Criminals-to-be were then compared with non-criminals on these measures of arousal. Criminals relative to non-criminal controls were found to have significantly lower resting heart rates both at the start and the end of the rest period, indicating reduced cardiovascular arousal in criminals (see Figure 11.1). Criminals also had significantly fewer non-specific skin conductance fluctuations (NSF) during the rest period, indicating reduced electrodermal arousal (see Figure 11.2). Criminals also had significantly more EEG power in the low frequency bands than non-criminals; in particular, they had significantly more power in the theta band, indicating cortical underarousal (see Figure 11.3).

Importantly, these arousal differences were not mediated by group differences in social and demographic factors (age, social class, academic ability, area of residence) since all relationships between these variables and arousal measures were small and non-significant. Furthermore, since EEG, heart rate and skin conductance arousal measures were uncorrelated in this sample (mean r –0.04), the findings of lower arousal on *all three* of these measures in criminals effectively constitutes three independent replications of the arousal–crime link. This appears to be the first study, prospective or nonprospective, to provide evidence for the role of both ANS and CNS underarousal in the development of criminal behaviour. Although prospective

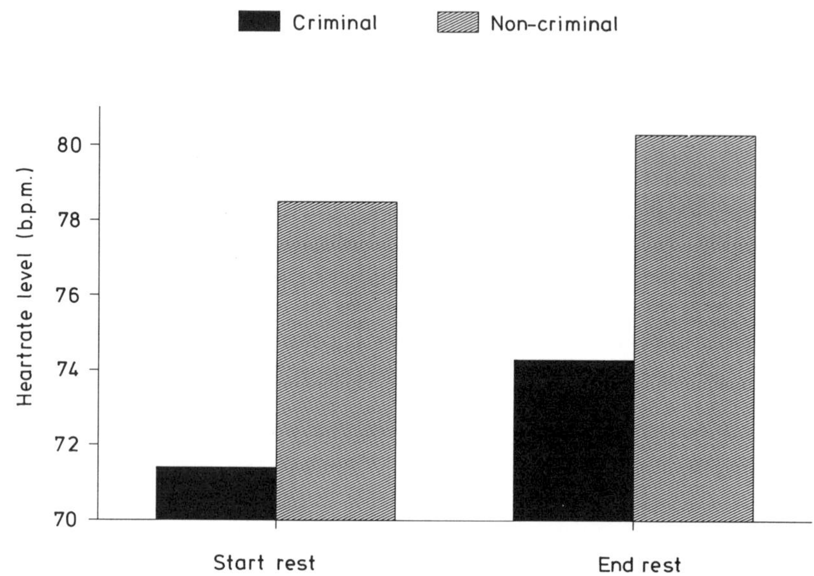

Figure 11.1. Heart rate levels in criminals-to-be and non-criminals at the start and end of the rest period.

Figure 11.2. Number of NSFs (non-specific skin conductance fluctuations) recorded during the rest period on right and left hands in criminals-to-be and non-criminals.

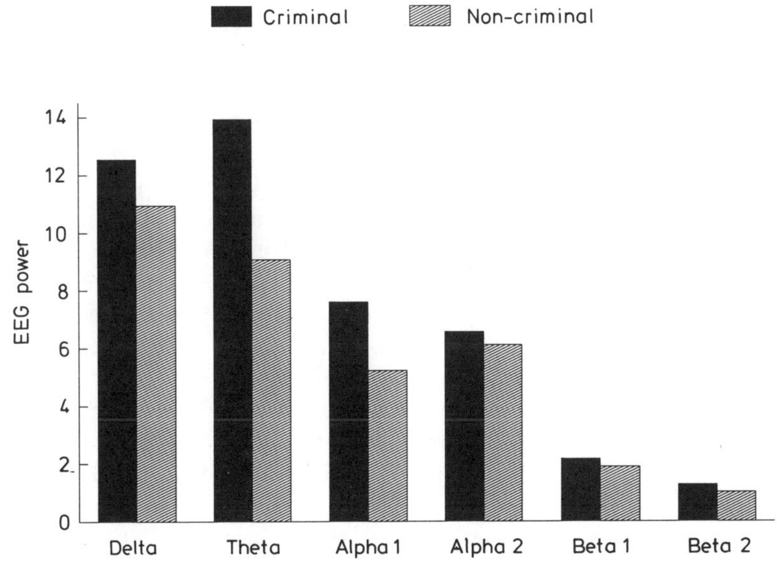

Figure 11.3. EEG power (in arbitrary units) across six frequency bands in criminals-to-be and non-criminals during the rest period.

studies cannot conclusively demonstrate causal relationships, these new findings are nevertheless consistent with the view that ANS and CNS under-arousal may play a role in the development of criminal behaviour.

The measures of arousal used in this study are in part genetically-determined. The finding of reduced arousal in criminals is therefore consistent with the view that the genetic predisposition to criminality may find its expression through ANS and CNS under-arousal. At a neuroanatomical level, the fact that levels of all three physiological systems are reduced suggests that a diffuse brainstem arousal mechanism may be dysfunctional in criminals.

These findings also have practical implications. Using only three psychophysiological variables (heart rate level, EEG theta activity, skin conductance non-specific fluctuations) as predictors in a discriminant function analysis, these variables were able to correctly classify 74.7% of all subjects, in contrast to chance levels of 50%. Furthermore, the false positive rate of 23.1% (i.e. 23.5% of non-criminals were incorrectly classified as criminals) is relatively small given the statistical difficulties in predicting events with low base rates. In conjunction with other social and psychological variables, measures of ANS and CNS under-arousal may facilitate the early prediction of later antisocial behaviour in addition to elucidating the aetiological basis of criminality.

The second psychophysiological paradigm in this study concerned the measurement of orienting deficits using skin conductance and heart rate measures (Raine, Venables and Williams, 1990b). Criminals-to-be were found to be characterized at age 15 by a reduced frequency of skin conductance responses to a series of 65 dB auditory orienting stimuli. Furthermore, 31% of criminals were characterized by electrodermal non-responding (no response to any of the orienting stimuli) in contrast to a rate of only 10% in non-criminal controls. These orienting deficits in the electrodermal system were also supported by findings of significantly smaller heart rate orienting responses to the same stimuli. Reduced orienting acitivity in criminals-to-be is consistent with the notion that antisocials have a deficit in the allocation of attentional resources to external stimuli (Raine and Venables, 1984b). Such a deficit may explain some early social and cognitive impairments in antisocial individuals, such as poor academic work, antisocial school behaviour, and difficulties in sustaining training courses and jobs.

Findings from the third psychophysiological paradigm suggest, however, that these attentional deficits seem likely to be specific to *passive* attend situations. In this third paradigm (Raine, Venables and Williams, 1990c), event-related potentials (ERPs) were recorded to stimuli which predicted the occurrence of an aversive tone. As such, these "warning" stimuli constitute "target" events characterized by *larger* N1 ERP amplitudes to these attended stimuli. Larger N1 amplitudes are interpreted as indicating enhanced early stimulus-set attention in criminals.

These findings are surprising and go against the classic notion that antisocial groups are characterized by across-the-board attentional deficits. They are, however, consistent with recent ERP studies into psychopathy and antisocial behaviour which indicate that in experimental situations which require *active* attention to short-term task-relevant events, antisocials show evidence of *greater* attentional processes as indicated by larger ERPs (e.g. Forth and Hare, 1989; Raine and Venables, 1988). Enhanced attentional focusing to events of interest would also be consistent with a sensation-seeking account of criminality (Quay, 1965) and also with a previous ERP research in criminality (see Raine 1989 for a review). Overly-focused short-term attention to events of interest may also relate to the undue emphasis on short-term gratification in criminals and psychopaths at the expense of the sustained attention required for a more stable, non-criminal lifestyle. One potentially important implication of these results is that interventions on antisocial populations may usefully focus on the type of attentional abilities and situations which give rise to performance superiorities in such subjects.

CONCLUDING COMMENTS

It will have become clear from the previous section on psychophysiology that attempts to make sense out of a relatively small number of psychophysiological studies can lead to either completely misleading speculations or else potentially valuable directives for future research. Inevitably the answer to whether these speculations are misleading or valuable will only be provided by empirical research directed at the questions raised above. Specific issues which do stand out as promising and deserving greater attention include those concerning female crime, mild levels of antisociality, frontal lobe dysfunction as a basis to schizoid psychopathy, prospective psychophysiological research, and psychopathic traits related to cheating reproductive strategies. While research into these specific issues would be useful, there remains a very definite need for studies which incorporate ideas and developments stemming from all the main areas covered above. As suggested in the introduction, cross-disciplinary research into antisocial behaviour is dependent on strong, integrated research within each discipline, and biological research can best contribute to such ventures when more researchers are prepared to cut across areas pertaining to biological psychology such as evolution, genetics, neuropsychology and psychophysiology. Finally, it must be recognized that antisociality is a pathological form of behaviour which has a strong developmental history, and that a developmental framework will be an essential part to a complete understanding of this behaviour. Bio-developmental studies of antisociality are sorely needed if we are to ever understand the mechanisms and processes by which such pernicious pathologies as psychopathy evolve from early childhood conduct problems.

REFERENCES

Andreasen, N.C. (1982) Negative symptoms in schizophrenia. *Archives of General Psychiatry*, **39**, 784–788.

Andreasen, N., Nasrallah, H.A., Dunn, V., Olson, S.C., Grove, W.M., Ehrhardt, J.C., Coffman, J.A. and Crossett, J.H.W. (1986) Structural abnormalities in the frontal system in schizophrenia. *Archives of General Psychiatry*, **43**, 136–144.

Baker, L.A. (1986) Estimating genetic correlations among discordant phenotypes: an analysis of criminal convictions and psychiatric hospital diagnoses in Danish adoptees. *Behaviour Genetics*, **16**, 127–142.

Bernstein, A.S., Frith, C.D., Gruzelier, J.H., Patterson, T., Straube, E., Venables, P.H. and Zahn, T.P. (1982) An analysis of the skin conductance orienting response in samples of American, British and German schizophrenics. *Biological Psychology*, **14**, 155–211.

Bohman, M. (1972) A study of adopted children, their background, environment and adjustment. *Acta Pediatrica Scandinavica*, **61**, 90–97.

Bohman, M., Cloninger, R., Sigvardsson, S. and von Knorring, A.L. (1982) Predisposition to petty criminality in Swedish adoptees. I. Genetic and environmental heterogeneity. *Archives of General Psychiatry*, **39**, 1233–1241.

Buchsbaum, A. (1975) Average evoked response augmenting/reducing in schizophrenia and affective disorders. In D.X. Freedman (ed.), *Biology of the Major Psychoses.* Research Publications of the Association of Research into Nervous and Mental Diseases, **54**, New York: Raven Press.

Buikhuisen, W. (1985) Crime, genetics and the criminal justice system. *Politics and the Life Sciences*, **4**, 103–107.

Buikhuisen, W., Bontekoe, E.H.M., Plas-Korenhoff, C. and van Buuren, S. (1984) Characteristics of criminals: the privileged offender. *International Journal of Law and Psychiatry*, **7**, 301–313.

Cadoret, R.J. (1978) Psychopathology in adopted-away offspring of biologic parents with antisocial behavior. *Archives of General Psychiatry*, **35**, 176–184.

Cadoret, R.J. and Cain, C. (1980) Sex differences in predictors of antisocial behavior in adoptees. *Archives of General Psychiatry*, **37**, 1171–1175.

Cadoret, R.J., Cain, C.A. and Crowe, R.R. (1983) Evidence for gene-environment interaction in the development of adolescent antisocial behavior. *Behavior Genetics*, **13**, 301–310.

Cadoret, R.J., O'Gorman, T.W., Troughton, E. and Heywood, E. (1985) Alcoholism and antisocial personality: interrelationships, genetic and environmental factors. *Archives of General Psychiatry*, **42**, 161–167.

Cadoret, R.J., Troughton, E. and O'Gorman, T.W. (1987) Genetic and environmental factors in alcohol abuse and antisocial personality. *Journal of Studies on Alcohol*, **48**, 1–8.

Christiansen, K.O. (1977) A preliminary study of criminality among twins. In S.A. Mednick and K.O. Christiansen (eds), *Biosocial Bases of Criminal Behavior*. New York: Gardner Press.

Clark, F. (1982) Relationship of electrodermal activity in three-year-olds to their levels of aggression at age nine: A study of physiologic substrates of temperament. Unpublished doctoral dissertation, University of Southern California.

Cleckley, H.C. (1976) *The Mask of Sanity* (5th edn.). St Louis: Mosby.

Cloninger, C.R., Christiansen, K.O., Reich, R. and Gottesman, I.I. (1978) Implications of sex differences in the prevalence of antisocial personality, alcoholism, and criminality for familial transmission. *Archives of General Psychiatry*, **35**, 941–951.

Cloninger, C.R., Reich, T. and Guze, S.B. (1975) The multifactorial model of disease transmission: II. Sex differences in the familial transmission of sociopathy (antisocial personality). *British Journal of Psychiatry*, **127**, 11–22.

Cloninger, C.R., Sigvardsson, S., Bohman, M. and von Knorring, A.L. (1982) Predisposition to petty criminality in Swedish adoptees. II. Cross-fostering analysis of gene-environmental interaction. *Archives of General Psychiatry*, **39**, 1242–1247.

Craft, M. (1966) *Psychopathic Disorders*. Oxford: Pergamon.

Crowe, R. (1974) An adoption study of antisocial personality. *Archives of General Psychiatry*, **31**, 785–791.

Damasio, A. (1979) The frontal lobes. In K.M. Heilman and E. Valenstein (eds), *Clinical Neuropsychology*. New York: Oxford University Press.

Davies, J.G.V. and Maliphant, R. (1971) Autonomic responses of male adolescents exhibiting refractory behaviour in school. *Journal of Child Psychology and Psychiatry*, **12**, 115–127.

Dawkins, R. (1976) *The Selfish Gene*. Oxford: Oxford University Press.

Devonshire, P.A., Howard, R.C. and Sellars, C. (1988) Frontal lobe functions and antisocial personality in mentally abnormal offenders. *Personality and Individual Differences*, **9**, 339–344.

Elliott, F.A. (1978) Neurological aspects of antisocial behavior. In W.H. Reid (ed.), *The Psychopath: a Comprehensive Study of Antisocial Disorders and Behavior*. New York: Brunner/Mazell.

Eysenck, H.J. (1977) *Crime and Personality*. 3rd edn. St. Albans: Paladin.

Flor-Henry, P. (1973) Psychiatric syndromes considered as manifestations of lateralised temporal-limbic dysfunction. In L. Latimer and K. Livingstone (eds), *Surgical Approaches in Psychiatry*. Lancaster: Medical and Technical.

Forth, A. and Hare, R.D. (1989) The contingent negative variation in psychopaths. *Psychophysiology*, **26**, 676–682.

Gornstein, E.E. (1982) Frontal lobe functions in psychopaths. *Journal of Theoretical Biology*, **7**, 1–16.

Hamilton, W.D. (1964) The genetic evolution of social behavior. *Journal of Theoretical Biology*, **7**, 1–16.

Hare, R.D. (1979) Psychopathy and laterality of cerebral function. *Journal of Abnormal Psychology*, **88**, 605–610.

Hare, R.D. (1980) A research scale for the assessment of psychopathy in clinical populations. *Personality and Individual Differences*, **1**, 111–120.

Hare, R.D. (1983) Diagnosis of antisocial personality disorder in two prison populations. *American Journal of Psychiatry*, **140**, 887–890.

Hare, R.D. (1984) Performance of psychopaths on cognitive tasks related to frontal lobe functions. *Journal of Abnormal Psychology*, **93**, 133–140.

Hare, R.D. (1985) Comparison of procedures for the assessment of psychopathy. *Journal of Consulting and Clinical Psychology*, **53**, 7–16.

Hare, R.D. and Forth, A.E. (1985) Psychopathy and lateral preference. *Journal of Abnormal Psychology*, **94**, 541–546.

Hare, R.D., Frazelle, J., Bus, J. and Jutai, J.W. (1980) Psychopathy and structure of primary mental abilities. *Journal of Behavioural Assessment*, **2**, 77–88.

Hare, J.D. and Jutai, J.W. (1983) Criminal history of the male psychopath: some preliminary data. In K.T. van Dusen and S.A. Mednick (eds), *Prospective Studies of Crime and Delinquency*. Boston: Kluwer-Nijhoff.

Hare, R.D. and Schalling, D. (eds) (1978) *Psychopathic Behavior: Approaches to Research.* Chichester: John Wiley & Sons.

Harpending, H. and Draper, P. (1988) Antisocial behavior and the other side of cultural evolution. In T.E. Moffitt and S.A. Mednick (eds), *Biological Contributions to Crime Causation.* Dordrecht: Martinus Nijhoff.

Heston, L.L. (1966) Psychiatric disorders in foster-home reared children of schizophrenic mothers. *British Journal of Psychiatry*, **112**, 819–825.

Hinton, J.W. (1983) *Dangerousness: Problems of Assessment and Prediction.* London: Allen & Unwin.

Holzman, P.S., Proctor, L.R. and Hughes, D.W. (1973) Eye tracking patterns in schizophrenia. *Science*, **181**, 179.

Howard, R.C. (1986) Psychopathy: a psychobiological perspective. *Personality and Individual Differences*, **7**, 795–806.

Hutchings, B. (1972) Genetic and Environmental Factors in Psychopathology and Criminality. University of London: M. Phil. thesis.

Hutchings, B. and Mednick, S.A. (1975) Registered criminality in the adoptive and biological parents of registered male adoptees. In R.R. Fieve, D. Rosenthal and H. Brill (eds), *Genetic Research in Psychiatry*. Baltimore: Johns Hopkins University Press.

Hutchings, B. and Mednick, S.A. (1977) Criminality in adoptees and their adoptive and biological parents. In S.A. Mednick and K.O. Christiansen (eds), *Biosocial Bases of Criminal Behavior.* New York: Gardner.

Kallman, F.J. (1938). *The Genetics of Schizophrenia.* New York: Locust Valley.

Kamin, L.J. (1974) *The Science and Politics of I.Q.* Harmondsworth: Penguin.

Levin, S. (1984) Frontal lobe dysfunctions in schizophrenia—I. Eye movement impairments. *Journal of Psychiatric Research*, **18**, 27–55.

Loeb, J. and Mednick, S.A. (1977) A prospective study of predictors of criminality, 3: Electrodermal response patterns. In S.A. Mednick and K.O. Christiansen (eds), *Biosocial Bases of Criminal Behaviour.* New York: Gardner.

Maynard Smith, J. (1976) Evolution and the theory of games. *American Scientist,* **64**, 41–45.

MacMillan, J. and Kofoed, L. (!984) Sociobiology and antisocial personality: an alternative perspective. *Journal of Nervous and Mental Disease,* **172**, 701–706.

McCord, W. and McCord, J. (1964) *The Psychopath: An Essay on the Criminal Mind.* Princeton: van Nostrand.

Mednick, S.A. (1978) Berkson's fallacy and high-risk research. In L.C. Wynne, R.L. Cromwell and S. Matthysse (eds), *The Nature of Schizophrenia: New Approaches to Research and Treatment.* New York: John Wiley & Sons.

Mednick, S.A. and Christiansen, K.O. (eds) (1977) *Biosocial Bases of Criminal Behavior.* New York: Gardner.

Mednick, S.A. and Finello, K.M. (1983) Biological factors and crime: implications for forensic psychiatry. *International Journal of Law and Psychiatry,* **6**, 1–15.

Mednick, S.A., Gabrielli, W.F. and Hutchings, B. (1983) Genetic influences in criminal behavior: evidence from an adoption cohort. In K.T. van Dusen and S.A. Mednick (eds), *Prospective Studies of Crime and Delinquency.* Boston: Kluwer Nijhoff.

Mednick, S.A. and Hutchings, B. (1978) Genetic and psychophysiological factors in asocial behaviour. In R.D. Hare and D. Schalling (eds), *Psychopathic Behaviour: Approaches to Research.* Chichester: John Wiley & Sons.

Mednick, S.A., Kirkegaard-Sorensen, L., Hutchings, B., Knop, J.M., Rosenberg, R. and Schulsinger, F. (1977) An example of bio-social interaction research: the interplay of socio-environmental and individual factors in the ethology of criminal behavior. In S.A. Mednick and K.O. Christiansen (eds), *Biosocial Bases of Criminal Behavior.* New York: Gardner.

Mednick, S.A., Moffitt, T.E. and Stack, S. (1989) *The Cause of Crime: New Biological Approaches.* New York: Cambridge University Press.

Mednick, S.A. and Volavka, J. (1980) Biology and crime. In N. Morris and M. Tonny (eds), *Crime and Justice: An Annual Review of Research.* Vol. 2. Chicago: University of Chicago Press.

Mednick, S.A., Volavka, J., Gabrielli, W.F. and Itil, T.M. (1981) EEG as a predictor of antisocial behavior. *Criminology,* **19**, 219–229.

Milner, B. (1963) Effects of different brain lesions on card sorting: the role of the frontal lobes. *Archives of Neurology,* **9**, 90–100.

Mitchell, D.A. (1988) Schizophrenia, electrodermal activity, and event-related potentials. Doctoral dissertation, University of York.

Moffitt, T.E. (1984) Genetic influences of parental psychiatric illness on violent and recidivistic criminal behavior. Unpublished doctoral dissertation, University of Southern California, Los Angeles.

Moffitt, T.E. (1988) Neuropsychology and self-reported early delinquency in an unselected birth cohort: a preliminary report from New Zealand. In T.E. Moffitt and S.A. Mednick (eds), *Biological Contributions to Crime Causation.* Dordrecht: Martinus Nijhoff.

Moffitt, T.E. and Mednick, S.A. (1988) *Biological Contributions to Crime Causation.* Dordrecht: Martinus Nijhoff.

Nachshon, I. (1983) Hemisphere dysfunction. In M.S. Myslobodsky (ed.), *Hemisyndromes: Psychobiology, Neurology and Psychiatry.* New York: Academic Press.

Newman, J.P., Pattersen, C.M. and Kosson, D.S. (1987) Response perseveration in psychopaths. *Journal of Abnormal Psychology,* **95**, 145–148.

Nuechterlein, K.H. and Dawson, M.E. (1984) Information processing and attentional functioning in the developmental course of schizophrenic disorders. *Schizophrenia Bulletin*, **10**, 204–232.

O'Connor, M., Foch, T., Sherry, T. and Plomin, R. (1980) A twin study of specific behavioural problems of socialisation as viewed by parents. *Journal of Abnormal and Clinical Psychology*, **8**, 189–199.

Petersen, I., Matousek, M., Mednick, S.A., Volavka, J. and Pollock, V. (1982) EEG antecedents of thievery. *Acta Psychiatrica Scandinavica*, **62**, 331–338.

Pritchard, W.S. (1986) Cognitive event-related potential correlates of schizophrenia. *Psychological Bulletin*, **100**, 43–66.

Quay, H.C. (1965) Psychopathic personality as pathological stimulation-seeking. *American Journal of Psychiatry*, **122**, 180–183.

Raine, A. (1985) A psychometric assessment of Hare's Checklist for Psychopathy on an English prison population. *British Journal of Clinical Psychology*, **24**, 247–258.

Raine, A. (1987a) Effect of early environment on electrodermal and cognitive correlates of schizotypy and psychopathy in criminals. *International Journal of Psychophysiology*, **4**, 277–287.

Raine, A. (1987b) Conjoint assessment of schizoid and psychopathic traits in criminals. Paper presented to the International Society for the Study of Individual Differences, Toronto, Canada, June.

Raine, A. (1988a) Antisocial behaviour and social psychophysiology. In H. Wagner (ed.), *Social Psychphysiology and Emotion: Theory and Clinical Applications*. London: John Wiley & Sons.

Raine, A. (1988b) Evoked potentials and antisocial behaviour. In T.E. Moffitt and S.A. Mednick (eds), *Biological Contributions to Crime Causation*. Dordrecht: Martinus Nijhoff.

Raine, A. (1989) Evoked potentials and psychopathy. *International Journal of Psychophysiology*, **8**, 1–16.

Raine, A. (1992) Schizotypal and borderline features in psychopathic criminals. *Personality and Individual Differences*.

Raine, A. and Venables, P.H. (1981) Classical conditioning and socialisation—A biosocial interaction. *Personality and Individual Differences*, **2**, 273–283.

Raine, A. and Venables, P.H. (1984a) Tonic heart rate level, social class and antisocial behaviour in adolescents. *Biological Psychology*, **18**, 123–132.

Raine, A. and Venables, P.H. (1984b) Electrodermal nonresponding, antisocial behaviour and schizoid tendencies in adolescents. *Psychophysiology*, **21**, 424–433.

Raine, A. and Venables, P.H. (1987) CNV, P3 evoked potentials and antisocial behavior. *Psychophysiology*, **24**, 191–199.

Raine, A. and Venables, P.H. (1988) Enhanced P3 evoked potentials and longer P3 recovery times in psychopaths. *Psychophysiology*, **25**, 30–38.

Raine, A. and Venables, P.H. (1990) Evoked potential augmenting-reducing in psychopaths and criminals with impaired smooth-pursuit eye movements. *Psychiatry Research*, **31**, 85–98.

Raine, A., Venables, P.H. and Williams, M. (1990a) Relationships between central and autonomic measures of arousal at age 15 and criminality at age 24. *Archives of General Psychiatry*, **47**, 1003–1007.

Raine, A., Venables, P.H. and Williams, M. (1990b) Autonomic orienting responses in 15-year-old male subjects and criminal behavior at age 24. *American Journal of Psychiatry*, **147**, 933–937.

Raine, A., Venables, P.H. and Williams, M. (1990c) Relationships between N1, P300 and contingent negative variation recorded at age 15 and criminal behavior at age 24. *Psychophysiology*, **27**, 567–574.

Reid, W.S. and Bottlinger, J. (1979) Genetic aspects of antisocial disorders. *The Hillside Journal of Clinical Psychiatry*, **1**, 87–95.

Robins, L. (1966) *Deviant Children Grown Up: A Sociobiological and Psychiatric Study of Sociopathic Personality*. Baltimore: The Williams & Wilkins Co.

Roth, W.T., Horvath, T.B., Pfefferbaum, A. and Kopell, B.S. (1980) Event-related potentials in schizophrenics. *Electroencephalography and Clinical Neurophysiology*, **48**, 127–139.

Rowe, D.C. (1983) Biometrical genetic models of self-reported delinquent behavior: a twin study. *Behavior Genetics*, **13**, 473–489.

Rutter, M. and Giller, H. (1983) *Juvenile Delinquency: Trends and Perspectives*. Harmondsworth: Penguin.

Schulsinger, F. (1972) Psychopathy: heredity and environment. *International Journal of Mental Health*, **1**, 190–206.

Sigvardsson, S., Cloninger, R., Bohman, R. and von Knorring, A.L. (1982) Predisposition to petty criminality in Swedish adoptees. III. Sex differences and validation of the male typology. *Archives of General Psychiatry*, **39**, 1248–1253.

Silverton, L. (1988a) The genetic relationship between antisocial behavior and schizophrenia: a review of the literature. In W. Buikhuisen (ed.), *Explaining Crime*. Leiden: Brill.

Silverton, L. (1988b) Crime and the schizophrenia spectrum: a study of three Danish cohorts. In T.E. Moffitt and S.A. Mednick (eds), *Biosocial Bases of Antisocial Behavior*. Dordrecht: Nijhoff.

Sutker, P.B., Moan, C.E. and Allain, A.N. (1983) Assessment of cognitive control in psychopathic and normal prisoners. *Journal of Behavioural Assessment*, **5**, 275–287.

Syndulko, K. (1978) Electrocortical investigations of sociopathy. In R.D. Hare and D. Schalling (eds), *Psychopathic Behaviour: Approaches to Research*. Chichester: John Wiley & Sons.

Taylor, M.A. and Abrams, R. (1984) Cognitive impairment in schizophrenia. *American Journal of Psychiatry*, **141**, 196–201.

Theorell, T., de Faire, U. and Fagrell, B. (1978) Cardiovascular reactions during psychiatric interview: a non-invasive study on a twin sample. *Journal of Human Stress*, **4**, 27–31.

Trivers, R.L. (1971) The evaluation of reciprocal altruism. *Quarterly Review of Biology*, **46**, 35–37.

Trivers, R.L. (1972) Parental investment and sexual selection. In B. Campbell (ed.), *Sexual Selection and the Descent of Man*. Chicago: Aldine.

Venables, P.H. and Raine, A. (1987) Biological theory. In B. McGurk, D. Thornton and M. Williams (eds), *Applying Psychology to Imprisonment*. London: HMSO.

Virkkunen, M., Nuutila, A. and Huusko, D. (1976) Effect of brain injury on social adaptability. *Acta Psychiatrica Scandinavica*, **53**, 168–172.

Volavka, J., Mednick, S.A., Gabrielli, W.F., Matousek, M. and Pollock, V.W. (1984) EEG and crime: evidence from longitudinal prospective studies. *Advances of Biological Psychiatry*, **15**, 97–101.

Wadsworth, M.E.J. (1976) Delinquency pulse rates and early emotional deprivation. *British Journal of Criminology*, **16**, 245–256.

Weinberger, D.R., Berman, K.F. and Zec, R.F. (1986) Physiologic dysfunction of dorsolateral prefrontal cortex in schizophrenia. I. Regional cerebral blood flow evidence. *Archives of General Psychiatry*, **43**, 114–124.

West, D.J. and Farrington, D.P. (1973) *Who Becomes Delinquent?* London: Heinemann.

Widom, C.P. (1978) A methodology for studying non-institutionalised psychopaths. In R.D. Hare and D. Schalling (eds), *Psychopathic Behaviour: Approaches to Research.* Chichester: John Wiley & Sons.

Widom, C.S. and Ames, A. (1988) Biology and female crime. In T.E. Moffitt and S.A. Mednick (eds), *Biological Contributions to Crime Causation.* Dordrecht: Martinus Nijhoff.

Wilson, E.O. (1975) *Sociobiology: A New Synthesis.* Cambridge Massachusetts: Harvard University Press.

Wilson, R.S. (1983) The Louisville Twin Study: Developmental synchronies in behaviour. *Child Development,* **54**, 298–316.

Yeudall, L.T., Fedora, O., Fedora, S. and Wardell, D. (1981) Neurosocial perspective on the assessment and etiology of persistent criminality. *Australian Journal of Forensic Science,* **13**, No. 4 and **14**, No. 1.

Yeudall, L.T. and Fromm-Auch, D. (1979) Neuropsychological impairments in various psychopathological populations. In J. Gruzelier and P. Flor-Henry (eds), *Hemisphere Asymmetries of Function in Psychopathology.* Amsterdam: Elsevier, North-Holland Biomedical Press.

Yeudall, L.T., Fromm-Auch, D. and Davies, P. (1982) Neuropsychological impairment in persistent delinquency. *Journal of Nervous and Mental Disease,* **170**, 257–265.

Chapter 12

Reversal Theory as a Biological Approach to Individual Differences

Michael J. Apter

Psychology Department, University of Chicago, 5848 South University Avenue, Chicago, Illinois 60637, USA

and

Sven Svebak

Department of Biological and Medical Psychology, Division of Somatic Psychology, Årstadvein 21, N-5009 Bergen, Norway

ABSTRACT

This chapter outlines some of the central concepts of reversal theory, including the concepts of metamotivation, telic and paratelic states, and state-dominance. It brings out how the concept of state-dominance introduces a whole new approach to the traditional state-versus-trait debate. Psychological research has been generated by the theory, and a survey is given of reports on electromyographic, cardiovascular, respiratory, and cortical activity. A number of theoretical and methodological issues are raised by reversal theory, and some of these issues are discussed in a final section.

Handbook of Individual Differences: Biological Perspectives
Edited by Anthony Gale and Michael W. Eysenck

INTRODUCTION: REVERSAL THEORY AND PSYCHOBIOLOGY

Reversal theory is a relative newcomer to the scene. While most of the approaches described in the present book have established themselves over a number of years, the first full text on reversal theory was published as recently as 1982 (Apter, 1982a). The aim of the present chapter is to introduce the theory, and show how it arises out of a certain dissatisfaction with some of the most influential ideas in the fields of personality, motivation, emotion and stress. There will not be sufficient space to describe the theory in all its aspects here, but enough will be presented to make clear some of the central ideas and, in particular, to review the psychophysiological research which has been generated by the theory. In the process, the biological aspects of the theory will be emphasized.

At this point, some of those already familiar with reversal theory may raise their eyebrows. After all, has not the general approach adopted by reversal theory been described as ''structural phenomenology'' (viz. Apter, 1981a; Apter, 1989; Murgatroyd and Apter, 1984)? Has it not been made clear that the starting point of reversal theory analyses is always subjective experience and the meanings which people assign to their feelings and activities? And does not the approach emphasize the way in which reference needs to be made to the subject's experience in the course of even the most rigorous of psychological experimentation? It may be helpful, therefore, for us to indicate at the very outset of this chapter the way in which reversal theory not only has biological aspects but may even be regarded as a biologically-based theory.

First, then, reversal theory regards mental processes as epiphenomena of biological processes (Apter, 1982a, chapter 13). If mental processes have structure, as the theory also claims, and such processes change over time according to various principles, then it is assumed that this is because the underlying neurophysiological and biochemical processes are at some level characterized by such structure and subject to such principles. So if the reversal theory approach is an ''inside-out'' one, in that it starts from the subjective and moves out to the objective, it is so in the sense that it is based on the belief that mental life provides a unique, and uniquely useful, window on neurophysiological functioning, and one which is likely to be ignored only to the detriment of the researcher. The reversal theory view that physiological processes cannot be meaningfully studied in isolation from the experience of the subject therefore is a short-hand way of saying that there are complex and high-level neural processes involved in even the simplest kind of task, and if they cannot yet (or ever) be identified at the neural level, their experiential concomitants *can* be discerned and investigated—and should be taken into account whenever possible.

Secondly, reversal theory is quite willing to accept that there are temperamental differences between people—that their nervous functioning differs in a variety of measureable respects, such as those studied by Strelau and his group (e.g. Strelau, 1983). But it adds that the sorts of low-level differences typically included in studies of temperament may be overlaid by higher-level neural programmes which are not so easily amenable to investigation, but which may play a larger part in determining individual differences at the more global level of organized purposeful behaviour.

Thirdly, in trying to understand various kinds of enigmatic behaviour, the perspective of reversal theory is essentially a Darwinian one. In particular, it asks about the evolutionary purpose of "gratuitous" behaviour—behaviour like that involved in religion and art, for example, which appears to play no obvious part in helping the species to survive (viz. Apter, 1982a, chapters 8 and 12). And it is very much concerned, especially in its clinical manifestations, with "paradoxical" behaviour—behaviour like drug-taking, gambling, vandalism and the like, which would appear to make the survival of the individual and his/her social group even *less* likely than it would otherwise have been. Again, the structures and dynamics of experience identified in reversal theory help to make sense of such biologically puzzling phenomena.

Perhaps the central theme of reversal theory is that intra-individual differences are as important as inter-individual differences and that the latter cannot be understood unless the former are also fully taken into account. This is a theme which cuts across many of the usual area demarcations in psychology. In particular, the theory suggests that there are different modes of functioning, or "programmes", available to each individual which that individual will switch—or "reverse"—between in the course of everyday life. And the difference between the psychological characteristics displayed in each of these modes within the individual may be greater than the difference between the psychological characteristics of two different individuals who are both operating within equivalent modes at a given time. It is therefore over-simple to try to characterize the personality of an individual in global terms which make no reference to the internal variations consequent on changes between different modes. Rather, the characteristics of each mode must also be studied within the individual (and also over populations). The characteristics of such a mode, or "metamotivational state" to use the reversal theory term, can be expected to be behavioural, phenomenological and biological, these different levels cohering to constitute a recognizable psychological identity.

METAMOTIVATIONAL STATES AND THE REVERSAL PHENOMENON

Let us then turn to some of the specific concepts and arguments of the theory itself. A convenient way to approach the theory is through a consideration of a central problem in motivation: that of the relationship between arousal level and hedonic tone. It should be understood from the outset that by arousal here will be meant "felt arousal"—that is, the subjective experience of being "worked up" or emotional. For the present we place in brackets the question of how this phenomenological arousal may relate to physiological arousal. The aim is first of all to make sense of the phenomenon of arousal at the level of meaningful experience, and only then (as will be described in a later section of the chapter) to see how the phenomenon disclosed by this analysis might be grounded in biological "reality". The hope, in proceeding in this way from the subjective to the objective, is to discover structures which may help to make sense of the complexity of psychophysiological data, and to indicate new directions for psychophysiological research.

In its approach to this question reversal theory differs markedly from optimal arousal theory, which of course has dominated research on arousal for a considerable period. Although optimal arousal theory, following Hebb and Thompson (1954), and Hebb (1955), has taken many different forms, all optimal arousal theorists appear to assume that there is only a single optimal point (or range) on the arousal dimension at a given time. Although there may be some gradual variation in which level is optimal at different times (e.g. times of the day), arousal is seen as essentially homeostatic. Reversal theory, by contrst, argues that there are two completely different and alternative systems, each with its own optimal point. In place of the notion of homeostasis, therefore, it substitutes the more complex notion of *bistability* (Apter, 1981b). Furthermore, it argues that these two optimal points or "preferred levels", are towards opposite ends of the arousal dimension. So instead of there being one level of preferred arousal to which the organism attempts to return, and which is felt as pleasant when obtained, reversal theory suggests that there are two such levels, only one of which is preferred at a given moment, this being the preferred level of the particular arousal system that is operative at that moment. Because the two alternative preferred levels are assumed to be towards *opposite* ends of the felt arousal dimension, switches between the systems involve discontinuous switches between opposites and are therefore referred to as *reversals.*

This idea can be made clear by reference to Figure 12.1, in which there are *two* hypothetical curves relating arousal to hedonic tone instead of the single curve of optimal arousal theory. Each of these curves relates to a different system or "state of mind", one of which may be thought of as "arousal-avoiding" and the other as "arousal-seeking". At any given level of actual experienced arousal, it is possible, according to the theory, to switch from the curve representing one of these systems to the curve representing the other—that is, a reversal may occur. One of the results of such a reversal may be a sudden change of hedonic tone in relation to the level of arousal experienced at that moment. Because the two systems are characterized by different ways

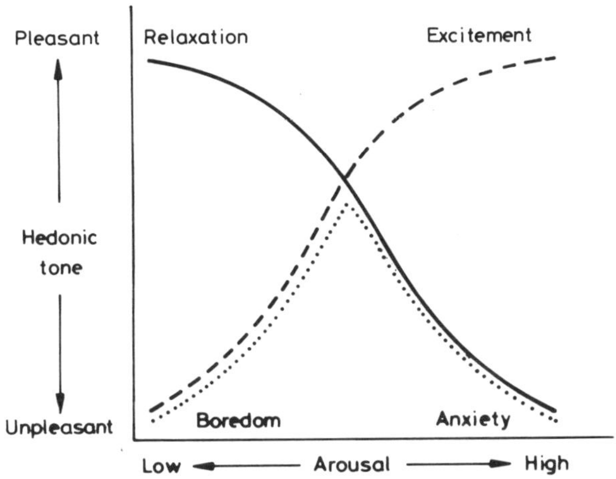

Figure 12.1. The two hypothetical curves which reversal theory suggests relate felt arousal to hedonic tone. The curve drawn with a continuous line represents the "arousal-avoiding" system, and the curve drawn with a discontinuous line represents the "arousal-seeking" system. (The dotted line represents the traditional optimal arousal curve.)

of *interpreting* a motivational phenomenon—arousal—they are described in reversal theory as *meta*motivational; and reversal from one to another such metamotivational system therefore constitutes a *meta*motivational reversal.

This view of the relationship between felt arousal and hedonic tone presents a number of advantages over the optimal arousal theory interpretation. These can be summarized as follows.

1. It accounts more easily than optimal arousal theory for the fact that on some occasions even *very high* arousal can be pleasant (e.g., during sexual behaviour, or watching football) and on other occasions even *very low* arousal can be pleasant (e.g., relaxing after a hard day's work).

2. It accounts for *four* nouns that describe the four different possible combinations of pleasant and unpleasant high and low levels of arousal—namely, excitement, anxiety, relaxation, and boredom—and it brings out the structural relationship between them. These four types of arousal are shown in the appropriate positions on the graph (Figure 12.1). By contrast, optimal arousal theory has difficulty in assimilating these four adjectives to its single curve and has to do so by making such unwarranted assumptions as that excitement is a lower form of arousal than anxiety (cf. Hebb, 1955).

3. Optimal arousal theory also implies that as arousal increases, excitement will always be felt before anxiety, and that it will always be felt after anxiety as arousal decreases—an implication for which there is no evidence and which would appear to be totally inconsistent with everyday experience.

4. It allows for the possibility of certain rapid changes in the way in which

arousal is felt. For example, it explains how anxiety can be converted almost instantaneously into excitement and vice versa. Like Zillmann's excitation-transfer theory (Zillmann, 1971), it helps to explain such psychological phenomena as the enjoyment of dangerous sport by suggesting that residual arousal is enjoyed as excitement after the danger which produced the arousal has been overcome.

The two different arousal-preference systems are, according to reversal theory, associated closely with (and may be regarded from one perspective as subsystems of) a more all-embracing pair of metamotivational systems, which have been labelled in the theory as "telic" and "paratelic" (from the Greek words "telic" meaning a "goal" and "para" meaning "alongside"). These two systems are most conveniently characterized in terms of the phenomenological states with which they are associated. The telic state is defined as a state of mind in which one conceives oneself to be pursuing an important goal, the behaviour being subsidiary and chosen to achieve the goal. The paratelic state of mind is one in which the orientation is toward the behaviour itself, together with its concomitant sensations, in this case any goal being conceived as subsidiary and essentially an excuse for the behaviour. In other words, there is a sense in which the goal is at a focus of the phenomenological field in the telic state and the ongoing activity is at the focus in the paratelic state. When a reversal does occur, this is somewhat analogous to a figure-ground perceptual reversal, with the figure being in one case a goal and in the other a form of activity.

For example, in walking somewhere in the telic state one will conceive of one's goal—e.g., to arrive in time for an interview—as of overriding importance, and if it begins to appear that one will not achieve this goal one will choose some other means (for example, take a taxi). If on the other hand one is walking somewhere in the paratelic state, then one's centre of interest is in enjoying the walk; and if in this case it turns out that one's destination is beyond one's reach in the time available, one will simply choose another destination while continuing with one's walk.

In the telic state, which is the state associated with low arousal preference, the state of mind is a serious one, and the concern is more likely to be with the future than the present; in this state the individual tries to plan ahead wherever possible. Anxiety arises if barriers to goal achievement occur, but the achievement of a goal produces relaxation. In the paratelic state, which is the state associated with high arousal preference, the state of mind is a more light-hearted or playful one in which the orientation is toward the present moment and its enjoyment; it is also characterized by a preference for spontaneity rather than planning. Intense experiences in this state are felt to be exciting, while a failure to achieve such intensity produces the experience of boredom.

Reversal theory, then, sees the telic and paratelic states as a bistable pair of opposite but complementary phenomenological states, each associated with its own underlying system, and with the continual possibility of reversal between these states/systems. Although these states are defined in terms of the primacy of goal or activity within experience, it will now be appreciated that the states themselves, and their underlying biological systems, are complex and involve a number of related characteristics or components.

What, then, are the factors which bring about, or facilitate, reversals between the telic and paratelic systems? Three general classes of such factors have been proposed:

1. *Contingent factors.* By this is meant events and situations which, when suitably interpreted by the individual, facilitate or induce a reversal. For example, a sudden physical danger may induce the telic system if it is not already in operation, while escape from such a danger may play a part in inducing the paratelic system; social cues like frowning may facilitate reversal to the telic system while cues like smiling and laughing may facilitate reversal to the paratelic; and some contexts, like a waiting-room at a hospital, will normally help to bring about a reversal into the telic mode whereas others, like the sports stadium, will normally help rather to bring the paratelic system into operation.

2. *Frustration.* The second general category is that of frustration of all kinds in achieving the satisfactions of the prevailing system, so that if the frustration is strong enough it will eventually induce the opposite system on its own or with the help of other factors. For example, if one is unable to achieve a serious goal one may switch at a certain point to the paratelic system and playfully fantasize goal achievement.

3. *Satiation.* By this is meant that there is an innate process which operates independently of contingent events and frustration in such a way as increasingly to facilitate reversal from the prevailing system over time. In other words, it builds up in strength until it is strong enough, with other factors, to bring about a reversal; and eventually it will become strong enough to bring about a reversal on its own even in the absence of other factors. Having brought about the reversal and dissipated its strength, it will start building up again in such a way as to help to induce a new reversal. So what is being suggested here is that there is an innate dynamic for change. In this the relationship between telic and paratelic systems is seen as not unlike that between waking and sleeping: when one has been awake long enough one will eventually go to sleep despite other factors, and when one has been asleep long enough one will eventually wake up if one has not been woken up in the meantime by some external occurrence.

One thing which this third postulate does is to show quite clearly that reversal theory is not a theory of situational specificity: because of the process of satiation it is quite possible to confront a certain situation in the telic system on one occasion and the paratelic system on another, and indeed to reverse backward and forward from one system to the other during the course of the same continuing activity. It will be realized from all this that reversal is conceived to be an involuntary process which occurs when the factors for change are, in combination, stronger than those which would inhibit it.

One general point about reversal theory, as should now be evident, is that it implies an inherent inconsistency and self-contradiction in human nature. At one moment a person may crave excitement and at another avoid exactly those arousing situations which he or she was so keen to experience a short time before; at one time he or she may experience his job as an obligation and at a later time experience the very same job as a kind of game. In such ways people differ not only from each other but from themselves at different times (and even when confronted by the same situation). In other words, there is a kind of internal dialectic, which underlies the changeability and complexity of human experience and behaviour.

However, this is not to deny that there are consistencies within individuals. One of these is the innate bias or tendency which they may have to be subject to one state or the other. This is known in reversal theory as "state-dominance" or simply "dominance". Thus the telic dominant individual is the person who is more likely at a given time, other things being equal, to be doing something which he or she conceives to be serious and important, attempting to avoid anxiety, and more likely to be seeing the current activity in a long-term perspective, than the paratelic dominant individual. The latter is more likely other things being equal, to be feeling and acting in a light-hearted, playful, and here-and-now oriented way, and looking for excitement. How far this is likely in each case will depend on the degree of telic or paratelic dominance involved, which in turn will depend on how susceptible the individual is to the factors listed above in relation to reversal in one direction rather than the other.

It must be emphasized, however, that telic/paratelic state-dominance is not a trait in the conventionally accepted sense, because telic dominant people will still be expected to spend certain periods in the paratelic system, and may be just as playful and excitement-seeking when this system is operating as paratelic dominant people; and paratelic dominant people will be expected to spend periods of time in the telic system, and may be just as serious and anxiety-avoiding when this system is operating as those who are telic dominant. At the same time, as we have pointed out above, the telic and paratelic systems are also not situationally dependent in any simple way, nor are they simple one-emotion states (like "anxiety"); and so reversal theory is not a state theory in the usual sense. Rather, it introduces a whole new approach to the traditional, and increasingly sterile, state-versus-trait debate.

It should be added that three other pairs of metamotivational systems have also been postulated in reversal theory: the negativism/conformity pair, the mastery/sympathy pair, and the autocentric/allocentric pair. The first of these concerns the opposite ways in which an individual can see her or himself to be acting in relation to external pressures (i.e. with them or against them).

The second is about the opposite ways in which transactions between self and other can be experienced (as controlling in the case of mastery, and caring or giving in the case of sympathy). The third concerns opposite ways of experiencing one's position in transactions with others: as being self-centred (autocentric) or other-centred (allocentric). More information on these and other reversal theory concepts like "cognitive synergy" (the experience of mutually contradictory properties in relationship to an object, person or situation) will be found for example in Apter (1982a), Apter (1989), Apter, Fontana and Murgatroyd (1985), and Apter, Kerr and Cowles (1988).

These concepts, taken together, allow reversal theory to provide a coherent and unitary explanation for a wide range of apparently diverse and unrelated phenomena. These include, for example, aesthetic experience (Apter, 1984a), sexual dysfunction and perversion (Apter and Smith, 1979a), gambling (Anderson and Brown, 1987), antisocial behaviour in childhood, adolescence, and old age (Apter, 1983), sport (Kerr, 1985), family interaction patterns (Apter and Smith, 1979b), the experience of religious states of mind (Apter, 1985), and the enjoyment of humour (Apter and Smith, 1977; Apter, 1982b). For instance, it is argued that humour is a special form of paratelic high arousal which is also characterized by a number of other specifiable subjective properties that have to do with cognitive synergy (Apter, 1982b).

Within the clinical context, what reversal theory does is to provide a general conceptual framework within which psychotherapy can be practised systematically. At the diagnostic level it provides a whole new classification system for disorders of the neurotic and personality type. In particular it suggests that there are a small number of major classes of psychopathology and that these can be defined in metamotivational terms (for more details, see Apter, 1982a, chapter 11; Apter, 1989; Murgatroyd and Apter, 1984). An appropriate form of therapy can then be chosen in the light of the nature of the presenting problem thus identified. The implications of this orientation have been discussed in more detail in relation particularly to crisis counselling (Murgatroyd, 1981), biofeedback (Svebak and Stoyva, 1980), and family therapy (Apter and Smith, 1979b).

EMPIRICAL RESEARCH ON REVERSAL THEORY

One of the ways in which the hypotheses of reversal theory has been investigated is through the development of empirical measures. In particular, a measure of telic dominance has been developed. This is the Telic Dominance Scale (TDS: Murgatroyd *et al.*, 1978) consisting of three subscales to measure serious-mindedness, planning-orientation and arousal-avoidance. This scale has now been used for a variety of purposes, experimental and applied, in many countries throughout the world and there are translations into a number of languages. As might be expected, some overlap has been found by various researchers between the TDS and other widely used psychometric instruments in the field of personality. In particular, significant correlations have been found by some workers between the arousal–avoidance subscale of the TDS and both the extraversion–introversion subscale of the EPI and Zuckerman's Sensation-Seeking Scale. However, the serious-mindedness subscale of the TDS (which can be regarded as the defining subscale) appears to be orthogonal to both the Zuckerman and the Eysenck scales (i.e. both the extraversion–introversion and the neuroticism subscales of the EPI), as well as other well-known personality measures such as Jenkins Activity Survey for type A/B behaviour (viz. Svebak and Apter, 1984). In general, therefore, the TDS seems to be, at least in part, sampling a psychological space which is not fully tapped by other major psychometric instruments. For more details of these and other psychometric studies the reader is referred to the review by Murgatroyd (1985) which also surveys the development, validation and applications of the TDS.

A conveniently simple measure of telic/paratelic states is also now available (Svebak and Murgatroyd, 1985), this indicating by means of a set of rating scales whether the telic or paratelic system is operating at a given moment in time.

If the sign of the strength of a theory is that it gives rise to unexpected discoveries that would not have been predicted by other theories, this representing what Lakatos (1974) has designated a progressive rather than degenerating research programme, then reversal theory may already be said to be showing signs of strength. Here, briefly, are two examples. First, reversal theory would predict that it is *not* the case that everyone is upset to some degree or another by so-called stress. (See Apter and Svebak, 1989; Svebak, 1988a, 1990a, for more extensive analyses of relations between stress, effort and emotions as seen from the reversal theory perspective.) On the contrary, reversal theory would make the surprising prediction that some persons, i.e. paratelic dominant individuals, would be likely to enjoy stress up to a certain point because this would cause higher arousal, and high levels of arousal are enjoyed by such individuals. (Above a certain point, however, the telic state would be likely to be induced even in those who are strongly paratelic dominant so that the effect would die away beyond these levels of stress.) Evidence consistent with this prediction has been presented by Martin (1985) and by Martin *et al.* (1987). They showed that for telic dominant subjects, the greater the stress, the greater the mood disturbance. But for paratelic dominant subjects, exactly the reverse relationship was found: up to a certain level of stress, the more the stress the better the mood. It was not that these subjects were simply less vulnerable to stress. They appeared to be thriving on it and positively enjoying it. Beyond this point the relationship became the same as that for telic dominant subjects, implying that increasing numbers of this group were reversing to the telic state as stress continued to build up.

Secondly, if people have a choice of a range of stimuli which can be placed along a dimension from highly arousing to highly de-arousing, reversal theory would predict that, because everyone at a given moment is either in the arousal-seeking or arousal-avoiding state, they will tend to choose stimuli from the extremes on such a dimension rather than more centrally-placed stimuli, and to switch from time to time from a preference for stimuli at one extreme to a preference for stimuli at the other. Using colour stimuli from across the spectrum, analysed for each individual in terms of how arousing or de-arousing each colour was for them personally, Walters, Apter and Svebak (1982) found that, when subjects (116 office workers) were asked to make colour preference choices at regular intervals during the working day (some of the subjects being tested for as many as eight days), they did indeed behave in the way expected—uniquely—by reversal theory. That is, they tended to choose either colours which they personally found highly arousing or highly de-arousing, ignoring intermediate colours, and to reverse from time to time from one relative extreme to the other.

We do not propose to review the whole of the research literature on reversal theory here (for which, see Apter, 1984b; Apter, 1989), but rather to focus on the psychophysiological research which has been carried out within the framework of the theory. If there are, as reversal theory claims on phenomenological grounds, two experientially distinct arousal dimensions, the question that arises is whether these two dimensions differ in measurable physiological ways. In other words, as experienced arousal increases and decreases, does it do so physiologically in ways which distinguish between opposite metamotivational states? If it can be demonstrated that it does so, then this would lend support to the reversal theory idea that there are overriding programmes, corresponding to metamotivational states, which co-ordinate activities throughout the nervous system from the highest neural to the lowest automatic functioning, and that these constitute psychological "identities" in their own right. Their existence might also then throw light on the notorious lack of correlations generally found between different physiological indicators of arousal level. At the same time, the question must be asked whether such physiological differences as are found may not be related to state-dominance—the innate tendency to be in one state or another—rather than to the states themselves, and so the possible effects of states and state-dominances have to be disentangled. It is to these questions that we turn in the next section.

PSYCHOPHYSIOLOGICAL RESEARCH

In 1982 Svebak and his students (Svebak, Storfjell and Dalen, 1982) reported the first psychophysiological experiment generated by reversal theory. They made use of a commercially available video game (a single-person car-racing simulation) which called upon continuous perceptual-motor co-ordination. Only minimal adjustments of a joystick held between two fingers of the preferred hand were required to perform the task. The task was performed twice, once with the threat of aversive, but not painful electric shocks for a high level of errors and once without this threat (counter-balanced over subjects).

The task was carefully selected to meet demands involving continuous perceptual monitoring and related motor responding, thus representing an experimental model which we have named the continuous perceptual-motor task paradigm. Many commercially available video games meet these task requirements, and are not unlike the tasks used by Malmo and his associates in the 1950s and 1960s (see e.g. Malmo, 1965) to investigate task-induced physiological changes. Also, video games are notoriously performed for fun as well as for serious purposes (e.g. the development of perceptual-motor and cognitive skills), and they therefore appeared in principle to be equally appealing to subjects performing in the telic and paratelic modes.

It was reasoned that threat of shock would help to induce the telic mode. In testing this it was necessary to avoid making explicit to the subject any actual level of errors which would lead to shock so that he or she would always remain under threat. (Actually, shocks were never given except during an initial procedure before the experiment proper, in which increasingly higher shock intensities were used to assess shock tolerance.) This threat manipulation therefore relied completely on the effect of the instruction.

It turned out that rating scales on task perception (level of difficulty, interestingness, and liking of the task) were not significantly altered by the threat manipulation. Rating scales on self-perception, however, indicated as expected a significant shift, on the average, toward the telic mode (serious-mindedness, planning orientation), and actual felt arousal also increased.

Parallel to this change in psychological state towards the telic mode and higher felt arousal in the threat condition, a number of tonic (slow) physiological changes were found to occur: the electromyographic (EMG) activity of the seemingly "*passive*" forearm flexor muscle (carpi radialis) increased over the course of the 150 seconds performance sessions (see the concept of "physiological gradient" proposed by Malmo, 1965), and threat of shock caused a more marked increase than occurred in the non-threat condition. Also, heart rate (HR) increased more with threat than without, and for this response system peak responses were reached early during task performance with reduced levels towards the end of the task. For respiratory activity (inspiration-expiration amplitude, frequency) changes paralleled those for the EMG gradient with the non-threat condition (i.e. peaking toward end of task), whereas threat of shock caused changes which were parallel to those for heart rate. (These overall patterns of tonic physiological changes have been replicated in other studies: see Svebak, 1982, 1986a; see also Myrtek, Dieterle and Brügner, 1990). It was, however, not possible to tell how far the observed differences were related to increased arousal or the movement towards the telic state, because these occurred concomitantly.

PSYCHOGENIC MUSCLE TENSION

In a follow-up experiment (Svebak, 1984), extreme groups of telic and paratelic dominant subjects were recruited by using the Telic Dominance Scale. (In fact, sub-scale scores on serious-mindedness were used because, as noted earlier, this component is held to be the defining aspect of the telic/paratelic distinction; see Apter, 1982a). In the light of the probabilistic nature of state-dominance, as seen by reversal theory, it was assumed that this extreme-group recruitment of subjects would increase the likelihood that subjects would be in the state corresponding to their state-dominance during the experimental session. In this way state could be manipulated without at the same time causing felt arousal changes, the hope being that this might allow the effects of state alone to be observed.

In this experiment, a continuous perceptual-motor task was performed five successive times with the instruction to make as few errors as possible. A "telic state measure" (TSM) consisting of a set of rating scales was completed at the end of each performance period. Results confirmed that serious-mindedness (as displayed by the telic dominant subject group) was significantly related to a tonic build-up of EMG activity in the "passive" forearm flexor over the course of task performance, the gradient being relatively shallow, if present at all, in paratelic dominant subjects. Interestingly, and in contrast, the playful state (paratelic dominant subject group) was associated with high phasic response amplitudes of the *active* forearm flexor EMG contingent upon changing the position of the joystick. Practice moderated the range of these state-specific EMG response patterns. Subjects maintained their dominant state during task performance, so that it was not possible, in the event, to distinguish the effects of state and state-dominance. But because rating scale scores reflecting felt level of arousal failed to discriminate between the two groups, it could be concluded that the physiological differences were more likely to be due to telic/paratelic differences (whether at the state or state-dominance level), than felt arousal changes. (Case illustrations of state-specific tonic and phasic response patterns for EMG are given in Figure 12.2)

It is a fairly common view that *phasic* (sudden, stimulus-elicited) response amplitudes remain quite constant when repeated, whereas attenuation of *tonic* (enduring, less stimulus-related) changes in baseline activity takes place within practice that allows for the development of coping skills (see, e.g., Ursin, 1978, p. 213). This view was challenged by the results reported by Svebak (1984) because practice caused attenuation of tonic as well as phasic task-related changes. In this respect, the classic distinction by Herrick (1927) between phasic activity, as mediated by the monosynaptic cortico-spinal

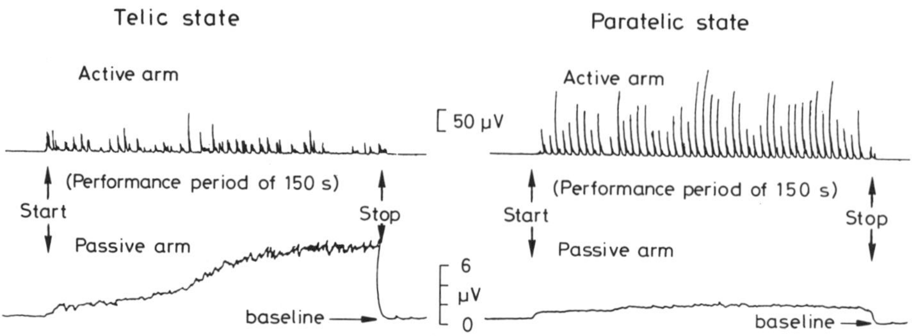

Figure 12.2. Illustrations of telic and paratelic state-specific tonic and phasic forearm EMG response patterns.

pyramidal pathway to skeletal muscles, and tonic activity, as mediated by the multisynaptic pathways to the skeletal muscles, also failed to gain straightforward support from the present findings.

Svebak (1986a) combined the extreme-group procedure and the threat of shock manipulation in the hope that at least some paratelic dominant subjects would reverse to the telic state in the course of the experiment, allowing a comparison of the effects of state and state-dominance. In the event there were not enough "cross-overs" of this kind to allow the comparison to be made, but the results substantiated the data from Svebak (1984) in relation to extreme groups, the telic dominant subjects, as before, displaying significantly steeper EMG gradients than the paratelic dominant subjects. The threat manipulation, however, did have the effect of reducing the phasic EMG responses in the paratelic dominant subjects, implying that the threat of shock did induce a more cautious response style in these subjects without inducing an overall reversal to the telic state.

It is a widespread view of laboratory experiments that they have little ecological validity, i.e. they do not relate much to the "real" world. Svebak and Murgatroyd (1985) showed that differences between telic and paratelic state-dominant groups of subjects performing continuous perceptual-motor laboratory tasks closely reflected lifestyle differences between the two groups, these being documented by structured interviews. This experiment again substantiated the main result of Svebak (1984) in relation to EMG gradients.

In a further attempt to disentangle the effects of state and state-dominance, Apter and Svebak (1986) recruited *moderate* rather than extreme groups of telic and paratelic dominant subjects, and used two manipulations: threat of shock for poor performance and monetary reward for good performance. Subjects played the game on four occasions, once with each of the manipulations and twice without either (the order being varied systematically). On this occasion a substantial proportion of the subjects in both groups did "cross over" to a state different from their dominance. Analysis of the results showed clearly that it was *state* rather than state-dominance, which related to tonic EMG changes in the "passive" forearm flexor muscle.

Consistent with this, Rimehaug and Svebak (1987) found that a constellation of the *telic state with negative hedonic tone* was significantly related to tonic increases of EMG activity in the biceps and triceps muscles of both the right and left upper arms. Their results were derived from a stratified distribution of subjects in relation to telic dominance performing a continuous perceptual-cognitive (rather than perceptual-motor) task, and these results therefore added generality to earlier findings from the passive forearm flexor muscle in the continuous perceptual-motor task paradigm.

In this way, the use of reversal theory as an approach to the measurement of EMG response patterns in continuous task performance has emerged as a promising line of research. This is not to overlook the role of genetical disposition in muscle physiology as a contributor to individual differences in muscle tension problems in real life, although our findings taken together suggest that the telic metamotivational state and negative affect are significant contributors to psychogenic muscle tension, if not to pain in the upper extremities.

The genetically given proportion of slow switch (Type I or aerobic) and fast twitch (Type II or anaerobic) muscle fibres was assessed in one recent study. Biopsy was performed in the right leg gastrocnemius muscle, in the area under the active EMG electrode site, after the performance of a perceptual-motor video task. A high proportion of slow twitch fibres turned out to be significantly correlated to high tonic EMG gradient responses during task performance which called upon movement of a joystick by the dominant forearm. The generalizability of this relationship extended to the EMG gradient also from the left leg and "passive" forearm (Svebak *et al.*, 1990). It is possible that extreme dominance of fast or slow twitch fibres represents a biological disposition towards a particular state dominance at the phenomenological level.

It has been a longstanding assumption that enduring states of muscle tension cause muscle pain (e.g. Malmo, 1965). From this perspective individuals who respond with marked EMG gradients (i.e. those who have a high proportion of fast-twitch muscle fibres) are at high risk of suffering musculoskeletal discomfort and pain. Two recent studies have failed to provide support for this assumption. High levels of pain in muscles of the neck and shoulders were associated with the experience of resentment and guilt, but not with anxiety. (Svebak *et al.*, 1991). It is argued in reversal theory that anxiety is experienced with high felt arousal in the telic state, i.e. the state where marked EMG gradients have been observed during task performance. The experience of resentment and guilt are seen as due to unsuccessful coping in other metamotivational states (Apter, 1988).

Furthermore, a recent study by Svebak, Anjia and Kårstø (submitted for publication) failed to show differences of tonic EMG levels (baseline and task-induced), as well as levels of anxiety, between fibromyalgia subjects and a group of matched controls.

CARDIOVASCULAR REACTIVITY

Reversal theory has initiated empirical research with a number of other physiological parameters than EMG, although this research is currently less extensive than that on EMG. Cardiovascular reactivity is one such area already included in the above reference to Svebak *et al.* (1982). They reported higher heart rate with than without threat of shock, but the shift toward the telic state as well as the improved performance with threat of shock left unsolved the role of increased arousal (and/or effort) versus metamotivational state as moderators of HR increase with threat of shock.

The experiment reported by Svebak (1986a) included measures of HR changes contingent upon the manipulation of threat of shock when extremely telic and paratelic state-dominant subjects performed a perceptual-motor task. Results showed that HR was low in the no-shock condition, in particular for the telic state-dominant group, and that threat of shock, not surprisingly, caused overall increase of HR reactivity in both groups. However, the telic state-dominant subjects showed particularly marked increases with threat of shock, this increase averaging around 40 beats per minute, and being significantly different from the increase in the paratelic dominant subjects. (See Figure 12.3 for illustration of this strong state-dominance effect.)

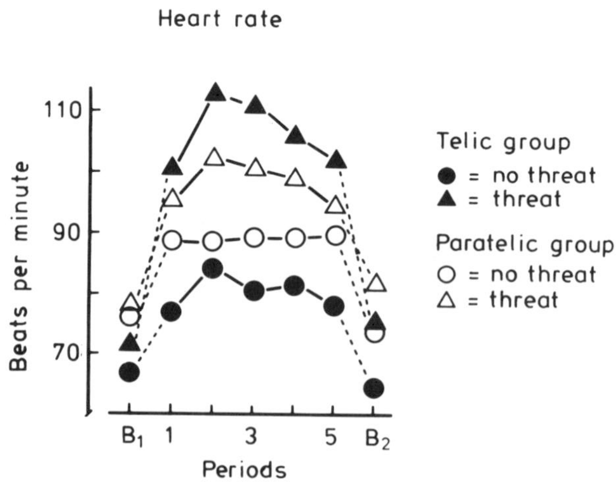

Figure 12.3. Heart rate changes of telic and paratelic state-dominant subjects under conditions of threat of shock and no threat, over a total period of 150 s. (Pre- and post-baseline rates are also shown.)

These findings implied that serious-mindedness plays an important role in tonic cardiovascular reactivity; and *effort expended in the telic state* might thus provoke cardiac activation above the level seen when effort is expended for fun (i.e. in the paratelic state), at least where physical workload is kept constant as between the telic and paratelic states. Moreover, these findings for HR emerged as completely independent of perceived task difficulty. They therefore challenge the view indicated by Turner and his associates (e.g. Carroll, Turner and Prasad, 1986) that task difficulty may play a major role in cardiac reactivity.

As noted earlier, Svebak and Apter (1984) reported orthogonality for serious-mindedness and coronary-prone Type A behaviour. Therefore, Svebak, Nordby and Ohman (1987) recruited 40 subjects representing factorial crossings of telic and paratelic state-dominance and Type A versus Type B behaviour. Results from this study, which used a perceptual-motor laboratory task, showed particularly high HR activation in telic dominant Type A individuals; in contrast, paratelic dominant Type B individuals showed the least reactive pattern of task-induced HR changes. Also, pulse transit time scores indicated higher systolic blood pressure increases in telic state-dominant Type A subjects than in paratelic state-dominant Type B individuals. Because the Type A behaviour pattern may be regarded as a lifestyle reflecting "chronic struggle", the results indicated therefore that telic state-dominance and high effort (chronic struggle) interact to cause particularly high cardiovascular reactivity in challenging perceptual-motor tasks. (See Svebak, 1988b, for a reversal theory definition of the coronary prone personality.)

Cardiac reactivity of a *phasic* nature has been observed in telic as well as paratelic state-dominant individuals when they were all in the *paratelic* state induced by watching a comedy film (Svebak and Apter, 1987). These marked phasic changes in HR were closely overlapping with laughter responses. However, they should be regarded as indirectly rather than directly reflecting the paratelic state because they were triggered by the mirthful laughter.

RESPIRATORY ACTIVITY

In Svebak *et al.* (1982), the experiment in which subjects played the video game under a threat and a no-threat condition, the threat condition produced increased inspiratory amplitudes along with the increased tendency of subjects to be in the telic state and to experience heightened arousal. Svebak and Murgatroyd (1985) and Svebak (1986b) both report data showing higher scores for inspiratory amplitude in telic-dominant subjects; and Svebak (1986b) showed that under the threat condition telic dominant subjects produced a significantly greater respiration rate than paratelic dominant subjects. These are all tonic effects. In contrast, mirthful laughter in the paratelic state (in both telic and paratelic dominant subjects) provoked massive phasic changes of respiratory activity (viz. Svebak, 1985a). Taken together, these experiments imply that the telic/paratelic distinction is one which enters into respiratory as well as other physiological functions, although the precise relationship of telic state, telic dominance, arousal and effort have yet to be determined.

One implication of this evidence might be that telic dominant people are more likely, other things being equal, to respond with hyperpnoea to threat. Svebak and Grossman (1985), consistent with this hypothesis, reported a positive association between scores reflecting degree of serious-mindedness and number of hyperventilation-related psychosomatic complaints; and threat of electric shock for inadequate performance in a perceptual-motor task amplified this positive association. The significance of these findings for the distinction between so-called generalized anxiety and panic disorder is not yet clear.

CORTICAL ACTIVITY

Svebak (1985b) recruited extreme groups of telic and paratelic dominant individuals for an experiment which investigated effects of self-induced breath-holding (hypopnoea) and excessive breathing (hyperpnoea) upon parietal EEG spectral power. Generally, paratelic dominant subjects revealed high spectral power scores (theta, alpha and beta), and their theta power was markedly *increased* in the left parietal area during hyperpnoea, and reduced in the right parietal area during hypopnoea. It has been argued elsewhere (Svebak, 1985b) that these results suggest relatively small parietal areas in synchronous processing as a characteristic of telic state-dominance. Conversely, relatively large parietal areas of synchronous processing were indicated among the paratelic state-dominant individuals. The relatively more complex nature of information processing in the telic mode, as compared with the paratelic mode (e.g. Apter, 1982a), would be consistent with these patterns of cortical power production.

The goal-directed nature of the telic mode of conscious processing bears relevance to the psychophysiology of event-related cortical potentials. Specifically, the so-called P300 potential is held to be a manifestation of an individual's ability to pay active attention to stimuli that are "task relevant" (see, e.g., Donchin, 1981). Svebak, Howard and Rimehaug (1987) suggested that the concept of "task relevance" involves more than merely a call upon attentional capacity to process unexpected events: motivational dispositions along the telic-paratelic dimension must play an important role as part of the interface between stimuli and related responses in P300 paradigms. They reported results from a forewarned "Go" and "NoGo" reaction time task where subjects dominated by a telic lifestyle showed particularly high P300 power scores in response to both "Go" and "NoGo" signals, few errors, and high number of "Go" responses that were within a preset reaction time window.

In this way, reversal theory has opened up a new approach to cortical processes. Future research will show the strength of association between metamotivational modes and cortical processing characteristics within the different lobes and hemispheres.

PSYCHOBIOLOGICAL RELATIONS IN SPORTS

Sport preferences represent a particularly interesting domain for the investigation of relations between biological disposition, metamotivational dominance, and overt behaviour patterns. Kerr has argued that telic dominance (serious-mindedness, planning orientation) facilitates the enjoyment of endurance sports (Kerr, 1985, 1987; Kerr and Lienden, 1987). Svebak and Kerr (1989) published evidence in support of this postulated association between sport preference and state dominance. They also reported data in support of a significant association between arousal avoidance and preference for safe sports (Kerr and Svebak, 1989).

These findings on relations between sport preference and metamotivational state-dominance are intriguing in light of the biological preconditions of expert performance in endurance (aerobic) and sprint (anaerobic) sports: a high proportion of aerobic (Type I) fibres are needed in the former, and a high proportion of anaerobic (Type II) fibres are needed in the latter, to reach the expert level (e.g. Fox, 1984).

Svebak (1990b) argued that enjoyment and excellence in sports are facilitated by a particular kind of triangular relationship: preference for endurance sports (enjoyment, excellence) is facilitated by telic state dominance and a high proportion of slow twitch (Type I) muscle fibres. In contrast, preference for explosive sports is facilitated by paratelic state-dominance and a high proportion of fast twitch (Type II) muscle fibres. The pattern of findings referred to above (including the relations between EMG gradients and fibre composition) are in concert with this assumption of state-based triangular relationships. Further support was reported recently by Braathen and Svebak (1990) who found marked EMG gradients in expert performers of endurance sports, whereas such gradients were practically absent in expert performers of explosive sports, when they all performed a perceptual-motor video task. The salience of such triangular relationships may, of course, prove to be weaker, and actual state, rather than state-dominance may prove more important, in less extreme subject samples recruited among amateurs.

SUMMARY OF PSYCHOPHYSIOLOGICAL FINDINGS

Much research is needed to replicate and extend the results reported here, and to explore the power of reversal theory as an approach to the psychobiology of individual differences. Still, so many promising results have already emerged that they indicate, in a preliminary way, a pattern of findings. This pattern of findings is summarized in Table 12.1.

For example, the significant association between state-dominance, tonic task-induced EMG changes, and skeletal muscle fibre composition is a real psychophysiological discovery. In this case a genetically coded biological difference between individuals has been reflected in differences at the level of a psychophysiological parameter (tonic EMG changes) as well as at the phenomenological level.

This research should be regarded as a challenge to the predominant approach in much of current psychophysiology which disregards the important role of phenomenology, and which persistently overemphasizes the signifi-

Table 12.1. Summary of findings which indicate response tendencies and biological characteristics in some physiological systems in relation to telic/paratelic characteristics (state or state-dominance).

	Metamotivation	
Dependent measures	Telic	Paratelic
1. Skeletal muscles		
(a) Tonic changes (passive)[1,2,3,4,5,6,13]	High	Low
(b) Phasic changes (active)[2,3,13]	Low	High
(c) Fibre composition[12]	Type I	Type II
2. Cardiovascular measures		
(a) Tonic heart rate changes (threat)[1,3,7]	High	Low
(b) Phasic heart rate changes (comedy)[8]	Low	High
(c) Pulse transit time[7]	Short	Long
3. Respiration rate (threat)[1,9]	High	Low
4. Respiration amplitude		
(a) Tonic changes (threat)[1,4,9]	High	Low
(b) Phasic changes (comedy)[8]	Low	High
5. Cortical activity		
(a) Area in synchrony[10]	Small	Large
(b) P300 amplitude[11]	Large	Small

[1] Svebak, Storfjell and Dalen (1982).
[2] Svebak (1984).
[3] Svebak (1986a).
[4] Svebak and Murgatroyd (1985).
[5] Apter and Svebak (1986).
[6] Rimehaug and Svebak (1987).
[7] Svebak, Nordby and Ohman (1987).
[8] Svebak and Apter (1987).
[9] Svebak (1986b).
[10] Svebak (1985a).
[11] Svebak, Howard and Rimehaug (1987).
[12] Svebak *et al.* (1990).
[13] Braathen and Svebak (1990).

cance of situational characteristics and enduring personality traits as sources of intra- and inter-individual variance in psychobiology.

SOME ISSUES RAISED BY REVERSAL THEORY

Reversal theory clearly differs from other theories of personality and individual differences in a number of fundamental respects, and it may be useful in this final section to review some of these differences. We shall do this by listing, and briefly discussing, a number of assumptions which are widespread in personality theory, including especially biologically-based personality theory, but which are directly challenged by reversal theory. We shall look specifically at three theoretical and three methodological assumptions, most of them assumptions which normally remain implicit and unexamined in personality theory and research.

THEORETICAL ISSUES

Motivational Processes are Homeostatic

By "homeostatic" here we do not mean to use the term in its original—but restricted—sense of the maintenance of physiological variables within limits. Rather, we mean it in the more general and abstract systems theory sense, of the maintenance of any specifiable variable within limits by the system which regulates that variable. Now in this sense every major theory of motivation, or theory of personality based on some notion of motivation, may be said to have been homeostatic. Whatever the variable which has been chosen by the theorist as the key variable, or type of variable in his or her scheme, the idea has been that the organism behaves in such a way as to attempt to maintain the values of such a variable within some preferred range. Whether we look at excitation in the Freudian sense, drive in Hull's sense, tension in the sense defined by Lewin, or the action-specific energy of Lorenz—to take some classic examples—the story is always essentially the same: if the value of the variable concerned exceeds some critical value, then certain psychological processes will be instigated (defence mechanisms, appetitive behaviour, etc.) which will tend to restore the variable to its preferred level. In a marginally more sophisticated way, optimal arousal theory supposes, as is well known, that the preferred range of values of the arousal variable is intermediate and that corrective action will be taken either when the actual value exceeds, or when it drops below, certain critical thresholds.

Reversal theory argues that, although optimal arousal may apply very well to a number of biological functions (e.g. the regulation of body temperature), all such schemes are inadequate when it comes to explaining the vagaries and vicissitudes of human experience and behaviour, and that something less simplistic is required. Accordingly it proposes that we move to the next degree of complexity and suggests that, for variables like felt arousal (and other variables which are identified in the theory) there may be *two* rather than one preferred range of values. In other words, it argues that it is time to move on from the unistability of homeostasis to the simplest kind of multistability: namely bistability.

In these terms, it is much too simple to ask what an individual's optimal level of arousal is: no psychologically healthy person spends all his or her life attempting to maintain only one preferred level. Rather, one must ascertain what are the different levels which are preferred at different times (which is accomplished in reversal theory research through the use of such measures as the Telic State Measure), and whether there are innate biases towards one preference rather than another (which may be accomplished through the use of such instruments as the Telic Dominance Scale). Indeed, a study by Fontana (1981) lent empirical support to the case of extreme state-dominance as a marker of psychopathology.

People are Essentially Self-consistent

Much of personality theory and research is based on the assumption that each individual displays a number of consistencies which characterize him or her, and that it is the job of the researcher to identify and measure these. Such consistencies are conceived of either as enduring personality traits or as situational characteristics. Again, reversal theory challenges this assumption and suggests that this emphasis on consistency produces a wooden and unlife-like picture of human beings. Instead, it asserts that people are, in important respects, inherently inconsistent.

Of course the situational-specificity viewpoint also implies a certain kind of inconsistency: people will be expected to behave in different ways in different situations. But the inconsistency proposed by reversal theory is much more radical than this. Reversal theory suggests that people will behave differently at different times *even in the same situation.* The reason for this is that there are a variety of forces that influence which metamotivational state the individual will be in at a given time, and the cues provided by the situation itself will only be one contributing factor. In particular, the reversal theory notion of satiation implies that there is an entirely internal dynamic which plays a part in determining metamotivational state, and this may well override situational influences at the time in question.

None of this is to deny that there are enduring biological characteristics which differentiate people and which affect their temperaments. But it is not enough to look at these alone, and theories which are based entirely on such characteristics will, in the reversal theory view, necessarily prove inadequate. For example, it may well be the case that arousal has a natural stability around some point on the arousal dimension, and that this point may vary over samples of different types of people. But reversal theory proposes that this low-level stability will be overlaid by higher-level metamotivational processes which specify different *preferred* levels. (For this reason the Telic State Measure differentiates between actual level of arousal as experienced at a given time and preferred level of arousal at that time—these two may frequently be very different.)

One might suggest from this point of view that certain types of psychopathology may arise where there is a misfit between the natural level of stability and the dominant preferred level, so that the two levels of the system are frequently in conflict. (Thus psychopathy might arise where the natural resting level of arousal is low and the preferred level usually high; and chronic anxiety might arise where the natural resting level is high and the preferred level usually low.) In suggesting this, it should be made clear that there is reason to suppose that the *preferred* level is also biologically determined in some way. This is to emphasize that even if personality is, in some sense, an entirely biological phenomenon, this does not mean that there cannot be conflicts between different levels of such a biological system.

Some such conflicts or misfits present problems for prevention of diseases dealt with in behavioural medicine. For example, adherence to aerobic exercise is likely to be poor in individuals with a genetically given predominance of fast-twitch (non-aerobic) muscle fibres. This means that prevention of, e.g., cardiovascular disease may have to include explosive (non-aerobic) types of exercise to assure better compliance in some individuals to a low-risk lifestyle. This also means that the activity repertoire of a healthy lifestyle should include alternatives that reflect state-based preferences.

Behaviour can be Predicted from a Knowledge of Enduring Personality Characteristics and Situational Demands

Whether the emphasis is placed on traits or on situations, or some blend of the two, personality theorists appear to be agreed that these are the two classes of factors which, in some way, determine behaviour. It is assumed therefore that a suitable knowledge of the nature of these two factors and the way in which they interact will eventually allow successful predictions to be made about behaviour. Reversal theory fundamentally disagrees with this assessment and suggests that there is a third, and critical, factor which needs to be included in any predictive equation: the factor of metamotivational state at the time in question.

An analogy may be helpful here. Suppose that we wanted to predict the speed and direction of a sailing ship. To do so we should certainly want to know certain things about the prevailing situation—in particular the speed and direction of winds and currents. And we should also want to know something about the enduring characteristics of the ship itself, such as its tonnage, length and overall design features. But even if we knew all this, our success in prediction would be small unless we also took into account something else. We should need to know which "mode" it was in; i.e., at the time in question we should need to know whether it was running or reaching, which is to say going before the wind or attempting to move obliquely against it. Now this is not situational because the ship can do either in any given condition. Neither is it a "trait" because it will change from time to time—the equivalent of "reversals" will occur. Of course this is an over-simple analogy, and there is no space here to argue it through in detail. The aim is simply to try to impart some feeling for the way in which the reversal theory approach attempts to "break up" certain ways of looking at personality which are prevalent in the field by adding a further important dimension of variation to the situation.

Let us now turn to the methodological assumptions which are challenged by reversal theory.

METHODOLOGICAL ISSUES

Personality can be used Unproblematically as an Independent Variable

Reversal theory suggests that manipulating the personality characteristics of experimental groups is not as straightforward as it has been assumed to be, at least if some of these characteristics display reversals in the reversal theory sense rather than remaining constant. The problem is that individual subjects will not necessarily be in the mode which is their typical mode in the course of everyday life, during the experiment itself. This is not the same as saying simply that the experimental situation may modify subjects' reactions in some way. It is to say something much stronger: some subjects may finish up in exactly the wrong groups. This implies at the very least that there should be some kind of *post-hoc* testing to see if subjects displayed the expected personality characteristics in the course of the experiment itself and did not become, temporarily, "people of the opposite kind".

A case in point would be an experiment carried out by the present authors (Apter and Svebak, 1986; see also Rimehaug and Svebak, 1987) and described in the previous section of this chapter, in which the dependent variable was EMG activity. Although moderately extreme groups of telic and paratelic dominant subjects were used, which state of mind, telic or paratelic, that subjects were in during the course of the experiment was assessed by means of a post-task "blind" interview with each subject. It was found not only that a substantial number of subjects had "crossed-over" in the sense that they performed the task in a state of mind opposite of that suggested by their dominance, but also that it was this state of mind rather than the more enduring personality dominance which predicted level of EMG activity.

Whether or not this general situation is true of characteristics other than those identified in reversal theory (for example, in relation to introversion/extraversion), we would suggest that metamotivational pairs of states like the telic and paratelic pair cannot be safely ignored in the design of psychophysiological experiments where the focus is on individual differences. More generally, there is the possibility that some biological predispositions, such as the genetically given bias toward a high proportion of slow-twitch muscle fibres, or a high natural resting level of arousal, present the exceptional case where a characteristic is maintained across the most diverse situations. In most psychophysiological experimental designs subjects are recruited by psychological criteria which we believe relate to characteristics whose stability is questionable, and systematic state-based psychophysiological response patterns are then at risk of being dealt with as "noise" unless a sensitive phenomenological assessment of state is part of the study.

It is Possible to Hold Personality Constant through Matching

This point complements the previous one. If there are problems in varying personality characteristics by means of tests of supposedly enduring features of personality, the same problem arises where different groups are chosen which avowedly display the *same* characteristics through matching, for example where the aim is to control subjects for personality while subjecting them to different manipulations. Now according to reversal theory, some subjects may change their personality characteristics in ways which contrast with the characteristics which they are supposed to have and, unless there is some form of *post-hoc* testing, there is no way of knowing whether the groups have remained comparable or not during the period of the experimental investigation (see Gale and Edwards, 1983), for a more extensive discussion at this point).

If reversal theory is correct in this, it may go some way towards throwing light on psychology's notorious problem of lack of replicability of findings. Replication may turn out to have been so difficult in certain areas of psychology, precisely because different experimenters and different conditions in these areas may have tended to induce different modes in subjects. It is possible to put this in a more positive way by suggesting that this provides the chance of making sense of such discrepancies by adding a new dimension of change.

In other areas, the problem may be of a rather different kind. If as it happens there *is* a comparability of mode between different experiments and different experimenters in a given area, the effect of this may be to narrow and bias all the conclusions. Thus if the subjects in a certain kind of experiment tend to be in the paratelic mode, then the results may reflect this mode alone. For example, in psychopharmacology experiments in which blood samples are taken, the taking of the sample will in most subjects, presumably, induce the telic mode (and, with it, anxiety). Any results of such a psychopharmacological experiment may therefore be specific to the telic mode alone and not generalisable beyond it.

Subjects can be used Straightforwardly as their Own Controls

If it is true, as has been argued throughout this chapter, that people change between different metamotivational states and, as a consequence, display dramatically different psychological characteristics at different times, then it is obvious that there must be problems also in using subjects as their own controls, even during the short period of an experiment (leave alone longer-term studies). Thus a subject may start an experiment in one metamotivational state and at some point (due to changes in the experimental conditions or task, or due to entirely internal processes), switch to an opposite state. Indeed, one may suppose that there may in some cases be switching back and forth throughout the whole duration of an experiment. Again, the only way of coping with this eventuality is through some form of *post-hoc* testing. It cannot simply be assumed that the subject has remained the same throughout. For example, Svebak and Apter (1987) discovered in this way that the effect of a comedy film was not just to change subjects' responses but to tend to bring all subjects into the same paratelic state, irrespective of whether they were telic or paratelic state-dominant. In this sense many subjects changed their "personality" in the course of the experiment.

In the first instance, reversal theory would claim that this problem in using subjects as their own controls is likely to be a problem in relation to those psychological characteristics involved in the pairs of metamotivational states identified in the theory. But at the same time this does at least raise as an issue the question of whether the same problem may not also relate more generally to other psychological characteristics. Is it possible, for example, that the extravert may become introvert under some conditions, and vice versa?

Whether or not these three methodological points might eventually form the foundation for a radical critique of experimental and psychometric methods, they would meanwhile certainly seem to imply the need for certain precautionary measures to be taken when working with human subjects. These might include: taking into account wherever possible subjects' subjective experience of the investigation, and in particular checking whether psychological manipulations have had the intended psychological effect (e.g. were "threats" threatening?); using state measures to test whether supposed personality characteristics have actually been brought into the investigation and whether they have remained constant throughout; and being open to the possibility that apparently inconsistent results may disclose intra-individual structure rather than being merely "noise". While much of the research carried out so far within the framework of reversal theory—such as that described earlier in the area of psychophysiology—might appear somewhat traditional in many respects, nevertheless one can see emerging in such research certain emphases which represent an attempt to come to terms with some of the methodological problems which have been thrown into sharp relief by the theory itself.

CONCLUSION

In conclusion, then, we can say that what reversal theory does is to introduce a new level of analysis to psychology: the metamotivational level. At the same time it introduces a new principle of change—that of reversal—which can be added to learning and maturation to widen the set of forces for change which psychologists might want to take into account in attempting to understand the complexity, changeability and variety of human behaviour. In particular, this new principle of change is one which can be used in the attempt to account systematically for those intra-individual differences which, outside the psychological laboratory, are so obvious a feature of human life. One of the main themes of reversal theory is that of the need to attend to these as much as to the inter-individual differences which have been at the focus of research for so long. Whether or not the particular ideas of reversal theory, in its present form, will stand the test of time, the theory does at the very least raise various critical issues for personality theory and the psychobiology of individual differences as well as pointing to potentially important new areas for research.

ACKNOWLEDGEMENTS

Our research which has been reviewed in this chapter was supported by grants from The British Council, Nato Science Foundation, the Norwegian Research Council for Social Science and the Humanities, and from the University of Bergen.

REFERENCES

Anderson, C. and Brown, R.I.F. (1987) Some applications of reversal theory to the explanation of gambling and gambling addictions. *Journal of Gambling Behaviour*, **3**, 179–189.

Apter, M.J. (1981a) The possibility of a structural phenomenology: the case of reversal theory. *Journal of Phenomenological Psychology*, **12**, 173–187.

Apter, M.J. (1981b) On the concept of bistability. *International Journal of General Systems*, **6**, 225–232.

Apter, M.J. (1982a) *The Experience of Motivation: The Theory of Psychological Reversals*. London and New York: Academic Press.

Apter, M.J. (1982b) Fawlty Towers: a reversal theory analysis of a popular television comedy series. *Journal of Popular Culture*, **16**, 128–138.

Apter, M.J. (1983) Negativism and the sense of identity. In G. Breakwell (ed.), *Threatened Identities* (pp. 75–90). London: John Wiley & Sons.

Apter, M.J. (1984a) Reversal theory, cognitive synergy, and the arts. In W.R. Crozier and A.J. Chapman (eds), *Cognitive Processes in the Perception of Art* (pp. 411–426). Amsterdam: North-Holland.

Apter, M.J. (1984b) Reversal theory and personality: a review. *Journal of Research in Personality*, **18**, 265–288.

Apter, M.J. (1985) Religious states of mind: a reversal theory interpretation. In L.B. Brown (ed.), *Advances in the Psychology of Religion* (pp. 62–75). Oxford: Pergamon Press.

Apter, M.J. (1988) Reversal theory as a theory of the emotions. In M.J. Apter, J.H. Kerr and M.P. Cowles (eds), *Progress in Reversal Theory* (pp. 43–62). Amsterdam: Elsevier.

Apter, M.J. (1989) *Reversal Theory: Motivation, Emotion and Personality*. London: Routledge.

Apter, M.J., Fontana, D. and Murgatroyd, S. (eds) (1985) *Reversal Theory: Applications and Developments*. Cardiff: University College Press.

Apter, M.J., Kerr, J.H. and Cowles, M.P. (eds) (1988). *Progress in Reversal Theory*. Amsterdam: North-Holland Press.

Apter, M.J. and Smith, K.C.P. (1977) Humour and the theory of psychological reversals. In A.J. Chapman and H.C. Foot (eds), *It's a Funny Thing, Humour* (pp. 95–100). Oxford: Pergamon Press.

Apter, M.J. and Smith, K.C.P. (1979a) Sexual behaviour and the theory of psychological reversals. In M. Cook and G. Wilson (eds), *Love and Attraction: An International Conference* (pp. 405–408). Oxford: Pergamon Press.

Apter, M.J. and Smith, K.C.P. (1979b) Psychological reversals: some new perspectives on the family and family communication. *Family Therapy*, **6**, 89–100.

Apter, M.J. and Svebak, S. (1986) The EMG gradient as a reflection of metamotivational state. *Scandinavian Journal of Psychology*, **27**, 209–219.

Apter, M.J. and Svebak, S. (1989) Stress from the reversal theory perspective. In C.D. Spielberger and J. Strelau (eds), *Stress and Emotion*, Vol. 12 (pp. 39–52). Washington DC: Hemisphere/McGraw-Hill.

Braathen, E.T. and Svebak, S. (1990) Task-induced tonic and phasic EMG response patterns and psychological predictors in elite performers of endurance and explosive sports. *International Journal of Psychophysiology*, **8**, 55–64.

Carroll, D., Turner, R. and Prasad, R. (1986) The effects of level of difficulty of mental arithmetic challenge on heart rate and oxygen consumption. *International Journal of Psychophysiology*, **4**, 167–173.

Donchin, E. (1981) Surprise! . . . Surprise? *Psychophysiology*, **18**, 493–513.

Fontana, D. (1981) Obsessionality and reversal theory. *British Journal of Clinical Psychology*, **20**, 299–300.

Fox, E.L. (1984) *Sport Physiology*. Philadelphia: Holt-Saunders.

Gale, A. and Edwards, J. (1983) Psychophysiology and individual differences: theory, research procedures and the interpretation of data. *Australian Journal of Psychology*, **35**, 361–379.

Hebb, D.O. (1955) Drives and the C.N.S. (conceptual nervous system). *Psychological Review*, **62**, 243–254.

Hebb, D.O. and Thompson, W.R. (1954) The social significance of animal studies. In G. Lindzey (ed.), *Handbook of Social Psychology*. Cambridge, MA.: Addison-Wesley.

Herrick, C.J. (1927) *An Introduction to Neurology* (4th edn). Philadelphia: Saunders.

Kerr, J.H. (1985) The experience of arousal: a new basis for studying arousal effects in sport. *Journal of Sports Sciences*, **3**, 169–179.

Kerr, J.H. (1987) Structural phenomenology, arousal and performance. *Journal of Human Movement Studies*, **13**, 211–229.

Kerr, J.H. and Lienden, J. van (1987) Telic dominance in master swimmers. *Scandinavian Journal of Sports Sciences*, **9**, 85–88.

Kerr, J.H. and Svebak, S. (1989) Motivational aspects of preference for and participation in 'risk' and 'safe' sports. *Personality and Individual Differences*, **10**, 789–800.

Lakatos, I. (1974) Falsification and the methodology of scientific research programmes. In I. Lakatos and A. Musgrave (eds), *Criticism and the Growth of Knowledge*. Cambridge: Cambridge University Press.

Malmo, R.B. (1965) Physiological gradients and behavior. *Psychological Bulletin*, **64**, 225–234.

Martin, R. (1985) Telic dominance, stress and moods. In M.J. Apter, D. Fontana and S. Murgatroyd (eds), *Reversal Theory: Applications and Developments* (pp. 59–71). Cardiff: University College Press.

Martin, R.A., Kuiper, N.A., Olinger, L.J., and Dobbin, J. (1987) Is stress always bad?: telic versus paratelic dominance as a stress moderating variable. *Journal of Personality and Social Psychology*, **53**, 970–982.

Murgatroyd, S. (1981) Reversal theory: a new perspective on crisis counselling. *British Journal of Guidance and Counselling*, **9**, 180–193.

Murgatroyd, S. (1985) The nature of telic dominance. In M.J. Apter, D. Fontana and S. Murgatroyd (eds), *Reversal Theory: Applications and Developments* (pp. 20–41). Cardiff: University College Press.

Murgatroyd, S. and Apter, M.J. (1984) Eclectic psychotherapy: a structural-phenomenological approach. In W. Dryden (ed.), *Individual Psychotherapy in Britain* (pp. 389–414). London: Harper & Row.

Murgatroyd, S., Rushton, C., Apter, M.J. and Ray, C. (1978) The development of the Telic Dominance Scale. *Journal of Personality Assessment*, **42**, 519–528.

Myrtek, M., Dieterle, W. and Brügner, G. (1990) Psychophysiological response patterns to variations of the experimental load of a reaction time task. *Journal of Psychophysiology*, **4**, 209–220.

Rimehaug, T. and Svebak, S. (1987) Psychogenic muscle tension: the significance of motivation and negative affect in perceptual-cognitive task performance. *International Journal of Psychophysiology*, **5**, 97–106.

Strelau, J. (1983) *Temperament—Personality—Activity*. London: Academic Press.

Svebak, S. (1982) The effect of task difficulty and threat of aversive electric shock upon tonic physiological changes. *Biological Psychology*, **14**, 113–128.

Svebak, S. (1984) Active and passive forearm flexor tension patterns in the continuous perceptual motor task paradigm: the significance of motivation. *International Journal of Psychophysiology*, **2**, 167–176.

Svebak, S. (1985a) Serious-mindedness and the effect of self-induced respiratory changes upon parietal EEG. *Biofeedback and Self-Regulation*, **10**, 49–62.

Svebak, S. (1985b) Psychophysiology and the paradoxes of felt arousal. In M.J. Apter, D. Fontana and S. Murgatroyd (eds), *Reversal Theory: Applications and Developments* (pp. 42–58). Cardiff: University College Press.

Svebak, S. (1986a) Cardiac and somatic activation in the continuous perceptual-motor task: the significance of threat and serious-mindedness. *International Journal of Psychophysiology*, **3**, 155–162.

Svebak, S. (1986b) Patterns of cardio-somatic-respiratory interaction in the continuous perceptual-motor task paradigm. In P. Grossman, K. Janssen and D. Vaitl (eds), *Cardiorespiratory and Cardiosomatic Psychophysiology* (pp. 219–230). New York: Plenum.

Svebak, S. (1988a) A state-based approach to the role of effort in experience of emotions. In V. Hamilton, G.H. Bower and N. Frijda (eds), *Cognitive Perspectives on Emotion and Motivation* (pp. 145–172). Dordrecht: Martinus Nijhoff.

Svebak, S. (1988b) Personality, stress and cardiovascular risk. In M.J. Apter, J. Kerr and M. Cowles (eds), *Progress in Reversal Theory* (pp. 163–172). Amsterdam: North-Holland Press.

Svebak, S. (1990a) The role of effort in stress and emotion. In C.D. Spielberger, Z. Kulcsar and J. Strelau (eds), *Stress and Emotion*, Vol. 13. Washington DC: Hemisphere/McGraw-Hill.

Svebak, S. (1990b) Sport and personality. In G.P.H. Hermans and W.L. Mosterd (eds), *Sport, Medicine, and Health* (pp. 87–96). Amsterdam: Excerpta Medica/Elsevier.

Svebak, S., Anjia, R. and Kårstø, S.I. (submitted for publication). Task-induced electromyographic changes in fibromyalgia patients and in controls.

Svebak, S. and Apter, M.J. (1984) Type A behaviour and its relation to telic dominance (seriousmindedness). *Scandinavian Journal of Psychology*, **25**, 161–167.

Svebak, S. and Apter, M.J. (1987) Laughter: an empirical test of some reversal theory hypotheses. *Scandinavian Journal of Psychology*, **28**, 189–198.

Svebak, S., Braathen, E.T., Sejersted, O.M., Bowim, B., Fauske, S. and Laberg, J.C. (1990) Biopsy assessment of fast and slow twitch muscle fibres: prediction of tonic EMG activation in perceptual-motor task performance. *Psychophysiology*, **27**, (suppl.), 568.

Svebak, S. and Grossman, P. (1985) The experience of psychosomatic symptoms in the hyperventilation provocation test and in non-hyperventilation tasks. *Scandinavian Journal of Psychology*, **26**, 327–335.

Svebak, S., Howard, R. and Rimehaug, T. (1987) P300 and quality of performance in a forewarned "Go-" "NoGo" reaction time task: the significance of goal-directed lifestyle and impulsivity. *Personality and Individual Differences*, **8**, 313–319.

Svebak, S. and Kerr, J.H. (1989) The role of impulsivity in preference for sports. *Personality and Individual Differences*, **10**, 51–58.

Svebak, S. and Murgatroyd, S. (1985) Metamotivational dominance: a multimethod validation of reversal theory constructs. *Journal of Personality and Social Psychology*, **48**, 107–116.

Svebak, S., Nordby, H. and Ohman, A. (1987) The personality of the cardiac responder: interaction of seriousmindedness and Type A behavior. *Biological Psychology*, **24**, 1–9.

Svebak, S., Storfjell, O. and Dalen, K. (1982) The effect of a threatening context upon motivation and task-induced physiological changes. *British Journal of Psychology*, **73**, 505–512.

Svebak, S. and Stoyva, J. (1980) High arousal can be pleasant and exciting: the theory of psychological reversals. *Biofeedback and Self Regulation*, **5**, 439–444.

Svebak, S., Ursin, H., Endresen, I., Hjelmen, A.M. and Apter, M.J. (1991). Back pain and the experience of stress, efforts and moods. *Psychology and Health*, **5**, 307–314.

Ursin, H. (1978) Activation, coping, and psychosomatics. In H. Ursin, E. Baade and S. Levine (eds), *Psychobiology of Stress: A Study of Coping Men*. New York: Academic Press.

Walters, J., Apter, M.J. and Svebak, S. (1982) Colour preference, arousal and the theory of psychological reversals. *Motivation and Emotion*, **6**, 193–215.
Zillmann, D. (1971) Excitation transfer in communication-mediated aggressive behavior. *Journal of Experimental Social Psychology*, **7**, 419–434.

Chapter 13

Gender Differences in Emotion

Antony S. R. Manstead
Department of Psychology, University of Manchester, Manchester M13 9PL, UK

ABSTRACT

This chapter reviews the evidence pertaining to gender differences in emotion from five lines of research: (1) psychophysiological research; (2) research on facial expressiveness; (3) research on the subjective experience of emotion; (4) research on emotional behaviour; and (5) research on accuracy in perceiving others' emotions. Although differences between males and females are found in each field, conclusions have to be tempered by the effect sizes typically observed: gender differences in emotion are often small, even where they have been shown to be consistent across relatively large numbers of studies. It is argued that these differences are currently better explained in terms of social psychological factors, rather than biological processes; however, the lack of programmatic research on this topic means that there is little research that bears directly on the issue of causation.

INTRODUCTION

One of the attributes traditionally ascribed to women, in Western cultures at least, is their greater emotionality relative to men. The Belk and Snell (1986) Beliefs about Women Scale (BAWS) was devised as an objective self-report measure of stereotypes about women. Of the sub-scales assessed by this measure, three were endorsed approximately equally by females and by males as

Handbook of Individual Differences: Biological Perspectives
Edited by Anthony Gale and Michael W. Eysenck

being characteristic of women: "Women have more emotional insight than men"; "Women are more interpersonal than men"; and "Women are less dominating than men". Each of these empirically established beliefs about women maps on to readily recognizable sex stereotypes: that women are "more in touch with their feelings" than men, and are thus more emotionally responsive and sensitive; that women are more oriented towards other persons and are thus better tuned to others' feelings and emotions than men are; and that women are less aggressive than men. The aim of this chapter is to provide a representative review of the evidence pertaining to such beliefs. Are women, indeed, more "emotional" than men? To address this question I shall review evidence under five rubrics:

(1) psychophysiological research;
(2) research on facial expressiveness;
(3) research on subjective experience;
(4) research on emotional behaviour (other than facial expression);
(5) research on accuracy in perceiving others' emotional states.

The chapter closes with a set of conclusions that can be drawn from the reviewed evidence.

There are some methodological points that should be made before proceeding to the evidence. The first concerns the magnitude of gender differences. Even where such differences have consistently been found on indices relating to emotion, they tend to be small in absolute terms, typically accounting for less than 5% of the variance on the measure in question. It is worth noting that gender differences on cognitive variables, such as verbal and spatial ability, are of an equivalent size (Deaux, 1984). This means, of course, that there is considerable overlap between the distributions of scores of male and female populations on psychological attributes. There is evidence that psychological differences associated with social class are much greater than those associated with sex of subject (Kornbrott, 1986; Newson and Newson, 1986), although such comparative data are not available for measures of emotion.

A related point concerns the reliability of measures of emotion. It is a well-established fact that single measures of any construct are less reliable than multiple measures (Epstein, 1980), although researchers have typically been rather insensitive to this issue. Because the majority of studies in this (as in other) fields of research use single indices of emotion, measured on one occasion and in specific circumstances, it is unwise to attach much theoretical significance to the findings of any one study, or even a small series of studies, especially in view of the fact that the effect attributable to gender is relatively small.

Another related problem concerns the possibility of interactions between sex of subject and other variables. Researchers have not addressed this problem systematically enough, preferring to look for main effects due to sex of subject than for interactions. Yet there are grounds for thinking that sex of subject will interact with, for example, sex of investigator (see Eagly and Carli, 1981; Gale and Baker, 1981; Rumenik, Capasso and Hendrick, 1977). Thus some effects that are attributed to sex of subject may in fact be due to the interaction of sex of subject with an uncontrolled variable. Alternatively, where researchers fail to find overall gender differences on indices of emotion, it may be that there are significant differences between subsets of male and female subjects.

These are some of the methodological problems that beset the study of differences in the psychological characteristics of males and females (for a fuller discussion, see Archer, 1987). Researchers are beginning to address the first two problems through the use of meta-analytic techniques (Glass, 1976; Rosenthal, 1984). Such techniques are not without their disadvantages; for example, they are relatively insensitive to differences in the quality of the studies across which they integrate. Nevertheless, they also have a number of advantages. These techniques almost invariably involve the computation of measures of effect size, which serves to heighten awareness of the fact that a statistically significant difference may be a small difference in absolute terms. Furthermore, by providing a means of statistically combining the results of many studies, meta-analysis helps to determine whether a difference is robust across specific measurement occasions and circumstances. However, the problem of interaction is one that in general is not being addressed. The difficulty here is that the number of variables with which subject sex could potentially interact is enormous. Although researchers should be guided by theory in their selection of candidate variables, it is a fact that much of the research reviewed in this chapter was not originally conducted in order to test one or other theory of gender differences. As Archer (1987) has noted, "The study of 'sex differences' has its roots in the field of individual differences research and has relied on the fortuitous discovery of statistically significant differences between men and women in studies whose theoretical focus was not concerned with sex differences" (p. 88).

RESEARCH EVIDENCE

PSYCHOPHYSIOLOGICAL RESEARCH

Nowhere is the lack of a clear theoretical rationale for the study of gender differences more apparent than in psychophysiological research. There is surprisingly little systematic research on gender differences in psychophysiological response to emotionally arousing stimuli and it is correspondingly difficult to draw clear inferences from those findings that have been reported. None the less, there is the semblance of a consistent difference between males and females across measures of electrodermal and cardiovascular functioning.

As far as *electrodermal responding* is concerned, several studies have found that males exhibit greater skin conductance (SC) responding than females. For example, Graham, Cohen and Shmavonian (1966) and Shmavonian, Yarmat and Cohen (1965) reported greater SC responding in males than in females in a classical conditioning procedure involving electric shock. Although Berger (1962) found no gender differences in electrodermal activity among subjects observing another person receiving shocks, Craig and Lowery (1969) found more skin resistance (SR) changes among males than among females when subjects watched others receiving shocks and McCracken (1969; cited in Buck, 1988) found higher SC levels in males than in females among subjects listening to time-compressed speech. It is worth noting that in the latter two studies, males reported a level of distress lower than that reported by females, despite their greater electrodermal responding. Commenting on such findings, Prokasy and Raskin (1973) have argued that females have smaller and/or less frequent electrodermal responses than males in many emotional situations, and that such a difference only becomes manifest after puberty.

Consistent with this conclusion are findings from a series of studies reported by Buck and his colleagues (Buck *et al.*, 1972; Buck, Miller and Caul, 1974; Buck, 1977). In the first two studies cited, adult female subjects tended to be below the median in SC responding whereas adult males tended to be above this median when viewing emotionally-loaded colour slides. In the third study, involving preschool children, there was no gender difference in SC responding to emotional slides. Also worth noting is a study of crowding reported by Nicosia *et al.* (1979), in which crowded men showed a marked increase in SC over time, whereas crowded women did not.

However, there are exceptions to this general trend for males to exhibit greater electrodermal activity than females. For example, Buck (1972) found that females exhibited greater SC responding than males when subjects were required to administer electric shocks to someone else; and Aronfreed, Messick and Diggory (1953) also found larger SC responses in females than in males when listening to "unpleasant words".

Evidence of gender differences in *cardiac activity* during emotional stimulation comes mainly from research on aggression. Here the evidence again points to the greater reactivity of male subjects. For example, Cantor, Zillmann and Einsiedel (1978) found that viewing violent movie excerpts elicited only modest excitatory reactions in females. McLean (1981; reported in Lang, 1984) examined subjects' cardiac responses to two versions of emotional scenarios. In one, subjects simply read a script and were instructed to imagine the scenario as vividly as possible; in the other, the scenario was enacted live as a ''mini-drama'', using trained actors and involving the subject as a participant observer. One scenario was designed to evoke fear, and concerned a live, poisonous snake; the other was intended to evoke anger, and cast the subject in the role of someone being berated by a tutor for lack of intelligence and poor examination performance. It was found that HR responses to these scenarios depended on their mode of presentation, their emotional content, and the subject's gender and imagery ability. Male good imagers responded more to the fear and anger dramas than did male poor imagers, but female good imagers, while responding much more to the fear scenario, did *not* differ from female poor imagers in response to the anger scenario. Thus female subjects showed reduced cardiac response to stimuli intended to arouse anger. Sapolsky, Stocking and Zillmann (1977) exposed male and female subjects to a provocation and then gave them the opportunity to aggress either immediately or after a 6 minute delay. During this delay period it was observed that females showed greater heart rate deceleration than males, reflecting more efficient physiological recovery from the provocation. It has been argued that such findings reflect the fact that women have learned to minimize the arousing effects of annoying or provocative stimuli (cf. Hokanson, 1970; Zillmann, 1979).

Further evidence of sex differences in cardiovascular responses comes from research on stress. Stimulated by the possible link between such sex differences and epidemiological evidence of sizeable sex differences in risk for coronary heart disease, Stoney, Davis and Matthews (1987) recently reported a meta-analytic review of all psychophysiological studies reported in English-language journals between 1965 and 1986. The meta-analysis yielded three major findings. First, females had higher resting heart rates (HR) than males, and tended to have higher HR increases during challenge. Second, males had higher resting systolic blood pressure (SBP) than females, and exhibited higher SBP changes during challenge. Third, the males had higher urinary epinephrine responses during stress. The authors note that:

> Taken together, the results provide some support for the hypothesis that men show greater physiological responses during acute behavioural stress than do women. Two caveats should be noted, however. First, the heart rate responses during stress were greater in women than in men, albeit not significantly so. Second, few investigations were available for analysis, and little research in this area has been programmatic (p. 129).

Another aspect of psychophysiological activity in which gender differences have been reported concerns autonomic self-perception. Katkin and his associates (Katkin, Blascovich and Goldband, 1981; Koenigsberg, Katkin and Blascovich, 1981) have studied individual differences in the ability to discriminate one's own heartbeat. In the Katkin procedure subjects are presented with one set of signals that have a fixed, invariant relationship to their own heartbeat, and another set of signals that have a variable relationship to own heartbeat. The subject's task is to discriminate correctly these two types of signal. In the Katkin, Blascovich and Goldband (1981) study, male and female subjects received 40 baseline trials followed by 120 trials in which they received veridical feedback on the correctness of their discrimination after each trial. Only male subjects showed any evidence of acquisition of heartbeat discrimination in the course of the feedback trials. The Koenigsberg, Katkin and Blascovich (1981) study was intended to examine whether the nature of the instructions given to subjects affected acquisition of heartbeat discrimination on 40 "retention" trials conducted after the feedback trials. "Experimental" subjects were given detailed instructions and extensive practice in the discrimination task, while "control" subjects were run under conditions replicating those obtaining in the Katkin, Blascovich and Goldband (1981) study. Under control conditions male subjects again showed significantly greater acquisition of heartbeat discrimination than did females; under experimental conditions, however, females did not differ from female controls but males performed much worse than male controls and more poorly than either female group. The authors concluded that male and female subjects use different cognitive strategies in learning heartbeat discrimination, such that instructions oriented towards an auditory discrimination strategy undermined the otherwise good acquisition displayed by male subjects while leaving female subjects unaffected.

Research using electromyography (EMG) to assess physiological response to emotional stimuli has generally shown that females exhibit greater facial EMG than males. In a series of studies, Schwartz and his associates (Schwartz, Ahern and Brown, 1979; Schwartz, Brown and Ahern, 1980; Schwartz *et al.*, 1976a; Schwartz *et al.*, 1976b; Schwartz *et al.*, 1978) have found that females, by comparison with males, tend to produce greater facial EMG, relative to rest, during affective imagery; to exhibit somewhat higher levels of corrugator activity (possibly indicative of greater sadness or concern) and lower levels of masseter activity (possibly indicative of less anger) during rest; and to generate larger facial EMG patterns when asked to pose overt expressions corresponding to different emotions. As we shall see in the next section of this chapter, these findings are consistent with research examining gender differences in facial expressiveness using different measurement techniques.

RESEARCH ON FACIAL EXPRESSIVENESS

Several studies have examined gender differences in so-called "spontaneous" facial expressiveness. The term "spontaneous" is used here to denote the fact that in such research "sender" subjects' facial reactions to emotional stimuli are covertly recorded (or relayed live via closed-circuit television) in order that other ("receiver") subjects can engage in the task of inferring the nature of the stimulus presented to the sender (e.g. Buck, Miller and Caul, 1974) or the nature of the sender's emotional response to that stimulus (e.g. Wagner, MacDonald and Manstead, 1986). For the sake of simplicity, these measures will hereafter be referred to as measures of "sending accuracy".

Consider first those studies involving adult subjects. Here there is consistent evidence that females' spontaneous facial responses to emotional stimuli (typically colour slides) are more accurately decoded by receiver subjects, by comparison with males' facial responses (Buck *et al.*, 1972; Buck, Miller and Caul, 1974; Fujita, Harper and Wiens, 1980; Gallagher and Shuntich, 1981).

Buck and his associates (Buck, Baron and Barrette, 1982; Buck *et al.*, 1980) have subjected video-tapes of spontaneous facial expressions to "segmentation analysis", a procedure in which observers are instructed to press a button whenever "something meaningful" occurs. The Buck *et al.* (1980) study found that sending accuracy was positively and significantly associated with the number of segmentation points noted by subjects in relation to the facial expressions of females; this was not the case with males' expressions. Thus the *amount* of "meaningful" facial/gestural activity exhibited by sender subjects is related to their sending accuracy in the case of females but not males.

In the Buck, Baron and Barrette (1982) study a more detailed analysis of segmentation points was performed, permitting the investigators to assess not just the number of segmentation points, but also the number of *consensual* segmentation points (CPs), where a CP is defined as a 1-second period which attracted in excess of one standard deviation above the average number of segmentation points per second given to that video sequence. Obviously, the greater the number of CPs, the more observers agree in their judgement of the location of meaningful behaviours. Furthermore, a second group of observer subjects were shown the same video-tape of facial expressions and told where CPs occurred; for each CP, these subjects had to judge whether it was based on a facial expression on the part of the sender, or related to some other behaviour such as head movement or postural change. The percentage of CPs judged to be facial expressions indicates the extent to which consensual judgements of meaningful behaviour involve facial expressions. In this study it was found that females' sending accuracy was significantly and positively correlated not only with the number of segmentation points (as in the earlier study) but also with the number of CPs; neither of these correlations was significant in the case of males. However, the percentage of CPs judged to be facial expressions was positively and significantly related to sending accuracy for males but not for females. These findings appear to indicate that sending accuracy, as reflected in the degree to which spontaneous facial expressiveness permits observers to make accurate inferences about the sender's state, is based upon different behaviours in males and females. It seems that among females, sending accuracy is related simply to the amount of meaningful activity, but that among males sending accuracy is related to the extent to which such activity involves facial expressions. As Buck (1984) observes, there appear to be qualitative as well as quantitative differences between males and females with regard to sending accuracy. Why this should be so is as yet unknown, and there is an obvious need for further research on this topic.

What is clear, however, is that the gender difference in spontaneous facial expressiveness observed in adults is not reliably found in infants and children. In two studies of preschoolers, Buck (1975, 1977) found a small gender difference in expressiveness, in that undergraduate receivers were more accurate in guessing the type of stimulus viewed by girls as compared with boys. However, there was no difference between girls' and boys' sending accuracy when the child's mother acted as the receiver. Field (1982) found no reliable gender differences in the facial expressiveness of neonates, and Yarczower and Daruns (1982) also found no gender differences in their study using children aged 6 or 12. These failures to find reliable gender differences among children suggest that the differences observed in adults are acquired relatively late in childhood, and may therefore be mediated by sex-role socialization. Consistent with such an interpretation is Buck's (1975, 1977) finding that sending accuracy tends to be inversely related with age among boys, but not girls—suggesting that spontaneous facial expressiveness in boys decreases as they get older.

It is one thing to speculate that gender differences in facial expressiveness are acquired, and quite another to provide evidence concerning the processes by which they are acquired. However, some progress has been made in pinpointing one such process. Malatesta and her colleagues (Malatesta and Haviland, 1982; Malatesta *et al.*, 1986; Malatesta and Lamb, 1987) have been exploring the role played by mothers' modelling of facial expressions and the way in which mothers respond contingently to their infants' facial expressions during the first two years of life. In the Malatesta and Haviland (1982) study, 60 mothers and their 3- to 6-month-old infants were video-taped during a 16-minute play period. Although male and female infants exhibited no significant difference in the type and rate of facial expression change, mothers were found to respond differentially to males and females. Mothers of male infants tended to match their child's expressions with similar expressions of their own, whereas mothers of female infants tended to follow their child's expressions with dissimilar expressions of their own. Mothers showed higher levels of contingent responding (especially contingent smiling) to the smiles of older versus younger male infants. However, the pattern was reversed for female infants, with mothers showing lower contingent responding to older versus younger females.

In the Malatesta and Lamb (1987) study, 58 2-year-olds and their mothers were video-taped during a 9-minute play period and in the "strange situation'' developed by Ainsworth and Wittig (1969). Mothers of male infants showed significant matching of infant sadness, unlike mothers of females. On the other hand, mothers of females showed significant matching of a ''pressed lip'' expression (thought to relate to anger suppression), whereas mothers of males tended to ignore this expression. Finally, when infants displayed full anger expressions, mothers of girls tended to ignore such expressions whereas mothers of boys did not.

The notion that such differential responding to male and female infants' expressions may have an impact on the infants' pattern of facial expression is supported by evidence from the longitudinal study reported by Malatesta *et al.* (1986). This research, spanning the period from 2 to 7 months of age, not only found further evidence of differential patterns of contingent responding and modelling on the part of mothers as a function of their infant's gender, but also found evidence that exposure to this differentiated pattern of stimulation in time results in different patterns of expressiveness. For example, modelling by mothers of joy and interest when the infant was 5 months old was predictive of increases in infant joy and interest expressions 2.5 months later.

The painstaking and pioneering research conducted by Malatesta and her associates is in need of replication but it points to the possibility that the ways in which males and females express emotion facially may elicit different reactions from caregivers even at a very early age. However, these differences do not appear to be sufficient in themselves to evoke a clear-cut gender difference in children's facial expressiveness, for as we have seen such a difference does not become reliable until children are into their teens. However, if this differentiated pattern of contingent responding is sufficient over time to provoke subtle differences in infants' facial displays of emotion, consider how much more powerful the more overt socialization effected at later ages, via verbal instruction, is likely to be. It also seems likely that same-sex peer groups will be important agents of socialization from puberty onwards, acting to reinforce behaviours consistent with culturally endorsed sex-roles. Children as young as 2–3 years attribute to a male doll the characteristic that ''he never cries'' (Kuhn, Nash and Bruchan, 1978), and by the time they are aged 5–8 children know many of the sex-stereotyped personality traits, including the ''feminine'' traits of emotionality (Best *et al.*, 1977). Given that overt socialization will tend to incorporate cultural beliefs about the appropriateness of overt emotional displays by males and females, it is hardly surprising that by adulthood males are less expressive than females in their spontaneous facial behaviours.

RESEARCH ON SUBJECTIVE EXPERIENCE OF EMOTION

Gender differences in subjective emotional experience are widely reported in the research literature. For example, questionnaire studies on children and adults tend to find that females experience more fear than males do (see Maccoby and Jacklin, 1974). One difficulty in knowing what to make of such findings is that those who are old enough to provide reliable responses to questionnaires are also sufficiently well socialized to have a fair idea of how appropriate it is for males and females to experience and express various emotions—including fear. Thus it is entirely possible (or even likely) that the way in which males and females respond to such questionnaires will, consciously or unconsciously, be influenced by their knowledge of sex stereotypes. The "greater fear" reported by females may simply reflect their greater willingness to admit to feeling fearful. Indeed, there is some evidence that scores on paper-and-pencil measures of fears and anxieties are inversely related to social desirability scores, indicating that those who report relatively few fears or anxieties tend to score higher on social desirability (Spiegler and Liebert, 1970; Wilson, 1967).

A further problem with questionnaire measures of negative emotionality such as anxiety, as Jahnke, Crannell and Morrissette (1964) have argued, is that it is difficult—if not impossible—to determine whether differences in the total scores of women and men reflect gender differences in underlying anxiety (or willingness to express anxiety) or are simply an artefact of the sex-typed content of the items included in the questionnaire measure. These authors point out that the Manifest Anxiety Scale, a very widely used self-report measure of anxiety, includes relatively few items that deal with the kinds of anxieties most likely to be experienced by men (such as anxiety over work-related matters). Hill and Sarason (1966) have made a similar point in relation to anxiety scales for children, and Maccoby and Jacklin (1974) suggest that as many as 10 of the 45 items of the General Anxiety Scale for Children are weighted towards fears more likely to be experienced by girls than boys.

Studies of the frequency of affective experience do not suffer from the possible problem of biased item content, but they do potentially suffer from the problem that observed gender differences may simply reflect differential willingness to report affective experience. It is interesting to note, then, that although some studies show that women report themselves as experiencing both positive and negative affect more frequently than men, the gender difference is rather greater in the case of negative affect (Bradburn, 1969; Harding, 1982). Indeed, in a study of over 3000 British adults, Warr and Payne (1982) found no overall gender difference in how much of the time on the previous day they had felt "pleased with things", but that 18% of women experienced "unpleasant emotional strain" on the previous day for about half the time or more, by contrast with 13% of men. The fact that gender differences are more reliably found in relation to *negative* emotional experience again raises the possibility that women may simply be more willing than men to confront and express such experience. A similar point applies to the one "non-trivial" gender difference in emotional experience observed in the large-scale cross-national study reported by Scherer, Wallbott and Summerfield (1986). Respondents were asked about joy, sadness, anger and fear, and with respect to subjective experience the only greater gender difference was that women reported more intense and longer-lasting experiences of *sadness*. One problem with interpreting such findings in terms of differential willingness to express or report negative affect is that women are more likely than men to be homemakers and to be engaged in child care. It is therefore possible that gender differences in reporting dysphoric affect stem partly or wholly from these differences in occupational roles. The average number of aversive events encountered by a woman who is a homemaker and/or mother may simply be greater than those encountered by a man in full-time employment. However, there is some additional evidence that men find it difficult to be open about dysphoric emotional experience. For example, in the research on marital satisfaction reported by Noller (1982), it was found that wives reported that they could often discern that their husbands were upset, but complained that it was difficult to get their husbands to express their feelings and to discuss why they felt upset.

It is worth noting, in passing, the fact that Scherer and his associates found no gender difference with regard to anger experiences, a finding that is consistent with earlier research by Averill (1982). This is interesting because (a) it emphasizes the point that the observed gender difference in negative emotionality does not apply to all negative emotions; and (b) it demonstrates that gender differences in aggressive behaviour, which will be discussed below, do not necessarily reflect differences in the subjective experience of anger.

Many psychological disorders have an affective component, so it is worth comparing women's and men's vulnerability to such disorders. Official statistics on psychological disorders should be interpreted cautiously, given that there are grounds for thinking that psychiatric diagnoses might vary according to whether the client is male or female. In a widely-cited study, Broverman *et al.* (1970) examined the possible influence of sex-role stereotypes on clinical diagnosis. Some clinicians were asked to rate a "healthy, mature, socially competent adult person" on a standard questionnaire listing personality traits. Other clinicians were asked to rate a man, also described as healthy, mature and socially competent; and a third group was asked to rate a similarly described woman. It was found that beliefs about what constituted a healthy "adult" were closer to the picture of the healthy male than that of the healthy female. If even a healthy female adult is seen by clinicians as differing from an "ideal" healthy adult, it is possible that women are more readily diagnosed as psychologically disordered than are men. Certainly, women are overrepresented in nearly all populations of persons using mental health services (see Cochrane, 1983; Miles, 1987). Archer and Lloyd (1985) report that women represented 58% of first admissions to mental hospitals and mental health units in England in 1979. Women are particularly over-represented in certain diagnostic categories: depressive psychosis and involutional melancholia (65%); psychoneurosis (66%); and senile and presenile psychoses (65%). The predominance of women in this last group can be attributed largely to their greater longevity. It should be noted that men are also over-represented in certain diagnostic categories: alcoholic psychosis (65%); alcoholism (72%); and drug dependence (69%). The overall predominance of women among psychiatric populations in the United States is also well established (e.g. Chesler, 1971; Gove, 1978; Guttentag, Salasin and Belle, 1980), and the general pattern of male and female representation in diagnostic categories is the same as in the UK.

It is clear, then, that women are on average more likely to be diagnosed as suffering from psychoneuroses and depression, two psychological disorders with a strong affective component. Do these higher morbidity rates for women reflect real differences between men's and women's subjective experiences, or do they simply reflect their differential willingness to express emotional problems and/or to seek help for them? Just as with the questionnaire studies of emotional experience mentioned above, a greater readiness on the part of women to admit that they are experiencing negative affect and/or to seek help in alleviating that negative affect may well contribute to the observed gender difference in morbidity. Hammen and Peters (1978) found that reactions to someone enacting a depressed role differed as a function of the person's sex: reactions to the depressed female were less negative than were reactions to the depressed male. Men's awareness of the relative unacceptability of emotional disorders such as depression in males may diminish their readiness to admit to such problems and to seek help in dealing with them. It has been estimated that as much as one quarter of the observed gender differences in psychological disorders could be due to such factors (see Kessler, Price and Wortman, 1985). Indeed, there is evidence that women more frequently seek help for emotional problems than men do (Phillips and Segal, 1969).

It seems unlikely that the observed gender differences in psychological disorders can be fully accounted for by invoking explanations based on women's greater willingness to acknowledge symptoms and/or to seek help. One possible explanation for such differences is that they reflect different strategies for coping with similar sorts of stressful life events; whereas women's "preferred" coping style is depressogenic in nature, men's "preferred" coping style involves drinking alcohol. Another possibility is one favoured by Gove and his colleagues, who have argued that such gender differences reflect real differences in the incidence of psychological disorders in men and women, and that these real differences in turn arise from sociocultural rather than biological factors (Gove, 1978; 1980; Gove and Tudor, 1973). An important basis for the argument that it is sociocultural factors that are responsible for gender differences in psychological disorder is the observation that married women exhibit greater susceptibility to such disorders whereas single, widowed or divorced women do not differ from their male counterparts (Gove, 1972; 1979; 1980). It is therefore reasoned that the social role played by women within marriage is stressful, because it gives rise to greater frustration, more constraint, less reward and ultimately to higher rates of psychological (and physical) illness than does the role played by married men.

It is worth noting, however, that general psychiatric admission rates among married patients in the USA are no longer appreciably higher for women than for men (see Bloom, Asher and White, 1978). Indeed, admission rates for inpatient facilities are generally higher for males, although those for outpatient facilities are somewhat higher for females (Bloom, Asher and White, 1978). Even when one compares diagnosis-specific admission rates in different marital status groups, there is relatively little evidence that being married results in greater depression among women than among men (Bloom, 1975). What is not in dispute is the fact that males suffer more than females following marital disruption (separation or divorce; Bloom, Asher and White, 1978) or bereavement (Stroebe and Stroebe, 1983). Although the fact that males are more adversely affected than females by separation, divorce or bereavement is consistent with Gove's social role hypothesis, there are alternative explanations. For example, males may be less willing or less well placed to elicit social support from others following marital disruption or bereavement (Stroebe and Stroebe, 1983).

A very different approach to the explanation of observed gender differences in psychological disorders is employed by those who emphasize the role of biological factors. Common to the diverse explanations that fall under this general heading is the assumption that sex hormones are important causal agents. For example, it has been suggested that the mood fluctuations experienced by many women premenstrually arise from progesterone deficiency or imbalance (Dalton, 1969; Hamburg and Lunde, 1966). However, direct measurement of levels of progesterone and other hormones such as oestradiol have failed to support such hypotheses. In a review of the evidence, Bancroft and Backstrom (1985) concluded that although there is a *prima facie* case for considering direct effects of progesterone and oestradiol on CNS activity, it is difficult to account for premenstrual mood changes in terms of varying levels of these two hormones. Furthermore, assessment of the supposedly therapeutic effects of hormonal intervention (e.g., through progesterone injection; Dalton, 1979) shows no evidence of improvement when double-blind procedures are followed (see Bancroft and Backstrom, 1985). Those who favour a more psychological or sociocultural explanation of premenstrual mood changes stress the role of negative beliefs about and attitudes to menstruation, and cognitive biases leading women to attribute to menstruation any negative affect experienced when they believe themselves to be premenstrual (see Parlee, 1988; Ruble and Brooks-Gunn, 1979). Whatever the basis of mood fluctuations during the menstrual cycle, it seems most unlikely that such fluctuations could account for the gender difference in the incidence of depression (see Weissman and Klermann, 1977). Research has also failed to support the notion that post-natal depression stems from hormonal changes at this time, such as the sudden fall in progesterone levels (Weldburn, 1980). Finally, some have argued that women's apparently greater vulnerability to depression at the time of menopause is the result of hormonal change (in this case, the decline in oestrogen levels; Dalton, 1979). However, Weissman (1979) concluded that the menopause is *not* associated with an increase in depression or any other psychological disorder; rather, it seems that depression in middle-aged women may result from factors such as the loss of maternal role (Bart, 1971) or stressful life events such as the death of a loved one (Greene, 1981) that tend to occur at the same general time as the menopause.

To summarize, there is evidence that women may be more inclined than men to experience dysphoric emotions such as fear, anxiety, sadness and depression. It is extremely difficult to determine whether these gender differences accurately reflect phenomenological differences in male and female emotionality but in the case of depression there appears to be some reason to believe that women are more prone than men to experience this type of negative affect. There is no satisfactory evidence that this gender difference has a biological basis. It seems possible that it is a reflection of the peculiar stresses experienced by women in fulfilling role obligations, although there is as yet no evidence that unequivocally supports this explanation.

RESEARCH ON EMOTIONAL BEHAVIOUR

As Maccoby and Jacklin (1974) have argued, a primary index of emotional disturbance in an infant is that he or she cries. These authors reviewed 21 studies of the frequency and duration of crying among children ranging in age from neonates to 5-year-olds, with the majority of studies focusing on the first year of life. The findings of these studies show no consistent evidence of a gender difference in frequency or duration of crying.

However, there is some evidence of a gender difference in reactions to frustration. Goodenough (1931) reported that the frequency of anger outbursts in boys and girls was similar up to the age of 18 months, but that beyond that age the frequency declined for girls and increased for boys. Studies of reactions to frustration tend to suggest that boys react more emotionally than girls do (see Maccoby and Jacklin, 1974). Maccoby and Feldman (1972) found that 2-year-old boys were more likely than their female peers to bang on the door through which their mother had departed, when left alone in a strange room. Martin (1981) observed 10-month-old children while their mothers were completing a questionnaire, and noted that boys seemed particularly unwilling to accept the mother's withdrawal of attention, and escalated the intensity of their demands for her attention if she failed to respond. Gunnar (1980) found that when 1-year-olds were prevented from controlling a frightening toy, boys were more likely than girls to become distressed.

Further evidence of gender differences in emotional behaviour comes from a review reported by Haviland and Malatesta (1981). These authors conclude that boys are more emotionally labile and more easily distressed than girls, at least during infancy. Girls, on the other hand, establish and maintain eye contact more than boys—and this difference appears to be maintained into adulthood. The authors suggest that the greater gazing behaviour of infant girls will promote feelings of closeness between mother and daughter, whereas the greater gaze aversion, irritability and inconsolability of male infants is likely to inhibit such feelings. Thus the different signals produced by male and female infants may elicit different responses from caregivers, and these differentiated patterns of response may underlie gender differences in emotional behaviour exhibited at later stages of development.

Research on aggressive behaviour has in general supported the stereotype that males are more aggressive than females. Before turning to the evidence, it is worth considering more closely what is meant by the term "aggression", and in particular how it relates to emotion. As Archer and Lloyd (1985) have noted, aggression is used sometimes to refer to "assertiveness" and sometimes as meaning "motivation to commit a violent act". These two meanings can be related, these authors go on to argue, "if we regard an assertive person as more ready to commit violent acts if his intentions are frustrated" (p. 126). It is only in the second sense of aggression, i.e., "motivation to commit a violent act" that emotion comes into play, in that anger can motivate and accompany aggressive behaviour. Much of the research on gender differences in aggression is not directly concerned with emotions, however. Rather, aggression is measured in terms of overt behaviour. Researchers usually observe the incidence of fighting, "rough and tumble play", or destructive acts in children; and the incidence of verbal aggression or the willingness to harm another person (e.g. by administering what are believed to be electric shocks) in adults.

Because aggression may or may not be motivated or accompanied by emotion (see Geen, 1990), this is not the appropriate context in which to review in great detail the research evidence on gender differences in aggression. In any case, the literature has been reviewed comprehensively by others (e.g. Eagly and Steffen, 1986; Frodi, Macauley and Thome, 1977; Hyde, 1984; Maccoby and Jacklin, 1974, 1980). What follows is therefore a brief overview.

Observational studies of children's behaviour typically show boys to be more aggressive than girls (Hyde, 1984). An example of such a study carried out on preschool children is the one reported by Smith and Green (1975). These investigators found that conflicts between boys were more frequent than those between girls or those between boys and girls. Although this finding is typical, it is worth noting that there was greater variation in the incidence of aggression *across* the 15 nursery schools, day nurseries and play groups studied than between boys and girls *within* these different settings (Henshall and McGuire, 1986). Nevertheless, the direction of the overall gender difference in this study is consistent with that found in other research (Hyde, 1984) and there is very little evidence of a reversal of the typical gender difference, even if one focuses on *verbal* rather than *physical* aggression.

Research on adults has yielded a somewhat less consistent pattern of findings, and it has been argued that this reflects the fact that situational variables become more important determinants of aggressive behaviour as age increases (Eagly and Steffen, 1986). The influential review of Frodi, Macauley and Thome (1977) concluded that the gender difference in aggression is dependent on several other factors, such as the mode of response available to the instigator, the gender of the target person, and emotional arousal. In relation to this last point, Frodi, Macauley and Thome argued that "women's aggressive behaviour must often be moderated by arousal of aggression anxiety over the propriety of such behaviour. It seems likely that a significant proportion of variation between (and probably within) the sexes can be accounted for by guilt or anxiety avoidance or arousal" (p. 645). Consistent with this argument, Eagly and Steffen (1986) found that women and men think differently about aggression and that these differential beliefs about the consequences of aggressive behaviour are important mediators of the gender difference in aggression. More specifically, "Women reported more guilt and anxiety as a consequence of aggression, more vigilance about the harm that aggression causes its victims, and more concern about the danger that aggression might bring to themselves" (p. 325).

Also relevant to this line of argument is a programme of research conducted by Hokanson and his colleagues (see Hokanson, 1970). In the context of simulated interaction with a peer, subjects were "attacked" by means of an electric shock administered by their partner. Subjects were free to respond to this attack by pressing one of three buttons: one delivered a shock to the partner; another delivered a reward; and the third delivered neither shock nor reward. A key dependent variable was systolic blood pressure. In males, it was found that recovery from the arousal induced by the partner's attacking behaviour was alleviated most rapidly following aggressive (i.e. shock) responses; recovery following non-aggressive responses was as slow as that in a control condition, where subjects were not given the opportunity to respond to the attack. However, females exhibited rapid autonomic recovery regardless of how they responded to the attack. Whichever of the three options they chose, recovery was significantly faster than it was in the control condition.

Commenting on this pattern of findings, Hokanson, Willers and Koropsak (1968) suggested that "Females undergo a set of learning experiences in which making nonaggressive responses to someone else's aggression is rewarded: in the specific sense of thereby effectively reducing the other person's aversive behaviour, and in the general sense that this behaviour conforms to cultural norms and expectations" (p. 388). To test this speculation, these investigators conducted an experiment involving three phases, during the first and third of which the subject's partner attacked him or her by administering electric shocks on trials determined via a random schedule. The subject could respond to such attacks by delivering a shock or a reward. In the second phase, however, the partner's attacks were contingent upon the sex and behaviour of the subject. Females were punished whenever they responded to shock by delivering a reward, and rewarded whenever they responded to shock by delivering another shock. For males this schedule of reinforcement was reversed. The results showed that during the first phase females showed faster autonomic recovery after reacting to shocks by delivering a reward, whereas males recovered faster after responding with a further shock. During the second phase this pattern was reversed, with females recovering more quickly after aggressive responses and males after non-aggressive responses. During the third phase males and females reverted fairly rapidly to the patterns of behaviour they exhibited during phase one. These findings are consistent with the view that the way in which an individual responds to annoyance and provocations is at least partly a function of learning (cf. Zillmann, 1979). In many cultures it seems that males and females are taught to react differently, in that annoyance-induced arousal in females dissipates as rapidly or more rapidly when they respond non-aggressively as when they respond aggressively, while such arousal in males dissipates more rapidly following aggressive responses than following non-aggressive responses. To the extent that aggression is a function of autonomic arousal (and there are circumstances under which it is not; see Zillmann, 1979), here is an acquired basis for the "typical" gender difference in aggression.

Archer and Lloyd (1985) point out that although laboratory-based research on adults suggests that the gender difference in aggression is small (albeit significant), a clearer picture emerges from studies of "real life" violence, such as violent crime, in which the perpetrator is almost always male. In the UK, for example, nearly ten times as many men as women are convicted for violence against other persons (*Social Trends*, 1984). It seems clear that willingness to commit violent acts against others is greater in men than in women.

The greater willingness of males to engage in aggressive and violent behaviour has attracted some theorists to biologically-based explanations that emphasize the role played by sex chromosomes in producing the gender difference. This has been investigated by studying the incidence of the XYY chromosomal pattern in populations of convicted violent criminals. Some reviews of this research (e.g. Kessler and Moos, 1970) have concluded that there is insufficient evidence to support the hypothesized relationship, while others (e.g. Nielsen and Christensen, 1974) conclude that the evidence points to such a relationship. In one of the most exhaustive studies of this issue, Witkin *et al.* (1976) examined XYYs drawn from the general population and compared them with XY controls from the same population. It was found that although XYYs had a higher mean rate of criminal convictions than XY controls, the frequency of crimes of violence was no higher among XYYs than among XYs. Thus the elevated crime rate of XYY males could not be accounted for in terms of aggression; rather, the data suggested that it might be related to low intelligence.

Another biological line of explanation comes from research on the relationship between sex hormones and aggression. There is evidence from studies of non-human species (reviewed by Maccoby and Jacklin, 1974) that prenatal exposure of females to androgens enhances aggressive behaviour; that post-natal administration of testosterone to females has a similar effect; and that more aggressive males tend to have higher levels of androgens. Archer and Lloyd (1985) note that much of this research used as subjects rats or mice—species in which the male is known to be more aggressive than the female—rather than gerbils or hamsters, species in which the female is as aggressive as or more aggressive than the male. They also question the relevance of research on rodents to theories about the biological basis of human gender differences in aggression. Nevertheless, Archer (personal communication) suggests that the following comparative argument currently has the most credibility. In a wide range of animals, increased aggressiveness is exhibited by males at puberty or on entering the breeding season, and this increase is likely to be in anticipation of fighting other males over resources necessary to, or useful for, reproduction. Since this makes functional sense over a wide range of animals, it might be worth looking for a similar phenomenon in humans. It remains to be seen whether there is a similar androgen-related effect on aggressiveness in boys at the time of puberty.

In humans, there are two main sources of evidence concerning the relationship between sex hormones and aggression. First, Money and Ehrhardt (1972) have compared girls who for one of a variety of reasons were exposed to androgens prenatally with a "normal" group of girls. This research strategy has also been followed by Reinisch (1981). Second, researchers such as Olweus *et al.* (1980) and Persky, Smith and Basu (1971) have examined the correlation between testosterone levels and various indices of aggression. Taken at face value, both lines of research tend to support the notion of a relationship between testosterone and aggression, but in each case problems of interpretation arise. In the research on girls exposed to androgens prenatally, it has been argued that the parents of these girls may have treated them differently than they would have treated "normal" girls; that at least some of the girls studied received relatively late surgical correction of genital abnormalities; and that much of the evidence concerning such girls is derived from questionnaires and interviews rather than direct observations of behaviour. The research on correlations between testosterone and aggression is obviously vulnerable to the argument that higher levels of testosterone may have *resulted from*, rather than caused, aggressive behaviour (cf. Mazur and Lamb, 1980). Such considerations weaken confidence in the conclusion that gender differences in human aggression are biologically caused.

The fact that it is very difficult, if not impossible, to produce evidence that unequivocally supports or refutes the hypothesis that human gender differences in aggression are biologically based is no accident. From birth onwards, boys and girls are treated differently (see Culp, Crook and Housley, 1983; Smith and Lloyd, 1978; Rubin, Provenzano and Luria, 1974) and the basis of this differential treatment is the sexual dimorphism that stems from chromosomal and hormonal differences between males and females. Biological and social influences are thus heavily confounded in the normal course of events, with the inevitable result that causal inference is seriously impeded. Even those who argue strongly that biological factors play a key role in determining gender differences in aggression recognize the impossibility of assigning causality in any straightforward manner:

> Women share with men the human capacity to heap all sorts of injury upon their fellows. And in almost every group that has been observed, there are some women who are fully as aggressive as the men. Furthermore, an individual's aggressive behavior is strengthened, weakened, redirected, or altered in form by his or her unique pattern of experiences. All we mean to argue is that there is a sex-linked differential readiness to respond in aggressive ways to the relevant experiences (Maccoby and Jacklin, 1974, p. 247).

Whatever the origin of the gender difference in human aggression, it is worth noting that it is at least partly inconsistent with the cultural stereotype that women are more emotional than men. The inconsistency is only partial in that aggression may or may not be accompanied by anger. Nevertheless, it is curious, as Shields (1987) has observed, that emotion in general is stereotypically associated with femaleness, whereas anger and aggression are stereotypically (and in the case of aggression, at least, to some extent veridically) associated with maleness.

RESEARCH ON RECOGNITION OF OTHERS' EMOTIONS

Studies of the ability to recognize non-verbally communicated affect comprise a fifth area of research on gender differences in emotion. Here, of course, the focus is not on gender differences in the individual who experiences or expresses the emotion, but rather on gender differences in the ability of observers to infer emotion from observations of others' non-verbal behaviours. Are women more accurate than men in decoding the emotional meaning of others' non-verbal behaviours? As Hall (1978) has pointed out, two influential reviews of the literature answered this question in the negative. Maccoby and Jacklin (1974) reviewed several relevant studies and concluded that "neither sex has greater ability to judge the reactions or intentions of others in any generalized sense" (p. 214). Hoffman (1977) arrived at a similar conclusion: ". . . when encountering someone in an emotional situation, both sexes are equally adept at assessing how that person feels" (p. 716).

However, Hall (1978, 1984) has conducted meta-analytic reviews of the research literature that point rather convincingly to a different conclusion. In her 1978 review of 75 studies published since 1923, Hall found a consistent and statistically reliable tendency for females to be better than males in decoding non-verbal expressions. Eighty-four per cent of the 61 studies in which the direction of the gender difference was reported found a difference in favour of women. From the 46 studies reporting appropriate statistics, Hall computed that the mean effect size (*d*; see Cohen, 1977) associated with this gender difference was 0.40 and highly significantly different from zero. Hall (1984) updated this analysis by reviewing 125 relevant studies. Of the 93 studies in which the direction of the gender difference was reported, 83% favoured women, and the mean effect size based on the 64 studies reporting appropriate statistics was 0.43. If one considers only those studies in which a statistically significant gender difference was observed, 33 of these favoured women and only two favoured men.

Confidence in the robustness of this gender difference is enhanced by the fact that very similar results emerged from a meta-analysis of 133 studies that were conducted in the course of the development of the Profile of Nonverbal Sensitivity (PONS) test (Rosenthal *et al.*, 1979). (Only 11 of these PONS studies were included in the 125 studies reviewed by Hall (1984), so the analysis of the PONS studies to all intents and purposes constitutes an independent meta-analysis.) Of the 133 PONS studies, 80% showed a gender difference favouring females, and the median effect size based on these studies was 0.41.

It is worth noting, however, that very few of the studies included in Hall's meta-analytic reviews were studies of the ability to decode *spontaneous* expression of emotion. As Hall (1978) noted, "the expressive stimuli in these studies were generated in a variety of ways. By far the most common method was to ask the sender or senders to express various emotions, while these expressions were photographed, audiotaped, and so forth" (p. 37). Furthermore, all the expressive stimuli included in the PONS test are of the "posed" variety. This tendency to use posed rather than spontaneous expressive stimuli obviously raises questions about the generalizability of the conclusion that females are better than males in decoding non-verbal cues. Clearly, expressive behaviour in everyday social interaction is not always (indeed, is perhaps only rarely) of the posed kind. It is important, then, to consider the extent to which the female advantage in decoding posed non-verbal cues generalizes to spontaneous cues. Some studies of gender differences in decoding spontaneous facial expressions (e.g. Buck *et al.*, 1972; Buck, Miller and Caul, 1974; Wagner, MacDonald and Manstead, 1986) have failed to find a significant female advantage. Furthermore, Fujita, Harper and Wiens (1980) found that although females were significantly better than males at decoding posed expressions, there was no significant gender difference in decoding spontaneous expressions.

A further issue arising from the Hall (1978) meta-analysis relates to the developmental course of the gender difference in decoding non-verbal cues. Hall concluded that the female advantage in judging non-verbal cues does not vary as a function of age. However, Eisenberg and Lennon (1983) have taken issue with this aspect of Hall's analysis. They review the findings of 15 studies on children's decoding of visual non-verbal cues and note that in only four out of 21 comparisons was there a significant or marginally significant difference favouring females, while one comparison revealed a significant male advantage. It is also worth noting that Eisenberg and Lennon review the findings of 23 studies of affective role taking, in which children are exposed to another's affective state by means of a story and/or pictures depicting a protagonist in an emotionally-arousing situation; here only three studies reported that girls scored significantly higher than boys, while one reported a significant difference in favour of males. On balance, then, there is little evidence to support the view that there are gender differences in the ability of children to recognize emotion in others on the basis of either non-verbal information or pictures and/or stories depicting someone in an emotionally-arousing situation.

A slightly different, but not unrelated, qualification of the general tendency for women to be superior to men in decoding non-verbal cues emerges from research conducted by Rosenthal and DePaulo (1979). They suggested that the female non-verbal decoding advantage might diminish as the non-verbal cues being decoded become less intended and less controllable by the sender. They reasoned that women may be more non-verbally "accommodating" than men, such that although they are more accurate in decoding *intended* cues, they will tend not to "eavesdrop" on non-verbal cues that the sender is not monitoring carefully and may not intend to emit. A key theoretical notion here is that of "leakage", a term coined by Ekman and Friesen (1969) to refer to the way in which some non-verbal behaviours can reveal a person's true feelings even when that person tries to conceal those feelings. Certain non-verbal channels are deemed to be "leakier" in this respect than others. For example, the face is a channel of communication that is typically highly informative about the sender's affective state; however, it is also a channel that can be monitored and controlled by the sender if he or she so wishes. It has been argued that other non-verbal channels, such as the body or the tone of one's voice, will often be more informative about the sender's affect when he or she is attempting to conceal it because these channels are monitored less carefully by the sender and cannot be controlled as effectively as the face. There is a body of empirical evidence confirming that body cues and tone of voice cues are leakier than facial cues (see DePaulo, Zuckerman and Rosenthal, 1980).

Rosenthal and DePaulo (1979) tested their suggestion about the relatively accommodating decoding style of women in a variety of ways. One of the most persuasive of these was a series of studies of the relationship between the size of the female decoding advantage and the leakiness of the channel being decoded. Here it was found that women's superiority over men systematically declined as the channels became leakier. This is consistent with the idea that women are more accommodating than men in their non-verbal decoding, refraining from accurately decoding the sender's less controllable cues (although there is no evidence that this style is *consciously* deployed). There is some evidence that those who are relatively good at decoding unintended non-verbal cues have less satisfactory personal relationships (Rosenthal *et al.*, 1979), and this was interpreted as showing that "knowing too much" about another person's state may disrupt one's relationship with him or her. If that interpretation is correct, it may be that women's relatively greater advantage in decoding less leaky non-verbal cues is part of their known general tendency to be more interpersonally accommodating than men.

Further evidence to support Rosenthal and DePaulo's thesis comes from research reported by Blanck *et al.* (1981), who examined the developmental acquisition of females' tendency to be non-verbally accommodating. In a cross-sectional study, these investigators showed that with increasing age, females lost their relative advantage in decoding cues from leaky channels, and gained an advantage in decoding cues from less leaky channels. Evidence from a 1-year longitudinal study of children aged between 11 and 14 also showed a tendency for females to lose their relative advantage in decoding leaky cues as they grew older. These findings were interpreted as supporting a socialization hypothesis that females learn to become non-verbally accommodating, presumably because they find that there are social costs in being adept at decoding unintended non-verbal cues and social rewards in being adept at decoding intended non-verbal cues.

On the basis of the research reviewed in this section, it seems reasonable to conclude that adult females have a consistent (albeit fairly small) advantage in decoding others' non-verbal expressions of emotion when these are posed, expressed intentionally, or are expressed in relatively less leaky channels, such as the face; and that this advantage decreases or even disappears when the non-verbal cues are spontaneous, expressed unintentionally, or are expressed in relatively more leaky channels, such as the body or tone of voice. To what extent this pattern of findings can be explained by invoking the argument that females are more non-verbally "accommodating" than males is open to question. First, to subsume all the evidence, one would have to assume that the apparent lack of consistent female advantage in decoding spontaneous facial expressions reflects the fact that such expressions contain more leaky cues than posed expressions. Admittedly, senders are less likely to monitor or control their facial expressions under spontaneous sending conditions, so there are some grounds for thinking that the face—normally regarded as the least leaky non-verbal channel—will be leaky when the expressions are spontaneous, but further research is needed to confirm this assumption. A second reservation concerns the explanatory value of the construct of "accommodatingness". A cynic might argue that this does little more than provide a shorthand description of the observed tendency for the female decoding advantage to be more apparent in some channels than in others. Although the Blanck *et al.* (1981) research suggests that the tendency for females to be non-verbally accommodating is acquired through experience, exactly how this occurs and why it should happen to females but not to males are matters in need of clarification.

CONCLUSIONS

In summary, this review of gender differences in emotion indicates:

(1) that males tend to exhibit higher levels of psychophysiological activity than females, with the important exception of facial EMG where the reverse applies;
(2) that females tend to be more facially expressive than males when exposed to emotionally-arousing stimuli;
(3) that gender differences in the subjective experience of emotion, while notoriously difficult to interpret, appear to be limited to a tendency for women to experience more dysphoric emotion—a tendency that is echoed by the fact that women are more likely than men to show unipolar depression;
(4) that there is relatively little evidence concerning gender differences in emotional behaviour other than aggression, where the evidence is that males are more likely to act aggressively;
(5) that in the realm of non-verbal decoding skills there is a tendency for females to be superior to males.

Any conclusions drawn from this pattern of findings must be tempered by an appreciation of the size of the differences involved. The mean effect size found in the Eagly and Steffen (1986) meta-analysis of the research on adult aggression was 0.29, which corresponds to a point-biserial correlation of 0.14 between gender and aggression. In other words, around 2% of the variance in aggressive behaviour observed in the studies reviewed by Eagly and Steffen can be accounted for in terms of the gender of the aggressor. The corresponding mean effect size reported by Hyde (1984) in her meta-analysis of the literature on children's aggression was 0.50, but even here just 5% of the variance is explained by gender. The mean effect sizes reported by Hall (1978, 1984) in her meta-analyses of the literature on non-verbal decoding skills were around 0.40, which indicates that roughly 4% of the variance in measures of such skills is accounted for by decoder gender. The largest gender difference observed in the present review is that associated with unipolar depression, where the mean female-to-male ratio is approximately 2 : 1 (Nolen-Hoeksema, 1987), but even in this case it is clear that gender is far from perfectly correlated with depression. The general point should be readily apparent: Gender differences in the realm of emotion are generally small even where they have been shown to be consistent across large numbers of studies; they invariably reflect differences between group means in sizeable populations and within these populations there will be substantial numbers of individual males and females whose scores on the measure in question do not reflect the overall mean difference between the groups.

With this in mind, we can turn to a consideration of the extent to which observed gender differences in emotion can be ascribed to biological factors. In the case of *psychophysiological indices*, there is no evidence that directly bears on this question. Although the Prokasy and Raskin (1973) observation that gender differences in electrodermal activity emerge after puberty may suggest that hormonal changes are involved, there is really insufficient evidence to be confident that these differences are confined to post-pubertal subjects and in any case such a pattern could equally well be explained by arguing that it reflects the differential socialization to which boys and girls are exposed. Gender differences in *facial expressiveness* are not reliably observed in infants or children, which casts some doubt on any explanation couched exclusively in genetic terms. On the other hand, there is evidence that male and female infants are exposed to differential socialization with regard to facial expressions, and that such exposure can influence subsequent expressiveness. Biological arguments have often been invoked to account for gender differences in *emotional experience*, and here the commonest type of argument relates to the emotional impact of hormonal fluctuations. However, neither direct assessment of hormonal levels nor double-blind evaluations of hormonal intervention therapy provide adequate support for this view. By contrast, there is some evidence implicating social and psychological factors, such as the conflicting role demands experienced by women (especially married women), the beliefs that women have about biological events such as menstruation and menopause, and the greater (relative to men) willingness of women to confront and express their experience of negative affect. A biological explanation of the observed gender difference in *aggression* commands more support. First, there is some evidence that exposure to androgens increases the likelihood of aggressive behaviour in many species of birds and mammals (and in some fish, amphibians and reptiles)—although the evidence relating to humans is equivocal; second, there is evidence that the gender difference is greater in children than in adults, which is broadly consistent with the view that biological regulation of aggression is overtaken by normative regulation in the course of socialization into adulthood (cf. Eagly and Steffen, 1986). As noted earlier, however, biological and social factors contributing to human aggression are often confounded, which makes assigning causality primarily to one factor or the other difficult, if at all possible. Finally, there is no evidence that the gender difference in *non-verbal decoding skill* is biologically based. Hall (1978) did tentatively suggest that women may be innately predisposed to be sensitive to non-verbal cues or to be rapid learners of their meaning, but as yet there is no evidence to support this argument. Indeed, there is little evidence in children of a gender difference in decoding non-verbal cues. There is also some evidence that the types of non-verbal cues decoded better by females than by males change between childhood and early adulthood, which suggests that non-verbal decoding skills are responsive to social reinforcement; one problem with a socialization explanation, however, is that there is no evidence that males and females receive differential reinforcement for non-verbal decoding.

In general, then, the small but consistent gender differences in emotion reviewed here are currently explained better in terms of social psychological processes than biological processes. However, the lack of programmatic research in many of the areas of research means that there is relatively little evidence that bears directly on issues of causation. Gender differences in emotion (as in other areas) are often not researched for their own sake; rather, they are observed in the course of research conducted chiefly for some other purpose. Serendipitous findings can help to establish whether or not there is a gender difference, but they are most unlikely to constitute evidence relevant to causation.

Given the small effect sizes associated with gender differences in emotion, it is worth reconsidering the value of research specifically focused on these differences. Rather than posing the question "How (or even why) do women and men differ in the realm of emotion?", it might be more productive to focus attention on individual differences in relationships among the different components of emotion, and only then consider whether these individual differences are related to gender. One of the abiding problems in emotion research is the fact that different indices of emotion (psychophysiological, self-report, facial expression, behavioural) are not related to each other in a straightforward manner; moreover, it seems that these relationships vary from individual to individual. For example, it has been argued by various investigators that the repression of overt expression of emotion may result in increased psychophysiological activity. Thus Fowles (1980) showed that behavioural inhibition in humans is associated with increased electrodermal activity; Waid and Orne (1982) have shown that highly "socialized" individuals, whose behaviour is more inhibited, exhibit higher SC levels than do their less socialized counterparts; similarly, Hare and his colleagues (see Hare, 1978) have demonstrated that sociopaths, whose behaviour is low in inhibition, tend to have lower SC levels than do normal individuals; investigators studying the relationship between spontaneous facial expressiveness and electrodermal activity have often reported negative between-subjects correlations (see Buck, 1979); and Pennebaker and Chew (1985) have demonstrated that the suppression of expressive behaviour that is associated with deception is correlated with an increase in electrodermal activity. There are grounds, then, for thinking that inhibition of overt expression of emotion leads to increased psychophysiological activity, and that individuals who chronically suppress emotional expression will tend to be more autonomically reactive than those who do not. Here is a basis for an individual differences analysis of emotion that links two key components of emotion; indeed, other components could be integrated into this analysis if the notion of "expression" were broadened to include any behavioural index of emotion, including self-report. Thus individuals who are willing to express emotion by communicating it to others in the form of uninhibited facial expression, self-report or other behaviours should in theory be characterized by low psychophysiological activity relative to those who are inhibited in expression.

It is also worth noting that a number of researchers have argued that the suppression of emotion can play a causal role in somatic illness (see, for example, Florin, Freudenberg and Hollaender, 1985; Malatesta, Jonas and Izard, 1987; Watson, Pettingale and Greer, 1984; Wirsching *et al.*, 1982). The fact that individual differences in style of emotional expression have been shown to be associated with illnesses as diverse as asthma, arthritis, eczema and cancer lends further importance to the search for an understanding of the relationships among variables such as temperament, socialization, expressiveness and physiological activity.

It should be apparent that the two broad types of expressive style outlined above appear to map on to what is currently known about gender differences in emotion. With the exception of situations likely to provoke aggression, males tend to be less expressive and more physiologically responsive than females. This is by no means a novel observation (see Buck, 1988) but it has not attracted systematic investigation—perhaps because of the relatively small effect sizes characteristic of gender differences in this area. Progress in understanding might be more rapid if researchers concentrated on specifying the developmental course of individual differences in expressive style, rather than emphasizing group differences between males and females. If, as current research suggests, differential socialization is a key factor underlying gender differences in emotion, these differences are liable to diminish as the socialization of males and females becomes more similar. It therefore seems prudent to develop and test an individual differences model of emotional expressivity without specific reference to gender. Having established the viability of such a model, researchers would be in a position to address the question of gender differences in emotion more coherently.

ACKNOWLEDGEMENTS

The author wishes to thank John Archer, Mike Eysenck, Tony Gale, Judith Hall, Carol Malatesta and Hugh Wagner for their comments on an earlier version of this chapter.

REFERENCES

Ainsworth, M.D.S. and Wittig, D.S. (1969) Attachment and exploratory behaviour of one year olds in a strange situation. In B.M. Foss (ed.), *Determinants of Infant Behaviour.* London: Methuen.

Archer, J. (1987) Beyond sex differences: comments on Borrill and Reid. *Bulletin of the British Psychological Society*, **40**, 88–90.

Archer, J. and Lloyd, B.B. (1985) *Sex and Gender.* Cambridge: Cambridge University Press.

Aronfreed, J.M., Messick, S.A. and Diggory, J.C. (1953) Re-examining emotionality and perceptual defense. *Journal of Personality*, **21**, 517–528.

Averill, J.R. (1982) *Anger and Aggression: An Essay on Emotion.* New York: Springer.

Bancroft, J. and Backstrom, T. (1985) Premenstrual syndrome. *Clinical Endocrinology*, **22**, 313–336.

Bart, P.B. (1971) Depression in middle-aged women. In V. Kornick and B.K. Moran (eds), *Women in Sexist Society.* New York: Basic Books.

Belk, S.S. and Snell, W.E. (1986) Beliefs about women: components and correlates. *Personality and Social Psychology Bulletin*, **12**, 403–413.

Berger, S.M. (1962) Conditioning through vicarous instigation. *Psychological Review*, **69**, 450–466.

Best, D.L., Williams, J.E., Cloud, J.M., Davis, S.W., Robertson, L.S., Edwards, J.R., Giles, H. and Fowles, J. (1977) Development of sex-trait stereotypes among young children in the United States, England, and Ireland. *Child Development*, **48**, 1375–1384.

Blanck, P.D., Rosenthal, R., Snodgrass, S.E., DePaulo, B.M. and Zuckerman, M. (1981) Sex differences in eavesdropping on nonverbal cues: developmental changes. *Journal of Personality and Social Psychology*, **41**, 391–396.

Bloom, B.L. (1975) *Changing Patterns of Psychiatric Care.* New York: Human Sciences Press.

Bloom, B.L., Asher, S.J. and White, S.W. (1978) Marital disruption as a stressor: a review and analysis. *Psychological Bulletin*, **85**, 867–894.

Bradburn, N.M. (1969) *The Structure of Psychological Well-Being.* Chicago: Aldine.

Broverman, I.K., Broverman, D.M., Clarkson, F.E., Rosenkrantz, P.S. and Vogel, S.R. (1970) Sex role stereotypes and clinical judgments of mental health. *Journal of Consulting and Clinical Psychology*, **34**, 1–7.

Buck, R. (1972) *Relationships between dissonance-reducing behaviour and tension measures following aggression*, Paper presented at the meeting of the Midwestern Psychological Association, Cleveland, 1972.

Buck, R. (1975) Nonverbal communication of affect in children. *Journal of Personality and Social Psychology*, **31**, 644–653.

Buck, R. (1977) Nonverbal communication of affect in preschool children: relationships with personality and skin conductance. *Journal of Personality and Social Psychology*, **35**, 225–236.

Buck, R. (1979) Individual differences in nonverbal sending accuracy and electrodermal responding: The externalizing-internalizing dimension. In R. Rosenthal (ed.), *Skill in Nonverbal Communication: Individual Differences.* Cambridge, MA: Oelgeschlager, Gunn and Hain.

Buck, R. (1984) *The Communication of Emotion.* New York: Guilford.

Buck, R. (1988) *Human Motivation and Emotion.* (2nd edition). New York: John Wiley & Sons.

Buck, R., Baron, R. and Barrette, R. (1982) Temporal organization of spontaneous emotional expression: a segmentation analysis. *Journal of Personality and Social Psychology*, **42**, 506–517.

Buck, R., Baron, R., Goodman N. and Shapiro, B. (1980) Unitization of spontaneous nonverbal behavior in the study of emotion communication. *Journal of Personality and Social Psychology*, **39**, 522–529.

Buck, R., Miller, R.E. and Caul, W.F. (1974) Sex, personality, and physiological variables in the communication of affect via facial expression. *Journal of Personality and Social Psychology*, **30**, 587–596.

Buck, R., Savin, V.J., Miller, R.E. and Caul, W.F. (1972) Communciation of affect through facial expressions in humans. *Journal of Personality and Social Psychology*, **23**, 362–371.

Cantor, J.R., Zillmann, D. and Einsiedel, E. (1978) Female responses to provocation after exposure to aggressive and erotic films. *Communication Research*, **5**, 395–412.

Chesler, P. (1971) Women as psychiatric and psychotherapeutic patients. *Journal of Marriage and the Family*, **33**, 746–759.

Cochrane, R. (1983) *The Social Creation of Mental Illness.* London: Longman.

Cohen, J. (1977) *Statistical Power Analysis for the Behavioural Sciences.* New York: Academic Press.

Craig, K. and Lowery, H.J. (1969) Heart rate components of conditioned vicarious autonomic responses. *Journal of Personality and Social Psychology*, **11**, 381–387.

Culp, R.E., Crook, A.S. and Housley, P.C. (1983) A comparison of observed and reported adult-infant interactions: Effects of perceived sex. *Sex Roles*, **9**, 475–479.

Dalton, K. (1969) *The Menstrual Cycle.* New York: Pantheon Books.

Dalton, K. (1979) *Once a Month.* London: Fontana.

Deaux, K. (1984) From individuals to social categories: analysis of a decade's research on gender. *American Psychologist*, **39**, 105–116.

DePaulo, B.M., Zuckerman, M. and Rosenthal, R. (1980) Detecting deception: modality effects. In L. Wheeler (ed.), *Review of Personality and Social Psychology, Vol. 1*, Beverly Hills, CA: Sage.

Eagly, A.H. and Carli, L.L. (1981) Sex of researchers and sex-typed communications as determinants of sex differences in influenceability: a meta-analysis of social influence studies. *Psychological Bulletin*, **90**, 1–20.

Eagly, A.H. and Steffen, V.J. (1986) Gender and aggressive behavior: a meta-analytic review of the social psychological literature. *Psychological Bulletin*, **100**, 309–330.

Eisenberg, N. and Lennon, R. (1983) Sex differences in empathy and related capacities. *Psychological Bulletin*, **94**, 100–131.

Ekman, P. and Friesen, W.V. (1969) Nonverbal leakage and clues to deception. *Psychiatry*, **32**, 88–105.

Epstein, S. (1980) The stablity of behavior: II. Implications for psychological research. *American Psychologist*, **35**, 790–807.

Field, T. (1982) Individual differences in the expressivity of neonates and young infants. In R.S. Feldman (ed.), *Development of Nonverbal Behavior in Children*. New York: Springer.

Florin, I., Freudenberg, G. and Hollaender, J. (1985) Facial expressions of emotion and physiologic reactions in children with bronchial asthma. *Psychosomatic Medicine*, **47**, 382–393.

Fowles, D.C. (1980) The three arousal model: implications of Gray's two-factor theory for heart rate, electrodermal activity, and psychopathy. *Psychophysiology*, **17**, 87–104.

Frodi, A., Macauley, J. and Thome, P.R. (1977) Are women always less aggressive than men? A review of the experimental literature. *Psychological Bulletin*, **84**, 634–660.

Fujita, B.N., Harper, R.G. and Wiens, A.N. (1980) Encoding-decoding of nonverbal emotional messages: Sex differences in spontaneous and enacted expressions. *Journal of Nonverbal Behaviour*, **4**, 131–145.

Gale, M.A. and Baker, S. (1981) In vivo or in vitro?: some effects of laboratory environments, with particular reference to the psychophysiology experiment. In M.J. Christie and P.G. Mellett (eds), *Approaches to Psychosomatics*. Chichester: Wiley.

Gallagher, D. and Shuntich, R.J. (1981) Encoding and decoding of nonverbal behavior through facial expressions. *Journal of Research in Personality*, **15**, 241–252.

Geen, R. (1990) *Human Aggression*. Milton Keynes: Open University Press.

Glass, G. (1976) Primary, secondary and meta-analysis of research. *Educational Research*, **5**, 3–8.

Goodenough, F.L. (1931) *Anger in Young Children*. Minneapolis, MN: University of Minnesota Press.

Gove, W.R. (1972) Sex roles, marital roles, and mental illness. *Social Forces*, **51**, 34–44.

Gove, W.R. (1978) Sex differences in mental illness among adult men and women: an evaluation of four questions raised regarding the evidence on the higher rates of women. *Social Science and Medicine*, **12**, 187–198.

Gove, W.R. (1979) Sex, marital status, and psychiatric treatment: A research note. *Social Forces*, **58**, 89–93.

Gove, W.R. (1980) Mental illness and psychiatric treatment among women. *Psychology of Women Quarterly*, **4**, 345–362.

Gove, W.R. and Tudor, J.F. (1973) Adult sex roles and mental illness. *American Journal of Sociology*, **78**, 812–835.

Graham, L., Cohen, S. and Shmavonian, G. (1966) Sex differences in autonomic responses during instrumental conditioning. *Psychosomatic Medicine*, **28**, 264–271.

Greene, J.G. (1981) Types of life-events in relation to symptoms at the climacterium. *Bulletin of the British Psychological Society*, **34**, 187.

Gunnar, M.R. (1980) Control, warning signals, and distress in infancy. *Child Development*, **51**, 262–265.

Guttentag, M., Salasin, S. and Belle, D. (eds) (1980) *The Mental Health of Women.* New York: Academic Press.

Hall, J.A. (1978) Gender effects in decoding nonverbal cues. *Psychological Bulletin,* **85**, 845–857.

Hall, J.A. (1984) *Nonverbal Sex Differences: Communication Accuracy and Expressive Style.* Baltimore, MD: Johns Hopkins University Press.

Hamburg, D.A. and Lunde, D.T. (1966) Sex hormones in the development of sex differences in human behaviour. In E.E. Maccoby (ed.), *The Development of Sex Differences.* Stanford: Stanford University Press.

Hammen, C.L. and Peters, S.D. (1978) Interpersonal consequences of depression: responses to men and women enacting a depressed role. *Journal of Abnormal Psychology,* **87**, 323–332.

Harding, S.D. (1982) Psychological well-being in Great Britain: an evaluation of the Bradburn affect balance scale. *Personality and Individual Differences,* **3**, 167–175.

Hare, R.D. (1978) Electrodermal and cardiovascular correlates of psychopathy. In R.D. Hare and D. Schalling (eds), *Psychopathic Behavior: Approaches to Research.* New York: John Wiley & Sons.

Haviland, J.H. and Malatesta, C.Z. (1981) The development of sex differences in nonverbal signals: fallacies, facts, and fantasies. In C. Mayo and N. Henley (eds), *Gender and Nonverbal Behavior.* New York: Springer.

Henshall, C. and McGuire, J. (1986) Gender development. In M. Richards and P. Light (eds), *Children of Social Worlds.* Cambridge: Polity Press.

Hill, K.T. and Sarason, S.B. (1966) The relation of test anxiety and defensiveness to test and school performance over the elementary-school years. *Monographs of the Society for Research in Child Development,* **31** (2), 1–76.

Hoffman, M.L. (1977) Sex differences in empathy and related behaviors. *Psychological Bulletin,* **84**, 712–722.

Hokanson, J.E. (1970) Psychophysiological evaluation of the catharsis hypothesis. In E.I. Megargee and J.E. Hokanson (eds), *The Dynamics of Aggression: Individual, Group, and International Analyses.* New York: Harper and Row.

Hokanson, J.E., Willers, K.R. and Koropsak, E. (1968) The modification of autonomic responses during aggressive interchange. *Journal of Personality,* **36**, 386–404.

Hyde, J.S. (1984) How large are gender differences in aggression? A developmental meta-analysis. *Developmental Psychology,* **20**, 722–736.

Jahnke, J.C., Crannell, C.W. and Morrissette, J.O. (1974) Sex differences and the MAS. *Educational and Psychological Measurement,* **24**, 309–312.

Katkin, E.S., Blascovich, J. and Goldband, S. (1981) Empirical assessment of visceral self-perception: individual and sex differences in the acquisition of heartbeat discrimination. *Journal of Personality and Social Psychology,* **40**, 1095–1101.

Kessler, R.C., Price, B.H. and Wortman, C.B. (1985) Social factors in psychopathology: stress, social support, and coping processes. *Annual Review of Psychology,* **36**, 531–572.

Kessler, S. and Moos, R.H. (1970) The XYY karotype and criminality: A review. *Journal of Psychiatric Research,* **7**, 153–170.

Koenigsberg, M.R., Katkin, E.S. and Blascovich, J. (1981) The effects of pretraining instructional set on the acquisition and maintenance of heartbeat detection in males and females. *Psychophysiology,* **18**, 196–197.

Kornbrott, D. (1986) *Women who excel in maths and science,* Paper presented at Conference on Women and Science and Technology, Lancashire Polytechnic, September, 1986.

Kuhn, D., Nash, S.C. and Bruchan, L. (1978) Sex role concept of two- and three-year olds. *Child Development,* **49**, 445–451.

Lang, P.J. (1984) Cognition in emotion: concept and action. In C.E. Izard, J. Kagan and R.B. Zajonc (eds), *Emotions, Cognition, and Behavior.* New York: Cambridge University Press.

Maccoby, E.E. and Feldman, S.S. (1972) Mother–infant attachment and stranger-reactions in the third year of life. *Monographs of the Society for Research in Child Development*, **37**(1), 1–86.

Maccoby, E.E. and Jacklin, C.N. (1974) *The Psychology of Sex Differences.* Stanford, CA: Stanford University Press.

Maccoby, E.E. and Jacklin, C.N. (1980) Sex differences in aggression: a rejoinder and reprise. *Child Development*, **51**, 964–980.

Malatesta, C.Z., Grigoryev, P., Lamb, C., Albin, M. and Culver, C. (1986) Emotion socialization and expressive development in preterm and full-term infants. *Child Development*, **57**, 316–330.

Malatesta, C.Z. and Haviland, J.M. (1982) Learning display rules: the socialization of emotion expression in infancy. *Child Development*, **53**, 991–1003.

Malatesta, C.Z., Jonas, R. and Izard, C.E. (1987) The relation between low facial expressivity during emotional arousal and somatic symptoms. *British Journal of Medical Psychology*, **60**, 169–180.

Malatesta, C.Z. and Lamb, C. (1987) *Emotion socialization during the second year*, Paper presented at the Annual Meeting of the American Psychological Association, New York: August, 1987.

Martin, J.A. (1981) A longitudinal study of the consequences of early mother–infant interaction: a micro-analytic approach. *Monographs of the Society for Research in Child Development*, **46**(3), 1–58.

Mazur, A. and Lamb, T.A. (1980) Testosterone, status, and mood in human males. *Hormones and Behavior*, **14**, 236–246.

Miles, A. (1987) *The Mentally Ill in Contemporary Society.* Oxford: Blackwell.

Money, J. and Ehrhardt, A.A. (1972) *Man and Woman, Boy and Girl.* Baltimore, MD: Johns Hopkins University Press.

Newson, J. and Newson, E. (1986) Family and sex roles in middle childhood. In D.J. Hargreaves and A.M. Colley (eds), *The Psychology of Sex Roles.* London: Harper and Row.

Nicosia, G.J., Hyman, D., Karlin, R.A., Epstein, Y.M. and Aiello, J.R. (1979) Effects of bodily contact on reactions to crowding. *Journal of Applied Social Psychology*, **9**, 508–523.

Nielsen, J. and Christensen, A.L. (1974) Thirty-five males with double Y chromosome. *Journal of Psychological Medicine*, **4**, 38–47.

Nolen-Hoeksema, S. (1987) Sex differences in unipolar depression: evidence and theory. *Psychological Bulletin*, **101**, 259–282.

Noller, P. (1982) Couple communication and marital satisfaction. *Australian Journal of Sex, Marriage and Family*, **3**, 69–75.

Olweus, D., Mattsson, A., Schallin, D. and Low, H. (1980) Testosterone, aggression, physical and personality dimensions in normal adolescent males. *Psychosomatic Medicine*, **42**, 253–269.

Parlee, M.B. (1988) Menstrual cycle changes in moods and emotions: causal and interpretive processes in the construction of emotions. In H.L. Wagner (ed.), *Social Psychophysiology and Emotion: Theory and Clinical Applications.* Chichester: John Wiley & Sons.

Pennebaker, J.W. and Chew, C.H. (1985) Behavioral inhibition and electrodermal activity during deception. *Journal of Personality and Social Psychology*, **49**, 1427–1433.

Persky, H., Smith, K.D. and Basu, G.K. (1971) Relation of psychologic measures of aggression and hostility to testosterone production in man. *Psychosomatic Medicine*, **33**, 265–277.

Phillips, D.L. and Segal, B.E. (1969) Sexual status and psychiatric symptoms. *American Sociological Review*, **34**, 58–72.

Prokasy, W. and Raskin, D. (1973) *Electrodermal Activity in Psychological Research.* New York: Academic Press.

Reinisch, J.M. (1981) Prenatal exposure to synthetic progestins increases potential for aggression in humans. *Science*, **211**, 1171–1173.

Rosenthal, R. (1984) *Meta-analytic Procedures for Social Research.* Beverly Hills, CA: Sage.

Rosenthal, R. and DePaulo, B.M. (1979) Sex differences in eavesdropping on nonverbal cues. *Journal of Personality and Social Psychology*, **37**, 273–285.

Rosenthal, R., Hall, J.A., DiMatteo, M.R., Rogers, P.L. and Archer, D. (1979) *Sensitivity to Nonverbal Communication: The PONS Test.* Baltimore, MD: Johns Hopkins University Press.

Rubin, J.Z., Provenzano, F.J. and Luria, Z. (1974) The eye of the beholder: parents' views on the sex of newborns. *American Journal of Orthopsychiatry*, **44**, 512–519.

Ruble, D.N. and Brooks-Gunn, J. (1979) Menstrual symptoms: a social cognition analysis. *Journal of Behavioral Medicine*, **2**, 171–194.

Rumenik, D.K., Capasso, D.R. and Hendrick, C. (1977) Experimenter sex effects in behavioral research. *Psychological Bulletin*, **84**, 852–877.

Sapolsky, B.S., Stocking, S.H. and Zillmann, D. (1977) Immediate vs. delayed retaliation in male and female adults. *Psychological Reports*, **40**, 197–198.

Scherer, K.R., Wallbott, H. and Summerfield, A.B. (1986) *Experiencing Emotion: A Cross-Cultural Study.* Cambridge: Cambridge University Press.

Schwartz, G.E., Ahern, G.L. and Brown, S.L. (1979) Lateralized facial muscle response to positive versus negative emotional stimuli. *Psychophysiology*, **16**, 561–571.

Schwartz, G.E., Brown, S.L. and Ahern, G.L. (1980) Facial muscle patterning and subjective experience during affective imagery: sex differences. *Psychophysiology*, **17**, 75–82.

Schwartz, G.E., Fair, P.L., Mandel, M.R., Salt, P., Mieske, M. and Klerman, G.L. (1978) Facial electromyography in the assessment of improvement in depression. *Psychosomatic Medicine*, **40**, 355–360.

Schwartz, G.E., Fair, P.L., Salt, P., Mandel, M.R. and Klerman, G.L. (1976a) Facial expression and imagery in depression: An electromyographic study. *Psychosomatic Medicine*, **38**, 337–347.

Schwartz, G.E., Fair, P.L., Salt, P., Mandel, M.R. and Klerman, G.L. (1976b) Facial muscle patterning to affective imagery in depressed and non-depressed subjects. *Science*, **192**, 489–491.

Shields, S.A. (1987) Women, men and the dilemma of emotion. In P. Shaver and C. Hendrick (eds), *Sex and Gender.* Beverly Hills, CA: Sage.

Shmavonian, B., Yarmat, A. and Cohen, S. (1965) Relations between the autonomic nervous system and central nervous system in age differences in behavior. In A.T. Welford and J.E. Birren (eds) *Behavior, Aging, and the Nervous System.* Springfield, IL: Charles C. Thomas.

Smith, C. and Lloyd, B.B. (1978) Maternal behavior and perceived sex of infant. *Child Development*, **49**, 1263–1265.

Smith, P.K. and Green, M. (1975) Aggressive behavior in English nurseries and play groups: sex differences and response of adults. *Child Development*, **46**, 211–214.

Social Trends (1984) London: HMSO.

Spiegler, M.D. and Liebert, R.M. (1970) Some correlates of self-reported fear. *Psychological Reports*, **26**, 691–695.
Stoney, C.M., Davis, M.C. and Matthews, K.A. (1987) Sex differences in physiological response to stress and in coronary heart disease: a causal link? *Psychophysiology*, **24**, 127–131.
Stroebe, M.S. and Stroebe, W. (1983) Who suffers more? Sex differences in health risks of the widowed. *Psychological Bulletin*, **93**, 279–301.
Wagner, H.L., MacDonald, C.J. and Manstead, A.S.R. (1986) Communication of individual emotions by spontaneous facial expressions. *Journal of Personality and Social Psychology*, **50**, 737–743.
Waid, W.W. and Orne, M.T. (1982) Reduced electrodermal response to conflict, failure to inhibit dominant behaviors, and delinquent processes. *Journal of Personality and Social Psychology*, **43**, 769–774.
Warr, P.B. and Payne, R. (1982) Experiences of strain and pleasure among British adults. *Social Science and Medicine*, **16**, 1691–1697.
Watson, M., Pettingale, K.W. and Greer, S. (1984) Emotional control and autonomic arousal in breast cancer patients. *Journal of Psychosomatic Research*, **28**, 467–474.
Weissman, M.M. (1979) The myth of involutional melancholia. *Journal of the American Medical Association*, **242**, 742–744.
Weissman, M.M. and Klerman, G.L. (1977) Sex differences in the epidemiology of depression. *Archives of General Psychiatry*, **34**, 89–111.
Weldburn, V. (1980) *Postnatal Depression*. London: Fontana.
Wilson, G.D. (1967) Social desirability and sex differences in expressed fear. *Behavior Research and Therapy*, **5**, 136–137.
Wirsching, M., Stierlin, H., Hoffman, F., Weber, G. and Wirsching, B. (1982) Psychological identification of breast cancer patients before biopsy. *Journal of Psychosomatic Research*, **26**, 1–10.
Witkin, H.A., Mednick, S.A., Schulsinger, F., Bakkestrom, E., Christiansen, K.O., Goodenough, D.R., Hirschhorn, K., Lundsteen, C., Owen, D.R., Philip, J., Rubin, D.B. and Stocking, M. (1976) Criminality in XYY and XXY men. *Science*, **193**, 547–555.
Yarczower, M. and Daruns, L. (1982) Social inhibition of spontaneous facial expressions in children. *Journal of Personality and Social Psychology*, **43**, 831–837.
Zillmann, D. (1979) *Hostility and Aggression*. Hillsdale, NJ: Erlbaum.

Index